July 9-12, 2018
Baltimore, MD, USA

**Association for
Computing Machinery**

Advancing Computing as a Science & Profession

HT '18

Proceedings of the 29th ACM Conference on
Hypertext and Social Media

Sponsored by:
ACM SIGWEB

In Cooperation with:
ACM SIGCHI

**Association for
Computing Machinery**

Advancing Computing as a Science & Profession

The Association for Computing Machinery
2 Penn Plaza, Suite 701
New York, New York 10121-0701

ISBN: 978-1-4503-5427-1 (Digital)

ISBN: 978-1-4503-6150-7 (Print)

Additional copies may be ordered prepaid from:

ACM Order Department
PO Box 30777
New York, NY 10087-0777, USA

Phone: 1-800-342-6626 (USA and Canada)
+1-212-626-0500 (Global)
Fax: +1-212-944-1318
E-mail: acmhelp@acm.org
Hours of Operation: 8:30 am – 4:30 pm ET

Chairs' Welcome

It is our great pleasure to welcome you to the 2018 ACM International Conference on Hypertext and Social Media (HT 2018) in Baltimore, Maryland, on July 9--12.

HT is a top-tier ACM conference in the areas of Hypertext and Social Media. Since 1987, it has successfully brought together leading researchers and developers from the community. It is concerned with all aspects of modern hypertext research, including social media, adaptation, personalization, recommendations, user modeling, linked data and semantic web, dynamic and computed hypertext, and its application in digital humanities, as well as the interplay between those aspects such as linking stories with data or linking people with resources.

HT 2018 continues to create an outstanding technical program consisting of research and demo paper presentations. The single-track conference brings together researchers working in topics including Algorithms and Methods for Social Media Analysis, Digital Humanities and Computational Social Science, Adaptive Hypertext and Recommendations, Semantic Web and Connected Data, Digital Storytelling and News, and Collaboration and Crowdsourcing.

In total, we have received 69 regular paper (10 pages) submissions reviewed by a group of 66 regular and 33 senior program committee members, who led the discussions. In the end, 19 regular papers (acceptance rate of 27%) were accepted with another 10 full papers accepted as short papers. Additionally, 3 of 16 short paper submissions were accepted. This year, for the first time, we also organized a "Blue Sky Ideas" track with the support of the Computing Community Consortium (CCC). This track received 5 submissions of which 3 were accepted and received partial travel support from CCC.

To help provide a broad perspective on current trends at the intersection of data science and society, the conference will host the following four, diverse keynote speakers: Leslie Sage, the Director of Data Science at DevResults; Seth Stephens-Davidowitz, the author of the NYT bestseller "Everybody Lies"; Elizabeth Kittrie, a Strategic Advisor for Data and Open Science at the National Library of Medicine (NLM); and Ben Zhao, the Neubauer Professor of Computer Science at the University of Chicago.

In addition to the scientific presentations and the keynotes, the pre-conference day on July 9 will also feature three focused workshops and a tutorial.

Organizing a conference such as HT requires the effort and the dedication and effort of many volunteers. We are grateful to an outstanding group of colleagues for serving on the organization team for generously contributing their time and energy, including especially registration chair (Thang Dinh), tutorial co-chairs (Miriam Redi and Pete Burnap), workshop co-chairs (Haewoon Kwak and Ujwal Gadiraju), data chair (Fabricio Benevenuto), web co-chairs (Sagar Joglekar and Kiran Garimella), publicity chair (Charlie Hargood), and publication chair (Kyungsik Han). The HT conference would have been impossible to organize without their volunteer spirit.

We also wish to thank the HT Steering Committee, especially Simon Harper, Yeliz Yesilada, and David Millard. Throughout the entire period of conference organization, we greatly benefited from the advice and mentoring given by them. Finally, we want to thank the hosting university, Towson University in Baltimore, MD and sponsors: ACM, SIGWEB, in cooperation with ACM SIGCHI.

We hope that you will find this program interesting and thought-provoking and that the conference will provide you with a valuable opportunity to share ideas with other fellow researchers and practitioners from institutions around the world.

Dongwon Lee
ACM HT'18 General Chair
Penn State University, U.S.A.

Nishanth Sastry
ACM HT'18 Program Co-Chairs
King's College London, UK

Ingmar Weber
ACM HT'18 Program Co-Chairs
QCRI, Qatar

Subrata Acharya
ACM HT'18 Local Co-Chairs
Towson University, U.S.A.

Nam Nguyen
ACM HT'18 Local Co-Chairs
Towson University, U.S.A.

Table of Contents

Session 4: User Behaviour

Session 5: Hypertext

Keynote IV

Session 6: Privacy, Bots and Automatic Methods

Session 7: News and Community Detection

Blue Sky Ideas

Tutorial

Author Index

ACM HT 2018 Organization

General Chair:	Dongwon Lee (Penn State University, USA)
Program Co-Chairs:	Nishanth Sastry (King's College London, UK)
	Ingmar Weber (QCRI, Qatar)
Local Co-Chairs:	Subrata Acharya (Towson University, USA)
	Nam Nguyen (Towson University, USA)
Publicity Chair:	Charlie Hargood (Bournemouth University, UK)
Registration Chair:	Thang Dinh (Virginia Commonwealth University, USA)
Tutorial Co-Chairs:	Pete Burnap (Cardiff University, UK)
	Miriam Redi (Bell Labs Cambridge, UK)
Workshop Co-Chairs:	Ujwal Gadiraju (L3S Research Center, Germany)
	Haewoon Kwak (QCRI, Qartar)
Data Chair:	Fabricio Benevenuto (UFMG, Brazil)
Publication Chair:	Kyungsik Han (Ajou University, Korea)
Senior Program Committee:	Dirk Ahlers (Norwegian University of Science and Technology, Norway)
	Martin Atzmueller (Tilburg University, Netherlands)
	Shlomo Berkovsky (CSIRO, Australia)
	Munmun De Choudhury (Georgia Institute of Technology, USA)
	Jana Diesner (University of Illinois at Urbana-Champaign, USA)
	Alexander Felfernig (Graz University of Technology, Austria)
	Emilio Ferrara (University of Southern California, USA)
	Niloy Ganguly (Indian Institute of Technology Kharagpur, India)
	Charlie Hargood (Bournemouth University, UK)
	Eelco Herder (Radboud University, Netherlands)
	Denis Helic (Graz University of Technology, Austria)
	Andreas Hotho (University of Wuerzburg, Germany)
	Geert-Jan Houben (Delft University of Technology, Netherland)
	Andreas Kaltenbrunner (NTENT, Spain)
	Florian Lemmerich (GESIS - Leibniz Institute for the Social Sciences & University of Koblenz-Landau, Germany)
	Luca Maria Aiello (Bell Labs Cambridge, UK)
	Wagner Meira Jr. (UFMG, Brazil)
	David Millard (University of Southampton, UK)
	Ethan Munson (University of Wisconsin-Milwaukee, USA)

External Reviewers: Mahdi Bohlouli

Anirban Chakraborty

Lukas Eberhard

Medhi Elahi

Ming Jiang

Patrick Kasper

Sarasi Lalithsena

Seokjun Lee

Enrico Mensa

Aditya Mogadala

Gary Munnelly

Fedelucio Narducci

Samuel Pecár

Ella Rabinovich

Rezvaneh Rezapour

Anna Sapienza

Junggab Son

Gabriele Sottocornola

Ivan Srba

Panagiotis Symeonidis

Pablo Torres-Tramon

Sponsor: sig web

In cooperation: SIGCHI

Lessons in Search Data

Seth Stephens-Davidowitz
seth.stephens@gmail.com

ABSTRACT

Seth will discuss what Google searches can teach us about racism, sexuality, mental illness, and other topics.

Detecting the Correlation between Sentiment and User-level as well as Text-Level Meta-data from Benchmark Corpora*

Shubhanshu Mishra
University of Illinois at Urbana-Champaign
School of Information Sciences
Champaign, Illinois
smishra8@illinois.edu

Jana Diesner
University of Illinois at Urbana-Champaign
School of Information Sciences
Champaign, Illinois
jdiesner@illinois.edu

ABSTRACT

Do tweets from users with similar Twitter characteristics have similar sentiments? What meta-data features of tweets and users correlate with tweet sentiment? In this paper, we address these two questions by analyzing six popular benchmark datasets where tweets are annotated with sentiment labels. We consider user-level as well as tweet-level meta-data features, and identify patterns and correlations of these feature with the log-odds for sentiment classes. We further strengthen our analysis by replicating this set of experiments on recent tweets from users present in our datasets; finding that most of the patterns are consistent across our analysis. Finally, we use our identified meta-data features as features for a sentiment classification algorithm, which results in around 2% increase in F1 score for sentiment classification, compared to text-only classifiers, along with a significant drop in KL-divergence. These results have potential to improve sentiment analysis applications on social media data.

CCS CONCEPTS

• **Information systems** → **Sentiment analysis**; *Social networks*;
• **Human-centered computing** → **Social media**; • **Computing methodologies** → *Supervised learning*;

KEYWORDS

Social media data, Social media meta-data, Sentiment analysis, Statistical analysis

ACM Reference Format:
Shubhanshu Mishra and Jana Diesner. 2018. Detecting the Correlation between Sentiment and User-level as well as Text-Level Meta-data from Benchmark Corpora. In *HT '18: 29th ACM Conference on Hypertext and Social Media, July 9–12, 2018, Baltimore, MD, USA*. ACM, New York, NY, USA, 9 pages. https://doi.org/10.1145/3209542.3209562

*Produces the permission block, and copyright information

1 INTRODUCTION

Sentiment prediction is a well-studied text classification problem [10, 20] that has mostly been applied to reviews, e.g., of movies [21, 23] and consumer products [20]. Sentiment analysis is also frequently used to identify the valence of social media posts and other types of text data [4, 6, 19]. Additionally, sentiment detected from text data has been shown to be useful for being correlated with or predicting individual as well as aggregated behavior, e.g., the political leaning of people [25] or stock market trends [3]. Many of these applications involve quantifying the distribution of sentiment classes, a task that is commonly referred to as sentiment quantification [5].

A major limitation of existing sentiment classification systems, when applied in the social media domain, is their reliance on mainly the text content of a post or tweet. However, platforms such as Twitter provide access to rich meta-data along with the text of the post. These meta-data include properties of social media posts and their authors, which may provide useful context for studying the sentiment conveyed in a tweet, and can complement the text features for the sentiment classification task. Earlier research has used tweet-based meta-data, such as the existence or number of URLs, hashtags, and mentions, as features for tweet sentiment classification [12, 13], as well as user-level meta-data for creating sentiment-based user networks [12]. However, there is a limited body of literature on using or incorporating meta-data of tweets for improving sentiment classification, and most of this prior work is based on non-public and non-standard datasets [24, 26]. With this paper, we aim to contribute to a more comprehensive understanding of the relationship between these meta-data features and the sentiment of tweets across multiple datasets. This work is enabled by the availability of large-scale standardized sentiment-annotated Twitter corpora, such as the Semantic Evaluation's Twitter sentiment task corpus [15, 16, 22], another recently available dataset of 1.6 million multilingual tweets [14], and a few other public datasets, which allow us to search for the existence of any meaningful relationships between the meta-data of tweets and tweet sentiment.

In this paper, we identify how various meta-data are (on average) related to the sentiment of tweets in existing sentiment annotated benchmark corpora. Our analysis is limited in that we identify patterns at an aggregate level across all datasets considered. However, we further support our observations by including additional data from users in our dataset, and observing the correlation between meta-data and sentiment (as predicted by a baseline classifier). The goal of this research is to understand the distribution of meta-data characteristics across these datasets, and to identify if these meta-data can reveal biases in sentiment annotation. Finally, we also detect how using these meta-data can help as features in a classifier to improve sentiment classifiers as well as sentiment quantification.

Our contributions with this paper are 1) an analysis of the relationship between sentiment (as per annotation) of tweets and tweet meta-data, 2) a validation of observed relationships between sentiment and meta-data by using additional tweets from users in benchmark data annotated with sentiment using a baseline classifier, 3) using the meta-data of tweets along with tweet text content for predicting sentiment, 4) a system called Meta-data Enhanced Sentiment Classification (MESC) for efficiently incorporating meta-data-based sentiment information of a tweet into existing text-based classifiers in a model-agnostic way, and 5) demonstrating the use of standard sentiment classification datasets for non-text-based sentiment analysis, thereby providing a baseline to compare other work against. The code reproducing this work as well as additional supplementary analysis is available at:
https://github.com/napsternxg/TwitterSentimentBenchmarks

2 BACKGROUND

Achieving high accuracy rates for sentiment classification is challenging, especially for social media data. This is evident from the top accuracy rates of state of the art systems, which are often below 90% for movie reviews [8, 23], and even lower for Twitter data [1, 15–18, 22]. One possible reason for this effect is the occasionally implicit assumption that the sentiment of a post is fully conveyed in the text; disregarding the text's context. Furthermore, sentiment classification models based on text do not necessarily perform well when applied across domains [13] due to factors such as diverse language use, concept evolution, and concept drift [11]. Recently, there has been an interest in quantifying the distribution of sentiment in a given collection of tweets [5, 15]. This topic deals with the focus of earlier studies on using aggregates of sentiment distributions to model changes in peopleâĂŹs mood[3], election results [25], reviews [2], and the stock market [3]. Our approach is methodologically closest to the research by Tan and colleagues [24], who used the full network of user follower, friend, and user mention along with the tweet text to infer the sentiment of tweets by using a computationally expensive graphical model. Our approach differs from that in several ways; for example, we only conduct analyses at the aggregate level of user and tweet meta-data, and our method can more easily be plugged into existing systems where text-based sentiment classification is already implemented.

3 DATA

Most existing sentiment datasets categorize the data into three classes, namely negative, neutral, and positive. We use the same set of labels for our analysis, and only consider datasets annotated with those labels. Additionally, we also consider a different set of binary class labels to identify if tweets are opinionated (either positive or negative) or non-opinionated (neutral). Furthermore, we selected only datasets with tweet IDs for each tweet label. This is important for collecting user and tweet-level meta-data using the Twitter API. Finally, to infer any meaningful relationship between meta-data and sentiment labels, we want to avoid any dataset specific idiosyncrasies in annotation and tweet distribution. We address this bias mitigation need by using sentiment labeled datasets from various

time periods, on different topics, and labeled by using different annotation guidelines and interfaces (but still the same classes). Using this approach, we hope to infer general relationships between tweet meta-data and sentiment labels after pooling the selected eligible datasets.

Based on our above-mentioned criteria, we identified six high quality, publicly available datasets as eligible for our analysis. The first dataset (referred to as SemEval) is from the recurring Twitter sentiment classification task of SemEval [15, 18, 22], and includes all training, development, and test data from 2013 throughout 2016. We only consider the data for the tasks where the goal was to classify tweet sentiment as either negative, neutral, or positive. The second dataset is a large collection of multilingual tweets from European countries from a study by Mozetič and colleagues [14]. We only work with the English tweets from this dataset. This dataset is available on the CLARIN data repository and therefore referred to as Clarin. The next two datasets, namely, Airline and GOP, were generated on the Crowdflower platform and hosted on Kaggle[1]. These two datasets include crowd sourced sentiment annotations for tweets about various Airlines as well as the first GOP debate of 2016. The final two datasets come from Saif and colleagues [23], and are about the Obama-McCain debate (referred as Obama) and healthcare (referred as Healthcare).

Our analysis considers user-level and tweet-level meta-data. Since the Twitter terms of service do not allow for tweet data to be (re-)distributed, we collected the tweet JSON data using the Twitter API, and then merged these data with the labels provided in each dataset. For evaluating the effect of meta-data features on tweet classification, we consider a training, development, and test split of each dataset. For the SemEval dataset, we use the provided training, development, and test splits, while for the other datasets, we create training, development, and test splits using a 72%, 8%, and 20% ratio of the datasets. The frequency of instances across the various datasets, labels, and data splits is presented in Table 1. Furthermore, the aggregate distribution of instances across the datasets and labels is presented in Figure 1a. This figure shows that our datasetś sizes are distributed across three orders of magnitude: large datasets with numbers of instances around 40K-60K, which include SemEval and Clarin, followed by smaller datasets, which are Airline and GOP, and finally, the smallest dataset of around 2K instances, namely Obama and Healthcare.

A major strength of the set of datasets that we consider is its temporal diversity, with tweet instances ranging from 2008 to 2016 (Figure 1). Both SemEval and Clarin were collected over lengthy time-periods (SemEval during 2011-16, Clarin during 2013-15) [14, 18]. However, the English tweets in the Clarin dataset are limited to 2014. The Healthcare dataset spans seven months between 2009-2010. The Airline dataset entails 2 days (2015), and the GOP (2015) and Obama (2008) datasets span 1 day each. All other datasets cover a shorter duration. A possible limitation with existing research on Twitter sentiment classification is the analysis of tweets from a specific period, which may result in a failure to capture trends across years as well as in overfitting on trends from a specific period. Using multiple datasets in this study aims at mitigating this issue.

---

[1]https://www.kaggle.com/crowdflower/datasets

Table 1: Distribution of the instances across datasets, labels, and data splits.

Dataset	Train			Development			Test			Total
Labels	Negative	Neutral	Positive	Negative	Neutral	Positive	Negative	Neutral	Positive	
Airline	5,515	1,843	1,467	613	205	163	1,532	512	408	12,258
Clarin	11,485	19,418	13,496	1,276	2,158	1,500	3,191	5,394	3,749	61,667
GOP	4,230	1,818	1,173	471	202	130	1,175	505	326	10,030
Healthcare	834	378	321	93	42	36	232	106	89	2,131
Obama	715	707	455	80	79	50	199	197	126	2,608
SemEval	4,313	13,031	11,405	479	1,448	1,268	1,198	3,620	3,169	39,931

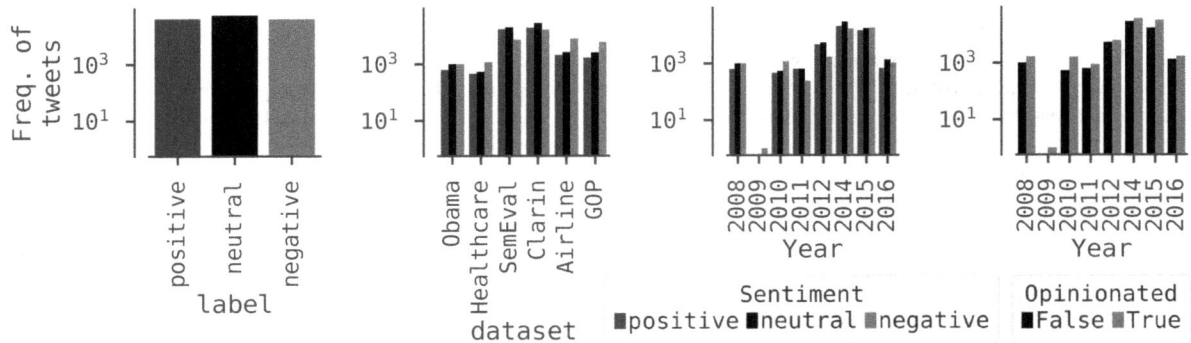

Figure 1: Frequency of sentiment labels across datasets and years. Opinionated tweet are either positive or negative.

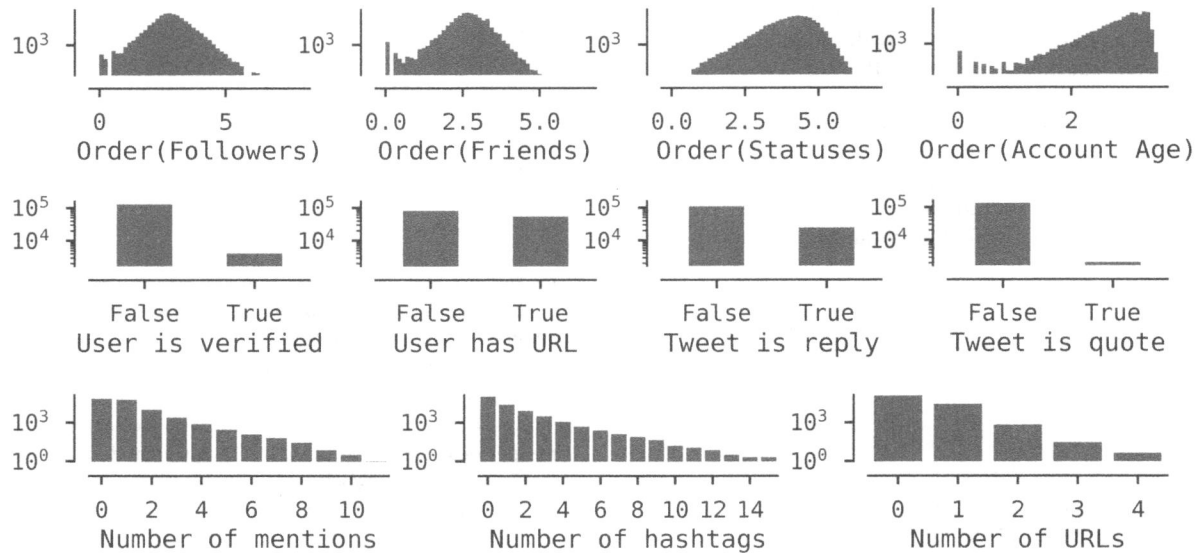

Figure 2: Frequency of user-level and tweet-level meta-data. $Order(x) = \log_{10}(x)$

For each tweet instance in our dataset, we extract a) user-level, and b) tweet-level meta-data from each tweet's JSON files. User meta-data includes number of statuses, followers, and friends, user account age (in days) based on account creation date and tweet creation date, if the user account is verified, and if the user profile has a URL. Tweet meta-data includes number of mentions, URLs, and hashtags, if the tweet is a retweet, and if the tweet quotes another tweet.

Since the distribution of the user-level meta-data is highly skewed and the tail of this distribution extends to large values, we transform the values by using a log transform with base 10, capturing their order. This allows our analysis to be robust to changes in meta-data values for user accounts over time as the log value changes are gradual compared to raw count changes. A distribution of the user and tweet meta-data is shown in Figure 2. Finally, a major advantage of jointly considering multiple datasets is that they are freer from selection and annotation biases than single sets with respect to the properties we are studying. It is common practice to perform the annotation task using only the text of the tweet [16], hence any bias in annotation because of user-level meta-data features being studied is less likely. We do acknowledge that the actual original tweet collections might still feature multiple types of sampling biases.

4 METHODS

In the following sections, we describe our methods for analyzing the relationship of sentiment with user and tweet level meta-data.

4.1 Relationship between sentiment and user meta-data

We define the following properties of a user and the respective measurement of these properties from the user meta-data:

(1) **Activity level** is measured in terms of the number of statuses posted by the user.
(2) **Social status** of a user is defined as the amount of incoming connections to the user on the platform, and measured as the number of followers of the user.
(3) **Social interest** of a user is defined as the amount of outgoing connections user make on the platform. The Twitter API defines this measure as the number of friends of a user. We measure it as the number of users that a user follows.
(4) **Account age** is measured as the number of days that the account has existed until the user posted a given tweet.
(5) **Profile authenticity** is measured using Twitter specific information, such as presence of a URL in the user profile, as well as the Twitter-provided verified user tag. This is a categorical measure.

As mentioned earlier, each numeric measure was analyzed using its order instead of the raw count. The order is defined as $f(x) = \log_{10}(1 + x)$, where x denotes the quantity being measured. We consider the order instead of the absolute value of the measure to prevent the effect of outliers on our analysis. We study the relationship between the sentiment of a tweet and its user-level meta-data using the log odds ratio (logOR) of the tweet belonging to a given class. Specifically, the log odds ratio of the correct class $C = 1$, for a meta-data value, $X = x$, relative to the meta-data value, $X = x_0$, is given as $logOR(x) = \ln(\frac{P(C=1|X=x)}{P(C=0|X=x)} / \frac{P(C=1|\bar{X}=x_0)}{P(C=0|X=x_0)})$. For the empirical analysis, the numeric attributes are partitioned into equal sized bins, and x_0 refers to the central bin. To investigate the interactive effect of correlated user meta-data features, we examine the relationship between the ratio of the numeric user meta-data features and the log odds ratio for a given class.

4.2 Relationship between sentiment and tweet meta-data

The tweet-level meta-data capture certain content properties of tweets. The placement of URLs, mentions, and hashtags can be aimed at providing evidence, shout-outs, and topical information, respectively. Furthermore, whether a tweet is a reply or quotes an existing status can provide an additional signal for the sentiment prediction. We study the relationship between the tweet-level meta-data features and sentiment class in the same way for the user-meta-data features.

4.3 Meta-data model

We use the user-level and tweet-level meta-data-based features to model the log odds of a tweet belonging to a specific class. We consider three settings: 1) only user-level meta-data features, 2) only tweet-level meta-data features, and 3) a linear combination of user and tweet-level meta-data features. We model the log odds of the tweet belonging to a given sentiment class by conditioning on all user/tweet/user+tweet level meta-data features. Numeric features are log transformed as described above. This is done by parameterizing a logistic regression model per class label; using a linear combination of the meta-data features. Based on the empirical relationship between the log odds and the meta-data features, certain features (e.g. social status, social influence, and activity level) are parametrized using an additional quadratic term. Models are fit on the aggregate of all datasets. We refer to the model with user and tweet meta-data features as the meta-data model.

4.4 MESC - Meta-data Enhanced Sentiment Classification

In this section, we describe our MESC system. The goal of this system is to seamlessly allow existing text-based classification systems to utilize meta-data-based attributes for enhancing the classification performance of existing text-based classifiers. We hypothesize that the sentiment class probabilities from the meta-data-based models can be used to enhance the prediction accuracy of text-based classifiers for social media texts. The MESC system runs through the following steps:

(1) Get the score (can be log probabilities or SVM score) for each sentiment class from the text-based model (**text model**).
(2) Get the score (can be log probabilities or SVM score) for each sentiment class from the meta-data model (**meta model**).
(3) Train a multinomial logistic regression model (**joint model**) using the class-based scores from the text model and the meta model as the only features.
(4) The final sentiment of the tweet is the one predicted by the joint model.

The framework described above considers the text model and meta-data model as black-box models, and is independent of the features used to train these models.

5 RESULTS

In this section, we describe the results obtained using our analysis methods.

5.1 Relationship between sentiment and user meta-data

The relationship between the log odds ratio of a tweet belonging to a given class based on various meta-data features is shown in Figure 3.

First, we discuss the correlation between a tweet user's activity level (order of statuses) with the sentiment label. We observe positive linear trend in the log odds ratio of a tweet being neutral with the activity level of its users. This might be partially explained by the fact that many of the accounts with high numbers of statuses are corporate or organizational accounts, e.g., @AmazonHelp, which has posted 1.25M statuses. These accounts might be less likely to engage in opinionated conversations. However, the relationship for low activity levels is highly variable, suggesting higher sentiment diversity in low activity users. Additionally, we observed that the overall relationship between activity and sentiment also holds for each of the individual datasets. Furthermore, tweets from users with mean activity level are more likely to be opinionated. Amongst the activity levels of opinionated users, we observe a quadratic relationship between the tweet being labeled as positive and the user having more than 10 tweets (order 1). This suggests that these median activity level users are more likely to tweet with positive sentiment, compared to others. However, no such trend is seen for the negative class, where the downward trend plateaus after the median activity level.

Second, we consider the effect of the user's social status (the order of the number of followers of the user) on predicting the sentiment of the tweet. Figure 3a shows a strong quadratic trend across all classes for this feature. Tweets from high follower accounts are more likely to be more neutral than opinionated.

Third, we examine the relationship between tweet sentiment and the users social interest (as quantified by the order of the number of followers of the user). Figure 3a shows a strong quadratic relationship between both variables for the positive class. Furthermore, as the order of number of friends increases, the tweets from those users are less likely to be neutral, and more likely to be negative after crossing the median value. This might reflect that users with extreme social interest (as defined in this paper, i.e., either very low or very high order of number of users they follow) are less likely to post positive tweets, while the average social interest users might be more likely to express positive sentiments.

Fourth, the account age significantly correlates with the sentiment classes: older accounts tend to post less positive or neutral tweets, and are more likely to post negative tweets. This might reflect veteran users who criticize issues or actively take part in social media conversations rather than just sharing neutral tweets.

Fifth, we study the user meta-data features that reflect profile authenticity (results shown in Figure 3b). We found that the presence of a URL in the user's profile is correlated with user postings being more neutral or positive, while the lack of a URL reflects a higher likelihood of negative tweets. Similarly, verified users are more likely to post neutral tweets compared to non-verified users. Both findings suggest that user authenticity is related to opinionated tweeting behavior. This trend might suggest that non-authentic users are more likely to share negatively perceived posts, while authentic profiles share more positive and neutral posts.

Finally, to test for the correlation of features, we further examined the Pearson correlation between the numeric features. We observe a positive correlation between measures of social status and social interest. We also observe a low positive correlation between social activity and social status. Based on this insight, we further examine the relationship between the sentiment class with the ratio of the numeric user-level meta-data features. These quantities are provided in Figure 4.

We found a strong relationship between the order of ratio of statuses and friends across all sentiment classes. Specifically, the log odds of neutral sentiment increases as the order of the ratio increases, while it decreases for negative sentiment. This reflects that for low order ratio neutral tweets are less likely compared to high order ratio. This may suggest that users with a high number of statuses compared to their number of friends are mostly sharing neutral (non-opinionated) content (like the @AmazonHelp account mentioned before).

5.2 Relationship between sentiment and tweet meta-data

We now turn to the relationship between tweet sentiment and tweet-level meta-data (Figure 3b). A distinct pattern can be seen between the number of URLs and the sentiment class: as the number of URLs increases, the probability of the tweet being neutral also increases. This might be partially accounted for by the fact that news agencies or blogging services share the URL of their content via Twitter. This results in most of these tweets being of neutral sentiment. Furthermore, the presence of a URL in non-neutral tweets is more likely to reflect a positive tweet. We also observe a decline in the probability of a negative tweet with an increase in the number of user mentions in a tweet. However, Figure 6b shows that tweets that are replies or direct quotes are more likely to be negative than neutral or positive.

5.3 Analysis with additional user tweets

The analyses up here have focused on sentiment-annotated data where the original annotators used the text of a given tweet to provide a sentiment label. One valid criticism of studying correlations between user meta-data and sentiment is that a tweet may exhibit multiple sentiments. However, in this study, we are only interested in the most common patterns of relationships between sentiments of tweets and its meta-data. Furthermore, we are not interested in causal analyses, but in the correlation between sentiment and meta-data features. More specifically, our current analysis is only reflective of the expected and most likely correlation of a user or tweet and the meta-data.

We conduct an additional set of experiments, this time based on data from all 110,388 users in our dataset and collect their most recent 200 tweets (for 98% of the users we were able to collect more than 190 tweets). The choice of the number of recent tweets was made to reduce the computational complexity of processing the data. We collected around 20 million tweets from the users in our dataset. Since this data was not annotated with sentiment, we decided to annotate it with a highly accurate lexicon and rule-based sentiment analysis system tailored for Twitter data (Vader Sentiment) [7]. Once the sentiment labels were assigned, we conducted the same

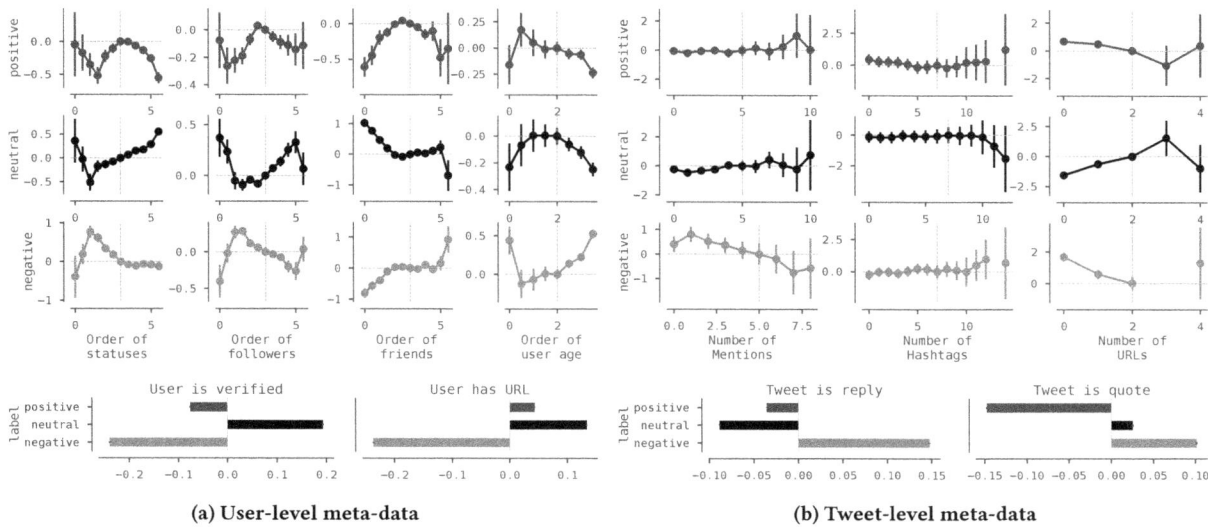

(a) User-level meta-data

(b) Tweet-level meta-data

Figure 3: Meta-data features vs. sentiment classes. Y-axis in top plots and X-axis in bottom plots, is log-odds ratio, with respect to point at dashed lines.

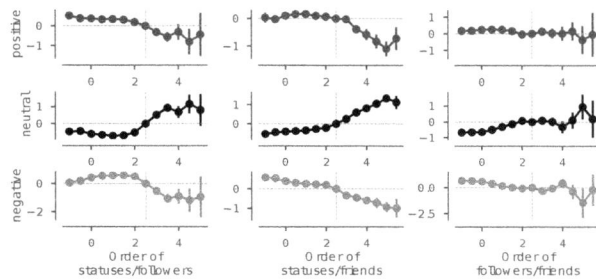

Figure 4: Ratio of user meta-data features vs. sentiment

analyses as before for the various meta-data feature categories. Our results are presented in Figure 5.

Among categorical attributes, the observed trends are consistent with our findings (Figure 3) for user-level attributes except for the correlation between positive sentiment and the user profile having a URL (see Figure 5a). For the latter case, the results show a reversal in the correlation, but this can be attributed to the low correlation in our original analysis. For tweet quotes, we see quite a different trend for the positive and negative label, which is likely to be caused by the classifier inaccuracy. Similar patterns persist for the numerical attributes: we observe similar but more noisy (compared to the human annotated data) patterns for all numerical user meta-data (Figure 5b). Note that these plots differ in the log odds ratio values from previous plots because of the selection of different baseline values. Another important point is the general trend for each of the curves, which are similar to those observed in the analysis based on the annotated data. Finally, we found that the patterns of ratio of user-level meta-data from our original data analysis are persistent in this version of the data. Figure 5c shows that the trends are similar to those observed in the original data,

with the exception of neutral sentiment for the statuses/followers plot.

5.4 Meta-data model

First, we consider the aggregated effect of using all user-level meta-data features in modeling the probability of a given sentiment of a tweet. Table 2 shows the model parameters for each sentiment class. The model parameters confirm the observation of high user activity levels being correlated with higher odds of neutral sentiment and low odds of negative or neutral sentiment (Figure 3a). Similarly, average activity levels are associated with a higher probability of positive as well as negative sentiments. Similarly, the relationships for social interest are also consistent with the earlier observation that greater social interest is related to more negative tweet sentiment. Additionally, we observe that the coefficients of social status are very small and not particularly significant for all sentiment classes. Furthermore, the strong relationship between profile authenticity and sentiment class holds true across all three sentiment classes. This confirms the earlier observation that profile authenticity might be correlated with tweet sentiment.

Second, we model all tweet-level meta-data measures (like the process used for the user meta-data) to study their cumulative effect on the odds of each sentiment class. Table 2 shows the model coefficients for each sentiment class. This model confirms our empirical observations: high numbers of URLs increase the probability of a neutral sentiment, while decreasing the probability of negative and positive sentiment. This effect is larger for negative sentiment. However, the trend is reversed for the number of user mentions. The tweet-level meta-data model associates large number of mentions with slightly higher odds of negative sentiment compared to positive and neutral sentiment. Furthermore, we observe a new pattern in the number of hashtags and the sentiment classes, indicating that higher numbers of hashtags are related to more negative sentiment.

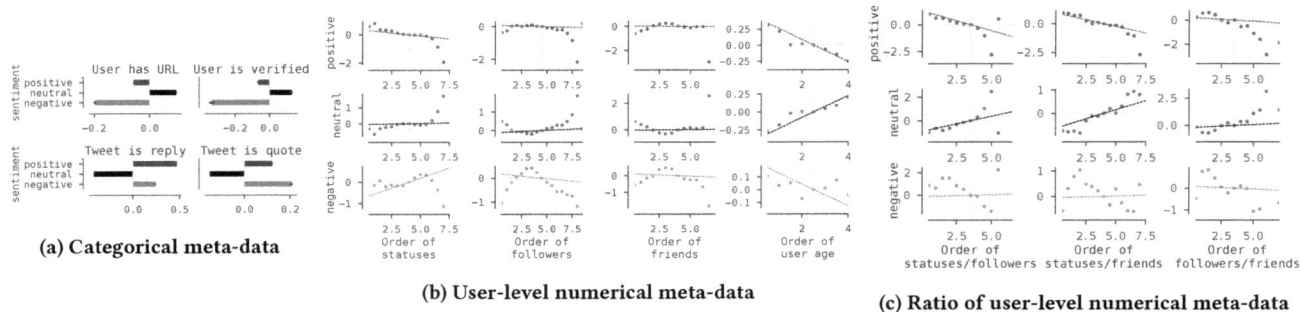

(a) Categorical meta-data

(b) User-level numerical meta-data

(c) Ratio of user-level numerical meta-data

Figure 5: Meta-data features vs. sentiment classes using recent 200 tweets for each user in the data. Sentiment predicted using VADER Sentiment [7]. X-axis in 5a, and Y-axis in 5b and 5c are log-odds ratio, with respect to point at the dashed lines.

Next, we consider the joint effect of the user and tweet-level meta-data on modelling the probability of the sentiment classes. Table 2 shows the coefficients of the joint model per class. We observe that the effects of the profile authenticity remain quite close to its value in the user meta-data models. We make the same observation for the activity levels, social interest effects, and the tweet meta-data measures. Overall, we observe that after controlling for all other factors, social status is less correlated with any of the sentiment classes.

5.5 Evaluation of the MESC system

In this section, we evaluate our MESC (Meta-data Enhanced Sentiment Classification) system using a simple text-based as well as our meta-data-based sentiment classifier. For the text model, we consider a unigram bag-of-words (BOW) model, where each word was lower-cased. We removed all user mentions, hashtags, and URLs from the tweet text. Finally, we use the TF-IDF (term-frequency * inverse-document frequency) weight for each unigram as the feature of each tweet. The text model is trained using a multinomial logistic regression, which is suitable for modelling the predicted probabilities for each sentiment class. For the meta model, we trained a multinomial logistic regression classifier using the user+tweet meta model features described above. Finally, the joint model uses a linear combination of the class scores (log probabilities) from the text and the meta model, as well as the pairwise products between the scores from the text and the meta model. Evaluation of sentiment classification was done using the overall accuracy, macro-averaged value for precision, recall, and F1 score. Table 3 shows that the joint model results in significant gains over the text-based model on all the datasets. The gain is especially evident for the Healthcare, GOP, and SemEval datasets, where the F1 score of the joint model on the test data increases by 8.5%, 4.2% and 1.9%, respectively. The lack of significant improvement on the Clarin dataset is probably because the simple text-based model is already performing at the level of inter annotator agreement between the tweets as reported in [14]. Finally, we studied the effect of using the joint model for quantifying the distribution of tweets. For this analysis, we only considered the test dataset, and compared the true class distribution to the predicted distribution of classes from the various models using Kullback-Leibler (KL) divergence [9] (a standard measure for measuring the distance between probability

distributions) as used in prior research [5]. Table 3 shows that the distributions produced by the joint model is closer to the true distribution compared to the text-based model. The overall evaluation of the models on the test data is presented in Table 3. We observe that the recall and F1 scores of the joint model are consistently higher than for the text model (by 0.5-4%), however, there is a slight dip in precision and accuracy. The lower precision and accuracy, whereas higher recall and F1, for the text joint models compared to text-based models reflects the ability of the joint models to correctly predict a larger proportion of labels at the cost of increasing the mistakes on these predictions.

6 DISCUSSION AND CONCLUSION

We have presented an analysis of the relationship between various meta-data features and the sentiment of tweets. Our findings suggest that certain user characteristics, such as their activity levels, profile authenticity, and the amount of profiles the users follow, can be highly correlated with the sentiment labels of tweets. Our proposed approach for integrating sentiment information correlated with meta-data into existing text-based classifiers results in a consistent increase in evaluation performance for sentiment classification and quantification tasks. We believe that this approach of using the meta-data-based sentiment correlation information of the tweets can serve as a prior for machine learning, which helps to improve the classification performance of text-based systems. This may be especially useful in cases where the tweet text has a high out of vocabulary (OOV) token rate. One major limitation of our approach is the usage of linear and pairwise combinations of prediction scores from the base model as well as the meta-data-based model. Although this approach results in a simple combination of models, more sophisticated approaches using deep neural networks can also be used for improving the prediction accuracy for the joint models. Furthermore, in our current experiments we used a standard unigram-based sentiment prediction model as a text model. It can be improved by using more sophisticated text classification algorithms based on current state of the art practices, thereby allowing us to further investigate the benefits of using meta-data models.

Another limitation of our analysis is the availability of labeled corpora that are annotated based on the text of the tweet. A more rigorous evaluation of our method could be done by annotating

Table 2: Feature weights for models of tweet sentiment based on user and tweet metadata. (*) marked coefficients are statistically NOT significant ($p > 0.005$)

Model types	User			Tweet			User + Tweet		
Labels	Negative	Neutral	Positive	Negative	Neutral	Positive	Negative	Neutral	Positive
Intercept	-0.79	0.02 *	-1.78	-0.85	-0.56	-0.69	-0.55	-0.36	-1.54
Activity level	-0.75	0.31	0.47	-	-	-	-0.72	0.28	0.47
Activity level ^2	0.08	-0.01 *	-0.08	-	-	-	0.08	-0.01 *	-0.08
Social status	-0.11 *	-0.09 *	0.17	-	-	-	-0.13	-0.04 *	0.13
Social status^2	0.00 *	0.01 *	-0.01 *	-	-	-	0.01 *	0.00 *	-0.00 *
Social interest	0.51	-0.6	0.34	-	-	-	0.27	-0.36	0.26
Social interest^2	-0.05	0.08	-0.07	-	-	-	-0.02 *	0.04	-0.05
Account age	0.34	-0.17	-0.13	-	-	-	0.37	-0.2	-0.13
User has URL	-0.32	0.22	0.07	-	-	-	-0.22	0.1	0.1
User verified	-0.11 *	0.26	-0.21	-	-	-	-0.15	0.29	-0.21
# Mentions	-	-	-	0.3	-0.07 *	-0.22	0.13	0.08 *	-0.23
# Hashtags	-	-	-	0.73	-0.22	-0.47	0.78	-0.24	-0.5
# URLs	-	-	-	-4.09	3.35	-0.73	-3.94	3.19	-0.67
Is reply	-	-	-	0.05 *	0.05	-0.1	0.03 *	0.06	-0.09
Is quote	-	-	-	1.17	-0.75	-0.05 *	1.1	-0.68	-0.05 *

Table 3: Evaluation scores of various models on the test split across all datasets. (Acc.=accuracy, P=precision, R=recall, F1=F1 score, KLD=KL divergence). Acc., P, R, F1 are measured as percentages and higher score means better. For KLD lower means better.

Dataset	Model	Acc.	P	R	F1	KLD
Airline	meta	63.9	61.1	36.8	32.8	0.663
	text	80.0	78.3	69.0	72.4	0.026
	joint	80.3	76.6	72.0	**74.0**	0.005
Clarin	meta	45.7	42.1	40.9	37.8	0.238
	text	64.1	64.5	62.2	62.9	0.012
	joint	64.1	64.0	63.0	**63.4**	0.000
GOP	meta	59.9	54.3	37.5	33.6	0.776
	text	66.4	63.7	51.4	53.6	0.111
	joint	65.6	59.9	56.5	**57.8**	0.006
Healthcare	meta	56.7	36.8	39.4	35.1	0.717
	text	64.2	71.3	49.5	51.0	0.233
	joint	65.6	61.6	58.3	**59.5**	0.007
Obama	meta	39.3	37.0	35.1	32.0	0.282
	text	61.5	64.8	59.7	60.9	0.030
	joint	62.3	63.2	61.6	**62.2**	0.002
SemEval	meta	47.0	31.0	36.2	33.0	0.845
	text	65.5	64.1	58.0	59.5	0.032
	joint	65.6	62.7	60.5	**61.4**	0.001

for complementing text-based sentiment analysis research of social media data, and the creation of standard datasets that capture these effects in detail. Finally, our results matter for the advancement of social media analytics: knowing expected tweet sentiments based on user-level meta-data enables a) the detection of outlier tweets, which may signal special relevance of individual data points, and b) the calibration of individual users within samples of multiple users. The second point can help to address a major issue with sampling biases for social media data, i.e., the normalization of individual users who have unexpectedly high or low sentiments in comparison to their user-level features. In classic survey research, identifying individual tendencies for responding in an overly positive or negative way is of high relevance, and such work can inform social media research. This paper offers a remedy for starting to fix this need. Finally, we provide code that can be used for reproducing the results along with supplementary analysis.

ACKNOWLEDGMENTS

This work was possible thanks to a Microsoft Azure Research Sponsorship awarded to the Shubhanshu Mishra. The views expressed in this paper are those of the authors. We would also like to thank Shadi Rezapour, Aseel Addawood, Ming Jiang, Chieh-Li Chin, and Ly Dinh from the iSchool at UIUC for their constructive feedback on this paper. We also thank the three anonymous reviewers for their feedback.

REFERENCES

[1] Ahmed Abbasi, Ammar Hassan, and Milan Dhar. 2014. Benchmarking Twitter Sentiment Analysis Tools. In *Proceedings of the Ninth International Conference on Language Resources and Evaluation (LREC'14)*. European Language Resources Association (ELRA), Reykjavik, Iceland. http://www.aclweb.org/anthology/L14-1406

[2] Sitaram Asur and Bernardo A. Huberman. 2010. Predicting the Future with Social Media. In *2010 IEEE/WIC/ACM International Conference on Web Intelligence and Intelligent Agent Technology*. IEEE, Toronto, Canada. https://doi.org/10.1109/wi-iat.2010.63

tweets based on both their meta-data and text content. This can help to better understand if the human annotators change their mind about the best fitting sentiment label when they also consider the meta-data of tweets. The methods we have described for studying correlation can also be applied to other social media corpora, such as Reddit or Wikipedia comments. We believe that our results can encourage the exploration of additional meta-data-based features

[3] Johan Bollen, Huina Mao, and Alberto Pepe. 2011. Modeling Public Mood and Emotion: Twitter Sentiment and Socio-Economic Phenomena. In *Proceedings of the Fifth International AAAI Conference on Weblogs and Social Media (ICWSM '11)*. AAAI, Barcelona, Spain. https://www.aaai.org/ocs/index.php/ICWSM/ICWSM11/paper/view/2826

[4] Rui Fan, Jichang Zhao, Yan Chen, and Ke Xu. 2014. Anger Is More Influential than Joy: Sentiment Correlation in Weibo. *PLOS ONE* 9, 10 (10 2014), 1–8. https://doi.org/10.1371/journal.pone.0110184

[5] W. Gao and F. Sebastiani. 2015. Tweet sentiment: From classification to quantification. In *2015 IEEE/ACM International Conference on Advances in Social Networks Analysis and Mining (ASONAM '15)*. IEEE, Paris, France, 97–104. https://doi.org/10.1145/2808797.2809327

[6] Alec Go, Richa Bhayani, and Lei Huang. 2009. Twitter Sentiment Classification using Distant Supervision. (2009). https://www.semanticscholar.org/paper/Twitter-Sentiment-Classification-using-Distant-Go-Bhayani/52e2bd533323ddf97073d034bae40a46eda55f34

[7] C. Hutto and Eric Gilbert. 2014. VADER: A Parsimonious Rule-Based Model for Sentiment Analysis of Social Media Text. In *Proceedings of the Eight International AAAI Conference on Weblogs and Social Media (ICWSM '14)*. AAAI, Ann Arbor, Michigan, USA. https://www.aaai.org/ocs/index.php/ICWSM/ICWSM14/paper/view/8109

[8] Yoon Kim. 2014. Convolutional Neural Networks for Sentence Classification. In *Proceedings of the 2014 Conference on Empirical Methods in Natural Language Processing (EMNLP '14)*. Association for Computational Linguistics, Doha, Qatar, 1746–1751. https://doi.org/10.3115/v1/D14-1181

[9] Richard A Leibler and S Kullback. 1951. On information and sufficiency. *Annals of Mathematical Statistics* 22, 1 (1951), 79–86.

[10] Bing Liu. 2011. *Opinion Mining and Sentiment Analysis*. Springer-Verlag Berlin Heidelberg, Berlin, Heidelberg. 459–526 pages. https://doi.org/10.1007/978-3-642-19460-3_11

[11] M. M. Masud, Q. Chen, L. Khan, C. Aggarwal, J. Gao, J. Han, and B. Thuraisingham. 2010. Addressing Concept-Evolution in Concept-Drifting Data Streams. In *2010 IEEE International Conference on Data Mining*. 929–934. https://doi.org/10.1109/ICDM.2010.160

[12] Shubhanshu Mishra, Sneha Agarwal, Jinlong Guo, Kirstin Phelps, Johna Picco, and Jana Diesner. 2014. Enthusiasm and support: alternative sentiment classification for social movements on social media. In *Proceedings of the 2014 ACM conference on WebScience (WebSci '14)*. ACM Press, Bloomington, Indiana, USA, 261–262. https://doi.org/10.1145/2615569.2615667

[13] Shubhanshu Mishra, Jana Diesner, Jason Byrne, and Elizabeth Surbeck. 2015. Sentiment Analysis with Incremental Human-in-the-Loop Learning and Lexical Resource Customization. In *Proceedings of the 26th ACM Conference on Hypertext & Social Media (HT '15)*. Guzelyurt, TRNC, Cyprus, 323–325. https://doi.org/10.1145/2700171.2791022

[14] Igor Mozetič, Miha Grčar, and Jasmina Smailović. 2016. Multilingual Twitter Sentiment Classification: The Role of Human Annotators. *PLOS ONE* 11, 5 (05 2016), 1–26. https://doi.org/10.1371/journal.pone.0155036

[15] Preslav Nakov, Alan Ritter, Sara Rosenthal, Fabrizio Sebastiani, and Veselin Stoyanov. 2016. SemEval-2016 Task 4: Sentiment Analysis in Twitter. In *Proceedings of the Tenth International Workshop on Semantic Evaluation (SemEval '16)*. Association for Computational Linguistics, Stroudsburg, PA, USA, 1–18. https://doi.org/10.18653/v1/S16-1001

[16] Preslav Nakov, Sara Rosenthal, Svetlana Kiritchenko, Saif M. Mohammad, Zornitsa Kozareva, Alan Ritter, Veselin Stoyanov, and Xiaodan Zhu. 2016. Developing a successful SemEval task in sentiment analysis of Twitter and other social media texts. *Language Resources and Evaluation* 50, 1 (jan 2016), 35–65. https://doi.org/10.1007/s10579-015-9328-1

[17] Preslav Nakov, Sara Rosenthal, Zornitsa Kozareva, Veselin Stoyanov, Alan Ritter, and Theresa Wilson. 2013. SemEval-2013 Task 2: Sentiment Analysis in Twitter. In *Proceedings of the Seventh International Workshop on Semantic Evaluation (SemEval '13)*. Association for Computational Linguistics, Atlanta, Georgia, USA, 312–320. http://www.aclweb.org/anthology/S13-2052

[18] Preslav Nakov, Sara Rosenthal, Zornitsa Kozareva, Veselin Stoyanov, Alan Ritter, and Theresa Wilson. 2013. SemEval-2013 Task 2: Sentiment Analysis in Twitter. In *Second Joint Conference on Lexical and Computational Semantics (*SEM), Volume 2: Proceedings of the Seventh International Workshop on Semantic Evaluation (SemEval '13)*. Association for Computational Linguistics, Atlanta, Georgia, USA, 312–320. http://www.aclweb.org/anthology/S13-2052

[19] Alexander Pak and Patrick Paroubek. 2010. Twitter as a Corpus for Sentiment Analysis and Opinion Mining. In *Proceedings of the Seventh conference on International Language Resources and Evaluation (LREC'10)*. European Languages Resources Association (ELRA), Valletta, Malta. http://www.aclweb.org/anthology/L10-1263

[20] Bo Pang and Lillian Lee. 2008. Opinion Mining and Sentiment Analysis. *Found. Trends Inf. Retr.* 2, 1-2 (Jan. 2008), 1–135. https://doi.org/10.1561/1500000011

[21] Bo Pang, Lillian Lee, and Shivakumar Vaithyanathan. 2002. Thumbs up? Sentiment Classification using Machine Learning Techniques. In *Proceedings of the 2002 Conference on Empirical Methods in Natural Language Processing (EMNLP '02)*. Philadelphia, PA, USA.

[22] Sara Rosenthal, Preslav Nakov, Svetlana Kiritchenko, Saif Mohammad, Alan Ritter, and Veselin Stoyanov. 2015. SemEval-2015 Task 10: Sentiment Analysis in Twitter. In *Proceedings of the 9th International Workshop on Semantic Evaluation (SemEval '15)*. Association for Computational Linguistics, Denver, Colorado, USA, 451–463. https://doi.org/10.18653/v1/S15-2078

[23] Richard Socher, Alex Perelygin, Jean Wu, Jason Chuang, Christopher D. Manning, Andrew Ng, and Christopher Potts. 2013. Recursive Deep Models for Semantic Compositionality Over a Sentiment Treebank. In *Proceedings of the 2013 Conference on Empirical Methods in Natural Language Processing (EMNLP '13)*. Association for Computational Linguistics, Seattle, Washington, USA, 1631–1642. http://www.aclweb.org/anthology/D13-1170

[24] Chenhao Tan, Lillian Lee, Jie Tang, Long Jiang, Ming Zhou, and Ping Li. 2011. User-level Sentiment Analysis Incorporating Social Networks. In *Proceedings of the 17th ACM SIGKDD International Conference on Knowledge Discovery and Data Mining (KDD '11) (KDD '11)*. ACM, San Diego, California, USA, 1397–1405. https://doi.org/10.1145/2020408.2020614

[25] Andranik Tumasjan, Timm Sprenger, Philipp Sandner, and Isabell Welpe. 2010. Predicting Elections with Twitter: What 140 Characters Reveal about Political Sentiment. In *Proceedings of the Fourth International AAAI Conference on Weblogs and Social Media (ICWSM '10)*. AAAI, Washington, DC, USA. https://www.aaai.org/ocs/index.php/ICWSM/ICWSM10/paper/view/1441

[26] Soroush Vosoughi, Helen Zhou, and deb roy. 2015. Enhanced Twitter Sentiment Classification Using Contextual Information. In *Proceedings of the 6th Workshop on Computational Approaches to Subjectivity, Sentiment and Social Media Analysis*. Association for Computational Linguistics, Lisboa, Portugal, 16–24. https://doi.org/10.18653/v1/W15-2904

Mining and Forecasting Career Trajectories of Music Artists

Shushan Arakelyan
USC Information Sciences Institute
shushan@isi.edu

Fred Morstatter
USC Information Sciences Institute
fredmors@isi.edu

Margaret Martin
USC Information Sciences Institute
mart586@usc.edu

Emilio Ferrara
USC Information Sciences Institute
ferrarae@isi.edu

Aram Galstyan
USC Information Sciences Institute
galstyan@isi.edu

ABSTRACT

Many musicians, from up-and-comers to established artists, rely heavily on performing live to promote and disseminate their music. To advertise live shows, artists often use concert discovery platforms that make it easier for their fans to track tour dates. In this paper, we ask whether digital traces of live performances generated on those platforms can be used to understand career trajectories of artists. First, we present a new dataset we constructed by cross-referencing data from such platforms. We then demonstrate how this dataset can be used to mine and predict important career milestones for the musicians, such as signing by a major music label, or performing at a certain venue. Finally, we perform a temporal analysis of the bipartite artist-venue graph, and demonstrate that high centrality on this graph is correlated with success.

CCS CONCEPTS

• **Information systems** → **Data mining**; *Web mining*; • **Networks** → **Online social networks**; • **Human-centered computing** → **Collaborative and social computing**; • **Computing methodologies** → *Machine learning approaches*; *Network science*;

KEYWORDS

networks, art and music, multidisciplinary topics and applications

ACM Reference Format:
Shushan Arakelyan, Fred Morstatter, Margaret Martin, Emilio Ferrara, and Aram Galstyan. 2018. Mining and Forecasting Career Trajectories of Music Artists. In *HT '18: 29th ACM Conference on Hypertext and Social Media, July 9–12, 2018, Baltimore, MD, USA*. ACM, New York, NY, USA, 9 pages. https://doi.org/10.1145/3209542.3209554

1 INTRODUCTION

Live performances are a crucial part of the life of a music artist. According to a recent industry report,[1] the revenues from live performances in the US have grown from \$8.72B in 2012 to \$9.94B in 2016, and are projected to reach almost \$12B by 2022. A recent study

---

[1] https://www.statista.com/statistics/491884/live-music-revenue-usa/

discovered a connection between live events and increased digital listenership [37] (which is the second highest source of income for a band after live performances). In light of this, it becomes increasingly more important for artists to be able to understand what milestones matter to accomplish the dream of a professional career: playing at top venues goes hand-in-hand with getting more digital listeners, which in turn may increase their likelihood of being signed with major music labels.

In this work, we aim to determine whether it is possible to model and predict these career trajectories under the emerging framework of *Science of Success* [9, 14]: recent work studying how careers in different fields, as well as individual and team success, can be predicted early by leveraging records of performance from digital traces. This data-driven framework has been applied to domains as diverse as education and academia [17, 21, 35], (e)sports [7, 8, 34, 39, 42], social media [3, 13, 24, 36], culture [2, 40], and even the entertainment industry [29, 33].

In light of these promising results, we pose the question: is it possible to find open data to understand and forecast careers and success in the music industry? To accommodate the increasing demand of music artists to get their message out to their fans, specialized sites like *Songkick* and *Discogs* have sprung up to create centralized repositories of music events and music artists. These sites contain rich metadata about the artists themselves as well as the concerts they perform. They allow the artists to attract interests in their concerts. Indirectly, this goldmine also allows researchers to model the music industry dynamics.

Research Problem

In this paper, we are interested in the problem of characterizing and understanding the career trajectories of the artists across different genres. Toward this goal, we analyze a large-scale longitudinal data of musical events occurring at various venues worldwide.

Specifically, we address the following research questions:

(1) Is the choice of venues where an artist performs correlated with the eventual success of that artist (for a given definition of success)? If so, can we leverage those correlations to forecast success?
(2) Can we predict which venues an artist/band will perform based on the history of his/her/their past performances?
(3) How do we measure the relative importance of performances in specific venues and their impact on career trajectories, and how do we jointly characterize *influential* artists and venues?

Contributions of this Work

Our main contributions are summarized as follows:

- We construct and present a new dataset by collecting all of the artists and concerts from the *Songkick* platform, and supplement this dataset with information from *Discogs*, which contains more granular details about the artists—such as their discographies.[2]
- We define a measure of success based on whether an artist has signed a contract with one of the major music record labels, and propose a forecasting task to differentiate between career trajectories of artist based on this measure of success.
- We demonstrate the viability of forecasting future performances of artists, and therefore their success, based on the history of past performances.
- We propose a centrality measure suited for the bipartite artist-venue network and demonstrate that it correlates strongly with the venue reputation.

The rest of the paper is organized as follows. After describing related work in Section 2, we describe the dataset in Section 3 and provide its basic statistics in Section 4. In Section 5 we define three related tasks - forecasting artist success, predicting future events by artist at specific venues, and identifying influential artists and venues - describe our approach for addressing those tasks, and present results. We conclude the paper by summarizing our main findings in Section 6.

2 RELATED WORK

Quantifying and forecasting success refers to the broader body of work that attempts to discover the patterns and performance trajectories that correlate with certain desirable outcomes: from forecasting highly-cited academic authors and papers [20, 38] to predicting future Nobel Prize winners [25], from uncovering successful fund-raising campaigns [27], to early identifying the next top model [29], or movie box office hit [11]. The new field of *Science of Success* brings a strong data-driven perspective on applied forecasting problems set in the real world.

Judge et al. [18] postulated that career success has intrinsic cues, like the person's own perception of success and self-satisfaction, and extrinsic ones, like awards, recognition or achievements. Since judgments about success in a creative profession like music are unavoidably subjective, we don't consider intrinsic factors and focus on objectively observable career accomplishments only.

Music industry criteria called "traditional markers of artist success" [12], like performance opportunities, labels, charts, awards, sales of recorded music or airplay, provide us with a number of possible directions for defining success of music artists. However, digitization has shaken these traditional markers—digital music has been linked to fall in record sales, airplay and charts no longer adequately measure popularity, given numerous streaming services and listenership outside of them—views on YouTube and/or illegal file-sharing. Given this, some researchers look at the popularity of music artists on digital delivery platforms like Last.fm, and formulate a forecasting problem to predict new song hits from the early adoption patterns of music listeners [33].

Success in post-digital music world can still be adequately represented by contracts with major labels. Music record labels are still important players in the industry—even though theoretically digital technologies allow artists to perform production, promotion and sales on their own, practically this doesn't happen very often [26]. Hence, in this work, forecasting success is operationalized as predicting the artists that are going to be signed by a major music recording label. To the best of our knowledge, this is a novel formulation that has not been presented in the literature before.

From a methodological perspective, our work is rooted on a blend of machine learning and network science techniques. We focus in particular on a broad class of problems often referred to as *link mining* (a.k.a. *link prediction*). Link mining is the problem of discovering new (unforeseen) edges in a graph. Typical possible applications are either network reconstruction [10, 15], or modeling the evolution of a network [5, 19, 41]. One common operationalization of link prediction is finding pairs of nodes that have high probability of being connected. This often translates into measuring node similarities, as mentioned by Liben-Nowell and Kleinberg [23]. However, other authors [22] noted that using traditional link prediction on bipartite graphs is not straightforward and often produces counterintuitive results. In order to address this shortcoming, some authors proposed modified similarity metrics [22, 23], or used techniques from recommender systems, such as low-rank matrix factorization and collaborative filtering [1, 6], and supervised learning approaches [4, 30]. We follow the example of those authors and use collaborative filtering and recommender systems inspired methods to perform link prediction for our task. In the results section, we will show how to leverage *BiRank* [16]—a modification to the *PageRank* [28] algorithm that tunes it towards bipartite graphs—to measure and predict the popularity of the artists and venues.

3 DATASET

SONGKICK[3] is a concert-discovery platform that aims to link fans to artists' events. It contains information about over 6 million concerts (and other music events like festivals), the artist(s) that perform at each event, and the venue where each event takes place. The "gigography" of an artist is the term that Songkick uses to refer to all of that artist's events.

Songkick data can be accessed through their website or via their API, which allows querying any artist's gigography. Songkick is our main repository of information for music events.

DISCOGS[4] is a music database that contains cross-referenced discographies of artists and labels. Each recording, artist, or label in Discogs can be uniquely identified by their IDs. Discogs provides separate data dumps[5] for artists, labels, and recordings. We used recordings data dump from May 1, 2017 to obtain artist and label IDs associated with each release. This data dump contains more than 8 million recordings. Most of the recordings have information about their release dates, and thus allow tracking the history of releases with different labels for each artist.

---

[2]The dataset is available at https://github.com/shushanarakelyan/forecasting_success

[3]https://www.songkick.com/
[4]https://www.discogs.com/
[5]https://data.discogs.com/

3.1 Data Collection

Songkick does not provide a lookup directory of artists, nor there is a direct mechanism to get all gigographies. For getting Songkick artist IDs we queried artist names present in Discogs' recordings data dump. As a result, all of the artists in our dataset have at least one recording on Discogs. This can be either self-recorded or recorded under a contract with a music label. This strategy avoids introduction of bias towards artists that did not publish any recordings, which are therefore excluded from our analysis.

The Songkick API call returns a list of possibly relevant artists, allowing for some inexact name matching. We processed the API output to retain data on artists that exactly matched the Discogs artist name.

From this name match we obtained artist IDs, and used them for another round of API calls, to get the gigographies of each artist. For each concert in the gigography, we extracted the following information: ID, date, city, country, state (if applicable), latitude and longitude of the venue, venue ID and venue name, name of the event and its popularity score as calculated by Songkick.

For every event there is information about billing for each artist, i.e., whether that artist was a headliner or a support artist at the concert. However, we did not consider headliners and support artists separately in the analysis presented further.

Collected data was organized into separate artist, event, and venue data frames. Each artist is indexed by its Songkick and Discogs IDs. Venues and events are indexed by their Songkick IDs. There are also several lists of cross-references: mapping venues to the events that happened there, and events to the venues where they took place. A similar mapping is available for events and artists, and releases and artists.

3.2 Data Preprocessing

Due to the fact that the goal of Songkick is connecting fans to their favorite artists through concerts, the platform puts less relevance on events that occurred prior to their inception. Songkick was founded in 2007 and there is a noticeable increase in the number of artists that have their earliest concerts recorded on Songkick in 2007 or later (see Figure 2 in the next section). For the sake of data completeness, we focus only on artists that have their first record of performance in 2007 or later. By doing so, we aim to retain only the artists who used Songkick to inform their fans about upcoming events, thus avoiding the use of possibly incorrect backdated data.

In this paper we consider an artist that has one or more recordings with one of the major labels (a.k.a., "Big Three"/Four/Five/Six),[6] or their subsidiaries, "successful", we provide a more detailed explanation for this choice in Section 5.1. Conveniently, each music record label in Discogs has information about its sub-labels and its parent label, if such exist. This allowed tracking all subsidiaries of the major labels. We assume the first time an artist releases a recording with such a label to be the change point in their career. We are interested in researching the trajectory of artists before the change point and ideally being able to forecast the change point.

Finally, we wanted to make sure that we have enough data about successful artists in the early stage of their career. Thus, in the last preprocessing step, we removed every artist and venue that

---

[6] https://en.wikipedia.org/wiki/Record_label#Major_labels

Table 1: Some of the most frequent n-grams extracted from sequences of artists' performances. Double-sided arrows indicate that these routes are frequently found in the data in both directions.

Frequent routes that artists follow
San Diego ↔ Los Angeles ↔ SF Bay Area ↔ Portland ↔ Seattle
Portland ↔ Seattle ↔ Boise ↔ Salt Lake City ↔ Denver
Chicago ↔ Toronto ↔ Montreal ↔ Boston/Cambridge ↔ New York
Washington ↔ Philadelphia ↔ New York ↔ Boston/Cambridge
London ↔ Birmingham ↔ Manchester ↔ Glasgow
Brisbane ↔ Sydney ↔ Melbourne ↔ Adelaide
Austin ↔ Houston ↔ New Orleans ↔ Atlanta

has less than 10 concerts associated with them before the change point. This also takes care of venues that may have been used for occasional events, or artists with short-lived careers.

4 STATISTICS

In the following we provide some statistical analysis of our dataset. The dataset contains 645,507 concerts, 13,912 artists, and 11,428 venues, collected for the time frame between 2007 and 2017. Artists in the dataset are associated with 39,641 distinct record labels, 286 of which are major labels, or their subsidiaries. One condition to be labeled as a "successful" artist in our study is to have recorded at least one album under any of these 286 recording labels.

Figure 1 depicts distributions of the number of concerts per artist and number of concerts per venue. Both distributions are very broad and heavy tailed, with few active artists and venues hosting many events, and a very large set of artists and venues associated with very few events.

In Figure 2 we show the dynamics of the number of events and number of artists from 1987 to 2017. As already mentioned, there is a significant increase in the number of artists that have their earliest concerts recorded on Songkick in 2007 or later. From Figure 2 it can be seen that the total number of concerts per year peaked in 2010.

Next, we look at the geographic distribution of venues in the dataset. There are 63 different countries with at least one event, which, for the mostÂăpart, are in North America and Europe. Almost half of all venues are located in the United States, where also more than half of all concerts happened. The second highest in both number of concerts and number of venues is the UK. Figure 3 demonstrates distribution of venues and concerts in the 10 most frequently occurring countries.

If we look at more granular information about geolocation of artists' performances we can get an insight on actual spatial trajectories of artists. Particularly, we can look for frequent subsequences among the sequences of performances of all artists. As displayed in Table 1, n-grams of length 4 and 5 show some frequent routes of

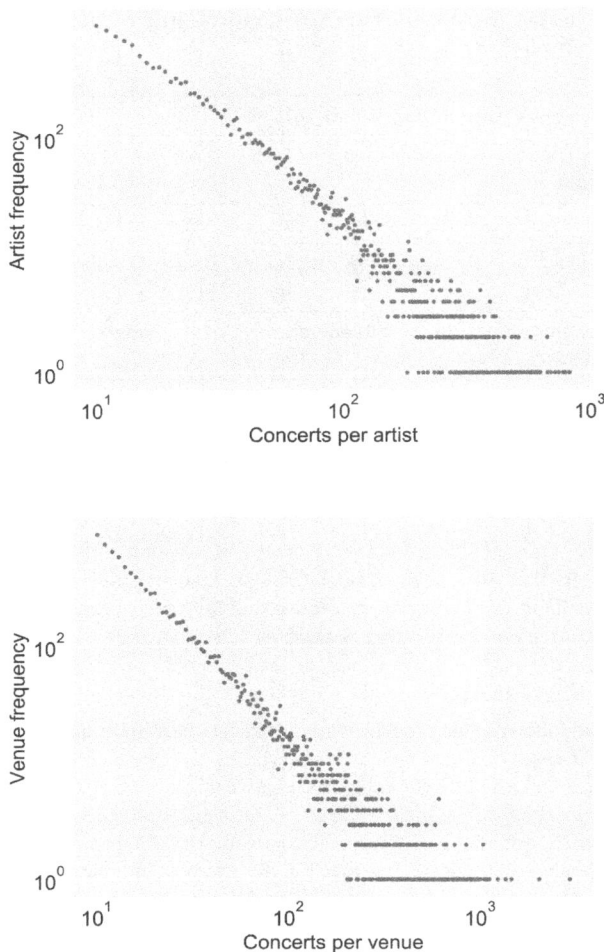

Figure 1: Heavy-tailed distributions of the number of concerts per artist (upper panel) and per venue (lower panel).

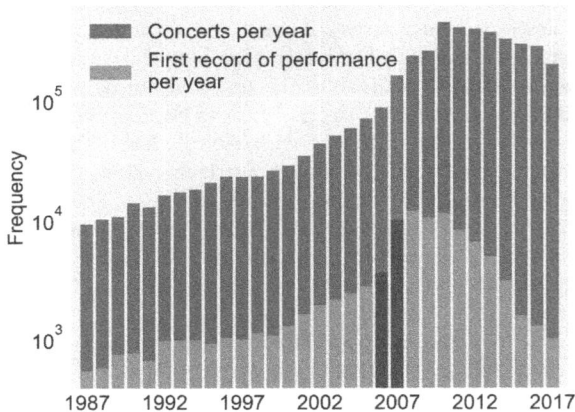

Figure 2: Total number of concerts per year in the dataset and number of artists that first appear on Songkick in a given year. The red bars illustrate the sudden change from 2006 to 2007 in the number of artists that first appeared on Songkick during those years. This can be explained by the fact that Songkick was founded in 2007. Data before 1987 are very limited thus not included in this illustration.

cities that artists take while touring. Following the distribution of the venues and concerts in the dataset, most frequent routes mostly include US cities. As demonstrated in Table 1, frequent routes contain clear patterns of artists performing in big cities on their way, while travelling from North to South or from East to West, etc.

5 ANALYSIS AND RESULTS

To better illustrate the idea that the music artist career trajectory can be predicted from artist-venue interactions we formulated the following 3 tasks, discussed next:

- Task 1: Forecasting artist success;
- Task 2: Event prediction;
- Task 3: Joint discovery of influential artists and venues.

In the next subsections, we describe each of those tasks in more details, elaborate on our approach for addressing them, and present our results.

5.1 Task 1: Forecasting Artist Success

Due to the nature of the partnership between artists and record companies, the bigger the recording label the more resources and opportunities it has to offer for its artists. Artists, nurtured by labels, have the chance to develop their sound, their craft, and their careers. Besides, record companies facilitate introductions to world-class producers, writers, and other performers, which can determine careers and bring huge rewards.

The recording industry has been marked by concentration and centralization for a while now. During the phase of consolidation in 1970s, most of the major labels were acquired by very few umbrella corporations or music groups. The Beatles, Frank Sinatra, Pink Floyd and even Maria Callas found prominence through those major record labels. From 1988 till 2012 the number of major record companies has decreased from six to three, as some of them got absorbed by the others. The remaining three major music groups, or the *Big Three* (Sony BMG, Universal Music Group, and Warner Music Group), have held a large share of the world music production since 2012.

Because of the influence and patronizing that the major labels provide, we consider artists that have a recording with either the parent major label, or one of its subsidiaries, as *successful*. We set to see if the rise to success can be predicted from a sequence of performances. Our goal in this task is, therefore, to identify successful artists from their career trajectories.

Ideally, we want to be able to identify such artists in a post-hoc manner. In other words, we want to detect the change that will lead

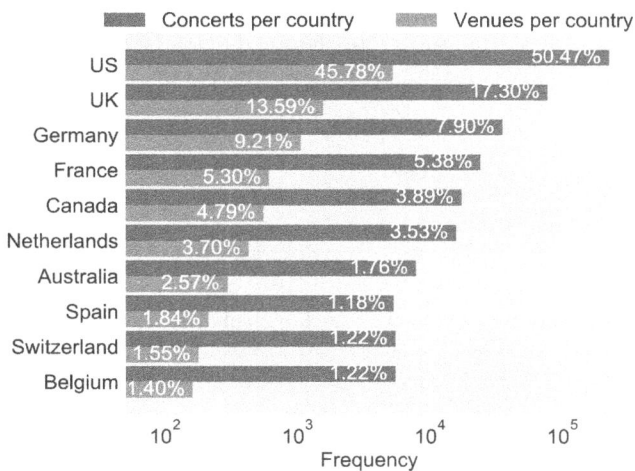

Figure 3: Log-scale distribution of concert frequencies in (i) the top 10 most active countries, and (ii) the number of distinct venues in those countries. A disproportionate preference toward English-speaking countries can be observed in the Songkick data, with United States, United Kingdom, and Australia cumulatively accounting for nearly 70% of the total events, and over 60% of the total venues.

to a release with a major label before the release itself happens. In the following discussion we refer to this task as *forecasting*.

We also consider the simpler task of discriminating artists that are already successful in our setup from the ones that are not. We refer to this task as *prediction*.

5.1.1 Experimental Setting. For both forecasting and prediction tasks we used the *affiliation matrix* of artists and venues. In such an affiliation matrix an artist is represented as a bag-of-words vector over the venues where the artist has performed. The entries in the matrix are the numbers of times the artists performed at the venue. We used those vectors as features for the prediction and forecasting tasks.

In the forecasting task for any artist we did not include any concert that happened after the artist released their first recording with a major music label. However, for the prediction task we included those performances too.

The classification labels (successful or not) were obtained by iterating over all the music labels that each artist has ever recorded with (this information was obtained from Discogs). If among these music labels there are either major ones or one of their subsidiaries, we assume that the artist was successful and label it as a positive instance—negative otherwise.

As a result of the procedure above, we labeled about 500 artists as successful, which is 3.6% of the total number. It is worth noting that our labeling procedure yields a highly unbalanced dataset where the positive instances (successful artists) are very infrequent: this is in line with the commonsense notion of popularity in the music

industry, where musicians that thrive with a professional career are exceptionally rare.

5.1.2 Metrics. A natural choice for evaluating a success forecasting or prediction task is classification accuracy. However, due to high imbalance in the data, we need metrics that are more sensitive and account for under-represented classes. Such metrics are Precision, Recall and F1 score, as well as ROC AUC score, which we used for evaluation.

5.1.3 Learning Models and Configuration. For Task 1, we defined three simple models described next, and used them to carry out the forecasting and predictions exercises.

Baseline: We can intuitively connect success of the artist to the number of their performances. We picked a baseline that would prove or disprove this scenario by using the number of concerts, scaled by the maximum number of concerts by an artist, as a proxy for probability for becoming successful.

Logistic Regression: As a base classifier in both prediction and forecasting experiments we used Logistic Regression from the scikit-learn library [31]. We used L_2 norm for regularization, and tuned one parameter, i.e., the inverse of regularization strength C.

SVD: Since the affiliation matrix we use has over 99% sparsity (percentage of zero entries), dimensionality reduction techniques could yield prediction performance improvements by transforming sparse data into dense. We performed dimensionality reduction using Singular Value Decomposition (SVD). Via cross-validation we discovered that best results are achieved when we use 750 components in prediction task and 1000 components in forecasting task.

For each model, we performed hyperparameter tuning via grid search with 3-fold cross validation on the training set. The results reported are obtained by using cross-validated average over 3 different train-test splits in 80-20 ratio.

5.1.4 Task Summary. The results for this task are presented in Table 2. Suggested baseline shows existing correlation between the number of concerts and prediction label, and this correlation is stronger in prediction task than in forecasting task. Next, simple logistic regression achieves 0.22 F1 score on the forecasting task and 0.4 on the prediction task. We can see that while reducing dimensions increase ROC AUC and F1 scores by several points in forecasting task, its improvement for prediction task is marginal.

The improvement in performance on the prediction task indicates there is a difference in distributions of artist performances before and after they record their first album with a major music label. This suggests the existence of change points in careers that are caused by recording with major labels, which corroborates our notion of artist's success. We expect that employing more sophisticated models for discovering change points would give better forecasting results.

5.2 Task 2: Event Prediction

Besides artist career trajectories, we are also interested in the overall dynamics of the network, where both venues and artists evolve and their influence changes as a result of constant interactions between venues and artists.

Table 2: Precision (P), Recall (R), F1-score and AUC for artist success forecasting (FCST) and prediction (PRED) tasks. We show results of logistic regression on full data (FCST/PRED LR) and with reduced dimensions (FCST/PRED LR+SVD)

Task	Model	P	R	F1	AUC
FCST	Baseline	0.07	0.26	0.11	0.60
FCST	LR	0.18	0.29	0.22	0.74
FCST	LR+SVD	0.18	0.35	0.23	0.78
PRED	Baseline	0.25	0.35	0.29	0.82
PRED	LR	0.36	0.45	0.40	0.86
PRED	LR+SVD	0.39	0.40	0.40	0.87

To see if we can explain part of those interactions, we formulate the artist-venue link prediction task. As in the forecasting artist success task, we consider here two configurations—*forecasting* and *prediction*. For this task we used the same affiliation network as in the previous task, but since we are interested in predicting new or hidden edges, we only use a binary affiliation matrix here.

In the previous task prediction experiments were performed to test whether or not our suggested definition of success is viable. For $(artist - venue)$ link mining task, however, we exercise prediction alongside to the forecasting to test for possible major temporal shifts in artists' behavior.

5.2.1 Experimental Setting. In the forecasting task, we looked for new $(artist, venue)$ links, or edges, based on the history of old ones. In particular, we used all performances from 2007 to 2015 as "history" (i.e., training data), and the performances in 2016 and 2017 as "future" (i.e., test set). We then went on and recursively removed all artists and venues that have less than 5 concerts associated with them in the training set. As a result we had 12,871 artists, 10,269 venues, 385,845 events in the training set and 43,122 events in the test set.

In the prediction task we kept the same set of artists and venues as described above for the forecasting task. We then randomly picked 20% of all links and hid them in the test data, using the remaining 80% for training purposes, similarly to a link prediction problem. Results reported are averaged over such three random splits. We binarized all the links as we are only interested in predicting new links, i.e. new venues, where artist performs.

5.2.2 Metrics. We measured the performance on this task using Area Under the Receiver Operating Characteristic curve (ROC AUC). One of the main advantages of this metric is the fact that it operates on rankings and is calculated for a range of thresholds, rather than prediction classes. This allows us to interchangeably use simple recommender system objectives for venue prediction.

5.2.3 Learning Models and Configuration. For Task 2, we decided to adopt some popular heuristic scores for link prediction, a simple matrix factorization technique and node similarity based model, all described in the following.

Heuristic scores: Likelihood of a link existing between a pair of nodes is often approximated in terms of the number of common direct neighbors of that pair. However, a score calculated in this

Table 3: Heuristic scores for link prediction in bipartite graph for node pair (u, v). $\mathcal{N}(u)$ indicates direct neighbors of node u, $\hat{\mathcal{N}}(u)$ indicates neighbors of neighbors of u.

Common Neighbors $(CN(u, v))$	$\|(\hat{\mathcal{N}}(u) \cap \mathcal{N}(v)) \cup (\hat{\mathcal{N}}(v) \cap \mathcal{N}(u))\|$
Jaccard's Coefficient	$\dfrac{CN(u,v)}{\|\hat{\mathcal{N}}(u) \cup \mathcal{N}(v) \cup \hat{\mathcal{N}}(v) \cup \mathcal{N}(u)\|}$
Preferential Attachment	$\|\mathcal{N}(u)\| \cdot \|\mathcal{N}(v)\|$

way will always be zero in a bipartite graph. Hence, we extended popular methods—Common Neighbors and Jaccard's coefficient—to use 2-hop neighbor sets of the pair instead of direct neighbors, as shown in Table 3, where $\mathcal{N}(u)$ is defined as the set of direct neighbors of node u, and $\hat{\mathcal{N}}(u) = \cup_{v \in \mathcal{N}(u)} \mathcal{N}(v)$ is the set of *neighbors of neighbors* of u. Another popular link prediction heuristic is Preferential attachment, which can be applied to a bipartite graph without any modifications.

Matrix factorization: Link mining in a bipartite graph can be naturally presented as a recommendation task. For each artist we have a list of "relevant" venues—the ones where the artist performed. Using methods for collaborative filtering we can find latent features or representations of venues that make them relevant for certain artists. Based on these hidden representations, we can then predict which venues are most relevant for the artist.

In this task, we used a simple yet popular collaborative filtering method based on matrix factorization—Singular Value Decomposition (SVD). To find the number of components for SVD, we used grid search—from 10 to 2000—and reported the result for 25.

Node similarity: Building and using graph representations is another approach that is often employed for link prediction. In our experiments we leveraged Deepwalk [32] for obtaining node representations and then used cosine similarity of a pair of nodes as an estimate for the probability of a link existing between them.[7]

Deepwalk is similar to training a Word2Vec model on a random walk sampled starting from every node in the graph. In our graph we gave preference to a larger number of short walks so we searched for the optimal number of walks of length 10. We report results for using 40 random walks. We then used cosine similarity of node representations as a proxy for probability of creating a new edge between those nodes.

Hyperparameters like number of hidden components in SVD and Deepwalk parameters in this task were only tuned for prediction task. We then used the same values for forecasting task. All parameters were estimated via grid search with 5-fold cross-validation, with 20% of all edges in each fold.

5.2.4 Task Summary. The results for the venue prediction task are presented in Table 4. As it can be seen, every method performs better on the prediction task than on forecasting, though for heuristic methods the improvement in performance is marginal. This hints that there might be a shift in artists' preferences for choosing a venue over time. It also indicates that while coarse statistics like Common Neighbors or Jaccard's coefficient are not affected much

---

[7] https://github.com/phanein/deepwalk

Table 4: Results for $(artist, venue)$ **link prediction task, measured in Area Under Receiver Operating Characteristics curve (AUC).**

Task	Model	AUC
FCST	Common Neighbors	0.87
FCST	Jaccard's coef	0.89
FCST	Preferential Attachment	0.79
FCST	SVD	0.81
FCST	Node similarity	0.84
PRED	Common Neighbors	0.91
PRED	Jaccard's coef	0.90
PRED	Preferential Attachment	0.84
PRED	SVD	0.91
PRED	Node similarity	0.90

by those shifts, slightly more sensitive methods like SVD and node similarity, that rely on the inner structure of the graph, are affected more. Yet, either that structure is not expressive, or the methods are not powerful enough, neither of those methods performs better than heuristic scores. Interestingly, four models out of five give performance of around 0.9 ROC AUC on prediction task. Out of all the methods we tried, Preferential Attachment has the lowest performance for both tasks.

5.3 Task 3: Joint Discovery of Influential Artists and Venues

In the previous tasks, we have attempted to classify an artist as about to be signed or not about to be signed. In this task we will investigate whether we can identify top artists and venues automatically by mining their performances.

To measure the popularity of the artists and venues, we leverage BiRank [16]. This algorithm is a modification to the PageRank [28] algorithm that tunes it towards bipartite graphs. The algorithm iteratively identifies influential venues by observing which influential artists play at them. Simultaneously, it measures influential artists by measuring their frequency of playing at influential venues.

Before running this algorithm, we set the initial ranking based upon the following measure:

$$g_i = \frac{\log(N_i + 1)}{\sum_{a \in \mathcal{A}} \log(N_a + 1)}, \quad (1)$$

where N_i measures the number of links to the node i, $\mathcal{A}$ is the set of artists in the dataset, and $i \in \mathcal{A}$. This constitutes the artist's initial score. Similarly, we compute:

$$g_j = \frac{\log(N_j + 1)}{\sum_{v \in \mathcal{V}} \log(N_v + 1)}, \quad (2)$$

where $\mathcal{V}$ is the set of venues and $j \in \mathcal{V}$. With this initial seed score, we proceed to run the BiRank algorithm to identify the most influential nodes in each set. Finally, it is important to note that there is a temporal weighting in the links. Each link in the adjacency matrix has a weight of δ^{2017-y_0}, where delta is the decay parameter (set to 0.85 in the experiments), and y_0 is the year of the first link.

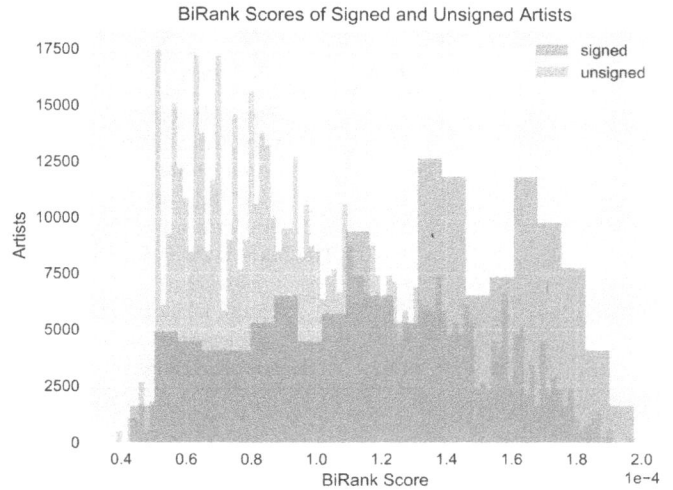

Figure 4: Histogram of signed and unsigned artists. Normalized to show relative frequency of BiRank scores.

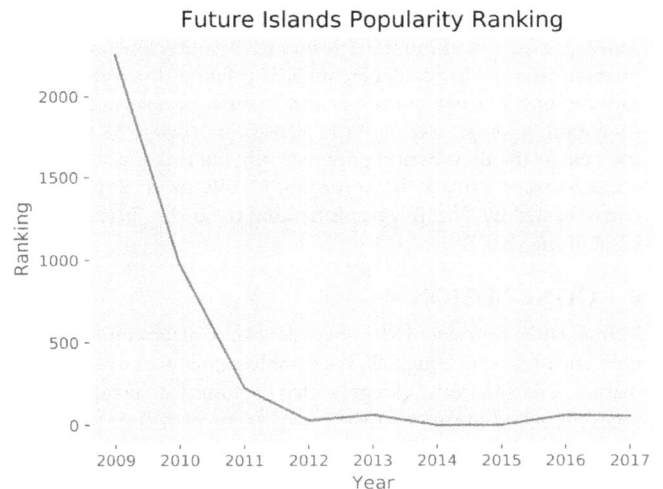

Figure 5: Trajectory of the group "Future Islands" through the lens of the BiRank score. The y-axis is the rank: lower is better. The BiRank score tracks the band's rise to popularity, culminating in the 2014 nomination of "breakthrough band of the year" by The Telegraph, suggesting that our framework can capture, and may predict, outstanding trajectories.

We subtract this number from 2017 as this is the most recent year in the dataset. This experimental setup closely resembles that of [16].

The results of this experiment can be seen in Table 5. These results seem to indicate promise for this method on our dataset. In the case of the venues, they correspond to some of the most popular venues in the world. As for the artists, the story is different. While they do not correspond to the most popular in terms of followers, these are the artists that have more performances in the dataset.

Table 5: The most influential nodes of each class identified by BiRank.

Rank	Artists	Venues
1	Frank Turner	The Observatory, Los Angeles, CA
2	Every Time I Die	The Masquerade, Atlanta, GA
3	Against Me!	The Bowery Ballroom, New York, NY
4	Reel Big Fish	Webster Hall, New York, NY
5	All Time Low	9:30 Club, Washington, DC
6	The Black Dahlia Murder	House of Blues, Boston / Cambridge, MA
7	Hatebreed	Theater of the Living Arts, Philadelphia, PA
8	Future Islands	The Middle East Downstairs, Boston / Cambridge, MA
9	Halestorm	Vienna Arena (Arena Wien), Vienna
10	Hawthorne Heights	Brudenell Social Club, Leeds

However, a natural question regarding the dynamics of BiRank is how indicative it is of artist success. To measure this phenomenon, we plot the histogram of BiRank scores for both signed and unsigned artists. This can be seen in Figure 4, where we see that the signed artists tend to have a higher BiRank score than unsigned artists.

The BiRank scores can also be useful for measuring the trajectory of an artist. By calculating the BiRank scores as previously indicated every year, with a three year moving window, we can observe the ranking of artists at different points in time. An example of this phenomenon can be seen in Figure 5. This figure shows the BiRank ranking of the artist "Future Island" over time. We can see that their ranking begins around the 2,300 mark. Over the course of the next years, their ranking dramatically improves, peaking with them being the top artist according to BiRank in 2014. This is corroborated by The Telegraph naming them the "breakthrough band of the year."[8]

6 CONCLUSION

In this paper we presented a novel dataset of artists and their live performances from Songkick. We complemented that data by information collected from Discogs, which contains full history of their recordings and releases. The dataset can be used for a variety of tasks which we exemplified by performing success forecasting and event prediction.

We proposed an operational definition of *success* - signing with a major label and/or their subsidiaries - and demonstrated that the event data contains useful information that can be leveraged to forecast artists' success with better than baseline accuracy. Similarly, we observed that by utilizing the underlying structure of this data, one can also predict whether an artist will have a concert in a particular venue. The performance of simple baseline models that we carried out in all three tasks indicates that much better results can be achieved with more carefully designed methods.

Finally, we illustrated how artist or venue influence can be measured based on analyzing a time-varying bipartite artist-venue graph. Specifically, we analyzed the evolution of the bipartite generalization of the Pagerank score, and demonstrated both qualitatively and quantitatively that its dynamics can be used to identify successful artists.

As future work, it will be interesting to perform more fine-grained analysis of all three tasks examined here. For instance, the results presented here were averaged across different genres. It is plausible, however, that analysis will yield (subtle) differences when conditioned on the genre. Similarly, our preliminary analysis of event sequence (as opposed to bag of word representation of events) yielded some interesting geographic patterns, which warrant further and more detailed studies.

Finally, we would like to point out two potentially important limitations of the present work. First, the definition of success used here, while operationally useful, is by no means comprehensive. Indeed, many artists who work with independent labels, or specialize in commercially less-viable genres, can still have very successful and celebrated careers. And second, we note that despite its demonstrated usefulness, the dataset presented here is not perfect and is likely to have some intrinsic biases, e.g., musicians might have varying incentives for joining platforms such as *Songkick* depending on the stage of their career. Identifying and potentially correcting for such biases is another important future task.

ACKNOWLEDGEMENTS

This research was supported in part by ARO (contract no. W911NF-12-R-0012) and DARPA (grant no. D16AP00115). This project does not necessarily reflect the position/policy of the Government; no official endorsement should be inferred. Approved for public release; unlimited distribution.

---

[8]www.telegraph.co.uk/culture/music/music-festivals/10975049/Latitude-Festival-2014-Future-Islands-the-breakthrough-band-of-the-year.html

REFERENCES

[1] Evrim Acar, Daniel M Dunlavy, and Tamara G Kolda. 2009. Link prediction on evolving data using matrix and tensor factorizations. In *Data Mining Workshops, 2009. ICDMW'09. IEEE International Conference on*. IEEE, 262–269.

[2] Santa Agreste, Pasquale De Meo, Emilio Ferrara, Sebastiano Piccolo, and Alessandro Provetti. 2015. Analysis of a heterogeneous social network of humans and cultural objects. *IEEE Transactions on Systems, Man and Cybernetics: Systems* 45, 4 (2015), 559–570.

[3] Roja Bandari, Sitaram Asur, and Bernardo A Huberman. 2012. The pulse of news in social media: Forecasting popularity. *ICWSM* 12 (2012), 26–33.

[4] Nesserine Benchettara, Rushed Kanawati, and Celine Rouveirol. 2010. Supervised machine learning applied to link prediction in bipartite social networks. In *Advances in Social Networks Analysis and Mining (ASONAM), 2010 International Conference on*. IEEE, 326–330.

[5] Catherine A Bliss, Morgan R Frank, Christopher M Danforth, and Peter Sheridan Dodds. 2014. An evolutionary algorithm approach to link prediction in dynamic social networks. *Journal of Computational Science* 5, 5 (2014), 750–764.

[6] Krisztian Buza and Ilona Galambos. 2013. An application of link prediction in bipartite graphs: Personalized blog feedback prediction. In *8th Japanese-Hungarian Symposium on Discrete Mathematics and Its Applications June*. 4–7.

[7] Paolo Cintia, Luca Pappalardo, and Dino Pedreschi. 2013. " Engine Matters": A First Large Scale Data Driven Study on Cyclists' Performance. In *Data Mining Workshops (ICDMW), 2013 IEEE 13th International Conference on*. IEEE, 147–153.

[8] Paolo Cintia, Salvatore Rinzivillo, and Luca Pappalardo. 2015. A network-based approach to evaluate the performance of football teams. In *Machine learning and data mining for sports analytics workshop, Porto, Portugal*.

[9] Aaron Clauset, Daniel B Larremore, and Roberta Sinatra. 2017. Data-driven predictions in the science of science. *Science* 355, 6324 (2017), 477–480.

[10] Aaron Clauset, Cristopher Moore, and Mark EJ Newman. 2008. Hierarchical structure and the prediction of missing links in networks. *Nature* 453, 7191 (2008), 98–101.

[11] Chrysanthos Dellarocas, Xiaoquan Michael Zhang, and Neveen F Awad. 2007. Exploring the value of online product reviews in forecasting sales: The case of motion pictures. *Journal of Interactive marketing* 21, 4 (2007), 23–45.

[12] M Evans et al. 2013. 'What Constitutes Artist Success in the Australian Music Industries?'. *International Journal of Music Business Research (IJMBR)* (2013).

[13] Emilio Ferrara, Roberto Interdonato, and Andrea Tagarelli. 2014. Online popularity and topical interests through the lens of instagram. In *Proceedings of the 25th ACM conference on Hypertext and social media*. ACM, 24–34.

[14] Santo Fortunato, Carl T Bergstrom, Katy Börner, James A Evans, Dirk Helbing, Staša Milojević, Alexander M Petersen, Filippo Radicchi, Roberta Sinatra, Brian Uzzi, et al. 2018. Science of science. *Science* 359, 6379 (2018), eaao0185.

[15] Roger Guimerà and Marta Sales-Pardo. 2009. Missing and spurious interactions and the reconstruction of complex networks. *Proceedings of the National Academy of Sciences* 106, 52 (2009), 22073–22078.

[16] Xiangnan He, Ming Gao, Min-Yen Kan, and Dingxian Wang. 2017. Birank: Towards ranking on bipartite graphs. *IEEE Transactions on Knowledge and Data Engineering* 29, 1 (2017), 57–71.

[17] Homa Hosseinimardi, Hsien-Te Kao, Kristina Lerman, and Emilio Ferrara. 2018. Discovering Hidden Structure in High Dimensional Human Behavioral Data via Tensor Factorization. In *HeteroNAM 2018: First International Workshop on Heterogeneous Networks Analysis and Mining*.

[18] Timothy A Judge, Chad A Higgins, Carl J Thoresen, and Murray R Barrick. 1999. The big five personality traits, general mental ability, and career success across the life span. *Personnel psychology* 52, 3 (1999), 621–652.

[19] Hisashi Kashima and Naoki Abe. 2006. A parameterized probabilistic model of network evolution for supervised link prediction. In *Data Mining, 2006. ICDM'06. Sixth International Conference on*. IEEE, 340–349.

[20] Qing Ke, Emilio Ferrara, Filippo Radicchi, and Alessandro Flammini. 2015. Defining and identifying Sleeping Beauties in science. *Proceedings of the National Academy of Sciences* 112, 24 (2015), 7426–7431.

[21] Gregor Kennedy, Carleton Coffrin, Paula De Barba, and Linda Corrin. 2015. Predicting success: how learners' prior knowledge, skills and activities predict MOOC performance. In *Proceedings of the Fifth International Conference on Learning Analytics And Knowledge*. ACM, 136–140.

[22] Jérôme Kunegis, Ernesto W De Luca, and Sahin Albayrak. 2010. The link prediction problem in bipartite networks. In *International Conference on Information Processing and Management of Uncertainty in Knowledge-based Systems*. Springer, 380–389.

[23] David Liben-Nowell and Jon Kleinberg. 2007. The link-prediction problem for social networks. *journal of the Association for Information Science and Technology* 58, 7 (2007), 1019–1031.

[24] Zongyang Ma, Aixin Sun, and Gao Cong. 2013. On predicting the popularity of newly emerging hashtags in twitter. *Journal of the Association for Information Science and Technology* 64, 7 (2013), 1399–1410.

[25] Amin Mazloumian, Young-Ho Eom, Dirk Helbing, Sergi Lozano, and Santo Fortunato. 2011. How citation boosts promote scientific paradigm shifts and nobel prizes. *PloS one* 6, 5 (2011), e18975.

[26] Rachel McLean, Paul G Oliver, and David W Wainwright. 2010. The myths of empowerment through information communication technologies: An exploration of the music industries and fan bases. *Management Decision* 48, 9 (2010), 1365–1377.

[27] Tanushree Mitra and Eric Gilbert. 2014. The language that gets people to give: Phrases that predict success on kickstarter. In *Proceedings of the 17th ACM conference on Computer supported cooperative work & social computing*. ACM, 49–61.

[28] Lawrence Page, Sergey Brin, Rajeev Motwani, and Terry Winograd. 1999. *The PageRank citation ranking: Bringing order to the web*. Technical Report. Stanford InfoLab.

[29] Jaehyuk Park, Giovanni Luca Ciampaglia, and Emilio Ferrara. 2016. Style in the age of instagram: Predicting success within the fashion industry using social media. In *Proceedings of the 19th ACM Conference on Computer-Supported Cooperative Work & Social Computing*. ACM, 64–73.

[30] Milen Pavlov and Ryutaro Ichise. 2007. Finding experts by link prediction in co-authorship networks. In *Proceedings of the 2nd International Conference on Finding Experts on the Web with Semantics-Volume 290*. CEUR-WS. org, 42–55.

[31] F. Pedregosa, G. Varoquaux, A. Gramfort, V. Michel, B. Thirion, O. Grisel, M. Blondel, P. Prettenhofer, R. Weiss, V. Dubourg, J. Vanderplas, A. Passos, D. Cournapeau, M. Brucher, M. Perrot, and E. Duchesnay. 2011. Scikit-learn: Machine Learning in Python. *Journal of Machine Learning Research* 12 (2011), 2825–2830.

[32] Bryan Perozzi, Rami Al-Rfou, and Steven Skiena. 2014. Deepwalk: Online learning of social representations. In *Proceedings of the 20th ACM SIGKDD international conference on Knowledge discovery and data mining*. ACM, 701–710.

[33] Giulio Rossetti, Letizia Milli, Fosca Giannotti, and Dino Pedreschi. 2017. Forecasting success via early adoptions analysis: A data-driven study. *PloS one* 12, 12 (2017), e0189096.

[34] Anna Sapienza, Hao Peng, and Emilio Ferrara. 2017. Performance Dynamics and Success in Online Games. In *2017 IEEE International Conference on Data Mining Workshops (ICDMW)*. 902–909.

[35] Roberta Sinatra, Dashun Wang, Pierre Deville, Chaoming Song, and Albert-László Barabási. 2016. Quantifying the evolution of individual scientific impact. *Science* 354, 6312 (2016), aaf5239.

[36] Gabor Szabo and Bernardo A Huberman. 2010. Predicting the popularity of online content. *Commun. ACM* 53, 8 (2010), 80–88.

[37] John Ternovski and Taha Yasseri. 2017. Social Complex Contagion in Music Listenership: A Natural Experiment with 1.3 Million Participants. *arXiv preprint arXiv:1711.05701* (2017).

[38] Dashun Wang, Chaoming Song, and Albert-László Barabási. 2013. Quantifying long-term scientific impact. *Science* 342, 6154 (2013), 127–132.

[39] Burcu Yucesoy and Albert-László Barabási. 2016. Untangling performance from success. *EPJ Data Science* 5, 1 (2016), 17.

[40] Burcu Yucesoy, Xindi Wang, Junming Huang, and Albert-László Barabási. 2018. Success in books: a big data approach to bestsellers. *EPJ Data Science* 7, 1 (2018), 7.

[41] Linhong Zhu, Dong Guo, Junming Yin, Greg Ver Steeg, and Aram Galstyan. 2016. Scalable temporal latent space inference for link prediction in dynamic social networks. *IEEE Transactions on Knowledge and Data Engineering* 28, 10 (2016), 2765–2777.

[42] Claudia Zuber, Marc Zibung, and Achim Conzelmann. 2015. Motivational patterns as an instrument for predicting success in promising young football players. *Journal of sports sciences* 33, 2 (2015), 160–168.

Predicting Twitter User Socioeconomic Attributes with Network and Language Information

Nikolaos Aletras
University of Sheffield
n.aletras@sheffield.ac.uk

Benjamin Paul Chamberlain
Imperial College London
Asos.com
benjamin.chamberlain@gmail.com

ABSTRACT

Inferring socioeconomic attributes of social media users such as occupation and income is an important problem in computational social science. Automated inference of such characteristics has applications in personalised recommender systems, targeted computational advertising and online political campaigning. While previous work has shown that language features can reliably predict socioeconomic attributes on Twitter, employing information coming from users' social networks has not yet been explored for such complex user characteristics. In this paper, we describe a method for predicting the occupational class and the income of Twitter users given information extracted from their extended networks by learning a low-dimensional vector representation of users, i.e. graph embeddings. We use this representation to train predictive models for occupational class and income. Results on two publicly available datasets show that our method consistently outperforms the state-of-the-art methods in both tasks. We also obtain further significant improvements when we combine graph embeddings with textual features, demonstrating that social network and language information are complementary.

KEYWORDS

social media, graph embeddings, user profiling

ACM Reference format:
Nikolaos Aletras and Benjamin Paul Chamberlain. 2018. Predicting Twitter User Socioeconomic Attributes with Network and Language Information. In *Proceedings of 29th ACM Conference on Hypertext and Social Media, Baltimore, MD, USA, July 9–12, 2018 (HT '18)*, 5 pages.
https://doi.org/10.1145/3209542.3209577

1 INTRODUCTION

The daily interaction of billions of users with online social platforms such as Facebook and Twitter has made available enormous amounts of user generated content. The plethora and diversity of this data (e.g. text, images or interactions with other users such as 'retweets' or 'likes') enables studies in computational social science [10, 26] to analyse human behaviour on a large scale and automatically infer user latent attributes.

Automatic inference of user characteristics includes studies on inferring age and gender [5, 39, 40], location [8, 11, 16], personality traits [21, 38, 45] and political orientation [9, 33, 44] inter alia. More recently, there has been a particular focus on inferring complex user socioeconomic characteristics such as occupational class [18, 27, 36], income [37, 45] and socioeconomic class [24, 31]. Apart from their importance in computational social science, such methods are also useful in downstream applications such as targeted advertising and online political campaigning.

Following the hypothesis that language is indicative of the social status of a person [3, 4, 23], previous research analysed user generated written content to derive text based features such as bag-of-words or clusters of words. These features are used to train predictive models for inferring socioeconomic attributes [27, 36]. Despite the fact that these methods have proved to perform well, they have not considered any relations and interactions between users. Moreover, there is a large proportion of inactive users that do not produce any content. For example, previous studies have shown that only around two thirds of the users are active (i.e. posted at least twice) on Twitter [19, 28]. This makes it impossible to solely utilise language based models to infer socioeconomic or other characteristics of inactive users.

A different approach to the problem is to include information from the social network structure. Socioeconomic status can be indicated by looking into the range and the composition of the social network of a person [6]. That is because people who belong to the same social circles often share common characteristics. This is known as social network homophily, i.e. the inclination of people towards developing social ties with similar others [25, 29]. Despite expected differences to real life social networks, it has been shown that online social networks, e.g. Facebook and Twitter, exhibit some levels of homophily [1, 21]. People that follow each other on Twitter usually share common topical interests [22, 46]. Previous work utilised the social network structure to infer user attributes such as gender and age, personality traits and sentiment [1, 21, 35, 41, 42], but not any socioeconomic attributes.

In this paper, we focus on using social network information to infer user's occupational class and income. Following that direction, we explore two hypotheses using data from Twitter: (1) a user's social network is indicative of their income and occupational class; and (2) the information from the social network structure and textual information are complementary. To answer these hypotheses, we extract information from a user's social network and encapsulate it in user graph embeddings [34, 43]. Graph embeddings place Twitter users in a vector space where similar users are likely to be close to each other. The user graph embeddings are treated as features to train linear and non-linear supervised models for predicting income and occupational class.

The major contributions of our paper are:

- To the best of our knowledge, this work is the first to introduce neural graph embeddings to predict income and occupational class on Twitter.
- Our model can be used to infer complex socioeconomic characteristics of inactive users, exploiting the fact that user graph embeddings do not rely on any textual information.
- We show that a user's social network and written content, i.e. tweets, contain complementary information. This is demonstrated by training models that combine both feature sets. Our evaluation on two standard, publicly available datasets of Twitter users that are labelled with occupational class and income shows that they outperform models using solely language or solely network information.
- Our proposed model achieves state-of-the-art performance in these two datasets of income and occupational class significantly outperforming models introduced by Preoţiuc-Pietro et al. [36, 37].

2 USER NEURAL GRAPH EMBEDDINGS

User neural graph embeddings are dense vector representations that position similar users close together in a high-dimensional Euclidean space. Neural embeddings are popular in natural language processing for learning vector representations of words [2, 30].

The only inputs required to learn word embedding models are sequences of words in documents and so the concept can be extended to network structured data using random walks to create sequences of vertices. In our case, vertices represent Twitter users and edges represent a follower/followee relationship, and we treat edges as if they were undirected. This is justified because Twitter is predominantly an interest graph [14] and a large body of research has shown that the homophily principle applies to users who express similar interests in social networks [7, 21, 42]. By treating the graph as undirected we ensure that all users that follow a common account (indicative of an interest) have a maximum path distance of two. Vertices are embedded by treating them exactly analogously to words in the text formulation of the model [34]. Extensions varying the nature of the random walks have been explored in LINE [43] and Node2vec [13]. The main justification for this idea is that social networks are a form of noisy measurement of a true underlying network. Random walks have been shown extensively to mitigate for false edges and infer the presence of missing ones [32].

2.1 Generating User Sequences and Contexts

Given a network of users connected with unweighted edges, random walks are generated by repeatedly sampling an integer uniformly from $\{1,2,\ldots,D_v\}$ where D_v is the vertex degree and moving to a new vertex. Concretely, for a random walk starting at vertex v_0 we would sample $x \sim U(\{1,2,\ldots,D_{v_0}\})$ where U is a uniform distribution and D_{v_0} is the degree of v_0. If $x = 1$ we move to the lowest indexed neighbour of v_0, append that vertex to the random walk and repeat the process at vertex v_1.

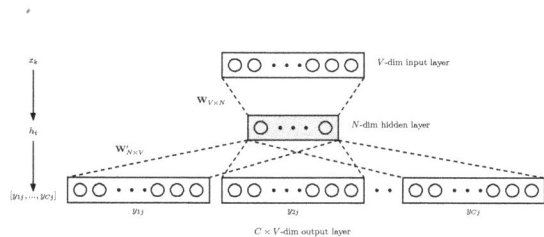

Figure 1: The Skipgram model uses two vector representations W and W' to predict the context vertices from a single input vertex.

2.2 The Skipgram Model on User Sequences

After we have sampled user sequences with random walks, we can use them to train user embeddings. There are several related embedding models, i.e. SkipGram and Continuous Bag of Words [30]. Here we adopt the SkipGram with Negative Sampling (SGNS) model that is depicted in Figure 1. The figure shows a shallow neural network with a single hidden layer and two separate vector representations labelled as **W** and **W'**. The input to SGNS is a sequence of users, which are mapped to (input, context) pairs by sliding a context window over the input sequences. The input user representation is in **W** and the neighbouring (i.e. context) users share a representation in **W'**. Users are initially randomly allocated within the two vector spaces and then the model is trained using Stochastic Gradient Descent (SGD). The objective function gives the probability of the context users given the input user, which is modelled by a softmax. We optimise the negative log likelihood given by

$$L = -\log p(w_{o,1}, w_{o,2}, w_{o,3}, \ldots, w_{o,C} \mid w_I) \quad (1)$$

$$= -\log \prod_{c=1}^{C} \frac{\exp \mathbf{v}_c'^T \mathbf{v}_I}{\sum_{j=1}^{V} \exp \mathbf{v}_j'^T \mathbf{v}_I} \quad (2)$$

where $w_{(.)}$ is a user and $\mathbf{v}_{(.)}$ and $\mathbf{v}_{(.)}'$ are the input and output vector representations of that user and C is the context size, typically ten. In practice, it is expensive to evaluate Equation (2) as the sum in the denominator is over all of the users in the network. Instead we use negative sampling, which is a form of Noise Contrastive Estimation (NCE) [15], to estimate the function by only evaluating a small number of negative samples in addition to the observed positive example. The gradient descent update rules for a user pair (w_I, w_O) with vector representations $(\mathbf{v}_I, \mathbf{v}_O')$ are found by applying the chain rule to Equation (2) and are given by

$$\mathbf{v}_j'^{new} = \begin{cases} \mathbf{v}_j'^{old} - \eta(\sigma(\mathbf{v}_j'^T \mathbf{v}_I) - t_j)\mathbf{v}_i, & w_j \in \chi \\ \mathbf{v}_j'^{old}, & \text{otherwise} \end{cases} \quad (3)$$

where $\chi = \{w_O\} \cup W_{neg}$. For the output representation and

$$\mathbf{v}_I^{new} = \mathbf{v}_I^{old} - \eta \sum_{j:w_j \in \chi} (\sigma(\mathbf{v}_j'^T \mathbf{v}_I) - t_j)\mathbf{v}_j' \quad (4)$$

for the input representation. In these equations t_j is an indicator variable that is one if and only if $w_j = w_O$ and zero otherwise, η is the SGD learning rate and W_{neg} is the set of negatively sampled

C	Title	U
1	Managers, Directors and Senior Officials	461
2	Professional Occupations	1615
3	Associate Profess. and Technical Occupations	950
4	Administrative and Secretarial Occupations	168
5	Skilled Trades Occupations	782
6	Caring, Leisure and Other Service Occup.	270
7	Sales and Customer Service Occupations	56
8	Process, Plant and Machine Operatives	192
9	Elementary Occupations	131
	Total	4625

Table 1: Distribution of users (U) across occupational classes (C).

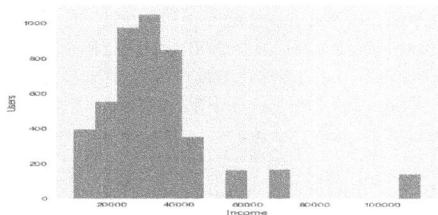

Figure 2: Distribution of users and income. Income is calculated in British pounds (£).

users. We follow [30] and draw W_{neg} from the distribution of users in the random walks raised to the power of $\frac{3}{4}$.

3 EXPERIMENTAL SETUP

3.1 Data

We experiment using two publicly available datasets that contain Twitter users mapped to their occupational class and income [36, 37]. The datasets contain the same group of 5,191 users in total. However, some of the accounts are not considered in our experiments since we were not able to extract their social network information. These accounts may have been deleted or become private since the release of the datasets. Therefore, we report results on a subset of the original set of users, i.e. 4,625 users, that are still publicly available.

Occupational Class. Users are mapped with an occupation using the Standard Occupation Classification (SOC) taxonomy devised by the Office of National Statistics in the UK, based on skill requirements. The SOC taxonomy has a hierarchical structure with 9 major groups (e.g managers or elementary occupations). Users in the dataset have been mapped to one of these major groups. Table 1 shows the distribution of users across the nine occupational classes. The Pearson's correlation between the original distribution of users and our subset distribution is 0.93.

Income. The occupational class of users has further been used as a proxy to infer their income from the Annual Survey of Hours and Earnings. The income represents the mean yearly earnings for 2013 in British Pounds (GBP) for each occupational class. Figure 2 shows

the distributions of users and income in the dataset. The mean user income in the original dataset is $32,509.74$, while the mean of the subset we use in our experiments is $32,727.92$.

3.2 Implementation of the Graph Embeddings

To construct graph embeddings we downloaded the Twitter IDs of everyone followed by the $4,625$ accounts. This produced a set of $3,925,702$ users in total. We considered only accounts followed by at least 10 users, which reduced the number of the unique accounts to $53,199$. To produce sequences of users we treat the edges of the Twitter graph as undirected and take 80 step random walks initiated at each vertex in this network.

The dimensionality of the embedding affects the performance in predictive tasks. We experimented with dimensionalities of 16, 32, 64 and 128 and chose the optimal value following a nested 10-fold cross-validation approach as in Preoţiuc-Pietro et al. [36, 37]. We found that the best performing embedding[1] dimensionality is 32. The user embeddings and the code to generate them are available to download from https://github.com/melifluos/income-prediction.

3.3 Predictive Models

Occupational Class. Predicting the occupational class of a user is defined as a 9-way classification task. Given a user feature representation, our goal is to assign the most probable class label. For that purpose, we use the graph embeddings as features and a concatenation of the graph embeddings with the topics introduced in [36] to train Logistic Regression (LR) [48], Support Vector Machines (SVM) [20] and Gaussian Process Classifiers (GPC) [47]. All of the classifiers[2] are trained following the one-vs-all approach[3].

Income. Inferring income is defined as a regression task. Given the user feature representation as input, we try to predict a real value representing the user's income. The goal is to minimise the absolute error between the actual and inferred income. We also compare three popular models: (1) linear regression (LR), (2) Support Vector Regression (SVR) [12], and (3) Gaussian Process Regression (GPR) [47].

4 RESULTS AND DISCUSSION

Tables 2 and 3 show the results obtained by the proposed models using the graph embeddings (*Graph*) and their combination (*Graph+Topics*) as feature representations for users. Note that models using *Topics* (i.e. word frequency of user's tweets in a set of 200 precomputed word clusters) and *Temporal Orientation* as features are the baseline methods presented in Preoţiuc-Pietro et al. [36, 37] and Hasanuzzaman et al. [17].[4] To compare against Preoţiuc-Pietro et al. [36, 37], we retrain these models using the user accounts in the dataset that are publicly available (see Subsection 3.1).

---

[1]During initial experimentation, we noticed that varying the length of the random walk between 40 and 100 did not substantially affect the quality of the embeddings.
[2]The Gaussian Process models are trained using GPy (http://github.com/SheffieldML/GPy). All the other models are trained using Scikit-learn (http://scikit-learn.org/).
[3]All the hyperparameters of the baseline predictive models using *Topics* as features are identical to the models presented in [36, 37]. We tune the hyperparameters of our proposed models (*Graph* and *Topics+Graph*) performing a nested 10-fold cross-validation, identical to the data splits used in previous work.
[4]Replicating the method of Hasanuzzaman et al. [17] was not possible, hence we report results only for income from their paper.

Occupational Class	
Method	**Accuracy (%)**
Majority Class	35.00
Preoţiuc-Pietro et al. [36]	
LR-Topics	46.57
SVM-Topics	49.47
GP-Topics	49.64
Ours	
LR-Graph	46.24
SVM-Graph	50.14
GP-Graph	50.44
LR-Graph+Topics	48.84
SVM-Graph+Topics	**52.00†**
GP-Graph+Topics	51.46†

Table 2: Accuracy of models in predicting user occupational class.† denotes statistical significant different (t-test, $p <$ 0.01) method to *GP-Topics*.

Income		
Method	**MAE (£)**	ρ
Preoţiuc-Pietro et al. [37]		
LR-Topics	10573	.50
SVR-Topics	9528	.59
GPR-Topics	9883	.60
Hasanuzzaman et al. [17]		
LR-Temporal Or.	10850	.45
GP-Temporal Or.	10235	.51
Ours		
LR-Graph	10811	.50
SVM-Graph	**9048‡**	.62
GP-Graph	9532	.63
LR-Graph+Topics	10326	.54
SVM-Graph+Topics	9072‡	**.64**
GP-Graph+Topics	9488	**.64**

Table 3: Mean Absolute Error (MAE) and Pearson's correlation coefficient (ρ) between actual and predicted income. ‡ denotes statistical significant different (t-test, $p < 0.001$) method to *SVM-Topics*.

Our best performing model using graph based features (*Graph*) achieves an accuracy of 50.44% in the occupational classification task. In income prediction, the MAE is $9,048$ and Pearson's correlation is 0.63. This implies that graph embeddings carry meaningful information about user's socioeconomic attributes making them an effective user representation. The graph embedding features perform consistently better than the textual features (*Topics*) for the majority of the predictive models on both tasks except for the LR model. This confirms our first hypothesis that information from the network structure of a user is indicative of socioeconomic attributes. Figure 3 shows a 2-d t-SNE plot of the best performing user embedding, where we observe many distinct "communities" of low and high income users that appear together. This confirms our assumption about the homophilic nature of the Twitter network.

The combination of user embeddings and topics (*Graph+Topics*) outperforms either feature set used individually. More specifically, our *GPC-Graph+Topics* model significantly outperforms (t-test, $p <$ 0.01) the previous state-of-the-art method, *GPC-Topics* introduced in Preoţiuc-Pietro et al. [36] on occupational classification. Moreover, our *SVR-Graph+Topics* model significantly outperforms ($p < 0.001$) the best baseline method, i.e. *SVM+Topics*. This confirms our second hypothesis that network structure and linguistic information are complementary.

The above findings shed light on the homophilic behaviour of users on Twitter. That might have further implications on user behaviour when selecting friends and forming social networks online. Our results suggest that a stronger bias might exist towards selecting friends with common socioeconomic backgrounds in contrast to common topics of interest and that needs to be explored further.

Non-linear models (i.e. SVM, SVR, GPC, GPR) achieve better results in inferring user socioeconomic attributes than linear (LR) models. While in the occupational classification task our best performing model is GPC, the best model in income inference is the SVR instead of GPR. This implies that model selection is important in these tasks.

An analysis of the errors in the occupational classification task shows that most misclassifications come from adjacent classes. For example, users in classes 1, 3 and 4 are mistakenly classified

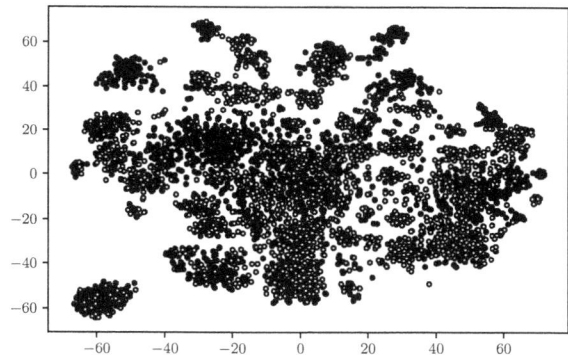

Figure 3: A t-SNE plot of the best performing user embedding (32D). Black and white represent users with above and below median income respectively.

as class 2. This happens because adjacent classes contain related occupations. However, we notice less dispersion of errors caused by other classes misclassified as class 2 when we use graph embeddings and the combination of graph embeddings and topics. This might be explained by the homophily of users' networks captured by graph embeddings.

5 CONCLUSIONS

We presented a method to predict user occupational class and income on Twitter. Information from a user's social network is represented by graph embeddings [34, 43] and is used to train predictive models. To the best of our knowledge, this work is the first to introduce graph embeddings for automatically inferring socioeconomic characteristics. We also demonstrated that user network and language information are complementary. That combination significantly improves predictive performance. Finally, our proposed models achieve state-of-the-art results in two standard datasets of income and occupational class, significantly outperforming previous methods.

REFERENCES

[1] Faiyaz Al Zamal, Wendy Liu, and Derek Ruths. 2012. Homophily and Latent Attribute Inference: Inferring Latent Attributes of Twitter Users from Neighbors. In *ICWSM*.

[2] Yoshua Bengio, Réjean Ducharme, Pascal Vincent, and Christian Jauvin. 2003. A Neural Probabilistic Language Model. *JMLR* 3 (2003), 1137–1155.

[3] Basil Bernstein. 1960. Language and social class. *The British Journal of Sociology* 11, 3 (1960), 271–276.

[4] Basil Bernstein. 2003. *Class, codes and control: Applied studies towards a sociology of language*. Vol. 2. Psychology Press.

[5] John D Burger, John Henderson, George Kim, and Guido Zarrella. 2011. Discriminating gender on Twitter. In *EMNLP*. 1301–1309.

[6] Karen E Campbell, Peter V Marsden, and Jeanne S Hurlbert. 1986. Social resources and socioeconomic status. *Social Networks* 8, 1 (1986), 97–117.

[7] Benjamin Chamberlain, Clive Humby, and Marc Peter Deisenroth. 2017. Probabilistic Inference of Twitter Users' Age based on What They Follow. In *ECML-PKDD*. 191–203.

[8] Zhiyuan Cheng, James Caverlee, and Kyumin Lee. 2010. You are where you tweet: a content-based approach to geo-locating Twitter users. In *CIKM*. 759–768.

[9] Raviv Cohen and Derek Ruths. 2013. Classifying political orientation on Twitter: It's not easy!. In *ICWSM*.

[10] Rosaria Conte, Nigel Gilbert, Giulia Bonelli, Claudio Cioffi-Revilla, Guillaume Deffuant, Janos Kertesz, Vittorio Loreto, Suzy Moat, Jean-Pierre Nadal, Anxo Sanchez, and others. 2012. Manifesto of computational social science. *European Physical Journal-Special Topics* 214 (2012), 325–346.

[11] Mark Dredze, Miles Osborne, and Prabhanjan Kambadur. 2016. Geolocation for Twitter: Timing Matters. In *NAACL-HLT*. 1064–1069.

[12] Harris Drucker, Christopher JC Burges, Linda Kaufman, Alex Smola, Vladimir Vapnik, and others. 1997. Support vector regression machines. In *NIPS*. 155–161.

[13] Aditya Grover and Jure Leskovec. 2016. node2vec: Scalable feature learning for networks. In *KDD*. 855–864.

[14] Pankaj Gupta, Ashish Goel, Jimmy Lin, Aneesh Sharma, Dong Wang, and Reza Zadeh. 2013. WTF: The Who to Follow Service at Twitter. In *WWW*. 505–514.

[15] Michael U Gutmann and Aapo Hyvärinen. 2012. Noise-contrastive estimation of unnormalized statistical models, with applications to natural image statistics. *JMLR* 13 (2012), 307–361.

[16] Bo Han, Paul Cook, and Timothy Baldwin. 2014. Text-based Twitter user geolocation prediction. *Journal of Artificial Intelligence Research* 49 (2014), 451–500.

[17] Mohammed Hasanuzzaman, Sabyasachi Kamila, Mandeep Kaur, Sriparna Saha, and Asif Ekbal. 2017. Temporal Orientation of Tweets for Predicting Income of Users. In *ACL*, Vol. 2. 659–665.

[18] Yanxiang Huang, Lele Yu, Xiang Wang, and Bin Cui. 2015. A multi-source integration framework for user occupation inference in social media systems. *WWW* (2015), 1247–1267.

[19] Bernardo Huberman, Daniel M Romero, and Fang Wu. 2008. Social networks that matter: Twitter under the microscope. *First Monday* 14, 1 (2008).

[20] Thorsten Joachims. 1998. Text categorization with support vector machines: Learning with many relevant features. In *ECML*. 137–142.

[21] Michal Kosinski, David Stillwell, and Thore Graepel. 2013. Private traits and attributes are predictable from digital records of human behavior. *PNAS* 110, 15 (2013), 5802–5805.

[22] Haewoon Kwak, Changhyun Lee, Hosung Park, and Sue Moon. 2010. What is Twitter, a social network or a news media?. In *WWW*. 591–600.

[23] William Labov. 2006. *The social stratification of English in New York city*. Cambridge University Press.

[24] Vasileios Lampos, Nikolaos Aletras, Jens K Geyti, Bin Zou, and Ingemar J Cox. 2016. Inferring the socioeconomic status of social media users based on behaviour and language. In *ECIR*. 689–695.

[25] Paul F Lazarsfeld, Robert K Merton, and others. 1954. Friendship as a social process: A substantive and methodological analysis. *Freedom and control in modern society* 18, 1 (1954), 18–66.

[26] David Lazer, Alex Sandy Pentland, Lada Adamic, Sinan Aral, Albert Laszlo Barabasi, Devon Brewer, Nicholas Christakis, Noshir Contractor, James Fowler, Myron Gutmann, and others. 2009. Life in the network: the coming age of computational social science. *Science* 323, 5915 (2009), 721.

[27] Jiwei Li, Alan Ritter, and Eduard H Hovy. 2014. Weakly Supervised User Profile Extraction from Twitter. In *ACL*. 165–174.

[28] Yabing Liu, Chloe Kliman-Silver, and Alan Mislove. 2014. The Tweets They Are a-Changin: Evolution of Twitter Users and Behavior. In *ICWSM*, Vol. 30. 5–314.

[29] Miller McPherson, Lynn Smith-Lovin, and James M Cook. 2001. Birds of a feather: Homophily in social networks. *Annual Review of Sociology* 27, 1 (2001), 415–444.

[30] Tomas Mikolov, Ilya Sutskever, Kai Chen, Greg S Corrado, and Jeff Dean. 2013. Distributed representations of words and phrases and their compositionality. In *NIPS*. 3111–3119.

[31] Renato Miranda Filho, Guilherme R Borges, Jussara M Almeida, and Gisele L Pappa. 2014. Inferring User Social Class in Online Social Networks. In *SNAKDD*.

[32] Lawrence Page, Sergey Brin, Rajeev Motwani, and Terry Winograd. 1999. *The PageRank citation ranking: Bringing order to the web*. Technical Report. Stanford InfoLab.

[33] Marco Pennacchiotti and Ana-Maria Popescu. 2011. A Machine Learning Approach to Twitter User Classification. In *ICWSM*. 281–288.

[34] Bryan Perozzi, Rami Al-Rfou, and Steven Skiena. 2014. Deepwalk: Online learning of social representations. In *KDD*. 701–710.

[35] Bryan Perozzi and Steven Skiena. 2015. Exact age prediction in social networks. In *WWW*. 91–92.

[36] Daniel Preoţiuc-Pietro, Vasileios Lampos, and Nikolaos Aletras. 2015. An analysis of the user occupational class through Twitter content. In *ACL-ICJNLP*.

[37] Daniel Preoţiuc-Pietro, Svitlana Volkova, Vasileios Lampos, Yoram Bachrach, and Nikolaos Aletras. 2015. Studying User Income through Language, Behaviour and Affect in Social Media. *PLOS ONE* 10, 9 (2015).

[38] Daniele Quercia, Michal Kosinski, David Stillwell, and Jon Crowcroft. 2011. Our Twitter profiles, our selves: Predicting personality with Twitter. In *SocialCom*. 180–185.

[39] Delip Rao, David Yarowsky, Abhishek Shreevats, and Manaswi Gupta. 2010. Classifying latent user attributes in twitter. In *SMUC*. 37–44.

[40] H. A. Schwartz, J. C. Eichstaedt, M. L. Kern, L. Dziurzynski, S. M. Ramones, M. Agrawal, A. Shah, M. Kosinski, D. Stillwell, M. EP Seligman, and others. 2013. Personality, gender, and age in the language of social media: The open-vocabulary approach. *PloS one* 8, 9 (2013).

[41] Jacopo Staiano, Bruno Lepri, Nadav Aharony, Fabio Pianesi, Nicu Sebe, and Alex Pentland. 2012. Friends don't lie: inferring personality traits from social network structure. In *UBICOMP*. 321–330.

[42] Chenhao Tan, Lillian Lee, Jie Tang, Long Jiang, Ming Zhou, and Ping Li. 2011. User-level sentiment analysis incorporating social networks. In *KDD*. 1397–1405.

[43] Jian Tang, Meng Qu, Mingzhe Wang, Ming Zhang, Jun Yan, and Qiaozhu Mei. 2015. Line: Large-scale information network embedding. In *WWW*. 1067–1077.

[44] A. Tumasjan, T. O. Sprenger, P. G. Sandner, and I. M Welpe. 2010. Predicting elections with Twitter: What 140 characters reveal about political sentiment. In *ICWSM*. 178–185.

[45] Svitlana Volkova and Yoram Bachrach. 2015. On predicting sociodemographic traits and emotions from communications in social networks and their implications to online self-disclosure. *Cyberpsychology, Behavior, and Social Networking* 18, 12 (2015), 726–736.

[46] Jianshu Weng, Ee-Peng Lim, Jing Jiang, and Qi He. 2010. Twitterrank: finding topic-sensitive influential twitterers. In *WSDM*. 261–270.

[47] Christopher KI Williams and Carl Edward Rasmussen. 1996. Gaussian processes for regression. In *NIPS*. 514–520.

[48] Hui Zou and Trevor Hastie. 2005. Regularization and variable selection via the elastic net. *Journal of the Royal Statistical Society: Series B (Statistical Methodology)* 67, 2 (2005), 301–320.

Joint Distributed Representation of Text and Structure of Semi-Structured Documents

Abhishek Laddha*
IBM Research, India
abladdha@in.ibm.com

Salil Joshi[#*]
American Express Big Data Labs
salilrajeev.joshi@aexp.com

Samiulla Shaikh
IBM Research, India
samiullas@in.ibm.com

Sameep Mehta
IBM Research, India
sameep.mehta@in.ibm.com

ABSTRACT

Majority of textual data over web is in the form of semi-structured documents. Thus, structural skeleton of such documents plays important role in determining the semantics of the data content. Presence of structure sometimes allows us to write simple rules to extract such information, but it may not be always possible due to flexibility in the structure and the frequency with which such structures are altered.

In this paper, we propose a joint modeling of text and the associated structure to effectively capture the semantics of the semi-structure documents. The model simultaneously learns the dense continuous representation for word tokens and the structure associated with them. We utilize the context of structures for projection such that similar structures containing semantically similar topics are close to each other in vector space. We explore two semantic text mining tasks over web data to test the effectiveness of our representation *viz.*, *document similarity*, and *table semantic component identification*. In context of traditional rule-based approaches, both these tasks demand rich, domain-specific knowledge sources, homogeneous schema for the documents, and rules that capture the semantics. On the other hand, our approach is unsupervised and resource conscious in nature. Despite of working without knowledge resources and large training data, it performs at par with state-of-the-art rule based and other unsupervised approaches.

CCS CONCEPTS

• **Information systems** → **Document representation**; Clustering and classification;

KEYWORDS

Semantic Document Representation, Document structure, Text mining, Classification and Clustering

---

[#]Work done while working for IBM Research, India until August 2017.
*Authors contributed equally.

ACM Reference Format:
Abhishek Laddha*, Salil Joshi[#*], Samiulla Shaikh, and Sameep Mehta. 2018. Joint Distributed Representation of Text and Structure of Semi-Structured Documents. In *HT '18: 29th ACM Conference on Hypertext and Social Media, July 9–12, 2018, Baltimore, MD, USA.* ACM, New York, NY, USA, 8 pages. https://doi.org/10.1145/3209542.3209551

1 INTRODUCTION

Vector representations had benefited the analytics on the unstructured text widely. Their potential in understanding the plain text were demonstrated successfully by the past efforts like [16]. The work was extended to represent words, sentences and documents efficiently [11, 15]. This line of exploration mainly targeted tasks performed on the plain text which is modeled as a word sequence. [8] showed that even the sequence of documents has useful information and proposed a hierarchical representation that captures this sequencing information.

Unlike the plain-text documents, semi-structured documents are usually HTML or XML formatted, *e.g.*, S.E.C. filings for companies in U.S.A, patent databases, *etc.* Extracting information from unstructured documents operates on flat text representation but semi-structure documents have a richer representation. They logically organize the information using structures, and hence algorithms should leverage such structural information. When it comes to extracting information from semi structured documents, generally the structure is either filtered out, or a fixed structure is assumed for writing extraction rules. The later only works where fixed structure of the documents of interest is known. The extraction rules too are specific to the given data, and can not be adapted for generalized tasks, where structure is not fixed. The important question that we are trying to address here is: can we come up with a generalized approach that can be applicable to the data sources not adhering to fixed structure, still captures the overall semantics resulting from the structure and the content. The primary aim of our work initiated from the need of using the structural information in combination with the text content, so that both of them work together to capture the closest intended meaning of the document.

With the aforementioned aim in mind, we proposed a joint distributed representation for the components of the semi-structured documents, where each component consists of the textual data and corresponding enclosing structure (*e.g.*, DOM path in case of HTML documents). Based on this representation, we experimented with two problems *viz.,*:

- Document similarity: Retrieving most similar documents for a given query document (useful to get the prior art in patent, checking plagiarism in research papers). Here, along with the content of the document, the structure also makes difference. If we ignore the structure, we might end up giving higher similarity scores to two patent documents that mention similar statements in different sections like prior art and core novelty. If we consider the structure, we can differentiate or relate such documents in a better way.
- Table Semantic Component Identification: The tables used in web documents are very flexible in terms of their structure. Automatically interpreting such tables can be tricky sometimes, especially when there are layers row-merges and column merges. Even the simplest non-merging cells can be header cells or data cells depending on the context.

Both these problems are dependent on the document structure but the degree to which the structure influences the tasks is substantially different, thereby testing the effectiveness of our representation under two distant settings. Document similarity is moderately structure dependent, but heavily influenced by the actual text, while in table cell classification, the structure has major influence as compared to the actual text content. The main contributions of our paper can be summarized as follows:

- We propose a neural network model which takes advantage of the structure of document together with text to learn the low-dimensional vector representation of documents/phrases. This is useful to extract information from structured part of document such as tables.
- The proposed approach captures the semantics of structure as well as text. The experimental results on *document similarity* and *table semantic component identification* task demonstrates the effectiveness of our approach.
- The proposed method is completely unsupervised and independent of any domain and language. It doesn't require domain-specific dictionaries, grammars and parser to extract information from web tables or to perform document similarity.

The rest of the paper is organized as follows - in Section 2, we present related literature, followed by a focused technical description of existing tools in Section 3. In Section 4, we formally describe our proposed model for joint learning of representation of structure and text. We describe datasets, experiments, and results in Section 5 along with a discussion on our interpretation of the results. Finally we conclude in Section 6 while briefly pointing out future directions for this work.

2 RELATED WORK

Representation of documents/phrases as continuous vector have been studied extensively. A very popular model for learning a neural language model was proposed in [2] which improves significantly over classical N-gram model. Their model could learn distributed representation for each word, and also provided probabilistic measure for various word sequences. This work has been followed by many others. [9] improves the word embedding by incorporating both local and global document context. In the seminal work, [15] describe two novel model architectures for computing continuous

vector representations of words from very large data sets. This later spawned a branch of work on its own, centered around representing a given context as a vector embedding, such as sentence, paragraph, or even document embeddings [11]. [16] describe modeling of phrases using a frequency based method. By sub-sampling the frequent words, they obtained significant speedup and could also learn more regular word representations. [8] describe model to learn the distributed representations for documents in data stream. [10, 12] used LSTM based auto-encoder to learn the sentence embeddings but LSTM based recurrent neural models are computationally expensive. Aforementioned neural modeling work focuses on textual content to derive context embedding. We draw extensions from these works in our approach by accommodating structural information from the document as explained subsequently.

There is another related thread of research which deals with the problem of extracting structured data (*e.g.* list of objects from tables) from web pages. [3, 5, 20] describes a system that extracts object records based on the tag tree structure. Various heuristic rules based around the tags (*e.g.*, <td>, <tr>, *etc.*) and attributes of structure (*e.g.*, rowspan, colspan, *etc.*) were proposed to discover the minimal object sub-tree and separator tags between objects. Heuristic based around the tags (*e.g.*, <td>, <tr>, *etc.*) and attributes of structure (*e.g.*, rowspan, colspan, *etc.*) are learned from manually labeled examples to identify the structure of table. Subsequently, cell information is classified either into labels using the string edit distance.

[13, 14] uses similarity of tree structure to cluster identical data records. Tag tree is partitioned into data regions and these segments are merged greedily using the tree edit distance matching information. [4] encodes the structured document as token string using tags. Repetitive patterns are identified from sub-string which occur multiple times in the token string. One common pitfall of these approaches comes in the form of nested data objects, where similarity based extraction fails to extract data. [6] proposed a framework named SystemT, which accepts the annotator specification in declarative format (AQL: Annotation Query Language). This work highlights that for industrial applications rule based systems are more suitable for their high precision in exchange of low recall.

Providing high quality rules is always a challenge, while machine learning approaches can quickly provide a classifier using labeled examples. [22, 23] trained a supervised classifier such as *Decision tree, SVM* based on the features constructed using tags, content and words of tables. [17] use conditional random field (CRFs) to classify different component of textual table. Preceding methods either require lots of training data or solely depends on the homogeneous structure of document for clustering. While we used an unsupervised method to learn the continuous representation of structure to extract the information from web pages.

3 BACKGROUND

In this section we provide a technical summary of existing methods for learning distributed vector representation for words and documents also known as embeddings. Our algorithm is fundamentally based on these existing representations.

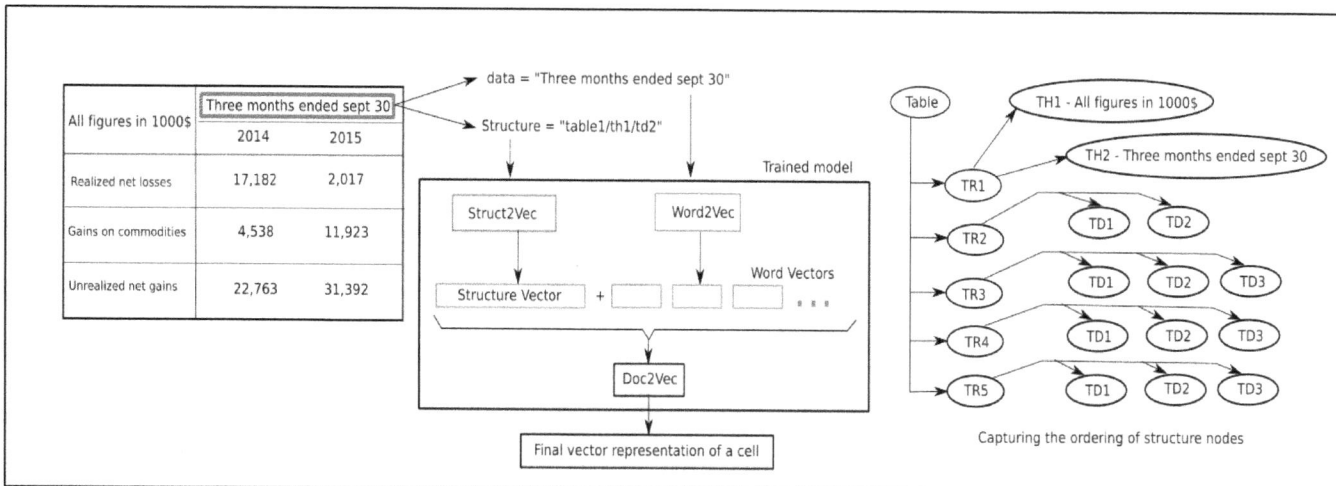

Figure 1: Example Table. HTML tree is used for constructing the structure vector and representation of data and structure are learned from the proposed model.

3.1 Continuous Skip-gram model

Continuous Bag of words (CBOW) and Skip-gram model are simplified version of neural language model which assumes that words that co-occur are statistically more dependent. CBOW model learns the probability distribution of a word given the fixed length preceding and succeeding set of words also know as context words. A log-linear classifier is learned for prediction where input is average of context word vectors. While skip-gram model predicts the context word based on the current word. Mathematically, the objective function of skip-gram model is as follows:

$$L = \sum_{x=1}^{X} -log\left(P\left(W_x^c | w_x\right)\right) \qquad (1)$$

where $W_x^c = \{w_{x-c}, \ldots, w_{x-1}, w_{x+1}, \ldots, w_{x+c}\}$ are the context words and the objective is to minimize the loss function L which is the negative log-likelihood of occurrence of context words given a word w_x. It assumes that context words are independent of each other given the current word. Probability of context word w_{x+j} given the current work w_x is $P(w_{x+j} | w_x)$ and defined as softmax

$$P(w_{x+j} | w_x) = \frac{exp(v_{w_x}^T v'_{w_{x+j}})}{\sum_{w'=1}^{V} exp(v_{w_x}^T v'_{w'})} \qquad (2)$$

where v_{w_x} and v'_{w_x} are input and output vector of word w_x. Further, skip-gram assumes that every context word is equally important and doesn't consider the ordering among the context words. After training the network, words which have similar meaning are mapped to similar position in vector space.

3.2 Paragraph Vector

[11] extended the CBOW and skip-gram models to represent longer documents such as paragraphs. Extending the idea of CBOW model, they concatenated a document vector along with the context words to predict the next word in the context. Document vector is shared for all the words of document and will have semantics of complete

paragraph after training. For new documents only document vector was updated and words vectors are kept constant. Similarly, extending the skip-gram model, they proposed a model which represent each document by a dense vector d_i which is trained to predict the words in the document. More formally, the objective function is

$$L = \sum_{i=1}^{D} -log\left(P\left(W_i | d_i\right)\right) \qquad (3)$$

where W_i are the words of the document and probability is calculated using the softmax function similar to Eq. 2.

4 SOLUTION DESIGN

In this section, we present our algorithm to learn a low-dimensional distributed representation of words, phrases, and the structural nodes together. Our approach is motivated by [11, 15, 16] where an unsupervised approach is employed to learn fixed length embedding of words and documents using the word order observed in the document. In addition to this, our models also takes structural information present in the documents. To be specific, similar to text, we model the probability of observing a specific structural node given the context of surrounding structural nodes and the underlying text. Figure 1 shows an example table where both structure and data of a cell in the table are used to learn the distributed representation of cell.

4.1 Notations

In the current problem setting, we assume that we are given a set of web documents $D = \{d_1, d_2, \ldots, d_M\}$, each document $d_i^w = \{w_{i,1}, w_{i,2}, \ldots, w_{i,N}\}$ consisting of N words and a hierarchical structure. Generally, web documents are in HTML/XML format which provides a tree structure and corresponding textual content is typically present under leaf nodes of tree [3]. Figure 1 shows an example tree structure of table where leaf elements of have the data of table. Tree structure can be translated into vectors using various techniques as described in Section 4.4, we refer to

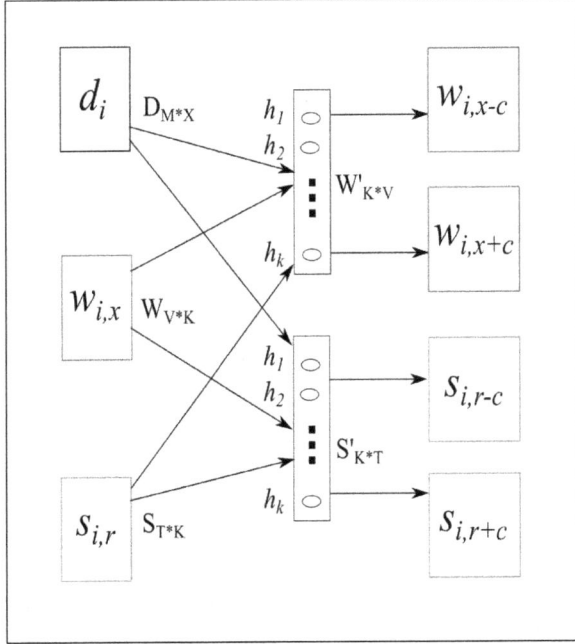

Figure 2: Main Architecture of our network. Input to the model is 1-hot encoding for word $w_{i,x}$, corresponding structure $s_{i,x}$ and document d_i. Outputs are 1-hot encoding of context word and hierarchical context structure in range $\{x-c, x+c\}$. $W_{V x K}$ transform the one-hot encoding of words into K-dimensional vector while $W'_{K x V}$ transforms back the K-dimensional vector into one-hot encoding of words.

those vectors as "structure vector". We obtained the ordering of leaf node structure vectors in the document $d_i^s = \{s_{i,1}, s_{i,2}, \ldots, s_{i,R}\}$ by performing in-order traversal of the tree. Note that each leaf elements can have a sequence of words which will have same structure vector. For *e.g.*, structure vector *table/th1/td2* shown in figure 1 have sequence of words "Three months ended sept 30". We call the subsequent structure in the ordering as "hierarchical context structure" to avoid confusion with structure of next word (which can have same structure as of current word). Let, the no. of unique words in vocabulary be V, no. of unique documents be M, unique structure vectors be T. We map each document, word and structure into low-dimension embedding vector of length K. During training we thus aim to learn the $(M + V + T) * K$ parameters.

4.2 Model Architecture

The architecture of the proposed model is shown in Figure 2. It is a two layer hierarchical neural network where one layer models the contexts of the structure while another layer models the contextual information of word sequences. The structure layer learns the neural language model of structure of document by predicting the hierarchical context structures given the current word and it's structure. The gist of the skip-gram model is to learn the semantic representation of words by participating the current word vector to predict the context words and it exploits a linguistic property that words that occur in similar context have similar semantic properties.

We followed similar notion for structure, based on the assumption that similar structures (those occurring in similar context of structures) have similar properties and words occurring under those structure will most probably belong to same semantic class. For *e.g.*, the words which are present in first column of table are most likely to be row header.

Further, we adopted the idea from [11] where each paragraph is mapped to unique vector and concatenation of paragraph vector and word vector is used to predict the context words. The intuition is that the paragraph vector will act as a common representation for the topic of paragraph. We employed a similar idea where each document is mapped to a unique vector and this document vector captures the topic of the overall document taking into account the relative position of text using the structural prediction. Document vector is shared among all the words of a document but not across the documents. For *e.g.*, each table cell is mapped to a vector which learns the representation of the data of the cell as well as the structural position of cell in the table.

Input to the model is the 3-hot encoding vector where each one hot encoding vector correspond to word, structure and document respectively and outputs are the context word probabilities and context structure probabilities. Formally, the objective function which we minimize is:

$$L = \sum_{i=1}^{|D|} \Bigg[\sum_{x=1}^{N} -log\, P\left(W_{i,x}^c | w_{i,x}, s_{i,x}, d_i\right)$$
$$+ \alpha \sum_{r=1}^{R} \sum_{w_x \in s_{i,r}} -log\, P\left(S_{i,r}^c | w_{i,x}, s_{i,r}, d_i\right) \Bigg] \quad (4)$$

where $W_{i,x}^c = \{w_{i,x-c}, \ldots, w_{i,x-1}, w_{i,x+1}, \ldots, w_{i,x+c}\}$ are context words except the current word $w_{i,x}$ and $S_{i,r}^c = \{s_{i,r-c}, \ldots, s_{i,r-1}, s_{i,r+1}, \ldots, s_{i,r+c}\}$ are hierarchical context structure except the current structural node $s_{i,r}$, $s_{i,x}$ is the structure of the current word and d_i is the document corresponding to context word. α specifies a trade-off between focusing on minimization of negative log-likelihood of structure sequence versus word sequences. Higher values of α will incorporate more importance to structure, depending upon the downstream task α could be fine-tuned. For *e.g.*, in the experiment section we have shown higher value of α is useful for "table semantic component identification" which mainly depends upon structural information for classification.

We assume that the prediction of context word and structure are independent of each other given the current word, structure and document. Hence conditional probability can be written as softmax function

$$P(w_{i,x+j} | w_{i,x}, s_{i,x}, d_i) = \frac{exp(u_{i,x}^T v'_{w_{i,x+j}})}{\sum_{w=1}^{V} exp(u_{i,x}^T v'_w)} \quad (5)$$

where $u_{i,x}$ is concatenation of input vector of $w_{i,x}$, $s_{i,x}$ and d_i, v'_w is output vector of word w. Similar to Eq. 5 probability of context structure (second part of Eq. 4) will be calculated by replacing the output vector of words (v'_w) to output vector of structures. Here, increasing the size of context c will improve the quality of model with the expense of higher computational cost.

An important point to note in Eq. 4 is that the context of structure is the next hierarchical structures in the document tree instead of the structure of next word. This captures the semantics among the structure, for *e.g.* in context of *Row Header* structures of *Data Cell* are more probable irrespective of text length. Finally, document vector is used to combine these vectors which can be consider as the global context for each document. Post training, the document vector acts as features in the classification task using any existing classifier or similarity between the document can be calculated directly as cosine distance between the vectors. One importance advantage of our model is that it is completely unsupervised and can work for tasks for which sufficient knowledge sources do not exist or enough labeled data is not available.

4.3 Model Optimization

We trained our neural network using the stochastic gradient descent where gradients are computed using back-propagation which is very suitable for large-scale problems. Calculating gradients is proportional to number of words in vocabulary and number of unique structure vectors which can be easily of the order of millions for large set of web documents available. An efficient alternative is described in [16] which uses the negative sampling approach. Instead of summing over all the words for calculating the gradient in each step it uses the certain negative samples to calculate the probability. Thus, our task becomes to distinguish the context word distribution from k negative samples distribution. For very large dataset, $k = \{2-5\}$ are enough for learning the good representation. We used negative sampling approach for calculating the context word probability as well as context structure probabilities.

4.4 Mapping Structure to the Vector space

Web document consists of text and tags which can be modeled as tag tree. A tag in a web document is marked by a tag name, all the internal nodes of a tree are tag nodes and all the leaf nodes are text nodes. Figure 1 shows an example tree which have internal nodes as tags and leaf node have data of table. We need some abstraction mechanism to translate the tree structure (HTML/XML) into vector. Since tags are the basic component for document representation and the tags themselves carry a certain structure information, it is intuitive to examine the tag token vector formed using the tree of document. For each leaf node there is a tag path, containing the ordered sequence of ancestor nodes in the tree. A simple approach would be to consider the tag path as a structure of text present in leaf node but it doesn't contain the information about the relative position of text in the document. For *e.g.*, both the <th> in figure 1 would have the same structure vector. We traversed the tree in breadth-first manner and label all the children of node corresponding to their enumerated number to capture the relative position of text among the leaf nodes. To generate the tag vector for any node in tree, ordered sequence of ancestor nodes are created where each ancestor node is appended by it's label in breadth first traversal.

```
<table>
  <tr> <th>All figures in 1000$ </th>
       <th> Three months ended sept 30 </th>
  </tr>
  <tr> <td>2014</td> <td>2015</td>
  </tr>
```

```
.
.
<\table>
```

For the table shown in Fig. 1 and corresponding HTML tree, tag structure for *"All figures in 1000$"* would be *"table/tr1/td1"* while tag structure of *"2014"* is *"table/tr2/td2"*. We formed the vocabulary of all the unique tag structure. These tag structures are converted to 1-hot encoding which we called as structure vector s_i of leaf node. The 1-hot encoded vectors along with the input documents are used to learn the continuous representation of the structure paths.

5 EXPERIMENTS

In this section, we describe the experimental evaluation of our proposed model, which we refer as Document-Structure model (doc+struct2vec). We evaluated our model on two popular application in data mining: (1) table semantic component identification, and (2) document similarity to understand the behavior of learned document vectors. In all the experiments, we use cosine distance to measure the similarity between embedding vectors. Further, all the embeddings are initialized using a uniform distribution from range $[-\frac{1}{K}, \frac{1}{K}]$, where K is the embedding size.

5.1 Table Semantic Component Identification

5.1.1 Task. [1] describe row class definitions for tables provided in web data. Our work follows similar definition, and we define following classes of interest over table cells:

(1) Row Header - A cell in the table that serves as a header for subsequent data cells in the same row
(2) Super Row Header - Cells that govern row header by providing higher level categorization
(3) Column Header - A cell in the table that serves as a header for subsequent data cells in the same column
(4) Super Column Header - Cells that provide higher level categorization of column header
(5) Data cell - Cells holding actual data content in the tables

To extract the structured information from table, it requires to assign appropriate class to each table cell. The inputs for the algorithm are the cell content and the encapsulating document structure (HTML structure in this case as shown in figure 1).

5.1.2 Dataset. We collected our dataset from Securities and Exchange Commission (S.E.C.) filings[1] for companies in U.S.A. We collected 131 web documents filing in HTML format and each file contains comprehensive summary of the company's financial performance. Since there is no predefined structure of documents, various ways are used to display the same information and different HTML tags are used to define the tables containing financial information. To extract information from these documents, each document is converted into DOM tree representation. Then all the subtrees containing the <table> tag are extracted and considered as separate tree. Here, we assumed that all table of document will have <table> tag. In general, following this assumption will give the high recall and low precision for detecting the tables because

---

[1]https://www.sec.gov/dera/data/financial-statement-data-sets.html

No. of structure	12,735
No. of Tables	12,452
Vocabulary Size	14,017
No. of table cell	72,310

Table 1: Dataset statistics for table semantic component identification task

<table> tags are also used for decorative purposes in HTML documents.

Next, for each tree, structure vector for leaf nodes are created as described in Section 4.4. To train the model as described in Section 4, we need to define what constituents the documents and ordering among the words. Here, every table cell is considered as document and document vector representation is learned based on the table cell content and structure. Table is traversed in row-major order to generate the sequence of words and sequence of structure is generated by taking the in-order traversal of tree and discarding all the internal nodes. Overall, we extracted 12, 452 tables from documents

Hyper-parameters	Table semantic component identification	Document similarity
context words window	2	3
# of negative samples	2	2
α	0.5	0.25
embedding size	300	300

Table 2: Hyper-parameters of tasks

and considered them as training data. Detailed Statistics of dataset is given in Table 1. In the pre-processing step, we tokenized the text using NLTK and removed the stop-words. Further, we replaced the words which appear very rarely (frequency = 1) with static token "UNK" and converted all numeric tokens into static token "NUM". All the hyper-parameters used for training are tuned using 5-fold cross validation and detailed in Table 2.

5.1.3 Experimental Procedure. After learning the vector representation, we used the following procedure for the classification of table cells. Training supervised classifier such as Logistic Regression or SVM requires lots of labeled data and it's absence makes this task non-trivial. To overcome the absence of sizable labeled data, we employed the approach similar to seed dictionaries [18].

We labeled certain number of seed words (4 words) for each category and measured the similarity of table cell with seed words. Each table cell is assigned to class with highest similarity (> 0.6) among the seed word. After assigning the classes to table cells using the similarity measure, we observed that there are cells whose similarity with seed words is very low and there is not enough confidence to assign a particular category. In that case we applied a post-processing step and used generic rules to assign the semantic categories. We used the following rules:

- If there is only one non-empty cell present in a row (excluding first few rows of table) and similarity with seed words is low then assign it to "Super row header" category.
- If more than half of the table cells are assigned to same category in a row then assign all the cell of that row to same category except the first non-empty cell.

All the results reported in Table 3 which have vector representation includes the post-processing step. To show the effectiveness of our model we compared the performance of the classification task with following strong baselines methods.

(1) **Rule Based Approach:** [6] proposed a framework named SystemT, which accepts the annotator specification in declarative format termed as *Annotation Query Language* (AQL). This work used dictionary based rules in order to achieve high precision expected by industrial applications.

(2) **word2vec:** [16] proposed a neural network based model to learn the distributed vector. After learning the word vectors, average of all the words of the document is used for document representation which is used as described above.

(3) **doc2vec:** [11] proposed a extension of [16] model to get a unique representation of each document.

(4) **doc+struct2vec:** Our model described in Section 4

For quantitative evaluation, we manually labeled a total of 1983 table cells from 35 tables and assigned one of 5 categories described above to each of the table cell. Labeling is done by 3 authors to avoid biases.

5.1.4 Result Discussion. Table 3 shows the result (Precision, Recall, F1-score) of classification task. Table 3 shows that doc2+struct2vec outperformed all the baselines significantly on the F-score metric for all classes. Rank of our method in recall metric is second in few classes while rule based system described in [6] has been best but requires dictionaries and organized structure which makes it a tedious task to on-board a new domain or language. Also, precision of rule based system is higher for few classes but at the expense of low recall while our model performed significantly better at F-score for all classes. We show here that by modeling the structural information, our domain independent approach performs better to the domain specific rule based approach [7].

Further, we observed that hybrid method with unsupervised doc+struct2vec and generic rules boosted the performance of unsupervised method substantially with minimum effort. Our model outperformed word2vec and doc2vec substantially, which shows that our model has successfully exploited the structure of document and relationship between them, resulting in improved performance. word2vec and doc2vec have considered only text of the data cell for the classification task, certain text such as 2014 (can be year or number) will always be classified as data cell since most of the numerical attributes belong to data cell category. While doc+struct2vec considered the structure of data cell as well to learn the representation of cell and able to distinguish between the column header (year 2014) and data cell (2014).

5.2 Document Similarity

5.2.1 Task. Semantic similarity between pair of document is defined as the distance between the conceptual likeness they exhibit. A common way of doing this is to transform the documents into tf-idf vectors, then compute the cosine similarity between them. Existing methods also resort to knowledge based distances where knowledge sources such as WordNet are typically used to define semantic similarity across tokens in the document. In contrast, we used neural embedding derived from structure as well as text of

Class	doc+struct2vec			word2vec			doc2vec			rule based		
	P	R	F	P	R	F	P	R	F	P	R	F
Column Header	82.75	71.11^1	76.49^1	89.02	54.07	67.28	76.34	52.59	62.28	**83.33**	66.67	74.07
Super Row Header	55.55	83.78^1	66.67^1	26.76	51.35	35.18	46.77	78.37	58.58	**77.77**	56.75	65.625
Super Column Header	**79.31**	48.93^3	60.52^1	30.23	**55.53**	39.09	47.82	23.04	31.42	59.52	53.19	56.17
Data Cell	**97.34**	89.99^2	93.49^1	94.56	89.99	92.91	96.44	89.86	93.04	88.02	**99.27**	93.30
Row Header	82.30	94.58^1	83.43^1	75.69	54.15	63.13	79.33	84.98	82.06	**97.05**	39.13	55.77
Total Micro	**92.78**	86.88^2	89.73^1	86.90	81.38	84.05	90.67	84.91	87.77	87.48	**87.48**	87.48
Total Macro	79.41	75.67^1	76.12^1	63.25	60.96	59.37	69.34	65.84	65.47	**81.14**	63.00	68.99

Table 3: Performance of table semantic component identification task with Precision, Recall, and F1 scores for different models. Superscript denotes the rank of our model for respective class and measure. Bold values denote the best score for each class and measure.

the document to compute similarity which is useful for class of documents for which sufficient knowledge sources are not available.

5.2.2 Dataset. We collected the patent documents from USPTO patent redbook bulk download, that provides the raw data[2] (*xml* format) starting from 1976. Each patent is assigned at least one class indicating the subject to which the invention relates and it's done manually while evaluating. For truthful evaluation of the novelty of the patent, it is essential to identify the prior art related to that technology. Thus, need to check similarity with all the previous patents and can help in avoiding patent infringement prior to developing new technology. Further, to study the particular technology it is requisite to classify the patent correctly to all the technologies for which it is relevant.

We collected all the granted patents of year 2016 and parsed them using the *xml* parser. We extracted all class labels of patents and considered only those patents which have a single class label. Further, to analyze the patent, we included the full text and struc-

Model	Accuracy score	V-measure score
Words as features	77.45	0.4215
word2vec	72.70	0.325825
doc2vec	76.44	0.5549
doc2vec + words	77.05	-
doc+struct2vec	78.40	**0.5723**
doc+struct2vec + word	**78.51**	-

Table 4: Results of various baselines on the v-measure score of clusters and accuracy on document classification task

ture involved in , <description>, <claims> tags. We extracted a total of 3978 utility patents belonging to top 10 classes and considered them as training data. This dataset has vocabulary size of $34,713$ and number of unique structures is 87 with average number of words in each document as 5456.

5.2.3 Experimental Procedure. In this task, each patent is considered as a document and separate tree structure is extracted for three tags (, <description>, <claims>). Structure vector for each node is constructed as described in Section 4.4. Each tag tree of one section of patent is large compared to a tables of previous task. Hence, we do not consider the ordering among the element of

[2]https://bulkdata.uspto.gov/

tree during breadth-first traversal and children are not numbered. It explains the decrease in total number of unique structure compared to previous task. Here, our aim is to capture the relative position of text present in various section of document instead of relative position of text in the same section. For *e.g.,* 'Claims' section of a patent contributes more to the semantics of document compared to 'Description', the aim is to take into account the respective weights instead of assigning equals weights to text tokens of each section. Data was further pre-processed as described in the previous task. In our experiments hyper-parameters are tuned on 5-fold cross-validated of classification task and are provided in Table 2.

Post training, we cluster the document vectors using the K-means algorithm. We evaluated these clusters using the V-measure score [19] which is harmonic mean between the homogeneity and completeness of clusters. [21] has shown that V-measure is biased when the number of clusters is large but since number of clusters are small we are using it. Class label of each document are considered as the true label for clusters. To compare our model we formed the following baseline by using all the words of the documents. We considered all the words as feature and used tf-idf to identify comparative importance of words in the document. Then, clustering was performed on updated tf-idf vectors, we refer to this baseline as "Words as features". We also compared our model with word2vec and doc2vec.

Since, we have a class label corresponding to each patent, we also used learned embedding of documents to perform supervised classification task. We trained a Logistic classifier with hyper-parameters tuned using a 5-fold cross validation. For comparison, we considered the same baselines as of clustering task. Additionally, for doc2vec and doc+struct2vec models, we concatenated the average word vectors with document vector ("doc2vec + words" and "doc+struct2vec + word" respectively) to assist in the classification task.

5.2.4 Result Discussion: Table 4 compares the clustering and classification results of various baselines. Low value of α for document similarity task is due to the fact that most patent document have uniform schema structurally. We think performance superiority of our model is due to learning of importance of different section while computing the overall semantic representation of the document. This also conforms with the low performance of word2vec model which was not able to distinguish between the importance of words in different sections which got further elevated due to averaging of word vectors. We observed that doc2vec performed significantly better than only words as features in the clustering task. We believe it is due to compact nature of continuous vector while feature length of "word as feature" is massive as vocabulary size and performed poorly. For clustering task, we haven't showed the result of models with concatenated word vector because it decreases the performance drastically as implied from low performance of "word2vec" model.

For classification, we observed that performance of "words as features" is similar to doc2vec because classifier has learned importance of words due to supervised nature. Our approach will be advantageous in case if we wanted to add more fine-grained classes. We can learn the document representation in unsupervised way and automatically relabel all the previous patent to maintain the consistency by computing similarity with few labeled patents for new class. While considering only words as features will not work with few labeled examples. Further, doc+struct2vec has outperformed all the other and this confirms our hypothesis about importance of document structure, as well as validates our implementation.

6 CONCLUSION

In this paper, we described a generic neural network model to learn the distributed representation of semi-structured documents in unsupervised manner. We learned the vector representation by predicting the surrounding word as well as context structure given the current word and structure. The structure vector capture the semantics of text contained within structure and statistically pattern among structure. We experimented on the S.E.C filing dataset to identify the semantically similar components of tables and document similarity on patent dataset using the compact representation. We showed that our method is competitive with state-of-the-art methods. Further, it doesn't require any predefined dictionaries or homogeneous schema of document which reduces the tedious task of forming rules for every domain and languages.

REFERENCES

[1] Marco D Adelfio and Hanan Samet. 2013. Schema extraction for tabular data on the web. *Proceedings of the VLDB Endowment* 6, 6 (2013), 421–432.
[2] Yoshua Bengio, Réjean Ducharme, Pascal Vincent, and Christian Jauvin. 2003. A neural probabilistic language model. *journal of machine learning research* 3, Feb (2003), 1137–1155.
[3] David Buttler, Ling Liu, and Calton Pu. 2001. A fully automated object extraction system for the World Wide Web. In *Distributed Computing Systems, 2001. 21st International Conference on*. IEEE, 361–370.
[4] Chia-Hui Chang and Shao-Chen Lui. 2001. IEPAD: information extraction based on pattern discovery. In *Proceedings of the 10th international conference on World Wide Web*. ACM, 681–688.
[5] Hsin-Hsi Chen, Shih-Chung Tsai, and Jin-He Tsai. 2000. Mining tables from large scale HTML texts. In *Proceedings of the 18th conference on Computational linguistics-Volume 1*. Association for Computational Linguistics, 166–172.
[6] Laura Chiticariu, Rajasekar Krishnamurthy, Yunyao Li, Sriram Raghavan, Frederick R Reiss, and Shivakumar Vaithyanathan. 2010. SystemT: an algebraic approach to declarative information extraction. In *Proceedings of the 48th Annual Meeting of the Association for Computational Linguistics*. Association for Computational Linguistics, 128–137.
[7] Laura Chiticariu, Yunyao Li, and Frederick R Reiss. 2013. Rule-based information extraction is dead! long live rule-based information extraction systems!. In *EMNLP*. 827–832.
[8] Nemanja Djuric, Hao Wu, Vladan Radosavljevic, Mihajlo Grbovic, and Narayan Bhamidipati. 2015. Hierarchical neural language models for joint representation of streaming documents and their content. In *Proceedings of the 24th International Conference on World Wide Web*. ACM, 248–255.
[9] Eric H Huang, Richard Socher, Christopher D Manning, and Andrew Y Ng. 2012. Improving word representations via global context and multiple word prototypes. In *Proceedings of the 50th Annual Meeting of the Association for Computational Linguistics: Long Papers-Volume 1*. Association for Computational Linguistics, 873–882.
[10] Ryan Kiros, Yukun Zhu, Ruslan R Salakhutdinov, Richard Zemel, Raquel Urtasun, Antonio Torralba, and Sanja Fidler. 2015. Skip-thought vectors. In *Advances in neural information processing systems*. 3294–3302.
[11] Quoc V Le and Tomas Mikolov. 2014. Distributed Representations of Sentences and Documents.. In *ICML*, Vol. 14. 1188–1196.
[12] Jiwei Li, Minh-Thang Luong, and Dan Jurafsky. 2015. A hierarchical neural autoencoder for paragraphs and documents. *arXiv preprint arXiv:1506.01057* (2015).
[13] Bing Liu, Robert Grossman, and Yanhong Zhai. 2003. Mining data records in web pages. In *Proceedings of the ninth ACM SIGKDD international conference on Knowledge discovery and data mining*. ACM, 601–606.
[14] Bing Liu and Yanhong Zhai. 2005. NET–a system for extracting web data from flat and nested data records. In *International Conference on Web Information Systems Engineering*. Springer, 487–495.
[15] Tomas Mikolov, Kai Chen, Greg Corrado, and Jeffrey Dean. 2013. Efficient estimation of word representations in vector space. *arXiv preprint arXiv:1301.3781* (2013).
[16] Tomas Mikolov, Ilya Sutskever, Kai Chen, Greg S Corrado, and Jeff Dean. 2013. Distributed representations of words and phrases and their compositionality. In *Advances in neural information processing systems*. 3111–3119.
[17] David Pinto, Andrew McCallum, Xing Wei, and W Bruce Croft. 2003. Table extraction using conditional random fields. In *Proceedings of the 26th annual international ACM SIGIR conference on Research and development in informaion retrieval*. ACM, 235–242.
[18] Duangmanee Pew Putthividhya and Junling Hu. 2011. Bootstrapped named entity recognition for product attribute extraction. In *Proceedings of the Conference on Empirical Methods in Natural Language Processing*. Association for Computational Linguistics, 1557–1567.
[19] Andrew Rosenberg and Julia Hirschberg. 2007. V-Measure: A Conditional Entropy-Based External Cluster Evaluation Measure.. In *EMNLP-CoNLL*, Vol. 7. 410–420.
[20] Ashwin Tengli, Yiming Yang, and Nian Li Ma. 2004. Learning table extraction from examples. In *Proceedings of the 20th international conference on Computational Linguistics*. Association for Computational Linguistics, 987.
[21] Jurgen Van Gael, Andreas Vlachos, and Zoubin Ghahramani. 2009. The infinite HMM for unsupervised PoS tagging. In *Proceedings of the 2009 Conference on Empirical Methods in Natural Language Processing: Volume 2-Volume 2*. Association for Computational Linguistics, 678–687.
[22] Yalin Wang and Jianying Hu. 2002. A machine learning based approach for table detection on the web. In *Proceedings of the 11th international conference on World Wide Web*. ACM, 242–250.
[23] Jeonghee Yi and Neel Sundaresan. 2000. A classifier for semi-structured documents. In *Proceedings of the sixth ACM SIGKDD international conference on Knowledge discovery and data mining*. ACM, 340–344.

As Stable As You Are: Re-ranking Search Results using Query-Drift Analysis

Haggai Roitman
IBM Research AI
Haifa, Israel
haggai@il.ibm.com

Ella Rabinovich
IBM Research AI
Haifa, Israel
ellak@il.ibm.com

Oren Sar Shalom*
Intuit
Hod Hasharon, Israel
oren.sarshalom@gmail.com

ABSTRACT

This work studies the merits of using query-drift analysis for search re-ranking. A relationship between the ability to *predict* the quality of a result list retrieved by an *arbitrary* method, as manifested by its estimated query-drift, and the ability to improve that method's initial retrieval by *re-ranking* documents in the list based on such prediction is established. A novel document property, termed "*aspect-stability*", is identified as the main enabler for transforming the output of an aspect-level query-drift analysis into concrete document scores for search re-ranking. Using an evaluation with various TREC corpora with common baseline retrieval methods, the potential of the proposed re-ranking approach is demonstrated.

ACM Reference Format:

Haggai Roitman, Ella Rabinovich, and Oren Sar Shalom. 2018. As Stable As You Are: Re-ranking Search Results using Query-Drift Analysis. In *HT '18: 29th ACM Conference on Hypertext and Social Media, July 9–12, 2018, Baltimore, MD, USA*. ACM, New York, NY, USA, 5 pages. https://doi.org/10.1145/3209542.3209567

1 INTRODUCTION

This work studies the problem of re-ranking a given document list, retrieved in response to a query, so as to improve retrieval effectiveness. To this end, a novel re-ranking approach is proposed based on query-drift analysis. A query-drift may occur when one or more aspects, which are irrelevant to the searched information need, are overemphasized in the retrieved result list, in the expense of relevant (and important) query aspects [3]. As a result, search quality may be negatively affected. Several methods have been suggested for estimating query-drift effects within a given retrieved result returned by some retrieval method in response to a given query [11, 12, 14, 17]. This work builds on top of such previous works, utilizing query-drift analysis for deriving a novel re-ranking approach. The proposed re-ranking approach is based on two main observations made in this work about the query-drift problem.

Observation 1: *By emphasizing the initial searched query towards a single specific aspect, that aspect's role in manifesting the*

---

*Work was done while the author was in IBM Research AI.

existence of a query-drift within the initial retrieved result and its marginal effect may be estimated.

The first observation directly builds on top of [3, 11]. As may be implied by this observation, a more refined, aspect-level, query-drift analysis may allow to trace those potential query aspects to which the underlying method is expected to provide better or worse performance.

Noting that query-drift analysis has been performed so far on a **whole** list-level [11, 12, 14, 17] rather than on an **individual** document-level, the second observation is stated as follows.

Observation 2: *While a result list as a whole may exhibit a query-drift, some subset of its retrieved documents may actually exhibit more moderate (to even no) query-drift effects.*

Further following this observation, in this work, a novel *document-level* query-drift analysis is proposed. A relationship is set between the ability to *predict* the quality of a result list retrieved by an *arbitrary* method via query-drift estimation and the ability to improve that method's initial retrieval by *re-ranking* documents in the list based on such prediction. Such a relationship is based on a novel document property, formally identified in this work and termed "**aspect-stability**". Moving from the original query to a single aspect-expanded query, an aspect-stable document strictly maintains its relative rank in both the initial and the aspect-response lists, as determined by the underlying retrieval method. Such documents are assumed to provide better answers to the query and basically characterize the durability of the underlying method to possible effects of query-drift. Hence, scores of documents that exhibit aspect-stable behavior are boosted for re-ranking.

A novel search re-ranking approach which is driven by the two above observations is proposed in this work. Using various TREC corpora and several common retrieval methods, the potential of this approach is demonstrated.

2 RELATED WORK

The classic re-ranking problem addressed in this work has been studied by many previous works. Several different approaches have been proposed, including usage of inter-document similarities [1, 10], induced structures [7, 9], score regularization [6], label propagation [16] and query performance prediction [13]. In this work, a novel re-ranking approach is proposed based on the combination of query-drift analysis and a new identified aspect-stability document property, which serves as the core source for re-scoring documents based on such analysis.

This work builds on top of [11]'s reference-list driven query performance prediction (QPP) framework. In [11], an automatic way in which pseudo-effective and pseudo-ineffective reference lists can be identified and selected using QPP methods was suggested.

Yet, [11] utilized such selection solely for the purpose of improving a given baseline QPP method's prediction quality. The approach taken in this work has a different goal, where the aim is to improve retrieval performance via search re-ranking by inducing a novel *document-level* robustness estimate.

3 IMPLEMENTATION

3.1 Preliminaries

Let q denote a query (*topic*), capturing some information need I_q, submitted to some retrieval method $\mathcal{M}$ over a corpus of documents $\mathcal{D}$. Let $D_q^{[k]} \subseteq \mathcal{D}$ denote the result list of the k highest ranked documents returned by method $\mathcal{M}$ in response to q. Let $Score_q(d)$ and $r_{d;q}$ further denote the score of document $d \in \mathcal{D}$ according to method $\mathcal{M}$ and its rank in $D_q^{[k]}$, respectively. For a given query q, let $\mathcal{A}_q$ denote a set of *topic aspects* (or aspects for short); each aspect $a \in \mathcal{A}_q$ encodes some possible facet of I_q.

3.2 Aspect-response lists generation

As a first step, for a given query q, its corresponding topic aspect set $\mathcal{A}_q$ is derived by considering the top-n candidate aspects a with the highest likelihood according to the RM3 model [8].

Using a term-at-a-time query expansion approach, for each given aspect $a \in \mathcal{A}_q$, its corresponding aspect-response is generated by expanding query q with that single aspect. Such expansion is simply implemented by adding the aspect as an additional disjunctive term to the query (i.e.: $q \vee a$). Let $D_{q \vee a}^{[k]}$ denote the aspect-response returned by method $\mathcal{M}$ given $q \vee a$, containing the top-k documents in $\mathcal{D}$ with the highest score $Score_{q \vee a}(d)$.

3.3 Aspect-response lists selection

Following Observation 1, the purpose of this step is to find a subset of aspects in $\mathcal{A}_q$ to which the underlying retrieval method $\mathcal{M}$ may provide reasonable performance. To this end, a **What-If Analysis** approach based on [11] is utilized and a subset of pseudo-effective aspect-lists $\{D_{q \vee a}^{[k]}\}$ is selected. For a given aspect $a \in \mathcal{A}_q$, let $\mathcal{P}_{rsp}(a)$ now denote the predicted quality of an aspect-response $D_{q \vee a}^{[k]}$ that was determined as pseudo-effective [11]. Following [11], we set $\mathcal{P}_{rsp}(a) \stackrel{def}{=} \mathcal{F}_a$, where $\mathcal{F}_a$ denotes the corresponding *Brown-Forsythe* test statistic value [2].

3.4 Aspect-stability document scoring

The next step utilizes the promising lists $\{D_{q \vee a}^{[k]}\}$ for re-ranking the documents in the initial retrieved list D_q.

3.4.1 Document aspect-stability criterion. Following Observation 2, a document $d \in D_q^{[k]}$ is now defined as "*aspect-stable*" with respect to a given aspect $a \in \mathcal{A}_q$, iff d is also included in $D_{q \vee a}^{[k]}$ and its initial rank in $D_q^{[k]}$ has not been downgraded by method $\mathcal{M}$ in $D_{q \vee a}^{[k]}$. For a given document $d \in D_q^{[k]}$, aspect $a \in \mathcal{A}_q$ and aspect-response $D_{q \vee a}^{[k]}$, let $\delta_{d;a}$ encode the fact that document d is aspect-stable (or not), i.e.:

$$\delta_{d;a} \stackrel{def}{=} \delta \left[d \in D_q^{[k]} \cap D_{q \vee a}^{[k]} \wedge r_{d;q \vee a} \le r_{d;q} \right] \quad (1)$$

As may be implied by this criterion, based on method $\mathcal{M}$ responses, a document that is aspect-stable may keep its relative quality with respect to the original information need I_q. In addition, such a document may provide a similar (relative) quality guarantee (and sometimes even a better one, i.e., when $r_{d;q \vee a} < r_{d;q}$) when being required to satisfy a specific aspect $a \in \mathcal{A}_q$; yet, still in the *context* of the original query q. Therefore, aspect-stability provides valuable *evidence* for a given document's ability to provide reasonable answer to a specific aspect of the main information need, yet not sacrificing its relative quality with respect to the original information need. Trying to generalize on such document property, this work hypothesizes that: *a document that remains stable with respect to more aspects of the main topic being queried I_q according to method $\mathcal{M}$, is a document that may provide a better response made by that same method for the original query q.*

3.4.2 Aspect-stable document rank scoring. The basic motivation behind the next $\mathcal{P}_{rank}(d; a)$ scoring component is that, aspect-stable documents that were originally ranked higher in $D_q^{[k]}$ should be more preferred. This is attributed to the fact that, the higher a document $d \in D_q^{[k]}$ rank is, the more strict is the aspect-stability criterion it must satisfy (see again Eq. 1). By satisfying a more stringent criterion for a given aspect $a \in \mathcal{A}_q$, such a document is assumed to provide a better answer to that specific aspect of the searched information need. Furthermore, for a given aspect $a \in \mathcal{A}_q$, the rank of an aspect-stable document $d \in D_q^{[k]} \cap D_{q \vee a}^{[k]}$ may actually be higher than its original rank (i.e., $r_{d;q \vee a} < r_{d;q}$). This would imply that, according to retrieval method $\mathcal{M}$, document d provides a better answer for aspect a relatively to at least one of the other documents that were previously ranked higher than d in $D_q^{[k]}$. Moreover, since document d is aspect-stable, this comes with minimum sacrifice of its ability to provide a potential relevant response to the original information need being searched. In accordance, the higher the gain in the document's rank is, the more important it should be.

The two aspect-stability document rank dimensions that were mentioned above are now captured by $\mathcal{P}_{rank}(d; a)$ using $\tau(l, r)$ as follows:

$$\mathcal{P}_{rank}(d; a) \stackrel{def}{=} \tau(k, r_{d;q}) \cdot \left(1 + \tau(r_{d;q}, r_{d;q \vee a}) \right), \quad (2)$$

where k is the number of documents in the initial list $D_q^{[k]}$ and $\tau(l, r) \stackrel{def}{=} \max \left(0, \frac{2(l+1-r)}{l(l+1)} \right)$.

3.4.3 Aspect-stability uniqueness scoring. Recall that, a document's aspect-stability may not be unique and may vary for different aspects in $\mathcal{A}_q$. For a given aspect $a \in \mathcal{A}_q$, the aspect-stability uniqueness of a given document $d \in D_q^{[k]} \cap D_{q \vee a}^{[k]}$ actually depends on the overall number of documents in $D_q^{[k]}$ that are also aspect-stable with respect to that same aspect. The fewer such documents, the more document d's aspect-stability would be unique, implying that it might be less sensitive to query-drift with respect to aspect *a*. Hence, such a document would be more preferable. The aspect-stability uniqueness of a given aspect $a \in \mathcal{A}_q$ is determined by the inverse frequency of documents in $D_q^{[k]}$ that are aspect-stable with respect to that aspect, i.e.:

$$\mathcal{P}_{uniq}(a) \stackrel{def}{=} \begin{cases} \log\left(\frac{1}{2} + \frac{k+2}{2 \cdot \sum_{d \in D_q^{[k]}} \delta_{d;a}}\right), & \sum_{d \in D_q^{[k]}} \delta_{d;a} > 0 \\ 0, & else \end{cases} \quad (3)$$

$\mathcal{P}_{uniq}(a)$ is maximized whenever $D_q^{[k]}$ includes only a single aspect-stable document and is further minimized whenever none of the documents in $D_q^{[k]}$ are aspect-stable. Moreover, the case where all the documents in $D_q^{[k]}$ are aspect-stable, is the case in which aspect a may not serve as a good differentiator between better or worse documents. Hence, in such a case, this aspect would contribute the least to the overall (re-)scoring of documents for re-ranking.

3.4.4 Combined aspect-stability scoring. The three basic scoring components (i.e., $\mathcal{P}_{rsp}(a)$, $\mathcal{P}_{rank}(d;a)$ and $\mathcal{P}_{uniq}(a)$) are combined together using their weighted power mean. Therefore, given a document $d \in D_q^{[k]}$ and aspect $a \in \mathcal{A}_q$, the overall aspect-stability score of that document is calculated as follows:

$$\varphi_{d;a}^{[\alpha,\beta]} \stackrel{def}{=} \delta_{d;a} \cdot \mathcal{P}_{rsp}(a)^\alpha \cdot \mathcal{P}_{rank}(d;a)^\beta \cdot \mathcal{P}_{uniq}(a)^{1-\alpha-\beta}, \quad (4)$$

where α and β are two coefficients such that $0 \le \alpha+\beta \le 1$, allowing to control the relative importance of each scoring component. Note that, the combined score strictly follows the aspect-stability criterion defined in Eq. 1 by further multiplying in $\delta_{d;a}$ (hence, $\delta_{d;a} = 0 \Rightarrow \varphi_{d;a}^{[\alpha,\beta]} = 0$).

3.5 Document re-ranking

The final re-ranking score of documents in $D_q^{[k]}$ is calculated by aggregating the aspect-stability scores obtained for the various aspects in $\mathcal{A}_q$. Such aggregation is implemented using a voting-based fusion approach [15]. Within such an approach, each aspect $a \in \mathcal{A}_q$ represents a single voter, whose aspect-response $D_{q\vee a}^{[k]}$ further represents that voter's opinion (or preference list) about the top-k documents in $\mathcal{D}$ that best satisfy the information need expressed in the expanded query $q \vee a$. To this end, for a given document $d \in D_{q\vee a}^{[k]}$, its corresponding score $Score_{q\vee a}(d)$ represents aspect a voter's opinion. For each aspect $a \in \mathcal{A}_q$, document scores $Score_{q\vee a}(d)$ are further sum-normalized [15]. Per voted document $d \in D_q^{[k]}$, various voters are assumed to have varying confidence about their vote which is (rank-wise) proportional to d's corresponding aspect-stability score $\varphi_{d;a}^{[\alpha,\beta]}$.

The overall aspect-stability score of a given document $d \in D_q^{[k]}$ (denoted $Score_q^{Stad}(d)$[1]) is calculated by summing all aspect voters scores, as follows:

---

[1]"Stad" is an abbreviation for **S**tability **T**o **A**spect-**D**rift.

Corpus	# of documents	Queries	Disks
WT10G	1,692,096	451-550	WT10g
ROBUST	528,155	301-450, 601-700	4&5-{CR}
AP	242,918	51-150	1-3
SJMN	90,257	51-150	3
WSJ	173,252	151-200	1-2

Table 1: TREC data used for experiments.

$$Score_q^{Stad}(d) \stackrel{def}{=} \sum_{a \in \mathcal{A}_q} \varphi_{d;a}^{[\alpha,\beta]} \cdot Score_{q\vee a}(d) \quad (5)$$

Noting that some documents $d \in D_q^{[k]}$ may appear in several aspect-responses, a further reward may be given to those documents that appear in more such lists; similarly in spirit to the CombMNZ fusion method [15]. Therefore, a refined aspect-stability score that further captures such fact is calculated as follows:

$$Score_q^{StadMNZ}(d) \stackrel{def}{=} MNZ(d) \cdot Score_q^{Stad}(d), \quad (6)$$

where $MNZ(d)$ is taken as the (log-scaled) number of aspect-responses that include a given document $d \in D_q^{[k]}$, in addition to its inclusion in $D_q^{[k]}$, i.e.:

$$MNZ(d) \stackrel{def}{=} \log\left(2 + \sum_{a \in \mathcal{A}_q} \delta\left[d \in D_{q\vee a}^{[k]}\right]\right) \quad (7)$$

The final re-ranking score of a given document $d \in D_q^{[k]}$ is obtained by multiplying (boosting) the original document's score $Score_q(d)$ with its aspect-stability score (i.e., either $Score_q^{Stad}(d)$ or $Score_q^{StadMNZ}(d)$).

4 EVALUATION

4.1 Setup

Datasets and baseline retrieval methods. The TREC corpora and queries used for the evaluation are specified in Table 1. These collections and queries were previously used by other re-ranking works (e.g., [7, 9, 10]). Titles of TREC topics were used as queries. The Apache Lucene[2] open source search library was used for indexing and searching documents. Documents and queries were processed using Lucene's English text analysis (i.e., tokenization, stemming, stopwords, etc.). Two common retrieval methods that are implemented within Lucene were chosen as baseline methods (i.e., possible instantiations of method $\mathcal{M}$) for search re-ranking. These methods are: query-likelihood (**QL**) with Dirichlet smoothing and Okapi-BM25 (**BM25**). The free parameters[3] of the two methods were tuned so as to *optimize MAP*.

Derivation of aspect set $\mathcal{A}_q$. The RM3 pseudo relevance feedback model [8] was used for deriving the initial query aspect-set $\mathcal{A}_q$ for each given query q, where the top-n terms with the highest likelihood were selected.

---

[2]http://lucene.apache.org
[3]For QL: (Dirichlet-smoothing parameter) $\mu \in \{100, 200, \ldots, 5000\}$. For BM25: $k1 \in \{0, 0.1, \ldots, 3.0\}$ and $b \in \{0, 0.1, \ldots, 2.0\}$.

	ROBUST				WT10G				AP				SJMN				WSJ			
	p@5	p@10	MRR	RI	p@5	p@10	MRR	RI	p@5	p@10	MRR	RI	p@5	p@10	MRR	RI	p@5	p@10	MRR	RI
QL(init)	49.2	44.0	67.6	–	36.4	30.9	57.7	–	44.6	41.9	59.5	–	36.1	32.4	56.3	–	54.2	47.9	72.1	–
+RM3	49.5	45.6	66.4	2.4	35.1	30.9	50.5	5.1	46.4	44.1	56.0	15.0	35.4	31.8	48.7	11.0	54.8	52.2	69.1	4.0
+CombSUM	49.3	44.1	67.2	1.2	38.0	31.8	59.1	3.3	45.4	43.1	58.4	2.1	36.6	33.1	56.9	1.1	55.4	49.4	76.2	6.2
+CombMNZ	49.3	44.2	67.2	1.0	38.2	31.9	59.1	4.4	45.4	43.0	58.5	2.1	36.6	33.1	56.9	1.1	55.4	49.4	76.2	6.2
+Stad	50.8	46.1^{abr}_c	67.5	3.7	$41.1r^a$	34.9^{abr}_{ce}	61.1	14.4	49.8^{abr}_c	48.1^{abr}_c	58.8	19.8	40.9^{abr}_c	37.8^{abr}_c	51.4	17.0	58.8^{abr}_c	52.9^{ab}_c	76.9	16.7
+StadMNZ	51.0^{br}_c	46.1^{abr}_c	67.6	4.5	$41.1r^a$	34.4^{abr}_c	61.1	14.4	49.8^{abr}_c	48.1^{abr}_c	58.8	19.8	40.9^{abr}_c	38.1^{abr}_c	51.4	17.0	58.3^{abr}_c	52.7^{ab}_c	76.9	16.7
BM25(init)	50.5	44.5	69.2	–	38.3	31.8	55.2	–	46.6	43.1	63.8	–	38.2	33.7	60.3	–	54.2	49.0	72.9	–
+RM3	50.2	45.9	66.6	4.3	36.7	31.7	51.3	6.1	48.0	45.9	60.2	9.0	35.4	32.4	52.4	4.0	55.2	52.0	70.7	12.0
+CombSUM	50.5	45.0	68.3	0.0	39.1	31.4	59.6	3.3	48.2	43.3	63.5	7.2	38.8	34.6	61.6	1.1	54.6	49.2	73.4	2.1
+CombMNZ	50.7	45.2	68.3	1.0	39.1	31.4	59.2	3.3	48.2	43.5	64.0	7.2	38.8	34.7	61.6	1.1	54.6	49.2	73.4	2.1
+Stad	51.9^{abr}	46.4^{abr}_c	69.1	5.7	38.9^r	32.2	56.6	7.6	49.9^r	47.5^{abr}_c	64.1	13.4	42.3^{abr}_c	36.2^{abr}_c	56.7	11.5	59.2^{abr}_c	55.0^{abr}_c	72.3	20.8
+StadMNZ	52.2^{abr}_c	46.7^{abr}_c	69.1	6.9	39.1^r	32.2	57.2	8.7	49.7^r	48.1^{abr}_c	64.8	12.4	42.3^{abr}_c	36.0^{abr}_{cd}	56.7	11.5	59.2^{abr}_c	55.0^{abr}_c	72.3	20.8

Table 2: Effectiveness of the proposed re-ranking approach. A bold faced value marks the best performance in a given setting. a, b, c, d, e and r mark a statistically significant difference in precision with init, CombSUM, CombMNZ, Stad, StadMNZ and RM3, respectively.

Free parameter tuning. Evaluation was conducted using an hold-out approach (two-fold cross validation). Accordingly, for each corpus $\mathcal{D}$, queries were separated into two disjoint and even-sized groups (folds). Next, free parameters were tuned using one group as a train set while the other group was used as a test set for evaluation, and vice versa. The average performance between the two test groups was measured.

Actual parameter configurations that were explored using each train set are described next. To derive $\mathcal{A}_q$, based on previous recommendations, the following two parameters were fixed: $\mu = 1000$ and $\lambda = 0.9$ [8]. Hence, only the number of top documents m in $D_q^{[k]}$ and the top RM3 terms n, used for inducing aspect set $\mathcal{A}_q$, were varied as follows: $m \in \{5, 10, \ldots, 100\}$ and $n \in \{50, 100, \ldots, 300\}$. Aspect-lists selection based on $\mathcal{A}_q$ was implemented according to Section 3.3. Furthermore, the following values for the two coefficients used in Eq. 4 were explored: $(\alpha, \beta) \in \{0, 0.1, \ldots, 1\} \times \{0, 0.1, \ldots, 1\}$ (such that $\alpha + \beta \leq 1$).

Evaluation. For each corpus $\mathcal{D}$ and query q, three initial lists $D_q^{[k]}$ were retrieved, one per each baseline method. Each list included the top $k = 100$ ranked documents according to each baseline method. Users usually tend to scan few documents in a given result list, and each document has a lower chance of being examined as the user scans further into the list [4]. Accordingly, our goal is to improve retrieval via result re-ranking, having relevant documents appear as early as possible in the result list. The effectiveness of the proposed re-ranking approach was, therefore, evaluated using the following measures: p@5, p@10, MRR at top-10 and Robustness Index (RI) at top-5 [7, 9, 10]. Statistically significant differences in performance were measured using the paired two-tailed t-test with a 95% confidence level.

4.2 Results

The effectiveness of the proposed re-ranking approach for the various TREC corpora and baseline retrieval methods is depicted in Table 2. The two document aspect-stability scoring methods that were defined in Eq. 6 and Eq. 7, which are used for boosting the initial document scores for re-ranking, are denoted **Stad** and **StadMNZ** in Table 2, respectively. The impact of the combination of the What-If Analysis approach to QPP (Step 2) and document aspect-stability scoring (Step 3) on the proposed re-ranking approach was further evaluated. For that, the combined aspect-stability score that was

defined in Eq. 4 was neutralized by setting $\varphi_{d;a}^{[\alpha,\beta]} = 1$ for every possible pair of document $d \in D_q^{[k]}$ and aspect $a \in \mathcal{A}_q$. This results in two additional baseline methods which reduce to the state-of-the-art **CombSUM** and **CombMNZ** fusion methods[4] [15]. These two fusion methods, therefore, may replace the proposed re-ranking approach's aspect-stability based scoring, which boosts the initial document scores for re-ranking in Eq. 6 and Eq. 7, respectively.

Following [5, 18], a robust query-expansion baseline was further implemented. This baseline re-ranked documents in the original list $D_q^{[k]}$ according to the **same** RM3 relevance model that was used for the initial aspect set $\mathcal{A}_q$ derivation. To this end, documents in $D_q^{[k]}$, were first scored according to their negative cross-entropy (similarity) RM3 score. Next, the RM3 score was multiplied in the original document score $Score_q(d)$ and the final re-ranking was obtained [5, 18].

Overall, both **Stad** and **StadMNZ** provided notable improvements compared to the initial retrieved lists (for both baseline retrieval methods and across all corpora); with an increase in p@5 of up to 13.3% and 10.7% for the **QL** and **BM25** baselines, respectively. A similar improvement trend was demonstrated for p@10. Comparing **Stad** and **StadMNZ** with their **CombSUM** and **CombMNZ** "counterparts" side by side, a notable impact on performance by using the proposed combination of What-If Analysis approach to QPP and document aspect-stability scoring (which is captured by $\varphi_{d;a}^{[\alpha,\beta]}$) was observed. Overall, up to 11.8% and 9.0% more boost in re-ranking effectiveness to that of **CombSUM** and **CombMNZ** was measured for the **QL** and **BM25** baselines, respectively. Such impact was observed both in absolute retrieval effectiveness terms (i.e., p@5 and p@10) and in retrieval robustness (with highly notable improvements in RI); yet, sometimes, with a slight sacrifice (but still a reasonable one) of the position of the first relevant document (according to the MRR measure). Finally, comparing **Stad** and **StadMNZ** side by side with the **RM3** baseline, demonstrates that, the former two methods are able to provide a much more robust query expansion solution, resulting in up to 19.8% and 11.1% more boost in re-ranking effectiveness, when the initial retrieval is based on the **QL** and **BM25** baselines, respectively.

---

[4]Following common practice, for these two methods, if a given document $d \notin D_q^{[k]} \cap D_{q \vee a}^{[k]}$, then $Score_{q \vee a}(d) = 0$ [15].

REFERENCES

[1] J. Baliński and C. Danilowicz. Re-ranking method based on inter-document distances. *Inf. Process. Manage.*, 41(4):759–775, July 2005.

[2] Morton B Brown and Alan B Forsythe. Robust tests for the equality of variances. *Journal of the American Statistical Association*, 69(346):364–367, 1974.

[3] C. Buckley. Why current ir engines fail. *In Proceedings of SIGIR '04.*

[4] N. Craswell, O. Zoeter, M. Taylor, and B. Ramsey. An experimental comparison of click position-bias models. In *Proceedings of WSDM '08.*

[5] F. Diaz. Condensed list relevance models. In *Proceedings of ICTIR '15.*

[6] F. Diaz. Regularizing ad hoc retrieval scores. *In Proceedings of CIKM '05.*

[7] O. Kurland and L. Lee. Pagerank without hyperlinks: Structural re-ranking using links induced by language models. *In Proceedings of SIGIR '05.*

[8] V. Lavrenko and W. B. Croft. Relevance based language models. *In Proceedings of SIGIR '01.*

[9] X. Liu and W. B. Croft. Cluster-based retrieval using language models. *In Proceedings of SIGIR '04*, pages 186–193, 2004.

[10] L. Meister, O. Kurland, and I. Gelfer Kalmanovich. Re-ranking search results using an additional retrieved list. *Inf. Retr.*, 14(4):413–437, August 2011.

[11] H. Roitman. An enhanced approach to query performance prediction using reference lists. In *Proceedings of SIGIR '17.*

[12] H. Roitman, S. Erera, and B. Weiner. Robust standard deviation estimation for query performance prediction. In *Proceedings of ICTIR '17.*

[13] H. Roitman, S. Hummel, and O. Kurland. Using the cross-entropy method to re-rank search results. *In Proceedings of SIGIR '14*, pages 839–842, 2014.

[14] A. Shtok, D. Kurland, O.and Carmel, F. Raiber, and G. Markovits. Predicting query performance by query-drift estimation. *ACM Trans. Inf. Syst.*, 30(2), May 2012.

[15] S. Wu. *Data fusion in information retrieval*, volume 13. Springer, 2012.

[16] L. Yang, D. Ji, G. Zhou, Y. Nie, and G. Xiao. Document re-ranking using cluster validation and label propagation. *In Proceedings of CIKM '06.*

[17] E. Yom-Tov, S. Fine, D. Carmel, and A. Darlow. Learning to estimate query difficulty: Including applications to missing content detection and distributed information retrieval. *In Proceedings of SIGIR '05*, pages 512–519, 2005.

[18] L. Zighelnic and O. Kurland. Query-drift prevention for robust query expansion. *In Proceedings of SIGIR '08.*

Embedding Networks with Edge Attributes

Palash Goyal
USC Information Sciences Institute
Marina Del Rey, CA
goyal@isi.edu

Homa Hosseinmardi
USC Information Sciences Institute
Marina Del Rey, CA
homahoss@isi.edu

Emilio Ferrara
USC Information Sciences Institute
Marina Del Rey, CA
ferrarae@isi.edu

Aram Galstyan
USC Information Sciences Institute
Marina Del Rey, CA
galstyan@isi.edu

ABSTRACT

Predicting links in information networks requires deep understanding and careful modeling of network structure. Network embedding, which aims to learn low-dimensional representations of nodes, has been used successfully for the task of link prediction in the past few decades. Existing methods utilize the observed edges in the network to model the interactions between nodes and learn representations which explain the behavior. In addition to the presence of edges, networks often have information which can be used to improve the embedding. For example, in author collaboration networks, the bag of words representing the abstract of co-authored paper can be used as edge attributes. In this paper, we propose a novel approach, which uses the edges and their associated labels to learn node embeddings. Our model jointly optimizes higher order node neighborhood, social roles and edge attributes reconstruction error using deep architecture which can model highly non-linear interactions. We demonstrate the efficacy of our model over existing state-of-the-art methods on two real world data sets. We observe that such attributes can improve the quality of embedding and yield better performance in link prediction.

KEYWORDS

Graph Embedding, Deep Learning, Network Representation

ACM Reference Format:
Palash Goyal, Homa Hosseinmardi, Emilio Ferrara, and Aram Galstyan. 2018. Embedding Networks with Edge Attributes. In *HT '18: 29th ACM Conference on Hypertext and Social Media, July 9–12, 2018, Baltimore, MD, USA*. ACM, New York, NY, USA, 5 pages. https://doi.org/10.1145/3209542.3209571

1 INTRODUCTION

Many real world problems can be formulated in terms of networks. For example, friendship in online community can be modeled as a friendship network [7] in which users are nodes and strength of friendship defines the weights of the links. Similarly, in biology, interactions of proteins can be modeled as a network and the connections in the network can be used to identify genes [28]. Other types of network include author collaboration network [8], router network [3] and language networks [14]. By nature, information networks are dynamic and constantly evolve. Understanding their evolution and predicting unforeseen links is a widely studied problem in this domain [19]. Over the past few decades, several techniques have been proposed to solve the link prediction problem. Common approaches include computing similarity between pairs of disconnected nodes using existing links [1, 15]. Some other methods use Bayesian models to learn inherent structure of the network [20]. Another class of models involve compute low-dimensional representation of each node and computing similarity between nodes in this space. Such methods, also referred as network embedding, have gained popularity in recent years [2, 5, 10, 22, 24, 27].

Network embedding methods studied so far learn latent representation from the links between the nodes [2, 5, 9, 22, 24, 27]. They define an objective function to preserve structure of the network characterized by certain properties and optimize it to obtain the embedding. Although many methods have been proposed to learn network embeddings from observed links, little attention has been given to utilize the metadata available with the network. For example, networks often have node and edge attributes which can be useful in predicting future links. Recently, some approaches have been proposed to incorporate node attributes in learning the representation [6, 12, 13]. However, these approaches do not consider edge attributes which can provide additional information about the network. For example, in collaboration networks in which authors are the nodes and edges represent presence of co-authored papers, the content of a co-authored paper can be used to characterize the interaction between the author nodes.

This work aims to bridge this gap and learn node representations capturing network structure and edge attributes in a unified manner. To this aim, we introduce *Edge Label Aware Network Embedding* (ELAINE) which uses a coupled deep autoencoder along with an edge attribute decoder to jointly optimize the reconstruction loss of network structure and edge attribute reconstruction. Our model is thus capable to learning non-linear manifold from the network. Furthermore, we input node similarity using random walk simulations and social roles metrics thus preserving higher order interactions between nodes and network roles. We evaluate our model on the task of link prediction. We show through our experiments that our model, ELAINE, effectively uses edge attributes and outperforms state-of-the-art embedding approaches. We show our results on two real world networks - an author collaboration network and an email communication network. We use meta data from publication abstracts and email content to inform our model.

Overall, we make three contributions. We propose ELAINE, a deep learning model which captures network structure and edge attributes. We show that edge attributes can help improve accuracy for the task of link prediction. Finally, we extend the deep architecture to preserve higher order proximity and social roles.

The rest of the paper is organized as follows. In Section 2, we provide the definitions required to understand the problem and models discussed next. We introduce our model in Section 3, and then describe our experimental setup and obtained results (Sections 4 and 5). Finally, in Section 6 we draw our conclusions and discuss potential applications and future research directions.

2 PROBLEM STATEMENT

We denote a weighted graph as $G(V, E)$ where V is the vertex set and E is the edge set. The weighted adjacency matrix of G is denoted by A. If $(i, j) \in E$, we have $A_{ij} > 0$ denoting the weight of edge (i, j); otherwise we have $A_{ij} = 0$. We use $\boldsymbol{a_i} = [A_{i,1}, \cdots, A_{i,n}]$ to denote the i-th row of the adjacency matrix. We use $E^a \in \mathbb{R}^{m \times p}$ to denote the edge attribute matrix and $\boldsymbol{e_{ij}^a} = [e_{ij1}^a, \cdots, e_{ijp}^a]$ to denote the attributes of edge (i, j), where p is the number of edge attributes.

We define our problem as follows: *Given a graph $G = (V, E)$ and associated edge attributes E^a, we aim to represent each node u in a low-dimensional vector space $\boldsymbol{y_u}$ by learning a mapping $f : \{V, E^a\} \rightarrow \mathbb{R}^d$, namely $\boldsymbol{y_v} = f(v, E^a) \; \forall v \in V$. We require that $d \ll n$ and the function f preserves some proximity measure defined on the graph G. Intuitively, if two nodes u and v are "similar" in graph G, their embedding $\boldsymbol{y_u}$ and $\boldsymbol{y_v}$ should be close to each other in the embedding space. We use the notation $f(G) \in \mathbb{R}^{n \times d}$ for the embedding matrix of all nodes in the graph G. Note that the embedding of an edge (u, v) is defined as $g(u, v) = [\boldsymbol{y_u}, \boldsymbol{y_v}]$, i.e. the concatenation of embeddings of nodes u and v. It can be written as $g : E \rightarrow \mathbb{R}^{2d}$. We use $g(u, v)$ to reconstruct the edge label $\boldsymbol{e_{uv}^a}$. This enables us to infer the missing edge labels by using the adjacency of the incident nodes.

3 ELAINE

We propose an edge label aware information network embedding method - ELAINE, which models l^{th}-order proximity, social role features and edge labels using a deep variational autoencoder. The core component of the model is based on a deep autoencoder which can be used to learn the network embedding by minimizing the following loss function:

$$L = \sum_{i=1}^{n} \|(\hat{\boldsymbol{a}}_i - \boldsymbol{a}_i) \odot \boldsymbol{\beta}_i\|_2^2 = \|(\hat{A} - A) \odot \mathcal{B}\|_F^2 \quad (1)$$

The objective function penalizes inaccurate reconstruction of node neighborhood. As many legitimate links are not observed in the networks, a weight $\boldsymbol{\beta}_i$ is traditionally used to impose more penalty on reconstruction of observed edges [29].

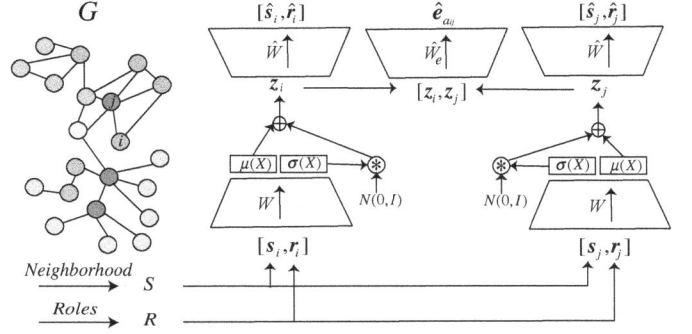

Figure 1: Edge label aware embedding model. ELAINE extracts higher order relations between nodes using random walks and social role based features. The coupled autoencoder jointly optimizes these features and edge attributes to obtain a unified representation.

Although the above model can learn network representations which can reconstruct the graph well, it suffers from four challenges. Firstly, as the model reconstructs the observed neighborhood of each vertex, it only preserves second order proximity of nodes. *Wang et. al.* [29] extend the model to preserve first order proximity but their model fails to capture higher order proximities. Concretely, if two nodes have disjoint neighborhoods the model will keep them apart regardless of the similarity of their neighborhoods. Secondly, the model is prone to overfitting leading to a satisfactory reconstruction performance but sub-par performance in tasks like link prediction and node classification. *Wang et. al.* [29] use l_1 and l_2 regularizers to address this issue but we show that using variational autoencoders can achieve better performance. Thirdly, the model does not explicitly capture social role information. Real world networks often have a role based structure understanding which can help with various prediction tasks. Lastly, the model does not consider edge labels. We show that incorporating edge label reconstruction leads to improved performance in various tasks.

To address the above challenges, we propose a random walk based deep variational autoencoder model with an objective to jointly optimize the higher order neighborhood, role based features and edge label reconstruction.

As we aim to find a low-dimensional manifold the original graph lies in, we want to learn a representation which is maximally informative of observed edges and edge labels. At the same time, as the autoencoder penalizes reconstruction error, it encourages perfect reconstruction at the cost of overfitting to the training data. This is in particular problematic for learning representations for graphs as networks are constructed from interactions which may be incomplete or noisy. We want to find embeddings which are robust to such noise and can help us in tasks such as link prediction and node classification. We propose to use variational autoencoder for graphs and illustrate in Section 5 that it can improve performance in different tasks. Variational autoencoders (VAEs) look at autoencoders from a generative network perspective and minimize the sum of two terms: (1) reconstruction loss and (2) KL-divergence of latent variable distribution and unit Gaussian, using backpropagation. The reconstruction variance controls the model generalization, which can be considered as the coefficient of KL-divergence loss.

3.1 Random Walks

Nodes in a network are related to each other via many degrees of connection. Some nodes have direct connections while others are connected through paths of varying lengths. A good embedding should preserve such higher order relations. Naively using node adjacency as the input, an autoencoder cannot achieve this. This is because the model then only considers the neighborhoods of nodes and does not explicitly capture the relations between these neighborhoods. To preserve higher order proximities, we obtain global distance based similarities of each node with the rest of the nodes. One way to obtain such a set of vectors is to use metrics such as Katz Index [16], Adamic Adar [1] and Common Neighbors [21]. Although such metrics capture global proximities accurately, their computation is inefficient and the time complexity is up to $O(n^3)$. We overcome the inefficiency by approximating them using random walks [4]. For each node i, we simulate k random walks each of length l. Each random walk, $\{v_{i,1}, v_{i,2} \ldots v_{i,l}\}$, from node i generates a node j with probability:

$$P(v_{i,j}|v_{i,j-1}) = \begin{cases} \frac{1}{d_{j-1}} & \text{if } (v_{i,j-1}, v_{i,j}) \in E \\ 0 & otherwise \end{cases}$$

where d_k is the degree of node k. Note that since a random walk of length l from node i is equivalent to a random walk of length $l-1$ for node $v_{i,1}$, generating k random walks of length l only requires $O(k)$ time each node.

3.2 Role preserving features

Social roles in a network are characterized by various local and global statistics. For example, high degree can be reflective of social importance. Broadly, we classify role discriminating features into two categories: (a) statistical features, and (b) edge attributes. We consider the following statistical features which have been shown to correlate with social roles[11]: (i) node's degree, (ii) weighted degree, (iii) clustering coefficient, (iv) eccentricity, (v) structural hole and (vi) local gatekeeper. We append these features with node's neighborhood as input to our model. Having such statistical features helps obtain an embedding which preserves social roles. Conversely, a node can take different roles with different neighbors (henceforth referred as interactive roles) which cannot be captured by such statistical features. For example, in a collaboration network, author i may take the role of Professor with his student j and colleague with another professor k. Identifying such distribution of roles can help model the network more accurately. For this we use the edge attributes which can be reflective of such interactions. Concretely, we consider the topics of conversation between nodes and jointly optimize their reconstruction of node neighborhood reconstruction.

3.3 Incorporating edge labels

Autoencoder defined above takes node neighborhood and statistical role preserving features as input and aims to reconstruct them. One possible approach to incorporate edge attributes is to aggregate them for each node and append them with other node features. The drawback of this approach is that information loss can incur following aggregation. Such aggregation cannot preserve interactive roles between nodes.

We propose to overcome this problem by coupling copies of autoencoders for nodes i and j. The model is composed of a coupled autoencoder and an edge attribute decoder, Figure 1. The intuition is to force the embeddings of nodes i and j to capture information pertaining to the attributes of the edge between them. This is ensured by adding the edge attribute reconstruction loss to the objective function. Thus, we learn model parameters by minimizing a loss function with the following terms:

Network structure reconstruction: The lth-order neighborhood of each node along with the social role preserving statistical features:

$$L_n = \|([\hat{S}, \hat{R}] - [S, R]) \odot \mathcal{B}\|_F^2,$$

where each row of $S \in \mathbb{R}^{n \times n}$ and $R \in \mathbb{R}^{n \times r}$ compose of neighborhood similarity and role statistics respectively. Henceforth, we will refer to $[\hat{S}, \hat{R}]$ by $\hat{F} \in \mathbb{R}^{n \times n+r}$ and $[S, R]$ by $F \in \mathbb{R}^{n \times n+r}$.

Edge label/attributes reconstruction: For each pair of nodes, we reconstruct the attributes of the edge between them, $L_e = \|\hat{E}^a - E^a\|_F^2$, where each row i of $E^a \in \mathbb{R}^{m \times p}$ is the vector of attributes of the ith edge . The overall objective function thus becomes

$$L = L_n + \alpha_1 L_e + L_{reg}, \tag{2}$$

where L_{reg} is the regularization on the weights. For our model, we use KL-divergence, Lasso and Ridge regularization.

To get the optimal parameters for the model defined above, we minimize the loss function L using stochastic gradient descent (SGD) [25] with Adaptive Moment Estimation (Adam)[17].

4 EXPERIMENTS

Here, we describe the data sets used and then discuss the baselines we use to compare our model and the evaluation metrics.

4.1 Datasets

Table 1: Dataset Statistics

Name	n	m	Avg. degree	# of edge attributes
Hep-th	7,980	21,036	5.27	100
Enron	145	912	12.58	10

We conduct experiments on the following real-world datasets to evaluate our proposed algorithm (summarized in Table 1):

Hep-th [8]: The original data set contains abstracts of papers in High Energy Physics Theory conference in the period from January 1993 to April 2003. We create a collaboration network for the first five years. We get the node labels using the Google Scholar API [1] to obtain university labels for each author. We apply NMF [26] on the set of abstracts to get topic distribution for each abstract. We aggregate the topic distribution of all the coauthored papers between two authors to get the edge attributes.

Enron [18]: This dataset contains emails among about 150 users, mostly senior management at Enron. We connect two users if they exchanged email(s). Edge attribute between node i and j is the extracted topics from each set of emails between them using NMF.

---

[1]https://pypi.python.org/pypi/scholarly/0.2

4.2 Baselines

We compare our model with the following state-of-the-art methods:

- *Graph Factorization* (GF) [2]: It factorizes the adjacency matrix with regularization.
- *Structural Deep Network Embedding* (SDNE) [29]: It uses deep autoencoder along with Laplacian Eigenmaps objective to preserve first and second order proximities.
- *Higher Order Proximity Preserving* [22] (HOPE): It factorizes the higher order similarity matrix between nodes using generalized singular value decomposition [23].
- *node2vec* [10]: It preserves higher order proximity by maximizing the probability of occurrence of subsequent nodes in fixed length biased random walks. They use shallow neural networks to obtain the embeddings. *DeepWalk* is a special case of *node2vec* with the random walk bias set to 0.

4.3 Metrics and Hyperparameters

In our experiments, we evaluate our model on link prediction. We use Mean Average Precision (MAP) as our metric. MAP averages the precision over all nodes. It can be written as $MAP = \frac{\sum_i AP(i)}{|V|}$, where

$AP(i) = \frac{\sum_k precision@k(i) \cdot \mathbb{I}\{E_{pred_i}(k) \in E_{gt_i}\}}{|\{k : E_{pred_i}(k) \in E_{gt_i}\}|}$ and $precision@k(i) = \frac{|E_{pred_i}(1:k) \cap E_{gt_i}|}{k}$.

For our model, we use two hidden layers for feature encoder and decoder with size [500, 300]. For the edge attribute decoder, we experiment with a single hidden layer with 1000 neurons and without any hidden layer. Optimal values of other hyperparameters are obtained using grid search over $[10^{-5}, 10^3]$ in factors of 10.

5 RESULTS AND ANALYSIS

In this section, we present results of our model on link prediction, and provide a comparison with baselines.

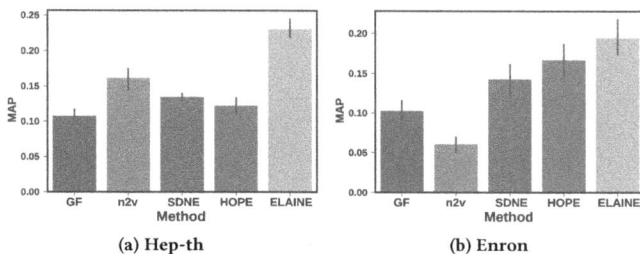

(a) Hep-th   (b) Enron

Figure 2: MAP of link prediction for different data sets.

Information networks are meant to capture the interactions in real world. This translation of interactions can be noisy and inaccurate. Predicting missing links in the constructed networks and links likely to occur in the future is an important and difficult task. We test our model on this link prediction task to understand the generalizability of our model. For each network, we randomly hide 20% of the network edges. We use the rest of the network to learn the embeddings of nodes and sort the likelihood of each unobserved edge to predict the missing links. As number of node pairs for a network of size N is $N(N-1)/2$, we randomly sample 1024 nodes

for evaluation (cf. [9]). We get 5 samples for each data set and report the mean and standard deviation of precision and MAP values.

Figures 2 illustrates the link prediction MAP values for the methods on data sets. We observe that our model significantly outperforms baselines on Hep-th. This implies that using the topic distribution of abstracts can help us understand the relation between authors. On Enron, we observe that gain in MAP isn't as significant as Hep-th but still improves over the baselines. This can be attributed to the characteristic of emails which tend to be more unstructured and noisy compared to abstracts of publications and hence more challenging to model. Furthermore, we observe that the performance of other models is not consistent over these two data sets. *node2vec* achieves best performance among the rest of the methods on Hep-th but performs poorly on Enron. Similarly, HOPE has high MAP value for Enron but is outperformed by SDNE and *node2vec* on Hep-th. Also, as our model extends deep autoencoders for edge attributes, to understand the importance edge attributes, we compare against SDNE which has similar architecture. We see that our model achieves significant gains over SDNE on both the data sets showing that our model can utilize edge attributes in different domains and improve link prediction performance.

6 CONCLUSION

In this work, we presented a novel method, ELAINE, which preserves network structure and edge attributes to obtain unified node representations. The model captures higher order proximities and social roles and can model non-linear network interactions. It uses a coupled deep autoencoder along with an edge attribute decoder to jointly optimize the reconstruction loss of network structure and edge attribute reconstruction. Our experiments demonstrate the efficacy of our model over two real world data sets including a collaboration network and an email network on the task of link prediction. In the future, we plan to extend our model to predict missing edge labels along with presence of edges. Furthermore, we believe that understanding dynamics of networks over time is an important tasks due to the nature of information spread. We thus want to extend our model to networks for which the edge attributes as well as the connections evolve. As our model uses a deep architecture, we see that the performance vastly depends on hyper parameters. We plan to study their behavior and develop a model which can automatically identify their optimal values. Another key direction is the choice of regularization. We observed improvement using a variational autoencoder and would like to understand the effect of regularization functions on the performance.

Acknowledgements. This work has been partly funded by the Defense Advanced Research Projects Agency (DARPA #W911NF-17-C-0094 and #D16AP00115), the Office of the Director of National Intelligence (ODNI), and the Intelligence Advanced Research Projects Activity (IARPA). The views and conclusions contained herein are those of the authors and should not be interpreted as necessarily representing the official policies, either expressed or implied, of DARPA, ODNI, IARPA, or the U.S. Government. The U.S. Government is authorized to reproduce and distribute reprints for governmental purposes notwithstanding any copyright annotation. The U.S. Government had no role in study design, data collection and analysis, decision to publish, or preparation of the manuscript.

REFERENCES

[1] Lada A Adamic and Eytan Adar. 2003. Friends and neighbors on the web. *Social networks* 25, 3 (2003), 211–230.

[2] Amr Ahmed, Nino Shervashidze, Shravan Narayanamurthy, Vanja Josifovski, and Alexander J Smola. 2013. Distributed large-scale natural graph factorization. In *Proceedings of the 22nd international conference on World Wide Web*. ACM, 37–48.

[3] Réka Albert, Hawoong Jeong, and Albert-László Barabási. 2000. Error and attack tolerance of complex networks. *nature* 406, 6794 (2000), 378–382.

[4] Lars Backstrom and Jure Leskovec. 2011. Supervised random walks: predicting and recommending links in social networks. In *Proceedings of the fourth ACM international conference on Web search and data mining*. ACM, 635–644.

[5] Shaosheng Cao, Wei Lu, and Qiongkai Xu. 2015. Grarep: Learning graph representations with global structural information. 891–900.

[6] Shiyu Chang, Wei Han, Jiliang Tang, Guo-Jun Qi, Charu C Aggarwal, and Thomas S Huang. 2015. Heterogeneous network embedding via deep architectures. In *Proceedings of the 21th ACM SIGKDD International Conference on Knowledge Discovery and Data Mining*. ACM, 119–128.

[7] Linton C Freeman. 2000. Visualizing social networks. *Journal of social structure* 1, 1 (2000), 4.

[8] Johannes Gehrke, Paul Ginsparg, and Jon Kleinberg. 2003. Overview of the 2003 KDD Cup. *ACM SIGKDD Explorations* 5, 2 (2003).

[9] Palash Goyal and Emilio Ferrara. 2018. Graph embedding techniques, applications, and performance: A survey. *Knowledge-Based Systems* (2018). https://doi.org/10.1016/j.knosys.2018.03.022

[10] Aditya Grover and Jure Leskovec. 2016. node2vec: Scalable feature learning for networks. In *Proceedings of the 22nd International Conference on Knowledge Discovery and Data Mining*. ACM, 855–864.

[11] Keith Henderson, Brian Gallagher, Tina Eliassi-Rad, Hanghang Tong, Sugato Basu, Leman Akoglu, Danai Koutra, Christos Faloutsos, and Lei Li. 2012. Rolx: structural role extraction & mining in large graphs. In *Proceedings of the 18th ACM SIGKDD international conference on Knowledge discovery and data mining*. ACM, 1231–1239.

[12] Xiao Huang, Jundong Li, and Xia Hu. 2017. Accelerated attributed network embedding. In *Proceedings of the 2017 SIAM International Conference on Data Mining*. SIAM, 633–641.

[13] Xiao Huang, Jundong Li, and Xia Hu. 2017. Label informed attributed network embedding. In *Proceedings of the Tenth ACM International Conference on Web Search and Data Mining*. ACM, 731–739.

[14] Ramon Ferrer i Cancho and Richard V Solé. 2001. The small world of human language. *Proceedings of the Royal Society of London B: Biological Sciences* 268, 1482 (2001), 2261–2265.

[15] Paul Jaccard. 1901. *Etude comparative de la distribution florale dans une portion des Alpes et du Jura*. Impr. Corbaz.

[16] Leo Katz. 1953. A new status index derived from sociometric analysis. *Psychometrika* 18, 1 (1953), 39–43.

[17] Diederik Kingma and Jimmy Ba. 2014. Adam: A method for stochastic optimization. *arXiv preprint arXiv:1412.6980* (2014).

[18] Bryan Klimt and Yiming Yang. 2004. The enron corpus: A new dataset for email classification research. In *European Conference on Machine Learning*. 217–226.

[19] David Liben-Nowell and Jon Kleinberg. 2007. The link-prediction problem for social networks. *journal of the Association for Information Science and Technology* 58, 7 (2007), 1019–1031.

[20] Kurt Miller, Michael I Jordan, and Thomas L Griffiths. 2009. Nonparametric latent feature models for link prediction. In *Advances in neural information processing systems*. 1276–1284.

[21] Mark EJ Newman. 2001. Clustering and preferential attachment in growing networks. *Physical review E* 64, 2 (2001), 025102.

[22] Mingdong Ou, Peng Cui, Jian Pei, Ziwei Zhang, and Wenwu Zhu. 2016. Asymmetric transitivity preserving graph embedding. In *Proc. of ACM SIGKDD*. 1105–1114.

[23] Christopher C Paige and Michael A Saunders. 1981. Towards a generalized singular value decomposition. *SIAM J. Numer. Anal.* 18, 3 (1981), 398–405.

[24] Bryan Perozzi, Rami Al-Rfou, and Steven Skiena. 2014. Deepwalk: Online learning of social representations. In *Proceedings 20th international conference on Knowledge discovery and data mining*. 701–710.

[25] David E Rumelhart, Geoffrey E Hinton, and Ronald J Williams. 1988. Neurocomputing: Foundations of research. *JA Anderson and E. Rosenfeld, Eds* (1988), 696–699.

[26] Suvrit Sra and Inderjit S Dhillon. 2006. Generalized nonnegative matrix approximations with Bregman divergences. In *Advances in neural information processing systems*. 283–290.

[27] Jian Tang, Meng Qu, Mingzhe Wang, Ming Zhang, Jun Yan, and Qiaozhu Mei. 2015. Line: Large-scale information network embedding. In *Proceedings 24th International Conference on World Wide Web*. 1067–1077.

[28] Athanasios Theocharidis, Stjin Van Dongen, Anton Enright, and Tom Freeman. 2009. Network visualization and analysis of gene expression data using BioLayout Express3D. *Nature protocols* 4 (2009), 1535–1550.

[29] Daixin Wang, Peng Cui, and Wenwu Zhu. 2016. Structural deep network embedding. In *Proceedings of the 22nd International Conference on Knowledge Discovery and Data Mining*. ACM, 1225–1234.

A Collaborative Filtering Method for Handling Diverse and Repetitive User-Item Interactions

Oren Sar Shalom*
Intuit, Israel
Bar Ilan University, Israel
oren.sarshalom@gmail.com

Haggai Roitman
IBM Research AI, Israel
haggai@il.ibm.com

Amihood Amir†
Bar Ilan University, Israel
Johns Hopkins University
amir@esc.biu.ac.il

Alexandros Karatzoglou
Telefonica Research, Spain
alexandros.karatzoglou@telefonica.com

ABSTRACT

Most collaborative filtering models assume that the interaction of users with items take a single form, e.g., only ratings or clicks or views. In fact, in most real-life recommendation scenarios, users interact with items in diverse ways. This in turn, generates complex usage data that contains multiple and diverse types of user feedback. In addition, within such a complex data setting, each user-item pair may occur more than once, implying on repetitive preferential user behaviors. In this work we tackle the problem of building a Collaborative Filtering model that takes into account such complex datasets. We propose a novel factor model, CDMF, that is capable of incorporating arbitrary and diverse feedback types without any prior domain knowledge. Moreover, CDMF is inherently capable of considering user-item repetitions. We evaluate CDMF against state-of-the-art methods with highly favorable results.

ACM Reference Format:
Oren Sar Shalom*, Haggai Roitman, Amihood Amir†, and Alexandros Karatzoglou. 2018. A Collaborative Filtering Method for Handling Diverse and Repetitive User-Item Interactions. In *HT '18: 29th ACM Conference on Hypertext and Social Media, July 9–12, 2018, Baltimore, MD, USA.* ACM, New York, NY, USA, 9 pages. https://doi.org/10.1145/3209542.3209550

1 INTRODUCTION

In most online recommendation settings user interactions with items can be quite complex and take multiple forms. For example, a user interested in some item may view its item page, then may add it to her "shopping cart", purchase it, write a review afterwards, etc. All in all, each user may have several interactions with an item, each such interaction defines a single *usage point*.

* This work was done while at IBM Research AI, Israel.
† Partially supported by ISF grant number 571/14.

Each usage point in such a complex data setting may record **multiple feedback types** that can be utilized for learning users' preferences. Feedback types can be diverse such as categorical, ordinal or numerical; discrete or continuous; explicit or implicit. For example, an item view event records a usage point that provides two feedback types: the type of the event itself (e.g., view_event) and the event's time (e.g., view_time). While the first feedback type is categorical, the second one is continuous. Both feedback types are further implicit. As another example, a usage point recorded for an item review_event may provide the additional feedback of review_rating, which is explicit and discrete.

Complex usage data may further include usage points of users that interacted with the same item more than once. Such **repetitive preferential behavior** can be utilized to enhance user preferences learning.

We next describe two motivating examples where complex usage data should be considered for enhanced item recommendation. Both examples are based on real-life use cases (and datasets) in our evaluation which require to handle usage points that record several diverse feedback types. In addition, usage points in these examples may include repetitive interactions of the same user-item pair over time.

Motivating Example 1: Professional social-networks. Let's now consider a career-oriented social networking site for professionals such as LinkedIn[1] or Xing[2]. A user that decides to look for a new career path can search relevant job postings. The user may click on any matching job posting, she can bookmark it, she may decide to apply to some job(s) or delete previously recommended job offers that are not relevant to her. In this example, four different categorial implicit feedback types may be gathered according to the type of action that the user performs with a given item. Moreover, these various event types may differently depend on their occurrence time. Therefore, the time of each event occurrence may be further utilized (e.g., click_time, bookmark_time, etc). All in all, using both the event type and its time as two different forms of feedback, eight different feedback types (two on each usage point) may be utilized for learning users' career preferences for potential jobs recommendation.

[1] https://www.linkedin.com/feed/
[2] https://www.xing.com/en

Motivating Example 2: Online shopping. Let's consider an online shop that sells various commodity items to users, e.g., food, digital appliances, cloths, music, etc. Within such a setting, each item purchase_event records a usage point in the user's purchase history. Each such usage point may further provide three additional forms of feedback, namely: purchase_price, purchase_amount and purchase_time. All three feedback types are implicit, where both price and time are further continuous and amount is discrete. Utilizing such additional feedback may help to reveal important item purchase preferences of each user. For example, a recommender system that utilizes such data may be able to learn that expensive items or those which are bought in larger quantities more significantly represent the user.

1.1 Utilizing complex usage data

Ideally, a Recommender System (RS) should handle complex (usage) data that includes multiple types of user feedback and also deal with repeated interactions of a user with an item. While it is evident that complex (usage) data may help to elevate item recommendation quality, surprisingly little attention has been given to utilizing such data. So far, most previous RS works have been mainly focused on either the rating prediction task or on implicit feedback modeling of a single type (e.g., views), possibly combined with a single source of explicit feedback [10, 25]. In addition, previous works were mostly tailored to **specific** domains, use cases, feedback types and their blends [2, 5, 11, 14, 18, 20]. Moreover, while some of these previous works have further considered user-item repetitions, the combination of the feedback recorded in various usage points have been applied so far using very naïve (and heuristic) data aggregation methods (e.g., summation [7, 10, 28]).

Accurately modeling the different types of interactions that users have with items and taking into account repetitive interactions has been shown to lead to better models of user preferences [10, 30]. For example, augmenting a recommender system with additional implicit feedback sources may help to elevate its accuracy in situations where explicit feedback is insufficient [10, 30]. Yet, modeling such data in a **generic** (domain-independent) way still remains a great challenge for RS practitioners.

1.2 Our contributions

Matrix Factorization (MF) is the most popular collaborative filtering method for implementing recommender systems [16]. Yet, existing MF methods cannot trivially model repeated user interactions with the same item, and typically fail to deal with usage points of different and multiple feedback types.

Trying to address this challenge, we propose a novel generic MF method for utilizing complex (usage) data for item recommendation. This method is domain independent, capable of utilizing diverse feedback sources, independently of their types, including an unbounded number of interactions between the same user-item pair. Specifically, we handle three different data phenomena:

(1) Usage points may be associated with a varied number of feedback types. For instance, a click event may be accompanied with time only while a purchase event with time and amount.

(2) The feedback types are diverse and may be of any kind such as categorical, ordinal or numerical; discrete or continuous; explicit or implicit.

(3) Users may interact with the same item multiple times.

2 COMPLEX DATA MATRIX FACTORIZATION

We term the method introduced in this work for tackling the multiple interactions and feedback challenge *Complex Data Matrix Factorization* (CDMF for short). CDMF simultaneously learns two sets of parameters. The first is the set of item vectors; the parameters in the second set allow to infer, for any given user, the *personalized weight* of each item in her interactions history. Combining the item vectors in the history of the user with the appropriate weights yields the current representation of the user.

2.1 Preliminaries

Let u denote a single user and let i denote a single item. Every user u may interact with any item i and let R_u denote the set of items in user u's interaction history. To capture the multi-feedback aspect of user interactions, we assume that each interaction may provide up to l different feedback types. We further assume that, a user may interact multiple times with any given item; each such interaction defines a single *usage point*. Such repetitive preferential behavior is actually quite common in real-life. For example, in the music domain, a user may listen to the same song again and again. Accordingly, let R_{ui} denote the sequence of usage points in user u's interaction history with a given item i; and let $R_{ui}^{(j)}$ denote the jth usage point in R_{ui}. Each usage point $R_{ui}^{(j)}$ is defined as a real vector of size l, with entry $R_{ui}^{(j)}[m]$ ($1 \le m \le l$) capturing the feedback obtained for the mth feedback type; If no such feedback exists, then we simply assign $R_{ui}^{(j)}[m] = 0$. For instance, a usage point of type review will have a non-zero value in the entry corresponding to rating; whereas usage points of other types will have a zero value in that entry. We can further have type-dependent time entries (e.g., purchase_time or click_time) when only one of them has a non-zero value.

In this work, we assume a latent factor model of users and items [16]. Hence, we associate each user u with a user-factors vector $p_u \in \mathbb{R}^f$, and each item i with an item-factors vector $q_i \in \mathbb{R}^f$. Using such a model, the predicted "score" of user u to item i is given by[3] $\hat{r}_{ui} = p_u^T q_i$. The score $\hat{r}_{ui}$ is assumed to correlate with the likelihood that the user will interact with the item.

2.2 User modeling

We now describe CDMF, that considers the various feedback types and multiple interactions with the same item. Similarly to [21] user u is not fitted directly to a parameter vector p_u. Instead, we model p_u as a function of the appropriate item vectors and their learned weights. This method significantly reduces the number of parameters in the model and hence is less prone to overfitting.

Since users choose to interact with items, and not the other way around, we concentrate only on modeling the importance of the items to the users. Let's assume, just for a moment, that the item

---

[3]We omit the bias terms for clarity of presentation.

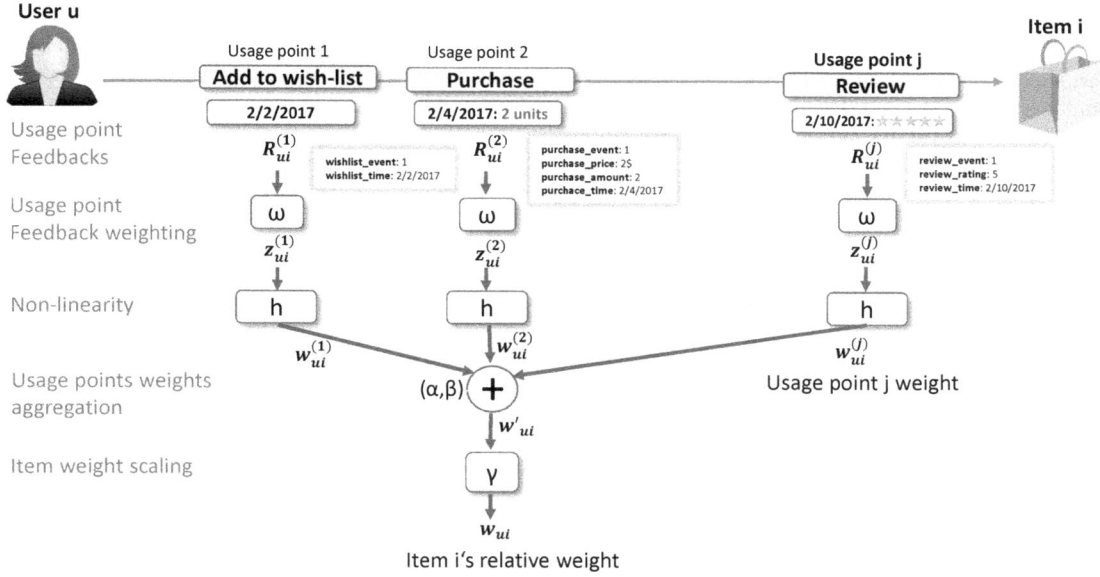

Figure 1: Illustration of item weighting in our approach. In this example, user u has three different usage points (interactions) with item i over time. Each such usage point provides different feedback types. The first usage point for example, records two implicit feedback types, wishlist_event (categorial) and wishlist_time (continuous), which document the fact that user u added item j to her wishlist and the time of such addition.

vectors $\{q_i\}$ are given. For a given user u, we now wish to estimate a new user-factors vector $\hat{p}_u$ that captures the *personalized weight* of each item $i \in R_u$ to user u; further denoted hereinafter as w_{ui} and termed *"item weight"*. The item weight indicates to what extent the item's latent features are correlated with the user's preferences.

Let us further assume, again just for a moment, that the item weights $\{w_{ui}\}$ are also given. From the definition of item weight, user u's vector p_u is modeled as the weighted average of the items in the user's history R_u:

$$\hat{p}_u = \frac{\sum_{i \in R_u} w_{ui} q_i}{\sum_{i \in R_u} w_{ui}} \tag{1}$$

We now relax both assumptions that the item weights $\{w_{ui}\}$ and the item vectors $\{q_i\}$ are given, and shall need to infer them.

2.3 Item weights estimation

Figure 1 illustrates the various steps in our approach for estimating the item weights w_{ui}. As an intermediate step, we first assume that each item weight w_{ui} depends on the relative importance of the different usage points in R_{ui}. Therefore, each usage point $R_{ui}^{(j)} \in R_{ui}$ may contribute differently to the overall weight w_{ui}, according to the different feedback types that were obtained at that usage point. Next, using a pooling approach, the weight w_{ui} is obtained by aggregating over all item i's usage point importance estimates.

2.3.1 Usage point weights estimation. We now define $\omega \in \mathbb{R}^l$, a real parameter vector, having entry $\omega[m]$ models the relative importance (weight) of the mth feedback type. Using such weights allows to capture situations in which different feedback types provide a variable level of "useful" evidence on user tastes (e.g., time

of event). In this work, we consider ω to be a global parameter. We note that, such a parameter can be individually derived for each user u (i.e., ω_u). Due to space considerations, we refrain from using this extension and leave this for future work.

Given ω, let $z_{ui}^{(j)}$ denote the relative importance of usage point $R_{ui}^{(j)}$ and is simply calculated as $z_{ui}^{(j)} = \omega^T R_{ui}^{(j)}$. We note that, while we choose a simple linear correlation for this purpose, any other function could be incorporated. Yet, we chose to use a simple one in order to focus on the novelty of our approach.

Mathematically, the usage point weights can be negative. However, in reality, negative weights do not seem to affect behavior. Thus, for sake of simplicity, we would like to consider only non-negative weights[4]. This would naturally mean that we take the maximum of the learned weight and 0. In our implementation 0 values cause infinite gradients, thus we take the maximum between the weight and some small constant real number τ. That is, we define: $h_\tau(x) = max\{x, \tau\}$, having $\tau = 0.01$ as the hyperparameter value of choice. Note that, the rectified linear unit (ReLU), a commonly used activation function[5] in Neural Networks, is a special case of this definition, with $\tau = 0$. We therefore model the weight of usage point $R_{ui}^{(j)}$ as: $w_{ui}^{(j)} = h_\tau(z_{ui}^{(j)})$.

2.3.2 Usage point weights aggregation. The overall weight w_{ui} is now obtained by aggregating over the usage point weights $\{w_{ui}^{(j)}\}$. We adopt a pooling approach for this purpose. Using such an approach allows to reduce an arbitrary number of features to a fixed

---

[4]This is not to be confused with the feedback type weights (i.e., ω), which can be negative.

[5]We also tried other activation functions like sigmoid. Yet, this one yielded the best results.

size, as we may have a variable number of usage point weights $\{w_{ui}^{(j)}\}$ based on the number of such points recorded in R_{ui} for each item i. The most popular pooling functions in neural networks are *max-pooling* and *average-pooling* [17]. That is, given a feature set, its max/average value is returned. We next make two observations that would allow us to design a data-driven pooling function.

First, we note that, the actual choice of a pooling operation may be domain-dependent. While in many recommendation scenarios, a reasonable assumption would be to emphasize more the highly weighted usage points, in some cases, the opposite may be true. For example, in the services domain, some user may use some service several times, but a single bad experience may determine the personalized weight of this service to that user. In this case, we may actually want to consider the minimum weight (i.e., min-pooling).

As a second observation, we note that, considering the length of item usage histories (i.e., $|R_{ui}|$) may be also important. On the one hand, interacting with the same item over and over again can imply a special importance of that item. As an example, considering the movies domain; the fact that a user has repeatedly seen a movie may be very significant. On the other hand, in the food retail domain, repeated purchases of the same item (e.g., bread, milk, etc.) have much less importance.

Motivated by these observations, we now introduce a more general pooling approach. Let α and β be two real parameters; the item weight w_{ui} is calculated as follows. We first calculate the unscaled weight:

$$w'_{ui} = \left\| \{w_{ui}^{(j)}\} \right\|_{\alpha} \cdot |R_{ui}|^{\beta}. \tag{2}$$

This weight function is composed of two parts. The first part is a L_{α}-norm [6], given by:

$$\left\| \{w_{ui}^{(j)}\} \right\|_{\alpha} = \left(\sum_{j=1}^{|R_{ui}|} w_{ui}^{(j)\alpha} \right)^{\frac{1}{\alpha}},$$

which aggregates over the weights of the different usage points. We note that, when $\alpha = 1$, we obtain the sum of usage point weights; as α increases, more emphasis is given to usage points with a higher weight $w_{ui}^{(j)}$; and as α approaches infinity, it is equivalent to taking the maximum weight. When $0 < \alpha < 1$ this is a definition of a distance, which is not a norm. Since $\|x\|_{\alpha} = 1/\|1/x\|_{-\alpha}$, then when $\alpha < 0$, as α decreases, more emphasis is given to usage points with a lower weight. In general, $\|x\|_{\alpha}$ with a learnable parameter α may be considered as a soft version of max- and min-pooling.

The second part of w'_{ui} allows to weigh each item i in proportion to the number of user u's interactions with item i (i.e., $|R_{ui}|$). Therefore, for $\beta > 0$, a higher importance is given to longer item interaction histories; for $\beta = 0$ we completely ignore this property; and for $\beta < 0$ shorter histories are preferred. This part increases the expressiveness of the pooling method, and allows, for example, to model average-pooling (having $\alpha = 1$ and $\beta = -1$). Note that, the commonly used sum-pooling [10] is a private case of this pooling method, having $\alpha = 1$ and $\beta = 0$.

2.3.3 Usage point weights scaling. Another domain-specific phenomenon that needs to be addressed is the following. There are some domains where a small sample of items in the history of the user is sufficient to determine her taste (e.g., in deciding movie tastes). In this case, considering only the most important items for each user would be beneficial as it will lower the level of noise in the system. On the other hand, there are domains with a vast number of items and tastes (e.g., food retail), where more items should be considered in order to model user preferences. A possible approach could be considering only the k most important items for each user. However, it may raise some open questions: how to set the appropriate value of k in each domain? how to personalize its value? and how to handle cases where the $(k+1)^{th}$ item is almost equal in importance to the kth item?

To cope with these questions, we designed a simple yet novel approach, that allows to learn the desired behavior from the data. We scale the weights of the items by raising them to a power γ, i.e.: $w_{ui} = (w'_{ui})^{\gamma}$, having γ as another learned parameter. In case few items are required to model users, the algorithm will assign a high value for γ. This would adjust the relative weight of the items in a non-linear way such that they differentiate in a drastic manner. In turn, few large weighed items will dominate the user tastes. On the other hand, as γ decreases, weight differences reduce and more items take a significant role in determining user tastes.

2.4 Learning the Parameters

We now describe how the various parameters introduced in the preceding sections (i.e., $\{q_i\}, \omega, \alpha, \beta, \gamma$) are learned. The common evaluation metrics in recommender systems are based on the same basic idea: *hide the last usage point of the user, and reward in case it was ranked high by the recommender* [3]. Motivated by that, in order to learn the various parameters, for each given user u, we first sort the usage points of **all** her item interactions histories R_{ui} chronologically and hide the last usage point; let i_p denote the item whose usage point was hidden. We then apply negative sampling proportional to the items popularity [6, 19] and pick an item $i_n \notin R_u$. The objective of the model is to maximize the log-likelihood of the hidden items. This objective is inspired by the *Bayesian Personalized Ranking* [23] (BPR) method. Yet, BPR maximizes the log-likelihood of the **whole item set in the history of the user** [23]. In contrast, our approach aims at modeling the current representation of the user in a manner that would directly maximize the likelihood of the **next interacted item**.

Formally, let $\hat{r}_u^p = \hat{p}_u^T q_{i_p}$ be the score of the hidden item based only on the revealed items in the corresponding user u's item interactions history (i.e., $R_u \setminus \{i_p\}$). Accordingly, let $\hat{r}_u^n = \hat{p}_u^T q_{i_n}$ be the score of the negative sample. Overall the (regularized) objective is to maximize the following[7]:

$$\max_{\Theta} \sum_{u \in TrainingSet} \ln \sigma(\hat{r}_u^p - \hat{r}_u^n) - \frac{\lambda}{2} \|\Theta\|^2, \tag{3}$$

where $\Theta = \{\{q_i\}, \omega, \alpha, \beta, \gamma\}$, $\sigma(x) = \frac{1}{1+e^{-x}}$ is the Sigmoid function and λ is the regularization coefficient. Since the weights w_{ui}

---

[6]Note that, by definition, $w_{ui}^{(j)}$ are all positive. Hence, we do not write their absolute value as required by the L_{α}-norm definition.

[7]We note that, hidden items with low importance may add noise to the learning. Yet, trying to differently weigh hidden items did not lead to any significant improvement.

and the users representations are computed in a feed-forward fashion, the learning is done using back-propagation with parameter tying [9]. Notice that, per each usage point an $O(1)$ computation is made and therefore the running time of the algorithm is linear with the number of usage points in the dataset.

We also tried to create meta-users, that contain a prefix of the usage points of the original items. Namely, let k be a hyper-parameter that controls the maximum number of meta-users allowed for a single real user. We define $s \leftarrow \min(k, |R_u| - 1)$. From each user we create s meta-users $u_1, \dots, u_s$, each meta-user u_t has the exact same usage points of u, but without the suffix of size $t - 1$. However, this approach did not lead to any statistically significant improvement, while increased the running time by a factor of k.

3 RELATED WORK

Most recommender systems have been designed to handle simple usage data that includes only a single type of user feedback for user preference learning [10, 25]. Few work have tried to incorporate several feedback types [4, 5, 7, 14, 18, 20, 28, 30–32]. Yet, such methods are still bounded to **specific domains and feedback types**. In addition, most of such methods were not designed to handle complex usage data that may include also **repetitive user-item interactions**; whereas those that have considered repetitions only applied very naïve data aggregation methods.

Among these methods, Koren [14] has proposed SVD++, an extended MF algorithm that combined explicit ratings with implicit feedback. Tang et al. [30] presented an empirical study on methods for incorporating multiple feedback types. Liu et al. [18] proposed a flexible personalized ranking framework that integrates a single explicit feedback type with one or more implicit feedback types. However, it requires *at least one explicit feedback type available*. Moreover, since the implicit feedback types are treated as binary values, they cannot be extended to continuous values.

Rendle [22] has developed *Factorization Machines* (FM), capable of processing rich user-item interaction vectors and to mimic most factorization models using feature engineering, and has obtained state-of-the-art results in context-aware recommendations [24]. FM can be used to model multiple feedback types settings, as it is able to incorporate diverse user-item interactions (e.g., having feedback types being modeled as context) and hence can capture complex usage behavior and to better model users and items.

Singh and Gordon [29] dealt with the problem of multiple relation types between entities (users and items in our case). They considered binary relationships, which can be extended to categorical relations as well. Parra and Amatriain [20] have trained a linear regression model using several feedback types to predict user ratings for music recommendation. In [26] they considered recency, popularity etc. to optimize recommended lists. Kordumova et al. [13] have trained a binary Naïve Bayes classifier using feedback features and classified newly items as either user "likes" or "dislikes". Yin et al. [31] recommended jokes to the JokeBox application users by augmenting explicit user votes with (implicit) pseudo-votes estimated from user application dwell times. Yu et al. [32] predicted item ratings in Heterogenous Information Netwroks by applying a Non-Negative MF method on several similarity matrices; each

matrix was induced by PathSim – a graph path based entity similarity measure. Shi et. al [28] have provided further improvement by considering explicit user ratings. Guo et. al [7] proposed an alternative recommendation approach based on a random-walk on the HIN hyper-graph. [27] considers multiple feedback types, but only for the users, while item modeling is done in a naive manner.

Finally, a couple of previous works [4, 5] have employed ensemble methods [1] as a post-processing step, used to combine the recommendations of several underlying recommenders, each trained over a single feedback type. Domingues et al. [5] have simply averaged the uni-feedback item scores obtained from several independent recommenders. Da Costa and Manzato [4] proposed an ensemble approach based on Rendle et al. [23] LearnBPR algorithm. However, these works could handle only categorical values.

3.1 Main Differences

Our work differs from previous works in several aspects. First, most previous work have focused on the implementation of **customized** recommender systems that require domain expertise. In addition, such methods rely on **specific feedback types** and their blends. Our approach, on the other hand, does not require any domain knowledge.

One of the cornerstones of our approach is the ability to learn how to handle multiple occurrences of the same user-item pair. Most previous works are oblivious to repetitions of the same user-item pair; whereas those that are not only apply naïve aggregations (e.g., summation) of feedback obtained from multiple usage points [7, 28].

Although continuous feedback types encode valuable data, most of previous work cannot handle such data (e.g., [4, 7, 18, 29, 30, 32]).

Finally, previous works such as [4, 5, 30] first applied several unimodal (single type) MF models and then trained a new model that combines them together. Using such an approach may result in base (MF) models that are **very limited**, as they are exposed to only a fraction of the usage points of each user and to a single feedback type. Having a model with a holistic view, would dramatically improve the recommender system's accuracy.

4 EVALUATION

We now describe the evaluation of our proposed CDMF approach.

4.1 Datasets

Our evaluation is based on three real-world datasets, and vary in the feedback types that are recorded. Therefore, they allow to evaluate the *robustness* of our approach.

The range of values of the feedback types may widely vary. For example, the typical range of "purchase price" might be significantly broader than the range of "purchase amount". We therefore Z-normalized the values of each feedback type.

Since the effect of time is user-dependent [15], across all datasets we Z-normalized the timestamps per user as well. Additionally, the effect of time on the importance of a usage point may vary among different event types. For example, the importance of a click event may be highly dependent on its freshness; on the other hand, a purchase event may capture long-term preferences and thus its importance is less correlated with freshness. For this reason, in all datasets we created a timestamp entry per each event type, when only one of them has a nonzero value.

4.1.1 RecSys Challenge 2016.
This dataset[8] (denoted as **RSC16**) contains interactions of Xing[9] users with job postings. In total there are $8,826,678$ interactions (usage points), by $784,687$ users with $1,029,480$ items (job postings). The interactions are divided into four event types: $7,183,038$ *click* events, $206,191$ add to *bookmark* events, $422,026$ click on *apply* button events and $1,015,423$ *delete* recommendations events. Each user interaction has a recorded timestamp. Therefore, usage points in this dataset may be associated with 8 possible feedback types. The challenge is to predict with which item a given user will interact with next. However, we would like to predict positive interactions only, and therefore, the hidden items in our test data do not contain interactions of type *delete recommendation*. Note that, since our method does not assume any domain knowledge, the training data does contain such interactions.

4.1.2 Ta-Feng.
This dataset[10] is a grocery shopping dataset released at ACM RecSys that contains 4 months of shopping transactions of various items from food, office supplies to furniture. Overall, there are $817,741$ transactions (purchase events) in this dataset, recorded for $32,266$ users and $23,812$ items. Each transaction provides 3 feedback types: *timestamp*, *price* and *amount*. The goal is to predict the next item that the user will purchase.

4.1.3 Yelp.
This dataset[11] contains about 1.5M *reviews* on a rating scale of 1 to 5 and 495,000 *tips* on more than 60,000 businesses made by about 367,000 users. The number of usage points in this dataset is 2,064,372. Each review has an associated *date* and each tip includes a *timestamp* and the *number of users who liked it*. This in all, translates to six different feedback types available within usage points of this dataset. Since we would like to predict positive interactions only, the hidden item in the test data do not contain usage points of type *reviews* with a rating lower than 3. Once again, since we do not assume any domain knowledge, the training data contains all usage points.

4.2 Setup

4.2.1 Baselines.
We compare CDMF to two baselines. The first, is the *Bayesian Personalized Ranking* (BPR) method [23], a state-of-the-art implicit feedback MF method that is capable of utilizing only a single feedback type. BPR is optimize for correctly ranking observed user-item interactions over non-observed ones. On each dataset, BPR was trained over uniform feedback usage points (i.e., all feedback events were considered with no type distinction). We note that this provided a much better performance compared to the alternative of training the same method using only a single feedback type. Following previous work [10, 23], *any* implicit feedback obtained in different usage points of a given (u, i) user-item pair was aggregated.

The second baseline is *Pairwise Ranking Factorization Machines* [8] (PRFM), a Factorization Machines [22] (FM) method with BPR loss

function. Compared to all previous related works that were mentioned in Section 3, the PRFM method is capable of handling multiple continuous feedback types in a domain independent way, similar to CDMF. An FM model essentially implements an 2-way tensor-factorization in the following model: $f(\mathbf{x}) = w_0 + \sum_{k=1}^{g} w_k x_k + \sum_{k=1}^{g} \sum_{j>k}^{g} \langle v_k, v_j \rangle x_k x_j$, where $\mathbf{x} \in \mathbb{R}^g$ is a feature vector, $w_0 \in \mathbb{R}$, $w \in \mathbb{R}^g$ and $V \in \mathbb{R}^{g \times f}$ are the model parameters. Let's assume that there are n_U users, n_I items and l possible feedback types in a given dataset; then, each usage point is represented as a sparse feature vector $\mathbf{x}$ of size $g = n_U + n_I + l$, where the non-zero values correspond to the appropriate user id, item id and feedback types. FMs can be also seen as a linear model with 2-way interactions in which the interaction parameters are factorized. The original formulation of FMs was used in conjunction with a regression loss function. To better reflect the fact that in recommender systems one is essentially looking for an optimal ranking of items based on preferences, a BPR pairwise ranking loss is utilized in the FM objective [8]. PRFM has been previously shown to outperform the BPR method and the basic FM method, including other rank-driven FM extensions (e.g., RankFM) [8]. Hence, PRFM serves as a strong baseline for comparison in our evaluation.

4.2.2 Evaluation Protocol & Measures.
Using each dataset, we evaluated our approach and the various baseline methods using an *"All But (Last) One"* protocol [3] (i.e., the hidden item belongs to the last usage point). Recommender systems usually present/display few items at once (e.g., 1-20), where the exact amount is system dependent. Hence the item a user may pick should be among the first few items on the list. Therefore, we chose several representative values for the size of the list k, namely $k \in \{1, 3, 5, 10, 20\}$. The first evaluation metric we used is **Success@k**, which returns 1 iff the hidden item is amongst the top-k items. Yet, this measure does not consider the actual rank of the item as long as it is amongst the top-k. Therefore, as a second metric we used the **MRR@k** (Mean Reciprocal Rank) which returns the inverse of the rank of the hidden item. **MRR@k** is zero if the rank of the item is above k. Note that, for $k = 1$, **Success@1** is same as **MRR@1**.

Since PRFM models the interactions between the item and the feedback types, at test time, it was given additional data. That is, the input for PRFM consists not only of the user id but also the feedback types of the next interaction, which is a *privileged information* comparing to the input of CDMF.

In all datasets, we randomly selected 70% of the users for the training set, 15% for the validation set and the remaining 15% for the test set. Following [10], since usually the goal of recommender systems is to recommend new items, we removed from the test set "trivial" hidden items, which already appeared in the history of the corresponding user in the training set.

4.2.3 Methods implementation.
We implemented the two baselines and CDMF using *TensorFlow*[12] employed with the *Adam* optimizer [12]. A useful heuristic, that was employed also on the baselines, was setting separate learning rates for the bias terms of the positive and negative items. The implementation code is available online[13]. The optimal dimensionality for both BPR and PRFM

---

[8]http://2016.recsyschallenge.com/
[9]https://www.xing.com/en
[10]http://www.bigdatalab.ac.cn/benchmark/bm/dd?data=Ta-Feng
[11]http://www.yelp.com/dataset_challenge

[12]https://www.tensorflow.org/
[13]Online link removed for anonymity.

Dataset/methods		Success@k					MRR@k			
		k=1	k=3	k=5	k=10	k=20	k=3	k=5	k=10	k=20
RSC16	BPR	.0008	.0047	.0091	.0172	.0300	.0024	.0034	.0045	.0054
	PRFM	.0007	.0062	.0128	.0257	.0434	.0028	.0060	.0060	.0072
	CDMF	**.0141**	**.0322**	**.0418**	**.0586**	**.0790**	**.0219**	**.0241**	**.0263**	**.0277**
Ta-Feng	BPR	.0040	.0100	.0180	.0338	.0542	.0067	.0085	.01058	.0119
	PRFM	.0173	**.0398**	**.0547**	**.0849**	**.1142**	**.0271**	**.0305**	**.0345**	**.0366**
	CDMF	**.0204**	.0361	.0469	.0718	.0909	**.0271**	.0296	.0330	.0343
Yelp	BPR	.0005	.0025	.0054	.0106	.0191	.0013	.0019	.0026	.0032
	PRFM	.0009	.0023	.0045	.0090	.0177	.0014	.0019	.0025	.0031
	CDMF	**.0033**	**.0127**	**.0199**	**.0352**	**.0595**	**.0072**	**.0089**	**.0109**	**.0125**

Table 1: Comparison of our approach with the two baselines. All reported CDMF numbers are statistically significant (paired two-tailed Student's t-test, $p < 10^{-4}$).

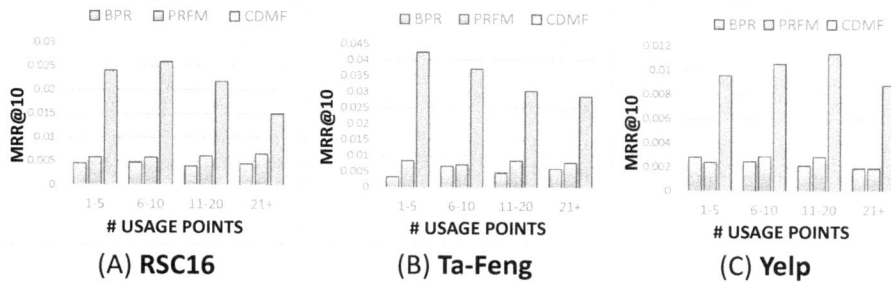

Figure 2: Comparison according to usage history size

baselines for the RSC16, Ta-Feng and Yelp datasets was 90, 40 and 50, respectively. In our evaluation we report the results using the same dimensionality configuration. In addition, the regularization parameter λ of all methods (i.e., the baselines and ours) was further tuned over the validation set (with $\lambda \in [0.001, 0.5]$).

4.3 Results

We now describe the results of our evaluation. We start with a comparison of CDMF with the two other baselines. We then analyze the effect of the user history size (i.e., number of different usage points) on recommendation performance. We next compare common pooling (aggregation) methods with CDMF's learnable pooling method for usage points' weights aggregation. Finally, we analyze the relative importance of each feedback type according to their weights that were learned by CDMF.

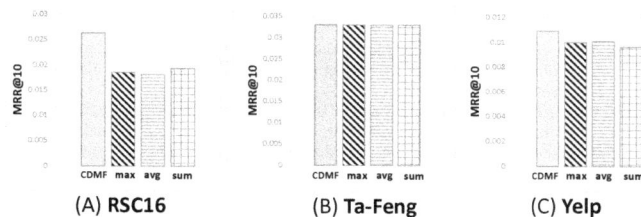

Figure 3: Comparison between CDMF's pooling method and other common (simple) pooling methods

4.3.1 Comparison with baseline methods. Table 1 reports on the main results of our evaluation. First we observe that, as expected across all datasets, the PRFM baseline was better than BPR. Here we note that, the significant difference between the two can be explained by the fact that BPR is basically a special case of PRFM, where the only 2-way interactions that are possible to be considered are direct user-item interactions.

In the Yelp and RSC2016 we observe that CDMF outperforms the two baselines by a large margin. This comes with no surprise, since CDMF is the first method so far that can handle the full complexity of these datasets. However, in the Ta-Feng dataset, for most values of k, CDMF is inferior to PRFM. This can be explained by the privileged data of PRFM. That is, at prediction time PRMF gets access to the additional information of purchase amount and price of the next purchased item. Both signals are indicative properties of the purchased item itself, and have a crucial impact on performance. This in contrast to the situation in the Yelp dataset, for example, where knowing whether the user wrote a tip or a review is not an indicative property of the interacted item.

4.3.2 Effect of user history size. We analyzed the effect of the number of usage points in a user's history on the various methods' performance. We separate the analysis into four different bins, each according to the number of usage points in a given user's history: $[1 - 5]$, $[6 - 10]$, $[10 - 20]$ and 21+. Figure 2 depicts the result of this analysis, having MRR@10 as the performance target. We observe that, in most cases, CDMF's relative advantage is when users have short histories, and it even outperforms PRMF in these bins in the

RSC16		Ta-Feng		Yelp	
Feedback	Weight	Feedback	Weight	Feedback	Weight
bookmark_event	1.012	purchase_price	.5787	tip_event	.8532
delete_event	.9830	purchace_event	.4447	review_time	.6716
apply_event	.9453	purchase_time	.2954	review_event	.6148
click_time	.6721	purchase_amount	.0596	tip_time	.3758
click_event	.5121			tip_likes	.0529
apply_time	.0308			review_rating	.0100
bookmark_time	.0296				
delete_time	.0259				

Table 2: Feedback type analysis

Ta-Feng dataset. This may be attributed to the fact that CDMF does not fit directly a parameter vector for each user (i.e., like more "traditional" MF methods utilize [16]), but infers such a model from the items in a given user's history. Therefore, this implies that, CDMF does not need many usage points in order to accurately model users, which may better help to mitigate the cold start problem in recommender systems.

4.3.3 Comparison between pooling methods. To recall, in order to obtain each item weight w_{ui}, CDMF employees a learned pooling method (modeled by the α and β parameters) which aggregates over the respective weights $\{w_{ui}^{(j)}\}$ of the different usage points. This in comparison to existing pooling methods which employ a rather simple approach, i.e., either max-, average- or sum-pooling. We evaluated the relative added contribution of using the learned pooling method over these baselines by further employing CDMF with each one of these baseline methods as an alternative pooling method. This is achieved by fixing the (α, β) parameters as follows: $(\infty, 0)$ for max-pooling; $(1, -1)$ for average-pooling; and $(1, 0)$ for sum-pooling.

Figure 3 now depicts, for each dataset, the comparison between CDMF's learnable pooling method and the baseline methods; having **MRR@10** as the performance target. As we can observe, in RSC16, the best performing method among the baseline methods was sum-pooling. Compared to this method, CDMF's method has provided about 36% improvement in performance. In the Yelp dataset, the best baseline method was average-pooling, to which CDMF's method further improved by 8%; In the Ta-Feng dataset, which belong to the grocery shopping domain, the difference between the various pooling methods is rather negligible. This is actually aligned with our established intuition (see again Section 2.3.2), as in this domain, repetitive interactions do not provide a significant signal on users' preferences.

4.3.4 Feedback type analysis. We now shortly discuss the analysis of the relative importance of the various feedback types on each dataset. We further present some anecdotal insights, as can be stemmed from Table 2. On each dataset, various feedback types are ranked according to their CDMF's inferred weight (ω_l).

In the RSC2016 dataset, a click event appears to be the least informative. It is also the most sensitive to freshness (i.e., the importance of a click decays rapidly as a function of the elapsed time, compared to the other event types). A counter intuitive example is the significant importance of delete events, which might have

been expected to be rather negative. This may be explained by the fact that, any deleted item was necessarily recommended by the Xing recommender system. The recommender suggests items for a reason, and therefore, even deleted items in this dataset are correlated with the users' preferences.

In the Ta-Feng dataset, purchased item's price got the highest weight among all feedback types. This implies that, users in this dataset are mostly characterized by the more expensive items they have purchased.

In the Yelp dataset, the very existence of a tip is more important than a review. This fact is consistent with common sense, as writing a free text tip takes more effort by users than selecting a 1-5 rating. Therefore, a tip reflects that an item is more important. Yet, tips seem to be more sensitive to time, implying that, as time passes by, a tip may lose its effect. Additionally, there is a slight positive correlation with the item importance and the number of likes a tip got. This may be since more effort is invested in writing tips that would gain more likes; and this in turn, implies on their importance. Another self-evident result is that, explicit ratings are positively correlated with item importance.

Finally, please note that, across all datasets and event types, the time feedbacks were always positive. This implies that, later events (i.e., those with a higher timestamp) provide a more accurate signal on the users' preferences.

REFERENCES

[1] Ariel Bar, Lior Rokach, Guy Shani, Bracha Shapira, and Alon Schclar. Improving simple collaborative filtering models using ensemble methods. In *Multiple Classifier Systems*, pages 1–12. Springer, 2013.

[2] Alejandro BellogíN, Iván Cantador, and Pablo Castells. A comparative study of heterogeneous item recommendations in social systems. *Information Sciences*, 221:142–169, 2013.

[3] John S. Breese, David Heckerman, and Carl Kadie. Empirical analysis of predictive algorithms for collaborative filtering. In *Proceedings of the Fourteenth Conference on Uncertainty in Artificial Intelligence*, UAI'98, pages 43–52, San Francisco, CA, USA, 1998. Morgan Kaufmann Publishers Inc.

[4] Arthur F. da Costa and Marcelo G. Manzato. Exploiting multimodal interactions in recommender systems with ensemble algorithms. *Inf. Syst.*, 56(C):120–132, March 2016.

[5] Marcos Aurélio Domingues, Fabien Gouyon, Alípio Mário Jorge, José Paulo Leal, João Vinagre, Luís Lemos, and Mohamed Sordo. Combining usage and content in an online music recommendation system for music in the long-tail. In *Proceedings of the 21st International Conference on World Wide Web*, WWW '12 Companion, pages 925–930, New York, NY, USA, 2012. ACM.

[6] G. Dror, N. Koenigstein, and Y. Koren. Web-scale media recommendation systems. *Proceedings of the IEEE*, 100(9):2722–2736, Sept 2012.

[7] Chun Guo and Xiaozhong Liu. Automatic feature generation on heterogeneous graph for music recommendation. In *Proceedings of the 38th International ACM SIGIR Conference on Research and Development in Information Retrieval*, SIGIR

'15, pages 807–810, New York, NY, USA, 2015. ACM.

[8] Weiyu Guo, Shu Wu, Liang Wang, and Tieniu Tan. Personalized ranking with pairwise factorization machines. *Neurocomputing*, 214:191–200, 2016.

[9] John J Hopfield. Neural networks and physical systems with emergent collective computational abilities. *Proceedings of the national academy of sciences*, 79(8):2554–2558, 1982.

[10] Yifan Hu, Yehuda Koren, and Chris Volinsky. Collaborative filtering for implicit feedback datasets. In *Proceedings of the 2008 Eighth IEEE International Conference on Data Mining*, ICDM '08, pages 263–272, Washington, DC, USA, 2008. IEEE Computer Society.

[11] Dietmar Jannach, Markus Zanker, and Matthias Fuchs. Leveraging multi-criteria customer feedback for satisfaction analysis and improved recommendations. *Information Technology & Tourism*, 14(2):119–149, 2014.

[12] Diederik Kingma and Jimmy Ba. Adam: A method for stochastic optimization. *arXiv preprint arXiv:1412.6980*, 2014.

[13] Suzana Kordumova, Ivana Kostadinovska, Mauro Barbieri, Verus Pronk, and Jan Korst. Personalized implicit learning in a music recommender system. In Paul De Bra, Alfred Kobsa, and David Chin, editors, *User Modeling, Adaptation, and Personalization*, volume 6075 of *Lecture Notes in Computer Science*, pages 351–362. Springer Berlin Heidelberg, 2010.

[14] Yehuda Koren. Factorization meets the neighborhood: A multifaceted collaborative filtering model. In *Proceedings of the 14th ACM SIGKDD International Conference on Knowledge Discovery and Data Mining*, KDD '08, pages 426–434, New York, NY, USA, 2008. ACM.

[15] Yehuda Koren. Collaborative filtering with temporal dynamics. In *Proceedings of the 15th ACM SIGKDD International Conference on Knowledge Discovery and Data Mining*, KDD '09, pages 447–456, New York, NY, USA, 2009. ACM.

[16] Yehuda Koren, Robert Bell, and Chris Volinsky. Matrix factorization techniques for recommender systems. *Computer*, 42(8):30–37, August 2009.

[17] Alex Krizhevsky, Ilya Sutskever, and Geoffrey E Hinton. Imagenet classification with deep convolutional neural networks. In *Advances in neural information processing systems*, pages 1097–1105, 2012.

[18] Jian Liu, Chuan Shi, Binbin Hu, Shenghua Liu, and S Yu Philip. Personalized ranking recommendation via integrating multiple feedbacks. In *Pacific-Asia Conference on Knowledge Discovery and Data Mining*, pages 131–143. Springer, 2017.

[19] Ulrich Paquet and Noam Koenigstein. One-class collaborative filtering with random graphs. In *Proceedings of the 22nd international conference on World Wide Web*, pages 999–1008, 2013.

[20] Denis Parra and Xavier Amatriain. Walk the talk: Analyzing the relation between implicit and explicit feedback for preference elicitation. In *Proceedings of UMAP'11*.

[21] Arkadiusz Paterek. Improving regularized singular value decomposition for collaborative filtering. In *Proceedings of KDD cup and workshop*, volume 2007,

pages 5–8, 2007.

[22] Steffen Rendle. Factorization machines with libfm. *ACM Trans. Intell. Syst. Technol.*, 3(3):57:1–57:22, May 2012.

[23] Steffen Rendle, Christoph Freudenthaler, Zeno Gantner, and Lars Schmidt-Thieme. Bpr: Bayesian personalized ranking from implicit feedback. In *Proceedings of the Twenty-Fifth Conference on Uncertainty in Artificial Intelligence*, UAI '09, pages 452–461, Arlington, Virginia, United States, 2009. AUAI Press.

[24] Steffen Rendle, Zeno Gantner, Christoph Freudenthaler, and Lars Schmidt-Thieme. Fast context-aware recommendations with factorization machines. In *Proceedings of the 34th international ACM SIGIR conference on Research and development in Information Retrieval*, pages 635–644, ACM, 2011.

[25] Francesco Ricci, Lior Rokach, Bracha Shapira, and Paul B. Kantor. *Recommender Systems Handbook*. Springer-Verlag New York, Inc., New York, NY, USA, 1st edition, 2010.

[26] Oren Sar Shalom, Noam Koenigstein, Ulrich Paquet, and Hastagiri P Vanchinathan. Beyond collaborative filtering: The list recommendation problem. In *Proceedings of the 25th International Conference on World Wide Web*, pages 63–72. International World Wide Web Conferences Steering Committee, 2016.

[27] Oren Sar Shalom, Haggai Roitman, Yishay Mansour, and Amir Amihood. A user re-modeling approach to item recommendation using complex usage data. In *Proceedings of the ACM SIGIR International Conference on Theory of Information Retrieval*, pages 201–208. ACM, 2017.

[28] Chuan Shi, Zhiqiang Zhang, Ping Luo, Philip S. Yu, Yading Yue, and Bin Wu. Semantic path based personalized recommendation on weighted heterogeneous information networks. In *Proceedings of the 24th ACM International on Conference on Information and Knowledge Management*, CIKM '15, pages 453–462, New York, NY, USA, 2015. ACM.

[29] Ajit P Singh and Geoffrey J Gordon. Relational learning via collective matrix factorization. In *Proceedings of the 14th ACM SIGKDD international conference on Knowledge discovery and data mining*, pages 650–658. ACM, 2008.

[30] Liang Tang, Bee-Chung Chen, Deepak Agarwal, and Bo Long. An empirical study on recommendation with multiple types of feedback. In *Proceedings of KDD'16*.

[31] Peifeng Yin, Ping Luo, Wang-Chien Lee, and Min Wang. Silence is also evidence: Interpreting dwell time for recommendation from psychological perspective. In *Proceedings of the 19th ACM SIGKDD International Conference on Knowledge Discovery and Data Mining*, KDD '13, pages 989–997, New York, NY, USA, 2013. ACM.

[32] Xiao Yu, Xiang Ren, Yizhou Sun, Quanquan Gu, Bradley Sturt, Urvashi Khandelwal, Brandon Norick, and Jiawei Han. Personalized entity recommendation: A heterogeneous information network approach. In *Proceedings of the 7th ACM International Conference on Web Search and Data Mining*, WSDM '14, pages 283–292. ACM, 2014.

Privacy-Aware Tag Recommendation for Image Sharing

Ashwini Tonge[1], Cornelia Caragea[1], Anna Squicciarini[2]
[1]Kansas State University, Manhattan, KS-66506
[2]Pennsylvania State University, University Park, PA-16801
atonge@ksu.edu,ccaragea@ksu.edu,asquicciarini@ist.psu.edu

ABSTRACT

Image tags are very important for indexing, sharing, searching, and surfacing images with private content that needs protection. As the tags are at the sole discretion of users, they tend to be noisy and incomplete. In this paper, we present a privacy-aware approach to automatic image tagging, which aims at improving the quality of user annotations, while also preserving the images' original privacy sharing patterns. Precisely, we recommend potential tags for each target image by mining privacy-aware tags from the most similar images of the target image obtained from a large collection. Experimental results show that privacy-aware approach is able to predict accurate tags that can improve the performance of a downstream application on image privacy prediction. Crowd-sourcing predicted tags exhibit the quality of the recommended tags.

KEYWORDS

Privacy-aware tag recommendation; Image tagging; Image's privacy

ACM Reference Format:
Ashwini Tonge[1], Cornelia Caragea[1], Anna Squicciarini[2]. 2018. Privacy-Aware Tag Recommendation for Image Sharing. In *HT '18: 29th ACM Conference on Hypertext and Social Media, July 9–12, 2018, Baltimore, MD, USA.* ACM, New York, NY, USA, 5 pages. https://doi.org/10.1145/3209542.3209574

1 INTRODUCTION

Images are constantly shared on social networking sites such as Facebook, Flickr, and Instagram. For instance, it is common to take photos at cocktail parties and upload them to social networking sites without much hesitation for self-promotion and personal sharing. However, when privacy settings are used inappropriately, these photos can potentially reveal a user's personal and social habits, resulting in unwanted disclosure and privacy violations [1, 20, 21, 33]. For example, malicious attackers can take advantage of these accidental leaks to launch context-aware or even impersonation attacks. Thus, several works [20–22, 27, 28, 30, 33] have been developed in an attempt to provide appropriate privacy settings for online images. Prior works on privacy prediction [20, 27, 29, 33] found that the tags associated with images are indicative of their sensitive content. Tags are also important for image-related applications such as indexing, sharing, searching, content detection and social discovery [5, 7]. Yet, the tags are at the sole discretion of users, and they tend to be noisy and incomplete [25]. Despite that many approaches to automatic image tagging have been developed [6, 12–14], none of these works considers the privacy aspect of an image while making the annotations and hence would not be sufficient for identifying images' private (or sensitive) content.

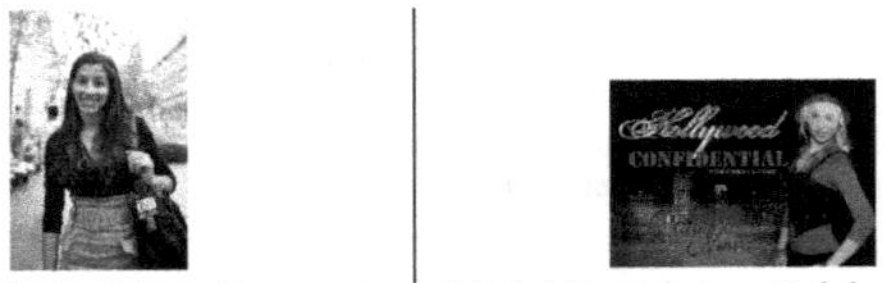

(a) *Private*: Style, Skirt, Corporate Pretty, Girl, Woman, Elegant | (b) *Public*: Sabrina, Celebrity, News Famous, Woman, Hollywood

Figure 1: Anecdotal evidence for privacy-aware user tags.

We posit that visually similar images can possess very different sets of tags if these images have different privacy orientations. For example, Figure 1 shows anecdotal evidence obtained from a Flickr dataset in which visually similar images of private and public classes display different sets of user tags. The picture of a woman that belongs to the private class in Figure 1(a) contains tags such as "Elegant," "Corporate," "Style," and "Pretty," whereas the picture of a woman that belongs to the public class in Figure 1(b) contains tags such as "Celebrity," "Famous," "News," and "Hollywood." Images are considered private if they belong to the private sphere (portraits, family, friends, home) or contain information that can not be shared (e.g., private documents) [33]. Figure 1 shows that the tags are correlated to image's privacy patterns [9, 22, 23] and are effective when access to the image content is not allowed since users may be reluctant to share the real images (revealing user's identity through the face, and friends, etc.) for visual content analysis. In such cases, privacy-aware tags can become good indicators of the privacy settings and improve the privacy prediction methods.

To this end, we ask the following questions and address them with our research agenda: *Can we develop an automated approach to recommend accurate image tags that can also take into account the sharing needs of the users for images in question? Can we make precise tag recommendations for newly uploaded images that have an incomplete set of user tags or no tags at all? Can these recommended tags help improve the privacy prediction performance?*

Contributions and Organization. We present a privacy-aware approach to image tagging [1], aimed at improving the quality of user tags, while also preserving the images' original privacy sharing patterns. Precisely, our approach recommends, based on collaborative filtering, potential tags for a target image by mining privacy-aware tags from the most similar images of a target image from a large collection. To evaluate the recommended tags, we employ crowd-sourcing to identify relevancy of the suggested tags to images. The results show that, although the user-input tags are noisy or incomplete, our approach can recommend accurate tags. We also

[1]The code is given at https://github.com/ashwinitonge/privacy-aware-tag-rec.git

HT '18, July 9–12, 2018, Baltimore, MD, USA

ACM ISBN 978-1-4503-5427-1/18/07...$15.00
https://doi.org/10.1145/3209542.3209574

investigate tag recommendation in a binary privacy setting, and show that the predicted tags can exhibit relevant cues for specific privacy settings (*public* or *private*) that can be used to improve the privacy prediction performance.

2 RELATED WORK

We briefly review the related work as follows.

Automatic Image Annotation: Many works on automatic image annotation have been proposed [4, 6, 10–14]. For example, Chen et al. [14] proposed an approach to image tagging, which learned two classifiers to predict tags: one that reconstructs the complete tag set from the tags available during training and the other that maps image features to the reconstructed tag set. Several works on tag recommendation for social discovery [2, 18] and image classification [2, 17, 32] in photo sharing sites (e.g. Flickr) typically trained classifiers for each tag using image's textual and/or visual features.

Collaborative Filtering: Our approach draws ideas from collaborative filtering (CF), and hence, we briefly review the most relevant works on CF here. Xu et al. [31] designed a CF approach to suggest high-quality tags for Web objects, according to several criteria (coverage, popularity, effort, uniformity). Authors consider that if two tags frequently co-occur when describing a specific object, they should also co-occur in the recommended set of tags. Recently, Peng et al. [15] generated joint item–tag recommendations for users, where the tags represent topics from an item (i.e., a web resource) in which the user may be interested.

Online Image Privacy: Several works analyzed users' posted data with respect to privacy. For example, Ahern et al. [1] studied the effectiveness of location information and tags in predicting privacy settings of images. They also conducted a study to verify whether the visual features are relevant to an image's privacy and found that content is one of the discriminatory factors affecting image privacy, especially for images depicting people. This supports the core idea underlying our work: that tags depicting private categories obtained from image content are pivotal for identifying the sensitive content from the search results. For example, tags such as "wedding," "bride," "people" describing a wedding event (private category) represent the private class. Jones and O'Neill [8] determined that people are more reluctant to share photos capturing social relationships than photos taken for functional purposes; certain settings such as work, bars, concerts cause users to share less. Zerr et al. [33] developed the PicAlert dataset to help detect private images. Recently, Tonge et al. [27, 29] showed the performance of automatically obtained image tags from the visual content using convolutional neural networks (CNN) for privacy prediction. Yet, these tags depicted objects or scenes given in the image and failed to capture the privacy characteristics of the image while generating the tags. To this end, we recommend privacy-aware tags for online images that have the potential to improve the set of user tags.

3 PRIVACY-AWARE TAG RECOMMENDATION

Our approach to recommending privacy-aware tags for newly posted images on content sharing websites is inspired from collaborative filtering (CF) [19]. Many images posted on the Web in recent years, facilitate the study of potential relationships between images. We leverages these relationships to exchange privacy-aware

---

Algorithm 1 Tag Recommendation

1: **Input**: A dataset $\mathcal{D} = \{I_1, \cdots, I_n\}$ of images and their tags $\{T_1, \cdots, T_m\}$; a target image I and its tags T; k the nearest neighbors of I from $\mathcal{D}$; r the number of tags to recommend.
2: **Output**: A set R of recommended tags for I.
3: $R \leftarrow \phi$; // the set of recommended tags, initially empty.
4: $S \leftarrow \phi$;
5: **if** $T = \phi$ **then** // if the set of tags is empty.
6:     $\mathbf{x} \leftarrow$ ImageContentEncoding(I); // deep features for I
7:     **for all** $I_j \in \mathcal{D}$ **do**
8:         $\mathbf{x}_j \leftarrow$ ImageContentEncoding(I_j); // deep features I_j
9:         $s_j \leftarrow$ similarity($\mathbf{x}, \mathbf{x}_j$); // visual content similarity
10:         $S \leftarrow S \cup (I_j, s_j)$; // store I_j and its similarity with I
11:     **end for**
12: **else**
13:     $\mathbf{x} \leftarrow$ ImageTagEncoding(I); // get tags' features of I
14:     **for all** $I_j \in \mathcal{D}$ **do**
15:         $\mathbf{x}_j \leftarrow$ ImageTagEncoding(I_j); // get tags' features of I_j
16:         $s_j \leftarrow$ similarity($\mathbf{x}, \mathbf{x}_j$); // compute the tags similarity
17:         $S \leftarrow S \cup (I_j, s_j)$; // store I_j and its similarity with I
18:     **end for**
19: **end if**
20: $S.similarities.sort()$; // sort images in decreasing order of similarity
21: $S \leftarrow$ top k (I_j, s_j) entries; // get k images with the highest similarities
22: $W \leftarrow$ TagRanking(S); // rank the tags from S images
23: $R \leftarrow r$ tags with the highest scores from W;
24: **return** R

---

tags between similar images. The analogy with conventional CF methods is that images correspond to users and tags correspond to items. We base our models on the assumption that *privacy-aware similar images possess similar tags*.

Algorithm 1 describes the process in detail. Recommendations are made for the target image based on the neighboring images' tags (as a privacy-aware weighted sum of occurrences of tags). A common problem in CF is the *cold start* problem [24]. In our case, this refers to images that have very few tags or no tags at all, and hence, there is not enough information available to find accurate nearest neighbors for a target image, based on tags. However, in our domain, images can be represented using two views: (1) visual content; and (2) tags. We take advantage of both the views. The input of the algorithm is a dataset $\mathcal{D} = \{I_1, \cdots, I_n\}$ of images and their tags, $\{T_1, \cdots, T_m\}$; a target image I and its set of tags T, which could be empty; k the number of nearest neighbors of I from $\mathcal{D}$; and r the number of tags to recommend. The output of the algorithm is a ranked list of r recommended tags for the target image. The algorithm starts by checking if the set of tags T of the target image I is empty (Alg. 1, line 5). If $T \neq \phi$, the similarities between I and all images in $\mathcal{D} \setminus \{I\}$ are computed based on images' tags (Alg. 1, lines 13-18). The top k most similar images to I are returned (Alg. 1, lines 20-21) and the candidate set that represents the union of the sets of tags extracted from these k similar images is ranked inside the subroutine for tag ranking (line 22) described in Algorithm 2. The highly ranked r tags from the candidate set are returned as recommended tags for the target image I (Alg. 1, line 23-24). If $T = \phi$ for image I, Alg. 1 recommends r tags based on the similarity computed using image content features (Alg. 1, lines 5-12). For each tag in the candidate set, we compute its score (or weight) as the privacy-aware sum of similarities between the target image and its neighbors (Alg. 2, lines 6-12). This weighting is based on the assumption that a "good" tag is likely to be exchanged

---

Algorithm 2 Tag Ranking

1: **function** TagRanking(S)
2:    $W \leftarrow \phi$; // the set of tags and their scores, initially empty.
3:    **for all** $I_j \in S$ **do**
4:        $T_j \leftarrow I_j.tags$ // get the set of tags of image I_j.
5:        $s_j \leftarrow I_j.similarity$ // similarity of target image and I_j.
6:        **for all** $t \in T_j$ **do**
7:            $w_t \leftarrow W.scoreOf(t)$ // w_t stores the score of t
8:            **if** w_t = null **then** // if tag t is not in W already
9:                $W \leftarrow W \cup (t, 0)$ // add t to W
10:           **end if**
11:           $w_t \leftarrow w_t + s_j \cdot P(t|pr)$ //score of t weighted by privacy
12:       **end for**
13:   **end for**
14:   $W.scores.sort()$ // sort the scores in W in the decreasing order.
15:   **return** W.
16: **end function**

---

between similar images. The weight of a tag t, w_t, is computed as:

$$w_t = \sum_{j \in S} c_{jt} \cdot s_j \cdot P(t|pr(I)) \qquad (1)$$

where S represents the k most similar images of I from $\mathcal{D}$, c_{jt} is 1 if tag t belongs to the tag set T_j of image I_j from S and 0 otherwise, and s_j is the similarity between image I_j and I. The probability $P(t|pr(I))$ is the likelihood of the tag t belonging to the privacy class (i.e., public or private) of the target image I. For instance, if the target image I is of private class then $P(t|pr(I))$ gives the probability of tag t belonging to the set of private images. The likelihood is calculated based on the dataset $\mathcal{D}$. We rely on the privacy likelihood of the tag instead of considering privacy as another parameter (referred as privacy-enforced similarity) in the image similarity because we desire privacy-aware tags without missing out on the high-quality tags. For example, using privacy-enforced similarity, for Figure 1(b) (given its public nature), tags such as "women," "girl" (inclined to private class) would not be suggested, whereas privacy-aware weights can obtain descriptive tags for both the image's content and privacy aspect of the image.

4 DATASET

Similar to prior works [20, 27, 33], that identified generic privacy patterns using tags, we verify if the recommended tags are indicative of the privacy classes and also validate their relevancy to the images' content. Thus, we evaluate the algorithm on Flickr images sampled from the PicAlert dataset [33]. PicAlert contains images on various subjects, which are manually labeled as *private* or *public*. We split the dataset into three subsets. The first two subsets, denoted as DS_1 and DS_2, for which we recommend tags, contain randomly sampled 3,689 and 500 images, respectively. The third dataset, $PicAlert_{8K}$, is a collection $\mathcal{D}$ of 8,000 images, labeled as private or public, that are used to recommend tags for the target images in DS_1 and DS_2. The ratio of public to private images in all datasets is 3 : 1. For privacy prediction, we use DS_1 to train Support Vector Machine (SVM) models on the recommended tags and use DS_2 to test these models. For each image I in DS_1 and DS_2, we randomly split its set of tags into two subsets (i.e., *visible* and *hidden*). The motivation behind using random split is that newly uploaded

image may have an incomplete and noisy set of user-input tags [25]. For both DS_1 and DS_2, we consider images with a number of user tags greater than 10 to have at least five visible tags to calculate an accurate similarity. After filtering the stop words, numbers, and URL, the size of the vocabulary is $\approx 19,000$.

5 EXPERIMENTS AND RESULTS

We evaluate the tags obtained by the proposed algorithm for images in DS_1 and DS_2, by transferring tags from their most similar images from $PicAlert_{8k}$ in two settings: *1) whether these tags hint to specific image privacy settings*; and *2) whether these tags are good enough to describe the content of an image*. Hence, we adopt two evaluation mechanisms: 1) we examine the performance of models trained on the recommended tags combined with the original tags (when available) for privacy prediction to determine their ability in identifying private content for online image sharing; and 2) we compare the suggested tags against the ground-truth, i.e., the *hidden* set of tags, and also evaluate their quality through crowd-sourcing.

Evaluation Setting. We generate five subsets of visible and hidden tags and report performance averaged over these five splits. For privacy prediction, we use SVM Weka implementation and Boolean features for tags, i.e., 1 if a tag is present and 0 otherwise.

5.1 Evaluation by Privacy Prediction

We study Alg. 1 in the setting where each image in DS_1 has a seed set of tags associated with it, i.e., $T \neq \phi$ (Alg. 1, lines 13-18). The similarity between images is computed between the *visible* tag set of a target image and all available tags from an image in $PicAlert_{8K}$. We experiment with $k = 2, \cdots, 10$ and $r = 5, \cdots, 20$, where k is the number of similar images, and r is the number of recommended tags (see Alg. 1). We show results for the best value of k i.e. $k = 10$.

Table 1 shows the performance obtained by the SVM models trained on the combination of recommended tags (rt) and visible tags (vt) (as we increase rt from 5 to 20) for the images in DS_1 and evaluated on the fixed set of visible tags of the images in DS_2 (for consistency). The

Features	Acc.%	F1	Pre.	Re.
vt	74.83	0.743	0.739	0.748
$vt\&rt(5)$	78.20	0.772	0.762	0.783
$vt\&rt(10)$	77.80	0.765	0.754	0.777
$vt\&rt(15)$	77.92	0.767	0.758	0.778
$vt\&rt(20)$	77.43	0.758	0.745	0.771

Table 1: Evaluation by privacy prediction, $T \neq \phi, k = 10$.

results show that the performance of privacy prediction improves when we add recommended tags to the set of visible tags. We get the best performance for $r = 5$ of F1-score of 0.772, whereas the SVM trained on only visible tags achieves 0.743 F1-measure, yielding an improvement of 3% in overall performance. We notice that generally, the performance increases with the decreasing value of r (best performance is given by $r = 5$ and $k = 10$). Due to the diverse nature of the data and a large vocabulary, a large r may introduce noise in the results. In the following experiments, we use $k = 10$.

5.2 Solution to the Cold Start Problem

Cold start is a challenging problem particularly in many CF approaches, where the absence of items (i.e., tags, in our case) that are used to bootstrap the algorithms may theoretically hinder the recommendations to be produced. Hence, we evaluate our approach in the setting where we assume that each image in DS_1 has no tags, i.e., $T = \phi$ and recommend tags from visually similar images (Alg. 1, lines 5-12). The similarity between two images is given as the cosine similarity of the corresponding feature vectors. We consider two types of image features extracted from a GoogLeNet CNN [26]: 1) *deep visual feature*, and 2) *deep tags*, due to their prior performance for privacy prediction [27, 30]. We extract visual features $pool_5$ from the layer named as "$pool_5/drop\_7x7\_s1$". For deep tags, we use the probability distribution over $1,000$ object categories for the input image obtained by applying the softmax function over the last fully-connected layer of the CNN. We consider the top k objects of highest probabilities as *deep tags*. We use the pre-trained GoogLeNet on a subset of the ImageNet dataset [16], which is distributed with the CAFFE framework for CNN [3].

Table 2 shows the privacy prediction performance obtained by the SVM trained on the privacy-aware tags recommended from visually similar images based on $pool_5$ ($pool_5(rt)$) and deep tags (DT(rt)) for the images in DS_1

Features	Acc.%	F1	Pre.	Re.
$pool_5(rt)$	75.74	0.743	0.729	0.757
DT(rt)	74.19	0.731	0.725	0.742
vt	74.83	0.743	0.739	0.748
DT	68.54	0.645	0.619	0.685

Table 2: Visual content similarity ($k = 10$).

and evaluated on the visible tags of the images in DS_2. The table also shows the performance of the models trained on visible tags alone (vt), if they would be available, and predicted deep tags (DT) of DS_1, as done in prior work [27]. The results show that the models trained on the recommended tags yield similar results to the models trained on visible tags (user-input tags – if we would know them). We obtain the best F1-score of 0.743 and recall of 0.757 with recommended tags $r = 5$. We observe that the models trained on tags recommended from visually similar images based on $pool_5$ ($pool_5(rt)$) outperform those trained on tags recommended from visually similar images based on deep tags (DT(rt)), which in turn, outperform the models trained on the deep tags (DT). The reason is that deep tags belong to only $1,000$ objects due to which many relevant tags (e.g. "walking" and "culture") can not be captured.

5.3   Quality Assessment of Recommended Tags

In the above experiments, we evaluated the effectiveness of recommended tags for privacy prediction. In this experiment, we determine whether the recommended tags describe an image's content appropriately. We compare the tags recommended using our privacy-aware weighting scheme against the ground-truth (i.e., *hidden* set of tags). Table 3 shows the performance (Precision@r) obtained for $r \in \{1, 2, 3, 4, 5, 10\}$ tags recommended for the images in DS_2 when compared against the gold-standard set (GS) of tags (those are hidden from the original user tags). We compute Precision as the total number of *recommended* and *relevant* tags over the number of tags recommended (i.e., r). The results show that the recommended tags achieve precision as high as 0.181 using gold-standard. The gold-standard set is nothing but a subset of user annotated tags, which may not provide all possible tags related to the image content. Hence, the gold-standard set may fail to capture

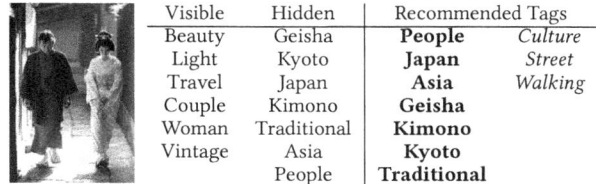

Visible	Hidden	Recommended Tags	
Beauty	Geisha	**People**	*Culture*
Light	Kyoto	**Japan**	*Street*
Travel	Japan	**Asia**	*Walking*
Couple	Kimono	**Geisha**	
Woman	Traditional	**Kimono**	
Vintage	Asia	**Kyoto**	
	People	**Traditional**	

Figure 2: Image with recommended tags, r=10.

highly relevant tags provided by the recommendation strategy. For example, in Figure 2, tags relevant to the image content (shown in italic) are recommended, but do not appear in the user-input tags.

Crowd-sourcing can be used to address the above limitation. We employ crowd-sourcing as follows: we use two annotators from the Amazon Mechanical Turk to determine if the recommended tags are relevant to the image content. For each tag, annotators were asked to choose between: *relevant*, *irrelevant* and *not sure*. To calculate precision values, we consider a tag as *Relevant* if at least one annotator marked it as *relevant*, i.e., the tags can be subjective and one annotator can observe more in an image than the other. Table 3 shows the performance ob-

r	GS	CS
1	0.177	0.855
2	0.181	0.761
3	0.181	0.755
4	0.172	0.703
5	0.174	0.691
10	0.155	0.633

Table 3: Quality evaluation of suggested tags.

tained through crowd-sourcing (CS). Note that the results of crowd-sourcing are higher than those obtained by relying only on *gold standard* to compute the performance. Precisely, through crowd-sourcing, the precision increased from 0.181 (GS) to 0.855, reassuring that the generated tags are relevant to image's content. The difference in the results can be justified as user tags tend to be noisy, incomplete, and may not relate to the image content [25].

6   CONCLUSIONS

We proposed privacy-aware image tagging, based on collaborative filtering, that can improve the original user-input tags while preserving the images' privacy. Although user tags are prone to noise, we were able to integrate them in our approach and recommend accurate tags. Importantly, we simulated the recommendation strategy for newly-posted images, which had no tags attached. This is a particularly challenging problem, as in many CF approaches, the absence of items (tags in our case) may theoretically hinder the recommendations to be produced, due to the lack of enough information available to find similar images to a target image. We achieve better performance for privacy prediction with recommended tags than the original set of user tags, which in turn indicate that the suggested tags comply to an image's privacy. We also conducted a user evaluation of recommended tags to inspect the quality of our privacy-aware recommended tags. The results show that the proposed approach is able to recommend highly relevant tags. In future, it would be interesting to study the algorithm for multiple sharing needs of users such as friends and family, by considering privacy likelihood with respect to multi-class privacy settings.

7   ACKNOWLEDGMENTS

This research is supported by NSF grant 1421970 and 1421776.

REFERENCES

[1] Shane Ahern, Dean Eckles, Nathaniel S. Good, Simon King, Mor Naaman, and Rahul Nair. 2007. Over-exposed?: privacy patterns and considerations in online and mobile photo sharing. In *CHI '07*.

[2] Hong-Ming Chen, Ming-Hsiu Chang, Ping-Chieh Chang, Ming-Chun Tien, Winston H. Hsu, and Ja-Ling Wu. 2008. SheepDog: group and tag recommendation for flickr photos by automatic search-based learning. In *MM '08*.

[3] Jeff Donahue, Yangqing Jia, Oriol Vinyals, Judy Hoffman, Ning Zhang, Eric Tzeng, and Trevor Darrell. 2013. DeCAF: A Deep Convolutional Activation Feature for Generic Visual Recognition. *CoRR* (2013).

[4] Yansong Feng and Mirella Lapata. 2008. Automatic Image Annotation Using Auxiliary Text Information. In *ACL-08: HLT*. Columbus, Ohio.

[5] Yue Gao, Meng Wang, Huanbo Luan, Jialie Shen, Shuicheng Yan, and Dacheng Tao. 2011. Tag-based Social Image Search with Visual-text Joint Hypergraph Learning. In *MM '11*. ACM, New York, NY, USA, 1517–1520.

[6] Matthieu Guillaumin, Thomas Mensink, Jakob Verbeek, and Cordelia Schmid. 2009. TagProp: Discriminative Metric Learning in Nearest Neighbor Models for Image Auto-Annotation. In *ICCV*.

[7] Livia Hollenstein and Ross Purves. 2010. Exploring place through user-generated content: Using Flickr tags to describe city cores. *J. Spatial Information Science* 1, 1 (2010), 21–48.

[8] Simon Jones and Eamonn O'Neill. 2011. Contextual dynamics of group-based sharing decisions (*CHI '11*). 10. https://doi.org/10.1145/1978942.1979200

[9] Peter Klemperer, Yuan Liang, Michelle Mazurek, Manya Sleeper, Blase Ur, Lujo Bauer, Lorrie F. Cranor, Nitin Gupta, and Michael Reiter. [n. d.]. Tag, you can see it! Using tags for access control in photo sharing. In *CHI'12*.

[10] Victor Lavrenko, R. Manmatha, and Jiwoon Jeon. 2004. A Model for Learning the Semantics of Pictures. In *NIPS 16*. MIT Press.

[11] Wee Leong, Rada Mihalcea, and Samer Hassan. 2010. Text Mining for Automatic Image Tagging (*COLING'10*).

[12] Jing Liu, Mingjing Li, Qingshan Liu, Hanqing Lu, and Songde Ma. 2009. Image Annotation via Graph Learning. *PR* (Feb. 2009), 11.

[13] Ameesh Makadia, Vladimir Pavlovic, and Sanjiv Kumar. 2008. *A New Baseline for Image Annotation*. Springer Berlin Heidelberg, 316–329.

[14] Kilian Q. Weinberger Minmin Chen, Alice Zheng. 2013. Fast Image Tagging. In *ICML*.

[15] Jing Peng, Daniel Dajun Zeng, Huimin Zhao, and Fei-yue Wang. 2010. Collaborative Filtering in Social Tagging Systems Based on Joint Item-tag Recommendations. In *CIKM '10*. ACM, 809–818. https://doi.org/10.1145/1871437.1871541

[16] Olga Russakovsky, Jia Deng, Hao Su, Jonathan Krause, Sanjeev Satheesh, Sean Ma, Zhiheng Huang, Andrej Karpathy, Aditya Khosla, Michael Bernstein, Alexander C. Berg, and Li Fei-Fei. 2014. ImageNet Large Scale Visual Recognition Challenge.. In *arXiv:1409.0575*.

[17] Jose San Pedro and Stefan Siersdorfer. 2009. Ranking and classifying attractiveness of photos in folksonomies (*WWW '09*). ACM, NY, USA.

[18] Neela Sawant. 2011. Modeling tagged photos for automatic image annotation (*MM '11*). ACM, 2.

[19] Yue Shi, Martha Larson, and Alan Hanjalic. 2014. Collaborative Filtering Beyond the User-Item Matrix: A Survey of the State of the Art and Future Challenges. *ACM Comput. Surv.*, Article 3 (May 2014), 45 pages. https://doi.org/10.1145/2556270

[20] Anna Squicciarini, Cornelia Caragea, and Rahul Balakavi. 2014. Analyzing Images' Privacy for the Modern Web (*HT '14*). ACM, NY, USA, 136–147.

[21] Anna Squicciarini, Cornelia Caragea, and Rahul Balakavi. 2017. Toward Automated Online Photo Privacy. *ACM Tran. on the Web* 11, 1, Article 2 (2017).

[22] Anna Squicciarini, Andrea Novelli, Dan Lin, Cornelia Caragea, and Haoti Zhong. 2017. From Tag to Protect: A Tag-Driven PolicyRecommender System for Image Sharing. In *PST '17*.

[23] Anna Squicciarini, Smitha Sundareswaran, Dan Lin, and Josh Wede. 2011. A3p: adaptive policy prediction for shared images over popular content sharing sites. In *HT '11*. ACM, 261–270.

[24] Xiaoyuan Su and Taghi M. Khoshgoftaar. 2009. A Survey of Collaborative Filtering Techniques. *Adv. in AI*, Article 4 (2009), 1 pages.

[25] H. Sundaram, L. Xie, M. De Choudhury, Y.R. Lin, and A. Natsev. 2012. Multimedia Semantics: Interactions Between Content and Community. *IEEE* 100, 9 (2012).

[26] Christian Szegedy, Wei Liu, Yangqing Jia, Pierre Sermanet, Scott Reed, Dragomir Anguelov, Dumitru Erhan, Vincent Vanhoucke, and Andrew Rabinovich. 2014. Going Deeper with Convolutions. *CoRR* abs/1409.4842 (2014).

[27] Ashwini Tonge and Cornelia Caragea. 2016. Image Privacy Prediction Using Deep Features. In *AAAI '16*.

[28] Ashwini Tonge and Cornelia Caragea. 2018. On the Use of "Deep" Features for Online Image Sharing. In *Companion Proceedings of The Web Conf.* 1317–1321.

[29] Ashwini Tonge, Cornelia Caragea, and Anna Squicciarini. 2018. Uncovering Scene Context for Predicting Privacy of Online Shared Images. In *AAAI '18*.

[30] Lam Tran, Deguang Kong, Hongxia Jin, and Ji Liu. 2016. Privacy-CNH: A Framework to Detect Photo Privacy with Convolutional Neural Network Using Hierarchical Features. In *AAAI '16*.

[31] Zhichen Xu, Yun Fu, Jianchang Mao, and Difu Su. 2006. Towards the semantic web: Collaborative tag suggestions. In *Collaborative Web Tagging Workshop*.

[32] J. Yu, D. Joshi, and J. Luo. 2009. Connecting people in photo-sharing sites by photo content and user annotations. In *ICME 2009*. IEEE.

[33] Sergej Zerr, Stefan Siersdorfer, Jonathon Hare, and Elena Demidova. 2012. Privacy-aware image classification and search. In *ACM SIGIR*. ACM, NY, USA.

Recommending Teammates with Deep Neural Networks*

Palash Goyal
USC Information Sciences Institute
Marina del Rey, CA, USA
goyal@isi.edu

Anna Sapienza
USC Information Sciences Institute
Marina del Rey, CA, USA
annas@isi.edu

Emilio Ferrara
USC Information Sciences Institute
Marina del Rey, CA, USA
ferrarae@isi.edu

ABSTRACT

The effects of team collaboration on performance have been explored in a variety of settings. Online games enable people with significantly different skills to cooperate and compete within a shared context. Players can affect teammates' performance either via direct communication or by influencing teammates' actions. Understanding such effects can help us provide insights into human behavior as well as make team recommendations. In this work, we aim at recommending teammates to each individual player for maximal skill growth. We study the effect of collaboration in online games using a large dataset from *Dota 2*, a popular Multiplayer Online Battle Arena game. To this aim, we construct an online co-play teammate network of players, whose links are weighted based on the gain in skill achieved due to team collaboration. We then use the performance network to devise a recommendation system based on a modified deep neural network autoencoder method.

CCS CONCEPTS

• **Information systems** → **Massively multiplayer online games**; **Data mining**; • **Computing methodologies** → **Neural networks**; **Factorization methods**;

KEYWORDS

recommendation system, link prediction, deep neural network, graph factorization, multiplayer online games, team formation

ACM Reference Format:
Palash Goyal, Anna Sapienza, and Emilio Ferrara. 2018. Recommending Teammates with Deep Neural Networks. In *HT '18: 29th ACM Conference on Hypertext and Social Media, July 9–12, 2018, Baltimore, MD, USA*. ACM, New York, NY, USA, 5 pages. https://doi.org/10.1145/3209542.3209569

1 INTRODUCTION

How is the performance of an individual affected by the interaction with peers? Psychologists and sociologists have researched this question for several decades in various contexts. Effect of coworkers on productivity at work [18], influence of students in a classroom [22], teammates effect in sports [5] are a few examples of

_____
*PG and AS contributed equally to this work.

such studies. These studies provide methods to measure influence in a collaborative setting and provide insights into the positive and negative effect of collaborations in various fields.

The advent of online games has opened new directions to explore. They provide unique challenges as the players often have minimal physical communication. The players collaborate in the virtual environment, the dynamics of which are often vastly different from the settings studied previously [14]. In online games, people from all over the world with varying backgrounds cooperate to achieve a common goal. Thus, they provide a suitable environment to analyze collaboration with higher diversity in individuals.

In this paper, we study a class of online games, called Multiplayer Online Battle Arena (MOBA) games, such as League of Legends (LoL), Defense of the Ancients 2 (Dota 2), Heroes of the Storm, and Paragon. In these games, two teams compete against each other to destroy the other team's base. At the start of the match each player chooses a character with a certain role and abilities. Broadly, the roles can be defensive or attacking. Players with defensive roles protect and cooperate with attacking players in a fight with the aim of moving forward towards the opponent's base. Therefore, both cooperation and influence of other players are intrinsic mechanisms of this genre of games, and can be either explicit or implicit: players can communicate through chat to shape the teammates' actions or can choose their moves based on their teammates' actions.

Prior research has shown that cooperation plays a key role in obtaining a high win rate in MOBA games [8, 24]. However, multiple factors can affect both cooperation and performance in this type of games. A great amount of work has been devoted to identify such factors, which can be broadly classified into two categories: 1) studies which use social interactions such as effect of friendship [17, 19] and frequency of co-play [15], and studies which focus on each player's choices, such as strategy, role, session length, and location of play [8, 9, 20, 24]. These studies show how each of these factors can have a significant impact on performance.

Although significant research has been done on identifying factors influencing a team's performance in MOBA games, the impact of such factors, and in particular the influence of cooperation on an individual's skills, needs further exploration. In the present work, we take a step in this direction and aim to understand and predict this impact. First, we note that performance of an individual and a team can greatly vary as players may have varying contribution to the outcome of a match. Thus, using the team's performance as measure for an individual can be misleading. Here, we thus take into account the individual skill level which is computed on the player's attributes and in-game performance. By using this measure of a player's performance, we study the effect of other players on the skill level of an individual over multiple matches in the well-known MOBA game Dota 2. To this aim, we construct a directed co-play network of players, the links of which exist if two players were teammates in the matches. Each directed link (u, v) is weighted based on the increase/decline of skill level of player v when playing with u. The network thus encompasses the cooperation effect aggregated over multiple matches. We finally study such a network and build a recommendation system for players. To this aim, we devise a modified deep neural network autoencoder that is able to predict the influence of teammates on each player.

In our experiments, we show that our teammate recommendation system can learn the inherent structure of the network and predict with high accuracy the teammates that are more beneficial to each player. To show this, we evaluate our autoencoder against a baseline model on the tasks of predicting an individual's skill gain and making player recommendations. We show that our model significantly outperforms the baseline and achieves an improvement of 9.00% on the former task. For player recommendations, the gain is instead 19.50%. We also compare our model against the widely used graph factorization model which does not achieve any significant gain over baseline. This shows that non-linear models are fundamental to capture the structure of co-play networks.

2 DATA COLLECTION AND PREPROCESSING

In the present work, we analyze data of Defense of the Ancient 2 (Dota 2), a popular MOBA game released in July 2013. We used *OpenDota* [7] to scrape the matches of Dota 2 in 2015. The overall dataset consists of 3,300,146 matches and 1,805,225 players. The game allows players to practice and play in different game modes. For the purpose of this study, we need to consider all the matches involving just human players. Therefore, we select the so called "Ranked" and "Public" matches. We further process this data to select matches for which there is no missing information. This step is done to avoid noisy and incomplete data samples. Finally, to understand the influence of teammates on an individual's performance, we compute the skill of players after each match in their history. Dota 2 has an internal matchmaking rank (MMR), which is a score defining each player skill that is updated any time the player conclude a match. However, the MMR is not disclosed by Dota 2 and thus, we use a proxy for players' skill level. Here, we use the TrueSkill [11] matchmaking system, developed by Microsoft. The TrueSkill value, as the Dota 2 MMR, has been designed for multiplayer team-based games such as MOBA games. It models players' skill through two values: the skill level and its certainty (i.e. a confidence interval for the skill level). The skill level changes accordingly to players performance in each match, while its confidence interval shrinks with the number of matches in the player's history. For a game setting like the one in Dota 2 (two teams of five players), the Trueskill requires at least 46 matches to accurately model the skill for a player.[1] Therefore, we further discard those players in our dataset having less than 46 matches. The preprocessing procedure leads to a final dataset consisting of all matches played by 87,155 players.

3 NETWORK GENERATION

We now explain the approach used to construct the co-play performance network. Here, nodes of the co-play network represent

players, while links reflect the TrueSkill score variations depending on the each player's teammate and aggregated over time.

Let us consider the set of 87,155 players in our post-processed Dota 2 dataset, and the related matches they played. For each player p, we define the player history to be the temporally ordered set $M_p = [m_0, m_1, \cdots, m_N]$ of matches played by p. As we consider just Public and Ranked matches in our dataset, matches are always composed by two opposing teams of 5 human players each, thus each match $m_i \in M_p$ can be further identified by a 4-tuple (t_1, t_2, t_3, t_4) of player's teammates.

Given a teammate t of player p in match $m_i \in M_p$, we define his/her influence on the performance of player p as the weight:

$$w_{pt, m_i} = ts_{m_i} - ts_{m_{i-1}}, \tag{1}$$

where, ts_{m_i} is the TrueSkill score of the player p after match $m_i \in M_p$. Thus, the weight w_{pt, m_i} captures the performance gain/loss of player p when playing with a given teammate t. This step generates as a result a set of directed links connecting together the players to their teammates in each match, and being characterized by the relative weights based on the fluctuations of TrueSkill level of players.

Next, we build the overall Performance Network, by aggregating the links connecting each couple of teammates in the network. Thus, the resulting Performance Network has a link between two nodes if the corresponding players were teammates at least once in the total temporal span of our dataset. Each link has a weight that is now defined as the sum of the weights given in (1). Thus, given player p and any possible teammate t in the network, their aggregated weight w_{pt} is equal to

$$w_{pt} = \sum_{i=0}^{N} w_{pt, m_i}, \tag{2}$$

where $w_{pt, m_i} = ts_{m_i} - ts_{m_{i-1}}$ if $t \in m_i$, and 0 otherwise. The resulting network has 87,155 nodes and 4,906,131 directed links with weights $w_{pt} \in [-0.58, 1.06]$.

The co-play performance network thus built may have unreliable weights. If two players play together just few times, the confidence we have on the corresponding weight is low. For example, if two players are teammates just one time their final weight only depends on that unique instance, and thus might lead to biased results. To tackle this issue, we further compute the distribution of the number of occurrences a couple of teammates plays together in our network and set a threshold based on these values. In particular, we decided to retain only pairs that played more than 2 matches together.

Finally, as many node embedding methods require a connected network as input [2], we extract the Largest Connected Component (LCC) of the performance network, which will be used for the performance prediction and evaluation. In particular, the LCC includes 38,563 nodes and 1,444,290 links. Consistently with the overall network, the weights of the LCC range from -0.58 to 1.06.

4 PERFORMANCE PREDICTION

In the following, we test whether the co-play performance network presents an underlying structure that can be leveraged to predict the performance gain of players with unknown teammates. To this aim, we evaluate both linear and non-linear models against a

---

[1]https://www.microsoft.com/en-us/research/project/trueskill-ranking-system/

baseline and show that our model achieves better performance in recommending teammates that maximize the skill of a player.

4.1 Problem Formulation

Let us consider the co-play performance network $G = (V, E)$ with weighted adjacency matrix W. A weighted link (i, j, w_{ij}) denotes that player i gets a performance variation of w_{ij} after playing with player j. We can formulate the recommendation problem as follows. Given an observed instance of a co-play performance network $G = (V, E)$ we want to predict the weight of each unobserved link $(i, j) \notin E$ and use this result to further recommend teammates to each player $i \in V$ by predicting the ranking of all other players $j \in V (\neq i)$.

4.2 Network Modeling

To predict the unobserved weights and recommend teammates to each player in our network, we assume that the co-play network we created contains information and hidden structures that can be used to forecast the influence, and thus the skill gain, of unseen pairs of players. To verify this assumption, we need a model that is able to capture such underlying structures.

To this aim, we modify a deep neural network autoencoder and we test its predictive power against two classes of approaches (both linear and non-linear) that are widely applied to build recommendation systems: (a) factorization based [1, 13, 21], and (b) deep neural network based [6, 12, 23].

4.2.1 Factorization.
Graph Factorization models for directed networks aim at finding a low-dimensional representation of the weighted adjacency matrix W. The adjacency matrix is indeed decomposed in two matrices $U \in \mathbb{R}^{n \times d}$ and $V \in \mathbb{R}^{n \times d}$ with number of hidden dimensions d such that the following function is minimized

$$f(U, V) = \sum_{(i,j) \in E} (w_{ij} - <u_i, v_j>)^2 + \frac{\lambda}{2}(\|u_i\|^2 + \|v_j\|^2)$$

Note that the sum is computed over the observed links to avoid of penalizing the unobserved one as overfitting to 0s would affect the predictions. Here, λ is chosen as a regularization parameter to give preference to simpler models for better generalization.

4.2.2 Traditional Autoencoder.
Autoencoders are unsupervised neural networks used to minimize the loss between reconstructed and input vectors. A traditional autoencoder is made of two main parts: (a) an encoder, which maps the input vector into low-dimensional latent variables; and, (b) a decoder, which maps the latent variables to an output vector. The reconstruction loss can be written as

$$L = \sum_{i=1}^{n} \|(\hat{x}_i - x_i)\|_2^2, \tag{3}$$

where x_is are the inputs and $\hat{x}_i = f(g(x_i))$. $f(.)$ and $g(.)$ are the decoder and encoder functions respectively. Deep autoencoders have recently been adapted to the network setting [6, 12, 23]. An algorithm proposed by *Wang et al.* [23] jointly optimizes the autoencoder reconstruction error and Laplacian Eigenmaps [4] error to learn representation for undirected networks. However, the "Traditional Autoencoder" equally penalizes observed and unobserved links in the network, while the model adapted to the network setting

cannot be generalized to the case of directed networks. Thus, we propose to modify the Traditional Autoencoder model to both take into account directed links and be able to find a low-dimensional representation in a network setting.

4.2.3 Teammate Autoencoder.
To model directed networks, we propose a modification of the Traditional Autoencoder model, that takes into account the adjacency matrix representing the directed network. Moreover, in this formulation we only penalize the observed links in the network, as our aim is to predict the weight and the corresponding ranking of the unobserved links. We then write our "Teammate Autoencoder" reconstruction loss as:

$$L = \sum_{i=1}^{n} \|(\hat{x}_i - x_i) \odot [a_{i,j}]_{j=1}^{n}\|_2^2, \tag{4}$$

where $a_{ij} = 1$ if $(i, j) \in E$, and 0 otherwise. Here, x_i represents i^{th} row the adjacency matrix and n is the number of nodes in the network. Minimizing this loss functions yields the neural network weights W and the learned representation of the network $Y \in \mathbb{R}^{n \times d}$.

4.3 Evaluation Framework

4.3.1 Experimental Setting.
To evaluate the performance of the models on the task of teammates' recommendation, we use a cross-validation framework. We randomly "hide" 20% of the weighted links and use the rest of the network to learn the embedding, i.e. the low-dimensional representation, of each player in the network. We then use each player's embedding to predict the weights of the unobserved links. As the number of player pairs is too large, we evaluate the models on multiple samples of the co-player performance networks (similar to [10, 16]) and report the mean and standard deviation of the used metrics. Instead of uniformly sampling the players as performed in [10, 16], we use random walks [3] with random restarts to generate sampled networks having similar degree and weight distributions as the original network.

4.3.2 Evaluation Metrics.
We use Mean Squared Error (*MSE*) and Mean Absolute Normalized Error (*MANE*) as evaluation metrics. *MSE* evaluates the accuracy of the predicted weights, whereas *MANE* evaluates the ranking obtained by the model.

First, we compute *MSE* to evaluate the error in the prediction of weights. It is defined as

$$MSE = \|w^{test} - w^{pred}\|^2,$$

where w_{test} is the list of weights of links in the test subnetwork, and w_{pred} is the list of weights predicted by the model.

Second, to test the models' recommendations for each player, we define the Mean Absolute Normalized Error (*MANE*), which computes the normalized difference between predicted and actual ranking of the test links among the observed links and averages over the nodes. Formally, it can be written as

$$MANE = \frac{\sum_{i=1}^{|V|} MANE(i)}{|V|},$$

where $MANE(i) = \frac{\sum_{j=1}^{|E_i^{test}|} |rank_i^{pred}(j) - rank_i^{test}(j)|}{|E_i^{train}||E_i^{test}|}$ and $rank_i^{pred}(j)$ represents the rank of the jth vertex in the list of weights predicted for the player i.

4.4 Results and Analysis

Here, we report the results achieved by the Graph Factorization, the Traditional Autoencoder and our Teammate Autoencoder. To this aim we first analyze the models' performance on the co-play performance network with respect to the MSE measure. In Fig. 1, we compare the models against an "average" baseline, where we compute the average performance of the players' couples observed in the training set and use it as a prediction for each hidden teammate link.

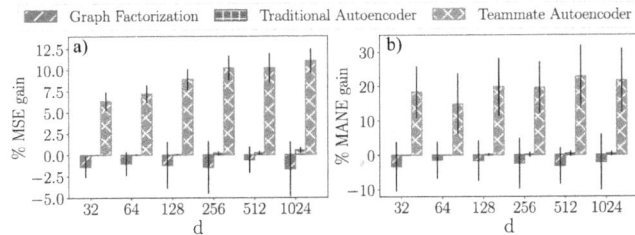

Figure 1: Performance results. a) Mean Squared Error (*MSE*) gain of models over average prediction. b) Mean Absolute Normalized Error (*MANE*) gain of models over average prediction.

Table 1: Mean and standard deviation of player performance prediction (*MSE*) and teammate recommendation (*MANE*) for $d = 1,024$ in the performance network.

	Baseline	GF	Autoencoder	Teammate Autoencoder
MSE	4.55/0.14	4.59/0.17	4.54/0.15	**4.15/0.14**
MANE	0.078/0.02	0.081/0.02	0.074/0.01	**0.059/0.008**

Fig. 1a shows the variation of the percentage of the *MSE* gain (average and standard deviation) while increasing the number of latent dimensions d for in each model. We can observe that the Graph Factorization model generally performs worse than the baseline, with values in the range $[-1.64\%, -0.56\%]$ and average of -1.2%. This suggests that the performance network of Dota 2 requires nonlinearity to capture its underlying structure. Nevertheless, a traditional non-linear model is not enough to outperform the baseline. The Traditional Autoencoder reaches indeed marginal improvements: its gain over the baseline is in the range of $[0.0\%, 0.55\%]$ and it reaches an average gain of 0.18%. On the contrast, our Teammate Autoencoder achieves substantial gain over the baseline across the whole spectrum. Moreover, its performance generally increases for higher dimensions, thus retaining more structural information. The MSE gain for different dimensions over the baseline of the Teammate Autoencoder spans between 6.34% and 11.06%, with an average gain over all dimensions of 9.00%. We also computed the MSE average over 10 runs and $d = 1,024$, shown in Tab. 1. We can observe that the value decreases from the baseline prediction of 4.55 to our Teammate Autoencoder prediction of 4.15.

We finally compare the models' performance in providing individual recommendations by analyzing the *MANE* metric. Fig. 1b shows the percentage of the *MANE* gain for different dimensions computed against the average baseline for the performance network. Analogously to the *MSE* case, the Graph Factorization performs worse than the baseline. Its values range indeed between -3.34%

and -1.48%, with an average gain of -2.37%, despite the increment in the number of dimensions. The Traditional Autoencoder achieves marginal gain over the baseline for dimensions higher than 128 ($[0.0\%, 0.37\%]$), and has an average gain over all dimensions of 0.16%. Our model attains instead significant percentage gain in individual recommendations over the baseline. It achieves an average percentage of *MANE* gain spanning from 14.81% to 22.78%, with an overall average of 19.50%. It is worth noting that the performance in this case does not monotonically increase with dimensions. This might imply that for individual recommendations the model overfits at higher dimensions. We report the average value of *MANE* in Tab. 1 for $d = 1,024$. Our model obtains average values of 0.059, compared to 0.078 of the average baseline.

In conclusion, our model achieves high performance on both tasks of predicting the unobserved weights of a co-play performance network and of recommending teammates that will have high impact in the skill gain of players, thus maximizing their performance when cooperating in a match.

5 CONCLUSIONS

In this work, we studied the influence of teammates on a player's performance in online games. Specifically, we achieved three goals: (i) we quantified the individual performance gain in online collaborative setting and studied the co-play network; (ii) we provided a framework to recommend teammates which maximize individual skill gain; and (iii) we illustrated the utility of a deep learning based recommendation model over linear models for this task.

For this purpose, we performed experiments on a popular Multiplayer Online Battle Arena game called Dota 2. We preprocessed the data to extract useful and robust information from the matches played in 2015. We used the Trueskill measure to track each individual's performance over matches and constructed a co-play performance network with players as nodes and aggregated gain in skill due to collaboration as the links' weights. Based on the network weights, we observed that players can have both adverse and positive effect on teammate's performance.

Thus, we developed a recommendation system for the co-play network based on a deep learning model. The model predicts performance gains for a set of players and uses the predictions to accurately recommend players which maximize skill gain of an individual. We compared our method against an average recommendation baseline, a traditional neural network autoencoder and a state-of-the-art graph factorization model. We showed our modified deep autoencoder model significantly outperforms the other models. Furthermore, we observed that the factorization based model only marginally improves over the average baseline showcasing the necessity of a complex non-linear model.

In the future, we plan to study the long term effect of a teammate on an individual's performance and evaluate our model on other online games and platforms. We also intend to test the model in real settings to directly evaluate the effect of our recommendations.

Acknowledgements. The authors are grateful to DARPA for support (grant #D16AP00115). This project may not reflect the position/policy of the Government; no official endorsement should be inferred. Approved for public release; unlimited distribution.

REFERENCES

[1] Amr Ahmed, Nino Shervashidze, Shravan Narayanamurthy, Vanja Josifovski, and Alexander J Smola. 2013. Distributed large-scale natural graph factorization. In *Proc. 22nd international conference on World Wide Web*. ACM, 37–48.

[2] Nesreen K Ahmed, Ryan A Rossi, Rong Zhou, John Boaz Lee, Xiangnan Kong, Theodore L Willke, and Hoda Eldardiry. 2017. A Framework for Generalizing Graph-based Representation Learning Methods. *arXiv:1709.04596* (2017).

[3] Lars Backstrom and Jure Leskovec. 2011. Supervised random walks: predicting and recommending links in social networks. In *WSDM'11*. ACM, 635–644.

[4] Mikhail Belkin and Partha Niyogi. 2001. Laplacian eigenmaps and spectral techniques for embedding and clustering. In *NIPS*, Vol. 14. 585–591.

[5] Kendrick T Brown, Tony N Brown, James S Jackson, Robert M Sellers, and Warde J Manuel. 2003. Teammates on and off the field? Contact with black teammates and the racial attitudes of white student athletes. *J. Appl. Soc. Psychol* 33, 7 (2003).

[6] Shaosheng Cao, Wei Lu, and Qiongkai Xu. 2016. Deep neural networks for learning graph representations. In *AAAI'16*. AAAI Press, 1145–1152.

[7] Albert Cui, Howard Chung, and Nicholas Hanson-Holtry. [n. d.]. YASP 3.5 Million Data Dump. ([n. d.]).

[8] Anders Drachen, Matthew Yancey, John Maguire, Derrek Chu, Iris Yuhui Wang, Tobias Mahlmann, Matthias Schubert, and Diego Klabajan. 2014. Skill-based differences in spatio-temporal team behaviour in defence of the ancients 2 (dota 2). In *Games media entertainment (GEM), 2014 IEEE*. IEEE, 1–8.

[9] Christoph Eggert, Marc Herrlich, Jan Smeddinck, and Rainer Malaka. 2015. Classification of player roles in the team-based multi-player game dota 2. In *International Conference on Entertainment Computing*. Springer, 112–125.

[10] Palash Goyal and Emilio Ferrara. 2018. Graph embedding techniques, applications, and performance: A survey. *Knowledge-Based Systems* (2018). https://doi.org/10.1016/j.knosys.2018.03.022

[11] Ralf Herbrich, Tom Minka, and Thore Graepel. 2007. TrueSkill: a Bayesian skill rating system. In *Advances in neural information processing systems*. 569–576.

[12] Thomas N Kipf and Max Welling. 2016. Variational Graph Auto-Encoders. *arXiv:1611.07308* (2016).

[13] Yehuda Koren, Robert Bell, and Chris Volinsky. 2009. Matrix factorization techniques for recommender systems. *Computer* 42, 8 (2009).

[14] Alex Leavitt, Brian C Keegan, and Joshua Clark. 2016. Ping to win?: Non-verbal communication and team performance in competitive online multiplayer games. In *Proc. Conference on Human Factors in Computing Systems*. ACM, 4337–4350.

[15] Alexandru Iosup, Ruud Van De Bovenkamp, Siqi Shen, Adele Lu Jia, and Fernando Kuipers. 2014. Analyzing implicit social networks in multiplayer online games. *IEEE Internet Computing* 18, 3 (2014), 36–44.

[16] Mingdong Ou, Peng Cui, Jian Pei, Ziwei Zhang, and Wenwu Zhu. 2016. Asymmetric transitivity preserving graph embedding. In *Proc. of ACM SIGKDD*. 1105–1114.

[17] Hyunsoo Park and Kyung-Joong Kim. 2014. Social network analysis of high-level players in multiplayer online battle arena game. In *Social Informatics*. 223–226.

[18] Jone L Pearce. 1993. Toward an organizational behavior of contract laborers: their psychological involvement and effects on employee co-workers. *Academy of Management Journal* 36, 5 (1993), 1082–1096.

[19] Nataliia Pobiedina, Julia Neidhardt, Maria del Carmen Calatrava Moreno, and Hannes Werthner. 2013. Ranking factors of team success. In *WWW*. 1185–1194.

[20] Anna Sapienza, Alessandro Bessi, and Emilio Ferrara. 2018. Non-negative tensor factorization for human behavioral pattern mining in online games. *Information* 9, 3 (2018), 66.

[21] Xiaoyuan Su and Taghi M Khoshgoftaar. 2009. A survey of collaborative filtering techniques. *Advances in artificial intelligence* 2009 (2009), 4.

[22] Tim Urdan and Erin Schoenfelder. 2006. Classroom effects on student motivation: Goal structures, social relationships, and competence beliefs. *Journal of school psychology* 44, 5 (2006), 331–349.

[23] Daixin Wang, Peng Cui, and Wenwu Zhu. 2016. Structural deep network embedding. In *Proc. 22nd SIGKDD*. ACM, 1225–1234.

[24] Pu Yang, Brent E Harrison, and David L Roberts. 2014. Identifying patterns in combat that are predictive of success in MOBA games.. In *FDG*.

Data and Design in International Development

Dr. Leslie Sage
DevResults
Washington, DC
leslie@devresults.com

ABSTRACT

Foreign aid is a $150 billion dollar industry[1], but the skills and tools for using data in international development are in their infancy. Herculean efforts to overhaul systems of agriculture, education, sanitation, and health go unexamined because collecting that information is hard. Governments and NGOs are tracking information that doesn't begin in electronic format, like school refurbishments and job trainings, then storing it in unstructured documents on inaccessible hard drives around the globe.

DevResults is a private software company with the objective of providing best-in-class tools for managing data in international development. The aim is to enable data-driven decision-making by international development practitioners and the communities they serve. If properly captured, shared, and interpreted, international development data offer insights on how to reduce disease, improve education, and lift people out of poverty.

DevResults is approaching this problem with a Software as a Service (SaaS) model, paired with consulting and training on designing metrics, structuring data, and using web-based tools. Over the last decade, DevResults has developed an iterative approach based on user feedback from thousands of users of over 100 product instances. This has produced an increasingly sophisticated application and complex data model as demand grows for linked, interoperable data. Among other lessons learned, DevResults has identified a key precept of only revealing complexity where needed, as organizations and users express a wide range of needs and capacities. The result is a commercially viable product that's modular in design. DevResults' software is in use at all organizational levels and has dramatically improved data management and analysis for user organizations.

CCS Concepts/ACM Classifiers

• General and reference~Measurement • Information systems~Relational database model • Information systems~Enterprise applications • Human-centered computing~Participatory design • Social and professional topics~Computing literacy

Author Keywords

International Development; Foreign Aid; Data Engineering; Interoperability; Emergent Complexity; Design

BIOGRAPHY

Leslie Sage is the Director of Data Science at DevResults. She has implemented data management software for use in over 60 countries by billion-dollar foreign aid organizations. In this capacity she has also systematized enterprise adoption, developed training curricula, and designed tools based on user input. Previously, she served as Deputy Data Director for the Obama Presidential Campaign 2012. Leslie earned her Ph.D. in Microvascular Physiology from the University of Bristol in England and her B.A. in Cognitive Science from Rice University in Houston.

REFERENCES

1. Organisation for Economic Co-operation and Development http://www.oecd.org/

Insecure Machine Learning Systems and Their Impact on the Web

Ben Y. Zhao
University of Chicago
Chicago, IL, USA
ravenben@cs.uchicago.edu

ABSTRACT

Increasingly powerful machine learning models are often seen as a panacea to a wide range of computational problems today.

There is an unsustainable level of excitement over recent results in solving systems problems using deep learning techniques, leading to a rush to deploy ML-based systems in countries around the world. In this talk, I will consider some of the negative implications of these powerful but opaque models from two angles. I will discuss vulnerabilities inherent in many of today's deep learning models, as well as the dangers of advanced ML tools used by malicious attackers. I believe that these critical issues must be addressed adequately before the wide-spread adoption of deep learning tools in today's security critical applications.

CCS Concepts

• Security and privacy~Web application security; Security and privacy~Human and societal aspects of security and privacy

Author Keywords

Deep learning; Adversarial Machine Learning

BIOGRAPHY

Ben Zhao is the Neubauer Professor of Computer Science at University of Chicago. He completed his PhD from Berkeley (2004) and his BS from Yale (1997). He is an ACM distinguished scientist, and recipient of the NSF CAREER award, MIT Technology Review's TR-35 Award (Young Innovators Under 35), ComputerWorld Magazine's Top 40 Tech Innovators award, Google Faculty award, and IEEE ITC Early Career Award. His work has been covered by media outlets such as Scientific American, New York Times, Boston Globe, LA Times, MIT Tech Review, and Slashdot. He has published more than 150 publications in areas of security and privacy, networked systems, wireless networks, data-mining and HCI. He recently served as TPC co-chair for the World Wide Web Conference (WWW 2016) and the upcoming ACM Internet Measurement Conference (IMC 2018).

HT'18, July 9-12, 2018, Baltimore, MD, USA.
© 2018 Copyright is held by the owner/author(s).
ACM ISBN 978-1-4503-5427-1/18/07.
DOI: https://doi.org/10.1145/3209542.3209544

Bootstrapping Web Archive Collections from Social Media

Alexander C. Nwala
Old Dominion University
Norfolk, Virginia, USA
anwala@cs.odu.edu

Michele C. Weigle
Old Dominion University
Norfolk, Virginia, USA
mweigle@cs.odu.edu

Michael L. Nelson
Old Dominion University
Norfolk, Virginia, USA
mln@cs.odu.edu

ABSTRACT

Human-generated collections of archived web pages are expensive to create, but provide a critical source of information for researchers studying historical events. Hand-selected collections of web pages about events shared by users on social media offer the opportunity for bootstrapping archived collections. We investigated if collections generated automatically and semi-automatically from social media sources such as Storify, Reddit, Twitter, and Wikipedia are similar to Archive-It human-generated collections. This is a challenging task because it requires comparing collections that may cater to different needs. It is also challenging to compare collections since there are many possible measures to use as a baseline for collection comparison: how does one narrow down this list to metrics that reflect if two collections are similar or dissimilar? We identified social media sources that may provide similar collections to Archive-It human-generated collections in two main steps. First, we explored the state of the art in collection comparison and defined a suite of seven measures (Collection Characterizing Suite - CCS) to describe the individual collections. Second, we calculated the distances between the CCS vectors of Archive-It collections and the CCS vectors of collections generated automatically and semi-automatically from social media sources, to identify social media collections most similar to Archive-It collections. The CCS distance comparison was done for three topics: "Ebola Virus," "Hurricane Harvey," and "2016 Pulse Nightclub Shooting." Our results showed that social media sources such as Reddit, Storify, Twitter, and Wikipedia produce collections that are similar to Archive-It collections. Consequently, curators may consider extracting URIs from these sources in order to begin or augment collections about various news topics.

CCS CONCEPTS

• **Information systems** → **Digital libraries and archives**;

KEYWORDS

Social Media, Collection evaluation, Web Archiving, News

ACM Reference Format:
Alexander C. Nwala, Michele C. Weigle, and Michael L. Nelson. 2018. Bootstrapping Web Archive Collections from Social Media. In *HT '18: 29th ACM*

Conference on Hypertext and Social Media, July 9–12, 2018, Baltimore, MD, USA. ACM, New York, NY, USA, 9 pages. https://doi.org/10.1145/3209542.3209560

1 INTRODUCTION AND BACKGROUND

Following the 2014 Ebola outbreak in West Africa [6], an archivist at the National Library of Medicine (NLM) collected seeds [26] on Archive-It (a service of the Internet Archive) for the *Ebola virus* outbreak. The seed list is an initial collection of URIs (Uniform Resource Identifiers) representing exemplar web pages for the topic and are subsequently crawled in order to discover more URIs. Human-generated seeds of archived web pages, such as the NLM Archive-It *Ebola virus* collection are time consuming to create. These collections are usually of a high quality because humans do a good job of filtering irrelevant documents. However, important events can unfold at a rapid pace, consequently, we cannot rely exclusively on experts to generate seeds. To cope with the problem of a shortage of curators amidst an abundance of world events, various organizations such as the Internet Archive (IA) routinely request for users to contribute links to seed Archive-It collections, e.g. the *2016 Pulse Nightclub Shooting* [18], the *2016 U.S. Presidential Election* [16], and the *Dakota Access Pipeline* [17] collections.

It is common practice for users on social media sites such as Storify, Reddit, Twitter, and Wikipedia to share hand-selected stories for events. For example, Table 2 juxtaposes seeds from an Archive-It collection and URIs extracted from Reddit and Wikipedia for the *Ebola virus* topic. We claim these kinds of collections created by social media users offer the opportunity for bootstrapping archived collections. In other words, the URIs extracted from such collections may augment curator-selected seeds for various news events.

To assess the validity of our claim, we investigated if Archive-It seeds are similar to collections created from social media sources for the following topics: "Ebola Virus," "Hurricane Harvey," and "2016 Pulse Nightclub Shooting." Comparing collections is not an easy task especially when the collections are about the same topic. For example, given two collections, e.g., the NLM Archive-It *Ebola virus* collection and a collection of local news stories about the Ebola outbreak from Guinea [24], how can one tell which is the "better" collection? This is a difficult question because both collections cater to different needs and answer different questions. Therefore, to address the problem of comparing collections, we defined a set of seven metrics - Collection Characterizing Suite (CCS) - that objectively characterize individual collections. Subsequently, multiple collections can be compared by computing the distances between their respective CCS vectors. Here is a complete list of the CCS metrics:

(1) Distribution of topics
(2) Distribution of sources (hostnames)

(3) Content diversity: Doc-Term matrix & List of Entity sets

(4) Temporal distribution: Publication and Content

(5) Source diversity: URI, Domain, Hostname, and Social media

(6) Collection exposure: Archival rate and Tweet index rate

(7) Target audience

Our contributions are as follows. First, we provide a suite of metrics for characterizing collections (CCS). Second, we demonstrate how to compare multiple collections. Third, we provide novel methods for instantiating the metrics in the CCS. Fourth, we used the CCS to compare collections from social media sources and Archive-It collections, showing that these collections are similar. As a result, we propose the extraction of URIs from social media sources to bootstrap archived collections.

Table 1: CCS Metrics derived from the transformation of Library Science Collection Evaluation Metrics

Library Science Metrics	CCS Metrics
Usage statistics, e.g., circulation and interlibrary loan statistics	Exposure (or popularity): 1. Archival rate 2. Tweet index rate Target audience (reading level)
Variety of library collection	Content diversity: 1. Document-Term matrix 2. Entity set matrix Source diversity (policies): URI, Hostname and Domain
Bibliographical set comparison	Distribution of sources (hosts)

2 RELATED WORK

There are many efforts addressing generating collections for specific topics through the use of a focused crawler [7]. Many of these methods require a system that decides whether or not a web page is relevant to the collection topic. Bergmark [3] used a classifier to determine if web pages belonged to various topics in science

Table 2: Sample of seed URIs from Archive-It *Ebola virus* collection, URIs extracted from Reddit SERP and comments for query "Ebola virus," and URIs extracted from the references of the Wikipedia *Ebola virus* document.

Title	URI
Archive-It (seed URIs)	
Eman Reports From Ebola Ground Zero...	http://blogs.plos.org/dnascience/2014/11/06/eman-reports-ebola-ground-zero/
Human rights and Ebola: the issue of quarantine...	http://blogs.plos.org/globalhealth/2014/11/ebola_and_human_rights/
2014-2016 Ebola Outbreak in West Africa...	http://www.cdc.gov/vhf/ebola/outbreaks/2014-west-africa/index.html
Reddit	
Management of Accidental Exposure to Ebola Virus...	http://jid.oxfordjournals.org/content/204/suppl_3/S785.long
Analysis of patient data from laboratories during...	http://journals.plos.org/plosntds/article?id=10.1371/journal.pntd.0005804
Monkey Meat and the Ebola Outbreak in Liberia...	https://youtu.be/XasTcDsDfMg
Wikipedia	
Proposal for a revised taxonomy of the...	https://www.ncbi.nlm.nih.gov/pmc/articles/PMC3074192
Ebola outbreak in Western Africa 2014...	https://www.ncbi.nlm.nih.gov/pmc/articles/PMC4313106
WHO - Ebola outbreak 2014-2015	http://www.who.int/csr/disease/ebola/en/

and mathematics. Farag et al. [10] used a similarity measure that relies on an event model representation of documents in order to determine if web pages were relevant to an event-based collection. Gossen et al. [13] introduced iCrawl, a focused crawler that crawls social media content in order to generate thematically and temporally coherent collections. Similar to focused crawling research, we considered adding the precision metric to the CCS as a means to quantify relevance, but excluded it because we cannot objectively evaluate precision for some collections since relevance can be subjective and there is often no gold standard data available. Also, it may be impossible to automate precision evaluation for arbitrary collections, because evaluating precision requires some notion of relevance. In the absence of these concerns, the user of the CCS may include the precision metric. Many focused crawling efforts did not address how the seeds used to initialize focused crawlers were generated, which is an important part of this work. We do not consider using focused crawlers to crawl seeds to discover more relevant URIs, but focus on how seeds can be generated by exploiting social media collections.

Other efforts related to building collections address the difficulty of seed selection. Schneider et al. [34] proposed the continuous selection of seeds for thematic collections about evolving events. Zheng et al. [39] proposed different seed selection algorithms and showed that different seeds may result in collections that are considered "good" or "bad." It is important to note that the discovery of seeds is not the focus of this work, instead we propose to extract seeds from social media collections such as Storify, Reddit, Twitter, and Wikipedia, to augment existing seed selection methods.

An important part of utilizing social media sources to bootstrap archived collections is assessing if the collections generated from social media sources are similar to expert-generated seeds, specifically Archive-It collections. To compare collections, we first proposed the CCS, a suite of seven metrics for characterizing individual collections. Collections are subsequently compared by a distance calculation between their respective CCS vectors. We considered research from Library and Web Sciences about collection evaluation in order to identify widely used metrics to include in the CCS.

In 1974, Bonn [4] presented different quantitative methods for evaluating various library collections and expressed the need for library collections to be varied in order to fulfill the needs of various academic programs. In the 1980s, the Research Libraries Group (RLG), a consortium of libraries in the U.S, published the RLG six (0-5) collecting levels [11, 14] to quantify the strength of collections. In summary, level 0 means the library collection is out of scope with respect to a subject, and level 5 means the collection is comprehensive. More recently (2004), Lesniaski provided a simplification [22] of White's brief tests [37] (comparing a short list of items to a library's collection) in order to make the test more adaptable by smaller college libraries. Additionally, he expressed the idea that there is not a single meaning of a "good" library collection since the meaning is defined by the user or target audience of the collection.

The questions proposed by the library sciences such as "How does one evaluate collection strength?" and "What is a good collection?" are applicable to the web domain. The solution offered by libraries to these questions (quantifying the strength of a collection) also inform the web domain through transformations. For example, the need for variety (or diversity) in library collections expressed by Bonn in 1974 is applicable to the web domain. Similarly, we included the *content diversity* metric in the CCS to capture the diversity expressed in web collections. Bonn also expressed the importance of evaluating library collections in order to see if they fulfill the needs of their community of users. Similarly, we included the *target audience* metric in order to estimate the audience a collection targets. Table 1 shows the CCS metrics derived from transforming library collection strength evaluation metrics.

Many solutions offered by libraries for quantifying collection strength can be summarized into two broad categories: collection-centered and use-centered [25]. Collection-centered methods include comparing a collection against an expert-provided gold standard bibliographical set. Use-centered methods include assigning the strength score to a collection based on circulation and interlibrary loan statistics, and patron surveys [15]. At web scale, a gold standard is often absent, but the collection-centered bibliographical set comparison practice informs our CCS *distribution of sources*, which reports the sources (hosts) that were sampled to build a collection. We believe the use-centered metric is a useful metric for approximating the exposure of a collection, which might approximate the popularity of the collection. Consequently, our CCS includes two metrics inspired by the use-centered metric for evaluating collection strength - *archival rates* and *tweet index rates*.

Risse et al. [32] surveyed social scientists, historical scientists, and legal experts in order to extract the requirements they find desirable for building collections. Some of the needs include topical dimension and time dimension, and the need to crawl social media sites. Topical dimension refers to the need to chronicle the evolution of an event over time. Consequently, our CCS includes a metric, *distribution of topics*, which gives insight about the various topics discussed in the collection. The time dimension is related to the topical dimension, but addresses the need to capture documents as events unfold. Some real world events have well-defined times e.g., a sports event and elections. Archivists often need the crawl duration to encompass the real world event time frame. Inspired by the time dimension metric, we added the *publication temporal* and *content temporal distribution* metrics to the suite. Social media is increasingly where the first reports of many events such as protests and popular uprising unfold, consequently, the CCS includes a *social media rate* as part of the broader *source diversity* metric for quantifying the amount of social media sources found in the collection.

3 BOOTSTRAPPING ARCHIVED COLLECTIONS FROM SOCIAL MEDIA

Archived collections begin with a list of URIs, or seeds, that share a common set of topics. The seeds are subsequently crawled to discover more URIs. We believe archived collections can be started or augmented by adding URIs extracted from social media collections from Storify, Reddit, Twitter, and Wikipedia.

Storify is a social media curation service that enables users to create *stories* which consist of hand-selected web resources such as URIs of news articles, images, videos, etc. Unfortunately, Storify

is scheduled to go out of service in May 2018 [36], but we are exploring other possible alternatives [19]. We can create a seed list by extracting the URIs from storify *stories* that are relevant to a collection topic. Twitter Moments is a service by Twitter that lets users create topical collections of tweets that may embed URIs and multimedia content. In addition to extracting URIs from the tweets in Twitter Moments collections, we can also generate collections automatically by searching Twitter for tweets related to a topic and extracting URIs from the tweets returned by the Twitter SERP (Search Engine Result Page). Reddit is a service that allows users to post URIs for various topics. Reddit users rate the URIs and post comments that may also include URIs. Reddit provides search, thus, the URIs from the Reddit SERP and their respective comments for relevant topics can be added to a seed list. The Wikipedia encyclopedia is a service that enables multiple contributors to create documents about various topics ranging from politics to science and technology. Wikipedia documents often include URIs of external references that are relevant to the document topic. For example, Table 2 consists of a sample of URIs extracted from the references of the Wikipedia document [38] about the *Ebola virus* event. A seed list for an archived collection can be generated with URIs extracted from the references of Wikipedia documents [21].

4 COLLECTION CHARACTERIZING SUITE

The CCS provides a means of characterizing individual collections and comparing multiple collections. The various metrics that make up the CCS can be instantiated in different ways - it is a template. Consequently, the main criteria considered for instantiating the various metric was generality.

4.1 Distribution of topics

A "topic" is informally defined as a group of words which frequently occur together. It provides a means to summarize collections and gives us some notion of what the collection is about. It is impractical to manually inspect all the web pages, especially for large collections, in order to discern aboutness, therefore, we need this measure to summarize collections. The *distribution of topics* is a ranked list of topics in a collection with the most frequent topics (most important summaries) at the top and the least frequent topics (least important summaries) at the bottom. A probabilistic language model assigns probabilities to a sequence of words that make up a topic. One goal of a language model is the assignment of high probabilities to frequent topics (or sentences) in a collection. Similarly, we adopted a variant of the n-gram language model. Since collections are organized around specific topics, web pages in the collection include these topics frequently in their vocabulary. For example, we would expect a collection about *sports* events to possess sports vocabulary, e.g., *football, basketball*, etc. Inspired by this characteristic of collections, we developed a method to derive the topical distribution of a collection by finding the n-grams in the collections with the highest frequency of occurrence in the collection. The method is described by Algorithm 1 and sample outputs are given in Table 6. Algorithm 1 leads to the possibility of splitting compound word n-grams. For example, given an *Ebola virus* collection, if we choose $n = 2$ to generate bigram topic distributions, it could result in a ranked list that includes "centers disease"

Algorithm 1 : Generate a distribution of n-grams (topics)

Input: A collection C of web pages ($|C| = N$), integers $n > 0$, & $m > 0$.
Output: A ranked list of m n−grams (topics); the n−grams with the highest frequencies at the top of the list.
function GENTOPICDIST(C, n, m)
   0. Represent each document $d_i \in C$ as a n−gram document
   1. Create a vocabulary vector $V \in \mathbb{Z}^{1 \times p}$, each entry v_i in V
   represents a unique n−gram from C (with p unique n−grams).
   2. Create a binary document term matrix $M \in \mathbb{Z}^{N \times p}$. Each row
   in M represents a document $d_i \in C$, and each
   column has 1 if $v_i \in d_i$, and 0 otherwise.
   3. Create a ranked list L. Populate L ($|L| \leq m$) with n−grams (v_i)
   with the highest frequencies of occurrence
   in M ($\max_{v_i \in V} \sum_{j=1}^{N} m_{j,i}$).
   Populate L with v_i in decreasing order of their frequencies.
   return L
end function

---

and "disease control". It is clear that both terms are part of the compound word (trigram) "centers disease control" (stopwords are removed). To solve this problem, we replace multiple lower-order (e.g., bigram) n-grams with their superset higher-order (e.g., trigram) n-grams.

4.2 Distribution of sources

Given a collection of web pages, the *distribution of sources* is a statistical summary of the various sources sampled in order to build the collection. For example, the NLM Archive-It *Ebola virus* collection consists of 18 (12.5%) web pages from *blogs.plos.org*, 14 (9.7%) from *cdc.gov*, and 11 (7.6%) from *twitter.com*. We may conclude that these are the three most influential sources in the collection.

The distribution of sources is instantiated with a simple enumeration of the frequencies of the various hosts that make up a collection. In order to make the description more compact, we chose to report the top 10 hosts that make up a collection, and what proportion of the collection the top 10 hosts account for. For example, the top 10 hosts in the NLM Archive-It *Ebola Virus* collection make up 50% of the collection.

4.3 Content diversity

Given a collection of web pages, the *content diversity* is defined as the degree of self-similarity of the content of the web pages in the collection. For example, if we sample a collection about a *shooting* event one hour after the event, we should expect a high degree of similarity in the web pages. Most of them are expected to report the location of the shooting, the casualty count, possible identity of the perpetrators, etc. However, one year after the event, we may see more diverse content, perhaps discussing the shooting in context to other shootings. The diversity of the content of such events increases with time.

The content diversity is a single metric which summarizes the degree of self-similarity of a collection. A diversity score of 0 means no diversity - duplicate web documents, and a diversity score of 1 means maximum diversity - mutually orthogonal vocabulary of documents.

The input to calculate a content diversity for an arbitrary collection is a *similarity matrix* D. The *similarity matrix* consists of the pairwise similarity of the web documents in the collection. We propose two ways of calculating the similarity between a pair of web pages corresponding with the two different ways of representing a collection. First, a collection may be represented as a *Document-Term matrix*: each row represents a document (web page), each column represents the TF or TFIDF value of a unigram in the collection vocabulary. In this representation, the similarity between a pair of documents is the cosine similarity measure. Second, a collection may be represented as a *List of Entity sets*: each document is represented as a set of entities of proper nouns for (people, location, organization, time, date, money, percent, and misc). The entities were extracted using the Stanford Named Entity Recognition System [12]. In this representation, we defined a new similarity measure - weighted Jaccard-Overlap similarity (Eqn. 1) measure to calculate the similarity between a pair of web documents, with a Jaccard weight ($\alpha \in [0, 1]$) of 0.4.

The weighted Jaccard-Overlap similarity $sim(A, B)$ between a pair of documents sets A and B is given by Eqn. 1, where β is the coefficient of similarity, defining the threshold two documents must reach to be considered similar. This threshold was empirically derived from a gold-standard dataset and set to 0.27.

$$sim(A, B) = \begin{cases} 1 & \text{, if } \alpha.J(A, B) + (1 - \alpha).O(A, B) \geq \beta \\ 0 & \text{, otherwise} \end{cases} \quad (1)$$

$J(A, B)$ is the Jaccard index of both documents, $J(A, B) = \frac{|A \cap B|}{|A \cup B|}$, and $O(A, B)$ is the Overlap coefficient of both documents, $O(A, B) = \frac{|A \cap B|}{min(|A|, |B|)}$.

Let a *similarity matrix* of n web pages in a collection be represented by $D \in \mathbb{R}^{n \times n}$, and an *all-ones matrix* $O \in \mathbb{R}^{n \times n}$. Given a square matrix, $N \in \mathbb{R}^{n \times n}$, with zeros on the main diagonal and ones everywhere else, for example, if $N \in \mathbb{R}^{3 \times 3}$,

$$N = \begin{bmatrix} 0 & 1 & 1 \\ 1 & 0 & 1 \\ 1 & 1 & 0 \end{bmatrix}, \text{ the content diversity score } d_c = 1 - \frac{||ND||_F}{||NO||_F}$$

where $||A||_F$ is the Frobenius norm: $||A||_F = \sqrt{\sum_{i=1}^{m} \sum_{j=1}^{n} |a_{i,j}|^2}$
Web documents consist of topics (groups of words that frequently occur together). This means multiple words that belong to the same topic tend to co-occur. We may not always consider our collection diverse by the mere presence of different words, especially if these words belong to the same topic. Instead, we may consider our collection diverse if it consists of different topics. Consequently, if we consider unigrams, we would reward diversity to different terms which occur together, even though they may belong to the same topic, i.e., no new information. The *Document-Term matrix* representation rewards diversity at the term level, while the *List of Entity sets* representation rewards diversity at the topic level.

4.4 Temporal distribution

The *publication temporal distribution* is an aggregation of publication dates that are used to timestamp web pages. The *content temporal distribution* is the collection of time references associated with events being discussed on web pages. The time information may be absolute, (e.g., "On Friday, Nov 17, 2017...") or relative (e.g.,

"Next month is..."). We normalize relative time information (e.g., if the reference date is "2017-11-17" we represent "next month" as "2017-12-17"). Temporal distributions enable the calculation of the collection age. The ages of web pages may be calculated with respect to the creation date of the collection to indicate how long web pages existed prior to being collected. A short duration between the publication date of web pages and the creation date of the collection may indicate that the curator intended to collect web pages following a recent event. Alternatively, the ages of documents may be calculated with respect to the current date to determine absolute ages of web pages.

The publication dates of web pages may provide useful information about the kinds of events discussed in the document. For example, stories concerning airport security before the September 11, 2001 terrorist attacks are not expected to discuss the TSA (Transportation Security Administration), because the TSA was founded on November 19, 2001. The publication date alone may not be sufficient to give us a full picture of the kinds of events discussed in a document, since documents often discuss events and include the dates of these events in their content. This may be relative, e.g., "last year" or absolute "on Jan 3rd, 2017." Therefore, we also have to pay attention to these dates.

We extract the publication dates of the documents in a collection to form the publication date distribution through the use of CarbonDate [33] which estimates the creation date of web pages based on information polled from multiple sources such as the document timestamps, web archives, Twitter, backlinks, etc. We extract the content dates with the aid of SUTime [8].

4.5 Source diversity

Similar to content diversity, the *source diversity* metric tells us whether a collection samples a single source, a handful of sources, or many sources. The URI source diversity metric [28], $d_{URI} \in [0, 1]$ tells us the rate of unique URIs; $d_{URI} = 0$ means the collection only has one distinct URI (duplicate web pages). On the other hand, if $d_{URI} = 1$, it means the collection is made up of unique URIs. We also explore source diversity at the domain (d_{domain}) and hostname ($d_{hostname}$) policies.

We deduplicated URIs in collections by trimming all parameters from the URIs as suggested by Brunelle et al. [5] before calculating source diversity. Given a policy set $P = \{URI, Domain, Hostname\}$ for a collection C, and the count of unique URIs in the collection U, the source diversity of a given policy d_p is given by Eqn. 2.

$$d_{p \in P} = \frac{U}{|C|}; d_p \in \left[\frac{1}{|C|}, 1\right] \qquad (2)$$

The normalized source diversity of a given policy d'_p is given by Eqn. 3.

$$d'_{p \in P} = \frac{d_p - \frac{1}{|C|}}{1 - \frac{1}{|C|}} = \frac{U - 1}{|C| - 1}; d'_p \in [0, 1] \qquad (3)$$

The social media diversity metric or social media rate quantifies the proportion of web pages in a collection that are from social media sites. We created a predefined list of social media domains: *twitter.com*, *facebook.com*, *youtube.com*, *instagram.com*, and *tumblr.com*. Given k URIs from social media domains in a collection C, the social media rate is $\frac{k}{|C|}$. For example, a collection composed

NLM (occurrence rate)	Reddit (occurrence rate)
"ebola outbreak west africa" (0.34)	"infected ebola virus disease" (0.25)
"guinea liberia sierra leone" (0.31)	"west africa" (0.21)
"cases ebola virus disease" (0.30)	"public health workers" (0.15)
"public health workers" (0.27)	"sierra leone" (0.15)
"centers disease control prevention" (0.15)	"united states" (0.14)

(a) Distribution of top five topics for NLM Archive-It and Reddit *Ebola virus* collections showing a similar topic distribution.

CCS Metric	NLM's Ebola Characterization	Reddit Ebola Characterization
Dist. of sources	Top 10 hosts fraction of collection: 50%	Top 10 hosts fraction of collection: 46%
Content diversity (Doc-Term matrix / Entity set)	(0.80 / 0.65)	(0.89 / 0.85)
Publication temporal dist. (Median age, where age: Creation date - Pub. date)	36 days	1,450 days (3.9 years)
Content temporal dist. (Median age)	1,144 days (3.1 years)	2,104 (5.8 years)
Source diversity (URI/ Hostname / Social media)	(1.0 / 0.34 / 0.07)	(0.98 / 0.53 / 0.12)
Collection exposure (Archival rate/ Tweet index rate)	(1.00 / 0.72)	(0.78 / 0.40)
Target audience (readability, Q1 / Median / Q3)	(0 / 0.57 / 1)	(0.14 / 0.57 / 0.85)

(b) CCS characterizations of NLM and Reddit *Ebola virus* collections

Table 3: Characterization of two collections Archive-It (144 URIs) and Reddit (150 URIs) *Ebola virus* collections. Each characterization describes the individual collection, juxtaposing multiple characterizations enables collection comparison.

of 3 URIs from Twitter, 2 from Facebook, and 5 from CNN, has a social media rate of $\frac{3+2}{10} = 0.5$.

4.6 Collection exposure

If a web page is "popular" (used widely), this means there is some need the document fulfills to a wide audience. We approximate popularity with the *collection exposure* metrics - *archival rate* and *tweet index rate*. In our previous work [31], we showed that collections of local news from local news organization, such as the *Caloosa Belle* newspaper (LaBelle, Florida USA), are less exposed, thus less popular than collections of news sources from mainstream news organizations, such as *CNN* and *The Washington Post*.

The archival rate of a collection C is the fraction of C that is archived. For example, if we found 10 archived stories from C (where $|C| = 50$), the archival rate of C is $\frac{10}{50} = 0.2$. Note that when comparing the archival rates of two collections, it is important to consider how old both collections are. For example, a collection A might have a much larger archival rate than a collection B only because A has much older documents than B, and as a result had the greater opportunity to be archived.

Popular (widely used) URIs are more likely to be archived than less popular URIs [1]. This means we could use the archival state of a URI to infer its popularity. This method will not be valid if every URI is archived (e.g. Archive-It seeds). If this were the case (all URIs archived), the magnitude of archived copies of a URI may indicate its popularity. The archive state of a web page can be measured using Memgator [2].

Similar to the archival rate, the tweet index rate of a collection C is the fraction of C found embedded in tweets. For example, if we found 40 URIs from C (where $|C| = 50$) embedded in tweets, the tweet index rate of C is $\frac{40}{50} = 0.8$. Also similar to archival rate, when comparing the tweet index rates of two collections, it is important to consider how old both collections are. For example, a collection A might have a much larger tweet index rate than a collection B only because A includes web pages that are much older than B, and as a result, had a greater opportunity to be tweeted. The tweet index state of a web page is set by searching Twitter for a tweet that embeds the page URI [27].

Similar to the archival rate, popular URIs are more likely to be shared on social media sites (e.g., Twitter) than less popular URIs. Consequently, the tweet index state (in tweet or not) of a web page may indicate the popularity or exposure of the web page. We may also be able to infer the popularity of a URI in a tweet by taking into account how often it is shared on Twitter. The tweet index rate is often a useful alternative to the archival rate when the collections to be compared have the same archival rate. For example, Archive-It seeds have a 100% archival rate. Likewise the archival rate provides an alternative when comparing collections with the same tweet index rates, for example, collections generated from Twitter have 100% tweet index rates.

4.7 Target audience

The *target audience* estimates the target users of the collection. This is not easy to achieve. Our premise is that the readability level of the documents in the collection is a reflection of the target audience. For example, if the reading level of a collection is at the 10th grade level, we conclude that the target audience starts from high school young adults and above. However, if the reading level is at the graduate level (16th grade) level, we may conclude the target audience might be professionals in a subject area.

The target audience of a collection provides important contextual information that may give insight about the composition of the collection, and may reflect the intent of the collection builder, such information is not often readily available.

We instantiate the target audience metric with readability measures. Readability measures estimate the reading level of documents through procedures that include counting syllables, words, and sentences. We employed widely used readability measures that output grade levels. These are the *Flesch-Kincaid Grade level* [20], *Coleman Liau index* [9], and the *Automated Readability index* [35]. For a single document, the readability score is the average score from the three readability measures (normalized between 0 and 1). The higher the readability score, the higher the grade level.

5 COLLECTION CHARACTERIZATION AND COMPARISON

In order to characterize a single collection with the CCS, we simply extract values for the metrics that make up the suite. These values collectively form a characterization for the collection. For example, Table 3 describes two collections. The first, the NLM Archive-It *Ebola Virus* collection, is an archived collection built manually by

an archivist at the NLM in October 2014. The second, the Reddit *Ebola Virus* collection, we built by issuing the query "ebola virus" to Reddit from *2017-07-25* to *2017-08-23* and extracting links from the Reddit SERPs and their respective comments. Let us consider both collections to see how the CCS describes both collections.

The top five topics from the NLM Archive-It collection show that the collection addresses issues arising from the Ebola virus outbreak in West Africa (Table 3a, topic 1) and that the main countries affected were Guinea, Liberia, and Sierra Leone (Table 3a, topic 2). Also two major players involved with the outbreak were public health workers and the Centers for Disease Control and Prevention (Table 3a, topic 4 & 5). The Reddit collection also mirrors this sentiment. Both collections are similarly characterized by the fraction of the collections the top 10 hosts make (Table 3b, Dist. of sources). Similarly, both collections target a similar audience (Table 3b, Target audience) since they have the same median normalized grade level of 0.57 (11th grade).

Table 4: Evaluation Dataset comprised of 129 collections from three Topics: "Ebola Virus," "Hurricane Harvey," and "2016 Pulse Nightclub shooting." WSDL represents the collections generated by the authors.

ID	Topic (URI Count)	Source (Author)	Creation Date	Extraction note
1	Ebola V... (144)	🅰 (NLM)	2014-10	Archive-It seeds
2	Ebola V... (669)	Ⓢ (WSDL)	2017-11-29	100 sub-collections (IDs 0-99) of URIs from 100 Storify *stories*
3	Ebola V... (669)	Ⓢ (WSDL)	2017-11-29	A Collection created by combining all links in Collection 2.
4	Ebola V... (155)	W (WSDL)	2017-07-25	URIs from references of *Ebola Virus* Wikipedia page
5	Ebola V... (153)	🔴 (WSDL)	2017-07-25 - 2017-08-23	URIs from Reddit (& comments) search for query: "Ebola Virus"
6	Ebola V... (152)	🐦 (WSDL)	2017-08-02 - 2017-11-28	URIs in tweets from Twitter search for query: "Ebola Virus"
7	Ebola V... (105)	G (WSDL)	2017-11-29	URIs from first 10 pages of Google, for query: "Ebola Virus"
8	Hurricane H...(44)	🅰 (IA)	2017-08	Archive-It seeds
9	Hurricane H...(151)	W (WSDL)	2017-09-02	URIs from references of *Hurricane Harvey* Wikipedia page
10	Hurricane H...(14)	Ⓞ (WSDL)	2017-12-08	2 sub-collections (IDs 0-1) of URIs from tweets in Twitter Moments
11	Hurricane H...(14)	Ⓞ (WSDL)	2017-12-08	A collection created by combining all URIs in Collection 10
12	Hurricane H...(94)	G (WSDL)	2017-09-02- 2017-11-29	URIs from first page of Google, for query: "Hurricane Harvey"
13	2016 Pulse...(151)	🅰 (IA)	2016-06	Archive-It seeds
14	2016 Pulse...(50)	Ⓞ (WSDL)	2017-12-08	5 sub-collections (IDs 0-4) of URIs from tweets from Twitter Moments
15	2016 Pulse...(50)	Ⓞ (WSDL)	2017-12-08	A collections created by combining URIs in Collection 14
16	Random (500)	UCI ML (Lichman, M)	2014-03-10 - 2014-08-10	10 sub-collections (IDs 0-9) of URIs or random news stories
Total	2,765 URIs			

Table 3b shows that the Reddit collection produced a higher content diversity for both collection representations (*Document-Term matrix* and *List of Entity sets*). The NLM Archive-It collection produced much newer web documents with a median publication age of 36 days, compared to the Reddit collection of 3.9 years. This suggests that the NLM Archive-It collection was created a few months after the Ebola event unfolded. Additionally, the Reddit collection sampled from more hosts (hostname source diversity - 0.53) and had more social media URIs (social media rate - 0.12) compared to the NLM Archive-It colleciton (hostname source diversity - 0.34, social media rate - 0.07). The NLM Archive-It collection indicated a higher exposure than the Reddit collection, with a higher archival rate of 1.0, compared to the 0.78 archival rate of the Reddit collection. The high archival rate of the Archive-It collection is no surprise because it is a collection of seeds; the seeds are meant to be crawled and archived. The NLM Archive-It collection also showed a higher tweet index rate (0.72) than the Reddit collection (0.40).

Table 5: List of collections most similar to three Archive-It collections and three random collections for the evaluation dataset topics.

Gold standard collections	Three most similar		
Ebola Virus (ebo.) [A] $ebo.1$	$ebo.5$ 0.17	$ebo.2.49$ 0.23	$ebo.2.57$ 0.25
Hurricane Harvey (hur.) [A] $hur.8$	$hur.12$ 0.27	$hur.11$ 0.32	$pul.15$ 0.34
2016 Pulse night.. (pul.) [A] $pul.13$	$pul.15$ 0.24	$pul.14.2$ 0.24	$pul.14.4$ 0.31
Random news stories 0 (ran.) [UCI ML] $ran.16.0$	$ran.16.8$ 0.16	$ran.16.5$ 0.19	$ran.16.4$ 0.22
Random news stories 1 (ran.) [UCI ML] $ran.16.1$	$ran.16.6$ 0.19	$ran.16.3$ 0.22	$ran.16.8$ 0.22
Random news stories 2 (ran.) [UCI ML] $ran.16.2$	$ran.16.3$ 0.22	$ran.16.4$ 0.22	$ran.16.5$ 0.22

6 EVALUATION

To assess if we could bootstrap archived collections from social media, we measured the distances between archived collections from Archive-It ([A]) and collections generated from social media sources: Storify ([S]), Reddit ([O]), Twitter Moments ([O]), Twitter SERP ([W]), and Wikipedia (W). The rationale for this is if collections created by extracting URIs from social media collections are similar (low distance) to expert-created collections on Archive-It, then we may start or augment archived collections with seeds extracted from social media sources.

We generated a dataset (Table 4) of 129 collections (2,765 URIs) from three topics: "Ebola Virus," "Hurricane Harvey," and "2016 Pulse Nightclub Shooting," and 10 collections (500 URIs) for random (multiple topics) news stories from the UCI news aggregator

Table 6: Dist. of top five Topics for Archive-It Collections.

2016 Pulse Nightclub Shooting	Hurricane Harvey
"pulse nightclub orlando florida"	"hurricane harvey photo"
"new york"	"27 2017 houston"
"en la comunidad"	"27 2017 photo"
"mass shooting"	"tropical storm harvey photo"
"omar mateen"	"corpus christi"

dataset [23]. Random collections ([UCI ML]) were included to assess if the CCS resulted in clusters of collections of common topics even in the presence of noise. We do not expect collections of random news stories to be more similar to archived collections than social media collections. Additionally, we included baseline collections generated by extracting URIs from Google ([G]). We believe most users primarily use Google to discover candidate URIs for their collections, so we included Google collections in order to quantify how these compare with social media and archived collections. Our previous work [30] showed that such collections change with time since search engines are biased to produce the latest documents.

The evaluation dataset collections were represented as a vector of CCS values, and a distance was calculated between Archive-It collections (Table 4, IDs 1, 8, and 13) and every other collection irrespective of the topics. The Euclidean distance metric was used (as opposed to cosine) to compute distance because the magnitudes of the respective CCS values in the collection vectors are significant. We normalized (0-1) the Euclidean distances since all possible maximum and minimum CCS values are known. Additionally, the CCS metrics were assessed to identify the metrics which provided the most information in distinguishing the collections. This was done by calculating the spread of values (standard deviation) of the individual CCS metrics for the collections.

We generated a CCS matrix for the evaluation dataset collections. The rows of the CCS matrix represented the collections and the columns represented the CCS metric values. The first and second columns represented the content diversity values calculated with the Document-Term matrix and List of Entity sets collection representations, respectively. The third column represented the URI source diversity, fourth - domain source diversity, fifth - hostname diversity, sixth - social media rate, seventh - collection exposure archival rate, eight - collection exposure tweet index rate, and ninth, the Jaccard similarity score of a given collection's top 10 n-gram distribution of topics to the Archive-It collection. The last column of the CCS matrix represented the normalized median reading level of the collection. Section 4 outlines how to extract the CCS metrics of all the entries, except the Jaccard similarity of the n-gram distribution of topics for two collections. The idea for this method is to find how similar two collections are in terms of their respective n-gram distribution of topics. In other words, if the collections are about a similar set of topics. We focused on finding similar collections based on the content of the collection and not the sources they sample from or the time the collection was built. Consequently, we excluded the distribution of sources and temporal distributions from the CCS vector.

7 RESULTS AND DISCUSSION

Each pictogram in Table 5 represents a collection expressed by an image of the collection source (section 6). The pictogram superscript represents the collection topic abbreviation followed by the collection ID (Table 4). The sub-collection ID follows the collection ID for Storify and Twitter Moments sub-collections. The subscript represents the normalized Euclidean distance of the collection to the specified Archive-It collection. For example, for the *Ebola Virus* topic, the Reddit (*ebo.5*) collection has the closest distance (0.17) to the Archive-It (*ebo.1*) collection.

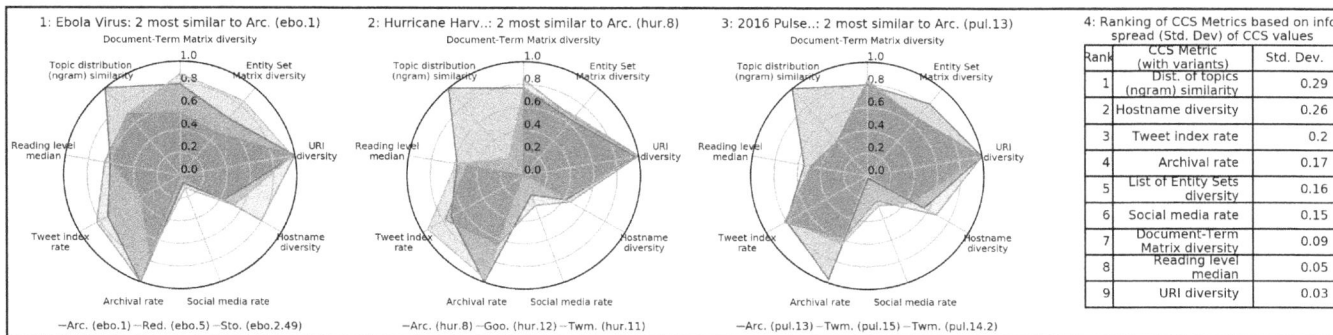

Figure 1: Distribution of CCS Metrics for pair of collections most similar to Archive-It collections (Chts. 1-3) and ranking of CCS Metrics based their respective informational values (Cht. 4).

Table 5 shows that the CCS resulted in the clustering of collections of similar topics with a distance ranging from 0.17 to 0.34 across all topics. The Reddit collection ($\mathbin{\textcircled{}}\ ebo.5_{0.17}$) was most similar to the Archive-It *Ebola Virus* collections ($\mathbin{\text{⬚}}\ ebo.1_0$). Since we had more Storify collections in our dataset, the Storify collections have a higher opportunity of outperforming (lowest distance) other collections. In fact, the Storify *Ebola Virus* collection ($\mathbin{\textcircled{}}ebo.3_{0.27}$) is 4.3 times the size of the Reddit collection, yet, the Reddit collection was most similar to the Archive-It collection. This suggests that the larger the collection may not always mean the better the collection. This result is potentially consequential: it suggests that we may consider Reddit as a collection source in the absence of Storify. The Google *Hurricane Harvey* collection ($\mathbin{\textcircled{G}}hur.12_{0.27}$) was most similar to the Archive-It *Hurricane Harvey* collection confirming our expectation that collections generated from Google may be similar to social media collections since users may use Google to discover URIs. The Twitter Moments *2016 Pulse nightclub shooting* collection ($\mathbin{\textcircled{}}pul.15_{0.34}$) was third most similar even though it has no topics in common with the Archive-It *Hurricane Harvey* collection (n-gram topic similarity of 0), indicating a strong similarity across other dimensions. This shows the need for taking topic similarity into consideration before collection comparison. Similarly, the Twitter Moments collections were most similar to the Archive-It *2016 Pulse nightclub shooting* collections.

Random collections were most similar to other random collections due a common set of properties random collections show: all the random collection produced high diversity values for *Document-Term matrix* (0.93 - 0.95) and *List of Entity sets* (0.88 - 1.0) representations. Also, they included no social media sources (social media rate - 0.0) and sampled from a diverse set of hosts (hostname diversity between 0.92 - 0.77).

Across the various topics, the distribution of topics (ngram similarity) CCS metric provided the most information to distinguish the collections, producing the highest variance or spread ($\sigma = 0.29$) across the collections (Fig. 1, Chrt 4). The radar plots (Fig. 1, Chrt 1-3) illustrates this variance. This suggests the importance of collection summaries in distinguishing collections. This was followed by the hostname diversity CCS metric ($\sigma = 0.26$), suggesting multiple ways collections sample hosts. The target audience (readability) and URI diversity provided the least information to distinguish the

collections: this may be explained by the idea that the documents in the collection target a common audience and have little or no duplicate links ($d_{URI} = 1$).

8 FUTURE WORK AND CONCLUSIONS

We believe the CCS of seven metrics can be expanded. Any new metric has to provide valuable information to a wide range of users since there are many measures one can easily extract from a collection.

To begin or augment expert-generated archived collections of web pages, we proposed extracting URIs from collections created by users on social media sites: Storify, Reddit, Twitter, and Wikipedia. This required us to assess the degree of similarity of the collections generated from social media sources and archived collection. To achieve such comparison, we developed a suite (CCS) of seven metrics that characterized individual collections. Multiple collections can be compared by computing the similarity or distances with respect to a given collection. The CCS metrics included widely used metrics motivated by the state of the art in collection evaluation such as distribution of topics, content diversity, and publication temporal distribution. We also provided and motivated additional metrics such as distribution of sources, content temporal distribution, source diversity, collection exposure, and target audience. The metrics provide valuable information such as a summary of the collection that indicates whether the collection is on topic and the degree of self similarity of the collection. We consider our collection characterizing suite as a template, and as such, may be realized in different ways, and provided novel options for instantiating the metrics. The CCS distance evaluation results showed that Archive-It collection and social media collections are similar with a distance ranging from 0.17 to 0.34, suggesting that we can start or augment the seed generation process of important events by extracting URIs from social media collections. Our evaluation dataset as well as source code that implements instantiations of the CCS are publicly available [29].

ACKNOWLEDGEMENTS

This work was made possible by IMLS LG-71-15-0077-15, and help from Christie Moffat at the National Library of Medicine.

REFERENCES

[1] Scott G Ainsworth, Ahmed Alsum, Hany SalahEldeen, Michele C Weigle, and Michael L Nelson. 2011. How much of the web is archived?. In *Proceedings of JCDL 2011*. 133–136.

[2] Sawood Alam and Michael L Nelson. 2016. MemGator-A portable concurrent memento aggregator: Cross-platform CLI and server binaries in Go. In *Proceedings of JCDL 2016*. 243–244.

[3] Donna Bergmark. 2002. Collection synthesis. In *Proceedings of JCDL 2002*. 253–262.

[4] George S Bonn. 1974. Evaluation of the Collection. *Library Trends* 22, 3 (1974), 265–304.

[5] Justin F Brunelle, Michele C Weigle, and Michael L Nelson. 2015. Archiving Deferred Representations Using a Two-Tiered Crawling Approach. *Proceedings of iPRES 2015* (2015).

[6] Centers for Disease Control and Prevention. 2016. 2014 Ebola Outbreak in West Africa - Case Counts. https://www.cdc.gov/vhf/ebola/outbreaks/2014-west-africa/case-counts.html.

[7] Soumen Chakrabarti, Martin Van den Berg, and Byron Dom. 1999. Focused crawling: a new approach to topic-specific Web resource discovery. *Computer Networks* 31, 11 (1999), 1623–1640.

[8] Angel X Chang and Christopher D Manning. 2012. Sutime: A library for recognizing and normalizing time expressions. In *LREC*. 3735–3740.

[9] Meri Coleman and Ta Lin Liau. 1975. A computer readability formula designed for machine scoring. *Journal of Applied Psychology* 60, 2 (1975), 283–284.

[10] Mohamed MG Farag, Sunshin Lee, and Edward A Fox. 2018. Focused crawler for events. *International Journal on Digital Libraries (IJDL)* 19, 1 (2018), 3–19. DOI: http://dx.doi.org/10.1007/s00799-016-0207-1

[11] Anthony W Ferguson, Joan Grant, and Joel S Rutstein. 1988. The RLG Conspectus: its uses and benefits. *College & Research Libraries* 49, 3 (1988), 197–206.

[12] Jenny Rose Finkel, Trond Grenager, and Christopher Manning. 2005. Incorporating Non-local Information into Information Extraction Systems by Gibbs Sampling. In *Proceedings of Association for Computational Linguistics (ACL 2005)*. 363–370.

[13] Gerhard Gossen, Elena Demidova, and Thomas Risse. 2015. iCrawl: Improving the freshness of web collections by integrating social web and focused crawling. In *Proceedings of JCDL 2015*. 75–84.

[14] Nancy E. Gwinn and Paul H. Mosher. 1983. Coordinating Collection Development: The RLG Conspectus. *College & Research Libraries* 44, 2 (1983), 128–140.

[15] Terese Heidenwolf. 1994. Evaluating an interdisciplinary research collection. *Collection Management* 18, 3-4 (1994), 33–48.

[16] Internet Archive. 2016. Help build an archive documenting responses to the 2016 U.S. presidential election at. https://twitter.com/internetarchive/status/797263535994613761.

[17] Internet Archive. 2016. What web pages should we save concerning DAPL? Tell us here:. https://twitter.com/internetarchive/status/806228431474028544.

[18] Internet Archive Global Events. 2016. 2016 Pulse Nightclub Shooting Web Archive. https://archive-it.org/collections/7570.

[19] Shawn M Jones. 2017. Where Can We Post Stories Summarizing Web Archive Collections? http://ws-dl.blogspot.com/2017/08/2017-08-11-where-can-we-post-stories.html.

[20] J Peter Kincaid, Robert P Fishburne Jr, Richard L Rogers, and Brad S Chissom. 1975. *Derivation of new readability formulas (automated readability index, fog count and flesch reading ease formula) for navy enlisted personnel*. Technical Report Research Branch Report 8-75. Naval Technical Training Command Millington TN Research Branch.

[21] Martin Klein, Lyudmila Balakireva, and Herbert Van de Sompel. 2018. Focused Crawl of Web Archives to Build Event Collections. In *Web Science Conference (WebSci 2018)*.

[22] David Lesniaski. 2004. Evaluating collections: a discussion and extension of Brief Tests of Collection Strength. *College & Undergraduate Libraries* 11, 1 (2004), 11–24.

[23] Moshe Lichman. 2013. UCI machine learning repository. http://archive.ics.uci.edu/ml.

[24] Local Memory Project. 2017. Ebola Virus Collection. http://www.localmemory.org/vis/collections/local-memory-project/queries/guinea-conakry-ebola-virus-10-2017-11-16.

[25] Barbara Lockett. 1989. *Guide to the evaluation of library collections*. American Library Association.

[26] National Library of Medicine. 2014. Global Health Events. https://archive-it.org/collections/4887.

[27] Alexander C Nwala. 2017. Finding URLs on Twitter - A simple recommendation. http://ws-dl.blogspot.com/2017/01/2017-01-23-finding-urls-on-twitter.html.

[28] Alexander C Nwala. 2018. An exploration of URL diversity measures. http://ws-dl.blogspot.com/2018/05/2018-05-04-exploration-of-url-diversity.html.

[29] Alexander C Nwala. 2018. Bootstrapping Web Archive Collections from Social Media - Git Repo. https://github.com/anwala/collection-characterizing-suite.

[30] Alexander C Nwala, Michele C Weigle, and Michael L Nelson. 2018. Scraping SERPs for Archival Seeds: It Matters When You Start. In *Proceedings of JCDL 2018*.

[31] Alexander C Nwala, Michele C Weigle, Adam B Ziegler, Anastasia Aizman, and Michael L Nelson. 2017. Local Memory Project: Providing Tools to Build Collections of Stories for Local Events from Local Sources. In *Proceedings of JCDL 2017*. 219–228.

[32] Thomas Risse, Elena Demidova, and Gerhard Gossen. 2014. What do you want to collect from the web. In *Proceedings of Building Web Observatories Workshop (BWOW 2014)*.

[33] Hany M SalahEldeen and Michael L Nelson. 2013. Carbon dating the web: estimating the age of web resources. In *Proceedings of WWW 2013*. 1075–1082.

[34] Steven M Schneider, Kirsten Foot, Michele Kimpton, and Gina Jones. 2003. Building thematic web collections: challenges and experiences from the September 11 Web Archive and the Election 2002 Web Archive. *Third Workshop on Web Archives* (2003), 77–94.

[35] Edgar A Smith and RJ Senter. 1967. *Automated readability index*. Technical Report AMRL-TR-66-220. AMRL-TR. Aerospace Medical Research Laboratories (US).

[36] Storify. 2017. Storify End-of-Life. https://archive.is/DOPFa.

[37] Howard D White. 1995. *Brief tests of collection strength: A methodology for all types of libraries*. Number 88.

[38] Wikipedia. 2018. Ebola virus. https://en.wikipedia.org/wiki/Ebola_virus.

[39] Shuyi Zheng, Pavel Dmitriev, and C Lee Giles. 2009. Graph based crawler seed selection. In *Proceedings of WWW 2009*. 1089–1090.

Studying the Spatio-Temporal Dynamics of Small-Scale Events in Twitter

Paul Mousset
IRIT, Université de Toulouse, CNRS
Toulouse, France
paul.mousset@irit.fr

Yoann Pitarch
IRIT, Université de Toulouse, CNRS
Toulouse, France
pitarch@irit.fr

Lynda Tamine
IRIT, Université de Toulouse, CNRS
Toulouse, France
tamine@irit.fr

ABSTRACT

Small-scale events are emerging as attractive objects of research. On Twitter, small-scale events represent weak sensors that report things happening in specific times and places. While previous work addressed the issue of detecting such events, very little is known so far about their inherent properties. In this paper, our main objective was to analyse the spatio-temporal peculiarities of small-scale events w.r.t different levels of location granularity, and to understand the general trend of their propagation along their lifetimes. Our findings suggest that (1) users involved in small-scale events mostly gravitate not significantly far from the geographical focus; (2) events do not exhibit major peaks; and (3) there exists distinct events that we can identify from users' posts that significantly differ from topic distribution, focus concentration and propagation distance perspectives across time.

CCS CONCEPTS

• **Computer systems organization** → **Embedded systems**; *Redundancy*; Robotics; • **Networks** → Network reliability;

KEYWORDS

Small-scale event; geo-tagged tweets; focus; entropy

ACM Reference Format:
Paul Mousset, Yoann Pitarch, and Lynda Tamine. 2018. Studying the Spatio-Temporal Dynamics of Small-Scale Events in Twitter. In *HT '18: 29th ACM Conference on Hypertext and Social Media, July 9–12, 2018, Baltimore, MD, USA.* ACM, New York, NY, USA, 9 pages. https://doi.org/10.1145/3209542.3209561

1 INTRODUCTION

Microblogging platforms such as Twitter provide active communication channels and a gold-mine of timely real-world information which has been shown to be highly effective for gaining knowledge about people's profiles [22], and opinions [16] to cite just a few. In particular, for events such as festivals, political campaigns, pandemics and crisis situations, user-generated micro-posts play a crucial role as social sensors by allowing the monitoring of users' activities and the provision of timely responses and

recommendations [12]. More specifically, event-related tweet streams provide valuable spatio-temporal data such as text messages with location mentions, the timestamp of the post and the geolocation of the user who posted the tweet. With the increasing connectivity of users through wireless networks and the wide use of mobile devices, geo-tagged tweets are currently created daily. This phenomena allowed the intensive use of Twitter data for detecting and monitoring both large-scale events (eg., earthquakes and epidemics) and small-scale events (eg., festivals, crimes and protests). An important body of early research focused on detecting, analysing and mining behavioural patterns from large-scale events (also called *global* events), which are bursty in the entire stream, impact a wide spatial area and trigger an important audience [6, 23]. Recently, there has been a growing research interest in detecting [1, 26, 30–32] and analysing [24, 25, 30] small-scale events. Unlike large-scale events, small-scale events (also called *local* or *localized* events) are generally micro-phenomena that stimulate people to post a low number of messages for a certain period of time in a local region. Such events play the roles of *weak signals* which have potential in several applications such as public order protection and traffic road assistance. However, the literature review reveals that very little has been understood so far about the spatio-temporal dynamics of such events [24, 25, 30]. A prior study [30] focused on the analysis of user physical network structure during two micro-events, namely a parking garage collapse in Atlanta and a church shooting in Wichita. The results mainly revealed that the event-related structure of the networks is not particularly more dense than the Twitter network structure and that central Twitterers are geographically central particularly in more spatially narrowed events. In [24, 25], authors examined the users' posts during two incidents which refer to small-scale events that result in damage or injuries. The authors found that different types of users (eg., journalists, organisation and citizens) report on the incidents and that citizens are generally faster than official sources in propagating tweet posts.

In this paper we pursue this line of research and report the findings of analyses that are designed to investigate the spatio-temporal dynamics of small-scale events. By using the focus and entropy measures, we thoroughly study the spatial and timely tweet post distributions of such events based on a wide set of event types automatically identified in geo-tagged tweet streams. Moreover, we consider locations at varying levels of granularity, from the borough to the Point Of Interest (POI) level. The key differences between close previous work [24, 25, 30] and ours are the following: (1) previous work focused on the analysis and comparison of network structure in the Twitter network vs. event-related network [30] and the identification of user types involved in the event [24, 25]. Moreover, the studies used limited samples of prior specific events (eg., incidents) in terms of number of tweets (655 event-related tweets used in [24, 25]), as well as number of events (2 events studied in [30]). In contrast, we deeply analyse the spatial narrowness of users involved in the events and study the propagation trend of their posts w.r.t varying levels of location; furthermore, our study relies on a significant number of event-related tweets (22832) as well as a significant number of events (410) belonging to a set of event types automatically identified from the users' posts. (2) We also examine the spatio-temporal evolution of small-scale events along their lifetime while the temporal dimension has not been addressed in previous work [24, 25, 30].

More specifically, our study is mainly designed for answering the following general questions: What is a rough estimate of the geographical impact of small-scale events in terms of situational-awareness among users? How do small-scale events evolve in time and space? Answering to these questions has many potential applications in improving the designing of better web tracking and searching services and helping both organisation and citizen better fulfill their information needs. For example, modelling the timely propagation of small-scale events from their *center of gravity* enables the development of more robust user's location estimators over time which can be useful for fine-grained location-based personalized information services [10] and designing more effective monitoring services allowing to better plan social events and offer user facilities [3]. A better understanding of their evolving spatio-temporal dispersion enables richer retrieval models answering location-based queries (eg., *What is happening at specific location X?*) that could improve the spatial extent of users' awareness during crisis situations. The analyses performed in our work directly address the following research questions:

> **RQ1:** What is the level of users' narrowness while posting small-scale event-related tweets?
> **RQ2:** How do location and time bound tweet propagation during small-scale events?
> **RQ3:** Can we identify and characterize event types with the tweet publications collected from users?

The remainder of this paper is organized as follows: Section 2 presents the related work. We detail the data and methods that are used in our analyses in Section 3. In Section 4, we report the findings of our study w.r.t the aforementioned research questions. We discuss the implications of our findings and conclude in Section 5.

2 RELATED WORK
2.1 Large-scale vs. small-scale event detection
To the best of our knowledge, there is no consensual definition of an *'event'* [20, 24]. One widely used definition has been introduced by the Topic Detection and Tracking (TDT) project which defines an event as *'an unique thing that happens at some point in time'* [13]. The main common facets of an event are time, place and audience as introduced by authors in [7] who define an event as a real-world occurrence with an associated time period, time-ordered messages discussing the occurrence during a period of time. According to spatial and social impacts, we can distinguish between large-scale events such as earthquakes and epidemics (also called *global* events)

and small-scale events such as crims, protests and festivals (also called *incidents*, *local* or *localized* events). While the former give rise to massive user-generated content and impact a wide spatial region, the latter lead to the posting of a low amount of content within a small region.

A number of early research work have investigated global event detection in Twitter [6, 23]. Related approaches fall in the document-based and feature-based categories. The key idea of document-based approaches relies on the association between document cluster based on a shared topic and the notion of event [2]. For instance, authors in [2] built events as clusters based on content similarity and user proximity. In feature-based approaches [11], the event detection algorithm rather relies on bursty features such as keywords and phrases. Such burstiness is captured as event signal wich is filtered and transformed (eg., using time-series) to identify events. The high connectivity of users through wireless networks and the wide availability of geo-tagged tweets nowadays gave rise to a recent emerging interest toward small-scale event detection which is particularly challenging given the low amount of induced posts [1, 26, 32]. The driving idea behind small-scale event detection algorithms is to identify joint geo-spatial and topical correlations in Twitter streams. The main underlying assumption is that, topical cohesion of even limited samples of tweets posted in a narrow geographical space, is a weak signal of event occurrence. Based on this general assumption, authors in [1] proposed the EVENTWEET algorithm which detects small-scale events by running four main stages: (1) determining time windows of bursty words; (2) identifying localized words by computing spatial entropy; (3) spatial clustering of localized words; and (4) associating each cluster with an event and then ranking events according to spatial coverage and burstiness measures. In the same spirit, the GEOBURST algorithm [32] relies on three main steps to detect small-scale events: (1) identifies representative tweets (called *pivots*) and associated geo-topic correlated tweets in slicing time windows; (2) compares the clusters of tweets to historical streaming tweets to identify bursty clusters of tweets among the candidate ones identified in the first stage; and (3) further identifies new pivots in successive windows.

2.2 Analysing spatio-temporal Twitter data
The prevalence of social media services such as Facebook and Twitter and the increasing use of mobile devices, have enabled the availability of a powerful source of streamed user-generated content about location and regional human behaviour. This motivates the spatio-temporal analysis of social media data for various purposes such as crisis management [21] and future prediction [5]. On Twitter, the literature review reveals that a large body of studies investigated the analysis of spatio-temporal metadata for different purposes [4, 14, 18, 27]. A first category of work have analysed the spatio-temporal properties of tweets to better understand their diffusion [4, 14] or discover spatio-temporal dependent topics that are addressed by Twitter users. For example, in [14], the authors mainly observed the joint phenomena of the high-locality of hashtags and their high-speed propagation over time.

Another category of work have used spatio-temporal data from Twitter to design web services such as automatic summarizers [19] or monitoring systems [3]. For instance, in [19], the authors developed an event summarizer called CEST that exploits Twitter geographical metadata mainly including POI. Once the event is detected, the *CEST* system provides a high-level picture of the spatial extent of the event as well as the distribution of positive vs. negative opinions embedded in the event-related tweets.

An other important category of work focused on mining from large-scale or small-scale events. Early work studied large-scale events through the examination of the regional trends and temporal patterns of users' behaviour to address medical concerns [18] or better manage emergency situations [27]. Lee et al. [18] designed a surveillance system for early prediction of seasonal disease outbreaks such as flu. Using tweet analytics about the timeline and geographical distribution of disease symptoms, the system can facilitate the monitoring of health resource allocation during epidemics. In [27], the authors analysed users' micro-posts across two disaster events that took place in the US: the Red River Floods and the Oklahoma Grassfires. They outlined that unlike in the overall tweet stream, there were a high proportion (more than 78%) of both geo-tagged tweets and location mentions in tweet texts during natural disasters which suggests that users are aware of the importance of geo-location information in collaboratively managing an emergency. Moreover, the analysis of the event time-line showed a clear picture of the spread of situational awareness among Twitterers. Other work, more close to ours focused on small-scale events, also called incidents in the specific case where they induce damage and injuries [24, 25, 30]. Their analysis mainly concerned the study of the impact of such events on the network structure [30] and the categorisation of user profiles (eg., organization, citizen) according to predefined event types such as crash and fire [24, 25]. The findings revealed that influencial users kept their roles in event-related networks [30] and that citizen were more importantly involved than officials in the event spread [24, 25].

3 STUDY DESIGN

3.1 Data

3.1.1 Twitter datasets. We analysed two collections of geo-tagged tweets related to New York City, and restricted our study to English-language tweets. The geotag provides latitude-longitude coordinates about the physical location of the associated Twitter user. To facilitate the analysis of multiple levels of location granularity, we used the latitude-longitude coordinates and mapped them to the borough and neighbourhood and to the most likely Place Of Interest (POI). To perform this mapping, we used a recent state-of-the art POI annotation method that relies on geo-tagged tweets [33]. We have particularly choosen New York City as the main location for a couple of reasons: (1) given the high number and the diversity of event types that might occur in New York; (2) the availability of rich resources that provide POI descriptions in New York City. The characteristics of the datasets are the following.

- The first dataset, which is referred to as NY2014, was released by Zhang et al. [32]. It consists of a sample of 2.4 million of tweets that were geo-tagged in New York and retrieved using the Twitter Streaming API[1] from 2014.08.01 to 2014.11.30.
- The second dataset was obtained by constantly monitoring the Twitter streams from 2016.06.18 to 2016.12.08 for 116

cities around the world, which included more than 65 million geo-tagged tweets. For this study, we extracted a sub-dataset, which is referred to as NY2016, that contains only geo-tagged tweets published in New York from 2016.10.01 to 2016.11.30. It contains approximately 2.98 million tweets.

3.1.2 Event labelling. The process of building a pool of small-scale events from the two datasets consisted in a 2-step task:

- *Step 1: Generating candidate small-scale events.* The objective of this step was to extract from the Twitter datasets clusters of representative event-related tweets. To achieve this objective without bias induced by the event detection algorithm, we used two state-of-the art event detection algorithms, namely the EVENTWEET [1] and GEOBURST algorithms [32]. In addition to our confidence in their effectiveness and efficiency, the main advantage of these algorithms is that they provide clusters of tweets and/or authoritative words that facilitate further human annotation. The generation of candidate small-scale events was run as follows:

  (1) Apply separately each of the EVENTWEET and GEOBURST algorithm on each dataset, namely the NY2014 and NY2016 datasets. More specifically: (i) we ran the GEOBURST algorithm using very similar parameters to those used by Zhang et al. [32]. More precisely, the kernel bandwith $h = 0.01$, the ranking parameter for balancing spatial and temporal burstiness $\eta = 0.5$ and the RWR similarity threshold $\delta = 0.01$ with sliding time windows of 6 hours, including 3 hours of overlapping time. (ii) we ran the EVENTWEET algorithm based on the partitioning of the whole space into NxN small grids with $N = 50$. At the end of this stage we obtained a pair of ranked lists of word clusters for each dataset.

  (2) With respect to our goal which consists in avoiding the bias induced by the event detection algorithm on the spatio-temporal properties of the tweets, we only selected a subset of common events that were detected by both algorithms as relevant candidate events. Instead of applying exact matching which is highly unlikely given the difference in the techniques used by the GEOBURST and EVENTWEET algorithms for tweet clustering, we applied an approximate matching based on a clustering similarity constrained by a threshold: the Szymkiewicz-Simpson overlap coefficient with a threshold set up to 0.5.

  This first step resulted in 1163 and 1802 event clusters for the NY2014 and NY2016 datasets respectively.

- *Step 2: Building the ground truth event datasets.* In the previous step we obtained a set of candidate small-scale events. However, given that the precision of each of the GEOBURST and EVENTWEET is less than 100%, human annotation was required to build the gold dataset. To this end, we set up a crowdsourced annotation tasks using CrowdFlower[2], which is a popular crowdsourcing platform. The objective of this task was to build the gold set of small-scale events from the candidate events which were represented as clusters of

---

[1]https://developer.twitter.com/

[2]http://www.crowdflower.com/

Table 1: Descriptive statistics of the NY2014 and NY2016 datasets.

	NY2014	NY2016
# small-scale events	278	132
Top 3 POIs	Metlife Stadium	Trump Tower
	Yankee Stadium	avits Center Shuttle
	Barclays Center	Barclays Center
Average duration	5h45	5h43
Duration standard deviation	2h25	2h24

Table 2: A sample of small-scale events identified in the pooled dataset.

Event	Dataset	Duration	# Tweets
NY Thanksgiving Parade	NY2014	17h30	723
Box fight (WWE)	NY2014	14h30	151
Hockey match	NY2016	5h16	28
Billy Joel concert	NY2016	3h27	10

authoritative tweets from the previous step. For this aim, we provided the crowdworkers with clusters of the 5 tweets with the highest authority scores and with the 10 most representative keywords. We asked them to judge whether each set of tweets corresponds to an event, and, if so, to judge whether it is a small-scale event. For the latter judgement, crowdworkers were instructed to follow the definition of a small-scale event that is given in [33] (called *local* event): "*a local event is a specific thing that occurs at a specific time and restricted to a narrow area (e.g., protest march, house fire, traffic jam*"). To ensure reliable task outcomes, we submitted the tasks to experienced crowdworkers with a high level of performance (Level = 3). The performance was assessed by the platform using an average measure of the correctness of their answers to the test questions over all the tasks they have performed. For additional quality control, for each task, we included predefined question-answer pairs as the gold standard. Only crowdworkers who achieved no less than 80% on the ground truth were finally recruited. Moreover, since it is likely that different workers have different levels of agreements, we assigned each task to 3 workers. The majority voting strategy was used to generate the final answer. We offered a payment of $0.05 per respondent for completing the survey.

At this stage, the gold set[3] for the NY2014 dataset (resp. the NY2016 dataset) consists of 378 (resp. 219) events including 278 small-scale events (resp. 132). More detailed statistics of the datasets are given in Table 1. Since the two datasets have similar values of both average duration and standard deviation, we pooled them into one dataset. Table 2 provides further statistics about a sample of human-annotated events.

3.2 Metrics

We detail below the metrics that were used in our study (which are similar to those used for analysing the geographic characteristics of YouTube videos [9]). It is worth to mention that the datasets contain geo-tagged tweets which provide spatial location of the Twitter users. Accordingly, tweet location mentioned below also refers to the location of the user who posted the tweet.

3.2.1 Geographical focus. Focus is concerned with how narrow the geographical space the event tweets deal with. For each event e and each location $l \in L$, we define the geographic focus, as the maximal probability of observing a tweet that is posted from or

discusses about a single location l.

$$F^e = \max_{l \in L} p_e^l \; ; \; p_e^l = \frac{|T_e^l|}{|T^e|} \tag{1}$$

where T^l is the set of tweet events that are geo-tagged at location l, T^e is the set of tweets related to event e and T_e^l is the subset of event tweets that are related to event e and geo-tagged at location l. The geographic focus inherently decreases with the propagation of the tweets that deal with event e. It is worth noting that an event for which the entire set of tweets are posted from the same location has a focus of 1.0. We can also measure the geographical focus over a time interval t, denoted as $F^e(t)$.

3.2.2 Event entropy. The entropy is concerned with how diverse the entire spatial distribution of the event is. The higher the entropy is, the more diverse the range of locations that are covered by the event. For instance, an event for which the entire set of tweets are posted from the single location has an entropy of 0.0. More generally, an event entropy value of H^e indicates that the event propagated almost evenly to 2^{H^e} locations.

$$H^e = -\sum_{l \in L} p_e^l \, log_2 \, p_e^l \tag{2}$$

Similar to the focus, we can measure the event entropy over a time interval t, denoted $H^e(t)$.

4 FINDINGS

4.1 Spatial coverage of users (RQ1)

Our objective here is to analyse the extent to which small-scale events have a meaningful geographical focus and how they propagate spatially w.r.t the different levels of spatial granularity: borough, neighbourhood and POI. To achieve this objective, we compute for each event the focus value F^e at each level. Figure 1(a) shows the related cumulative distributions (CDF) of focus values. By observing the two coarsest levels, namely, neighbourhood and borough, we conjecture that the users involved in the events are almost all restricted to the same borough and to very few neighbourhoods. Indeed, for 97% of events, at least 90% of the tweets are posted from the same borough ($F^e \geq 0.90$), and for half (49%) of the events, at least 90% of the tweets originate from a single neighbourhood ($F^e \geq 0.90$). However, at the POI level, tweets are more diffuse. Only 70% of events have at least half of their tweets posted from a single POI ($F^e \geq 0.50$); more generally, with the distribution being nearly linear, the focus values seem to be uniformly distributed.

---

[3]Dataset is available at https://doi.org/10.6084/m9.figshare.c.4089605

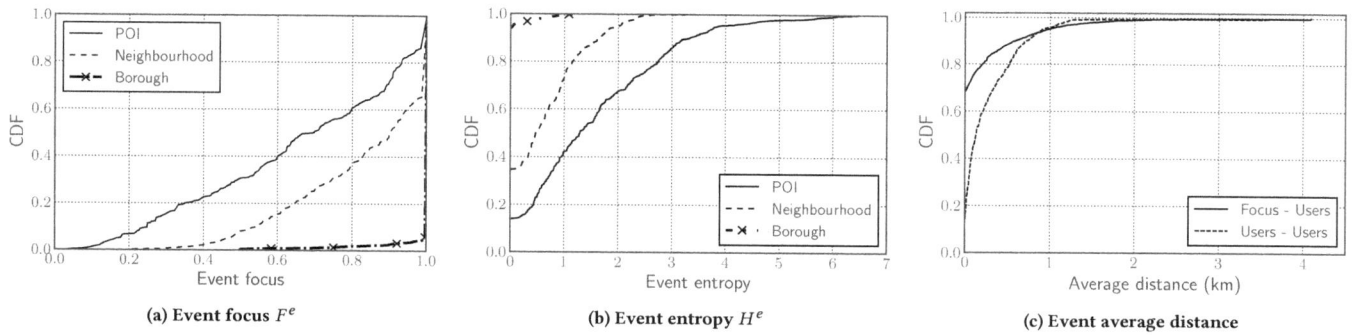

Figure 1: Cumulative Distribution Function (CDF) of event focus, entropy and average distance.

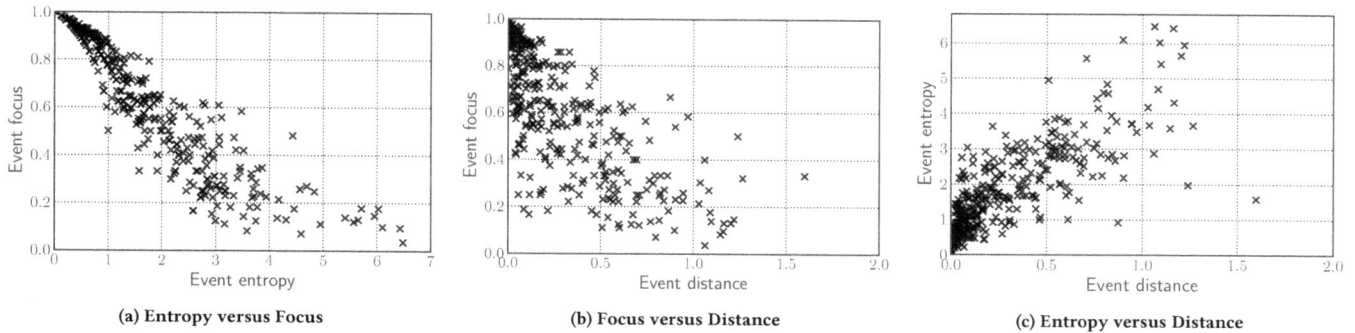

Figure 2: Correlation between Focus, Entropy and Distance at POI level.

Beyond the focus, we analyse the event propagation across locations. To do so, we examine the event entropy values, H^e, which are plotted in Figure 1(b). As can be observed, events are mostly limited to a single neighbourhood (75%) or borough (99%). At the POI level, approximately 42% of the events mainly involve a single POI ($H^e < 1$). Thus, the majority of small-scale events (53%) involves from 2 to 16 POIs, ($1 \leq H^e \leq 4$). This observation confirms our previous result about the spatial narrowness of the users.

So far, we used focus and entropy metrics to provide insights into event epicentres and propagation trends. However, no clues are provided about the geographic area over which events propagate. To fill this gap, we compute for each event both the user-user distance and the user-focus distance using the standard Haversine distance tailored for longitude-latitude coordinates[4]. Figure 1(c) reports the cumulative distribution of the average distance values w.r.t user-user distance (dashed line) and focus-user distance (solid line). Looking at the user-user average distances, we can see that 80% of the events have an average distance of less than 500 metres. Thus, users' locations are mostly very close to one another which confirms the narrowness of the influence areas of small-scale events. From the examination of the focus-user distance values, we can note that 88.3% of tweets are posted less than 500 metres from the focus, and only 4.85% are posted from more than 1,000 metres away. To sum up, the further away from the focus users are, the fewer

posted tweets there are. This suggests that most of users who post event tweets *gravitate* around the geographical focus.

We finally analyse the potential relationships between the event geographical influence which is represented by the focus, the event propagation, which is represented by the entropy and the spatial proximity of users, represented by the distance. Building on previous results that indicated that event dispersion over POI is more important, we plotted the correlations between those measures w.r.t POI. Figure 2 reports the pairwise correlations between these metrics which were computed using the Pearson coefficient. Figure 2(a) shows a strong negative correlation (-0.92) between entropy and focus as can be expected from the previous observations about the narrowness of the event-related area around the focus. Turning our attention to the correlations between focus and distance (Figure 2(b)) and between entropy and distance (Figure 2(c)), we note that when the distance between users increases, the intensity of the focus decreases, which leads to a negative correlation (-0.64), and the entropy increases, which leads to a positive correlation (0.69). In summary, the more scattered an event is, the less the users concentrate around a single POI, and the more tweets are propagated over several locations.

4.2 Spatio-temporal dynamic trends (RQ2)

Here, we cross the spatial and temporal perspectives with the aim of investigating the evolving spatial properties of events across their lifetimes. Our practical objective is to provide some insights into how quickly and how long small-scale events propagate. To achieve

---

[4]http://www.movable-type.co.uk/scripts/latlong.html

Table 3: Ratio of events w.r.t their duration.

Duration	Percentage
0 – 3 h	6.59%
3 – 6 h	66.83%
6 – 9 h	20.00%
9 + h	6.58%

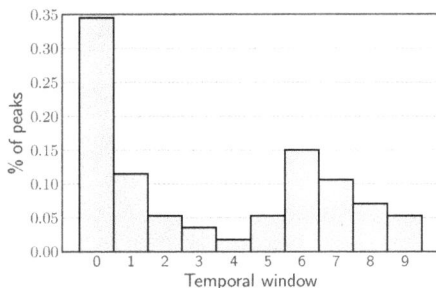

Figure 3: Ratio of peak occurrence in non-stationary events.

this objective, first we focus on the study of event temporalities to investigate the presence vs. absence of differences in event lifetimes and then cross the spatial and temporal dimensions to understand the event propagation trend.

4.2.1 Analysis of event temporalities. Our aim here is to analyse the temporal evolution of events. Accordingly, we first identify the relevant temporal window to be used in the study. Based on the average duration of events ($\sim 5\,h$) and standard deviation ($\sim 2\,h$), we split the events into intervals of 3h durations, as shown in Table 3. The results show that most events (66.83%) last between 3h and 6h and that very few are short (6.59%) or very long (6.58%). By cross-looking at the event size -in terms of number of posted tweets- per range of duration, we found a moderate positive correlation (Pearson coefficient correlation = 0.613). This suggests that tweet publications during an event have the same trend as the event does.

To gain a clear understanding of this observation, we split each event into 10 windows of equal-size and then, for each window, computed the number of tweets that were posted during the temporal interval. We studied the stationarity of the resulting time series using the Kwiatkowski Phillips Schmidt Shin (KPSS) test [17]. We found that only 28% of events are non-stationary ($p < 0.05$) which suggests the presence of peaks. For those non-stationary temporal series, we further determined the temporal windows within which the peaks occur (Figure 3). We can see that approximately 35% of the *candidate peaks* (which represent $\sim 9\%$ of the overall events) appear at the *birth* of the event. This observation seems to be quite obvious because the latter is mechanically used to detect the event itself. To check this feeling, we computed the statistical differences in the propagation trends of events with peaks and those without peaks using focus, entropy and location-based feature values. We used the Welch's t-test [28] which does not assume equal population variance. Table 4 provides a summary of these feature

values and the associated standard statistical indicators. The significance of the difference between feature means as determined by the obtained *p-value* and the level of significance are respectively reported in the last two rows of Table 4. We can observe that no significant difference has been reported for each of the studied features. Combining all these observations about temporal users' tweet publication, we hypothesize that, unlike for global events, the notion of peaks does not really make sense for small-scale events. Thus we consider all the events at the same level of interest in the following spatio-temporal analysis.

Table 4: Comparison of events with peak vs. without peak.

Level POI	# Events	Focus	Entropy	Distance User - User	Distance Focus - User
Events with peak	113	0.65	1.78	0.313	0.201
Events without peak	297	0.66	1.52	0.271	0,169
t-test p-value	-	0.803	0.108	0.401	0.386
Test significance	-	=	=	=	=

4.2.2 Analysis of spatio-temporal event trends. Our objective at this stage is to understand the spatio-temporal dynamics of events. In light of our objective, we split the events into 10 windows of equal-size and calculate the average entropy, $H^e(t)$, and focus, $F^e(t)$, for each temporal window. The results are shown in Figure 4. Looking specifically first at the entropy, we observe at the neighbourhood level, the entropy slightly increases (from 0.31 to 0.64) which indicates that small-scale events do not really propagate through different neighbourhoods. Therefore, events remain confined within less than 2 neighbourhoods, on average. At the POI level, when the events begin, tweets are posted from a limited number of POIs (less than 2 POIs on average since $H^e(0) = 0.59$). Then, the events tend to quickly propagate to approximately 2 locations in the first half of the event duration ($H^e(5) = 1.13$), before stabilizing thereafter at approximately 3 POIs ($H^e(9) = 1.59$). To measure the impact of the entropy increase on the concentration of tweets that are published within the same location, we turn our attention to the evolution of the average geographical focus. At the beginning of an event (i.e., during the first temporal window), the focus values are high: 88% and 78% at the neighbourhood and POI levels respectively. They slightly decrease as the event unfolds and stabilizes

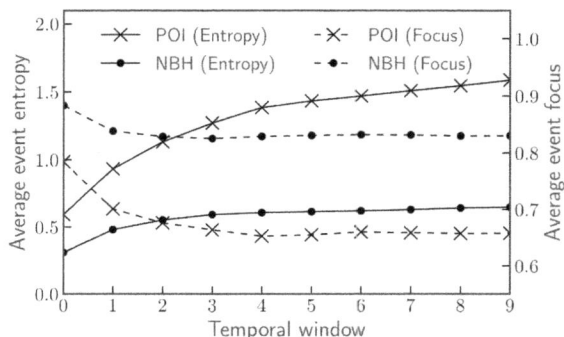

Figure 4: Average event entropy $H^e(t)$ and focus $F^e(t)$ evolution over time.

when reaching half of the event duration. Finally, 83% (resp. 66%) of tweets are posted from the focus at the neighbourhood (resp. POI) level. Moreover, we note that the coarser the level, the faster the focus values stabilize. Despite this drop in focus, the latter is still informative at any time of the event since it systematically attracts more than 50% of tweets ($F^e \geq 0.5$) regardless of the spatial level or the temporal window. Combining our observations about entropy and focus dynamics as highlighted from results, we conjecture that the more scattered an event is, the less a single location draws most of the users' attention.

4.3 Event types (RQ3)

Our practical objective here is twofold: (1) investigate wether specific types of events can emerge from the users' posts; (2) characterise the event types (if present) w.r.t topical and audience features.

4.3.1 Identification of event types. Building on previous results, we consider results at POI level only, and use the focus as a criterion for event categorization. More specifically, we split the events into 5 clusters according to their focus values and compute the average entropy and distance per event cluster and per temporal window as shown in Figure 5. Points labelled with 0 are associated with the first temporal window whereas points labelled with 9 are associated with the last window[5]. At a general glance, we can see that the clusters follow the same pattern: the distance values slightly increase during the event lifetime whereas the entropy quickly increases until half of the event duration and then remains stable. However a deeper analysis identifies three types of events from this result. The first type (solid line) consists of the 21% of events belonging to the 2 top clusters in Figure 5 that are associated with low focus values ($0 \leq F^e \leq 0.4$) and labelled as *Group A*. Events belonging to this type are spread between approximately 2 POIs from the beginning ($H^e(0) > 1.11$) and continue to propagate across 8 to 20 POIs during their lifetimes ($3.05 < H^e(9) < 4.34$). Moreover, they also spatially spread based on the increase in the average distance between users. These events are dynamic events that reach a wide audience since they propagate to both multiple locations and multiple geographic areas. The second type of events (dashed line) consists of the 37% of events belonging to the 2 median event clusters in Figure 5 that are associated with moderate focus values ($0.4 \leq F^e \leq 0.8$) and labelled as *Group B*. They globally remain concentrated within the same area, i.e., the distance slightly increases, but they spread over several locations. They arise in less than 2 POIs ($H^e(0) < 1$) and propagate quickly across 2 to 4 POIs ($1.14 < H^e(3) < 1.71$) for the first third of the event duration. For the remaining lifetimes, the events no longer propagate (i.e., their entropies remain stable). Finally, the third type of events (no line) consists of the 42% of events belonging to the cluster at the bottom in Figure 5 that have high focus values ($0.8 \leq F^e \leq 1$) and labelled as *Group C*. Events that fall within this group are very localized bringing people together in a single POI. Their entropies and distances do not change during the event.

4.3.2 Characterisation of event types. To gain better insights from the event types identified from the previous analysis, we performed a qualitative analysis at the topical level enhanced with a quantitative analysis of audience (in terms of number of users involved in events). Basically speaking, a topic is a common subject

[5]For the sake of readability, labels associated with intermediate windows are omitted.

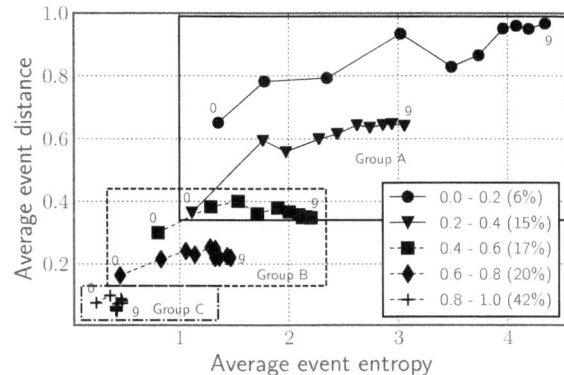

Figure 5: Evolution of the averaged distance and entropy values at POI level.

discussed in the Twitter stream. Given that the datasets used in our study are geo-tagged in New York City and that we are interested in event topics, we used the topic labels of the NY Times medium as already done in previous work on Twitter datasets [34]. The topic categories are *Arts, World, Business, Sports, Style, Technology and Science, Health, Education* and *Travel*. To perform the topic labelling task, we first built 3 event groups (*Group A, Group B, Group C*) by splitting the original event dataset per event type identified previously. Then we applied in each event group the Latent Dirichlet Allocation (LDA) model [8] to the meta-documents built from the tweets belonging to each event and then tuned the optimal number of topics using the perplexity measure [8]. We reached a minimal perplexity value of 27.6, 20.1 and 17.3 at 30 topics respectively for *Group A, Group B* and *Group C*. Each topic from the 90 automatically extracted LDA topics (30 topics extracted from each group) was labeled by 4 human assessors who were instructed to define topic labels w.r.t the NY Times topic categories if relevant and to assign to the '*Other*' topic category if no relevant NY topic category matched the LDA topic. Assessors' agreement was estimated using the Fleiss Kappa cœfficient and revealed a moderate agreement with value of 59.68%. A final topic category has been assigned to each event by applying the majority voting strategy. To have a picture of the group characteristics at the event level, we mapped the group topics to event topics by using the LDA inference algorithm [8] and then computed for each group the distribution of events and audience w.r.t each topic category, as shown in Figure 6. From a general view, we can see that apart from the '*Other*' category, the topics extracted from all the event groups are mostly related to *Arts* (resp. 48%, 28%, 28% for group A, B and C) and *Sports* (resp. 14%, 21%, 52% for group A, B and C). The observation about the relative high size of the '*Other*' category is consistent with previous work which have shown that Twitter streams give rise to specific topics that do not always fit with standard categorical topics [29, 34]. Thus, we further asked the annotators to assign Twitter labels as provided in [34] to the events belonging to the '*Other*' category. The annotation performed with a moderate Fleiss Kappa agreement of 56.87% showed that most of the topics belong to the '*Family and life*' category (resp. 55%, 56% and 97% events for Group A, B, and C) which is one of top hot topics addressed in Twitter including highly

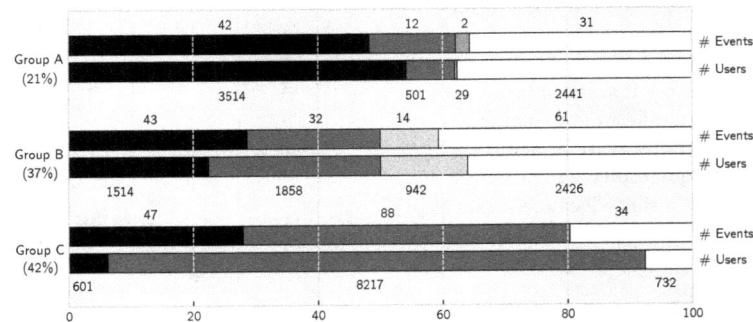

Figure 6: Distribution of number of users and number of tweets w.r.t event groups and topics.

personal and opinionated tweets. We can also observe from Figure 6 the following: (1) *Group A* is characterised with the lowest number of events (21%) and the highest average audience per event[6] (74). *Group A* seems to represent a set of few important events since they are moreover spatially spread as shown in the previous analysis. (2) In *Group B*, the average audience is less important (45) than in *Group A* but users are involved in a higher number of events (37%) and address more diverse topics including *Art*, *Sport*, *Politic* and *Other*. Combining this observation with the spatial analysis, we expect that events in this group are more likely to be less important events in wide-open spaces. (3) *Group C* includes the highest proportion of events (42%) with an average audience per event higher than in *Group B* (56, but still lower than in *Group A*), with however comparable topic diversity. Combining these observations with the spatial narrowness of users involved in this group of events suggests that *Group C* includes numerous and topically diverse micro-events with a low spatial impact. A qualitative annotation of a sample of events allowed us to confirm our expectations. For instance the *Global citizen festival* and the *Race of the cure* events which are well known periodic events in the US fall into the *Group A*, the *Tennis US Open* and the *NY Comic Con* fall into the Group B, while we found numerous private concerts and soccer matches in the *Group C*.

5   CONCLUSION AND IMPLICATIONS

In this paper, we analysed the spatio-temporal dynamics of small-scale events. Our primary objective was to determine the perimeters of their geographical social impacts at different levels of location granularity, and to gain understanding of their audience and the general trends of their propagation along their lifetimes. Our results suggest the following trends:

- In response to **RQ1**, the results show that the focus is a significant origin location from which users post their tweets, particularly at coarser levels of location granularity. Moreover, even if events propagate over several locations, they mostly reach narrow regions. Building on these findings, one relevant practical implication that we envision is the design of information seeking algorithms that are able to timely and automatically enlarge the event propagation diameter

---

[6]Ratio between total number of users and total number of events in the group.

by rooting event mentions to users who are located in narrowed regions. User's location, if not explicitly provided, could either be inferred using improved state-of-the art algorithms for tweet geo-location [15]. This would increase the situational awareness particularly during security incidents.

- In response to **RQ2**, we found that the temporal series of events are mostly stable which suggests the absence of significant peaks. We also found that evently timely evolve from diverse locations and quickly stabilize not significantly far from the focus. A relevant research opportunity that arises from this study is to examine these findings alongside previous research findings about large-scale event detection [6] to design novel algorithms that can jointly detect both weak and strong signals in Twitter streams considering appropriate spatio-temporal distribution and density of posts. Such general detectors can provide means for monitoring people' activities (eg., for public order maintenance purpose).

- In response to **RQ3**, we found that we can detect distinct types of events with evolutions that are significantly different according to audience, focus concentration and propagation distance trends over time. Based on these findings, the implications for further theoretical investigation is to develop models for predicting event type based on the event-related features. Event type prediction would be a prior step to the development of an automatic visual summarization method that would give a high-level picture of what is happening in a region.

Our study has some limitations. First, we only used the focus, entropy and distance metrics to report the analysis results. Although these measures are the primary metrics that are used for the spatio-temporal analysis of events, they are still insufficient for revealing other relevant facets such as propagation rate. Second, enlarging the spatio-temporal scope of our study to other cities and during different periods might give better insights about the generalisability of our findings. This investigation is planned for future work.

ACKNOWLEDGMENTS

This research was supported by IRIT and ATOS research program under ANRT CIFRE grant agreement.

REFERENCES

[1] Hamed Abdelhaq, Christian Sengstock, and Michael Gertz. 2013. Eventweet: Online localized event detection from twitter. *PVLDB Endowment* 6, 12 (2013), 1326–1329.
[2] Charuc C. Aggarwal and Karthik Subbian. 2012. Event Detection in Social Streams. In *Proceedings of the 2012 SIAM International Conference on Data Mining (SDM'12)*. SIAM, 624–635.
[3] Paolo Arcaini, Gloria Bordogna, Dino Ienco, and Simone Sterlacchini. 2016. User-driven geo-temporal density-based exploration of periodic and not periodic events reported in social networks. *Information Sciences* 340-341 (2016), 122 – 143.
[4] Sebastien Ardon, Amitabha Bagchi, Anirban Mahanti, Amit Ruhela, Aaditeshwar Seth, Rudra Mohan Tripathy, and Sipat Triukose. 2013. Spatio-temporal and Events Based Analysis of Topic Popularity in Twitter. In *The 22nd ACM International Conference on Information and Knowledge Management (CIKM '13)*. ACM, 219–228.
[5] Sitaram Asur and Bernardo A. Huberman. 2010. Predicting the Future with Social Media. In *Proceedings of the 2010 IEEE/WIC/ACM International Conference on Web Intelligence and Intelligent Agent Technology (WI-IAT '10)*. IEEE, 492–499.
[6] Farzindar Atefeh and Wael Khreich. 2015. A survey of techniques for event detection in twitter. *Computational Intelligence* 31, 1 (2015), 132–164.
[7] Hila Becker, Mor Naaman, and Luis Gravano. 2011. Beyond Trending Topics: Real-World Event Identification on Twitter.. In *Proceedings of the Fifth International Conference on Weblogs and Social Media (ICWSM'11)*. AAAI, 438–441.
[8] David M. Blei, Andrew Y. Ng, and Michael I. Jordan. JMLR'03. Latent Dirichlet Allocation. *Journal of Machine Learning Research* 3 (JMLR'03), 993–1022.
[9] Anders Brodersen, Salvatore Scellato, and Mirjam Wattenhofer. 2012. YouTube Around the World: Geographic Popularity of Videos. In *Proceedings of the 21st World Wide Web Conference 2012 (WWW'12)*. ACM, 241–250.
[10] Zhiyuan Cheng, James Caverlee, and Kyumin Lee. 2010. You Are Where You Tweet: A Content-based Approach to Geo-locating Twitter Users. In *Proceedings of the 19th ACM Conference on Information and Knowledge Management (CIKM '10)*. ACM, 759–768.
[11] Gabriel Pui Cheong Fung, Jeffrey Xu Yu, Philip S. Yu, and Hongjun Lu. 2005. Parameter Free Bursty Events Detection in Text Streams. In *Proceedings of the 31st International Conference on Very Large Data Bases (VLDB '05)*. ACM, 181–192.
[12] Bo Hu and Martin Ester. 2013. Spatial Topic Modeling in Online Social Media for Location Recommendation. In *Seventh ACM Conference on Recommender Systems (RecSys '13)*. ACM, 25–32.
[13] Allan James, Carbonell Jaime, Doddington George, Yamron Jonathan, and Yang Yiming. 1998. Topic Detection and Tracking Pilot Study Final Report. In *DARPA Broadcast News Transcription and Under standing Workshop (BNTUW '98)*. Morgan Kaufmann Publishers, 194–218.
[14] Krishna Y. Kamath, James Caverlee, Kyumin Lee, and Zhiyuan Cheng. 2013. Spatio-temporal Dynamics of Online Memes: A Study of Geo-tagged Tweets. In *The 22nd International World Wide Web Conference (WWW '13)*. ACM, 667–678.
[15] Sheila Kinsella, Vanessa Murdock, and Neil O'Hare. 2011. "I'M Eating a Sandwich in Glasgow": Modeling Locations with Tweets. In *Proceedings of the 3rd International CIKM Workshop on Search and Mining User-Generated Contents (SMUC '11)*. ACM, 61–68.
[16] Efthymios Kouloumpis, Theresa Wilson, and Johanna D Moore. 2011. Twitter sentiment analysis: The good the bad and the omg! *Icwsm* 11 (2011), 538–541.
[17] Denis Kwiatkowski, Peter C.B. Phillips, Peter Schmidt, and Yongcheol Shin. 1992. Testing the null hypothesis of stationarity against the alternative of a unit root: How sure are we that economic time series have a unit root? *Journal of Econometrics* 54, 1 (1992), 159 – 178.
[18] Kathy Lee, Ankit Agrawal, and Alok Choudhary. 2013. Real-time Disease Surveillance Using Twitter Data: Demonstration on Flu and Cancer. In *The 19th ACM SIGKDD International Conference on Knowledge Discovery and Data Mining (KDD '13)*. ACM, 1474–1477.
[19] Deepa Mallela, Dirk Ahlers, and Maria Soledad Pera. 2017. Mining Twitter Features for Event Summarization and Rating. In *Proceedings of the International Conference on Web Intelligence (WI '17)*. ACM, 615–622.
[20] Andrew J. McMinn, Yashar Moshfeghi, and Joemon M. Jose. 2013. Building a Large-scale Corpus for Evaluating Event Detection on Twitter. In *The 22nd ACM International Conference on Information and Knowledge Management (CIKM '13)*. ACM, 409–418.
[21] Stuart E Middleton, Lee Middleton, and Stefano Modafferi. 2014. Real-time crisis mapping of natural disasters using social media. *IEEE Intelligent Systems* 29, 2 (2014), 9–17.
[22] Alan Mislove, Bimal Viswanath, Krishna P. Gummadi, and Peter Druschel. 2010. You Are Who You Know: Inferring User Profiles in Online Social Networks. In *Proceedings of the Third International Conference on Web Search and Web Data Mining (WSDM '10)*. ACM, 251–260.
[23] Takeshi Sakaki, Makoto Okazaki, and Yutaka Matsuo. 2010. Earthquake Shakes Twitter Users: Real-time Event Detection by Social Sensors. In *Proceedings of the 19th International Conference on World Wide Web (WWW '10)*. ACM, 851–860.
[24] Axel Schulz, Eneldo Loza Mencía, and Benedikt Schmidt. 2016. A Rapid-prototyping Framework for Extracting Small-scale Incident-related Information in Microblogs. *Information Systems* 57, C (2016), 88–110.
[25] Axel Schulz and Petar Ristoski. 2013. The Car that Hit The Burning House: Understanding Small Scale Incident Related Information in Microblogs. In *Proceedings of the Seventh International Conference on Weblogs and Social Media (ICWSM'13)*. AAAI, 11–14.
[26] Axel Schulz, Benedikt Schmidt, and Thorsten Strufe. 2015. Small-Scale Incident Detection Based on Microposts. In *Proceedings of the 26th ACM Conference on Hypertext & Social Media (HT'15)*. ACM, 3–12.
[27] Sarah Vieweg, Amanda L. Hughes, Kate Starbird, and Leysia Palen. 2010. Microblogging During Two Natural Hazards Events: What Twitter May Contribute to Situational Awareness. In *Proceedings of the 28th International Conference on Human Factors in Computing Systems (CHI '10)*. ACM, 1079–1088.
[28] B. L. Welch. 1947. The Generalization of Student's Problem When Several Different Population Variance Are Involved. *Biometrika* 34, 1-2 (1947), 28–35.
[29] David Wilkinson and Mike Thelwall. JASIST'12. Trending Twitter topics in English: An international comparison. *Journal of the American Society for Information Science and Technology* (JASIST'12), 1631–1646.
[30] Sarita Yardi and danah boyd. 2010. Tweeting from the Town Square: Measuring Geographic Local Networks. In *Proceedings of the Fourth International Conference on Weblogs and Social Media (ICWSM'10)*. AAAI, 194–201.
[31] Chao Zhang, Liyuan Liu, Dongming Lei, Quan Yuan, Honglei Zhuang, Tim Hanratty, and Jiawei Han. 2017. TrioVecEvent: Embedding-Based Online Local Event Detection in Geo-Tagged Tweet Streams. In *Proceedings of the 23rd ACM SIGKDD International Conference on Knowledge Discovery and Data Mining (KDD '17)*. 595–604.
[32] Chao Zhang, Guangyu Zhou, Quan Yuan, Honglei Zhuang, Yu Zheng, Lance Kaplan, Shaowen Wang, and Jiawei Han. 2016. GeoBurst: Real-Time Local Event Detection in Geo-Tagged Tweet Streams. In *Proceedings of the 39th International ACM SIGIR conference on Research and Development in Information Retrieval (SIGIR '16)*. ACM, 513–522.
[33] Kaiqi Zhao, Gao Cong, and Aixin Sun. 2016. Annotating Points of Interest with Geo-tagged Tweets. In *Proceedings of the 2016 ACM on Conference on Information and Knowledge Management (CIKM'16)*. ACM, 417–426.
[34] Wayne Xin Zhao, Jing Jiang, Jianshu Weng, Jing He, Ee-Peng Lim, Hongfei Yan, and Xiaoming Li. 2011. Comparing Twitter and Traditional Media Using Topic Models. In *Proceedings of the 33rd European Conference on Advances in Information Retrieval (ECIR'11)*. ACM, 338–349.

The Utility Problem of Web Content Popularity Prediction

Nuno Moniz
LIAAD - INESC Tec
University of Porto
Porto, Portugal
nmmoniz@inesctec.pt

Luís Torgo
Faculty of Computer Science
Dalhousie University
Halifax, Canada
ltorgo@dal.ca

ABSTRACT

The ability to generate and share content on social media platforms has changed the Internet. With the growing rate of content generation, efforts have been directed at making sense of such data. One of the most researched problem concerns predicting web content popularity. We argue that the evolution of state-of-the-art approaches has been optimized towards improving the predictability of average behaviour of data: items with low levels of popularity. We demonstrate this effect using a utility-based framework for evaluating numerical web content popularity prediction tasks, focusing on highly popular items. Additionally, it is demonstrated that gains in predictive and ranking ability of such type of cases can be obtained via naïve approaches, based on strategies to tackle imbalanced domains learning tasks.

KEYWORDS

Machine learning, Social networking sites, Social recommendation

ACM Reference format:
Nuno Moniz and Luís Torgo. 2018. The Utility Problem of Web Content Popularity Prediction. In *Proceedings of 29th ACM Conference on Hypertext and Social Media, Baltimore, MD, USA, July 9–12, 2018 (HT '18)*, 5 pages.
https://doi.org/10.1145/3209542.3209573

1 INTRODUCTION

One of the most challenging tasks involving web content concerns accurately forecasting the degree of interest shown by users [14], i.e. popularity. Popularity is described by heavy-tail distributions [14], which would not be a problem if under-represented items were not relevant. However, prediction tasks in this domain are very concerned with accurately predicting such cases, i.e. with high popularity levels, since they probably should be suggested to users.

This non-standard learning scenario of data imbalance and non-uniform domain preferences is commonly described as imbalanced domain learning [3]. Solving such tasks is an interesting and open issue, considered to be one of the most important problems in machine learning and data mining [18]. However, the majority of previous work concerning prediction of web content popularity

has addressed this problem as a standard learning task, assuming balanced distributions and/or uniform domain preferences.

This paper provides a study of numerical web content popularity prediction approaches and their ability to forecast and rank highly popular web content. This study includes the analysis of 5 previously proposed prediction approaches, and 2 new proposals based on strategies to tackle imbalanced domain learning tasks. Experimental evaluation efforts are focused on the online news type of social media data.

2 WEB CONTENT POPULARITY

Web content popularity prediction tasks focus on two separate settings: *i) a priori*, and *ii) a posteriori* prediction. The first concerns the prediction of items' popularity before or upon their publication, and the second after they are published. Data mining tasks used to formalize this prediction problem include classification [12], regression [2], time series forecasting [10], and others. Tatar et al. [14] provide a survey on web content popularity prediction. This paper is based on the analysis of approaches to the problem of *a posteriori* and numerical prediction of web content popularity, i.e. regression or time series forecasting tasks.

Szabo and Huberman [13] propose two statistics-based approaches, the constant scaling and the log-linear approaches. The constant scaling approach uses a time-dependent factor similar to a growth factor, which is multiplied by the popularity of all the items chosen for prediction. The log-linear approach explores the linear relationship of popularity values at a given timeslice (sampling intervals) and their final value, using logarithmic transformations. Pinto et al. [13] propose two approaches focusing on the dynamics of items' popularity. The first is a multivariate linear regression model, denoting each timeslice as a popularity *delta*, i.e. the difference in popularity between consecutive intervals. The second extends the multivariate linear model by accounting for the similarity of cases, using Radial Basis Functions. Tatar et al. [15] and Asur and Huberman [2] rely on linear models to learn the dynamics of popularity. The former proposes a direct approach, where the model represents the relation between the popularity of items in a training set w.r.t. a given timeslice, and their final popularity. The latter extends this direct approach by including features related to sentiment analysis.

3 PROBLEM DEFINITION

This work addresses two main tasks: *i)* identifying highly popular items by predicting its popularity, and *ii)* transforming this knowledge into rankings considering both recency and popularity.

The first task can be modelled as a non-standard regression problem (due to its focus on rare cases with extreme values). The unknown function $\hat{y}()$ we want to approximate performs the mapping between the popularity p_j^t of a given item n_j for a given alive-time t, and its final popularity, $p_j^{t_f}$. The alive-time t of the story will be henceforth called a timeslice, and the final timeslice is represented by t_f (*i.e.* two days). We set the duration of each timeslice to 20 minutes (*e.g.* timeslice 1 represents 0-20 minutes of alive-time, timeslice 6 represents 100-120 minutes).

The second task consists in generating rankings using the predictions of the approaches to the previous task and evaluating them. The objective of this second task is to confirm that it is possible to generate timely suggestions of highly popular web content.

3.1 Utility-Based Regression

Unlike standard learning tasks, web content popularity prediction may concern a scenario where users assign different levels of relevance to distinct types of cases. To enable tasks of evaluation, comparison and model selection in such scenarios, Ribeiro [11] proposes the utility-based regression framework, which is based on two concepts: *i)* relevance functions, and *ii)* utility surfaces.

Ribeiro [11] proposes the use of relevance functions to assign relevance scores to each of the values in a given target variable, concerning a given domain: $\phi(Y) : \mathcal{Y} \rightarrow [0, 1]$. This is carried out via interpolation of relevance using Piecewise Cubic Hermite Interpolating Polynomials [5] (*pchip*) method. The interpolation uses control points generated via box plot statistics [17]: the median of Y receives a relevance score of 0; the lower and upper whiskers a relevance score of 1; and all outliers a relevance score of 1. In addition, users may establish relevance thresholds, t_R, representing a boundary for the user-definition of relevant values.

Based on the concept of relevance functions, Ribeiro [11] defines the principle of utility for imbalanced domain regression tasks. Unlike standard regression tasks, where utility is considered a function of the error of predictions, utility-based regression considers utility as a function of such errors and the relevance of both predicted ($\hat{y}$) and true (y) values, bounded by -1 and 1. Using this process, one is able to obtain utility functions for continuous domains, also denoted as *utility surfaces*. In this paper, utility surfaces are generated via a rule-based approach proposed by Moniz et al. [8].

4 PREDICTION MODELS

In *a posteriori* prediction tasks it is commonly assumed that one possesses a set of cases C describing the dynamics of their popularity evolution (training set), and that the objective is to predict the final popularity values of a second set of cases P, for which the evolution of popularity is known until a given timeslice t (test set).

In the first moments, it may be difficult to distinguish which observations relate to cases that will obtain a high level of popularity. Given the focus of standard learning algorithms in optimizing models towards the average behaviour of the data, these will only be able to detect relevant cases that obtain high levels of popularity in a short amount of time. This problem can be tackled if learning algorithms are altered to be more sensitive to such cases early on. In this paper, we present two algorithm-based methods [3] of altered kernel regression and k-nearest neighbour approaches, using a biased case selection procedure: instead of basing the prediction of cases on overall statistics (e.g. the average slope), the objective of the proposals is to implement this process locally.

4.1 Kernel-Based Approach

The first proposal is based on the concept of kernel regression [9]. The objective is to capture the local popularity dynamics of items using locally weighted averages. This relates to the procedure of case selection, where distinct training cases should provide a differentiated contribution to the prediction of future values, depending on their distance w.r.t. the target case. To achieve this outcome, a distance factor is introduced in the training case selection process. This allows the selection of cases that have similar levels of popularity w.r.t. the target prediction case, at a given timeslice t. Concerning the definition of the interval, this proposal uses the interquartile range (IQR). Given that the distribution of popularity may vary in consecutive timeslices, the value of IQR is calculated for each timeslice t and is denoted as IQR_t, where $t \in (1, \cdots, t_f)$.

Given a case for prediction p_j in timeslice t, the kernel-based approach formulates the predictive problem as $\hat{p}_j^{t_f} = f(p_j^t, C^t)$, where $\hat{p}_j^{t_f}$ is the predicted value of popularity for the item p_j in the final timeslice t_f, p_j^t is the level of popularity at the reference time (time of prediction), and C^t represent the popularity values of cases from a given training set C in timeslice t. By using the value of the target case at the reference time (p_j^t), a procedure is applied to obtain a set of indexes A_j^t representing cases that are within the interval of IQR_t to target case p_j^t.

Then, the weight of cases W_a^t is defined as the inverse distance between the popularity at timeslice t for each case c_a^t where $a \in A_j^t$, and the popularity value of the target case p_j^t. These values are normalized into a $[0, 1]$ scale. Using the train cases considered similar to the target case, and their calculated weights, the prediction of the popularity value at the final timeslice t_f for a given case p_j^t is

carried out as $\hat{p}_j^{t_f} = \frac{\sum_a w_a \times c_a^{t_f}}{\sum_a w_a}, a \in A, c \in C^t$

4.2 kNN-Based Approach

The second proposal is based on the k-nearest neighbour algorithm [1] (*k*NN). Typical settings of the method operate by deriving a subset of k train cases presenting the smallest distance to the target case. Using this subset, the predictions are given by the average of their target values. In comparison to the original kNN algorithm, instead of providing a fixed number of neighbours k, in the proposed kNN-based approach this value is given by the number of cases in a training set that, at timeslice t, have a similar popularity value w.r.t. the target case, i.e. within IQR_t distance.

The formalization of the kNN-based approach is very similar to the formalization of the kernel-based approach. The main difference between these two approaches is the non-use of weights. Disregarding the influence of such factors, the formalization of the kNN-based approach is given by the following, concerning a given target case p_j and the prediction of its final popularity value w.r.t. to the reference timeslice t:

$$\hat{p}_j^{t_f} = \frac{\sum_a c_a^{t_f}}{|A_j^t|}, a \in A_j^t, c \in C^T. \qquad (1)$$

5 EXPERIMENTAL STUDY

The objectives of this study are *i)* to assess the predictive ability of proposals on web content popularity prediction concerning highly popular items; *ii)* to compare the results with the common evaluation approach in previous work, where it is implied that users consider each item equally important; and *iii)* to draw conclusions on which formalization provides the best outcome in terms of the rankings generated by the prediction models, in a timely manner. We use a recent data set [7] (available in UCI) concerning online news and its popularity in social media platforms. It contains 93,239 news items from a timespan of 8 months, concerning four topics: *economy, microsoft, obama* and *palestine*. News items were obtained from top-100 rankings (20 minutes interval) in Google News and Yahoo! News, and popularity observations concern social media platforms Facebook, Google+ and LinkedIn.

5.1 Methods

Baseline methods used in the experimental evaluation of prediction models include the constant scaling (*ConstScale*) and log-linear (*Linear-log*) proposals made by Szabo and Huberman [13], the multivariate linear regression (*ML*) proposal and its extension using features by the application of Radial Basis Function (*MRBF*), by Pinto et al. [10], and the linear regression approach using sentiment analysis features (*LM*) proposed by Asur and Huberman [2]. These proposals are described in Section 2. Concerning the *LM* model, the authors use a distribution parameter as a predictive feature, which in this paper is defined as the accumulated popularity of the web content item, until the moment of prediction.

Concerning baselines used for evaluating the ranking task, the effectiveness of the proposed prediction models in generating timely news rankings is compared to three baseline strategies: *Time*, where news are ranked by time of publication with the most recent first; *Live*, where news are ranked by the amount of popularity accumulated until the reference time (time of prediction); and *Source*, where news are ranked by the average final popularity of news items from their news outlet, available in the train set.

5.2 Evaluation Methodology

The evaluation of the predictive ability of models in this experimental study is based in two metrics: *i)* the root mean squared error and *ii)* a utility-based F-Score [11]. The root mean squared error (*RMSE*) is a standard evaluation metric accounting for squared prediction errors, assuming uniform domain preferences. The utility-based F-Score (F_1^u) is based on the precision/recall evaluation framework commonly used in classification tasks. Based on the previously detailed concepts of relevance and utility (Section 3.1), we resort to the proposal presented by Moniz et al. [8] for regression tasks with imbalanced domains. In this paper t_R is set to 0.9, denoting approximately 10% of the items as highly relevant, in each topic of the data set. To evaluate the ranking task, the Normalized Discounted Cumulative Gain [6] (*NDCG@k*) metric is used and k is defined as 10 (*NDCG@10*). For metric estimations, the Monte Carlo simulation [16] method is used with 20 repetitions, 50% of cases as training set and the subsequent 25% as test set.

5.3 Predictive Modelling Results

This section provides evidence to address two of the objectives of this study: *i)* to assess the predictive ability of previousprediction approaches concerning highly popular web content, and *ii)* to compare such results with the common evaluation approach (e.g. *RMSE*). This study focuses on the predictive ability of approaches in the first 3 timeslices, i.e. first hour after publication. Results from different prediction models are compared according to the guidelines provided by Demšar [4], and illustrated in Figures 1 and 2 concerning the *RMSE* and the F_1^u metrics, respectively.

Results obtained with the *RMSE* metric show that the best predictive approaches for the first 3 timeslices are *ConstScale*, *ML* and *knn* models, and the proposed algorithm-based method *knn* is capable of obtaining good results, presenting one of the best overall predictive approaches. As for the F_1^u metric, results show an advantage of the proposed methods w.r.t. previous work. This confirms the intuition motivating our proposals, concerning the issues of previous approaches and the influence of the imbalanced distribution of web content popularity. We should note that although *Linear-log* models show poor predictive performance concerning *RMSE*, they present a considerable advantage to other methods in predicting highly popular content. Conversely, the best approach according to the *RMSE* metric, *ConstScale*, presents the worst outcome w.r.t. F_1^u.

Given the outcome of the experiments and the objectives for this evaluation, results show that regarding the prediction of highly popular items shortly after publication: *i)* the proposed algorithm-based methods present the best overall results; and *ii)* the optimization of web content popularity prediction models using standard evaluation metrics can lead to an over-estimation of their ability in predicting highly popular web content.

5.4 Ranking Results

This section presents the results concerning the second task formalized in Section 3, and the third objective of this study: which formalization of the predictive task provides the best outcome in terms of the rankings generated by prediction models, in a timely manner. Unlike the previous experiment, train and test cases are the top-100 item rankings from Google News and Yahoo! News. Prediction models use news items data included in rankings of the train set, and predictions report to items from rankings in a test set. News items in the test set are not used to build prediction models, to avoid overfitting. Estimations of the *NDCG@10* metric are compared according to the guidelines by Demšar [4], illustrated in Figure 3.

Results show that the algorithm-level methods proposed in this paper are capable of obtaining an advantage over previous proposals to the problem of web content popularity prediction. Also, results are coherent in terms of the models providing the worst ranking outcome. These include the *ML*, *MRBF* models, and the *Time* baseline (ranks items by recency). However, discrepancies between results when using data from Google News or Yahoo! News should be studied further. For example, while the *Linear-log* approach is evaluated as one of the top-performers concerning Google News rankings data, this is not true for Yahoo! News rankings, and the inverse situation is reported regarding the *LM* model. Also, results show that the baseline *Live* provides an advantage

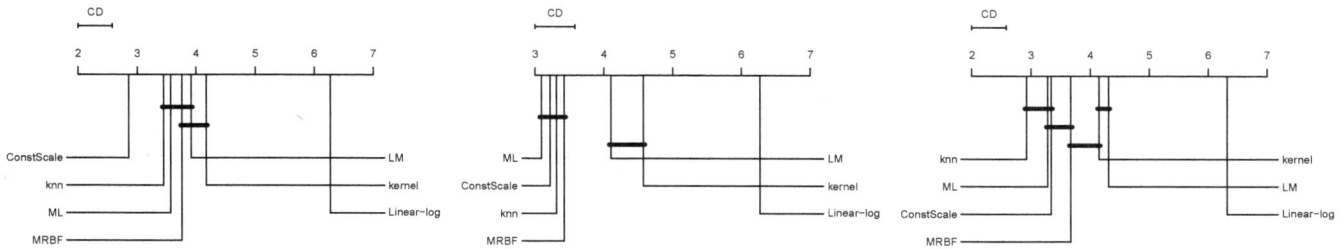

Figure 1: Critical difference diagram concerning the results of the evaluation metric *RMSE* for models in *a posteriori* prediction in the first (left), second (center) and third (right) timeslices.

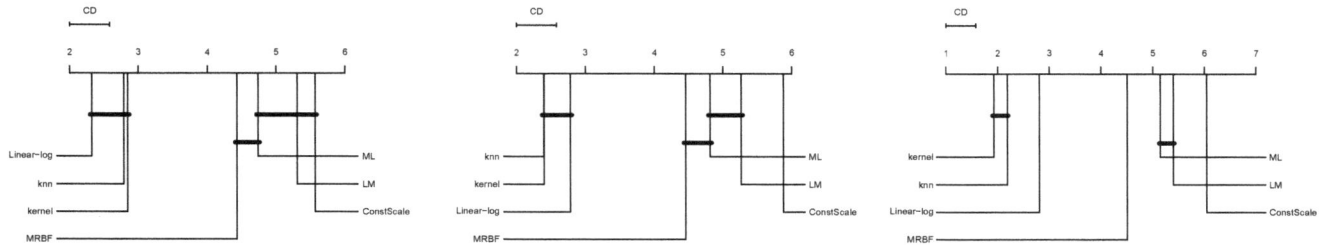

Figure 2: Critical difference diagram concerning the results of the evaluation metric F_1^u for models in *a posteriori* prediction in the first (left), second (center) and third (right) timeslices.

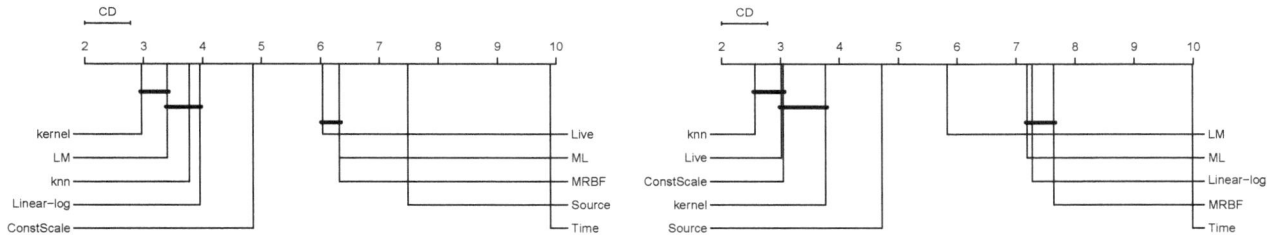

Figure 3: Critical difference diagram concerning rankings generated by all prediction approaches and baselines, using Google News (left) and Yahoo! News (right) rankings, according to the *NDCG@10* evaluation metric.

over all the approaches tested when using Yahoo! News data, with the exception of the proposed *knn* approach.

6 CONCLUSIONS AND OUTLOOK

In this paper, an experimental study on the ability of web content popularity prediction approaches in forecasting and ranking highly popular items is presented. The objectives are *i)* to assess the ability of web content popularity prediction models in forecasting highly popular web content, *ii)* to compare such results with the standard evaluation approach used in previous work, and *iii)* to conclude which formalization provides the best outcome concerning the generation of timely rankings. Results show that previous proposals which obtain the best results in predicting the average behaviour of the data are also those with the worst performance in predicting the popularity of highly relevant cases, concerning the first 3 timeslices, i.e. first hour after publication. Also, it shows that the predictive

approaches proposed in this paper provide the best predictive ability concerning the target cases. Rankings generated by the outcome of prediction models also confirm that the proposed approaches obtain the best results in terms of a timely suggestion of highly popular content.

For the sake of reproducible science, code and data necessary to replicate our results are available in https://tinyurl.com/y6wejrbm.

ACKNOWLEDGMENTS

This work is financed by the ERDF – European Regional Development Fund through the COMPETE 2020 Programme within project POCI-01-0145-FEDER-006961, and by National Funds through the FCT – Fundação para a Ciência e a Tecnologia (Portuguese Foundation for Science and Technology) as part of project UID/EEA/50014/2013.

REFERENCES

[1] N. S. Altman. 1992. An Introduction to Kernel and Nearest-Neighbor Nonparametric Regression. *The American Statistician* 46, 3 (1992), 175–185.

[2] S. Asur and B. A. Huberman. 2010. Predicting the Future with Social Media. In *Proc. of 2010 Int. Conf. on Web Intelligence and Intelligent Agent Technology (WI-IAT '10)*. IEEE Computer Society, Washington, DC, USA, 492–499.

[3] P. Branco, L. Torgo, and R. P. Ribeiro. 2016. A Survey of Predictive Modeling on Imbalanced Domains. *ACM Comput. Surv.* 49, 2, Article 31 (Aug. 2016).

[4] J. Demšar. 2006. Statistical comparisons of classifiers over multiple data sets. *JMLR* 7, Jan (2006), 1–30.

[5] R. L. Dougherty, A. Edelman, and J. M. Hyman. 1989. Nonnegativity-, Monotonicity-, or Convexity-Preserving Cubic and Quintic Hermite Interpolation. *Math. Comp.* 52, 186 (1989), 471–494. https://doi.org/10.2307/2008477

[6] K. Järvelin and J. Kekäläinen. 2000. IR Evaluation Methods for Retrieving Highly Relevant Documents. In *Proc. of the 23rd ACM SIGIR*. 41–48. https://doi.org/10.1145/345508.345545

[7] N. Moniz and L. Torgo. 2018. Multi-Source Social Feedback of Online News Feeds. *CoRR* abs/1801.07055 (2018).

[8] N. Moniz, L. Torgo, M. Eirinaki, and P. Branco. 2017. A Framework for Recommendation of Highly Popular News Lacking Social Feedback. *New Generation Computing* 35, 4 (2017), 417–450.

[9] E. A. Nadaraya. 1964. On Estimating Regression. *Theory of Probability & Its Applications* 9, 1 (1964), 141–142.

[10] H. Pinto, J. M. Almeida, and M. A. Gonçalves. 2013. Using Early View Patterns to Predict the Popularity of Youtube Videos. In *Proc. of 6th ACM Int. Conf. WSDM (WSDM '13)*. ACM, New York, NY, USA, 365–374.

[11] R. Ribeiro. 2011. *Utility-based Regression*. Ph.D. Dissertation. Dep. Computer Science, Faculty of Sciences - University of Porto.

[12] B. Shulman, A. Sharma, and D. Cosley. 2016. Predictability of Popularity: Gaps between Prediction and Understanding. In *Proc. of 10th ICWSM*. AAAI, Cologne, Germany, 348–357.

[13] G. Szabo and B. A. Huberman. 2010. Predicting the Popularity of Online Content. *Commun. ACM* 53, 8 (Aug. 2010), 80–88.

[14] A. Tatar, M. D. de Amorim, S. Fdida, and P. Antoniadis. 2014. A survey on predicting the popularity of web content. *JIAS* 5, 1 (2014), 1–20.

[15] A. Tatar, J. Leguay, P. Antoniadis, A. Limbourg, M. D. de Amorim, and S. Fdida. 2011. Predicting the Popularity of Online Articles Based on User Comments. In *Proc. of 2011 WIMS (WIMS '11)*. ACM, New York, NY, USA, Article 67.

[16] L. Torgo. 2014. An Infra-Structure for Performance Estimation and Experimental Comparison of Predictive Models in R. *CoRR* abs/1412.0436 (2014), 1–40.

[17] J. W. Tukey. 1977. *Exploratory Data Analysis*. Addison-Wesley, Princeton, NJ.

[18] Q. Yang and X. Wu. 2006. 10 challenging problems in data mining research. *Int. J. of Inf. Tech. & Dec. Mak.* 05, 04 (2006), 597–604.

Know Thy Neighbors, and More!
Studying the Role of Context in Entity Recommendation

Sumit Bhatia
IBM Research AI
New Delhi, India
sumitbhatia@in.ibm.com

Harit Vishwakarma
IBM Research AI
Bangalore, India
harivish@in.ibm.com

ABSTRACT

Knowledge Graphs capture the semantic relations between real-world entities and can thus, allow end-users to explore different *aspects* of an entity of interest by traversing through the edges in the graph. Most of the state-of-the-art methods in entity recommendation are limited in the sense that they allow users to search only in the immediate neighborhood of the entity of interest. This is majorly due to efficiency reasons as the search space increases exponentially as we move further away from the entity of interest in the graph. Often, users perform the search task in the context of an information need and we investigate the role this *context* can play in overcoming the scalability issue and improving knowledge graph exploration. Intuitively, only a small subset of entities in the graph are relevant to a users' interest. We show how can we efficiently select this sub-set by utilizing contextual clues and using graph-theoretic measures to further re-rank this set to offer highly relevant graph exploration capabilities to end-users.

CCS CONCEPTS

• **Information systems** → **Probabilistic retrieval models**; **Retrieval tasks and goals**; *Web searching and information discovery*; *Content ranking*; *Personalization*; Enterprise information systems;

KEYWORDS

entity Search; entity recommendation; entity retrieval; contextual entity recommendation; contextual exploration; knowledge graph exploration; information discovery

ACM Reference Format:
Sumit Bhatia and Harit Vishwakarma. 2018. Know Thy Neighbors, and More! Studying the Role of Context in Entity Recommendation. In *HT '18: 29th ACM Conference on Hypertext and Social Media, July 9–12, 2018, Baltimore, MD, USA.* ACM, New York, NY, USA, 9 pages. https://doi.org/10.1145/3209542.3209548

1 INTRODUCTION

A large fraction of web search queries are entity-centric and contain at least one named entity mention such as names of places, persons, movies, etc. (estimates vary from 40% [27] to 60% [36]). Further,

users are often interested in knowing and exploring about a topic of interest rather than obtaining instant answers [12]. To achieve this goal, they perform more exploratory and investigative searches [29] that are often open-ended and gain a better understanding of the topic while interacting with the system [48]. In addition to web search, such entity-oriented exploration tasks are also common in enterprise and domain specific settings [10] such as finding entities related to an entity of interest [9], exploring relations between drugs and genes [19], or studying connections between different criminals and terrorists [42]. In such exploratory tasks, *context* plays a key role in determining the information to be presented to the user. For example, a user interested in knowing more about *Elon Musk* in context of *Tesla Motors* will be interested in a different set of entities than a user who is more interested in *SpaceX*, the space exploration company.

Most of the existing work on such entity-oriented search and exploration (covered in detail in Section 2) have studied entity search or recommendation in context of Web Search [11, 12] where the features derived from query logs and session statistics are used to recommend entities related to the input entity specified by the user; or in *ad-hoc* entity retrieval setting where the focus is on retrieving entities embedded in documents [7, 13, 17, 18]. Such methods rely solely on the textual information present in documents containing entity mentions where the information present is often ambiguous and unstructured and thus, it is harder to utilize the interactions between related entities present in different documents [30].

Recent advancements in semantic search technology have made structured knowledge bases such as DBPedia [5], Yago [44], etc. a critical component of modern information management systems. Many large scale knowledge graphs are often constructed automatically using machine-learned information extraction techniques [4, 15] and can thus also be used in domain specific applications such as finance [40], healthcare [34], cybersecurity [21]. In such knowledge graphs, nodes represent real world concepts or *entities* and their relationships with other such entities are represented as edges in the graph. This structured representation about real world concepts (entities) can help overcome the shortcomings of text-based methods for entity-oriented tasks. For example, in context of recommender systems, variants of personalized page ranks over user and item graphs have been shown to capture indirect relationships in the graph and thus, improving recommendation accuracy [24, 50]. However, one major shortcoming of such graph-based methods is scalability [30] as the number of entities to evaluate increases exponentially with the distance from the seed entity. Consequently, for typical knowledge graphs that contain millions of entities, most graph based methods only work in the immediate neighborhood of the input entity or at most up to one hop neighborhood [2, 3, 6, 25] ignoring the useful information present in the rest of the graph.

We posit that the *context* in which the user performs a search or exploration task can be utilized to overcome the shortcomings of existing graph based methods in terms of scalability. Specifically, we argue that the contextual information can be employed to increase the search space over the whole graph, instead of just the direct neighborhood of the input entity. If we can filter the entities of the graph by their relevance to the context, graph structure based approaches can then be efficiently used to re-rank this much smaller, yet highly relevant sub-set of the graph. To test this hypothesis, we focus on the problem of entity-oriented search over knowledge graphs where the user is interested in finding entities relevant to an input entity in context of an information need. For example, a user researching about the Turkish Warrior *Timur* might be interested in knowing entities (places, people, etc.) relevant to *Timur's conquest of Persia*. Thus, the user specifies *Timur* as the input entity, and *Timur's conquest of Persia* as the context and the system returns a list of relevant entities to the user.

We describe a probabilistic formulation that takes into account the contextual information of the entities and then combines it with graph structural features to produce a final list of entities ranked by their relevance to the input entity (Section 3). Experiments conducted using a knowledge graph created out of Wikipedia articles and queries selected from the Wikistream dataset (Section 4) showed that *incorporating contextual information does help* – we are able to find lot more relevant entities beyond the direct neighborhood of the input entity. Further, a combination of graph-based features and contextual information also helps in pushing more relevant entities to the top of result list.

2 RELATED WORK

2.1 Entity Relatedness and Finding Related Entities

Wikipedia, with its rich semantic data and extensive hyperlink structure, has been extensively used for measuring relatedness between two entities (or concepts). Just as the Google Similarity Distance [16] is defined over Google's web graph, Milne and Witten[31] described a measure for computing entity relatedness by utilizing the hyperlink structure in Wikipedia articles [31] and used it for predicting missing links in Wikipedia [32]. Strube and Ponzetto [43] utilized the category hierarchy as provided by Wikipedia to compute relatedness between two entities.

Text Retrieval Evaluation Conference (TREC) introduced a related entity finding (REF) track [7] with an objective to develop benchmark collections and evaluation measures for *entity-oriented* search tasks. Given an input query and a description of users' search intents, the systems were required to produce a ranked list of homepages representing target entities. The REF track, thus, did not take into account the structured relationships between entities and focused only on the content present in entity homepages. In context of TREC REF task, Bron et al. [13, 14] describe the use of co-occurrence statistics for ranking related entities. Fang and Luo [18] describe a probabilistic model for ranking related entities that utilizes Wordnet concepts for estimating the type information of target entities. Raghavan et al. [37] use the context around entity

mentions to build *entity langugae models* and use these models to perform related entity finding task. These methods, however, rely mostly on the textual information present in entity homepages and thus, do not utilize the semantic information otherwise present in a knowledge graph.

2.2 Entity Recommendation in Web Search and Other Information Retrieval Systems:

Blanco et al. [12] study the problem of entity recommendations in Web search. Given an input entity, they used a learning to rank approach to rank entities using co-occurrence based features derived from search query logs, tags in flickr and twitter, in addition to graph theoretic features derived from the graph created out of hyperlinks in web pages. Bin et al. [11] incorporate the click data for entity panes shown to users in their entity recommendation system for web search users. Reinanda et al. [39] identify and extract different aspects of an entity from query logs and use these aspects to improve query recommendations to search users.

As examples of domain-specific applications of utilizing knowledge graphs, Fokoue et al. [19, 20] proposed a framework to predict drug-drug interactions through similarity based link prediction.

In context of semantic knowledge bases, Wang et al. [47] and Zhang et al. [51] proposed time aware entity recommendation methods that are developed on the intuition that relationship between entities evolve over time (e.g. *married* relationship between two persons is valid only for a specific period in time). Tran et al. [45] improve upon such models by recommending topic and time sensitive results. However, like other link prediction and recommendation methods, they also limited their models to direct neighbors of the input entity whereas the focus of present work is to study how context can be utilized to efficiently increase the search space to include entities that may not be directly connected.

3 PROPOSED APPROACH

We first describe the problem setting and present a mathematical formulation of the contextual entity recommendation problem. We then describe our proposed probabilistic framework and describe different components of the framework in detail.

3.1 Problem Formulation

Let $G = \{\mathcal{E}, \mathcal{R}\}$ be a knowledge graph with $\mathcal{E} = \{e_1, e_2, \ldots, e_n\}$ as the set of entities (nodes) and $\mathcal{R} = \{r_1, r_2, \ldots, r_m\}$ as the set of relationships (edge set). Let $\mathcal{D}$ be the underlying document corpus. For each edge $r \in \mathcal{R}$, $\mathcal{P}_r = \{p_{r1}, p_{r2}, \ldots, p_{rk}\}$, is the set of passages in $\mathcal{D}$ that contain mentions of relationship r. This passage set is generally available for automatically constructed knowledge bases [10, 15] as these methods output the portions of text from which a specific relationship is identified. Even in manually curated knowledge graphs, these passages can be identified by using entity-linking techniques [33].

Next, consider a user who wants to explore this graph. The user specifies a starting query entity e_q and the text context C, and would like to see entities from the graph relevant to entity e_q in context, C. For example, the user may be interested in knowing entities relevant to Steve Jobs in context of pixar animation. In such a case, an entity like Steve Wozniak is not relevant for the user even though it is a very important entity for Steve Jobs, whereas, Edwin Catmull, a Pixar executive is highly relevant, even though Steve Jobs and Edwin Catmull are weakly connected in the graph.

Mathematically, having observed the input entity e_q and context C, we are interested in computing the probability of observing a target entity e, i.e, $P(e|e_q, C)$.

Application of Bayes' Theorem yields

$$P(e|e_q, C) \propto P(e)P(e_q, C|e) \qquad (1)$$

Here, the denominator $P(e_q, C)$ can be ignored as it is constant for all target entities and will not alter the relative ranking of target entities. Assuming e_q and C to be independent, the above equation can be written as follows.

$$P(e|e_q, C) \propto \underbrace{P(e)}_{\text{entity prior}} \times \underbrace{P(e_q|e)}_{\text{entity affinity}} \times \underbrace{P(C|e)}_{\text{context relevance}} \qquad (2)$$

Note that the above formulation clearly separates the probability computation into three components – prior probability of target entity, affinity between target and query entity and relevance of target entity in context C. While the prior and entity affinity components can be computed using structural properties of the graph, context relevance can be computed using the underlying document corpus $\mathcal{D}$. We discuss in detail the choices for the different components of the model in the following sub-sections.

3.2 Entity Prior

This component measures the prior probability of observing the entity e and is independent of the input query e_q and context C. Intuitively, in absence of any input information, an entity that has connections with many other entities in the graph has a higher probability of being observed than an isolated entity. Therefore, we define the entity-prior in terms of degree of each entity as follows:

$$P(e) = \frac{d(e)}{2|\mathcal{R}|} \qquad (3)$$

Here $d(e)$ denotes the degree (in-degree + out-degree) of e and $\mathcal{R}$ is the number of edges in the knowledge graph. Note that this is a valid probability distribution and sums to 1 when summed over all the entities, since $\Sigma_e d(e) = 2|\mathcal{R}|$. This prior assigns high score to entities that are connected to a large number of other entities and also helps in reducing the scores of noisy or erroneous entities (present in the graph as a result of imperfect automatic knowledge extraction methods) that typically have very few connections.

3.3 Entity Affinity

Entity affinity captures the likelihood of association between two given entities and is a measure of semantic relatedness between them. We can exploit the knowledge graph to compute the affinities and capture the rich structural information available in the graph.

We assume $P(e_q|e)$ is same as $P(e|e_q)$. This allows us to model entity-affinity as a measure of similarity. While the relatedness between two entities in the graph can be captured using multiple ways, we study following three widely studied relatedness measures.

Adamic-Adar (AA): It was originally proposed to predict whether one person is likely to be associated with another in an academic social network constructed from web-pages [2]. Empirically, this measure has been shown to perform better than many other common neighbors based similarity metrics such as common neighbors count, Jaccard and cosine similarities for link-prediction in social networks [26]. It is based on the intuition that if two persons are similar then they will share many common "friends" between them. Moreover, a person who is connected to a few is weighted more than the person connected to many, since connections with such less popular nodes are more informative and discriminative. In terms of a graph, two nodes are highly similar if they have many common neighbors which are not connected to a large number of other nodes. For example, the fact that both Steve Jobs and Bill gates share United States as a common neighbor is not very informative and should not contribute heavily in determining their relatedness as there are many other entities in the graph that have connections with United States. Hence, it is important to assign low weights to popular nodes, which is a major shortcoming of some of the other neighborhood based measures like cosine similarity and Jaccard similarity. Formally Adamic-Adar similarity $AA(u, v)$ between two nodes $u, v \in \mathcal{E}$ is defined as following:

$$AA(u, v) = \sum_{x \in N(u) \cap N(v)} \frac{1}{\log(|N(x)|)} \qquad (4)$$

Here $N(w)$ denotes the set of nodes to which there are outgoing edges from w in the knowledge graph $\mathcal{G}$. Note that it is computationally inexpensive hence can be used with very large graphs easily.

Milne-Witten (MW): It was introduced to compute semantic relatedness between Wikipedia articles using only the hyper-link structure (graph) between the articles [32]. The basic intuition behind this measure is that two Wikipedia articles are topically related if there are many Wikipedia articles that link to both of them. It has been successfully applied to a variety of tasks related to Wikipedia data such as for measuring semantic associativity between Wikipedia concepts for entity disambiguation [38] and entity linking tasks [41].

Formally Milne-Witten similarity $MW(u, v)$ between two nodes $u, v \in \mathcal{E}$ is defined as following:

$$MW(u, v) = \frac{\log\left(\max(|N'(u)|, |N'(v)|)\right) - \log\left(|N'(u) \cap N'(v)|\right)}{\log\left(|\mathcal{E}|\right) - \log\left(\min(|N'(u)|, |N'(v)|)\right)} \qquad (5)$$

Here $N'(w)$ denotes the set of nodes having outgoing edges to w.

Note that just like Adamic-Adar and other neighborhood based methods, this measure also relies only on the neighborhood information of input entities and is therefore, easy to compute even on large graphs. However, this limitation prevents use of these measures for computing relatedness of entities that share no common neighbors. Consequently, the search space for these methods is limited to the second-hop neighbors of the query entity, however in practice there could be many relevant entities that lie beyond the second hop neighborhood. Further, since these methods utilize information only about the common neighbors and ignore longer path between entities, these methods are limited in capturing complete structural similarity induced by the graph.

SimRank: To overcome the limitations discussed above, we used the `SimRank` algorithm proposed by Jeh and Widom [22] that is based on the intuition that "two nodes are related if they are related to similar nodes". Note that this recursive definition of SimRank allows us to capture arbitrarily long paths and compute structural similarities between entities that are farther away in the graph. In contrast to the neighborhood based similarity scores it can measure similarities among nodes that don't share any common neighbors. Thus, it allows us to look beyond first and second hop neighbors of a given node and has been empirically applied to a variety of tasks such as predicting links in social networks [26].

Formally, `SimRank` $SR(u, v)$ for any two vertices $u, v \in \mathcal{E}$ is defined as following.

$$SR_\gamma(u, v) = \begin{cases} 1, & \text{if } u = v \\ \gamma \cdot \frac{\sum_{x \in N'(u)} \sum_{y \in N'(v)} SR_\gamma(x, y)}{|N'(u)| \cdot |N'(v)|}, & \text{otherwise} \end{cases} \quad (6)$$

Here, $\gamma \in (0, 1)$ is a constant called decay factor, which assigns a lower weight to far-away nodes in the graph. Typically $\gamma = 0.8$ has been used in literature. The above equation defines SimRank in a recursive fashion such that the SimRank between two nodes u and v is computed as a function of pair-wise SimRank score computed between their neighbors. The base case, as represented by the first part of above equation, denotes that an entity is maximally similar to itself.

SimRank Computation: As is evident from Equation 6, recursive computation of SimRank is computationally inefficient and it is infeasible to compute it for large graphs. As a result, fast and scalable approximation algorithms have been proposed in literature for efficient SimRank computation. We used one such recently proposed single pair SimRank algorithm [23] based on random walks and monte carlo simulations for our implementation. Its time complexity is $O(TR)$, where R is the number of random walks simulated and T is the maximum steps up to which the walks are performed.

Normalization to Probabilities: The above graph based affinity scores are not valid probabilities hence we have to normalize them appropriately. Let $S(x, y)$ be a similarity measure between nodes x and y. Then a normalized version is as follows:

$$P(x|y) = \frac{1 + S(x, y)}{\sum_{z \in \mathcal{E}} S(z, y) + |\mathcal{E}|} \quad (7)$$

Note here that the denominator requires us to compute the similarity function over all pairs of entities x and y which may not always be feasible due to the size of the graph. However, we also note that the denominator remains same for all the entities in the graph, and here can be ignored as we are only interested in relative ranking of the entities.

3.4 Context Relevance

This component measures the relevance of the target entity to the context in which the search/exploration task is being performed. As discussed previously, this is a crucial component of our proposed framework as it can help us in identifying a shortlist of contextually relevant entities that can then be re-ranked to produce the final result list. In our problem setting, the context is represented as a set of terms input by the user (Section 3). Assuming that the context terms are observed independently of each other, the component $P(C|e)$ can be estimated as follows:

$$P(C|e) = \prod_{c \in C} P(c|e) \quad (8)$$

Here, $c \in C$ are the constituent terms of context C.

In order to compute the probability of the term c given the entity e, we built a *context document* for each entity in the graph by utilizing the relationship passage sets described in Section 3. Intuitively, the probability of observing a context term given an entity is higher if that term appears frequently with mentions of the input entity in the underlying corpus. If $\mathcal{R}_e = \{r_{e1}, r_{e2}, \ldots, r_{en}\}$ be the set of relationships in which entity e is involved, and $P_{r_{ei}}$ is the set of passages from which r_{ei} was extracted, the context document for entity e is defined as follows:

$$CD(e) = \bigcup_{r_{ei} \in \mathcal{R}_e} P_{r_{ei}} \quad (9)$$

Thus, a context document for an entity is the concatenation of all the passages from the text corpus from which a relation involving the entity was extracted. Once the context document of the entity is build, the probability of observing a term given the entity can be estimated using a unigram language model for the context document [28, Chapter 12] as follows:

$$P(c|e) = P(c|CD(e)) = \frac{tf(c) + 1}{|CD(e)| + |V|} \quad (10)$$

Here, tfc is the term frequency of term c in the context document and $|V|$ is the total number of terms in the vocabulary. Note that the factor of one in numerator is added for smoothing purposes to prevent zero probabilities for terms not present in the context document [28, Chapter 12].

As an example, consider the entity `Steve jobs` that has many relationships with different Apple products (`iPhone`, `iPod`, `iPad`, `Macintosh`, etc.). Words occurring in passages from which these relationships are extracted are representative of different *contexts* in which `Steve jobs` appears (such as design, development, invention, functioning, etc.). Likewise, `Steve Jobs` has many relationships with different executives like `Tim Cook`, `Eddie Cue`, `Jonathan Ive`, etc. and words occurring in relationship passages with these entities will be different than those occurring with Apple products. Thus, the context document for `Steve Jobs` will capture different terms representative of different *contexts* relevant to `Steve Jobs`. Also note that these words do not correspond to named entities and hence, are not present in the graph but will be captured in the context document for `Steve Jobs`.

3.5 Final Scoring Function and Variations:

Finally, we plug-in the above prior, entity-affinity and context relevance scores in Equation 2 and take log to arrive at the following final ranking function:

$$score(e|e_q, C) = \log P(e) + \log(1 + S(e_q|e)) + \log P(C|e) \quad (11)$$

Method	Score Function
Context (C)	$\log P(C|e)$
Degree (D)	$\log P(e)$
D+Adamic-Adar(AA)	$\log P(e) + \log(1 + AA(e_q, e))$
D+Milne-Witten(MW)	$\log P(e) + \log(1 + MW(e_q, e))$
D + SimRank (SR)	$\log P(e) + \log(1 + SR(e_q, e))$
D + C + AA	$\log P(e) + \log(1 + AA(e_q, e)) + \log P(C|e)$
D + C + MW	$\log P(e) + \log(1 + MW(e_q, e)) + \log P(C|e)$
D + C + SR	$\log P(e) + \log(1 + SR(e_q, e)) + \log P(C|e)$

Table 1: Summary of methods with their corresponding score functions for ranking.

This scoring function allows us to obtain different variations which are summarized in Table-1. There are three sections in the table, first is just the context based method and it doesn't use any information from the knowledge graph and relies completely on the results from the text corpus, the second section is of purely graph based methods that use only the graph based scores to rank the entities. The third group combines the above two, i.e. it combines both the graph based features and context relevance. In the next Section, we use these variations to study the impact of different components of the ranking function (Equation 11).

4 EXPERIMENTS

In this section we describe the data and query set we used for evaluation. We provide details about the knowledge graph and entity language model construction. We describe a new dataset for this task that we constructed using the WikiStream dataset [49]. Implementation details of the scores mentioned in the Equation 11 are discussed. We show comparison of methods utilizing only the context information, graph based scores, and combinations of these using well known performance measures. We also study the distribution of relevant entities at different path lengths from the query entity to understand the importance of entities at different distances.

4.1 Data Description

4.1.1 Text Corpus: We use dump of the English Wikipedia as our background text corpus $\mathcal{D}$ as it is a snapshot of the general open domain knowledge about the World. It has around 5 million articles and is used to construct our knowledge graph and entity context documents as described next.

Knowledge Graph: We use a semantic graph constructed from the text of all articles in Wikipedia by automatically extracting the entities and their relations by using Statistical Information and Relation Extraction (SIRE) toolkit [15]. Even though there exist popular knowledge bases like DBPedia that contain high quality data, we chose to construct a semantic graph using automated means as such a graph will be closer to many practical real world scenarios where high quality curated graphs are often not available and one has to resort to automatic methods of constructing knowledge bases. Our graph contains more than 30 millions entities and 192 million

distinct relationships in comparison to 4.5 million entities and 70 million relationships in DBpedia.

Entity Context Documents: We construct the context documents for all 30 million+ extracted entities in our knowledge graph and indexed them using the Indri Language Modeling Toolkit as provided by the Lemur project [1].

Indexing Entity Context Documents: To efficiently search the documents relevant in a given context we use Indri search engine of the Lemur project. Indri is efficient, scalable and gives highly accurate search results [46]. In addition Indri also gives the likelihood score for each result it returns, which we can use for `context-relevance` score. In the indexing process we use a standard stopwords list as provided by the Onix text retrieval toolkit[1] and krovetz stemmer as implemented in Indri.

4.2 Query Set

We create the query set by using the recently released WikiStream dataset [49] following an approach similar to the one followed by Tran et al. [45]. Entity mentions on a Wikipedia page are often linked to their respective Wikipedia pages and users often click on these linked Wikipedia pages to read more about these related entities. Further, since the articles in Wikipedia are often categorized into sub-topics, an entity link mentioned in a specific section of the article and clicked frequently by the users can be considered a proxy for relevance of the clicked entity to the source entity in context of the sub-topic/aspect. For example, "Pixar and Disney" section on Steve Jobs' Wikipedia article contains links to Lucasfilm, Bob Iger, Michael Eisner, etc. – entities relevant to Steve Jobs in context of Disney and Pixar, even though, they may not be deemed relevant otherwise. The WikiStream dataset is created by processing Wikipedia request logs for the month of February 2015 and consists of $< referer, resource >$ pairs where *resource* is a Wikipedia article and a *referer* could be another Wikipedia article, or some other external source (request coming from search engines, other web pages, etc.). We extracted all the click pairs from the click stream logs where the referrer and resource were Wikipedia entities and mapped the click pairs with the title of the sub-section where the entity was mentioned giving us $< inputentity, context >$ pairs to use as query and an associated list of clicked entities as our answer set. Hence we have a collection of tuples (query entity, context, relevant entities) and we randomly select a subset of 50 such tuples and refer it by `WikiContext` dataset in the following sections. Table 2 presents some example queries from our dataset. The complete list of queries, context, and relevant entities used in our experiments can be accessed at http://sumitbhatia.net/source/datasets.html.

4.3 Scores Computation

4.3.1 Context Score: We search for relevant documents (entities) in the given context C by using C as input query to Indri. It returns a list of documents most relevant to the given query but note that in the corpus each indexed document corresponds to an entity. As a result, we obtain a ranked list of contextually relevant entities. Indri also provides log probability score for each output entry denoting its relevance to the query. We use this score as the Context relevance score defined in equation 2. From the

---

[1]http://www.lextek.com/manuals/onix/stopwords1.html

Input Entity	Context	Example Answer Entities
Lee H. Oswald	John F. Kennedy and J. D. Tippit Shootings	James Tague, John Connally, Texas Theatre
Timur	Campaign Against The Tughlaq Dynasty	Delhi Sultanate, Sultan Nasir-U Din Mehmud
Martina Hingis	Injuries and Hiatus From Tennis	Williams Sisters, Hopman Cup
Art Modell	As Principal Owner of Baltimore Ravens 1996-2004	Ted Marchibroda, Brian Billick
Art Modell	As Cleveland Browns owner 1961–1995	Paul Brown, Blanton Collie

Table 2: Example queries from the WikiContext dataset.

results returned by Indri we select top-100 entities and compute the entity-affinity scores for these shortlisted entities.

*4.3.2 **Graph Scores:*** We compute graph scores between the query entity (source entity) and the target entities (shortlisted based on their relevance to context). Similarity measures like Adamic-Adar, Milne-Witten etc. can be computed easily by simple neighborhood queries. However SimRank computation requires backward random walks starting from the source and target entities each. Since it is a Monte Carlo based method, we have to take many samples of the walk in order to get a good approximation. We store the full graph in-memory so that random walks could be simulated efficiently. We use $\gamma = 0.8$, number of random walks (samples) $R = 200$ and maximum distance $T = 10$, for SimRank computation between the source and target entities.

4.4 Evaluation Protocol

We first retrieve top-100 entities based on the context from the entity docs indexed using Indri. This gives us candidate entities relevant to the context and limits the search space as well. We compute the degree score for these entities and the graph based similarity scores between the target entity and the candidate entities. The candidate entities are re-ranked using different combinations of scores listed in Table- 1. We then evaluate the quality of results by comparing against the automatically obtained ground truth and relevance scores obtained from human evaluators. We are interested in Top-5, Top-10 and Top-25 final entities obtained after re-ranking the candidate set.

We report Mean Reciprocal Rank (MRR), Normalized Discounted Cumulative Gain (NDCG), Precision and Recall @K to evaluate the effectiveness of context and graph based entity retrieval components. We first re-rank the top-100 candidate entities by different scores and then compute the measures by taking top-k results of the re-ranked list. We report the average of each performance metric over all the queries in the given query set.

4.5 Results and Discussions

We evaluate the quality of results obtained from different methods and also study the relevance of entities beyond neighborhood. We evaluate results on this dataset against the automated ground truth as well as the ground truth obtained from manual labeling for all 50 queries.

4.5.1 *Automated Ground Truth:*

Note that in the automatically extracted ground truth, graded relevance judgments are not available. Hence we can't compute NDCG in this case and report Precision, Recall and MRR in Table-3. It can be observed from the table that the combination (D+C+SR) outperforms pure Context and pure graph based methods across all metrics. Note that the pure graph based methods lack the context relevance scores hence their performance is not as good as just the context based method as they produce a *static* ranking that remains same for different contexts. The context based method, while capable of finding contextually relevant entities, suffers from not utilizing the similarity information induced by rich graph structure. Augmenting the context based method with graph structural information produces consistently better results providing support for our hypothesis that incorporating contextual clues to graph based similarity measures can help retrieve more relevant entities.

4.5.2 *Manual Ground Truth:*

In the automatically constructed ground truth created from the WikiStream dataset, relevance judgments for all the entities are not available for all the entities retrieved by different methods. Therefore, we obtained relevance labels for top 100 shortlisted entities for each query from two human judges for better evaluation and comparison of the results obtained by different methods. The judges were presented with the query entity, context and the Top-100 shortlisted entities in random order and were asked to assign labels from {0 : irrelevant, 1 : relevant, 2 : highly relevant} for each result entity. In case of disagreements, the final judgments were aggregated by selecting the minimum value of the two judgments for each result entity. Table-4 reports the numbers on these aggregated relevance labels. Once again, similar observations to Table 3 can be made. We note that the method (D+C+SR) consistently outperforms other methods – it not only finds more relevant entities, it is able to produce a better ranking as indicated by higher NDCG values. Moreover, the gap in performance when compared to other methods is also significant.

4.5.3 *Per Query Performance Comparison*

. Next, we study how the best performing method (D+C+SR) performs against the second best method D+C+AA and just the Context based method C. We take the difference between the performance metrics (Δ Precision @10, ΔRecall @10, ΔNDCG @10) obtained by D+C+SR and C, D+C+AA for all 50 queries in the dataset. We sort these Δ values and plot them on bar plots, shown in Figure-1. These values are computed on the manually obtained ground truth. We observe that D+C+SR performs better than the C and D+C+AA methods in terms of precision and recall @10 for around 20 queries and around 30 queries for NDCG @10. Thus, on an average, more queries are benefited by combining contextual and graph based measures than using either of them in isolation. We also note that in general, gains for queries that benefit from the combination are

	@5			@10			@25		
	P	R	MRR	P	R	MRR	P	R	MRR
Context (C)	0.116	0.116	0.212	0.104	0.208	0.241	0.062	0.312	0.251
Degree (D)	0.080	0.080	0.170	0.064	0.128	0.195	0.054	0.268	0.212
D + Adamic Adar(AA)	0.096	0.096	0.194	0.082	0.164	0.226	0.063	0.316	0.239
D + Milne Witten(MW)	0.080	0.080	0.169	0.060	0.120	0.189	0.051	0.256	0.208
D + SimRank (SR)	0.112	0.112	0.195	0.094	0.188	0.227	0.063	0.316	0.237
D + C + AA	0.100	0.100	0.215	0.094	0.188	0.253	**0.066**	0.328	0.269
D + C + MW	0.088	0.088	0.204	0.074	0.148	0.227	0.060	0.300	0.247
D + C + SR	**0.124**	**0.124**	**0.225**	**0.112**	**0.224**	**0.262**	**0.066**	**0.332**	**0.270**

Table 3: Wiki Results with automated ground truth

	@5				@10				@25			
	P	R	NDCG	MRR	P	R	NDCG	MRR	P	R	NDCG	MRR
Context (C)	0.212	0.081	0.105	0.277	0.236	0.187	0.170	0.313	0.210	0.410	0.270	0.317
Degree (D)	0.164	0.070	0.083	0.289	0.194	0.166	0.142	0.327	0.189	0.407	0.243	0.339
D + Adamic Adar(AA)	0.208	0.101	0.118	0.355	0.228	0.217	0.189	0.379	0.206	0.439	0.286	0.386
D + Milne Witten(MW)	0.156	0.068	0.079	0.275	0.188	0.163	0.137	0.315	0.182	0.382	0.232	0.325
D + SimRank (SR)	0.264	0.151	0.171	0.384	0.244	0.255	0.233	0.412	0.217	0.455	0.328	0.414
D + C + AA	0.224	0.110	0.137	0.353	0.230	0.219	0.204	0.382	0.213	0.444	0.304	0.387
D + C + MW	0.180	0.074	0.094	0.330	0.198	0.172	0.151	0.362	0.200	0.425	0.259	0.374
D + C + SR	**0.308**	**0.170**	**0.192**	**0.398**	**0.278**	**0.275**	**0.258**	**0.423**	**0.226**	**0.470**	**0.349**	**0.426**

Table 4: Results on WikiContext Dataset with manually obtained ground truth.

more than the loss in performance for few queries increasing the overall performance. We also observe that while both *D+C+AA* and *D+C+SR* achieve better performance when compared with just using the context, the gains are more prominent for the *D+C+SR* method. Given that Adamic Adar (AA) impacts only the entities that share common neighbors with the input entity while SimRank has no such limitation, better performance achieved by SimRank once again lends weight to the importance of going beyond the 1-hop or 2-hop neighborhood of input entity for finding contextually relevant entities.

4.5.4 *Contributions of non-neighbors:*

Next, in order to understand how many relevant entities are found beyond the immediate neighborhood, we compute the lengths of shortest paths from the query entity to all the relevant entities in the contextually relevant shortlist (top-100 entities). We then re-rank these entities by the SimRank based *D+C+SR* method and compute the distribution of different path lengths for top 10, 50 and 100 positions. The results are summarized in Figure-2. We observe that there exist a significant number of relevant entities beyond the immediate neighbors (Path Length = 1). Methods like `Adamic-Adar` and `Milne-Witten` are based on common neighbors and hence they can find entities only till path length = 2. As we see in the plot there is significant fraction of relevant entities at path length greater than 2 and this increases as we increase the value of K. For $K = 100$, only 30% of relevant entities are found in the immediate

neighborhood and about 20% of relevant entities lie at a path length of 3 – a significant number that is never evaluated by traditional neighborhood methods.

5 CONCLUSIONS AND FUTURE WORK

We studied the problem of finding relevant entities that the end-user might want to explore given an input entity and context specified as text keywords. We argued that utilizing this context information can help overcome the scalability problem of standard graph based approaches of entity recommendation. We showed how context can be employed in producing a focused shortlist of relevant entities by performing a fast search over the complete graph and then computing graph based features only on this much smaller set. Experiments conducted over a knowledge graph created out of Wikipedia articles showed that by utilizing contextual information helps retrieve more relevant entities, and combining with graph features improves the ranking performance. We also found that a significant fraction of relevant entities lie outside the immediate neighborhood of input entities, thus corroborating our initial hypothesis. Since most of the existing work on entity recommendation has focused on immediate neighborhood of the input entity, explaining how the recommended entities are connected to the input entity was not crucial. Our future work will focus on developing methods for explaining how the entities that are not directly connected to input entities are relevant to the input entity. For this, both graph based methods (such as path

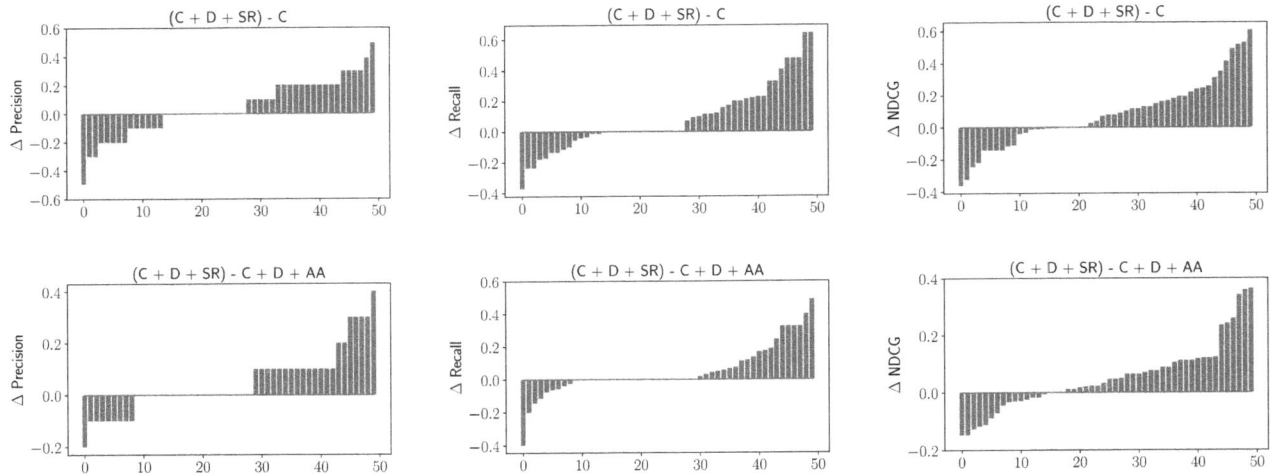

Figure 1: Bar plot showing performance difference per query. X-axis represents queries and bars represent the difference between Precision, Recall, NDCG @10 in the order left to right. First row shows the performance difference between ensemble of Context, Degree Prior and SimRank (C + D + SR) and only the Context (C) while the second row shows comparison against ensemble with Adamic Adar (AA)

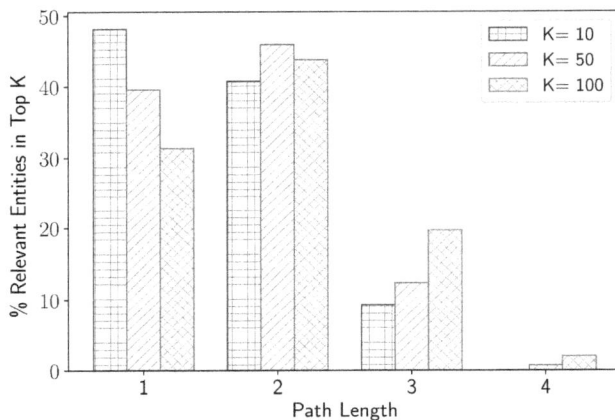

Figure 2: Bar plot showing percentage of relevant entities at different path lengths for Top-K entities ranked by (D + C + SR)

ranking [3, 35]) can be utilized as well as textual explanations [8] by utilizing the relationships passages could be produced.

REFERENCES

[1] 2000. The Lemur Toolkit. https://www.lemurproject.org/. Accessed: 2018-01-31.
[2] Lada A Adamic and Eytan Adar. 2003. Friends and neighbors on the Web. *Social Networks* 25, 3 (2003), 211 – 230. https://doi.org/10.1016/S0378-8733(03)00009-1
[3] Nitish Aggarwal, Sumit Bhatia, and Vinith Misra. 2016. Connecting the Dots: Explaining Relationships Between Unconnected Entities in a Knowledge Graph. In *The Semantic Web - ESWC 2016 Satellite Events, Heraklion, Crete, Greece, May 29 - June 2, 2016, Revised Selected Papers*. 35–39. https://doi.org/10.1007/978-3-319-47602-5_8
[4] Gabor Angeli, Melvin Jose Johnson Premkumar, and Christopher D Manning. 2015. Leveraging linguistic structure for open domain information extraction. In *Proceedings of the 53rd Annual Meeting of the Association for Computational Linguistics and the 7th International Joint Conference on Natural Language Processing (Volume 1: Long Papers)*, Vol. 1. 344–354.
[5] Sören Auer, Christian Bizer, Georgi Kobilarov, Jens Lehmann, Richard Cyganiak, and Zachary Ives. 2007. Dbpedia: A nucleus for a web of open data. In *The semantic web*. Springer, 722–735.
[6] Lars Backstrom and Jure Leskovec. 2011. Supervised Random Walks: Predicting and Recommending Links in Social Networks. In *Proceedings of the Fourth ACM International Conference on Web Search and Data Mining (WSDM '11)*. ACM, New York, NY, USA, 635–644. https://doi.org/10.1145/1935826.1935914
[7] Krisztian Balog, Arjen P de Vries, Pavel Serdyukov, Paul Thomas, and Thijs Westerveld. 2009. Overview of the TREC 2009 entity track. In *In Proceedings of the Eighteenth Text REtrieval Conference*.
[8] Sumit Bhatia, Purusharth Dwivedi, and Avneet Kaur. 2018. Tell Me Why Is It So? Explaining Knowledge Graph Relationships by Finding Descriptive Support Passages. *CoRR* abs/1803.06555 (2018). arXiv:1803.06555 http://arxiv.org/abs/1803.06555
[9] Sumit Bhatia, Alok Goel, Elizabeth Bowen, and Anshu Jain. 2016. Separating Wheat from the Chaff - A Relationship Ranking Algorithm. In *The Semantic Web - ESWC 2016 Satellite Events, Heraklion, Crete, Greece, May 29 - June 2, 2016, Revised Selected Papers (Lecture Notes in Computer Science)*, Harald Sack, Giuseppe Rizzo 0002, Nadine Steinmetz, Dunja Mladenic, Sören Auer, and Christoph Lange 0002 (Eds.), Vol. 9989. 79–83.
[10] Sumit Bhatia, Nidhi Rajshree, Anshu Jain, and Nitish Aggarwal. 2017. Tools and Infrastructure for Supporting Enterprise Knowledge Graphs. In *International Conference on Advanced Data Mining and Applications*. Springer, 846–852.
[11] Bin Bi, Hao Ma, Bo-June Paul Hsu, Wei Chu, Kuansan Wang, and Junghoo Cho. 2015. Learning to recommend related entities to search users. In *Proceedings of the Eighth ACM International Conference on Web Search and Data Mining*. ACM, 139–148.
[12] Roi Blanco, Berkant Barla Cambazoglu, Peter Mika, and Nicolas Torzec. 2013. Entity Recommendations in Web Search. In *Proceedings of the 12th International Semantic Web Conference - Part II (ISWC '13)*. Springer-Verlag New York, Inc., New York, NY, USA, 33–48. https://doi.org/10.1007/978-3-642-41338-4_3
[13] Marc Bron, Krisztian Balog, and Maarten De Rijke. 2010. Ranking related entities: components and analyses. In *Proceedings of the 19th ACM international conference on Information and knowledge management*. ACM, 1079–1088.
[14] Marc Bron, Krisztian Balog, and Maarten de Rijke. 2009. *Related entity finding based on co-occurrence*. Technical Report. AMSTERDAM UNIV (NETHERLANDS).
[15] Vittorio Castelli, Hema Raghavan, Radu Florian, Ding-Jung Han, Xiaoqiang Luo, and Salim Roukos. 2012. Distilling and Exploring Nuggets from a Corpus. In *Proceedings of the 35th International ACM SIGIR Conference on Research and Development in Information Retrieval (SIGIR '12)*. ACM, New York, NY, USA, 1006–1006. https://doi.org/10.1145/2348283.2348431

[16] Rudi L Cilibrasi and Paul MB Vitanyi. 2007. The google similarity distance. *IEEE Transactions on knowledge and data engineering* 19, 3 (2007).

[17] Gianluca Demartini, Tereza Iofciu, and Arjen P. De Vries. 2010. Overview of the INEX 2009 Entity Ranking Track. In *Proceedings of the Focused Retrieval and Evaluation, and 8th International Conference on Initiative for the Evaluation of XML Retrieval (INEX'09)*. Springer-Verlag, Berlin, Heidelberg, 254–264. http://dl.acm.org/citation.cfm?id=1881065.1881096

[18] Yi Fang and Luo Si. 2015. Related entity finding by unified probabilistic models. *World Wide Web* 18, 3 (2015), 521–543.

[19] Achille Fokoue, Oktie Hassanzadeh, Mohammad Sadoghi, and Ping Zhang. 2016. Predicting Drug-Drug Interactions Through Similarity-Based Link Prediction Over Web Data. In *Proceedings of the 25th International Conference Companion on World Wide Web (WWW '16 Companion)*. International World Wide Web Conferences Steering Committee, Republic and Canton of Geneva, Switzerland, 175–178. https://doi.org/10.1145/2872518.2890532

[20] Achille Fokoue, Mohammad Sadoghi, Oktie Hassanzadeh, and Ping Zhang. 2016. Predicting Drug-Drug Interactions Through Large-Scale Similarity-Based Link Prediction. In *Proceedings of the 13th International Conference on The Semantic Web. Latest Advances and New Domains - Volume 9678*. Springer-Verlag New York, Inc., New York, NY, USA, 774–789. https://doi.org/10.1007/978-3-319-34129-3_47

[21] Michael Iannacone, Shawn Bohn, Grant Nakamura, John Gerth, Kelly Huffer, Robert Bridges, Erik Ferragut, and John Goodall. 2015. Developing an Ontology for Cyber Security Knowledge Graphs. In *Proceedings of the 10th Annual Cyber and Information Security Research Conference (CISR '15)*. ACM, New York, NY, USA, Article 12, 4 pages.

[22] Glen Jeh and Jennifer Widom. 2002. SimRank: a measure of structural-context similarity. In *KDD '02: Proceedings of the eighth ACM SIGKDD international conference on Knowledge discovery and data mining*. ACM Press, New York, NY, USA, 538–543. https://doi.org/10.1145/775047.775126

[23] Mitsuru Kusumoto, Takanori Maehara, and Ken-ichi Kawarabayashi. 2014. Scalable Similarity Search for SimRank. In *Proceedings of the 2014 ACM SIGMOD International Conference on Management of Data (SIGMOD '14)*. ACM, New York, NY, USA, 325–336. https://doi.org/10.1145/2588555.2610526

[24] Sangkeun Lee, Sang-il Song, Minsuk Kahng, Dongjoo Lee, and Sang-goo Lee. 2011. Random walk based entity ranking on graph for multidimensional recommendation. In *Proceedings of the fifth ACM conference on Recommender systems*. ACM, 93–100.

[25] Jure Leskovec, Lars Backstrom, Ravi Kumar, and Andrew Tomkins. 2008. Microscopic Evolution of Social Networks. In *Proceedings of the 14th ACM SIGKDD International Conference on Knowledge Discovery and Data Mining (KDD '08)*. ACM, New York, NY, USA, 462–470. https://doi.org/10.1145/1401890.1401948

[26] David Liben-Nowell and Jon Kleinberg. 2003. The Link Prediction Problem for Social Networks. In *Proceedings of the Twelfth International Conference on Information and Knowledge Management (CIKM '03)*. ACM, New York, NY, USA, 556–559. https://doi.org/10.1145/956863.956972

[27] Thomas Lin, Patrick Pantel, Michael Gamon, Anitha Kannan, and Ariel Fuxman. 2012. Active Objects: Actions for Entity-Centric Search. In *World Wide Web*. ACM. http://research.microsoft.com/apps/pubs/default.aspx?id=161389

[28] Christopher D. Manning, Prabhakar Raghavan, and Hinrich Schütze. 2008. *Introduction to Information Retrieval*. Cambridge University Press, New York, NY, USA.

[29] Gary Marchionini. 2006. Exploratory Search: From Finding to Understanding. *Commun. ACM* 49, 4 (April 2006), 41–46.

[30] Alexander H. Miller, Adam Fisch, Jesse Dodge, Amir-Hossein Karimi, Antoine Bordes, and Jason Weston. 2016. Key-Value Memory Networks for Directly Reading Documents. In *Proceedings of the 2016 Conference on Empirical Methods in Natural Language Processing, EMNLP 2016, Austin, Texas, USA, November 1-4, 2016*. 1400–1409. http://aclweb.org/anthology/D/D16/D16-1147.pdf

[31] David Milne and Ian H. Witten. 2008. An Effective, Low-Cost Measure of Semantic Relatedness Obtained from Wikipedia Links. In *In Proceedings of AAAI 2008*.

[32] David Milne and Ian H. Witten. 2008. Learning to Link with Wikipedia. In *Proceedings of the 17th ACM Conference on Information and Knowledge Management*

(CIKM '08). ACM, New York, NY, USA, 509–518. https://doi.org/10.1145/1458082.1458150

[33] Andrea Moro, Alessandro Raganato, and Roberto Navigli. 2014. Entity linking meets word sense disambiguation: a unified approach. *Transactions of the Association for Computational Linguistics* 2 (2014), 231–244.

[34] Meenakshi Nagarajan et al. 2015. Predicting Future Scientific Discoveries Based on a Networked Analysis of the Past Literature. In *KDD (KDD '15)*. 2019–2028.

[35] Giuseppe Pirrò. 2015. Explaining and Suggesting Relatedness in Knowledge Graphs. In *The Semantic Web - ISWC 2015 - 14th International Semantic Web Conference, Bethlehem, PA, USA, October 11-15, 2015, Proceedings, Part I*. 622–639.

[36] Jeffrey Pound, Peter Mika, and Hugo Zaragoza. 2010. Ad-hoc Object Retrieval in the Web of Data. In *WWW '10*. 771–780.

[37] Hema Raghavan, James Allan, and Andrew McCallum. 2004. An Exploration of Entity Models, Collective Classification and Relation Description. In *Proceedings of the Second International Workshop on Link Analysis and Group*. 1–10.

[38] Lev Ratinov, Dan Roth, Doug Downey, and Mike Anderson. 2011. Local and Global Algorithms for Disambiguation to Wikipedia. In *Proceedings of the 49th Annual Meeting of the Association for Computational Linguistics: Human Language Technologies - Volume 1 (HLT '11)*. Association for Computational Linguistics, Stroudsburg, PA, USA, 1375–1384.

[39] Ridho Reinanda, Edgar Meij, and Maarten de Rijke. 2015. Mining, ranking and recommending entity aspects. In *Proceedings of the 38th International ACM SIGIR Conference on Research and Development in Information Retrieval*. ACM, 263–272.

[40] Tong Ruan, Lijuan Xue, Haofen Wang, Fanghuai Hu, Liang Zhao, and Jun Ding. 2016. Building and Exploring an Enterprise Knowledge Graph for Investment Analysis. In *International Semantic Web Conference*. Springer, 418–436.

[41] Wei Shen, Jianyong Wang, Ping Luo, and Min Wang. 2012. LINDEN: Linking named entities with knowledge base via semantic knowledge. (04 2012).

[42] Amit Sheth, Boanerges Aleman-Meza, I Budak Arpinar, Clemens Bertram, et al. 2005. Semantic association identification and knowledge discovery for national security applications. *Journal of Database Management* 16, 1 (2005), 33.

[43] Michael Strube and Simone Paolo Ponzetto. 2006. WikiRelate! Computing semantic relatedness using Wikipedia. In *AAAI*, Vol. 6. 1419–1424.

[44] Fabian M Suchanek, Gjergji Kasneci, and Gerhard Weikum. 2007. Yago: a core of semantic knowledge. In *WWW*. 697–706.

[45] Nam Khanh Tran, Tuan Tran, and Claudia Niederée. 2017. Beyond Time: Dynamic Context-Aware Entity Recommendation. In *The Semantic Web: 14th International Conference, ESWC 2017, Portorož, Slovenia, May 28 – June 1, 2017, Proceedings, Part I*, Eva Blomqvist, Diana Maynard, Aldo Gangemi, Rinke Hoekstra, Pascal Hitzler, and Olaf Hartig (Eds.). Springer International Publishing, Cham, 353–368. https://doi.org/10.1007/978-3-319-58068-5_22

[46] Howard Turtle, Yatish Hegde, and S Rowe. 2012. Yet another comparison of lucene and indri performance. In *SIGIR 2012 Workshop on Open Source Information Retrieval*.

[47] Yafang Wang, Mingjie Zhu, Lizhen Qu, Marc Spaniol, and Gerhard Weikum. 2010. Timely YAGO: Harvesting, Querying, and Visualizing Temporal Knowledge from Wikipedia. In *Proceedings of the 13th International Conference on Extending Database Technology (EDBT '10)*. ACM, New York, NY, USA, 697–700. https://doi.org/10.1145/1739041.1739130

[48] Ryen W White and Resa A Roth. 2009. Exploratory search: Beyond the query-response paradigm. *Synthesis lectures on information concepts, retrieval, and services* 1, 1 (2009), 1–98.

[49] Ellery Wulczyn and Dario Taraborelli. 2015. Wikipedia Clickstream. figshare.doi: 10.6084/m9.figshare.1305770.

[50] Xiao Yu, Xiang Ren, Yizhou Sun, Quanquan Gu, Bradley Sturt, Urvashi Khandelwal, Brandon Norick, and Jiawei Han. 2014. Personalized entity recommendation: A heterogeneous information network approach. In *Proceedings of the 7th ACM international conference on Web search and data mining*. ACM, 283–292.

[51] Lei Zhang, Achim Rettinger, and Ji Zhang. 2016. A Probabilistic Model for Time-Aware Entity Recommendation. In *The Semantic Web – ISWC 2016*, Paul Groth, Elena Simperl, Alasdair Gray, Marta Sabou, Markus Krötzsch, Freddy Lecue, Fabian Flöck, and Yolanda Gil (Eds.). Springer International Publishing, Cham, 598–614.

Content Driven Enrichment of Formal Text using Concept Definitions and Applications

Abhinav Jain
IBM Research India
abhinavj@in.ibm.com

Nitin Gupta
IBM Research India
ngupta47@in.ibm.com

Shashank Mujumdar
IBM Research India
shamujum@in.ibm.com

Sameep Mehta
IBM Research India
sameepmehta@in.ibm.com

Rishi Madhok
Delhi Technological University
rishimadhok96@gmail.com

ABSTRACT

Formal text is objective, unambiguous and tends to have complex sentence construction intended to be understood by the target demographic. However, in the absence of domain knowledge it is imperative to define key concepts and their relationship in the text for correct interpretation for general readers. To address this, we propose a text enrichment framework that identifies the key concepts from input text, highlights definitions and fetches the definition from external data sources in case the concept is undefined. Beyond concept definitions, the system enriches the input text with concept applications and a pre-requisite concept graph that showcases the inter-dependency within the extracted concepts. While the problem of learning definition statements is attempted in literature, the task of learning application statements is novel. We manually annotated a dataset for training a deep learning network for identifying application statements in text. We quantitatively compared the results of both application and definition identification models with standard baselines. To validate the utility of the proposed framework for general readers, we report enrichment accuracy and show promising results.

CCS CONCEPTS

• **Computing methodologies** → **Information extraction**; *Supervised learning by classification*; Neural networks; • **Applied computing** → *E-learning*;

KEYWORDS

Content Enrichment; Key Concepts; Concept Graph; Definition Extraction; Application Identification; Deep Learning

ACM Reference Format:
Abhinav Jain, Nitin Gupta, Shashank Mujumdar, Sameep Mehta, and Rishi Madhok. 2018. Content Driven Enrichment of Formal Text using Concept Definitions and Applications. In *HT '18: 29th ACM Conference on Hypertext and Social Media, July 9–12, 2018, Baltimore, MD, USA*. ACM, New York, NY, USA, 5 pages. https://doi.org/10.1145/3209542.3209566

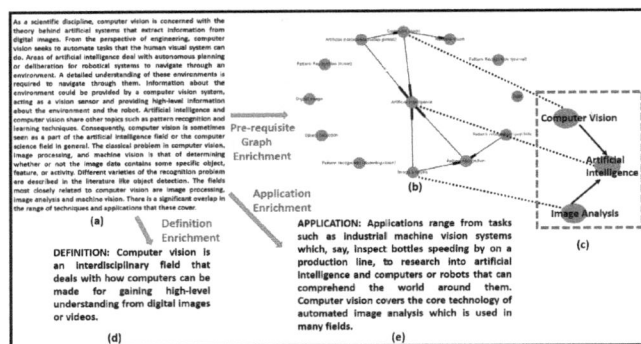

Figure 1: Output of enrichment system for formal text on Computer Vision which is undefined. (a) Input Text, (b)-(c) Pre-requisite graph, (d) Extracted Definition, and (e) Applications of key-concept "Computer Vision".

1 INTRODUCTION

Formal texts are characterized by coherency and completion, used to communicate knowledge. They contain technical terms which we call as key concepts. For example, consider an excerpt from a space and astronomy article *"What is dark matter?"*. *"Dark matter may be made of baryonic or non-baryonic matter. To hold the elements of the universe together, dark matter must make up approximately 80 percent of its matter. Most scientists think that dark matter is composed of non-baryonic matter. The candidates for this are Neutralinos, massive hypothetical particles heavier and slower than neutrinos and sterile neutrinos."* The article is intriguing but filled with key concepts such as *"baryonic matter"*, *"neutralinos"* and *"sterile neutrinos"* for which descriptions are left out. With the exception of textbooks, formal text in daily usage (for example scientific articles, blogs etc.) lacks explanation of key concepts for the sake of brevity. In the absence of domain knowledge, it is difficult for readers to understand these key concepts within text and their relationships which leads to an incomplete semantic understanding of the presented text. We aim to solve this problem through a content enrichment system that analyzes the input text to conditionally enrich them with information in accordance with reader's discretion. We have sourced the information from Wikipedia. Wikipedia is a collaborative and open-source medium with reliable information on general topics referenced from verifiable and notable sources. Although we equip our enrichment framework by sourcing information from Wikipedia, we propose an overall enrichment framework that can be easily extended to any available information source. For an average reader, we want to mitigate the cumbersome problem of searching the missing information through heaps of text via high quality augmentations in the form of definitions, real-life applications [6] and inter key-concept relationships that can provide more clarity to a key concept. By relationships, we mean scenarios where a concept X requires prior knowledge of the concept Y. The aforementioned augmentations are crucial for understanding a technical concept irrespective of reader's expertise in the corresponding domain.

In this work, we develop a framework for enrichment of formal text that consists of the following modules- (i) key-concepts extraction, (ii) definition identification, (iii) application identification, (iv) concept graph generation. The definition identification module checks for the presence of definitions for the extracted key-concepts and fetches the definitions of undefined key-concepts. The application identification module operates similarly to enrich the text with application statements. The concept graph generation module provides an overview of the pre-requisite relationships between extracted key-concepts to help the reader to understand the concept dependencies. The main contributions of our work are:

- We present a novel framework to conditionally enrich formal text with supplementary material that includes definitions, applications and concept graphs sourced from Wikipedia.
- Our method for definition and application identification utilizes LSTM networks and CNNs for sentence-level feature learning under a supervised setting.
- We created a (1) labeled dataset for learning application statements in formal text (2) datasets of formal text snippets obtained from *Scientific Articles* and lecture notes obtained from *MITOpenCourseware* to ascertain the effectiveness of our overall enrichment system.

2 RELATED WORK

One of the earliest approaches for enriching formal text, identified key-concepts and enriched the text with links to authoritative material [2], [1] found on Wikipedia. However, the semantics of the content and the text being enriched is ignored by both of these works. Another line of work has been explored in prior art to enrich formal text by providing a concept map. An approach is proposed in [8] that models concepts in vector space using their related concepts. An RefD score is proposed that measures the difference in the way the related concepts refer to each other. In [5], the method utilized cross-entropy and information flow separately to infer concept dependency relations. A method that jointly optimizes the two subproblems - key concept extraction and concept relationship identification for concept map extraction is proposed in [14].

Identifying definition statements from formal text has also attracted a lot of attention in the community. Some of the earliest approaches used hand-engineered features for their automatic extraction. For example, in [10], method proposed identifies star-patterns and word-class lattices from text for automatic definition extraction. A compendium of word level features for a weakly-supervised bootstrapping approach to classify sentences is proposed in [3]. To automate the learning of features for definition extraction, [7] models the problem as a supervised classification task, using LSTM

to generate these features and outperforms non-Deep Learning based approaches.

The prior art partly addresses some of the challenges for enrichment of formal text. We combine some of these previous efforts and address some of their shortcomings to build a content-driven enrichment system for formal text. Specifically, we enrich the input formal text as seen in Fig. 1. In the next section, we present the details of the proposed framework.

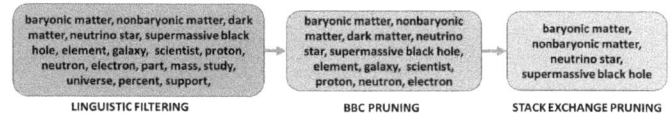

Figure 2: Key concept extraction output after every stage for the sample text shown in Table 1(a).

3 METHODOLOGY

Our overall methodology to enrich any input text consists of three phases. The initial phase extracts key concepts from the formal text, the second phase identifies the need for enrichment of these concepts, and the final phase conditionally enriches the input text with key concepts' definition and applications. This phase additionally generates a concept map from the input text which organizes key concepts based on their pre-requisite relationship with each other. We present the details of individual system components below.

3.1 Key Concepts Extraction

Extracting key concepts by exploiting training data limits the domain to work on. Thus in this section, we present a generic pipeline to reliably extract them from any input text.

Linguistic Filtering: The input text is first POS tagged using Stanford POS tagger [13]. Tagging is needed by linguistic filters that permit only specific strings for extraction without which strings such as *of the*, *is a* will also be extracted. We use following filters [2] - (i) P1 $= C^*N$, (ii) P2 $= (C^*NP)^?(C^*N)$ and (iii) P3 $= A^*N^+$ where N refers to a noun, P a preposition, A an adjective, and $C = A|N$.

Pruning: We leverage the word count dictionary of 90 million words BBC corpus [12] which is an up-to-date representation of general-science related vocabulary to identify stop-list of words such as good, day, voting, state, please, etc. It is further essential to filter candidate concepts such that they pertain to technical key concepts that may occur in formal text and require enrichment. In order to do so, we propose pruning using a corpus of such technical terms constructed using "tags" from StackExchange, SE. SE tags are used to annotate questions with a specific key concept that those questions pertain to. The SE Corpus approximately contains 60,000 tags from fields such as Mathematics, Physics, Electrical Engineering, Chemistry, Biology, Signal Processing etc. We illustrate the above stages in Fig. 2. Ultimately, we obtain a set of pruned key-concepts, $C = \{c_1, ..., c_N\}$, for which the need of enrichment is determined in the next phase.

3.2 Key Concept to Sentence Matching

Sentences quoting key-concept's definitions and applications have key-concepts as their subjects. Hence, we ensure unique association

Table 1: Excerpt from sample formal texts with annotation for some of the extracted key concepts (shown in bold).

Text
Studies of other galaxies in the 1950s first indicated that the universe contained more matter than seen by the naked eye. Support for dark matter has grown, and although no solid direct evidence of dark matter has been detected, there have been strong possibilities in recent years. The familiar material of the universe, known as **baryonic matter**, is composed of protons, neutrons and electrons. Dark matter may be made of baryonic or **non-baryonic matter**. To hold the elements of the universe together, dark matter must make up approximately 80 percent of its matter. The missing matter could simply be more challenging to detect, made up of regular, baryonic matter. Potential candidates include dim brown dwarfs, white dwarfs and **neutrino stars**. **Supermassive black holes** could also be part of the difference.

Key Concepts	Definition	Application
Baryonic matter	Yes	No
Supermassive black holes	No	No

i.e. one-to-one mapping between sentences and key-concepts for subsequent identifications. For example, *"The laws of thermodynamics define fundamental physical quantities (temperature, energy, and entropy) that characterize thermodynamic systems at thermal equilibrium."* has *"laws of thermodynamics"* as its subject since the sentences is its definition but not of key-concept *"thermal equilibrium"* which is merely mentioned in the sentence. For this, a set of sentences, S_i for every key-concept, c_i is created which contains all the sentences from the input text that have c_i as their subject using Stanford's Dependency Parser [4].

3.3 Application/Definition Identification

We formulate the identification phases as supervised binary classification problems. For every key-concept $c_i \in C$, we determine whether any sentence in S_i possesses a certain structure that marks the existence of concept's application or definition. Instead of hand-engineering these patterns, we employ Neural Networks to learn them from a carefully annotated dataset. We use CNN with LSTM because it excels at learning the spatial structure in input data. Our application and definition datasets have one-dimensional spatial structure in the sequence of words and the CNN should be able to pick out invariant features from the positive samples. These learned spatial features may then be learned as sequences by an LSTM layer. We have the following methodology executed on $\forall s_i \in S_i \forall c_i$:

(1) **Word Embeddings**: We encode Top-N frequent words as 300-dimensional GLOVE[11] vector embeddings.

(2) **Sentence Embeddings**: We add a one-dimensional CNN and max pooling layer after the Embedding layer which then feeds the consolidated features to the LSTM.

(3) **Classification**: Ultimately, LSTM feeds the learned sentence embedding to a dense network with logistic regression classifier which predicts labels of sentences in S_i. This overall learning is done on a carefully handcrafted dataset for which details are provided in Section 4.1.

3.4 Enrichment

After identification of key concepts, we mine Wikipedia's content to enrich the input text. We first provide the user with a pre-requisite relationship based concept map for better understanding of hierarchy present amongst identified key-concepts. Then we provide enrichment in terms of definitions and applications.

Pre-requisite Relationship Identification: We define the "pre-requisite structure" for a corpus as a graph, where nodes are key-concepts to comprehend, and a directed edge A → B corresponds to the assertion that "understanding A is a prerequisite to understanding". We identify the pre-request relationship between two key-concepts A and B by equally weighing the sum of the following similarity measures: (1) **RefD score** [8] using a threshold of $\theta = 0.02$ to determine the direction and existence of edge between A and B and (2) **Wikipedia link based Semantic Similarity** [15] to measure the semantic relatedness between A and B using the idea that if two concepts occur on the same page, they are more likely to be related to each other.

Enrichment with Definitions and Applications: For definitional enrichment, we deploy our definition and Application identification module on key-concept's Wikipedia page and identify those sentences which qualify as concept's definition and application.

Model	Prec(%)		Recall(%)		F1(%)	
	App^n	Def^n	App^n	Def^n	App^n	Def^n
LSTM	**88.09**	92.78	82.40	88.73	84.72	90.39
CNN	84.42	92.05	83.17	**92.79**	83.70	92.40
CNN-LSTM	87.21	**93.56**	**83.73**	92.25	**85.31**	**92.83**

Table 2: Performance of different models trained on Application and Definition Identification Model Training Datasets

4 RESULTS AND DISCUSSION

4.1 Tasks and Datasets

Definition Identification Model Training Dataset: We used the dataset provided by [9] to train our CNN-LSTM network for Definition Identification task. The dataset consists of 1,908 definitional sentences and 2,711 non definitional sentences created from Wikipedia which consists of domain-independent samples to prevent any kind of bias during learning. This makes the dataset apt for our purpose of enrichment of formal text because of its eligibility for domain-independent use.

Application Identification Model Training Dataset: Authors of the paper manually created and reviewed the annotated dataset from Wikipedia which consists of 3,000 positive candidates and 3,702 negative candidates for Application Identification task. We identified generic patterns within sentences which were classified as applications of key-concepts. Every positive candidate consists of (i) the key-concept being applied, (ii) a verb phrase showing how the key-concept is being applied and (iii) the field where the key-concept is being applied. Consider the following sentences:

(1) [*Scenery generators*]$_{concept}$ [are commonly used in] [*movies, animations and video games*]$_{fields}$.

(2) [*The COS cell lines*]$_{concept}$ [are often used by] [*biologists when studying the monkey virus SV40*]$_{field}$.

(3) [*In the production of semiconductor materials and devices,*]$_{field}$ [*octafluorocyclobutane*]$_{concept}$ [serves] as a deposition gas.

System Evaluation Dataset: To evaluate the overall effectiveness of our enrichment system, we created following Ground Truth datasets: (1) Lectured notes from MIT Open Courseware on 'Physics', 'Chemistry', 'Algebra' and 'Algorithms'. They contain a total of 80 educational texts (15 pages each and 10-15 key-concepts per page) and (2) 'Articles' dataset which consists of 100 articles(15-20 concepts each) from multitude of science magazines. Excerpt from some sample text is shown in Table 1. Lecture notes dataset have significant number of defined concepts in topics such as 'Probability', 'Chemical Reactions' etc but lacks their real-life applications. On the contrary "Articles" dataset is rich with formal texts targeted for specific demographics lacking definitions of many key-concepts.

		Ground Truth	
		Enrichment Required	Enrichment Not Required
Proposed Method	Enrichment Provided	*TP*	*FN*
	Enrichment Not Provided	*FP*	*TN*

Table 3: Notions for Enrichment Accuracy metrics

4.2 Evaluation Metrics

Model Learning: We evaluated the performance of all the learned models during 10-fold cross validation on definitions' and applications' dataset using Precision, Recall and F1-measure.

Enrichment System: To evaluate the performance of our enrichment system, we have the following metrics:

- **Key Concept Extraction (KCE)** : KCE, the first phase of our enrichment system is evaluated using using usual notions of Precision and Recall.
- **Overall Enrichment Accuracy (EA)**: Identification and Extraction phase is collectively evaluated using EA which is calculated using following notions of True/ False Positives/Negatives 3.

$$EA = \frac{TP + TN}{TP + TN + FP + FN} \qquad (1)$$

4.3 Experiment Settings

Training : We trained the models using 10-fold cross validation. We restricted the Definition and Applications dataset to Top-1000 and Top-5000 frequent words respectively. GLOVE vector embeddings constituted the embedding layer. Following are the architectural details of different models stacked on top of the embedding layer:
(1) LSTM: LSTM (h=300 units) → Dropout, DL($p_{dropout}$ = 0.2).
(2) CNN: Convolution Layer, CL(mask size=5, filter maps=128) → Max-Pooling Layer, ML(size=2) → CL(5, 64) → ML(2)
(3) CNN-LSTM: CL(5, 128) → ML(2) → LSTM(h=300) → DL(p=0.2).

The CNN layers used ReLU for activation. For training, we used Adam Optimizer to minimize log loss. A batch size of 32 was chosen, vanilla-LSTM model was trained for 3 epochs, CNN-model for 10 epochs and CNN-LSTM for 5 epochs.

Overall Testing : (a) Extract key-concepts, (b) Create $S_i \forall c_i$ using concept-sentence matching. (c) Run all identification models

on $S_i \forall c_i$. (d) Obtain concept-dependency graph. (e) Based on (c), run identification model to mine relevant information from Wikipedia.

Pruning Phase	Prec(%)		Recall(%)		F1(%)	
	Edu	*Art*	*Edu*	*Art*	*Edu*	*Art*
LF	19.44	13.23	90.34	92.59	31.99	23.15
BBC Pruning	26.20	19.1	87.75	90.1	40.36	31.53
StackExchange	53.20	32.38	81.37	82.92	64.34	46.57
WikiRecall	78.68	72.04	76.35	81.71	77.50	76.57

Table 4: Performance of KCE phases in sequential order

4.4 Results

We report the results of all the KCE phases in Table 4. Linguistic filtering does not have 100% recall because of maximal string matching. For example, 'isotherm' as a concept is ignored as it is part of the string 'validity of freundlich isotherm'. BBC pruning improves precision, but there is a small decrement in recall because of pruning of concepts like "Moore Voting" as it has a common(frequent) word 'Voting' in it. We observe that SE tags increases the precision due to the richness in terms of technical concepts they provide, however, we extract some additional unneeded concepts that may be technically sound but not relevant to the context of the text thus leading to increasing cognitive burden, redundancy and irrelevant data. This trade off however depends on how well the SE tag corpus is related to the context of the text. In Wikipedia based recall, we retain only those concepts which have corresponding Wikipedia articles. It is not part of our Key-concept extraction phase. However, we observe a decrease in recall due to unavailability of concepts' Wikipages. To showcase the effectiveness of SE pruning, we computed the results for Wikipedia based pruning without it: *Prec* : 75.81%, *Recall* : 75.46% and *F*1 : 75.64%. From Table 2, it is quite evident from the results that the CNN-LSTM model preformed better as expected on both the datasets. Finally, we report EA for Definitions: 77.17% and 78.57% and Applications: 75.14% and 81.81% on Lectured Notes and Articles dataset respectively. For qualitative analysis, Fig. 1 represents the output of our enrichment system for formal text on "Computer Vision". The text neither contains its definition nor its applications, our system realizes this need and fetches them. Also, our system provides a concept graph to visualize the dependencies like understanding of "Computer Vision" is crucial before understanding "Artificial Intelligence".

5 CONCLUSION

We proposed a novel framework to enrich formal text with supplementary material. In the proposed approach, we extract key-concepts from text, identify the enrichment need using Deep Learning and finally enrich the text with definitions, applications and a pre-requisite concept graph to make the comprehension of the text easier. We also prepared the System Evaluation and Applications dataset. Lastly, we have done a quantitative analysis of the enrichment results to measure the effectiveness of our proposed framework. In future, we would like to validate the effectiveness of our enrichment framework on users with varying expertise by conducting a user study.

REFERENCES

[1] Rakesh Agrawal, Sreenivas Gollapudi, Anitha Kannan, and Krishnaram Kenthapadi. 2011. Identifying enrichment candidates in textbooks. In *WWW*. ACM.

[2] Rakesh Agrawal, Sreenivas Gollapudi, Krishnaram Kenthapadi, Nitish Srivastava, and Raja Velu. 2010. Enriching textbooks through data mining. In *DEV*. ACM.

[3] Luis Espinosa Anke, Horacio Saggion, and Francesco Ronzano. 2015. Weakly supervised definition extraction. In *RANLP*.

[4] Danqi Chen and Christopher Manning. 2014. A fast and accurate dependency parser using neural networks. In *EMNLP*.

[5] Jonathan Gordon, Linhong Zhu, Aram Galstyan, Prem Natarajan, and Gully Burns. 2016. Modeling Concept Dependencies in a Scientific Corpus.. In *ACL*. ACM.

[6] Clyde Freeman Herreid. 1994. Case Studies in Science–A Novel Method of Science Education. *Journal of College Science Teaching* 23, 4 (1994).

[7] SiLiang Li, Bin Xu, and Tong Lee Chung. 2016. Definition Extraction with LSTM Recurrent Neural Networks. In *CCL*. Springer.

[8] Chen Liang, Zhaohui Wu, Wenyi Huang, and C Lee Giles. 2015. Measuring Prerequisite Relations Among Concepts.. In *EMNLP*. ACL.

[9] Roberto Navigli and Paola Velardi. 2010. Learning word-class lattices for definition and hypernym extraction. In *ACL*. ACM.

[10] Roberto Navigli, Paola Velardi, Juana María Ruiz-Martínez, et al. 2010. An Annotated Dataset for Extracting Definitions and Hypernyms from the Web.. In *LREC*.

[11] Jeffrey Pennington, Richard Socher, and Christopher Manning. 2014. Glove: Global vectors for word representation. In *EMNLP*. ACL.

[12] Tzipora Rakedzon, Elad Segev, Noam Chapnik, Roy Yosef, and Ayelet Baram-Tsabari. 2017. Automatic jargon identifier for scientists engaging with the public and science communication educators. *PloS one* 12, 8 (2017).

[13] Kristina Toutanova, Dan Klein, Christopher D Manning, and Yoram Singer. 2003. Feature-rich part-of-speech tagging with a cyclic dependency network. In *NAACL*. ACL.

[14] Shuting Wang, Alexander Ororbia, Zhaohui Wu, Kyle Williams, Chen Liang, Bart Pursel, and C Lee Giles. 2016. Using prerequisites to extract concept maps fromtextbooks. In *CIKM*. ACM.

[15] Ian H Witten and David N Milne. 2008. An effective, low-cost measure of semantic relatedness obtained from Wikipedia links. (2008).

Modeling Semantics Between Programming Codes and Annotations

Yihan Lu
Arizona State University
Tempe, Arizona
lyihan@asu.edu

I-Han Hsiao
Arizona State University
Tempe, Arizona
Sharon.Hsiao@asu.edu

ABSTRACT

It is a common practice for programmers to leave annotations during program development. Most of the annotated documentations are predominantly being used as the archive of the coding events for limited developers. We hypothesize that these annotations captured mass amount of valuable information which can be utilized to identify similar codes or to examine code quality. However, due to the annotating behaviors vary and the language composition can be complex, this work sets out to investigate a systematic method to examine the annotation semantics and their relations with codes. We designed a semantic parser to extract concepts from codes and the corresponding annotations. Additionally, text mining techniques are applied to summarize linguistic features from the annotations. We then build models to predict concepts in programming code annotations. Results show that the proposed semantic modeling method achieved a higher performance compared to a random guessed baseline.

CCS CONCEPTS

• **Social and professional topics** → **Computing education**; **Computer science education**; **Software engineering education**; **Student assessment**; • **Theory of computation** → **Machine learning theory**; **Online learning theory**; **Query learning**; *Boolean function learning*; • **Applied computing** → **Computer-assisted instruction**; • **Information systems** → *Nearest-neighbor search*;

KEYWORDS

Coding concept detection, Programming semantics, Text based classification, Semantic modeling

ACM Reference Format:
Yihan Lu and I-Han Hsiao. 2018. Modeling Semantics Between Programming Codes and Annotations. In *HT '18: 29th ACM Conference on Hypertext and Social Media, July 9–12, 2018, Baltimore, MD, USA.* ACM, New York, NY, USA, 5 pages. https://doi.org/10.1145/3209542.3209578

1 INTRODUCTION

Programming is a problem-solving adventure for programming learners. It involves a variety of complex cognitive activities, from

conceptual knowledge construction to basic structural operations, including program design, programming understanding, modifying, debugging, and documenting. Among all the activities, it is a common practice for programmers to leave annotations during program development. The annotation content can range from code descriptions, uses and unused of codes, expected/unexpected outcomes, copyrights, logics, limitations, comments on the implementation, etc. Most of the annotated documentations are predominantly being used as the archive of the coding events for limited developers. We hypothesize that these annotations captured mass amount of valuable information based on the types, purposes, understandings and locations. This information can be further used to reduce the cognitive load [9] for coders. Therefore, by extracting and modeling the semantics of the annotations could enable multiple applications in the educational context, for instance, further estimation of the coder's intention, examination of the problem-solving approaches, example code recommendations, etc [1]. However, dissecting the annotation semantics is not a trivial task. Due to the annotating behaviors and languages complexities, one can annotate a single line of code or a block of codes; one can leave plain English or a combination of natural languages with the programming languages. Therefore, this work sets out to investigate a systematic method to examine the annotation semantics and their relations with codes. We proposed a semantic modeling method, to extract concepts from codes and the corresponding annotations. Additionally, text mining techniques are applied to summarize linguistic features from the annotations. Combining the semantic and pragmatic features, we then build models to predict concepts in programming code and annotation. The following paper will give a short summary on related works and detail description on the semantic modeling method. Finally, the evaluation results and discussions are presented.

2 LITERATURE REVIEW

There have been a few studies investigated the relations between natural languages and programming languages. A parser-based code example recommender was developed by Singh [10] for educational purpose. Tan et al. [11] used the comment and code annotation to detect bugs. Corazza [2] researched the coherence between comments and the corresponding codes. Hsiao et al. [5] evaluated a variation of topic model by integrating NLP-based short texts and programming language syntactical features. Such method has been applied to extract semantics from programming exams [6] and programming discussion forums [4]. Haixun et al. attempted to extract semantic knowledge from short text [7]. From the study, they also indicated the difficulties in understanding short text, including the lack of syntax elements, the shortage in state-of-the-art tagging, and the impact of noise. Another study conducted by Howard

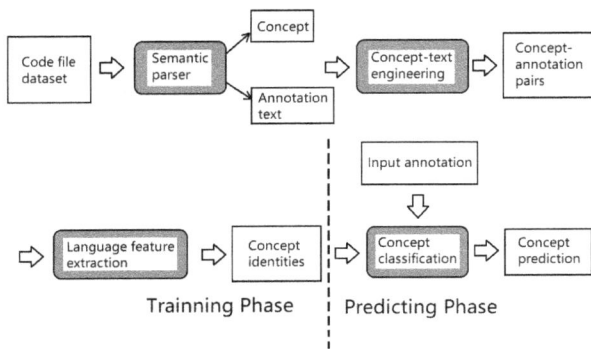

Figure 1: Workflow of methodology.

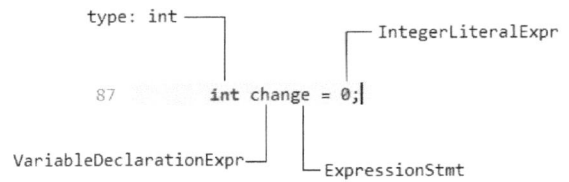

Figure 2: Example of concept extraction from a code line.

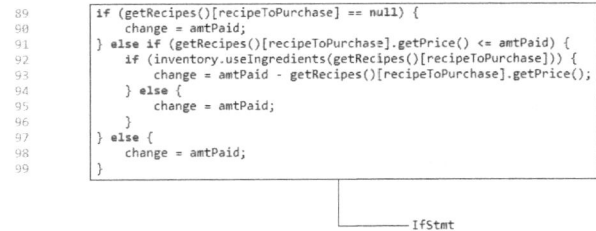

Figure 3: Example of Concept belongs to a block of code.

aimed to identify semantically similar words from comment-code mappings [4], which utilized a mapping method similar to ours, but focused on the connection between annotations and function signatures.

In our work, we design a programming language parser that analyzes code and annotation connections and extracts concepts from the context. The capability to preserve the code and annotation connections permits to capture the semantic meaning of the code in a finer-grained level, because the scale of code analysis is ranged from the whole code file to each single word.

3 METHODOLOGY

3.1 General Workflow

In this work, we propose a method to extract the connection between programming code concepts and annotation linguistic features, which help to predict the concepts involved in the source code based on its annotation text. The methodology includes two phases: training and predicting. In the training phase, the algorithm takes a set of code documents including code and corresponding annotations as input, and abstracts concepts in code with language feature identities; in the predicting phase, the algorithm takes an annotation text as input and predicts related concepts according to language feature identities detected. This work is based on the following assumptions: (1) Source codes with similar concepts would share similar terms in annotations; (2) Each concept would have identical textual feature in its related annotations; (3) Concepts with high occurrence frequency would be easier to identify from annotations; (4) Concepts frequently involved in annotations would be easier to identify from annotations. Based on these assumptions, we developed a concept identity extraction method with four main technical parts: code concept extraction, code-annotation engineering, annotation linguistic feature extracting, and concept classification. Figure 1 is the general work flow.

3.2 Code Concept Extraction

The first step of this work is to extract code concepts from code blocks. The methodology of concept extraction utilizes programming semantic parser. This technique recursively scans programming code, identifies structure, and detects concepts in code line or block. Figure 2 is an example of concept extraction in a single line.

Besides the names of concept, this method also records the line range of each occurrence. In the last example, all four concepts belong to the line 87. A concept could also belong to a range of lines. In Figure 3, the concept "IfStmt" belongs to a block of code from line 89 to 99.

After concept extraction, each code file is turned into a set of concepts with line ranges in the file.

3.3 Code & Annotation Engineering

To capture code and annotation connection semantics, the adjacency relation is extracted from the line range of concepts and annotations.

Annotation text is extracted from code file with line range, and each annotation text is matched to a set of concepts according to adjacency relations. As shown in Figure 4, there are three types of line range adjacency.

3.4 Concept Identity Extraction

In this step, each annotation text is processed as a natural language document to extract linguistic features. After punctuation removal, stop-words removal, and stemming, we transform the documents into a document-term matrix, and apply tf-idf algorithm on the matrix to determine the representativeness for each term in each document. For example, in Figure 5 the content of *doc1* is:

"Add a separator to the supplied menu. The separator will only be added, if additional items are added using addAction."

```
                                                                      (1)
// These are in-line comments just before the method definitition
if (constDec.getComment() != null){
    if (this.comments == null){
        this.comments = "";//initialize string as empty    (2)
    }
    this.comments += constDec.getComment().getContent();
}
                                                                      (3)
// Recursively loop through child nodes and make a dictionary
this.parseBody(constDec.getBlock());
```

Figure 4: Three types of adjacency: (1) comments before a block of code statement; (2) comments follow the termination of the code in the same line; (3) comments before a single line of code.

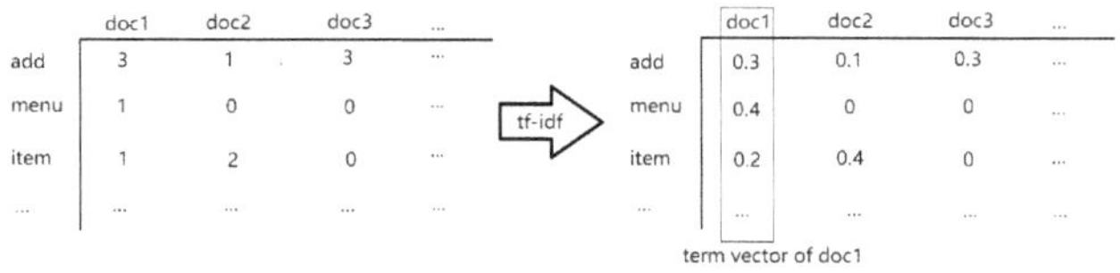

Figure 5: An example of applying tf-idf on document-term matrix; The term vector of doc1 is highlighted.

The term vector of doc1 is initiated as Fig. 5 on the left. After applying tf-idf, the values in term vector of doc1 turn into fractions as Figure 5 on the right. Since the term "menu" does not appear in other documents, its representativeness is higher than the other terms for doc1.

In the document-term matrix, each document d is transformed into a numerical term vector V_d, where each element in V_d is a tf-idf value of a term. For concept C, assume the set of documents containing concept C is:

$$S_c = \{d_1, d_2, ...d_k\} \quad (1)$$

The corresponding term vectors of S_C are:

$$M_C = \{V_{d1}, V_{d2}, ...V_{dk}\} \quad (2)$$

In order to remove the concept frequency bias, the identity of concept is normalized. The normalized center of S_C, namely V_C, is defined to be the linguistic feature identity of concept C.

$$V_C = \frac{\overline{M_C}}{|\overline{M_C}|} \quad (3)$$

Then for all concepts $\{C_1, C_2, ...C_n\}$, the matrix formed by their linguistic feature identity $\{V_{C1}, V_{C2}, ...V_{Cn}\}$ is defined to be the concept identity matrix M. Take concept "AssignExpr" as example, it is involved in the set of documents:

$$S_{AssignExpr} = \{doc3, doc4, doc6, ...\} \quad (4)$$

Their term vectors are:

$$M_{AssignExpr} = \{V_{doc3}, V_{doc4}, V_{doc6}, ...\}$$
$$= \{(0.1, 0.3, 0.5, ...), (0, 0.1, 0.1, ...), (0, 0, 0, ...), ...\} \quad (5)$$

Table 1: Descriptive statistics of the java projects in the dataset, N_f (number of java files), N_a (number of annotations).

Java project	N_f	N_a
CoffeeMaker	7	73
JFreeChart 6.0	86	1130
JfreeChart 7.1	127	1641
JhotDraw	569	5019

The normalized center of these vectors is:

$$V_{AssignExpr} = \frac{\overline{M_{AssignExpr}}}{|\overline{M_{AssignExpr}}|}$$
$$= \frac{(0.03, 0.3, 0.012, ...)}{0.12} = (0.25, 2.5, 0.1, ...) \quad (6)$$

$V_{AssignExpr}$ is the identity of the concept "AssignExpr", which is also part of the concept identity matrix $M = \{V_{C1}, V_{C2}, ...V_{Cn}\}$. After this part, the training phase is finished.

3.5 Concept Classification

After processing the code data set into concept identity matrix, we can predict concepts involved given a descriptive text of a source code. Assume the given text is T, which is formed by a series of terms. After natural linguistic feature extraction, T is transformed into a term vector V_T. Consider the dot product as the similarity between two vectors, by calculating

$$Sim_T = M * V_T \quad (7)$$

The similarity between V_T and each concept identity is represented as a single fraction in $SimV_T$.

To determine whether a concept is involved, the similarity of between a text and a concept is compared with a cut-off related to the concept. Noting "#" as the length of a vector and S as the whole document set, the cut-off of concept C is defined as follows:

$$Cut_C = V_{C_{\lfloor \#V_C * \frac{\#S_C}{\#S} \rfloor}} \quad (8)$$

In this way, a high frequency concept is more likely to be determined as involve.

3.6 Dataset

To evaluate the method, we reused the data set of Corazza's work [2]. This data set is open source online [8], which includes 799 files from four java projects (Table 1).

3381 different concepts are detected from the data set and 8520 annotations are extracted from the files together with corresponding code pieces.

These open source java projects are chosen because their annotation coverage is relatively high, and the annotation contents are descriptive to the corresponding codes.

(a) f1 value distribution of prediction

(b) f1 value distribution of baseline

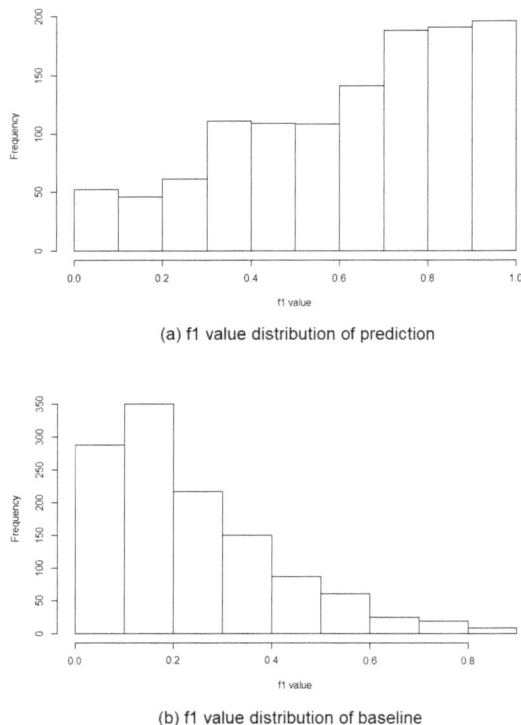

Figure 6: Comparison between proposed method and baseline.

4 EVALUATION AND DISCUSSION

4.1 Annotation Concept Prediction Evaluation

In this section, we compare our method with a baseline conducted with random prediction algorithm [3]. Given any annotation text, the random prediction will determine whether a concept is involved randomly according to the concept occurrence rate. For example, a concept appears in 60% code pieces in the dataset, then the baseline has a 60% chance to label this concept as involved without analyzing the annotation. This baseline is valid for our prediction algorithm since it reflects the scale of information the annotation can provide to predict code concepts. After applying concept prediction on the dataset, each code piece has a set of predicted concepts based on its announcement. The prediction is evaluated by comparing with the truth, then every code piece has a precision, accuracy, and f1 value. Figure 6 compares the f1 value distribution of proposed method with baseline. The performance of proposed method ($\overline{f1}$=0.64, sd=0.27) is significantly better than baseline ($\overline{f1}$=0.12, sd=0.09).

4.2 Concept Frequency vs. Prediction Accuracy

Another evaluation is from the perspective of concept, since it is necessary to examine whether every concept can be predicted with a stable performance, especially the concepts with lower frequency in code dataset. In the prediction result, every concept is connected to a set of code pieces. By comparing the prediction to the truth, every concept has a precision, accuracy, and f1 value. The relation

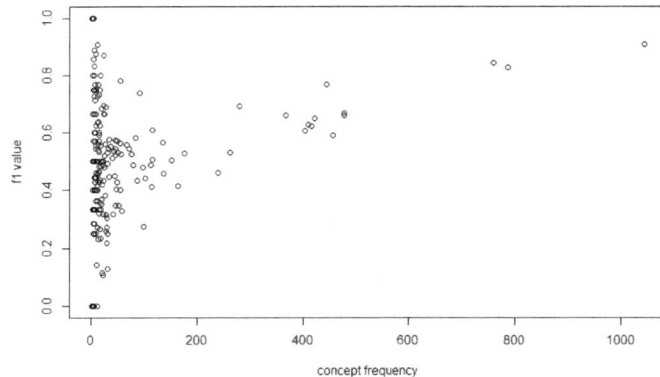

Figure 7: The relation between concept frequency and f1 value

between concept frequency and f1 value in Figure 7 indicates the f1 value of low frequency concepts is not stable compare to high frequency concepts, while the average f1 value increases with concept frequency.

5 SUMMARY $ FUTURE WORK

In this work we proposed a semantic modeling method to extract concepts from codes and the corresponding annotations. Text mining techniques are applied to summarize linguistic features from the annotations. After combining the semantic and pragmatic features, we then build models to predict concepts in programming code according to given annotation. The evaluation result shows this concept prediction has a higher performance compare to random guess as baseline; The performance is higher and more stable on high frequency concepts in code.

There are several limitations in this work. According to the evaluation, the performance of concept detection is not stable on low frequency concepts. One solution on this shortage is to filter low frequency concepts and provide concept identities with high confidence. Another potential improvement is in the linguistic feature extraction part. More NLP based techniques can be used including "semantic distance" and "semantic network". However, the potential of this method is still promising. One application of this method is the "example code recommending" in programming education, in which a student just need to provide the textual description of the code he/she wants to write, then the method will predict the concepts involved, and provide relevant code examples for the student to refer.

REFERENCES

[1] Robert K Atkinson, Sharon J Derry, Alexander Renkl, and Donald Wortham. 2000. Learning from examples: Instructional principles from the worked examples research. *Review of educational research* 70, 2 (2000), 181–214.
[2] Anna Corazza, Valerio Maggio, and Giuseppe Scanniello. 2015. On the coherence between comments and implementations in source code. In *Software Engineering and Advanced Applications (SEAA), 2015 41st Euromicro Conference on*. IEEE, 76–83.

[3] R Don Horner and Donald M Baer. 1978. Multiple-probe technique: A variation of the multiple baseline. *Journal of Applied Behavior Analysis* 11, 1 (1978), 189–196.

[4] Matthew J Howard, Samir Gupta, Lori Pollock, and K Vijay-Shanker. 2013. Automatically mining software-based, semantically-similar words from comment-code mappings. In *Proceedings of the 10th Working Conference on Mining Software Repositories*. IEEE Press, 377–386.

[5] I-Han Hsiao and Piyush Awasthi. 2015. Topic facet modeling: semantic visual analytics for online discussion forums. In *Proceedings of the Fifth International Conference on Learning Analytics And Knowledge*. ACM, 231–235.

[6] I-Han Hsiao and Yi-Ling Lin. 2017. Enriching programming content semantics: An evaluation of visual analytics approach. *Computers in Human Behavior* 72 (2017), 771–782.

[7] Wen Hua, Zhongyuan Wang, Haixun Wang, Kai Zheng, and Xiaofang Zhou. 2017. Understand short texts by harvesting and analyzing semantic knowledge. *IEEE transactions on Knowledge and data Engineering* 29, 3 (2017), 499–512.

[8] Valerio Maggio. 2015. Comments and Implementations—A Public Benchmark. http://www2.unibas.it/gscanniello/coherence

[9] Jan L Plass, Roxana Moreno, and Roland Brünken. 2010. *Cognitive load theory*. Cambridge University Press.

[10] Shashank Singh. 2017. *CodeReco-A Semantic Java Method Recommender*. Ph.D. Dissertation. Arizona State University.

[11] Lin Tan, Yuanyuan Zhou, and Yoann Padioleau. 2011. aComment: mining annotations from comments and code to detect interrupt related concurrency bugs. In *Software Engineering (ICSE), 2011 33rd International Conference on*. IEEE, 11–20.

IntelliEye: Enhancing MOOC Learners' Video Watching Experience through Real-Time Attention Tracking

Tarmo Robal
Tallinn University of Technology
Tallinn, Estonia
tarmo.robal@ttu.ee

Yue Zhao, Christoph Lofi, Claudia Hauff*
Delft University of Technology
Delft, Netherlands
{y.zhao-1,c.lofi,c.hauff}@tudelft.nl

ABSTRACT

Massive Open Online Courses (MOOCs) have become an attractive opportunity for people around the world to gain knowledge and skills. Despite the initial enthusiasm of the first wave of MOOCs and the subsequent research efforts, MOOCs today suffer from retention issues: many MOOC learners start but do not finish. A main culprit is the lack of oversight and directions: learners need to be skilled in self-regulated learning to monitor themselves and their progress, keep their focus and plan their learning. Many learners lack such skills and as a consequence do not succeed in their chosen MOOC. Many of today's MOOCs are centered around video lectures, which provide ample opportunities for learners to become distracted and lose their attention without realizing it. If we were able to detect learners' loss of attention in real-time, we would be able to intervene and ideally return learners' attention to the video. This is the scenario we investigate: we designed a privacy-aware system (IntelliEye) that makes use of learners' Webcam feeds to determine—in real-time—when they no longer pay attention to the lecture videos. IntelliEye makes learners aware of their attention loss via visual and auditory cues. We deployed IntelliEye in a MOOC across a period of 74 days and explore to what extent MOOC learners accept it as part of their learning and to what extent it influences learners' behaviour. IntelliEye is open-sourced at https://github.com/Yue-ZHAO/IntelliEye.

KEYWORDS

MOOCs; online learning; IntelliEye

ACM Reference Format:
Tarmo Robal and Yue Zhao, Christoph Lofi, Claudia Hauff. 2018. IntelliEye: Enhancing MOOC Learners' Video Watching Experience through Real-Time Attention Tracking. In *HT'18: 29th ACM Conference on Hypertext & Social Media, July 9–12, 2018, Baltimore, MD, USA*. ACM, New York, NY, USA, 9 pages. https://doi.org/10.1145/3209542.3209547

---

*The first and second author of this paper contributed equally.

---

1 INTRODUCTION

In 2011, the *MOOC revolution* began: Stanford University offered the first MOOC on Artificial Intelligence followed by more than 160,000 learners worldwide. The idea of MOOCs quickly spread. A major motivation behind MOOCs is the provision of ubiquitous learning to people from all walks of live. Today, MOOCs are being offered by many world-renowned universities on platforms such as Coursera, FutureLearn and edX[1], reaching millions of learners. At the same time, the initial predictions of this revolution have not come to pass—MOOCs today suffer from a lack of retention with usually less than 10% (in extreme cases < 1%) of learners succeeding [9]. Examining the current nature of MOOCs reveals an important clue as to why they fail to realize their potential: although they offer flexibility, and scale, they do not involve truly novel technologies. Most MOOCs today revolve around a large number of videos[2] and automatically graded quizzes and little else. This setup (largely chosen for its inherent scalability), requires learners to be skilled in *self-regulated learning* [21], that is, to monitor themselves and their progress, keep their focus and plan their learning. Many learners lack such skills and as a consequence do not succeed. In this paper we present IntelliEye, a system we designed to directly tackle the "loss of focus" issue during MOOC lecture video watching by detecting it in real-time and alerting the learner to it. We focus our efforts on the video watching activity as (i) learners spend a large portion of their time in a MOOC on it; (ii) learners are prone to lose their focus even in short lecture videos of six to ten minutes [30], a common video length in MOOCs; (iii) video watching is a rather passive activity which provides ample opportunities for learners to become distracted—and engage in "heavy media multitasking" [13] by reading their emails, surfing the Web, etc.—and lose their focus often without realizing it; and (iv) inattention has been shown to be significantly and negatively correlated with learning efficiency [26].

How exactly can we detect learners' loss of focus *in real-time* and *at scale*? How can we alert the learner to her loss of focus? One answer to these questions lies in the ubiquitous availability of Webcams in today's laptops: IntelliEye employs the Webcam feed to observe learners' activities during their time on the MOOC platform and intervenes (e.g. by delivering an auditory signal) if it detects a loss of focus. All of these actions are performed by IntelliEye in a *privacy-aware* manner: none of the data or computations leaves a user's machine. Prior works [1, 2, 18, 30] exploited eye-tracking to determine a user's attention state, though these studies were either conducted with commercial high-quality hardware eye-tracking devices and/or well-settled experimental lab conditions [30]. In contrast, in our work we make use of commonly available Webcams

---

[1]https://www.edx.org/
[2]The MOOC we deploy IntelliEye in contains 104 lecture videos.

and deploy IntelliEye "in the wild", to 2, 612 MOOC learners in an actual MOOC, instead of a controlled lab study.

We conduct our analyses of IntelliEye's use along three dimensions: (1) the **technological capabilities** of MOOC learners' hardware, (2) the **acceptance** of IntelliEye by MOOC learners, and, (3) the **effect** of IntelliEye on MOOC learners' behaviour. Specifically, we investigate the following research questions:

RQ1 To what extent is MOOC learners' hardware capable to enable the usage of technologically advanced widgets such as IntelliEye?

RQ2 To what extent do MOOC learners accept technology that is designed to aid their learning but at the same time is likely to be perceived as privacy-invading (even though it is not)? Are certain types of MOOC learners (e.g. young learners, or highly educated ones) more likely to accept this technology than others?

RQ3 What impact does IntelliEye have on learners' behaviours and actions? To what extent does IntelliEye affect learners' video watching behaviour?

Our main findings can be summarized as follows:

- We find that most learners (78%) use hardware and software setups which are capable to support such widgets, making the wide-spread adoption of our approach realistic from a technological point of view.
- The majority of learners (67%) with capable setups is reluctant to allow the use of Webcam-based attention tracking techniques, citing as main reasons privacy concerns and the lack of perceived usefulness of such a tool.
- Among the learners using IntelliEye we observe (i) high levels of inattention (on average one inattention episode occurs every 36 seconds—a significantly higher rate than reported in previous lab studies) and (ii) an adaptation of learners' behaviour towards the technology (learners in conditions that disturb the learner when inattention occurs exhibit fewer inattention episodes than learners in a condition that provides less disturbance).

2 RELATED WORK

Attention Loss in the Learning Process

Identifying and tracking learners' loss of attention in the classroom has been explored in a myriad of ways since the 1960s, including the analysis of students' notes [7, 15], the observation of inattention behaviors (by observers, stationed at the back of the classroom) [8], the retention of course content [16], probes (requiring participants to record their attention at particular given points in time) [12, 27] and self-reports (requiring participants to report when they become aware of their loss of attention) [3]. A common belief was that learners' attention decreases considerably after 10-15 minutes into the lecture [27]. Later, Wilson and Korn [29] challenged this claim and argued that more research is needed, a call picked up by Bunce et al. [3] who found that learners start losing their attention early on in higher-education lectures and may cycle through several attention states within 9-12 minute course segments.

With the advent of online learning, the issue of attention loss, how to measure it and how it compares to classroom attention lapses received renewed attention. Different studies have shown that in online learning environments (often simulated in lab settings where participants watch lecture videos), attention lapses may be even more frequent than in the classroom setting. Risko et al. [23] used three one hour video-recorded lectures with various topics (psychology, economics, and classics) in their experiments, probing participants four times throughout each video. The attention-loss frequency was found to be 43%. In addition, a significant negative correlation between test performance and loss of attention was found. Szpunar et al. [28] studied the impact of interpolated tests on learners' loss of attention within online lectures, asking participants to watch a 21-minute video lecture (4 segments with 5.5 minutes per segment) and report their loss of attention in response to random probes (one per segment). In their study, the loss of attention frequency was about 40%. Loh et al. [13] also applied probes to measure learners' loss of attention, finding a positive correlation between media multitasking activity and learners' loss of attention (average frequency of 32%) whilst watching video lectures. Based on these considerably high loss of attention frequencies we conclude that reducing loss of attention in online learning is an important approach to improve learning outcomes.

Automatic Detection of Attention Loss

Inspired by the eye-mind link effect [22], a number of previous studies [1, 2, 18] focused on the automatic detection of learners' loss of attention by means of gaze data. In [1, 2], Bixler and D'Mello investigated the detection of learners' loss of attention during computerized reading. To generate the ground truth, the study participants were asked to manually report their loss of attention when an auditory probe (i.e. a beep) was triggered. Based on those reports, the loss of attention frequency ranged from 24% to 30%. During the experiment, gaze data was collected using a dedicated eye-tracker. Mills et al. [18] asked study participants to watch a 32 minute, non-educational movie and self-report their loss of attention throughout. In order to detect loss of attention automatically, statistical features and the relationship between gaze and video content were considered. In contrast to [1, 2], the authors mainly focused on the relationship between a participant's gaze and areas of interest (AOIs), specific areas in the video a participant should be interested in. Zhao et al. [30] presented a method to detect inattention similar to the studies in [18], but optimized for a MOOC setting (including the use of a Webcam alongside a high-quality eye-tracker). All mentioned approaches relying on the eye-mind link share two common issues: (i) they are usually unable to provide real-time feedback as they are trained on eye-gaze recordings with sparse manually provided labels (e.g., most approaches have a label frequency of 30-60 seconds, which directly translates into a detection delay of similar length), and (ii) the reported accuracy is too low for practical application (e.g., [30] reports detection accuracy between 14%-35%). Lastly, we note that besides the eye-mind link, another recent direction is the use of heart rate data (measured for instance by tracking fingertip transparency changes [20]) to infer learners' attention.

MOOC Interventions

We now discuss MOOC interventions, especially those geared towards video watching and towards improving self-regulated learning. Existing research on MOOC videos is largely concerned with the question of what makes a MOOC video engaging and attractive to learners; examples include the overlay of an instructor's face over the lecture slides [10], shorter video segments instead of one long lecture video [6], and the overlay of an instructor's gaze to enable learners to more easily follow the video content [25].

Few works have considered the issue of self-regulated learning in MOOCs, largely because this requires approaches that are personalized and reactive towards each individual learner. Simply informing learners about the best strategies for self-regulated learning at the beginning of a MOOC is not sufficient [11]. Davis et al. [5] recently designed a visual "personalized feedback system" that enables learners to learn how well they are doing compared to successful passers from a previous MOOC edition (in terms of time spent on the platform, their summative assessment scores and so on). This comparison, even though this feedback moment was rare (once a week), enabled learners to self-regulate their learning better, leading to significantly higher completion rates for learners exposed to the feedback system. A prior study by Davis et al. [4] had indicated that non-compliance among learners is a difficult obstacle in very simple interventions: the authors had included an extra question in each week of a MOOC, asking learners to write about their study plans (and thus make learners think about those plans). Few learners saw the benefit of this question (it was ungraded) and thus very few complied.

Overall, we have shown that attention lapses are a regular occurrence in the classroom and occur with even greater frequency in online learning, where learners are prone to digital multitasking. We have also presented some drawbacks of sophisticated eyetracking-based attention loss detectors (accuracy and timeliness of detection) and finally we have pointed out the difficulty of bringing self-regulated learning into the MOOC scenario due to learners' non-compliance. In response to these findings we have designed IntelliEye, a robust attention loss (by using face detection as a proxy) detector that requires no additional actions by the learners beyond what they usually do on a MOOC platform, provides personalized feedback, is privacy-aware and detects a loss of attention in near-real-time (with at most 2 seconds delay).

3 INTELLIEYE

3.1 Architecture

The goal of IntelliEye is to provide real-time feedback on learner's attention, and is based on a set of heuristics *reliably implementable* on a wide variety of hardware setups: (1) if the browser tab/window containing the lecture video is not visible to the learner, IntelliEye triggers an inattention event; (2) we assume a learner is inattentive if her face cannot be detected for a period of time, i.e. we employ face tracking as a robust proxy of attention tracking[3]; (3) if the face tracking module detects a loss of the face we consider the mouse movements as a safety check: if no face is detected but the mouse is being moved, no event is triggered.

The resulting high-level architecture is shown in Figure 1. We implemented IntelliEye in JavaScript, as the edX platform allows custom JavaScript to be embedded in course modules—thus providing us with an easy way to "ship" IntelliEye to all learners

in our MOOC. As visible in Figure 1, IntelliEye resides exclusively on the client to ensure learners' privacy; usage logs are send to our dedicated IntelliEye log server for the purpose of evaluating IntelliEye, though this communication is not necessary for IntelliEye to function. This setup requires IntelliEye to be light-weight and resource-saving as all computations are carried out on the learner's device and within the resource limits of a common Web browser. We now describe the seven architecture modules that IntelliEye consists off.

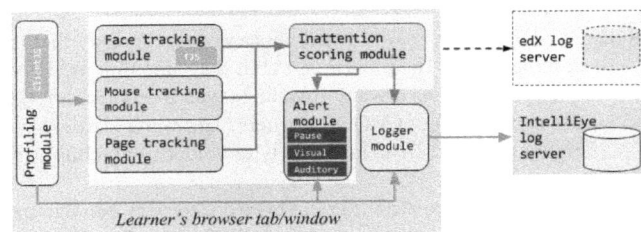

Figure 1: IntelliEye's high-level architecture. The profiling and logger modules are always active; the attention tracking and alerting modules are only enabled if supported setup is detected and learner has granted access to Webcam feed.

3.1.1 Profiling Module. In order to provide a smooth user experience for MOOC learners we limit the full usage of IntelliEye to devices that fulfill certain device setup requirements, a situation we call *supported setup*. We rely on the ClientJS[4] library to determine the device type, operating system and browser version of the learner's device and activate the inattention tracking modules only if a supported setup is detected. The requirements are as follows:

(1) The device is not a mobile device and is not running iOS or Android, due to their incompatibility with IntelliEye.
(2) The browser used is either: Chrome 54+ (i.e. version 54 or higher), Firefox 45+ or Opera 41+ to ensure the availability of JavaScript dependencies necessary for IntelliEye.
(3) The device has at least one usable Webcam as detected via the Media Capture and Streams API.

If the profiling yields an *unsupported setup*, a log entry is sent to our IntelliEye log server and no further modules are activated.

The profiling module is also responsible for extracting the learner's edX user ID, which in turn determines which alert type the learner receives in our experiments.

3.1.2 Face Tracking Module. In IntelliEye, we use face tracking to proxy inattention detection, thus aiming at overcoming the reported shortcomings of gaze tracking with respect to response time and reliability: if a learner's face is not visible in front of the screen when a lecture video is playing, we argue that she is likely not paying attention.

We initially experimented with two open-source libraries for this purpose—WebGazer.js[5] and tracking.js [14][6] (or TJS for short)—and investigated their suitability for Webcam-based inattention detection using face tracking in a user study with 20 participants [24]. As an upper bound, we also included the high-end

---

[3]We note that this is a lower-bound for inattention, as learners watching the video may still not pay attention.

[4]https://github.com/jackspirou/clientjs
[5]https://webgazer.cs.brown.edu
[6]https://trackingjs.com

hardware eye-tracker Tobii X2-30 Compact. We evaluated all three setups using fifty behaviours that learners typically execute in front of their computer; thirty-five of those behaviours should lead to a face detection loss (such as *Check your phone*; *Look right for 10 seconds*) and fifteen should not (e.g. *Reposition yourself in the chair*; *Scratch the top of your head*). During the study the participants were asked to perform each of the fifty tasks in turn. The study showed that only TJS has a competitive accuracy: it is able to detect 77.8% (compared to Webgazer.js's 14.8%) of the face hit/face miss behaviours that the Tobii X2-30 Compact was identifying correctly. We also measured the delay in detecting inattention, i.e. the difference in seconds between the behaviour being performed by a study participant and the inattention being detected: $0.6 \pm 1.1s$ for TJS and $1.3 \pm 1.0s$ for Webgazer.js. Based on these results, we chose TJS as our face detection library.

The module performs face presence detection (via TJS) from the Webcam feed every 250ms and reports a boolean (face present or absent) to the *Inattention scoring module*. We chose this time interval not to overburden the computational resources of the learner's device.

3.1.3 Mouse Tracking Module.
This module acts as a sanity check for the face tracking module: if the face tracking module reports loss of a face and the learner is still moving the mouse in the active MOOC window, we assume that the face tracking module misclassified the situation and do not raise an inattention alert. This module tracks the absence or presence of mouse movements every 250ms and reports it to the *Inattention scoring module*.

3.1.4 Page Tracking Module.
This module tracks the visibility of the browser window or tab that contains the edX page (and thus the lecture video) using the document.hidden() Web API call. A value is produced every 250ms and forwarded to the *Inattention scoring module*.

3.1.5 Inattention Scoring Module.
This module estimates inattention of a learner by aggregating the data obtained from the tracking modules based on the heuristics already introduced at the start of § 3.1: a learner is inattentive if her face is not trackable unless there is mouse movement and the video player browser window is visible. The input from the three scoring modules is aggregated over a sliding time window of five seconds—we chose this time window based on our user study with 50 typical activities during MOOC video watching, where we found the longest activity to take approximately five seconds. Recall that each module has a fixed sampling rate of 250 ms, and thus our sliding window takes into account 20 measurement points from each tracking module.

More formally, the input to this module are the boolean values (i) for face presence $\mathcal{F} = (..., f_{n-20}, f_{n-19}, ..., f_n)$, (ii) mouse movement $\mathcal{M} = (..., m_{n-20}, m_{n-19}, ..., m_n)$, and (iii) page visibility $\mathcal{V} = (..., v_{n-20}, v_{n-19}, ..., v_n)$. To conserve computational resources, the module computes the attention state once a second. Algorithm 1 outlines the inattention decision process employed by the *Inattention Scoring module*. In essence, a weighted score is computed for the face presence and mouse movement values (lines 3 & 4), giving higher weights to more recent values. The visibility score of the video window is simply the last recorded value (line 5). Lines 6-9 compute face-tracking trends over time. The role of

the face-tracking trend computation is to minimize the volume of false positives driven by learner behaviour, in particular sudden movements, bad position in front of the Webcam, or a temporary short time failure of TJS in detecting the face in Webcam video feed. Lines 10-11 show the rules the module employs to determine inattention based on the predefined threshold (which represents the minimum accepted score that is considered as attention, in our case $\mathcal{L} = 2.92$), computed scores and the trend. The threshold and rules are another outcome of our user study—they led to the highest accuracy in distinguishing between attention and inattention behaviours [24].

Algorithm 1 Inattention detection mechanism in IntelliEye

Require: $\mathcal{F}, \mathcal{M}, \mathcal{V}, \mathcal{L}$ — threshold value, $\mathcal{S}$—scores for $\mathcal{F}, \mathcal{M}, \mathcal{V}$
$\mathcal{T} = (t_1, t_2, ..., t_k)$ score queue of the trending functionality;

1: $inAttention \leftarrow False$
2: $n \leftarrow 20$
3: $S_F \leftarrow \sum_i f_{n-i}(n-i)/n$
4: $S_M \leftarrow \sum_i m_{n-i}(n-i)/n$
5: $S_V \leftarrow v_n$
6: $trend_F \leftarrow 0$
7: $T.dequeue(t_1); T.enqueue(t_k \leftarrow S_F)$
8: $(t_k > t_{k-1}) \Rightarrow trend_F \leftarrow 1$
9: $(t_k < t_{k-1}) \wedge (t_{k-1} < t_{k-2}) \Rightarrow trend_F \leftarrow -1$
10: $Q \leftarrow (S_F < L \wedge trend_F < 1)$
11: $(Q \wedge S_M < L \wedge S_V) \vee (Q \wedge \neg S_V) \vee (S_F > L \wedge \neg S_V) \Rightarrow inAttention \leftarrow True$

Note that the level of thresholding ($\mathcal{L}$) determines the sensitivity of IntelliEye—lowering the value will make the system less rigorous, increasing this value will on the other hand increase system responsiveness to learner behaviour.

3.1.6 Alert Module.
We explored three different mechanisms—with varying levels of disruption—to raise learners' awareness about their detected loss of attention; none of these requiring an action from the user beyond returning their attention to the video at hand. In our experiment each learner is assigned to a single alert type, depending on their edX user ID detected by the *Profiling module*.

Pausing the video: When attention loss is detected IntelliEye will pause the currently playing lecture video. Once IntelliEye detects re-gained attention on the video, playing is resumed. At what position playing is resumed depends on *how long* the learner was not paying attention since pausing. The video is rewound to between 0 and 10 seconds before the attention loss was detected; we define three different configurations: (i) if the inattention period is less than 1.5 seconds, the video continues from where it was paused as it would be annoying for a learner to review content just seen and available in her short-time memory, but also to avoid repetitive 'rewind-and-play' situations; (ii) if the inattention lasted more than 10 seconds, the video is rewound 10 seconds which is the approximate lower level of human short-time memory (reported in between 10-30 seconds [17, 19]); and (iii) in all other cases it is rewound 3 seconds—rewind a little for rapid recall in case of distraction. This scheme ensures that the video will restart at a familiar point for the learner. The drawback of this mechanism is the severity of false alerts as the video will pause and thus the learner is disturbed if inattention was falsely determined.

Auditory alert: In this setup, the video keeps playing but an additional sound effect (a bell ring) is played repeatedly as long as inattention is detected. This setup is not as "annoying" as falsely pausing the video, but can still substantially disturb the learner.

Visual alert: In this version, `IntelliEye` visually alerts the learner by repeatedly flashing a red border around the video as long as inattention is detected. Figure 3 shows an example of this alert. This scenario is the least intrusive in case `IntelliEye` falsely detects inattention. It may also be the least effective, as learners who look away from the screen or minimize the browser tab/window will not be able to view the alert.

3.1.7 Logger Module. This module is responsible for logging `IntelliEye`'s usage. These logs are sent to our dedicated log server. Specifically, the following actions lead to logging (for log entries with categorical values we list all possible values within {...}):

Loading: When `IntelliEye` is loaded due to a learner accessing a course subsection[7] containing one or more video units we log (`timestamp, alertType {pause, visual, auditory}, userID, deviceSetup`).

Video status change: Every change in the video's status (e.g. from paused to play) for a learner with supported setup leads to a log of the form (`videoID, timestamp, videoStatus {play, pause, seek, end}, videoTime, videoLength, videoSpeed, subtitles {on, off}, fullScreen {on, off}`). The `videoTime` entry refers to the point in time within the video the status changed.

IntelliEye status change: When a learner with a supported setup changes the status of `IntelliEye` (e.g. from disabled to enabled), we log (`videoID, timestamp, videoTime, videoLength, IntelliEyeStatus {allow, disallow, start, pause, resume, end}`). Information on the video is logged as most interactions with `IntelliEye` occur within the edX video player (cf. §3.2).

Inattention status change: This log event occurs when for a learner with a supported setup the attention status changes: (`videoID, timestamp, videoTime, videoLength, inattention {start, stop}`). Here, `start` indicates that inattention has been detected. The next event is generated when the status changes back to attention again (`stop`). As long as the inattention state is maintained, no further log events are generated.

Finally, we note that beyond the `IntelliEye` logs (cf. Figure 1), we also have access to the official edX logs, which contain information on all common actions learners perform within a MOOC on the edX platform such as quiz submissions, forum entries, clicks, views, and so on—data we use in some of our analyses.

3.2 User Interface

Having described `IntelliEye`'s architecture, we now turn to its user interface. Figure 2 shows `IntelliEye`'s welcome screen (potentially shown every time a MOOC learner opens a course subsection with one or more video units), describing its capabilities, and the positive impact it can have on learning. The learner has four choices: (i) to enable `IntelliEye` for this particular video only, (ii) to disable `IntelliEye` for this video only, (iii) to enable `IntelliEye` for all

videos, and, (iv) to disable `IntelliEye` for all videos. If a learner opts for (iv), we ask the her for feedback on the decision (*"You have disabled IntelliEye. Please tell us why."*).

Once a learner enables `IntelliEye`, the face tracking module attempts to access the Webcam feed, which in all supported browsers triggers a dialogue controlled by the browser (*Will you allow edx.org to use your camera?*); once the learner chooses *Allow*, `IntelliEye` is fully functioning.

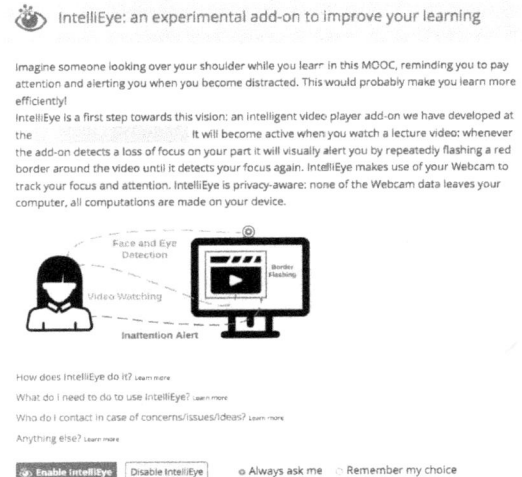

Figure 2: IntelliEye welcome screen.

Figure 3 shows how `IntelliEye` embeds itself in the edX video player. Here the learner can return to the welcome screen and change her enable/disable decisions (via the "eye" icon) and switch `IntelliEye` on or off on the fly. `IntelliEye`'s status is visible at all times: either 'Active' (`IntelliEye` is enabled, the video is not playing at the moment), 'Playing' (`IntelliEye` is enabled), or 'Not Active' (`IntelliEye` is disabled). Note that this change in the video player interface is only visible to learners with a supported setup. Learners on non-supported setups will receive the original edX video player without alterations.

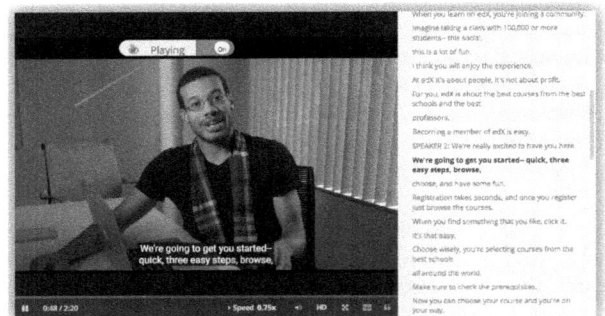

Figure 3: IntelliEye's video player interface (arrow) embedded in the edX video player widget. The red hue around the video player is the visual alert we experiment with.

[7]A set of course elements semantically belonging together, cf. §4.

110

4 MOOC SETTING

We deployed `IntelliEye` in the MOOC *Introduction to Aeronautical Engineering (AE1110x)* offered by TU Delft on the edX platform. The MOOC's target population are learners who are looking for a first introduction to this particular field of engineering. The MOOC requires around 80-90 hours of work and consists of 104 videos and 332 automatically graded summative assessment questions. The MOOC is *self-paced*, that is, the MOOC is available for learners to enroll for up to 11 months. In contrast to the more common six to ten week MOOCs, learners can set their own schedule and their own pace. The MOOC was opened for enrollment on May 1, 2017 and remained so until March 31, 2018. `IntelliEye` was deployed for ten weeks (October 5, 2017 to December 17, 2017); it was available for all videos within the MOOC. A total of 2,612 different learners visited the MOOC during the deployment period and were exposed to `IntelliEye`. We deployed `IntelliEye` in three different variants according to the manner of alerting learners to their lack of attention: video pause, auditory alert and visual alert (§ 3.1.6). We conducted an inter-subject study: each learner was randomly assigned (based on their learner ID) to one of the three conditions. Once assigned, a learner remained in that condition throughout the experiment. Table 1 shows the distribution of the 2,612 learners across the three conditions.

Before turning to the analyses section, we introduce the relevant concepts and definitions:

Course subsection: on the edX platform, a course subsection refers to a sequence of course units (such as video units, quiz units and text units) that are grouped together, most likely because they all relate to the same topic. As an example, one of the subsections in our MOOC consists of the following sequence: video →video →text →quiz →video →quiz →text.

Session: refers to a sequence of logs from a single learner (active on a single device), with no more than thirty minutes time difference between consecutive log entries. This means that after thirty minutes of inactivity in the MOOC, we assume a new "learning" session starts (if the learner becomes active again). We combine the logs we retrieved from our `IntelliEye` log server with those collected by edX.

Supported session: refers to a session with a supported setup.

Unsupported session: a session without a supported setup.

Video session: a session in which at least one video was being played by the learner, regardless of the length of video playing.

IntelliEye session: refers to a supported session which is also a video session, and in which `IntelliEye` was running (which means that the learner did accept the terms of use and played a video while `IntelliEye` was active).

Non-IntelliEye session: a supported session which is also a video session, and in which `IntelliEye` is not active while the video was playing (this either means that the learner did not accept the terms of use, or manually disabled `IntelliEye`).

5 EMPIRICAL EVALUATION

5.1 RQ1: Technological Capabilities

The first question we consider is to what extent our MOOC learners (who, according to their edX profiles, hail from 138 different

countries) have a supported device setup: according to Table 1, 78% of learners (across all three alert types) log in at least once with a device supported in `IntelliEye`. Among those 563 learners (22%) who never have a supported session, 223 of them only access the course with a mobile device (that is 9% of the overall learner population). If we drill down on the 340 learners with unsupported sessions on non-mobile devices, the most common reason is an outdated browser we do not support (e.g. Chrome 52, IE 11, Safari 10 and Safari 11), followed by the lack of a Webcam (in 118 cases). We do not observe a particular skew towards certain countries or regions; learners from India (104 learners) and learners from the US (93 learners) have the largest number of unsupported setups, which are also the two countries where most learners hail from (484 learners from India and 334 from the US).

Table 1: Learners exposed to `IntelliEye`. Shown is the number of learners: (i) in each alert type condition, (ii) with at least one session with supported setup, (iii) who used `IntelliEye` at least once, and (iv) not accepting `IntelliEye`.

Alert Types	#Exposed Learners	#Learners with 1+ Supported Sessions	#Learners with 1+ IntelliEye Session	#Learners without IntelliEye Session
Video pause	861	681	214	467
Auditory alert	902	703	208	495
Visual alert	849	665	236	429
Total	2612	2049	658	1391
% of total	–	78%	25%	53%

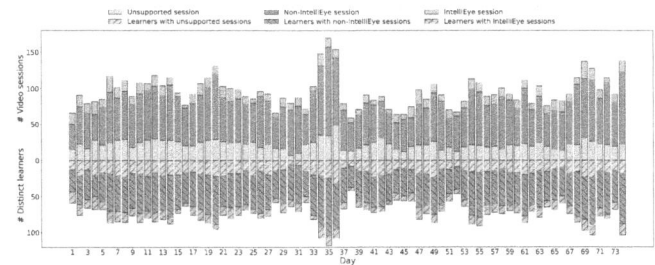

Figure 4: Distribution of video sessions and unique learners. A learner may be listed in more than one session type.

5.2 RQ2: Acceptance of `IntelliEye`

Having established that our hardware requirements are reasonable, we now turn to `IntelliEye`'s acceptance, i.e., are learners willing to enable a widget which observes them via a Webcam. As Table 1 shows, 32% of learners (658 out of 2049) with at least one supported session activate `IntelliEye` at least once.

We had two hypotheses on who engages with our intervention: (1) younger learners are more likely to engage than older ones, and (2) more active learners are more likely to engage than less active ones. To explore these hypotheses we computed various metrics for three different user groups (learners that do not engage with `IntelliEye`, learners that have one or two `IntelliEye` sessions and learners that have three or more `IntelliEye` sessions) as shown in Table 2[8]. We observe significant differences across

---

[8]Note that all our analyses consider the 74 days of `IntelliEye`'s deployment only, i.e. the number of sessions, the quiz scores, etc. are only computed for that time period.

Table 2: Learner attributes partitioned according to the use of IntelliEye (choices made on welcome page are not considered in grouping). Only learners with at least one supported video session are considered. * indicates Student's t-test significance at $p < 0.05$ level. † and ‡ indicate Mann-Whitney U test significance at $p < 0.05$ and $p < 0.01$ levels respectively.

	Number of IntelliEye sessions		
	None	1-2	3+
Number of learners	1030	623	35
Median age	23	21^{*None}	22
Median prior education	Associate degree	High school ^{*None}	High school ^{*None}
Median av. session length (min)	27.77	27.44	$35.17^{†None,1-2}$
Median #sessions	3	3	$12^{‡None,1-2}$
Median quiz score	3.0	$3.0^{†None}$	$7.0^{‡None,1-2}$
Median minutes video watching	21.78	21.87	$102.82^{‡None,1-2}$
Median minutes on platform	94.56	90.83	$542.04^{‡None,1-2}$

almost all metrics (the exception being age) between those learners not (or hardly) using IntelliEye and those using IntelliEye three or more times. The number of learners in each group though—highly skewed with more than 1,600 learners in the not/hardly using IntelliEye groups and 35 learners in the remaining group—has to serve here as a point of caution. Based on these results, IntelliEye appears to be used most often by learners who are already engaged—a finding which is inline with prior MOOC interventions, e.g. [4, 5].

Next, we consider the use of IntelliEye across time (Figure 4): for each day of our experiment we plot the number of learners exposed to IntelliEye and whether they have IntelliEye or non-IntelliEye session. The usage of IntelliEye neither increases nor decreases significantly over time.

In Table 3 we take a look at learners' decisions of enabling or disabling IntelliEye in subsequent video sessions. Learners that enabled IntelliEye in a video session, did so again with a probability of 0.35 (6% of learners chose to enable IntelliEye for all sessions, 29% chose to enable IntelliEye for just the next video session). After enabling IntelliEye in a video session, 21% decided to permanently disable IntelliEye in the next session. We discuss the main reasons for this decision at the end of this section. Learners that disabled IntelliEye in their video session were very unlikely to change their decision in the next video session with 97% of learners sticking to their disable decision.

Next, we consider for *how long* learners are using IntelliEye during their video sessions: do they use IntelliEye continuously or do they disable it after some time? For all the IntelliEye sessions in which IntelliEye is enabled initially (725 sessions from 557 distinct learners), we condense the video session time (which includes video watching as well as other activities on the platform) to video watching time only, based on the edX log data. We then proceed to determine whether IntelliEye was consistently enabled throughout, or whether it was disabled in the first, second or the last third of the video. We find (Table 4) that mostly IntelliEye is either switched off very early or employed throughout a session. Few learners disable it well into the video watching experience (beyond the first third of the video). Learners that received the pause alert are more likely to disable IntelliEye than learners in the

other alert groups; learners in the visual alert condition are most likely to keep IntelliEye enabled, reflecting the various levels of disturbance the alerts cause.

Table 3: IntelliEye usage transition probabilities between subsequent video sessions; E=Enabled, D=Disabled, EF=Enabled Forever, DF=Disabled Forever.

Decision $v(i)$	Decision $v(i+1)$			
	E	D	EF	DF
IntelliEye enabled	0.29	0.43	0.06	0.21
IntelliEye disabled	0.03	0.68	0.00	0.28

As a last analysis of this research question, we focus on the reasons learners provided when disabling IntelliEye. Of the 938 learners (248 of them have at least one IntelliEye session) who chose to disable IntelliEye forever, 379 provided us with reasons for their decision. With an open card sort we sorted the provided reasons into eight categories shown in Table 5. As the vast majority of learners reported a single reason, for the few (< 10) learners who provided a number of reasons we selected the one they were most vocal about. Most commonly (35%) learners cited themselves as not needing help to self-regulate their learning (*I never lose my attention because the lecture and the whole course are very interesting.*).

22% of the learners mentioned a non-functioning Webcam (e.g. *Because my camera doesn't work well*; *Webcam and audio are easily accessible with WebRTC so I cover and disable it.*), followed by 17% with privacy concerns (e.g. *I feel awkward being observed and controlled.*; *I don't like the idea of having the webcam on.*) and 9% with IntelliEye not performing as expected [9]. Interestingly, conscious multitasking was mentioned several times (*I'm multi-tasking while doing this.*), showing that at least some learners are very much aware of their learning behaviour and what IntelliEye is supposed to do for them. Among the 27 learners who report being disturbed by the alerts, 12 learners received the pause and 12 learners the auditory alert. Overall, this feedback shows that IntelliEye works reasonably well (only 34 out of 248 learners using IntelliEye at least once reported issues) and that the largest issue facing future use of IntelliEye is learners' *perception* of not requiring an attention tracker during their learning, followed by privacy concerns.

Table 4: Number of sessions with IntelliEye initially enabled grouped by the time it is switched off in the session.

Disabled during	Pause	Auditory alert	Visual alert
1st third of a session	48%	44%	35%
2nd third of a session	6%	10%	7%
Last third of a session	7%	6%	6%
Enabled throughout	39%	39%	52%
Total # sessions	242	207	276

5.3 RQ3: Impact of IntelliEye

We now investigate the impact of IntelliEye on learners over time and explore whether learners change their video watching behaviour over time. Specifically, we consider all learners with at least two IntelliEye sessions (the most active learner in our dataset has six IntelliEye sessions); for each learner we bin her

---

[9] We note that one possible reason is our lack of a calibration step: to make IntelliEye easy to use and accessible we did not impose one; IntelliEye assumes the learner to be facing the screen and the Webcam.

Table 5: Reasons provided for disabling IntelliEye forever.

Reason	#Learners	[%]
Attention tracking not perceived as useful/needed	131	35%
Webcam not functioning	83	22%
Privacy concerns	64	17%
IntelliEye not working well	34	9%
Disturbed by alerts	27	7%
Conscious facing away from the screen	14	4%
Hardware/Internet connection too slow	14	4%
Conscious multitasking	6	2%
Uncomfortable feeling	6	2%
Σ	379	40%
No reason provided	559	60%

sessions into two bins (the first half and the second half). We then proceed to compute for each bin (i) the average number of minutes lecture videos were played, (ii) the average attention duration and inattention duration detected by IntelliEye, and, (iii) the average number of inattention alerts occurring per minute of video watching. The results are shown in Table 6. Recall that according to the literature, inattention occurs frequently in video watching, though the manner of investigating this (through probes issued at certain times to study participants) [13, 23, 28] does not allow us to draw minute-by-minute conclusions. In contrast, in our work we can now make a statement to this effect: the average number of inattention alerts varies between 0.84 and 2.86 per minute (the latter means that on average a learner gets distracted every 21 seconds in the visual alert condition!). Across all conditions, on average 1.65 inattention alerts are triggered per minute (i.e. one every 36 seconds on average). Interestingly, learners are quickly able to adapt their behaviour towards the offered technology: while the learners in the visual alert type are often alerted (in a manner that is easy to ignore), the learners in the auditory alert conditions receive significantly fewer alerts (cf. row *Mean #inattention per min*); similarly, learners in the pause and auditory alert conditions have significantly shorter inattention spans (cf. row *Mean avg. inattention duration*) than those in the visual condition. As learners were assigned to the conditions randomly we are confident that this behavioural adaptation is due to the different types of alerts.

When comparing the statistics for the two session bins (to detect trends over time), we do not observe a significant decrease over time in the number of inattention triggers per minute and the duration of inattention. There are a number of reasons that can explain this outcome (e.g. as the material becomes more difficult over time, maintaining the same attention levels may already be a success), we will leave this investigation to future work.

6   CONCLUSIONS

In this paper, we have tackled an issue that is inhibiting successful learning in MOOCs: learners' ability to self-regulate their learning. We have designed IntelliEye to increase learners' attention while watching MOOC lecture videos by alerting learners to their loss of attention (approximated through face tracking via Webcam feeds) in real-time. To re-gain learner attention, we trialed three types of interventions—pausing the video with automatic resume once the learner is focusing on the video again, an auditory alert to call learners to attention, and a visual alert around the video widget.

Table 6: Overview of the impact of IntelliEye on learners' behaviors. There are 37 (pause), 27 (auditory) and 41 (visual) learners in each group. † indicates significance at $p < 0.05$ level between the first half and the second half of the IntelliEye sessions (Mann-Whitney U test). * indicates significance at $p < 0.05$ level between the marked group and the visual alert group (Mann-Whitney U test).

Metrics	Alert type	First 50% IntelliEye sessions	Last 50% IntelliEye sessions
Mean avg. video playing length (min)	Pausing	11.93(9.46)	15.96(13.38)*
	Auditory alert	13.38(10.43)	16.16(13.17)
	Visual alert	17.15(16.21)	24.68(20.38)†
Mean avg. attention duration (min)	Pausing	6.71(7.09)	6.70(8.94)
	Auditory alert	9.38(8.76)	9.04(12.13)
	Visual alert	9.33(9.40)	12.53(17.35)
Mean avg. inattention duration (min)	Pausing	0.62(1.45)*	0.50(1.25)
	Auditory alert	0.45(1.94)*	1.07(4.93)*
	Visual alert	3.69(9.03)	3.46(5.29)
Mean avg. #inattention per min	Pausing	1.30(1.96)	1.50(2.13)
	Auditory alert	0.84(2.05)*	0.93(2.14)*
	Visual alert	2.86(4.31)	2.13(3.24)

To explore the viability and acceptance of learners towards such an assistive system, IntelliEye was deployed in an engineering MOOC across a 74-day period to 2, 612 learners.

Our analyses explored three issues: (1) the technological capabilities of our MOOC learners' hardware, (2) the acceptance of IntelliEye by MOOC learners, and, (3) the effect of IntelliEye on MOOC learners' behaviour. We found the vast majority of learners (78%) to possess hardware capable of running IntelliEye; we found fewer—though still a considerable number—learners willing to try such an assistive tool (32% of all learners with supported setups) and among those that did use IntelliEye we determined extremely high levels of inattention, on average 1.65 inattention events per minute (i.e. on avg. inattention arises every 36 seconds).

Learners learnt to adapt their behaviour as needed: learners in the pausing/auditory conditions had significantly fewer inattention events than learners in the non-disruptive visual alert condition. This though, did not yet translate into learning gains. Learners that opted not to use IntelliEye often did not see a need for it and were concerned about their privacy.

Considering the facts that we observe high levels of inattention and that learners once they make a decision on the tool's usage do not change that decision, we need to put more effort into the initial "sign-up" phase of such a tool in future work.

With IntelliEye being the first of its kind to address the learner (in)attention problem in MOOCs in real-time and by relying on non-calibrated common Webcams and open-source face tracking, we have shown that there is a potential for such a system. In our future work, we will extend the deployment of IntelliEye to a larger audience and a wider variety of MOOCs. We will investigate learner incentives and compliance issues to increase the awareness and acceptance of our approach.

ACKNOWLEDGEMENTS

This research has been partially supported by the EU Widening Twinning project TUTORIAL, the Leiden-Delft-Erasmus Centre for Education & Learning and NWO project SearchX (639.022.722).

Session 4: User Behaviour

HT '18, July 9–12, 2018, Baltimore, MD, USA

REFERENCES

[1] Robert Bixler and Sidney D'Mello. 2014. Toward fully automated person-independent detection of mind wandering. In *UMAP'14*. Springer, 37–48.

[2] Robert Bixler and Sidney D'Mello. 2016. Automatic gaze-based user-independent detection of mind wandering during computerized reading. *User Modeling and User-Adapted Interaction* 26, 1 (2016), 33–68.

[3] Diane M Bunce, Elizabeth A Flens, and Kelly Y Neiles. 2010. How long can students pay attention in class? A study of student attention decline using clickers. *Journal of Chemical Education* 87, 12 (2010), 1438–1443.

[4] Dan Davis, Guanliang Chen, Tim Van der Zee, Claudia Hauff, and Geert-Jan Houben. 2016. Retrieval practice and study planning in moocs: Exploring classroom-based self-regulated learning strategies at scale. In *European Conference on Technology Enhanced Learning*. Springer, 57–71.

[5] Dan Davis, Ioana Jivet, René F Kizilcec, Guanliang Chen, Claudia Hauff, and Geert-Jan Houben. 2017. Follow the successful crowd: raising MOOC completion rates through social comparison at scale.. In *LAK*. 454–463.

[6] Philip J Guo, Juho Kim, and Rob Rubin. 2014. How video production affects student engagement: An empirical study of mooc videos. In *Proceedings of the first ACM conference on Learning@ scale conference*. ACM, 41–50.

[7] James Hartley and Alan CameronâĽŬ. 1967. Some observations on the efficiency of lecturing. *Educational Review* 20, 1 (1967), 30–37.

[8] Alex H Johnstone and Frederick Percival. 1976. Attention breaks in lectures. *Education in chemistry* 13, 2 (1976), 49–50.

[9] Katy Jordan. 2014. Initial trends in enrolment and completion of massive open online courses. *The International Review of Research in Open and Distributed Learning* 15, 1 (2014).

[10] René F Kizilcec, Kathryn Papadopoulos, and Lalida Sritanyaratana. 2014. Showing face in video instruction: effects on information retention, visual attention, and affect. In *Proceedings of the SIGCHI conference on human factors in computing systems*. ACM, 2095–2102.

[11] René F Kizilcec, Mar Pérez-Sanagustín, and Jorge J Maldonado. 2016. Recommending self-regulated learning strategies does not improve performance in a MOOC. In *Proceedings of the Third (2016) ACM Conference on Learning@ Scale*. ACM, 101–104.

[12] Sophie I Lindquist and John P McLean. 2011. Daydreaming and its correlates in an educational environment. *Learning and Individual Differences* 21, 2 (2011), 158–167.

[13] Kep Kee Loh, Benjamin Zhi Hui Tan, and Stephen Wee Hun Lim. 2016. Media multitasking predicts video-recorded lecture learning performance through mind wandering tendencies. *Computers in Human Behavior* 63 (2016), 943–947.

[14] Eduardo Lundgren, Thiago Rocha, Zeno Rocha, Pablo Carvalho, and Maira Bello. 2015. tracking. js: A modern approach for Computer Vision on the web. *Online].*

[15] H Maddox and Elizabeth Hoole. 1975. Performance decrement in the lecture. *Educational Review* 28, 1 (1975), 17–30.

[16] John McLeish. 1968. *The lecture method*. Cambridge Institute of Education.

[17] George A Miller. 1956. The magical number seven, plus or minus two: some limits on our capacity for processing information. *Psychological review* 6a3, 2 (1956), 81.

[18] Caitlin Mills, Robert Bixler, Xinyi Wang, and Sidney K D'Mello. 2016. Automatic Gaze-Based Detection of Mind Wandering during Narrative Film Comprehension. In *EDM'16*. 30–37.

[19] Lloyd Peterson and Margaret Jean Peterson. 1959. Short-term retention of individual verbal items. *Journal of experimental psychology* 58, 3 (1959), 193.

[20] Phuong Pham and Jingtao Wang. 2015. AttentiveLearner: improving mobile MOOC learning via implicit heart rate tracking. In *International Conference on Artificial Intelligence in Education*. Springer, 367–376.

[21] Paul R Pintrich and Elisabeth V De Groot. 1990. Motivational and self-regulated learning components of classroom academic performance. *Journal of educational psychology* 82, 1 (1990), 33.

[22] Keith Rayner. 1998. Eye movements in reading and information processing: 20 years of research. *Psychological bulletin* 124, 3 (1998), 372–422.

[23] Evan F Risko, Nicola Anderson, Amara Sarwal, Megan Engelhardt, and Alan Kingstone. 2012. Everyday attention: variation in mind wandering and memory in a lecture. *Applied Cognitive Psychology* 26, 2 (2012), 234–242.

[24] Tarmo Robal, Yue Zhao, Christoph Lofi, and Claudia Hauff. 2018. Webcam-based Attention Tracking in Online Learning: A Feasibility Study. In *23rd International Conference on Intelligent User Interfaces*. ACM, 189–197.

[25] Kshitij Sharma, Patrick Jermann, and Pierre Dillenbourg. 2015. Displaying Teacher's Gaze in a MOOC: Effects on Students' Video Navigation Patterns. In *Design for Teaching and Learning in a Networked World*. Springer, 325–338.

[26] Jonathan Smallwood, Daniel J Fishman, and Jonathan W Schooler. 2007. Counting the cost of an absent mind: Mind wandering as an underrecognized influence on educational performance. *Psychonomic bulletin & review* 14, 2 (2007), 230–236.

[27] John Stuart and RJD Rutherford. 1978. Medical student concentration during lectures. *The lancet* 312, 8088 (1978), 514–516.

[28] Karl K Szpunar, Novall Y Khan, and Daniel L Schacter. 2013. Interpolated memory tests reduce mind wandering and improve learning of online lectures. *Proceedings of the National Academy of Sciences* 110, 16 (2013), 6313–6317.

[29] Karen Wilson and James H Korn. 2007. Attention during lectures: Beyond ten minutes. *Teaching of Psychology* 34, 2 (2007), 85–89.

[30] Yue Zhao, Christoph Lofi, and Claudia Hauff. 2017. Scalable Mind-Wandering Detection for MOOCs: A Webcam-Based Approach. In *European Conference on Technology Enhanced Learning*. Springer, 330–344.

Dosegljivo: https://trackingjs. com/[Dostopano 30. 5. 2016] (2015).

SimilarHITs: Revealing the Role of Task Similarity in Microtask Crowdsourcing

Alan Aipe
IIT Patna
Patna, Bihar, India
alan.me14@iitp.ac.in

Ujwal Gadiraju
L3S Research Center,
Leibniz Universität Hannover
Hannover, Germany
gadiraju@L3S.de

ABSTRACT

Workers in microtask crowdsourcing systems typically consume different types of tasks. Task consumption is driven by the self-selection of workers in the most popular platforms such as Amazon Mechanical Turk and CrowdFlower. Workers typically complete tasks one after another in a chain. Prior works have revealed the impact of ordering tasks while considering aspects such as task complexity. However, little is understood about the benefits of considering task similarity in microtask chains.

In this paper, we investigate the role of task similarity in microtask crowdsourcing and how it affects market dynamics. We identified different dimensions that affect the perception of task similarity among workers, and propose a supervised machine learning model to predict the overall task similarity of a task pair. Leveraging task similarity, we studied the effects of similarity on worker retention, satisfaction, boredom and fatigue. We reveal the impact of chaining tasks according to their similarity on worker accuracy and their task completion time. Our findings enrich the current understanding of crowd work and bear important implications on structuring workflow.

CCS CONCEPTS

• **Information systems** → **World Wide Web**; • **Human-centered computing**; • **Computing methodologies** → *Machine learning*;

KEYWORDS

Crowdsourcing; Microtasks; Task Similarity; Workers; Performance

ACM Reference Format:
Alan Aipe and Ujwal Gadiraju. 2018. SimilarHITs: Revealing the Role of Task Similarity in Microtask Crowdsourcing. In *HT '18: 29th ACM Conference on Hypertext and Social Media, July 9–12, 2018, Baltimore, MD, USA*. ACM, New York, NY, USA, 8 pages. https://doi.org/10.1145/3209542.3209558

1 INTRODUCTION

Crowdsourcing has evolved rapidly over the last decade and presently accounts for a multi-million dollar marketplace. There is a wide variety of Human Intelligence Tasks (HITs) which are typically crowdsourced. Thousands of diverse workers with different motivations complete HITs on crowdsourcing platforms based on availability, their eligibility to participate, and a number of other variables that drive the market dynamics [9]. In such a diverse environment, the role of parameters affecting efficiency and accuracy of workers gain significance and need to be studied in order to improve the overall effectiveness of the paradigm [15]. Task consumption in microtask crowdsourcing platforms is largely driven by a self-selection process, where workers meeting the required eligibility criteria select the tasks that they prefer to work on. Moreover, prior works have established that, during the course of completion of a variety of tasks, workers tend to perform better with experience due to learning effects [8, 11]. Thus, understanding the factors that drive dynamics of learning and devising intelligent task chaining techniques can augment the quality of contribution of workers in microtask crowdsourcing platforms.

In this paper, we focus on understanding the similarity between HITs and the role of task similarity in shaping market dynamics and outcomes. The study commences by identifying different similarity dimensions and their influence on overall similarity of a task pair. Using the above dimensions as key ingredients, we propose a supervised machine learning model to predict similarity of any given task pair. After this, we move forward and investigate the effects of task similarity on significant parameters like worker satisfaction, boredom, fatigue, and task completion time.

Definition : The *similarity* of a task pair can be defined as the degree of resemblance between two tasks, i.e., the extent to which they are identical in nature.

Research Questions and Original Contributions. This paper aims at filling this knowledge gap by contributing novel insights on the nature and importance of task similarity in microtask crowdsourcing. By combining qualitative and quantitative analysis, we seek to answer the following research questions.

> **RQ1**: What are the different dimensions of similarity between two HITs? How much influence does each dimension have on the perceived similarity of a HIT pair?

Through a study of 100 workers on CrowdFlower (Study I), we identified key dimensions of similarity between microtasks and their corresponding influence in the overall task similarity perception of workers.

> **RQ2**: How can we model the overall similarity between two HITs?

We used a supervised machine learning model and proposed features to predict the workflow and topic similarity of any given task pair. Building on our findings from Study I, we propose a weighted sum of task similarity over individual dimensions as the overall task similarity of a pair of tasks from a holistic standpoint. Our proposed stochastic gradient descent regressor model results in predicting task similarity accurately, with a mean average error of 0.68.

> **RQ3**: What is the effect of task similarity on worker retention, worker satisfaction, boredom and fatigue?

Our studies reveal that ordering tasks in a chain according to overall task similarity results in improved accuracy, but at the cost of inducing boredom.

2 RELATED LITERATURE

2.1 Task Chaining and Complexity

Crowdsourcing microtasks are small units of work designed to be completed one bit at a time, eventually contributing to a much larger goal. Although they can be performed in isolation, in practice people often complete them one after another, in a chain [4]. Prior research has shown that task ordering or chaining has a profound impact on worker performance [4, 21]. This is because transitions between consecutive cognitive tasks have measurable effects on ongoing mental processes. Related literature in psychology suggests that the contribution ability of workers tends to wane and become more error-prone while switching between tasks, when compared to a single task scenario. This can be accounted by re-configuration of physical and psychological parameters to adapt to new task at hand [19, 25].

Task complexity has undoubtedly turned out to be an integral parameter driving the performance of workers on crowdsourcing platforms. Research work in the field of task chaining with respect to complexity revealed that lead-up microtasks have a significant impact on momentum and performance of workers performing a final task. Authors also proved that while the same operation chains aid in the efficiency of simple microtasks, same content chains might help alleviate mental burden on more complex microtasks [4, 26]. Therefore, task chaining has to be operationalized with a broader set of dimensions under consideration. In this paper, we extend such prior work by investigating the role of task similarity in microtask chains. In contrast to prior works, we propose a holistic definition of task similarity between a pair of tasks.

2.2 Workflows and Task Clarity

Task Clarity is also perceived as a worthwhile parameter affecting worker performance. Several authors have stressed about the positive impact of task design, clear instructions and descriptions on the quality of crowdsourced work. As per studies carried out in this domain [14], clarity was found to have direct relationship with cognitive load experienced by workers pursuing a continuous sequence of tasks, thus forming a quantifiable influence on performance.

Workflow of tasks can potentially affect worker performance in task chains. Task workflows can be defined as a sequence of steps that are required to be performed in order to complete a given task. Frequently, a task requester experiments with several alternative workflows to accomplish the task, but choose a single one for the production runs that workers can follow. Several works in the past have addressed the importance of good workflows. Workflows that create short-term goals have been shown to help workers by increasing the perceived likelihood of success [1, 10]. Lin, Mausam and Weld showed that selecting a single best workflow is suboptimal, because alternative workflows can compose synergistically to attain higher quality results [17]. Moreover, collaborative workflows have also been explored to bring about better overall performance [3].

Recent work has sought to improve workers' experiences with microtasks by inserting micro-diversions to provide timely relief during long chains [6]. Large organizations have explored re-designing assembly lines to build task specialization while still enabling task switching and creativity [2]. On crowd platforms, priming effects [20] and monetary interventions [27] can also improve performance.

In summary, prior works have touched upon some of the similarity dimensions individually and its effects on engagement of workers. Moreover it has also portrayed the importance of task chaining in a macro-scale crowdsourcing environment. In this paper, we build on the current understanding of crowd work and conceptualize task similarity as a worthwhile parameter in microtask crowdsourcing.

3 STUDY I : DIMENSIONS OF SIMILARITY

In this pilot study, we aimed to identify different dimensions of task similarity and their influence on the overall perceived similarity of a task pair (**RQ1**).

3.1 Methodology

To address **RQ1**, we manually identified a set of different dimensions based on which two tasks can be considered to be similar. These dimensions included the *workflow* of tasks (i.e., the steps required to complete the tasks successfully), *topic* of tasks (i.e., the topic(s) related to the content of the task), *time required* to complete the tasks, *time available* to complete the tasks, *batch size* of tasks, the associated monetary *reward*, *type of data* in the tasks (i.e., text, images, audio/video), task *metadata* such as title, description and keywords, and the *country* of origin of the task requesters. In light of prior works, we also considered similarity based on task types (proposed via a goal-oriented taxonomy of microtasks [12]), similarity based on task complexity [26], and on task clarity [14]. The different dimensions we considered are presented in Table 1.

We then designed and deployed a survey on the CrowdFlower[1] platform. In this survey, workers were asked to rate the influence of

---

[1] https://crowdflower.com/

different dimensions on the overall perceived similarity of a generic task pair, on a 7-point Likert scale (from *1: No Influence* to *7: High Influence*). In an open-ended question, workers were also asked to suggest any missing dimensions and the extent to which such dimensions influenced the overall similarity of a task pair. In order to detect untrustworthy workers and ensure reliability of responses, the survey was designed by following the guidelines proposed by Gadiraju et al. for running crowdsourced surveys [13]. To further ensure reliability, we restricted the participation of workers to *Level-3 workers*[2] on CrowdFlower.

On average, workers took 3.68 minutes to complete the survey and were compensated at an hourly rate of 7 USD. Responses from 100 different high quality workers were thus collected and aggregated, obtaining the following results.

3.2 Results

Workers in general did not mention any influential dimension of similarity that they felt was not reflected in the set of 12 similarity dimensions presented to them. Therefore, we limit our analysis to these. To compare the effect of the similarity dimensions on the overall perceived similarity of a pair of tasks, we computed a one-way between workers ANOVA across the 12 similarity dimensions considered. We found significant differences in the influence of the dimensions on the overall perceived similarity across the 12 conditions at the $p < .001$ level; $F(11, 1199) = 10.479$. Post-hoc comparisons using the Tukey-HSD test revealed that workers believe the *task type* of tasks and *workflow* influence their perception of similarity to a significantly greater extent[3] than *task complexity***, *reward***, *batch size***, *time required***, *time available***, and *country of requester***. Workers believe that the *type of data* in tasks influences their perception of similarity to a significantly greater extent than *time required**, *time available**, and *country of requester***. We found that the *topic* and *metadata* of the tasks were significantly more influential dimensions of similarity in comparison to the *country of requesters***. Finally, *task complexity* and the associated monetary *reward* were deemed to be significantly more influential in determining the overall task similarity than the *type of data* in tasks*.

Having identified a set of dimensions that influence the overall perception of task similarity, we aim to model task similarity between a pair of tasks next.

4 STUDY II : MODELING TASK SIMILARITY

In this study, we aim to propose a supervised machine learning model to predict overall similarity of a task pair (**RQ2**).

4.1 Methodology

To address **RQ2**, we adopted the following steps:
(1) Establishing ground truth for perceived task similarity.
(2) Modeling overall similarity of a task pair based on the different dimensions of similarity studied earlier.

---

[2]*Level-3 contributors* on CrowdFlower comprise workers who completed over 100 test questions across hundreds of different types of tasks, and have a near perfect overall accuracy.
[3]** denotes statistical significance at the $p < .01$ level, and * denotes significance at the $p < .05$ level.

Table 1: Different similarity dimensions and their influence on the overall task similarity (aggregated from 100 distinct judgments on a 7-point Likert-scale).

Similarity Dimension	Influence (on 7-point scale)
Task Type (w.r.t. goal [12])	5.51 ± 1.42
Workflow	5.33 ± 1.32
Task Clarity	5.32 ± 1.42
Task Complexity	5.30 ± 1.36
Reward	5.30 ± 1.64
Topic	5.28 ± 1.56
Datatype	5.04 ± 1.37
Metadata	4.84 ± 1.40
Batch Size	4.53 ± 1.60
Time Required	4.29 ± 1.91
Time Available	4.25 ± 1.67
Country of Requester	3.83 ± 1.88

(3) Learning a supervised model to predict overall similarity of a task pair.

Establishing Ground Truth

To train a supervised model, we needed to establish ground truth for the overall task similarity between pairs of tasks. For this purpose, we considered the publicly available dataset of tasks sampled from Amazon Mechanical Turk used by Yang et al. to model task complexity in their work [26]. The dataset comprises of 61 distinct tasks of different types, as shown in Table 2.

Table 2: Tasks in the AMT dataset [26].

Task Type	#Tasks (in%)
Survey	6.60%
Content Creation	31.15%
Content Access	6.60%
Interpretation and Analysis	27.87%
Verification and Validation	3.30%
Information Finding	22.95%
Other	1.60%

We re-instantiated all 61 tasks and hosted them on an external server. Next, we designed and deployed a task on CrowdFlower to acquire similarity ratings from workers on different task pairs. We considered all possible pairs from the set of 61 tasks in the AMT dataset, resulting in 1,891 task pairs. In each case, workers were provided with links to the pair of tasks, asked to explore the tasks and then rate the (i) *workflow similarity*, and (ii) *topic similarity* of the given pair. To detect untrustworthy workers and ensure reliability of responses, we included test questions with priorly know answers [13, 22]. We also restricted the participation to *Level-3* workers on CrowdFlower. We gathered 3 responses for each task pair, and workers were compensated with monetary rewards at the hourly rate of 7.5 USD. Task pairs corresponding to at least one response from an unreliable worker (who failed to answer at least one test question correctly) were discarded. Thus, 1,877 task pairs were selected for learning the model.

Task Similarity Based on Individual Dimensions

Next, we computed the similarity of the task pairs with respect to each of the individual dimensions described earlier.

Task type similarity: The goal-oriented task types of each of the 61 tasks in the dataset were determined according to the taxonomy proposed by previous work [12]. Considering two generic tasks P and Q, with their corresponding task types, we compute the task type similarity $TTS(P,Q)$ as follows –

$$TTS(P,Q) = \begin{cases} 1 & \text{if the task types of } P \text{ and } Q \text{ are different} \\ 7 & \text{otherwise} \end{cases} \quad (1)$$

We use the extremities of the 7-point Likert scale used to build our ground truth to ensure adequate distinction between a pair of tasks, even if tasks are identical with respect to all other dimensions.

Workflow similarity: We propose a supervised machine learning model for computing workflow similarity between two tasks. To learn the model, we rely on the workflow similarity labels acquired from workers for each task pair as described earlier. Considering tasks P and Q, the similarity between the task pair based on each parameter (shown in Table 3) except the goal-oriented task type were calculated as follows –

$$S_i(P,Q) = 4 - 6f(\cosh(1 + |u^2 - v^2|)) \quad (2)$$

where u denotes the absolute value of parameter i of P, v denotes the absolute value of parameter i of Q and f denotes the mean normalization function. Our rationale behind choosing such a function was to ensure a considerable difference in similarity scores even after mean normalization of the difference. As *cosh* is a monotonously increasing function with steeper slopes at higher values, the mean normalized value of task P will not be in the close neighborhood of that of task Q. Task type similarity was calculated using *Eq. 1*. These similarity values were fed into a stochastic gradient descent (SGD) regressor as features, in order to predict the workflow similarity. We experimented with other regression models like support vector machine but SGD regressor was found to give least mean average error.

To evaluate the model, we compared the workflow similarity obtained from the regressor, to the ground truth aggregated from the responses of workers collected earlier. We found that the mean average error (*MAE*) observed was 0.63 on the 7-point Likert scale (approx. 9% error). Thus, the proposed model can efficiently capture workflow similarity of a task pair.

Table 3: Predicting workflow and topic similarity using supervised machine learning models. *MAE* represents the mean average error in prediction on a 7-point scale.

Dimension	Workflow	Topic
Model	SGD Regressor	SGD Regressor
Parameters	Task type, effort, time required, reward, time available, link count, image count, title length, description length, goal clarity, role clarity	top–5 topics related to task, title length, description length, title quality, description quality, language quality
MAE	0.63	0.7

Table 4: Glossary of features used to predict workflow and topic similarity between a task pair.

Feature	Definition
Task type	Goal-oriented task type of a given task [12]
Effort	Cognitive load experienced by workers during the course of the task [26]
Time Required	Time required to successfully complete the task
Reward	Monetary reward obtained after successful completion of the task
Time available	Time alloted by requester to complete the task
Link count	Number of web links in the task definition
Image count	Number of images associated with the task
Title length	Number of characters in the title of the task
Description length	Number of characters in the description of the task
Goal clarity	Extent to which the objective of a task is clear to workers [14]
Role clarity	Extent to which the steps or activities to be carried out in the task are clear [14]
Quality	Measure of understandable information carried by given entity with respect to the task

Topic similarity: We propose a supervised model to compute the topic similarity of a task pair. We rely on the topic similarity labels acquired from workers for each task pair as described earlier, to learn the model. We adopted the same approach as in case of determining *workflow similarity* between a task pair, using the different parameters shown in Table 3. We found that the proposed model is capable of predicting topic similarity with a mean average error (*MAE*) of 0.7 on 7-point scale (approx. 10% error).

Task clarity similarity: We use the task clarity model proposed in previous work by Gadiraju et al. to obtain task clarity scores for all tasks in the dataset [14]. We compute the task clarity similarity using *Eq. 2*.

Task complexity similarity: Similarly, we use the task complexity model proposed in previous work by Yang et al. to obtain task complexity scores for all tasks in the dataset [26]. We compute the task complexity similarity using *Eq. 2*.

Datatype similarity: Data associated with tasks can be of different media types; audio, image, video, textual in nature, or a combination of these media types. Therefore considering tasks P and Q, similarity (*DS*) with respect to data associated with tasks can be calculated as follows –

$$DS(P,Q) = 1 + 6J(u,v) \quad (3)$$

where u and v denotes set of type of data associated with P and Q respectively and $J(u,v)$ denotes Jaccard similarity of set u and v. The use of Jaccard similarity in this context is supported by the fact that the type of data involved in a particular task can be expressed as a set.

Similarity w.r.t. other dimensions: The absolute value of other dimensions like reward, batch size, task completion time, available time, etc. of the 61 tasks in the AMT dataset, were available along with the data used to compute similarities based on the aforementioned dimensions. Thus, similarity of a task pair with respect to these objective dimensions can be calculated using *Eq. 2*.

4.2 Computing the Overall Task Similarity

Based on our findings from Study I addressing **RQ1**, the overall similarity of a task pair can be computed as the weighted mean of similarities with respect to each of the individual dimensions described earlier (with their corresponding influences as weights). Considering two tasks P and Q, the overall task similarity S between the task pair can be obtained as follows –

$$S(P,Q) = \frac{\Sigma_i w(i) d(i)}{\Sigma_i w(i)} \qquad (4)$$

where $d(i)$ denotes the similarity score with respect to i^{th} dimension and $w(i)$ denotes its corresponding influence (as shown in Table 1).

4.2.1 Results. By computing the overall similarity of task pairs as described above, and leveraging the workflow and topic similarity prediction models, we were able to predict overall similarity of a task pair with an mean average error (*MAE*) of 0.68 on a 7-point Likert scale. This suggests that our proposed model can efficiently capture overall similarity of a task pair.

5 STUDY III : IMPACT OF TASK SIMILARITY

In this section, we aim to investigate the impact of task similarity in microtask chains on aspects such as worker retention, worker satisfaction, boredom, and fatigue.

5.1 Methodology and Task Design

To address **RQ3** and understand the impact of task similarity on microtask chains, we considered three different conditions;

- *Similar* – In this condition, tasks are chained such that each subsequent task has a high overall task similarity with respect to the preceding task.
- *Dissimilar* – In this condition, tasks are chained such that each subsequent task in the chain has a low overall task similarity with respect to the preceding task.
- *Random* – In this condition, tasks are randomly chained irrespective of their overall task similarity with respect to each other.

First, we determined *similar* and *dissimilar* tasks by using the similarity scores obtained from Study II, with the help of $k-means$ clustering. Next, we created distinct chains of 10 tasks each according to the three conditions described earlier. Tasks in the first chain were *similar* to each other, those in the second chain were *dissimilar* to each other while the third chain consisted of tasks selected at *random*. Table 5 presents example excerpts of task chains in the three conditions; similar, dissimilar and random).

With an aim to study the impact of task similarity in microtask chains on several aspects pertaining to workers, we deployed three different microtask chains (*similar*, *dissimilar*, and *random*) in otherwise identical fashion on CrowdFlower. Workers were asked to complete as many tasks in the chain as they wished to, with a constraint of the first 4 tasks being mandatory. We did so to ensure a bare minimum number of tasks being completed in the microtask chains by workers, that we could still reliably analyze in case of poor worker retention. After completing at least the mandatory first 4 tasks in the chain, workers were asked to answer questions

Table 5: Example excerpts of *similar*, *dissimilar*, and *random* task chains. In this example, the first task in each of the three chains is selected to be the same, to better illustrate the difference in task similarity along the task chains in the different conditions.

Condition	Tasks in the Chain (first 4 of 10 tasks are shown)
Similar	(1). Find a consumable product given on a particular website (2). Find duplicate buisness names from a website (3). Find official URL of an organization (4). Find public URL of a given image ... (10)
Dissimilar	(1). Find a consumable product given on a particular website (2). Find punctuation errors in a sentence (3). Transcribe an audio clip (4). Find address of a particular store or boutique ... (10)
Random	(1). Find a consumable product given on a particular website (2). Find punctuation errors in a sentence (3). Rate a story with respect to its description quality (4). Find official URL of organization ... (10)

regarding their *satisfaction*, *boredom*, and *fatigue* on a 7-point Likert scale. Finally, workers were also asked to rate the *overall similarity* of tasks in the chain. To ensure reliability of responses and promote high quality, we restricted the participation to *level-3* workers on CrowdFlower in each of the three microtask chain conditions. Responses from 100 distinct workers were collected and analyzed for each microtask chain condition. Workers were compensated according to the number of tasks they completed at an hourly rate of 7.5 USD.

To understand the overall impact of chaining tasks based on task similarity on the perception of workers, we acquired responses about their *satisfaction* with the tasks on a 7-point Likert scale from *1: Highly Disappointed* to *7: Highly Satisfied*. Similarly, we acquired self-reported assessments of worker *boredom* (from *1: Not Bored At All* to *7: Highly Bored*) and *fatigue* (from *1: Not Tired At All* to *7: Very Tired*), to better analyze the impact of task similarity in microtask chains. Prior works in other domains have investigated boredom [5, 23] and fatigue [16] of workers from the physical and cognitive standpoint. These works found that underutilization of cognitive resources is related to misdirection of attention resources, leading to boredom. Authors showed that fatigue can affect workers doing batches of monotonous tasks, risking a reduced well-being, and creating lower quality, unreliable data as a result. This has also formed the basis of several works in crowdsourcing that have focused on improving worker retention/engagement by reducing boredom/fatigue [7, 18, 24]. While prior works dealing with retention in microtask crowdsourcing have focused on batches of similar tasks with respect to a single dimension of similarity (that of the task objective, for example a batch of image tagging tasks), we investigate boredom, fatigue and worker retention based on our holistic definition of *overall task similarity*.

To verify the authenticity of task similarity in our task chain conditions, we also acquired responses from workers regarding their perceived task similarity of the set of tasks they completed in the chain (from *1: Highly Dissimilar* to *7: Highly Similar*).

5.2 Results

5.2.1 Worker Retention. Worker retention can be defined as the fraction of tasks that workers complete on average, from a given batch of tasks available to them. Since the first 4 of the available 10 tasks were made mandatory, we analyze worker retention in the remaining tasks in the batch. Figure 1 presents the percentage of workers who completed a given number of tasks in the chain across the three conditions.

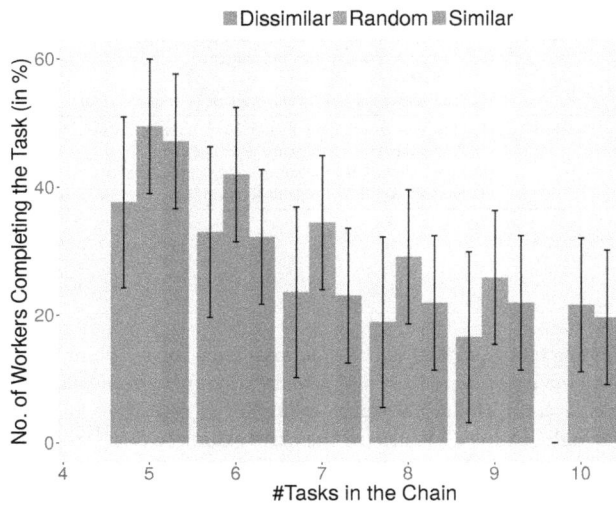

Figure 1: Average worker retention across the different task chains. Tasks 1–4 in each task chain were mandatory.

Interestingly, we found that on average worker retention is greatest in the task chain with the *random* task similarity condition ($M=33.69, SD=10.48$), when compared to that in the task chain with *similar* condition ($M=27.59, SD=10.53$), and the task chain with *dissimilar* task similarity condition ($M=21.57, SD=13.34$). We conducted a one-way between workers ANOVA to compare the effect of task similarity in microtask chains on the worker retention across the three conditions. We did not find a significant effect of task similarity in the chains on worker retention.

We note that in the *random* condition 21.5% of the workers completed all the tasks available to them, compared to 19.54% of workers in the *similar* condition. In contrast, not a single worker completed all the 10 tasks available to them in the *dissimilar* condition; 16.47% of workers completed 9 tasks. We reason that the *random* condition resulted in greater worker retention due to a balance between arousing worker interest through dissimilar tasks and maintaining continuity through similar tasks. Prior works that have suggested micro-diversions or breaks to increase worker engagement lend support to this finding [6, 24].

5.2.2 Worker Accuracy. We analyzed the accuracy of workers across the different task chain conditions, and conducted a one-way between workers ANOVA to measure the effect of task similarity in the microtask chain on the accuracy of workers. We found a significant effect of task similarity in the chain on the accuracy of workers

across the three conditions at the $p < .001$ level; $F(2,261)=30.35$. Post-hoc comparisons using the Tukey-HSD test revealed that workers in the *similar* condition performed with a significantly higher accuracy on average ($M=79.68, SD=16.96$), in comparison to workers in the *dissimilar* condition ($M=61.42, SD=16.68$), and those in the *random* group ($M=70.32, SD=12.11$) with $p < .01$. We also found that workers in the *random* condition performed significantly more accurately than those in the *dissimilar* condition with $p < .01$.

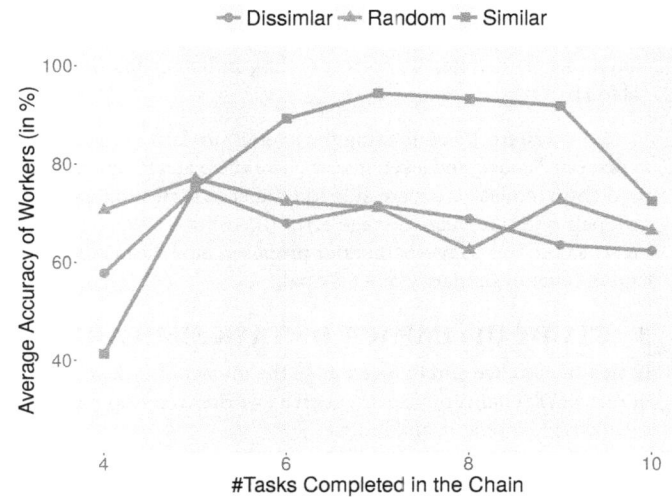

Figure 2: Average accuracy of workers with respect to the number of tasks they completed, across the different task chain conditions. Tasks 1–4 in each chain were mandatory.

Figure 2 presents the average accuracy of workers with respect to the number of tasks they completed in the chain across the three different task similarity conditions. We found that the average accuracy of workers in the *similar* condition is comparatively higher than those in the other conditions, when considering workers who completed 5 or more tasks in the chain of 10 tasks.

5.2.3 Task Completion Time. To compare the effect of task similarity on the task completion time of workers across the different conditions, we conducted a one-way between workers ANOVA. Results confirmed a significant effect of task similarity on the task completion time of workers at the $p < .001$ level; $F(2, 297) = 18.99$. Post-hoc comparisons revealed that workers take significantly more time on average to complete the task chains corresponding to the *dissimilar* ($M=15.67$ mins, $SD=6.57$) and *random* ($M=15.51$ mins, $SD=1.83$) conditions when compared to the *similar* condition ($M=11.77$ mins, $SD=5.55$) at the $p < .01$ level. Since worker retention varied across the different conditions (i.e., workers completed different number of tasks in the different conditions on average), we also computed the average time workers took to complete a single task in the chain. Once again, we found that workers in the *dissimilar* condition took more time to complete a single task ($M=2.21$ mins, $SD=1.04$) than workers in the *similar* ($M=2.13$ mins, $SD=1.21$), or the *random* condition ($M=2.02$ mins, $SD=1.08$). These differences were not found to be statistically significant.

5.2.4 Overall Task Similarity and Worker Satisfaction. Next, we analyzed the responses of workers to the questions regarding their perception of the overall task clarity of the task chains, and their corresponding satisfaction on 7-point scales. Our findings are presented in Figure 3. We found that workers rated the overall task clarity of tasks in the *similar* chain to be higher (*M=3.82, SD=1.67*) than that in the *dissimilar* (*M=3.61, SD=1.65*) or *random* chain (*M=3.67, SD=1.47*). Workers exhibited a higher satisfaction with tasks in the *random* chain (*M=5.49, SD=1.31*) in comparison to those in *similar* (*M=5.06, SD=1.62*) and *dissimilar* chains (*M=5.16, SD=1.41*). However, multiple T-tests revealed a lack of statistical significance between these comparisons.

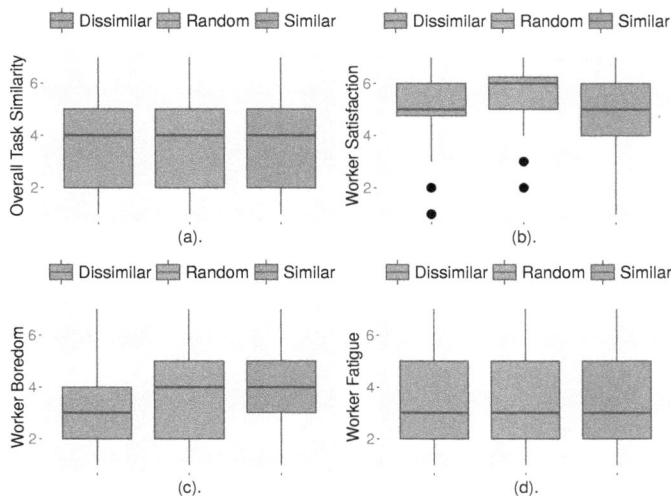

Figure 3: A comparison of the perceived (a). overall task similarity, (b). worker satisfaction, (c). worker boredom, and (d). worker fatigue across the three task chain conditions.

5.2.5 Boredom and Fatigue. We found that workers in the *similar* task chain (*M=3.38, SD=1.78*) experienced the most fatigue while those performing the *dissimilar* tasks experienced the least fatigue (*M=3.16, SD=1.80*). Workers in the *random* chain corresponded to a fatigue of (*M=3.37, SD=1.74*). We did not find a statistically significant difference between these comparisons using a one-way between workers ANOVA.

We conducted another one-way between workers ANOVA to compare the effect of task similarity in chains on worker boredom. Results confirmed a significant effect of task similarity on boredom at the $p < .05$ level; $F(2,297) = 3.068$. Post-hoc comparisons using the Tukey-HSD test confirmed that workers experience most boredom while completing a chain of *similar* tasks (*M=3.90, SD=1.64*), followed by chain of *random* tasks (*M=3.30, SD=1.75*) and least while doing a chain of *dissimilar* tasks (*M=3.58, SD=1.72*). The difference between the boredom experienced by workers in the *similar* and *dissimilar* chain conditions was found to be statistically significant at the $p < .05$ level. This is in line with our intuitive expectations as discussed earlier. Prior studies in behavioral psychology prove that repeatedly performing tasks which are similar to each other reduces the interest of workers and induces boredom [5, 23].

6 CONCLUSIONS AND FUTURE WORK

In this paper, we investigated the role of task similarity in microtask chains and how it affects worker performance. We successfully identified different similarity dimensions and their influences. Using a supervised model, we were able to model overall task similarity of a task pair. Next, we studied the impact of task similarity in microtask chains on worker retention, satisfaction, boredom and fatigue.

Our studies reveal that ordering tasks in a chain according to overall task similarity results in improved accuracy, but at the cost of inducing boredom. This paper points at the necessity of striking a balance between similarity and dissimilarity in a chain of tasks so as to bring forth better engagement of workers. Our findings enrich the current understanding of crowd work and bear important implications on structuring workflow. Further studies into the similarity dimensions will help us in striking a better balance during task chaining and is reserved for future work.

ACKNOWLEDGEMENTS
This research has been supported in part by the European Commission within the H2020-ICT-2015 Programme (*Analytics For Everyday Learning* (AFEL) project, Grant Agreement No. 687916).

REFERENCES
[1] David S Ackerman and Barbara L Gross. 2005. My instructor made me do it: Task characteristics of procrastination. *Journal of Marketing education* 27, 1 (2005), 5–13.
[2] Paul S Adler, Barbara Goldoftas, and David I Levine. 1999. Flexibility versus efficiency? A case study of model changeovers in the Toyota production system. *Organization Science* 10, 1 (1999), 43–68.
[3] Vamshi Ambati, Stephan Vogel, and Jaime Carbonell. 2012. Collaborative workflow for crowdsourcing translation. In *Proceedings of the ACM 2012 conference on Computer Supported Cooperative Work*. ACM, 1191–1194.
[4] Carrie J Cai, Shamsi T Iqbal, and Jaime Teevan. 2016. Chain reactions: The impact of order on microtask chains. In *Proceedings of the 2016 CHI Conference on Human Factors in Computing Systems*. ACM, 3143–3154.
[5] Jonathan SA Carriere, J Allan Cheyne, and Daniel Smilek. 2008. Everyday attention lapses and memory failures: The affective consequences of mindlessness. *Consciousness and cognition* 17, 3 (2008), 835–847.
[6] Peng Dai, Jeffrey M. Rzeszotarski, Praveen Paritosh, and Ed H. Chi. 2015. And Now for Something Completely Different: Improving Crowdsourcing Workflows with Micro-Diversions. In *Proceedings of the 18th ACM Conference on Computer Supported Cooperative Work & Social Computing, CSCW 2015, Vancouver, BC, Canada, March 14 - 18, 2015*. 628–638.
[7] Peng Dai, Jeffrey M Rzeszotarski, Praveen Paritosh, and Ed H Chi. 2015. And now for something completely different: Improving crowdsourcing workflows with micro-diversions. In *Proceedings of the 18th ACM Conference on Computer Supported Cooperative Work & Social Computing*. ACM, 628–638.
[8] Djellel Eddine Difallah, Michele Catasta, Gianluca Demartini, and Philippe Cudré-Mauroux. 2014. Scaling-up the crowd: Micro-task pricing schemes for worker retention and latency improvement. In *Second AAAI Conference on Human Computation and Crowdsourcing*.
[9] Djellel Eddine Difallah, Michele Catasta, Gianluca Demartini, Panagiotis G. Ipeirotis, and Philippe Cudré-Mauroux. 2015. The Dynamics of Micro-Task Crowdsourcing: The Case of Amazon MTurk. In *Proceedings of the 24th International Conference on World Wide Web, WWW 2015, Florence, Italy, May 18-22, 2015*. 238–247.
[10] Joseph R Ferrari, Judith L Johnson, and William G McCown. 1995. Procrastination research. In *Procrastination and Task Avoidance*. Springer, 21–46.
[11] Ujwal Gadiraju and Stefan Dietze. 2017. Improving learning through achievement priming in crowdsourced information finding microtasks. In *Proceedings of the Seventh International Learning Analytics & Knowledge Conference, Vancouver, BC, Canada, March 13-17, 2017*. 105–114.
[12] Ujwal Gadiraju, Ricardo Kawase, and Stefan Dietze. 2014. A taxonomy of microtasks on the web. In *25th ACM Conference on Hypertext and Social Media, HT '14, Santiago, Chile, September 1-4, 2014*. 218–223.
[13] Ujwal Gadiraju, Ricardo Kawase, Stefan Dietze, and Gianluca Demartini. 2015. Understanding malicious behavior in crowdsourcing platforms: The case of online

surveys. In *Proceedings of the 33rd Annual ACM Conference on Human Factors in Computing Systems*. ACM, 1631–1640.

[14] Ujwal Gadiraju, Jie Yang, and Alessandro Bozzon. 2017. Clarity is a Worthwhile Quality: On the Role of Task Clarity in Microtask Crowdsourcing. In *Proceedings of the 28th ACM Conference on Hypertext and Social Media, HT 2017, Prague, Czech Republic, July 4-7, 2017*. 5–14.

[15] Aniket Kittur, Jeffrey V Nickerson, Michael Bernstein, Elizabeth Gerber, Aaron Shaw, John Zimmerman, Matt Lease, and John Horton. 2013. The future of crowd work. In *Proceedings of the 2013 conference on Computer supported cooperative work*. ACM, 1301–1318.

[16] Gerald P Krueger. 1989. Sustained work, fatigue, sleep loss and performance: A review of the issues. *Work & Stress* 3, 2 (1989), 129–141.

[17] Christopher H Lin, Daniel S Weld, et al. 2012. Dynamically switching between synergistic workflows for crowdsourcing. In *Workshops at the Twenty-Sixth AAAI Conference on Artificial Intelligence*.

[18] Andrew Mao, Ece Kamar, and Eric Horvitz. 2013. Why stop now? predicting worker engagement in online crowdsourcing. In *First AAAI Conference on Human Computation and Crowdsourcing*.

[19] Stephen Monsell. 2003. Task switching. *Trends in cognitive sciences* 7, 3 (2003), 134–140.

[20] Robert R Morris, Mira Dontcheva, and Elizabeth M Gerber. 2012. Priming for better performance in microtask crowdsourcing environments. *IEEE Internet Computing* 16, 5 (2012), 13–19.

[21] Edward Newell and Derek Ruths. 2016. How one microtask affects another. In *Proceedings of the 2016 CHI Conference on Human Factors in Computing Systems*. ACM, 3155–3166.

[22] David Oleson, Alexander Sorokin, Greg P Laughlin, Vaughn Hester, John Le, and Lukas Biewald. 2011. Programmatic Gold: Targeted and Scalable Quality Assurance in Crowdsourcing. *Human computation* 11, 11 (2011).

[23] Nathalie Pattyn, Xavier Neyt, David Henderickx, and Eric Soetens. 2008. Psychophysiological investigation of vigilance decrement: boredom or cognitive fatigue? *Physiology & Behavior* 93, 1 (2008), 369–378.

[24] Jeffrey M Rzeszotarski, Ed Chi, Praveen Paritosh, and Peng Dai. 2013. Inserting micro-breaks into crowdsourcing workflows. In *First AAAI Conference on Human Computation and Crowdsourcing*.

[25] Glenn Wylie and Alan Allport. 2000. Task switching and the measurement of "switch costs". *Psychological research* 63, 3 (2000), 212–233.

[26] Jie Yang, Judith Redi, Gianluca Demartini, and Alessandro Bozzon. 2016. Modeling Task Complexity in Crowdsourcing. In *In Proceedings of The Fourth AAAI Conference on Human Computation and Crowdsourcing (HCOMP 2016)*. 249–258.

[27] Ming Yin, Yiling Chen, and Yu-An Sun. 2014. Monetary interventions in crowdsourcing task switching. In *Second AAAI Conference on Human Computation and Crowdsourcing*.

Penny Auctions are Predictable

Predicting and Profiling User Behavior on DealDash

†Xinyi Zhang, §Shawn Shan, †Shiliang Tang, §Haitao Zheng, §Ben Y. Zhao

{xyzhang,shiliang_tang}@cs.ucsb.edu,{shansixioing,htzheng,ravenben}@cs.uchicago.edu

†UC Santa Barbara, §University of Chicago

ABSTRACT

We study user behavior and the predictability of penny auctions, auction sites often criticized for misrepresenting themselves as low-price auction marketplaces. Using a 166-day trace of 134,568 auctions involving 174 million bids on DealDash, the largest penny auction site in service, we show that a) both the timing and source of bids are highly predictable, and b) users are easily classified into clear behavioral groups by their bidding behavior, and such behaviors correlate highly with the eventual profitability of their bidding strategies. This suggests that penny auction sites are vulnerable to modeling and adversarial attacks.

CCS CONCEPTS

• **Applied computing** → **Online auctions**; • **Human-centered computing** → *User models*;

KEYWORDS

online auctions; user behavior; sequence prediction; clustering

ACM Reference Format:
†Xinyi Zhang, §Shawn Shan, †Shiliang Tang, §Haitao Zheng, §Ben Y. Zhao. 2018. Penny Auctions are Predictable: Predicting and Profiling User Behavior on DealDash. In *HT '18: 29th ACM Conference on Hypertext and Social Media, July 9–12, 2018, Baltimore, MD, USA.* ACM, New York, NY, USA, 5 pages. https://doi.org/10.1145/3209542.3209576

1 INTRODUCTION

Penny auctions, also known as pay-per-bid auctions, are auctions in which all participants must pay a bidding fee each time they place an incremental bid. Each auction starts with a small reserve price, and a countdown timer. Each new bid increments the current price by a small fixed amount and resets the timer. When the timer expires, the participant who placed the last bid wins the auction and purchases the item with the final auction price. Penny auctions are often criticized for their misleading advertisement [9] where they use an auction's final price as the cost of the auctioned item, when, in fact, the majority of the revenue comes from the prices paid for each bid.

The unique structure of penny auctions is designed to generate revenue from all users, both winners and losers. They are seen as exploiting human psychological tendencies such as risk-seeking behavior [18] and the sunk-cost fallacy [3]. However, the mechanisms used, i.e. short bid timer and small incremental bids, impose specific constraints on the auction process itself. A natural question arises, do these mechanisms encourage the formation of fundamental processes driving bidding behavior? And if so, do such behaviors produce predictable patterns that can be modeled and predicted using modern machine learning tools? Success could signal the possibility of designing adversarial bidding algorithms that consistently win auctions with minimal cost of bids.

Our work tries to answer these initial questions, by studying empirical traces of bids in auctions on DealDash, the largest and one of the oldest penny auctions online today. We record details of bids and outcomes for all DealDash auctions over a 166-day period, totaling 134,568 auctions with 174 million bids from 101,936 unique users.

Using analysis of this trace, our goal is to answer two key questions. First, we want to understand what types of patterns exist in bidding behavior in DealDash auctions, and if these patterns make the overall bidding process predictable using modern machine learning models. Second, we want to understand what, if any, common strategies exist in bidding behavior, and how such strategies fare in quantifiable terms. We want to identify the most successful strategies, as a first step towards developing adversarial bidding algorithms for penny auctions.

Our analysis and experiments produce some surprising results. First, our analysis shows that most users optimize their bids in accordance with the pay-per-bid auction structure. Nearly all bids come at the last possible second before timer expiration. Users tend to exhibit repetitive bidding behavior across auctions, making sequences of bids in each auction highly predictable. Second, we use similarity analysis to cluster bidders by their bidding behavior, and identify five key categories, defined by the dominant bidding strategy most commonly observed in their bidders. Mapping these bidding behaviors to auction outcomes shows that, unsurprisingly, aggressive and persistent bidders win a disproportionally high number of auctions, and earn significant gains per auction. In contrast, low-activity bidders or those limited by budget win fewer auctions per user, and generally have trouble recouping their losses from paying for bids, resulting in net loss.

We believe our work is the first to empirically study the predictability of bidding behavior in penny auctions. Our results suggest that these systems can be gamed by adversarial strategies using bid predictions from machine learning prediction models.

2 BACKGROUND & RELATED WORK

DealDash. DealDash [1] is one of the largest and longest-running penny auction websites (since 2009). Its functionality is typical of other penny auctions. On DealDash, the typical bid fee is 12-15 cents, and the fixed price increment is restricted to 1 cent. The countdown clock expires in 10 seconds. DealDash supports a buy-it-now function, by which a losing bidder can purchase the item with a posted retail price and have all the previously placed bids refunded. DealDash also provides a helper function called BidBuddy, which is a script that takes a fixed amount of budget from the participant and automatically place bids whenever the countdown clock reaches 1 second and someone else holds the last bid.

Related Work. Prior work noted that penny auctions are very profitable for the sellers [3, 18]. Most studies of penny auctions aim at finding theoretical explanations of the high revenue, *e.g.*, information asymmetry [8], risk-loving nature of bidders [18] and sunk cost fallacy [3]. Other studies have made great effort to predict the final price of an auction, either statically [11, 21] or dynamically [13, 22], using machine learning and various modeling tools.

While significant progress has been made on developing economic models on auction process and auctioneer profits, few have examined individual bidder behavior in these systems. In contrast, our work predicts whether a bid will appear and who will place the bid, which is more similar to individual behavior models for sequence synthesis done on small-scale English auctions [6, 17].

Some studies have identified different types bidding behavior in "traditional" auction settings such as English or Dutch auctions. The behaviors identified include jumping [10], snipping [4, 19], evaluating [5], participatory [5], strategic exiting [2] and shilling [20]. To the best of our knowledge, our work is the first to systematically identify bidding behavior used in penny auction settings.

3 INITIAL ANALYSIS

We begin by describing our data collection methodology and our dataset. Then we perform preliminary analysis to understand the bidding activities on DealDash. This provides the context for in-depth studies in later sections.

3.1 Data Collection

We collect all observed auctions from DealDash over a 166-day period, from October 19th, 2017 to April 3rd, 2018. In total, we obtained complete history for 134,568 auctions. Each auction contains the name of the item, the buy-it-now price, the starting time and each bid placed during the auction. For each bid, we record the ID of the user placing this bid, and the time of the bid. We extracted 101,936 unique users from a total of 174,076,943 bids.

To verify the completeness of our dataset, we launched two sets of crawlers from two distinct sets of IP addresses. We find that 99.7% of all observed auctions are identified by both crawlers. It is thus safe to conclude that we have covered most or all of the auctions that a typical DealDash user would see.

3.2 Preliminary Analysis

For an initial understanding of the user behaviors in penny auctions, we start by answering a few basic questions.

When are bids placed? In DealDash, the countdown timer expires in 10 seconds. When looking at how long users waited before placing their bids, Figure 1 shows that the majority of bids (81.6%) are placed at the very last second. The reason of this is twofold. First, it is in the users' best interest to wait until the last seconds in hope of someone else being impatient enough to do the bidding for them. Second, DealDash provides a functionality called *BidBuddy* which automatically place bids for the user at the last second.

How many bids do you need to win? We look at the number of bids placed by users in an auction, as well as the winning users. As shown in Figure 2, half of the users place more than an average of 20 bids per auction. To win an auction, more bids need to be placed. Only 8.1% of the users can win an auction with less than 10 bids. In half of the auctions, more than 21.3% of all bids are placed by the auction winner. This shows that winning an auction is more than being at the right place at the right time. It takes repeated bids to convince the other bidders to give up. In Section 5, we delve into detail about the behavior patterns of auction winners.

How much does an auction winner gain? As discussed in Section 1, the actual savings from penny auction are often unclear to users. We examine how much money is "won" in each DealDash auction. When calculating the value of the item won, we estimate the retail price using the price of the same item offered on Amazon.com. Note that the price of each bid ranges from 12 to 15 cents. Here we use 12 cents as an estimation of the bid cost for each user. Using 13, 14 or 15 cents per auction produces similar results.

Figure 3 shows a CDF of the proportion of money paid by the winners and all participants during each auction. In the majority of the cases, even after accounting for the price of bids, the winner pays significantly less than retail for the item won. Half of the winners win the item after spending 12.3% of the retail price. Even accounting for bids placed by the losing bidders, DealDash is only able to generate profit out of 32.5% of the auctions. One thing to note is that certain bidders will pay more than the retail price to win auctions. For example, a user called "leilani2" placed 169,223 bids on a Lawn Mower with retail price of $3,099. The bids would cost approximately $20,307. This behavior is commonly associated with power bidders [15]. Power bidders establish a reputation by not giving up an auction even when the price goes unreasonably high. They hope that experienced users will learn to avoid the power bidders, and they can then win auctions at a very low price. We show in Section 5 that in the case of DealDash, most power bidders still need to put in a large number of bids to win auctions.

4 BID PREDICTION

In this section we study the predictability of bidders in penny auctions. We achieve this by building machine learning models to predict bidding behavior and evaluating them using our DealDash traces. More specifically, we use n-gram [7] and recurrent neural network (2-layer LSTM [12]) models, and show that bidding behavior in penny auctions are actually highly predictable.

4.1 Methodology

Our prediction models use a sequence-based framework. An auction with n bids forms a sequence $S = (U_1, U_2, ..., U_n, End)$, where

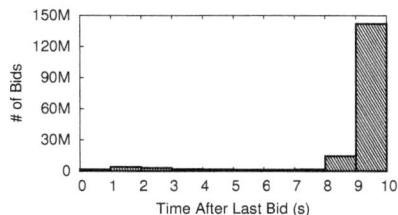

Figure 1: Distribution of time waited until the next bid.

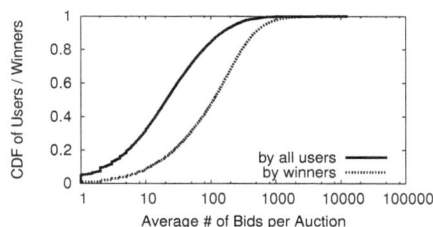

Figure 2: Bids placed per auction, for auctions winners or across all bidders.

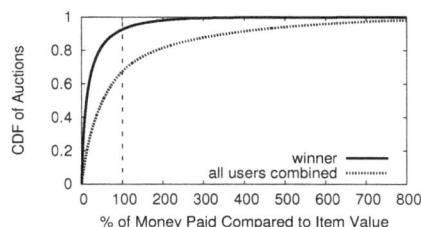

Figure 3: Distribution of price paid relative to product value.

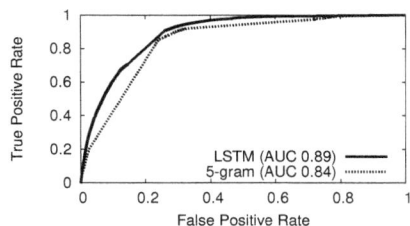

Figure 4: ROC-curve for predicting whether an auction will end.

	AUC	Top-1 Accuracy	Perplexity
3-gram	0.831	0.875	**1.557**
4-gram	0.843	0.886	1.653
5-gram	**0.844**	0.890	1.827
6-gram	0.839	**0.891**	2.063
7-gram	0.831	0.890	2.318
LSTM	0.890	0.900	1.259

Table 1: AUC in predicting auction ending. Top-1 accuracy and perplexity in predicting next bidder.

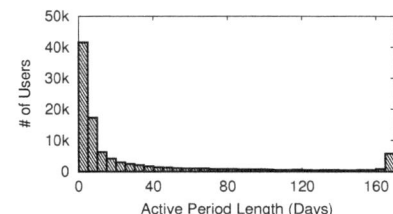

Figure 5: Distribution of time gap between each users' first and last bid.

U_i is the username of the user who placed the ith bid in the auction, and *End* is a token that indicates auction has ended. Our model takes in any subsequence $(U_1, U_2, ..., U_k)$ where $k \le n$ and predicts the value of S_{k+1}, either the username of the $k + 1^{th}$ bidder or that the auction has ended.

A bidder who has recently placed a bid in an auction is likely to bid again soon. Hence, we introduce the concept of "relative position," as the position difference between the current bid and the most recent bid placed by the same user. We can then transform a bidding sequence into a sequence of relative positions of the bidder who placed each bid. When a user has not previously placed any bid in the auction, her relative position will be regarded as infinite.

For example, a bidding sequence $S = (A, B, A, C, B, A, End)$ can be transformed into $S_{rel} = (Inf, Inf, 2, Inf, 3, 3, End)$, which is then used in prediction. We find the performance is better when we treat different relative positions as separate classes instead of as a numeric value. Given that most relative bids (95.5%) are below 20, we enforce a cap of 20 on the maximum relative position. Experiments show different threshold values of 10, 20 and 50 have minimal impact on prediction results.

4.2 Prediction Results

We separate our data trace by time, auctions that concluded at least 14 days before the end of the trace (120,671 auctions), and auctions taking place during the last 14 days (13,842 auctions). We use the older auctions for training, and the newer auctions for testing.

We first use the probability on the class "End" to predict whether an auction will end or not. In Table 1, the best performing n-gram model is 5-gram with an AUC of 0.844. The LSTM model beats it by a large margin with an AUC of 0.890, as shown in Figure 4.

We evaluate bidder prediction using top-1 accuracy, which is the percent of time our model correctly predicts whom the next bidder is. As shown in Table 1, the LSTM achieves a slightly higher top-1 accuracy of 0.900. In addition, we evaluated each model's

perplexity. It is formulated as $\exp(-\sum_i (\log p_i)/n)$, where p_i is the predicted probability of the i-th relative position in the test set of n bids. A lower perplexity indicates a better model. LSTM significantly outperforms the rest.

The high accuracy in bid prediction indicates strong underlying processes that drive bidder behavior. Next, we will try to identify these underlying behavior patterns, and show how these behaviors lead to the failure or success of a penny auction bidder.

5 PROFILING USER BIDDING BEHAVIOR

To identify behavior patterns underlying how users bid, we cluster users based on similarity in statistical features of their bidding history, and then analyze the bidding performance of each cluster.

5.1 Clustering Methodology

Users' bidding patterns manifest only when there is sufficient bidding history. With 19.3% of users joining only one auction, user activity is highly skewed. As shown in Figure 5, users fall into two distinct types. The ones who played for a short period and quit, and those who are active for most of the crawling period. This high user churn is common in penny auction sites [23]. Using Figure 5, we thus filter out users who are active for less than 128 days, which we call *short-term bidders*. This leaves us with 9,105 users.

We quantify user behavior using the following features with the aim of capturing behaviors relevant to bidding performance while removing correlation between features.

- **Number of auctions.** Activity level of a user defined by number of auctions user has participated in.
- **Bids per auction.** Average number of bids placed by the user in each auction.
- **Bid response time.** Average time gap between a user's bid and the prior bid.

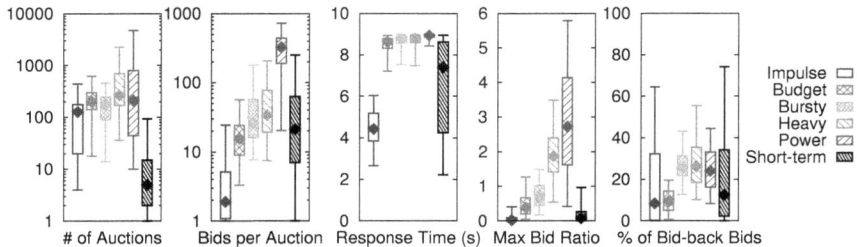

Figure 6: Distribution of feature value for each cluster and for short-term bidders. We depict each distribution with box plot quantiles (5%, 25%, 50%, 75%, 95%).

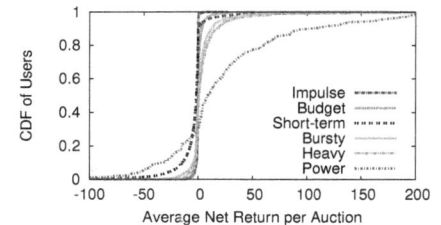

Figure 7: Distribution of earnings per auction for different types of bidders.

- **Max bid ratio.** Maximum ratio of value of bids placed against the value of the product, across all auctions participated in by the user. A value above 1 means the bidder paid more in bids than the value of the product in at least one auction.
- **Bid-back rate.** Bid-back is when a user is out-bid and she places the immediate next bid. This measures the user's aggressiveness in auctions.

We compute the feature vector for each user (z-score normalized), and measure the Euclidean distance between user pairs. We then applied Divisive Hierarchical Clustering [14] to cluster the 9,105 active users. When breaking the users into five clusters, we achieves the best clustering quality as indicated by modularity [16].

5.2 Cluster Analysis

We manually label each cluster based on the feature values they exhibit, as shown in Figure 6. To measure performance, we show, in Figure 7, on average how much each user is wining from each auction. Each user's net return is calculated as the total worth of items won in auctions minus the final auction price and minus the cost of bids.

- Impulse Bidders (9.79% of users). Contrary to common practice, these users do not wait until the last second to place their bids. Instead, their bids are placed at random points during the countdown, with a median wait time of 4.4 seconds. Most in this group failed to make money from auctions, losing a median of $0.20 per auction.
- Budget Bidders (55.8%). They only place a few bids in each auction, and rarely bid back when outbid. These users are not aggressive enough, and most win less than 1% of the auctions they join. This is the user cluster with the largest median net loss, losing more than $0.47 per auction.
- Bursty Bidders (19.6%). These users avoid spending too many bids in any auction, but are still able to maintain a high bid-back rate. They tend to concentrate their bids to a short period, either ending in winning the auction or running out of bids. Most users in this group produce net gains, with a median return of $0.48 per auction.
- Heavy Bidders (12.5%). These users join a lot of auctions and are willing to place substantial number of bids to win the auction. Median return per auction is $0.63.
- Power Bidders (2.22%). They are similar to heavy bidders, but place an order of magnitude more bids, characterized by a high max bid ratio. Given more bids placed per auction, it

is unsurprising that they are much more likely to win their auctions, with a median of 14.8% chance of winning. Median return per auction for these users is $9.38.

By observing the clusters, we find that most DealDash bidders are actually losing money, while a small number of winners earn significant profit. The most successful users (power bidders and heavy bidders) win 13.08% and 27.00% of all auctions, despite making up less than 15% of the long-term user population. While other groups win their share of auctions, they lose far more auctions, and are generally unable to recoup their losses from the cost of bids.

6 DISCUSSION AND CONCLUSIONS

Our analysis of penny auctions and their users focused on two things, the predictability of sequential bids in auctions, and identifying common bidding behaviors in penny auctions and the results of these behaviors.

There are two takeaways from our results. First, we find that penny auctions are surprisingly predictable. Due to both the awareness of last second bidding strategies and scripts that follow them, bidding is highly periodic. In addition, users tend to exhibit highly periodic bidding behavior, which is easily captured by n-gram models, and slightly more accurately using LSTM models. Together, they suggest that the sequence of bids and timing can both be predicted with reasonable accuracy. Second, we find that most bidders tend to fall into one of a handful of clear behavioral categories, based on how patient they are, how aggressive they are, and how much money they have and are willing to use to win. We show that the large majority of users lose money, and the winnings go disproportionately to a small portion of the users (mostly power bidders willing and able to use large bid volumes to win auctions).

Finally, our results suggest that penny auctions themselves could possibly be gamed adversarially. It seems intuitive that drawing from our results, a reasonably complex model could emulate power bidder behavior, and use predictions to gain a significant advantage over its competitors and profit. We leave the development of such a model and adversarial algorithm to future work.

ACKNOWLEDGMENTS

We wish to thank our anonymous reviewers for their constructive feedback. This project was supported by NSF grants CNS-1527939 and CNS-1705042. Any opinions, findings, and conclusions or recommendations expressed in this material are those of the authors and do not necessarily reflect the views of any funding agencies.

REFERENCES

[1] 2017. DealDash. (October 2017). https://dealdash.com/.

[2] Corey M Angst, Ritu Agarwal, and Jason Kuruzovich. 2008. Bid or buy? Individual shopping traits as predictors of strategic exit in on-line auctions. *International Journal of Electronic Commerce* 13, 1 (2008), 59–84.

[3] Ned Augenblick. 2015. The sunk-cost fallacy in penny auctions. *The Review of Economic Studies* 83, 1 (2015), 58–86.

[4] Matt Backus, Thomas Blake, Dimitriy V Masterov, and Steven Tadelis. 2015. Is Sniping A Problem For Online Auction Markets?. In *Proc. of WWW*.

[5] Ravi Bapna, Paulo Goes, Alok Gupta, and Yiwei Jin. 2004. User heterogeneity and its impact on electronic auction market design: An empirical exploration. *Mis Quarterly* (2004), 21–43.

[6] Eric T Bradlow and Young-Hoon Park. 2007. Bayesian estimation of bid sequences in internet auctions using a generalized record-breaking model. *Marketing Science* 26, 2 (2007), 218–229.

[7] Peter F Brown, Peter V Desouza, Robert L Mercer, Vincent J Della Pietra, and Jenifer C Lai. 1992. Class-based n-gram models of natural language. *Computational linguistics* 18, 4 (1992), 467–479.

[8] John W Byers, Michael Mitzenmacher, and Georgios Zervas. 2010. Information asymmetries in pay-per-bid auctions. In *Proc. of ACM EC*.

[9] Patrick Collinson. 2017. Six auction sites' ads banned over misleading savings claims. The Guardian. (February 2017). https://www.theguardian.com/money/2017/feb/22/auction-sites-ads-banned-claims-madbid-asa.

[10] Robert F Easley and Rafael Tenorio. 2004. Jump bidding strategies in internet auctions. *Management Science* 50, 10 (2004), 1407–1419.

[11] Rayid Ghani. 2005. Price prediction and insurance for online auctions. In *Proc. of KDD*.

[12] Sepp Hochreiter and Jürgen Schmidhuber. 1997. Long short-term memory. *Neural computation* 9, 8 (1997), 1735–1780.

[13] Wolfgang Jank, Galit Shmueli, and Shanshan Wang. 2006. Dynamic, real-time forecasting of online auctions via functional models. In *Proc. of KDD*.

[14] Leonard Kaufman and Peter J Rousseeuw. 2009. *Finding groups in data: an introduction to cluster analysis*. Vol. 344. John Wiley & Sons.

[15] David R Konkel. 2012. Costing a Pretty Penny: Online Penny Auctions Revive the Pestilence of Unregulated Lotteries. *Seattle University Law Review* 36 (2012), 1967.

[16] Mark EJ Newman. 2006. Modularity and community structure in networks. *PNAS* 103, 23 (2006), 8577–8582.

[17] Young-Hoon Park and Eric T Bradlow. 2005. An integrated model for bidding behavior in Internet auctions: Whether, who, when, and how much. *Journal of Marketing Research* 42, 4 (2005), 470–482.

[18] Brennan C Platt, Joseph Price, and Henry Tappen. 2013. The role of risk preferences in pay-to-bid auctions. *Management Science* 59, 9 (2013), 2117–2134.

[19] Alvin E Roth and Axel Ockenfels. 2002. Last-minute bidding and the rules for ending second-price auctions: Evidence from eBay and Amazon auctions on the Internet. *American Economic Review* 92, 4 (2002), 1093–1103.

[20] Jarrod Trevathan and Wayne Read. 2009. Detecting shill bidding in online English auctions. *Handbook of research on social and organizational liabilities in information security* 46 (2009), 446–470.

[21] Dennis Van Heijst, Rob Potharst, and Michiel van Wezel. 2008. A support system for predicting eBay end prices. *Decision Support Systems* 44, 4 (2008), 970–982.

[22] Shanshan Wang, Wolfgang Jank, and Galit Shmueli. 2008. Explaining and forecasting online auction prices and their dynamics using functional data analysis. *Journal of Business & Economic Statistics* 26, 2 (2008), 144–160.

[23] Zhongmin Wang and Minbo Xu. 2016. Selling a dollar for more than a dollar? Evidence from online penny auctions. *Information Economics and Policy* 36 (2016), 53–68.

The StoryPlaces Platform: Building a Web-Based Locative Hypertext System

Charlie Hargood
Creative Technology
Bournemouth University
chargood@bournemouth.ac.uk

Mark J. Weal
Web and Internet Science
University of Southampton
mjw@ecs.soton.ac.uk

David E. Millard
Web and Internet Science
University of Southampton
dem@ecs.soton.ac.uk

ABSTRACT

Locative narrative systems have been a popular area of research for nearly two decades, but they are often bespoke systems, developed for particular deployments, or to demonstrate novel technologies. This has meant that they are short-lived, the narratives have been constructed by the creators of the system, and that the barrier to creating locative experiences has remained high due to a lack of common tools.

We set out to create a platform based on the commonalities of these historic systems, with a focus on hypertext structure, and designed to enable locative based narratives to be created, deployed, and experienced in-the-wild.

The result is StoryPlaces, an open source locative hypertext platform and authoring tool designed around a sculptural hypertext engine and built with existing Web technologies. As well as providing an open platform for future development, StoryPlaces also offers novelty in its management of location, including the separation of location and nodes, of descriptions from locations, and of content from pages, as well as being designed to have run-time caching and disconnection resilience. It also advances the state of the art in sculptural hypertext systems delivery through conditional functions, and nested, geographic and temporal conditions.

The StoryPlaces platform has been used for the public deployment of over twenty locative narratives, and demonstrates the effectiveness of a general platform for delivering complex locative narrative experiences. In this paper we describe the process of creating the platform and our insights on the design of locative hypertext platforms.

CCS CONCEPTS

• **Human-centered computing** → **Hypertext/hypermedia**;

KEYWORDS

Location-Based Narrative, Sculptural Hypertext

ACM Reference Format:
Charlie Hargood, Mark J. Weal, and David E. Millard. 2018. The StoryPlaces Platform: Building a Web-Based Locative Hypertext System. In *HT'18: 29th ACM Conference on Hypertext & Social Media, July 9–12, 2018, Baltimore, MD, USA*. ACM, New York, NY, USA, 8 pages. https://doi.org/10.1145/3209542.3209559

1 INTRODUCTION

In 2017 Claus Atzenbeck told the hypertext research community that "research on traditional hypertext systems has been fading out over the past decade" [2] - something that very much appears to be true. The early concepts such as Memex [12] and projects like Xanadu [27], led to later systems such as Hypercard [32] and StorySpace [5, 8], which in turn inspired the Hypertext ideas of the 90s such as MICROCOSM [18], and adaptive hypertext in Interbook [10] and AHA [14], as well as "strange Hypertext" experiments such as CardShark [3]. But since then there has been little in the way of new hypertext infrastructure presented in the literature save for a new version of StorySpace [6] and Atzenbeck's own system ODIN [2]. In contrast there have been a number of commercial tools that have become popular in the interactive fiction community, such as Twine[1] and Inform[2].

The rise of the Web undeniably had an impact but these examples show us there is still much to learn from Hypertext implementations in a post Web world. In 1999 Mark Bernstein asked us "Where are the hypertexts?", nearly twenty years later we might ask "Where are the hypertext systems?".

StoryPlaces[3], as a research project, sought to better understand locative narrative (interactive stories that are contextually aware and respond to the readers location). It followed work seeking a generic model for all location aware narrative [25] and has worked both to understanding the poetics of location based narrative [29], its hypertextual patterns and structures [20], and the impact on the writing process [23]. During the project three story deployments were made each delivering 6 stories written by a combination of volunteer and paid authors in three different UK cities (Southampton, Bournemouth, and London) - alongside another experimental story created as part of a reflection on the writing process [20]. These stories were delivered using the StoryPlaces platform - a new generic sculptural hypertext system.

In this paper we present the StoryPlaces platform, its features and innovations, the rationale behind its design, and the lessons learned in the engineering of a new generic sculptural hypertext platform.

---

[1] http://twinery.org/ as of 17/4/18
[2] http://inform7.com/ as of 17/4/18
[3] http://storyplaces.soton.ac.uk/ as of 31/1/2018

2 BACKGROUND ON LOCATIVE NARRATIVE

Early locative systems often took the form of tour guides, linking a database of information to specific locations in the environment to create personalised pages designed to be read in-situ [9]. Early systems such as GUIDE had to deal with relatively inaccurate location data [13], adopting strategies where the user was involved in choosing the correct location from a shortlist generated by the application, but later systems could rely on more stable location technologies such as GPS, and the research focus moved to the experience itself. This often took the form of narrative experiences such as a mosaic of personal stories [28] or historical plays that unfold in a given location [7]. The potential of these sorts of experience for heritage applications has been noted for both navigation and education [19], as well as considered as a way of augmenting more conventional exhibition spaces [21].

Educational applications of locative hypertext have also been popular. The Chawton House project combined digital information with physical activities for schoolchildren in the grounds of a period house [34], for example giving children information about the use of a particular area, and then asking the children to write a poem in their notebooks about the household interacting in that space. Other systems use digital activities supported directly by the system, for example 'Gaius' Day in Egnathia' [1] asks users to collect location-based clues that draws them through the exploration of Egnathia, an ancient Roman city in Southern Italy.

Research has also explored how the real world can be incorporated into the digital experience. In 'University of Death' [11] players collect and use real world props alongside digital clues to progress. Augmented Reality is a popular approach - 'Viking Ghost Hunt' [26] allows players to hunt ghosts on the streets of Dublin, using AR technology to visualize their targets. AR can also be used to present information overlaid over real world targets, or even to recreate historical buildings and places using the device [17].

StoryPlaces is concerned with applications that are closer to interactive fiction, with a focus on story and interactive structure. These locative narrative experiences have been termed locative literature' [22] or 'ambient literature'[16]. Some examples, such as the 'iLand of Madeira', have simple structure, in the case of iLand relying on a mosaic of story nodes that are gradually revealed to the reader [15]. Other examples use more complex rules and draw on not only reader choices but contextual information, for example 'San Servolo, travel into the memory of an island', which considers not only location but also weather [30].

Locative literature can be conceptualised as a *Sculptural Hypertext* system, where all nodes are potentially linked, but those links are 'sculpted away' based on rules that are compared to the readers' state [4, 35]. Sculptural hypertext is a good fit for locative systems, as location can be modeled as part of the users state, allowing location to be incorporated seamlessly alongside logical rules (for example, 'Node C is visible once you have read Node B, and you are standing in the Courtyard'. Sculptural Hypertext has been shown to support linear, branching, and open locative structures (described as Canyons, Deltas, and Plains) which when combined are sufficient to describe a wide range of location-based narratives [25]. It is this model that drives the StoryPlaces Platform, and enables it to support a wide range of locative experiences.

3 THE STORYPLACES PROJECT AND DESIGN PROCESS

StoryPlaces was a two and a half year Leverhulme Trust funded project investigating the structures, poetics, impact, and application of locative narratives. Its name is a deliberate homage to Storyspace [5, 6, 8] and one of its key contributors (Mark Bernstein) who did much to establish the idea of sculptural hypertext [3]. The project was an interdisciplinary collaboration between the authors as computer scientists, literary academics, and writers. Locative fiction has largely existed within bespoke systems created for individual stories. This is expensive, forces authors to acquire technical skills or require collaborators, and is often not sustainable in the long term as maintenance for each application only lasts as long as its initial deployment. A general framework for locative narrative supported by an authoring tool could unlock the creation of locative narrative to a wider base of writers, create a technological standard for longer term community maintenance as an open source project, and provide a platform for the StoryPlaces project to create a range of stories to support its own investigation into locative fiction.

The framework was designed based on a combination of participatory design, co-operative inquiry, and systematic review. The sculptural model was based on the previous work *Canyons, Deltas, and Plains* - as common structures of locative narratives that could potentially support the majority of systems described in the literature [25]. Initial low-fi experiments with creative writers writing locative fiction revealed a number of common patterns and also confirmed the suitability of sculptural hypertext as an underlying model [20]. Following this the team worked with both engineers and writers in a participatory design process to create interface components and explore the requirements from both a technical and artistic point of view. As part of this process, and in the spirit of co-operative inquiry [31], we also personally explored the process of authoring a locative narrative itself [23]. The direct experience of working with the form provided insights into the challenges authors face, which aided later workshops with authors, leading us to create a toolkit of advice for authors to help them balance the demands of story, structure, and landscape [29].

The research and design process went in parallel with iterative development on the technology. First in the form of a server and web-based reading client, used for the project's public deployments, and then later including an authoring tool that encapsulated the lessons learned about designing locative narratives. These are detailed in the next Section.

4 THE STORYPLACES PLATFORM

The StoryPlaces platform is an open source generic platform for delivering locative hypertext. Its development followed, and builds upon, the CDP locative narrative model [25]. The framework is made up of three individual applications: *reading-tool, authoring-tool,* and *server*.

4.1 Architecture

While the *server* functions as host, storage, and validator for content, the *reading-tool* and *authoring-tool* provide the interface and control to content for different modes of usage. The *authoring-tool* is for

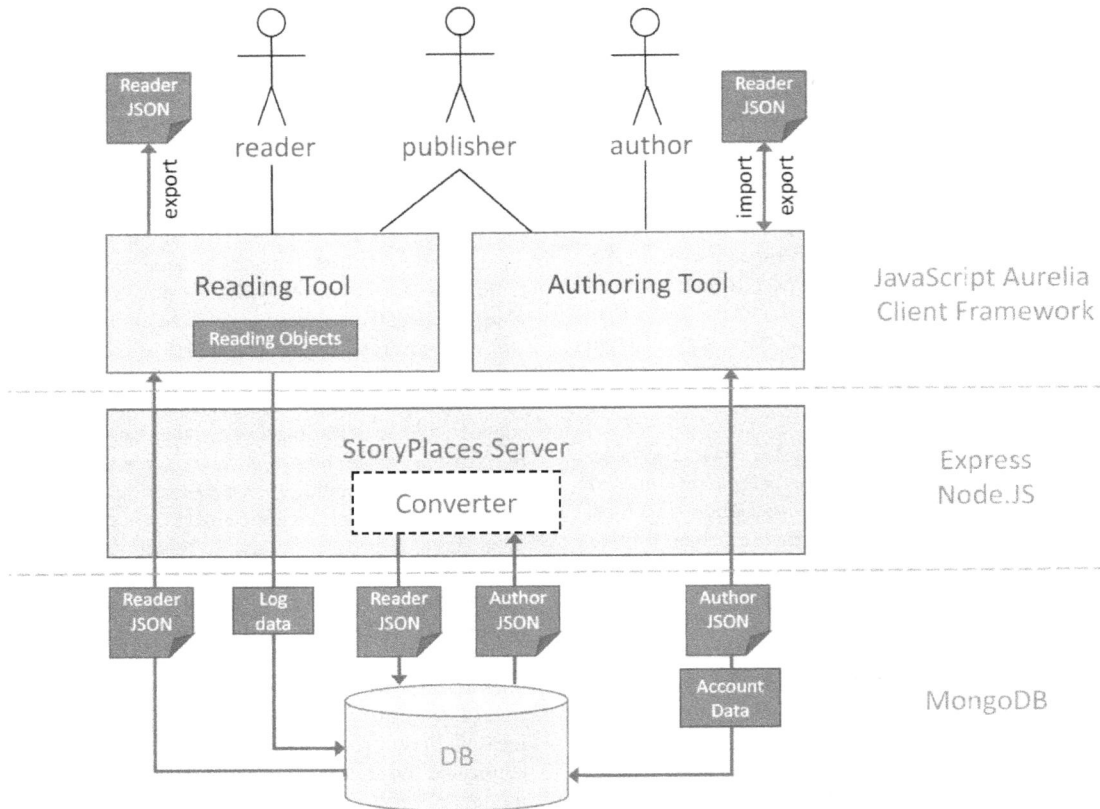

Figure 1: The Storyplaces Architecture, User Interaction, and Data Flow

the management, creation, and editing of stories, while the *reading-tool* is for reading published content. Authors authenticate with the *server* using a Google account. This allows their stories to be stored centrally by the server and potentially published to others. Readers are anonymous, so their reading state (stories started and progress) are held locally within their web client using cookies and only uploaded to the server for analysis purposes. A sequence of usage for StoryPlaces might be summarised as follows:

(1) **Author** creates a story using the *authoring-tool* which is stored on the *server*
(2) **Author** uses the *authoring-tool* to create a preview of the story and tests it using the *reading-tool*
(3) **Author** refines their story using the *authoring-tool* and marks it as ready for publication; updates *server*
(4) **Publisher** reviews the story and may publish through the *authoring-tool*; updates *server*
(5) **Reader** encounters the story on the *reading-tool* which loads from the *server* and selects it for reading
(6) **Reader** creates a Reading for the story which is held locally in their instance of the *reading-tool*
(7) **Reader** opens the reading and reads the story, their reading state is stored locally in the *reading-tool*, and usage data is logged on the *server*

The architecture of the StoryPlaces platform, and the flow of data between its parts, is summarised in Figure 1. The authoring tool uses an extended version of the Story JSON format, which includes additional information used to scaffold the creation of the stories (for example, information used to support pattern based authoring - an approach discussed in more depth in previous work [24]). When the story is published (either in a limited way by the author for testing, or in a more permanent way by the publisher for others to discover) a converter within the server transforms the Author JSON into Reader JSON, which can then be served to the Reading Tool. Openness was an important design goal, and so the author allows Reader JSON to be imported/exported using the authoring tool, and the reading tool also allows Reader JSON to be exported.

4.2 Implementation

StoryPlaces is powered by a flexible Sculptural Hypertext engine that resides in the *reading-tool*. Sculptural Hypertext can be compared to a state machine defined by pages, rules, and constraints. Consequently the StoryPlaces **Story** object is modeled in terms of *Pages* with *Conditions* that determine their visibility, and *Functions* which may be executed by pages to change the state, thus changing page visibility.

The StoryPlaces **Reading** object stores the current state information, which serves as the instance of a users specific reading of a

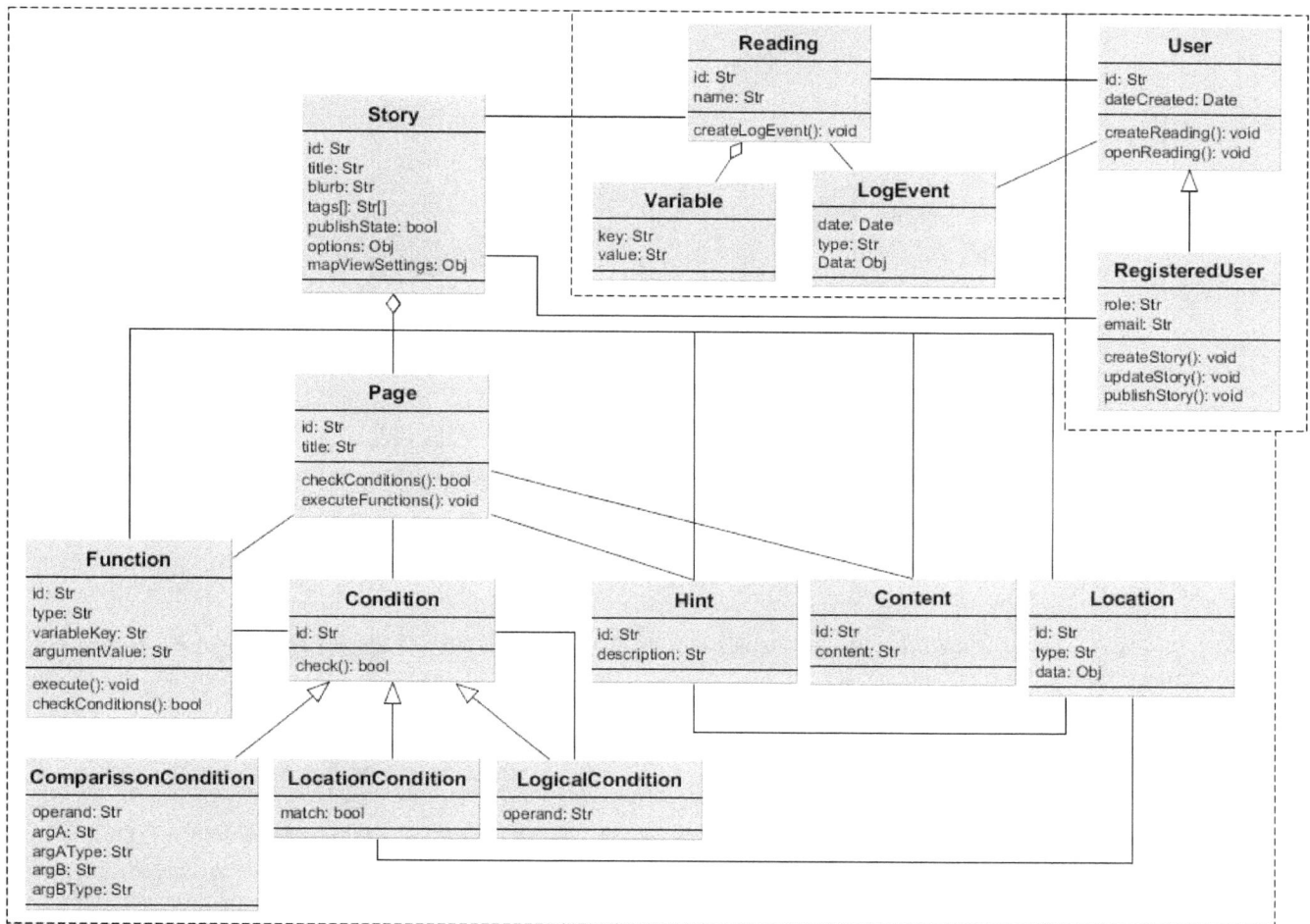

Figure 2: The Storyplaces Schema as a class diagram depicting the story model, runtime elements, and user elements

particular story. Readings are made up of a reference both to **User** and **Story**, and contain a list of *Variables* which are key-value pairs of strings read by *Conditions* and written to by *Functions*. Finally **User** and **LogEvent** complete the first order objects, handling user role and identity, and logging of actions within the system.

The *Condition* object was separated into three types: *ComparisonCondition*, *LocationCondition*, and *LogicalCondition*. *ComparisonConditions* handle standard Sculptural Hypertext constraints - comparing variables. *LocationConditions* serve the inherently locative aspect of the medium the system works with, this is a contextually aware constraint that utilises a *Location* object, and considers whether the user currently satisfies this based on data and sensors available. At present StoryPlaces defines location within or outside of a defined GPS centered circle. However, the *Location* object is extensible. Finally *LogicalCondition* enabled the construction of more complex logical statements by taking reference to other *Conditions* and a defined logical function such as AND or OR. Through the use of all three types the engine can support sculptural hypertext with largely limitless complexity in structure through logical

hierarchies of variable comparisons and location checks. While *Pages* make reference to *Conditions* in a way typical of sculptural hypertext, StoryPlaces also allows the *Functions* on *Pages* to have *Conditions* controlling their execution and the changes of state. The combination of conditional functions and logical hierarchies of conditions serves to provide the sculptural hypertext engine with a fully functioning state machine.

Pages also reference *Hint* and *Content* objects. Locative Narrative is unlike most hypertexts in that it demands its reader satisfies location conditions during the reading. The Reading Tool therefore can give readers guidance on where potential pages are; these are pages where the comparison and logical conditions are met, but the location conditions are not. The reader can then move to that location to open and read the page. The *Hint* object describes how these potential pages should be described to the user. StoryPlaces currently supports textual directions and points on a map (the points are defined using their own Location object, and therefore need not match the Location conditions themselves). *Content* objects deals with the actual content of a page, specifying its text

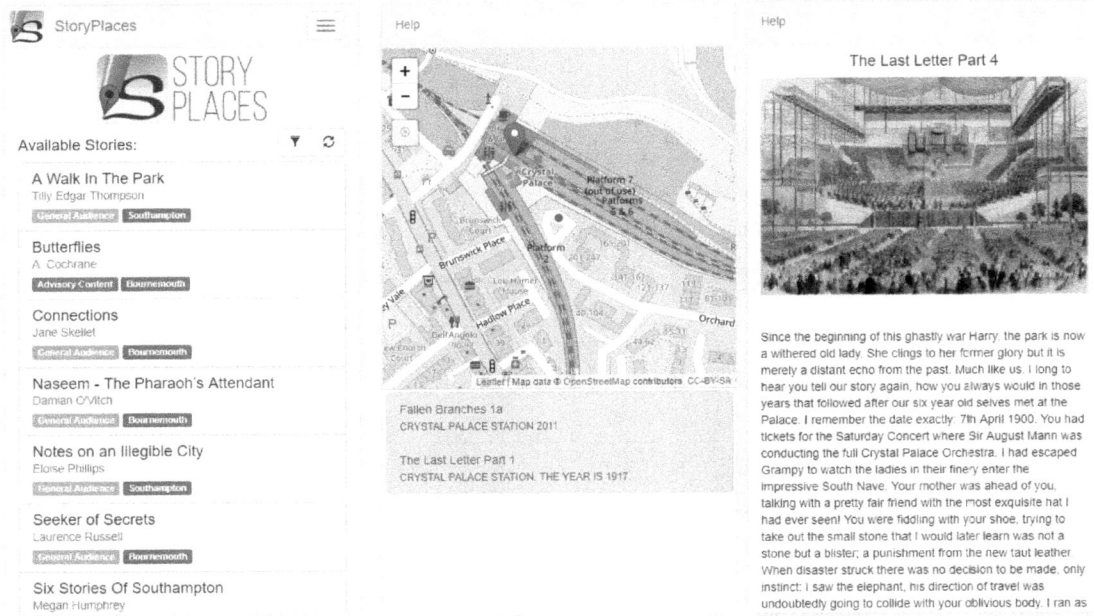

Figure 3: Three screenshots of the StoryPlaces reading tool displaying (from left to right) selecting a story, navigating to a location during a reading, and reading a page

and any multimedia (currently images, audio, and video are supported). StoryPlaces is therefore unusual in that it does not view a node (a Page) as a wrapper for content, but rather as a relationship object that binds together content, conditions, functions, and hints. This will be explored further in Section 5.2. Beyond this structural schema many objects also include more mundane meta data such as titles for *Page* and **Story**, blurb and tags for **Story**, and name for **Reading**. The entirety of our Sculptural Hypertext engine schema is summarized in a slightly simplified class diagram in figure 2.

The StoryPlaces Platform has been implemented as a node.js web application with the reading tool and authoring tool implemented in the Aurelia JavaScript client framework. Web applications are able to access hardware such as the camera and GPS on mobile devices while ensuring a degree of platform neutrality between Android, iOS, and any other mobile operating system outside of browser compatibility. Web applications also avoid the barrier of working with OS application distribution services such as the app store, and allow StoryPlaces to be accessed on both mobile and more conventional devices through the use of responsive CSS. This is especially useful as both tools allow location to be spoofed, so stories can be authored and tested on a desktop machine as well as in-situ.

The StoryPlaces server is implemented using node.js, express.js, a mongoose schema, and operates a mongo database for its objects. It exposes an API which allows its client applications CRUD access to its objects. The reader-tool and authoring-tool client side applications are implemented principally in aurelia.js and make use of open street map for their map based applications. Figure 3 displays screenshots of the implemented reader-tool on a mobile device, and

Figure 4 shows the authoring tool on a desktop device. StoryPlaces is fully open source and available under the MIT license.

5 HYPERTEXT SYSTEM INNOVATIONS

StoryPlaces is unusual as a generic web-based hypertext system that is focused on location. The platform therefore demonstrates several innovations in both its treatment of location within its hypertext model, and in the power of its sculptural model and engine.

5.1 Building upon the Sculptural Premise

Nearly two decades ago the idea of sculptural hypertext sought to demonstrate that hypertext could arise out of a system that "sculpted away" links at runtime [4, 35], similarly to the way that 'guard fields' controlled the availability of links in the StorySpace system - in essence a sculptural hypertext is one where every node is linked to every other, but each of those links has guard fields. The latest version of StorySpace (version 3) contains a sculptural engine, and extends the power of guard fields to include nested logical structures, such as '(visited(A) & unvisited(B)) | clicked(Anne)' to mean true if the reader has visited node A but not B, or if they have previously clicked the word Anne [6].

StoryPlaces hierarchy of constraints has similar expressive power, allowing *arbitrary nested constraints* comprised of logical or comparative statements. It also includes locative constraints, meaning it is possible to mix logical and location requirements. For example, to express that a page is visible if the reader is in the garden, or if they have previously met Anne and are in the driveway. The use of contextual constraints extends to time, and StoryPlaces supports *time-based constraints* in the form of checks against

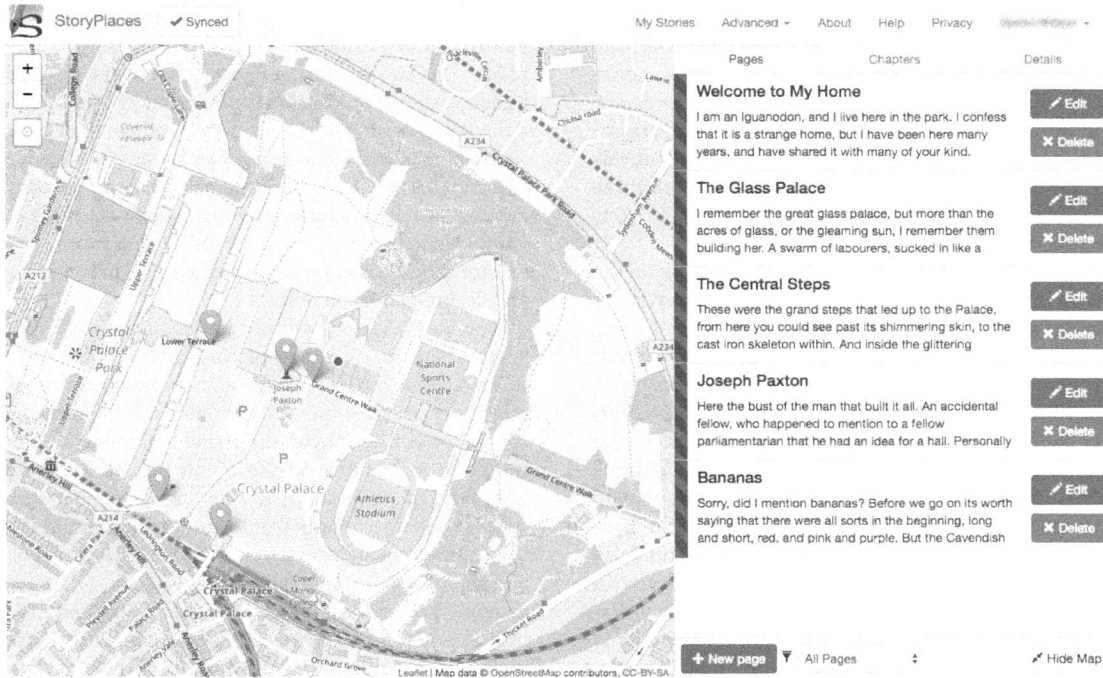

Figure 4: The StoryPlaces authoring tool (username blurred)

time frames that are either absolute (e.g. can only be accessed from 11.00-13.00) or relative to user action (e.g. only available 1 hour after reading node 6). Time and location are two examples of contextual constraints that rely on information beyond the system itself, other examples - such as weather or social media context - would be possible, but remain as future work.

Previous sculptural hypertext systems have often made constraints a part of the page itself (for example as an embedded statement in a domain specific language), but StoryPlaces keeps its conditions and functions outside of the page where they are referenced by the page via ID. Thus in StoryPlaces complex constraints are in fact an explicit named hierarchy of JSON objects. This makes reusing complex constraints easy, as all constraints are first class and can be referenced, but does make creating complex constraints by hand cumbersome (although this is easily hidden behind a GUI interface in the authoring tool).

One of the things that we have observed when working with StoryPlaces is that these constraints encourage a much more complex structure than a normal branching narrative. For example, we can begin to see intricate networks of dependent nodes in two of the larger StoryPlaces stories: Isle of Brine [23] and Fallen Branches [29], that would be cumbersome to create using calligraphic models.

StoryPlace's functions allow for the simple manipulation of variables (via set and increment), the system also supports *conditional functions*, which are functions with their own constraints that limit when they are activated. This allows for a greater degree of author control over state changes and avoids the need for duplicated pages with differing functions for different conditions. For example,

imagine that we want to move to Act 2 once all five of our main characters have been encountered, regardless of the order in which they were met; using conditional functions we can do this by creating a function that increments the Act, and placing a constraint on it that is a check that character count is 5. We can now attach this function to every page in Act 1, and it will only trigger once the condition is met. Without conditional functions we would have had to duplicate the five pages that introduce the main characters so that there is a second version that replaces the first when the other four have been met, and which changes the Act.

5.2 Locative Demands

Sculptural hypertext lends itself to locative narrative as it more easy supports open structures with many possible navigational paths, which is a good match for readers navigating a physical environment [20, 25]. But, location does make certain demands of the hypertext model.

We have already described how *LocationConditions* serve to expand the scope of hypertext state from the text itself to the users context. LocationConditions reference a Location object which defines an area. In StoryPlaces these are *first class locations* detached from their conditions and referenced by ID. This means that a story includes a set of locations that are defined independently of the content and logical rules of the story, these locations could therefore be easy swapped for alternatives, instantly remapping a story onto a new area. At present this is not supported by the reader, but can be done directly with the JSON story definitions.

StoryPlaces also uses *first class content*, also referenced by ID. This is because it is sometimes conceptually easier to model different states as different nodes that share the same content, rather than as a single node with very complex constraints. This was particularly useful for Isle of Brine [23] where a thread of narrative was replicated in three Acts set in entirely different areas, but was only visible to the reader in their current Act. In this case three nodes were created to account for the three states in the three Acts but only a single content object was necessary.

Unlike a traditional hypertext where a user selects a link on the screen, navigation in StoryPlaces is done through a combination of screen and physical navigation. Thus guidance is necessary to help the user find locations in their environment to trigger new content. Although StoryPlaces uses a map, this is theoretically possible in a number of ways, and therefore StoryPlaces also *separates hints from locations*, using the Hint object to direct readers rather the location information attached to the constraints. StoryPlaces hints can contain both a textual direction (that is shown on the screen) and a GPS location (that is shown on the map), but modeling these explicitly means that they are used at the authors discretion and it is perfectly possible to have a node with no hint, or a hint with the description or the location missing. To our knowledge StoryPlaces is the first locative system to have separated direction hints from actual location and given authors this control. It also creates a conceptual place in the model where more sophisticated hint information could be placed in future iterations of the software (such as audio cues, or AR models).

Finally, as a system designed to be used in-the-wild and on-the-move StoryPlaces cannot make the same sort of assumptions about users' connectivity as more traditional desktop hypertext systems. Consequently StoryPlaces undertakes *client-side caching for disconnection resilience*, creating a local cache of the story, content and usage data for later synchronization in the event of loss of connectivity. This is applied in the authoring tool as well as the reader, which will hold a queue of changes locally and resync with the server once connectivity has been restored. Browser based local storage limits prevent StoryPlaces from caching all media, however the system is typically able to cache the story structure, text, and images client side. This does not include audio and video due to the storage limits, which represents a future challenge for these types of web-based application.

6 CONCLUSIONS AND FUTURE WORK

In this paper we have presented the StoryPlaces Platform - a generic web-based locative hypertext system with a powerful Sculptural Hypertext engine. StoryPlaces is the first general platform for locative narrative, and a rare example of a new and novel hypertext system [2].

The StoryPlaces Platform has been used to create and deliver 21 different stories in various locations across the UK (6 in Southampton, 7 in Bournemouth, 6 in London, 1 in Exeter, and 1 in Tiree). The majority (18) of these stories were released at launch events in their host cities where they were publicly advertised through local partners and attended by the general public. The stories include linear works, branching narratives, open narratives, short stories of 20 minutes and long stories of 4 hours, text based works,

audio works, and mixed media works. Our readers have been a mixture of academics, reading group members, and the general public. Our authors have included 2 members of the research team, 3 commissioned professional authors, and 17 volunteer writers with a mixture of professional, academic and amateur backgrounds.

The StoryPlaces Platform is open source software comprised of two web-based clients (the *reading-tool*, and *authoring-tool*) implemented in the JavaScript Aurelia framework, that communicate with a Node.JS *server*, using the JSON data format, and MongoDB for storage. The clients use responsive CSS to render to both mobile and desktop environments.

The StoryPlaces Platform demonstrates both an evolution of Sculptural Hypertext, and an innovative response to the demands of locative narrative. Specifically its sculptural engine supports arbitrarily complex (nested) conditions, conditional functions, and contextual constraints (in the form of temporal and location conditions). To deal with locations the hypertext model separates locations from pages (potentially allowing remapping of stories to new spaces), separates hints from locations (meaning that directions to locations are independent of the definition of those locations), and separates content from pages (treating pages, or nodes, as a mapping between content, constraints, hints, and functions, rather than as a wrapper for content). The system also supports runtime caching for both reading and authoring tools in order to provide disconnection resilience.

Our Future work includes both software developments and new locative applications. Work is currently underway to use the framework to recreate a number of classical locative experiences from the research literature whose own bespoke systems have fallen out of maintenance and functionality - this includes 'The Chawton House Project' [34], and 'iLand of Madeira' [15] with permission from the original authors.

Further work is also required to explore alternative interfaces for reading, and understand their impact on the reader experience. For example, StoryPlaces' current reliance on screen-based navigation takes the reader's attention, distracting them from their surroundings. It's possible that an audio based interface may provide a less demanding alternative that would allow users to spend more time looking at the locations themselves rather than their device. We are also considering options that would allow for the platform to support location in other ways, including classifications of locations that are not tied to one specific GPS point, allowing stories to be mapped dynamically to new areas as required. Finally while locative narrative (and a majority of hypertext) is designed as an individual experience we are also exploring how the StoryPlaces' sculptural engine might be extended to support multi-participant narratives, where sculptural state is shared between several readers, meaning that a readers' experience is affected by the choices of others [33].

Our hope is that the StoryPlaces Platform will lower the barriers for authors who want to experiment with locative literature, and act as an extensible software platform that can be used by researchers and developers for further experimentation into what is possible with locative storytelling.

7 ACKNOWLEDGMENTS

This work was undertaken as part of the StoryPlaces project funded by The Leverhulme Trust (RPG-2014-388). We would like to acknowledge the assistance of our co-designers and developers who have contributed to the StoryPlaces project: Verity Hunt, Heather Packer, Petros Papadopoulos, Yvonne Howard, Will May, Phillip Hoare, James Jordan, Patrick McSweeney, Andrew Day, Kevin Puplett, Callum Spawforth, Victoria Dawson, James Cole, and Katie Lyons.

REFERENCES

[1] C Ardito, P Buono, M.F Costabile, R Lanzilotti, and T. Pederson. 2007. Mobile games to foster the learning of history at archaeological sites. *Visual Languages and Human-Centric Computing* (2007).

[2] Claus Atzenbeck, Thomas Schedel, Manolis Tzagarakis, Daniel Roßner, and Lucas Mages. 2017. Revisiting Hypertext Infrastructure. In *Proceedings of the 28th ACM Conference on Hypertext and Social Media*. ACM, 35–44.

[3] Mark Bernstein. 1998. Patterns of Hypertext. In *Proceedings of the Ninth ACM Conference on Hypertext and Hypermedia*. ACM, New York, NY, USA, 21–29.

[4] Mark Bernstein. 2001. Card shark and thespis: exotic tools for hypertext narrative. In *Proceedings of the twelfth ACM conference on Hypertext and Hypermedia*.

[5] Mark Bernstein. 2002. Storyspace 1. In *Proceedings of the thirteenth ACM conference on Hypertext and hypermedia*. ACM, 172–181.

[6] Mark Bernstein. 2016. Storyspace 3. In *Proceedings of the 27th ACM Conference on Hypertext and Social Media*. ACM, New York, NY, USA.

[7] M. Blythe, J. Reid, P. Wright, and E. Geelhoed. 2006. Interdisciplinary criticism: analysing the experience of riot! a location-sensitive digital narrative. *Behaviour & Information Technology* 25, 2 (2006), 127–139.

[8] Jay David Bolter and Michael Joyce. 1987. Hypertext and creative writing. In *Proceedings of the ACM conference on Hypertext*. ACM, 41–50.

[9] J. Broadbent and P. Marti. 1997. Location aware mobile interactive guides: usability issues. In *Proceedings of the Fourth International Conference on Hypermedia and Interactivity in Museums*. 162–172.

[10] Peter Brusilovsky, John Eklund, and Elmar Schwarz. 1998. Web-based education for all: a tool for development adaptive courseware. *Computer Networks and ISDN Systems* 30, 1-7 (1998), 291–300.

[11] B.S. Bunting, J. Hughes, and T. Hetland. 2012. The Player as Author: Exploring the Effects of Mobile Gaming and the Location-Aware Interface on Storytelling. *Future Internet* 4, 1 (2012), 142–160.

[12] Vannevar Bush et al. 1945. As we may think. *The atlantic monthly* 176, 1 (1945), 101–108.

[13] N Davies, K Cheverst, K Mitchell, and A Efrat. 2001. Using and determining location in a context-sensitive tour guide. *Computer* 34, 8 (2001), 35–41.

[14] Paul De Bra, David Smits, and Natalia Stash. 2006. The design of AHA!. In *Proceedings of the seventeenth conference on Hypertext and hypermedia*. ACM, 133–134.

[15] Mara Dionisio, Valentina Nisi, and Jos P. Van Leeuwen. 2010. The iLand of Madeira Location Aware Multimedia Stories. In *Proceedings of the Third Joint Conference on Interactive Digital Storytelling (ICIDS'10)*. Springer-Verlag, Berlin, Heidelberg, 147–152.

[16] Jonathan Dovey. 2016. Ambient literature: Writing probability. *Ubiquitous Computing, Complexity and Culture* (2016), 141–154.

[17] Mihai Duguleana, Raffaello Brodi, Florin Girbacia, Cristian Postelnicu, Octavian Machidon, and Marcello Carrozzino. 2016. Time-Travelling with Mobile Augmented Reality: A Case Study on the Piazza dei Miracoli. In *Digital Heritage. Progress in Cultural Heritage: Documentation, Preservation, and Protection*, Marinos Ioannides, Eleanor Fink, Antonia Moropoulou, Monika Hagedorn-Saupe, Antonella Fresa, Gunnar Liestøl, Vlatka Rajcic, and Pierre Grussenmeyer (Eds.). Springer International Publishing, Cham, 902–912.

[18] Andrew M Fountain, Wendy Hall, Ian Heath, and Hugh C Davis. 1990. MICROCOSM: An Open Model for Hypermedia with Dynamic Linking.. In *ECHT*. 298–311.

[19] Chiara Garau and Emiliano Ilardi. 2014. The âĂŢNon-PlacesâĂŤ Meet the âĂŢPlaces:âĂŤ Virtual Tours on Smartphones for the Enhancement of Cultural Heritage. *Journal of Urban Technology* 21, 1 (2014), 79–91. https://doi.org/10.1080/10630732.2014.884384 arXiv:https://doi.org/10.1080/10630732.2014.884384

[20] Charlie Hargood, Verity Hunt, Mark Weal, and David E. Millard. 2016. Patterns of Sculptural Hypertext in Location Based Narratives. In *Proceedings of the 27th ACM Conference on Hypertext and Social Media*. ACM, New York, NY, USA.

[21] Fotis Liarokapis, Panagiotis Petridis, Daniel Andrews, and Sara de Freitas. 2017. *Multimodal Serious Games Technologies for Cultural Heritage*. Springer International Publishing, Cham, 371–392. https://doi.org/10.1007/978-3-319-49607-8_15

[22] Anders Sundnes Løvlie. 2009. Poetic Augmented Reality: Place-bound Literature in Locative Media. In *Proceedings of the 13th International MindTrek Conference: Everyday Life in the Ubiquitous Era (MindTrek '09)*. ACM, New York, NY, USA, 19–28. https://doi.org/10.1145/1621841.1621847

[23] David E. Millard and Charlie Hargood. 2017. Tiree tales: a co-operative inquiry into the poetics of location-based narratives. In *Proceedings of the 28th ACM Conference on Hypertext and Social Media*.

[24] David E Millard, Charlie Hargood, Yvonne Howard, and Heather Packer. 2017. The StoryPlaces Authoring Tool: Pattern Centric Authoring. In *Authoring for Interactive Storytelling 2017 Workshop @ ICIDS 2017*.

[25] David E. Millard, Charlie Hargood, Michael O. Jewell, and Mark J. Weal. 2013. Canyons, Deltas and Plains: Towards a Unified Sculptural Model of Location-based Hypertext. In *Proceedings of the 24th ACM Conference on Hypertext and Social Media*. ACM, New York, NY, USA, 109–118.

[26] K. Naliuka, T. Carrigy, N. Paterson, and M. Haahr. 2010. A narrative architecture for story-driven location-based mobile games. In *New Horizons in Web-Based Learning*. Springer, 11–20.

[27] Theodor Holm Nelson. 1999. The unfinished revolution and Xanadu. *ACM Computing Surveys (CSUR)* 31, 4es (1999), 37.

[28] V. Nisi, I. Oakley, and M. Haahr. 2008. Location-aware multimedia stories: turning spaces into places. *Universidade Cátolica Portuguesa* (2008), 72–93.

[29] Heather S Packer, Charlie Hargood, Yvonne Howard, Petros Papadopoulos, and David E Millard. 2017. Developing a WriterâĂŹs Toolkit for Interactive Locative Storytelling. In *International Conference on Interactive Digital Storytelling*. Springer, 63–74.

[30] F. Pittarello. 2011. Designing a context-aware architecture for emotionally engaging mobile storytelling. *IFIP Conference on Human-Computer Interaction* (2011), 144–151.

[31] Peter Reason and Hilary Bradbury. 2005. *Handbook of action research: Concise paperback edition*. Sage.

[32] Ted Smith and Steve Bernhardt. 1988. Expectations and experiences with Hyper-Card: a pilot study. In *Proceedings of the 6th annual international conference on Systems documentation*. ACM, 47–56.

[33] Callum Spawforth and David Millard. 2017. A framework for multi-participant narratives based on multiplayer game interactions. In *International Conference on Interactive Digital Storytelling*. Springer. https://eprints.soton.ac.uk/414445/

[34] M.J. Weal, D. Cruickshank, D.T. Michaelides, D.E. Millard, D.C.D. Roure, K. Howland, and G. Fitzpatrick. 2007. A card based metaphor for organising pervasive educational experiences. In *Pervasive Computing and Communications Workshops, 2007*. IEEE, 165–170.

[35] Mark J. Weal, David E. Millard, Danius T. Michaelides, and David C. De Roure. 2001. Building Narrative Structures Using Context Based Linking. In *In Hypertext '01. Procddings of the Twelfth ACM conference on Hypertext, Aarhus, Denmark*. 37–38.

Narrative Plot Comparison Based on a Bag-of-actors Document Model

Sharath Srivatsa
International Institute of Information Technology
Bangalore, India
sharath.srivatsa@iiitb.org

Srinath Srinivasa
International Institute of Information Technology
Bangalore, India
sri@iiitb.ac.in

ABSTRACT

Comparing documents based on their semantic plot structure or narrative is an important problem in several application areas. Approaches based on information retrieval methods, latent semantic indexing, sentence embedding, and topic modeling are inadequate to capture the structural elements of the narrative. In this work, we present an abstract "bag-of-actors" document model, meant for comparing, indexing and retrieving documents based on their narrative structures. This model is based on resolving the main entities or actors in the plot, and the corresponding actions associated with them. We use this to compare movie plot summaries from IMDB (Internet Movie Database) to identify movie plots that are remakes or were inspired by one another. Evaluation over a wide range of movie plots from different genres, show encouraging results.

KEYWORDS

narratives, narrative document model, bag of actors model, plot comparison algorithm, narrative storage and ranked retrieval

ACM Reference Format:
Sharath Srivatsa and Srinath Srinivasa. 2018. Narrative Plot Comparison Based on a Bag-of-actors Document Model. In *HT '18: 29th ACM Conference on Hypertext and Social Media, July 9–12, 2018, Baltimore, MD, USA*. ACM, New York, NY, USA, 9 pages. https://doi.org/10.1145/3209542.3209556

1 INTRODUCTION

In several application areas, there is a need to compare documents based on similarity in the underlying storyline – or the document narrative. For example, an accident insurance claim that narrates the accident in question may need to be compared with similar accident situations from past claims. Similarly, a lawyer studying the story of a legal contention, may need to compare this story with similar stories from earlier cases, to see how the law was applied.

In such cases, conventional text mining methods may prove to be insufficient. Documents with similar narratives may have vastly different terms representing the story. Their topic distribution may also be different, depending on the exposition style of the narrative. A similar message can be conveyed using vastly different vocabulary

and illustrative cases, making the problem of comparing narratives non-trivial.

In the study of Narratives, the semantic structure of documents are modeled as comprising of "the underlying sequence of story-world events (called the *fabula*), as well as their selection and ordering in the surface rendering of the story (called the *syuzhet*)" [4]. The *syuzhet* is in turn, modeled as comprising of two components: the *plot* and the *exposition*. The plot refers to the main "story" of the narrative, while the exposition refers to the *style* in which the story is narrated.

While several research efforts have addressed computational modeling of narratives [15, 17], they have mostly focused on formal representation of the fabula. To the best of our knowledge, there is a dearth of research – especially from a *data management* perspective – addressing representation, comparison, indexing and retrieval of narratives from a corpus.

In this work, we propose an abstract model of documents that represents elements of their narrative as actors attributed with their expressions. We extract sets of events in which actors are referred, infer expressions that are part of the events, attribute expressions to corresponding actors and create a set of actors and associated expressions. This model, called "bag-of-actors" is amenable to storage, retrieval and comparison, akin to a conventional information retrieval platform. We hypothesize that, a given narrative is said to be similar to another if both of them have similar attributed expressions of actors (the plot), despite vastly different styles of narration.

Our problem is restricted to comparing, storing, indexing and retrieval of documents based on their narrative. We are not interested in interpreting the storyline, which requires a formal representation of the fabula.

Based on these motivations, a plot is represented as a "bag-of-actors" where, an "actor" in turn, is defined as a role-player entity (including non-person entities), whose characterization is based on the actions it performs.

Actors are identified and scored based on collections of actions that are associated with an entity. The actions of the actors are extracted based on computing co-reference resolutions. Similarity between actors are computed by comparing similarity in their action groups. For this, we use the WordNet LIN [20] similarity score. Semantic equivalence between actors is established by maximizing the likelihood of similarity in the action groups of all actors in the same candidate equivalence class.

Indexing of documents based on their narratives is performed by building a hypernym tree of the expressions in their bag of actors model. Retrieval is performed based on matching expressions in the query document with the hypernym tree, and ranking of results is based on where in the hypernym tree do the expressions match.

2 RELATED WORK

A popular computational model for representing narratives is the Story Intention Graph (SIG) [4, 13]. A SIG narrative model consists of three interconnected layers namely: Text, Timeline and Interpretative layers. Narratives are modeled through relationships between basic units. Based on the patterns of SIG encodings, narratives are categorized in to 80 pre-defined scenario classes like "Gain," "Promise Broken," "Unintended Harm," etc. The scenario classes express narrative tropes in terms of SIG relations. SIG captures both temporal and agentive or actor or entity relationships in the narrative document. Analogical similarity between narratives can be deduced by using all or part of SIG encodings. Three approaches to analogy detection are suggested: Propositional similarity, Static analogy detection and Dynamic analogy discovery. Propositional similarity uses only timeline layer for detection. Static analogy detection is a top-down approach where encoding is mapped to one of pre-defined scenario patterns and analogy is inferred. Dynamic analogy detection is a bottom-up approach where analogy is inferred through largest isomorphic subgraph. An application called Scheherazade[1] is also freely available where stories can be encoded in to SIG.

There is a strong overlap between the goals of a SIG and our purpose which makes it a good representation tool for comparison at a deeper level. However, while the SIG presents a formal model to represent a narrative, this formal data structure has to be manually created from the text. The SIG is primarily meant for computationally *comparing* narratives, rather than creating the model itself. Due to this reason, SIGs were not useful for our problem. The authors are also unaware of any approaches based on SIGs that can be used to index and retrieve documents based on narratives.

Another computational model for representing narratives is the Abstract Meaning Representation (AMR) graph [1, 6]. AMR represents each sentence as a rooted, directed, acyclic graph that describes the following meaning: "who is doing what to whom." AMR graphs can be represented as collections of triples of the form (I, ARG_0, ARG_1), where I is the instance of the property or action ("what"), while ARG_0 represents the doer ("who") and ARG_1 represents the doee ("whom"). The purpose of AMR was to create a English sembank, where sentences are paired with their simple readable logical meanings. With a large English sembank, semantic parsers can be built similar to syntactic parsers.

Many computational parsers also exist that automatically generate AMRs from English text [21]. In Flanigan et al. [6], a deterministic graph-based parser for AMRs, called JAMR is proposed[2].

However, when we used AMR outputs from JAMR for comparing narratives, we found that sentence-level mapping of meaning is too fine-grained to capture the essence of the plot. Different exposition styles of the same story resulted in vastly different AMRs. To the best of our knowledge, there is no easy way of pruning the AMRs to obtain the essence of the plot. Hence, even AMRs were not suitable for our problem.

Sentence-level semantic similarity computation has attracted significant research interest [5, 9, 14, 18]. These methods can be broadly divided into classical approaches based on constructing formal linguistic structures of sentences; and the more recent deep-learning approaches based on computing sentence embeddings and neural network based comparison.

However, as with the case with AMRs, sentence-level comparisons based on both classical approaches and deep-learning approaches are ineffective in capturing the essence of the plot. Sentence level comparisons are susceptible to variations in exposition styles, and the same story narrated in different styles, are considered different.

In Halpin et al. [8], an approach to analyze plots of rewritten stories is presented. This was devised to develop a system called *"Story Station"* which would provide guidance in writing, to children aged between 10-12 years. An exemplar story was narrated to children by a narrator and children were asked to articulate the story in their own words. A corpus of 103 stories rewritten by children were used to evaluate the approach. Plot comparison of rewritten and exemplar stories was done by finding equivalence of lemmatized tokens of events, using WordNet and events order. Rewritten stories with similar events and events order were rated high. The goal of this approach is close to our approach as we are measuring plot similarity using events or expressions or actions. We presume that in this study events order was considered since the purpose was to improve writing skills. For our purpose of narrative plot comparison we assume event order is not important and with only quantified similarity between events associated with entities or subjects or actors, plots similarity of narratives can be achieved.

In Miller et al. [16], similarity between entities across narratives is computed by matching events across the narratives. Synthesizing similarity between entities is termed as *alignment*. Events are extracted and event sets are created manually. Events are related through computing an abstract hypernym of tokens appearing in the event text. Entities in event sets are related through adjacency matrix if they appear in events related by a hypernym. The adjacency matrix results in a graph of entities as nodes and edges as hypernym relation. From these graphs, using network analysis approaches, similarity between all entities of narrative document is computed. In our approach we are extracting entities from co-reference resolution and aligning entities through similarity of bag-of-disambiguated tokens from expressions associated with entities.

Reiter et al. [22] presents an unsupervised and automated narrative structure discovery approach evaluated on ritual description and folktale narratives corpus. A narrative is represented as a graph with entities as nodes and edges as relationship between them. The story is first represented as a sequence of events, and entities referred in a single event are related. Model is constructed using FrameNet for event re-construction, co-reference resolution to relate entities across narrative document and WordNet sense to compare events at a higher abstract level. Three alignment algorithms are proposed, Sequence alignment to align chains of sequences from narrative documents, Graph based predicate alignment to align by similar predicate argument structures of events from narrative documents and Bayesian model merging to align using Hidden

---

[1]Scheherazade SIG tool: http://www.cs.columbia.edu/~delson/software.shtml
[2]JAMR: https://github.com/jflanigan/jamr

Markov Models (HMM) in event sequences from narrative documents. While there is a lot of similarity with this and our proposed approach, the motivation in our approach is not so much on alignment, but on comparison, indexing, and search over a corpus based on narratives.

3   COMPARING PLOTS OF NARRATIVES

A *narrative* is defined to be made of two elements – the story *plot* and its *exposition*. Similarity in narratives is defined as the problem of computing similarity between the plots, despite different styles of exposition.

A popular way of representing a plot is by using the sequence of its major events recorded in the fabula. However, this not only requires modeling the fabula, but also different exposition styles may narrate the same plot by representing its events in different sequences. Automatically identifying semantic ordering of events in the plot is a non-trivial problem. Added to this is the requirement that the model is amenable for storage and effective retrieval from a corpus when searching for similar narratives.

Due to these motivations, we narrow down the essence of a plot to the following elements: the primary *actors* of the plot, and the set of *expressions* or *actions* that characterize the actors. In other words, the essence of a plot is distilled to: *who* are involved in the plot and *what* do they do. An actor represents any entity (including non-person entities, like a country or an organization), that plays a central role in the plot. Each actor is characterized by a set of expressions that represent the role played by the actor in this plot.

Formally, we conceptualize a *hermeneutic universe* in which narratives are defined as comprising of two types of elements: *Actors* and *Expressions*. The set *Actors* represents the set of all key roleplayer entities, and the set *Expressions* make up the set of key actions and characterizations that apply to actors.

A narrative N, represented as a bag-of-actors is a set of tuples of the form:

$$N = \{(e_i, exSet_i) \mid e_i \in Actors, exSet_i \in \mathcal{P}(Expressions)\} \quad (1)$$

Here e_i is an entity or actor that plays a significant role in the story, and $exSet_i$ denotes a set of "expressions" that characterize the actor. For a given narrative N, its set of actors are denoted by $actors(N)$ and for a given actor a, its characterization is denoted by $expressions(a)$.

Each expression $x_j \in exSet_i$ is of the form:

$$x_j = \{t_1, t_2, \ldots, t_n\}$$

where each t_i is a sense-disambiguated term representing a noun or a reified verb phrase, that characterizes the expression. Each t_i is of the form: *Word#POS#SenseIndex*, where *Word* is a noun or the noun counterpart of the verb appearing in the expression, *POS* is the part-of-speech tag, and *SenseIndex* is the WordNet sense index of the nearest meaning with which the *Word* is used in the expression x_j. We use the Wordnet SenseRelate[3] library to disambiguate the sense.

Actors and expressions are compared using the WordNet LIN [11, 12, 19] similarity measure. LIN gives a similarity score of 1 when

[3]Wordnet SenseRelate:
http://search.cpan.org/~tpederse/WordNet-SenseRelate-AllWords-0.19/lib/WordNet/SenseRelate/AllWords.pm

the provided tokens match the term and the sense. When the terms and/or sense do not match, LIN returns a similarity measure based on the information content (IC) of the respective words and that of their least common subsumer (LCS) in the hypernym tree that subsumes them.

Given two expressions x_1 and x_2 as sets of corresponding tokens, and with $|x_1| = m$ and $|x_2| = n$, similarity between them is computed as follows:

$$sim_{Ex}(x_1, x_2) = \underset{\substack{a \neq b \neq \ldots \neq c \\ and \\ x \neq y \neq \ldots \neq z}}{\arg \max} \left(\frac{lin(t_{1_a}, t_{2_x}) + \ldots + lin(t_{1_c}, t_{2_z})}{min(n, m)} \right) \quad (2)$$

Here, all tokens of the form t_{1x} belong to x_1 and tokens of the form t_{2x} belong to x_2. The similarity computation is modeled as a maximal matching problem between tokens of the first expression and the second. It is implemented in the form of a greedy knapsack algorithm [23].

In other words, similarity between expressions is computed as a maximal matching between the tokens and their senses, representing the respective expressions.

Similarity between actors, called the sim_{act} measure, is computed in an analogous fashion, by computing a maximal matching between expressions associated with the respective actors. The same structure, as outlined in Eq. 2 is used, except that the LIN similarity measure is replaced by the sim_{Ex} measure between expressions. Given two actors a_1, a_2, their similarity is computed as:

$$sim_{act}(a_1, a_2) = \underset{\substack{a \neq b \neq \ldots \neq c \\ and \\ x \neq y \neq \ldots \neq z}}{\arg \max} \left(\frac{sim_{Ex}(t_{1_a}, t_{2_x}) + \ldots + sim_{Ex}(t_{1_c}, t_{2_z})}{min(n, m)} \right)$$

$$(3)$$

where $\forall x, t_{1x} \in expressions(a_1)$ and $t_{2x} \in expressions(a_2)$.

Finally, similarity between narratives, called the sim_N measure is also computed in an analogous fashion, by treating each narrative as a bag of actors. The equation structure as outlined in Eq. 2 is used, except that the LIN similarity function is replaced by the sim_{act} function. Given two narratives N_1 and N_2, their similarity is given by:

$$sim_N(N_1, N_2) = \underset{\substack{a \neq b \neq \ldots \neq c \\ and \\ x \neq y \neq \ldots \neq z}}{\arg \max} \left(\frac{sim_{act}(a_{1_a}, a_{2_x}) + \ldots + sim_{act}(a_{1_c}, a_{2_z})}{min(n, m)} \right)$$

$$(4)$$

where $\forall x, a_{1x} \in actors(N_1)$, and $a_{2x} \in actors(N_2)$.

The proposed bag-of-actors model computes an optimal matching between elements of two narratives, based on the overlap in information content of actions mentioned in the narratives and the elements with which the actions are associated with. This is explained as follows.

WordNet LIN score between two terms t_i and t_j is computed as follows:

$$LIN(t_i, t_j) = \frac{2IC(LCS(t_i, t_j))}{IC(t_i) + IC(t_j)} \quad (5)$$

where $IC(t) = -\log P(t)$ is a corpus based measure of the specificity of concept t. When the LIN score is maximized across two sets of tokens representing actions from two plots, it maximizes their similarity in terms of the specificity of the actions that characterize the plots.

A unique set of sense-disambiguated terms from expressions are used to compute sim_{Ex}. This results in an $m \times n$ matrix of LIN scores between terms. With unique pair of terms the matrix would have row-rank of m and column-rank of n. With all row vectors and column vectors being linearly independent, sets of row and column vectors constitute a matroid – a generalized notion of linear independence in vector spaces. It is shown that with a matroid, greedy knapsack computation results in an optimal set of independent elements (Whitney [24], Kun [10]). Since each expression is associated with a single actor, matchings of actors in sim_{act} also constitute an optimal, independent set. A similar argument can be used for sim_N as long as the actors identified from the narrative are independent of one another.

Extracting actors and expressions. The bag-of-actors based comparison model proposed above depends upon reliable identification of actors and association of relevant expressions with the actors.

Identification of actors and expressions are performed by parsing the document on a sentence level, to identify actors and expressions. Actors across sentences are linked using the Stanford NLP neural co-reference resolution system (Clark and Manning [2, 3]) with an average F1 score of 65.73 on CoNLL 2012 English Test Data. F1 score is harmonic mean of precision and recall, and an unbiased average. Our observation was that, for example, if an actor appears in seven sentences, we would get groups of five and two sentences resulting in an error of two actors while there is only one actor and there would be always one set with major number of sentences. Since we are achieving co-reference resolution of candidate narratives on same system, the error introduced is symmetric and will not affect the narrative comparative score (computed from Eq. 3 and 4) and with a better average F1 score co-reference resolution system the comparative score would be more and symmetrical across all comparisons with no effect on conclusion of similarity and dissimilarity derived from current system.

Expressions are extracted from *constituency parse trees* of sentences. Constituency parse trees break sentences into sub-phrases with words as leaf nodes and phrase types as inner nodes. These are contrasted with "dependency parse trees" that depict grammatical relation between words. With our requirement to extract phrases from sentences, constituency parsed trees of sentences was an obvious choice. Fig. 1 shows an example constituency parse tree of second sentence from Narrative-1 in Table 1. Leaf nodes are tokens in the sentence, and inner nodes are Part-Of-Speech tags from Penn Treebank tagset[4]. In Fig. 1, it can be observed that entity (the NP) is associated with two verbal phrases (VP) or expressions.

Co-reference resolution results in set of tuples of entity mention and its associated sentence numbers set. For each entity, with sentence numbers and parse tree of sentences, expressions are extracted. Verbal phrases (VP) are minimal semantic units of expressions, and best attempt is made to extract verbal phrases associated

[4]Penn Treebank Project POS Tags: https://www.ling.upenn.edu/courses/Fall_2003/ling001/penn_treebank_pos.html

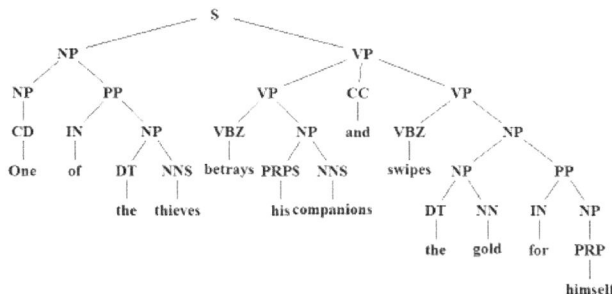

Figure 1: Example constituency parse tree of second sentence "One of the thieves betrays his companions and swipes the gold for himself" from Narrative-1 in *Table 1*

with entity mentions. If verbal phrase do not form an obvious part of sentence then complete sentence is considered as expression of the entity. Verbal phrases are extracted in sentence instances which have an entity (NP or NNP) and verbal phrase (VP) as siblings; or when entity is the object of verbal phrase. Specific steps to extract expressions is presented in Algorithm 1.

Algorithm 1: Entity expressions extraction **EnEx**

Input: A finite sentence Parse Tree set ordered by sentence sequence number in narrative document $P = \{p_1, p_2, \ldots, p_n\}$
Input: A finite tuple set of entity and associated sentence number set
$En = \{(e_1, \{i, \ldots\}), (e_2, \{j, \ldots\}), \ldots, (e_l, \{k, \ldots\})\}$ where
$1 <= i \ldots, j \ldots, k \ldots <= n$ and $|n|$ is Total Number of sentences
Output: A finite tuple set of entity and associated expression set
$Ex = \{(e_1, \{ex_i, \ldots\}), (e_2, \{ex_j, \ldots\}), \ldots, (e_l, \{ex_k, \ldots\})\}$ where
$|En| = |Ex|$ and $(e_l, |\{k, \ldots\}|) \in En = (e_l, |\{ex_k, \ldots\}|) \in Ex$

1   $Ex \leftarrow \emptyset$
2   **foreach** *tuple* $(e_l, \{k, \ldots\}) \in En$ **do**
3      $ex \leftarrow \emptyset$
4   **foreach** t *in* $\{k, \ldots\}$ **do**
5   **if** *Entity e_l sibling of Verbal Phrase(VP) in p_t* **then** $ex \leftarrow ex \cup VP$
6
7   **else if** *Entity e_l is part of complete Sentence(S) in p_t* **then**
            $ex \leftarrow ex \cup S$
8
9   **else if** *Entity e_l is object of Verbal Phrase(cVP) in p_t* **then**
            $ex \leftarrow ex \cup cVP$
10
11      $Ex \leftarrow Ex \cup (e_l, ex)$
12   **return** Ex

In Table 1 a set of three narratives is presented as an example. Narrative-1 and Narrative-2 have a similar plot, while the plot for Narrative-3 is different. Entities and their reference sentence numbers are extracted using Stanford co-reference resolution system and these are inputs to Algorithm 1, which extracts expression or action text associated with each entity from sentences and outputs tuples of entity and expression set. Table 2 shows entities and extracted expressions of all three narratives in Table 1. Tokens in expressions are disambiguated to find the nearest sense with which they are used in the expression. Table 3 shows disambiguated tokens of two example expressions. Similarity score between sense

---

Algorithm 2: Common computation method to find maximum likelihood similarity scores between:
1. Two expressions through similarity scores matrix of disambiguated tokens,
2. Two entities through similarity scores matrix of expressions.
3. Two narratives through similarity scores matrix of entities.
MaxLkl(M: Matrix of tokens or expressions or entities similarity scores)

Input: $n \times m$ Matrix M where $1 <= i <= n$ and $1 <= j <= m$ and $0 <= a_{ij} <= 100$
Output: Maximum likelihood match score Mlk where $0 <= Mlk <= 100$

1 $Mlk \leftarrow 0$
2 $k \leftarrow min(n, m)$
3 **while** $k > 0$ **do**
4 | $a_{ij} = maxOf(M)$
5 | $Mlk \leftarrow Mlk + a_{ij}$
6 | **for** $c \leftarrow 1$ *to* m **do**
7 | | $a_{ic} = -1$
8 | **for** $r \leftarrow 1$ *to* n **do**
9 | | $a_{rj} = -1$
10 | $k \leftarrow k - 1$
11 $Mlk \leftarrow Mlk/minOf(n, m)$
12 **return** Mlk

Algorithm 3: Compute maximum likelihood narrative similarity score

---

Input: A finite sentence Parse Tree set ordered by sentence sequence number in 1st narrative document $P_1 = \{p_{1_1}, p_{2_1}, \ldots, p_{n_1}\}$
Input: A finite sentence Parse Tree set ordered by sentence sequence number in 2nd narrative document $P_2 = \{p_{1_2}, p_{2_2}, \ldots, p_{n_2}\}$
Input: A finite tuple set of entity and associated expressions in 1st narrative document
$En_1 = \{(e_{1_1}, \{i_1, \ldots\}), (e_{2_1}, \{j_1, \ldots\}), \ldots, (e_{l_1}, \{k_1, \ldots\})\}$
where $1 <= i_1 \ldots, j_1 \ldots, k_1 \ldots <= n_1$
Input: A finite tuple set of entity and associated expressions in 2nd narrative document
$En_2 = \{(e_{1_2}, \{i_2, \ldots\}), (e_{2_2}, \{j_2, \ldots\}), \ldots, (e_{l_2}, \{k_2, \ldots\})\}$
where $1 <= i_2 \ldots, j_2 \ldots, k_2 \ldots <= n_2$
Output: Maximum likelihood narrative similarity score NSim where $0 <= NSim <= 100$

1 $Ex_1 \leftarrow \textbf{EnEx}(P_1, En_1)$
2 $Ex_2 \leftarrow \textbf{EnEx}(P_2, En_2)$
3 $EntitySim[][] \leftarrow null$
4 **foreach** *tuple* $(e_u, \{ex_{u_i}, \ldots, ex_{u_j}\}) \in Ex_1$ **do**
5 | **foreach** *tuple* $(e_v, \{ex_{v_i}, \ldots, ex_{v_j}\}) \in Ex_2$ **do**
6 | | $ExpSim[][] \leftarrow null$
7 | | **foreach** $ex_y in\{ex_{u_i} \ldots, ex_{u_j}\}$ **do**
8 | | | $arr_1[] \leftarrow \textbf{getDisAmbiguatedTokens}(ex_y)$
9 | | | **foreach** $ex_z in\{ex_{v_i} \ldots, ex_{v_j}\}$ **do**
10 | | | | $arr_2[] \leftarrow \textbf{getDisAmbiguatedTokens}(ex_z)$
11 | | | | $tokensSim[][] \leftarrow null$
12 | | | | **foreach** $t_1 in arr_1$ **do**
13 | | | | | **foreach** $t_2 in arr_2$ **do**
14 | | | | | | $tokensSim[][] \leftarrow \textbf{LIN}(t_1, t_2) \times 100$
15 | | | | $ExpSim[][] \leftarrow \textbf{MaxLkl}(tokensSim[][])$
16 | | $EntitySim[][] \leftarrow \textbf{MaxLkl}(ExpSim[][])$
17 $NSim \leftarrow \textbf{MaxLkl}(EntitySim[][])$
18 **return** $NSim$

---

attributed tokens is computed using Lin similarity measure. Similarity between expressions, entities and narrative plots are computed using maximum likelihood computation as shown in Algorithm 2.

Tables 4, 5 and 6 shows examples of expression, entity and narrative plot similarity scoring respectively. Algorithm 3 shows all steps involved in computing similarity between two narratives from parse trees of sentences in narrative and tuples of entities and associated sentence numbers. Narrative similarity score is the range of 0 to 100.

3.1 Storage, Retrieval and Ranking of Narratives

While the comparison model outlined in Algorithm 3 can compare narrative similarity given two documents, the larger problem is to retrieve candidate documents for comparison from a corpus of documents. Given an input document with a story, it is impractical to compare it pairwise against all documents in a large corpus.

In order to address this, we propose a variant of the conventional inverted index model for indexing documents, called the *hypernym index*.

An inverted index is in the form of a "postings list," where each element in the list represents a term and points to a set of documents that contain the term. Formally, a term listing in a posting post is given by:

$$postings(t) = \{(d_i, s_i) \mid d_i \in D, s_i \in \mathcal{R}\} \quad (6)$$

Here D is the document corpus, and s_i is a real-valued score that identifies the importance of term t in document d_i. In a conventional inverted index, the score is typically represented as the tf-idf value (term frequency, inverse document frequency), indicating relevance of the term in the document.

In order to index documents for narrative comparison, we index the tokens obtained from extracting expressions associated with actors. For each sense disambiguated token t, a hypernym tree is constructed by retrieving hypernym synsets token from immediate hypernym till a root node in the WordNet taxonomy. An hypernym of a sense-attributed token has a IS-A relationship with the token. A token can have more than one hypernyms or hypernym synset. All possible hypernym trees are considered, with the token forming the leaf node in several hypernym paths to the root node in WordNet taxonomy.

The token and each of its hypernym ancestor is then indexed in the postings list. The score for the token t would be the tf-idf value of t for any given document. The score for any hypernym ancestor h for a given document d is computed as:

$$s_i(h, d) = \gamma^k \cdot tfidf(t, d) \quad (7)$$

Here, $0 \leq \gamma \leq 1$ is a decay factor, and k is the height of the hypernym ancestor h with from the leaf node t. If there already exists a postings entry for document d for hypernym term h, then the computed score is added to the existing score. Hence, if a document d comprises of terms "school" and "company," both of which have a common hypernym "organization," then the score for "organization" would be contributed by a decay value of the tf-idf scores of both "school" and "company." Furthermore, if the term "organization" itself were to be present in document d, then its own tf-idf score would be added to the overall score.

Table 1: Set of narratives for analysis

Narrative-1

In Venice, Italy, a team of expert thieves pulls a daring heist of 35 million dollars in bars of gold. One of the thieves betrays his companions and swipes the gold for himself. One year later, in Los Angeles, the surviving team members create a smart and devious plan to steal back the gold and get their revenge on the traitor.

Narrative-2

A group of players consisting of a con-man, a con-woman, an illusionist, explosives expert, professional hacker and disguise master have a mission to steal gold for their dreams. Their plan succeeds but are double-crossed by their own member. Through losses and a new ally, they try to have their revenge and gold back. But will they succeed this time?

Narrative-3

John and Clark are back as the buddy cops on their toughest job so far. "Mr.A" is an international thief who has planned to steal a priceless artifact in New York and the police have got to nab him. But Mr.A manages to steal the artifact and elude the police. He finds his match in Katie and they form a partnership. They move on to Rio for their next job, with John and Clark hot on their trail. Mr.A whose actual name is Smith, and Katie are drawn towards each other but little does Smith know of Katie's little secret

Table 2: Extracted entities and expressions of narratives in _Table 1_

Narrative	Extracted entities from narrative	Expressions associated with entities
Narrative-1	Entity 1: "the gold for himself" in sentence 2	steal back the gold
		swipes the gold for himself
	Entity 2: "the surviving team members" in sentence 3	get their revenge on the traitor
		create a smart and devious plan to steal back the gold and get their revenge on the traitor
	Entity 3: "One of the thieves" in sentence 2	betrays his companions and swipes the gold for himself
		betrays his companions
		swipes the gold for himself
Narrative-2	Entity 1: "A group of players consisting of a con-man, a con-woman, an illusionist, explosives expert, professional hacker and disguise master" in sentence 1	steal gold for their dreams
		have a mission to steal gold for their dreams
		succeeds but are double-crossed by their own member
		succeed this time
		double-crossed by their own member
		try to have their revenge and gold back
		have their revenge and gold back
Narrative-3	Entity 1: "Mr.A" in sentence 3	is an international thief who has planned to steal a priceless artifact in New York
		manages to steal the artifact and elude the police
		finds his match in Katie
	Entity 2: "John and Clark" in sentence 1	are back as the buddy cops on their toughest job so far
	Entity 3: "Clark" in sentence 1	are back as the buddy cops on their toughest job so far
	Entity 4: "an international thief who has planned to steal a priceless artifact in New York" in sentence 2	is an international thief who has planned to steal a priceless artifact in New York
	Entity 5: "a priceless artifact" in sentence 2	steal a priceless artifact in New York
		steal the artifact
	Entity 6: "the police" in sentence 2	have got to nab him
		elude the police
	Entity 7: "Katie 's" in sentence 6	move on to Rio for their next job
		finds his match in Katie
		know of Katie 's little secret
		form a partnership

Given a query document, we use the hypernym index to retrieve candidate documents that are likely to be similar in terms of their narrative. In order to do this, we first parse the query document d_q and obtain all the sense-disambiguated tokens representing expressions. We then compute the hypernym trees for each of the tokens obtained.

For every term t_q in the set of query tokens and their hypernyms, we retrieve the set of all documents that have a non-zero score for the term. The weight of the retrieval is added to the pre-existing score if any, for the document.

$$score(d_i) = score(d_i) + \gamma^k \cdot s_i(t_q, d_i) \qquad (8)$$

Here, t_q is the query term which is either a token or its hypernym, γ is the same decay factor as earlier, and k is the distance of t_q from the leaf token k whose hypernym ancestors are being queried. $score(d_i)$ is the total score for document d_i obtained from all query terms, which is initialized to zero.

The retrieved documents are ordered in descending order of their total scores, and the top 90 percent of retrievals were chosen as candidates for narrative comparison. The final ranking of query results is based on the bag-of-actors similarity score from Algorithm 3 on the set of candidates.

4 EVALUATION

To validate the approach we compiled a test collection of 24 sets, each with three plot narratives of movies authored in IMDB by movie enthusiasts. Each movie plot in IMDB is associated to one or more genres. In each set of three narratives, two narratives were of movies that were remakes of one another. The third plot was a movie with a different story line, but in the same genre, with the same overall motif of the story, and with several overlapping keywords to one of the other two story lines. With these 24 sets we validated the scoring approach. In each set, similarity score between remade movie plots was expected to be higher than other two combinations.

We compiled one large set of 72 narratives from 24 sets used in scoring approach validation and used it as the corpus for testing the storage-retrieval-ranking methods. With input narrative being one of the two similar narratives from scoring approach sets, we expected the other similar narrative in the set to be listed among the top five ranked retrievals – ideally, as the top ranked narrative.

In 24 sets of three narratives each, where two were known to be having similar plots, the bag-of-actors model correctly identified 20 out of 24 test sets as remakes.

Since the third narrative in the test set also belonged to the same genre with the same story motif, we needed a control parameter against which to compare the performance of the algorithm. For this, we created a team of 10 human evaluators, coming from graduate school and professional environments, and were familiar with the concept of narrative similarity and movie remakes.

Evaluators were asked to score similarity between each pair of narratives in a test set of three narratives. Their scores, which were values between 0 to 10, were converted into categorical classes as shown in Table 7.

Table 7: Human evaluation score ranges

Categories	Score ranges
Similar	8 to 10
Near Similar	4 to 7
Dissimilar	0 to 3

Results from the algorithm were also converted to 72 categorical values where in each set, the higher scoring pair was labelled "similar", the second highest being labeled "near similar" and the lowest scoring pair as "dissimilar."

We used this transformed data to compute three performance measures. Our objective here was to measure whether the results from the algorithm can be deemed indistinguishable from human judgment. This is computed as the agreement score using the Fleiss' kappa (Fleiss [7]) metric. In a second form of agreement computation, scores from the 10 evaluators were consolidated to one score, by labelling a pair as "similar" if 6 or more evaluators have agreed to be similar, or "dissimilar" otherwise. This was then compared with the result of the algorithm using the F1 measure. In a third evaluation, agreement among a set of scores were computed as given in Eq. 9.

$$agreement_i = \frac{\max(|similar|, |dissimilar|)}{No. of results} \qquad (9)$$

Here, $|similar|$ and $|dissimilar|$ is the sizes of the set of all scores labeled "similar" and "dissimilar" respectively across the 10 evaluators. Two Confidence Intervals (CIs) of agreement scores was computed – first, by excluding the algorithm result from the human evaluation results; and the second, by including the algorithm results with ten human evaluation results. Table 8 lists scores of all three performance measures.

Table 8: Performance evaluation scores

Metric	Score
Fleiss' kappa	0.7042
F1 Score	0.7917
95% Confidence Interval of agreements (Eq. 9) (ten evaluations)	0.82 to 0.88
95% Confidence Interval of agreements (Eq. 9) (ten evaluations and algorithm)	0.82 to 0.88

A positive Fleiss' kappa score indicates agreement, and a score of 0.7042 indicates a significant adequate agreement between the algorithm and with ten human evaluations. F1 score represents the harmonic mean of precision and recall, and we obtained a score of 0.7917, which indicates a high agreement. The 95% Confidence Interval (CI) of agreement scores (Eq. 9) excluding and including algorithm results was identical, further indicating that the algorithm results are as good as results from a collection of human judgments.

Retrieval and Ranking evaluation. We evaluated the retrieval mechanism over a corpus made from the 72 documents collated for the earlier evaluation activity. Each of the documents were then provided as a query, that returned a ranked list of results with the query document itself (which was in the corpus) as the first result. We removed the first result and measured the rank order of the document which was known a priori, to have a similar narrative.

Table 3: Disambiguation Example

Expressions	Disambiguated Tokens
create a smart and devious plan to steal back the gold and get their revenge on the traitor	plan#n#1, back#n#5, gold#n#3, revenge#n#1, traitor#n#1
steal gold for their dreams	steal#n#2, gold#n#3, dream#n#1

Table 4: Similarity matrix between two expressions. Normalized score 46.27 .

	steal#n#2	gold#n#3	dream#n#1
plan#n#1	0.00	0.09	**0.39**
back#n#5	0.00	0.06	0.00
gold#n#3	0.00	**1.00**	0.08
revenge#n#1	0.00	0.08	0.21
traitor#n#1	0.00	0.06	0.00

$$sim_{Ex} = \frac{(1.0 + 0.39) * 100}{min(3, 5)}$$

Table 5: Similarity matrix between two entities Narrative-1: Entity 1 and Narrative-2: Entity 1. Normalized score 75.00

	double-crossed by their own member	have a mission to steal gold for their dreams	have their revenge and gold back	steal gold for their dreams	succeed this time	succeeds but are double-crossed by their own member	try to have their revenge and gold back
steal back the gold	6.94	50.00	**100.00**	50.00	9.14	6.94	100.00
swipes the gold for himself	6.68	**50.00**	50.00	50.00	9.14	6.68	50.00

$$sim_{act} = \frac{(100.0 + 50.0)}{min(2, 7)}$$

Table 6: Similarity matrix between two narratives Narrative-1 and Narrative-2 . Normalized score 75.00

	A group of players consisting of a con-man , a con-woman , an illusionist , explosives expert , professional hacker and disguise master in sentence 1
the gold for himself in sentence 2	**75.00**
One of the thieves in sentence 2	34.5
the surviving team members in sentence 3	60.74

$$sim_N = \frac{75.00}{min(1, 3)}$$

From 72 indexed narratives on an average 23 documents with a IS-A relationship were retrieved for 48 narrative documents known to be having similar narrative in the index. The search for similar narrative was narrowed to 32% of indexed narratives and with scoring approach ranking (Algorithm 3) similar narrative appeared among top five ranks in 30 out of 48 cases. With these metrics of narrowing and ranking the storage-retrieval-ranking method is promising to scale.

Given that the narrative with a similar plot was already known, we computed the rank precision score for retrieval-ranking method. Given that query i gave a set of k_i candidates, where correct answer was at rank r_i, the ranked precision score across all queries was computed as:

$$precision = average\left(\frac{k_i - r_i + 1}{k_i}\right) \quad where \quad i = 1 \dots 48 \quad (10)$$

Over the set of 48 query documents presented, an average ranked precision score of 0.6893 was noted.

5 CONCLUSIONS AND FUTURE WORK

The primary contribution in this work is to explore the modeling of the essential elements of a narrative in a way that is amenable to effective comparison, storage and retrieval. Towards this end, we find that representing a story by its set of key actors, and characterizing actors with their corresponding actions, offer an encouraging perspective into the concept of narrative modeling across different exposition styles.

The comparison, indexing and retrieval methods presented are fairly straightforward. It is definitely possible to enhance them with newer advances in models for semantic representation, indexing and retrieval. However, we believe that regardless of the sophistication of the semantic representation, an underlying abstraction of a narrative as a bag-of-actors as a suitable model for the narrative search problem, will continue to hold.

Our next goal is to improve the accuracy and sophistication of the storage-retrieval-ranking approach, and evolve a mechanism for absolute measures of similarity between narratives. The latter would obviate the need for a unrelated narrative to be used as a control baseline to reason about the similarity scores between two narratives.

Bag-of-actors model proved to be good measure to indicate plot similarity of narratives. Given broad variations in exposition styles of narratives, we believe our approach would result in good measure of plot similarity between narratives.

REFERENCES

[1] Laura Banarescu, Claire Bonial, Shu Cai, Madalina Georgescu, Kira Griffitt, Ulf Hermjakob, Kevin Knight, Philipp Koehn, Martha Palmer, and Nathan Schneider. 2012. Abstract meaning representation (AMR) 1.0 specification. In *Parsing on Freebase from Question-Answer Pairs. In Proceedings of the 2013 Conference on Empirical Methods in Natural Language Processing. Seattle: ACL.* 1533–1544.

[2] Kevin Clark and Christopher D Manning. 2016. Deep reinforcement learning for mention-ranking coreference models. *arXiv preprint arXiv:1609.08667* (2016).

[3] Kevin Clark and Christopher D Manning. 2016. Improving coreference resolution by learning entity-level distributed representations. *arXiv preprint arXiv:1606.01323* (2016).

[4] David K Elson. 2012. Detecting story analogies from annotations of time, action and agency. In *Proceedings of the LREC 2012 Workshop on Computational Models of Narrative, Istanbul, Turkey.*

[5] Rafael Ferreira, Rafael Dueire Lins, Fred Freitas, Bruno Avila, Steven J Simske, and Marcelo Riss. 2014. A new sentence similarity method based on a three-layer sentence representation. In *Web Intelligence (WI) and Intelligent Agent Technologies (IAT), 2014 IEEE/WIC/ACM International Joint Conferences on*, Vol. 1. IEEE, 110–117.

[6] Jeffrey Flanigan, Sam Thomson, Jaime G Carbonell, Chris Dyer, and Noah A Smith. 2014. A discriminative graph-based parser for the abstract meaning representation. (2014).

[7] Joseph L Fleiss. 1971. Measuring nominal scale agreement among many raters. *Psychological bulletin* 76, 5 (1971), 378.

[8] Harry Halpin, Johanna D Moore, and Judy Robertson. 2004. Automatic Analysis of Plot for Story Rewriting.. In *EMNLP.* 127–133.

[9] Aminul Islam and Diana Inkpen. 2008. Semantic Text Similarity Using Corpus-based Word Similarity and String Similarity. *ACM Trans. Knowl. Discov. Data* 2, 2, Article 10 (July 2008), 25 pages. https://doi.org/10.1145/1376815.1376819

[10] Jeremy Kun. 2014. When Greedy Algorithms are Perfect: the Matroid. https://jeremykun.com/2014/08/26/when-greedy-algorithms-are-perfect-the-matroid/

[11] Dekang Lin. 1998. Automatic retrieval and clustering of similar words. In *Proceedings of the 17th international conference on Computational linguistics-Volume 2*. Association for Computational Linguistics, 768–774.

[12] Dekang Lin. 1998. An Information-Theoretic Definition of Similarity. In *Proceedings of the Fifteenth International Conference on Machine Learning (ICML '98)*. Morgan Kaufmann Publishers Inc., San Francisco, CA, USA, 296–304. http://dl.acm.org/citation.cfm?id=645527.657297

[13] Stephanie M Lukin, Kevin Bowden, Casey Barackman, and Marilyn A Walker. 2016. PersonaBank: A Corpus of Personal Narratives and Their Story Intention Graphs.. In *LREC.*

[14] Tomas Mikolov, Ilya Sutskever, Kai Chen, Greg S Corrado, and Jeff Dean. 2013. Distributed representations of words and phrases and their compositionality. In *Advances in neural information processing systems.* 3111–3119.

[15] Ben Miller, Antonio Lieto, Rémi Ronfard, Stephen Ware, and Mark Finlayson. 2016. Proceedings of the 7th Workshop on Computational Models of Narrative. In *7th Workshop on Computational Models of Narrative (CMN 2016)*, Vol. 53.

[16] Ben Miller, Ayush Shrestha, Jennifer Olive, and Shakthidhar Gopavaram. 2015. Cross-Document Narrative Frame Alignment. In *OASIcs-OpenAccess Series in Informatics*, Vol. 45. Schloss Dagstuhl-Leibniz-Zentrum fuer Informatik.

[17] Erik T. Mueller. 2013. Computational models of narrative. *Sprache und Datenverarbeitung, Special Issue on Formal and Computational Models of Narrative* 37, 1-2 (2013), 11–39.

[18] Hamid Palangi, Li Deng, Yelong Shen, Jianfeng Gao, Xiaodong He, Jianshu Chen, Xinying Song, and Rabab Ward. 2016. Deep Sentence Embedding Using Long Short-term Memory Networks: Analysis and Application to Information Retrieval. *IEEE/ACM Trans. Audio, Speech and Lang. Proc.* 24, 4 (April 2016), 694–707. http://dl.acm.org/citation.cfm?id=2992449.2992457

[19] Patrick Pantel and Dekang Lin. 2002. Discovering word senses from text. In *Proceedings of the eighth ACM SIGKDD international conference on Knowledge discovery and data mining*. ACM, 613–619.

[20] Ted Pedersen, Siddharth Patwardhan, and Jason Michelizzi. 2004. WordNet:: Similarity: measuring the relatedness of concepts. In *Demonstration papers at HLT-NAACL 2004*. Association for Computational Linguistics, 38–41.

[21] Michael Pust, Ulf Hermjakob, Kevin Knight, Daniel Marcu, and Jonathan May. 2015. Parsing English into abstract meaning representation using syntax-based machine translation. *Training* 10 (2015), 218–021.

[22] Nils Reiter, Anette Frank, and Oliver Hellwig. 2014. An NLP-based cross-document approach to narrative structure discovery. *Literary and Linguistic Computing* 29, 4 (2014), 583–605.

[23] Eric W Weisstein. [n. d.]. Knapsack Problem. From MathWorld–A Wolfram Web Resource. http://mathworld.wolfram.com/KnapsackProblem.html.

[24] Hassler Whitney. 1935. On the abstract properties of linear dependence. *American Journal of Mathematics* 57, 3 (1935), 509–533.

Mother – An Integrated Approach to Hypertext Domains

Claus Atzenbeck*
Hof University
Institute of Information Systems
Hof, Germany
claus.atzenbeck@iisys.de

Daniel Roßner
Hof University
Institute of Information Systems
Hof, Germany
daniel.rossner@iisys.de

Manolis Tzagarakis
University of Patras
Department of Economics
Rion, Greece
tzagara@upatras.gr

ABSTRACT

The idea to associate information with so-called *links* was developed by hypertext pioneers in the 1960s. In the 1990s the *Dexter Hypertext Reference Model* was developed with the goal to provide a general model for node-link hypertext systems. In the 1990s and 2000s there were important steps made for hypertext infrastructures, which led to *component-based open hypermedia systems* (CB-OHS).

In this paper we provide a detailed description of node-link structures. We argue that Dexter does not match the need of CB-OHS, as it supports a mix of multiple structure domains. Based on the implementation of link support in our system *Mother* we demonstrate how Dexter needs to be tailored accordingly. We further describe Mother's ability of node-link structures to interoperate with other available structure services and vice versa.

CCS CONCEPTS

• **Human-centered computing** → **Hypertext / hypermedia**; • **Software and its engineering** → *Software infrastructure*;

KEYWORDS

hypertext infrastructure; open hypermedia systems; CB-OHS; navigational hypertext; Mother; Asgard; Midgard; Hel

ACM Reference Format:
Claus Atzenbeck, Daniel Roßner, and Manolis Tzagarakis. 2018. Mother – An Integrated Approach to Hypertext Domains. In *HT '18: 29th ACM Conference on Hypertext and Social Media, July 9–12, 2018, Baltimore, MD, USA*. ACM, New York, NY, USA, 5 pages. https://doi.org/10.1145/3209542.3209570

1 INTRODUCTION

People have been referencing texts since they invented writing. The idea to associate information with so-called *links* was developed much later: A little more than 70 years ago, Vannevar Bush, who is referenced in the scientific community as one of the "fathers of hypertext", proposed the idea of "associative trails" in his system Memex [6]. This idea was adopted and further developed by various computer scientists, e. g., Doug Engelbart [11] or Ted Nelson [28]. In the 1980s many academic and commercial systems became available. including KMS [1] or NoteCards [16]. Their main paradigm is based

on nodes interconnected via links. Because users can "navigate" from node to node, this type of hypertext is called *navigational hypertext*. In the late 1980s the *Dexter Hypertext Reference Model* [14] finally provided a general model of node-link hypertext systems.

Although other hypertext paradigms (such as spatial hypertext [20] or argumentation support [7]) have been introduced about the same time, the predominant association mechanism was and still is navigational hypertext. Its level of awareness further increased by the raising popularity of the World Wide Web in the 1990s.

At that time research on hypertext systems evolved even beyond today's WWW. Examples include *Hyper-G* [22] or *Microcosm* [18]. In an interview Andy van Dam describes the Web even as "the lowest common denominator of hypertext" [3]. By the end of the 1990s and early 2000s systems like *Construct* [43] or *Callimachus* [40] also supported non-navigational structures. Due to their open and component-based architecture they were called *Component-based Open Hypermedia Systems* (CB-OHS). These systems – as a consequence of supporting navigational and non-navigational structures within the same framework – raised the issue of interoperating structure services, i. e., combining different structure services.

Years later, our system (which we call *Mother*) with its structure-aware layer *Asgard* [4] became the first component-based open hypermedia system that was built primarily with the most challenging to handle hypertext structure type in mind: spatial structures. In this paper we describe Mother's support for navigational structures and its ability to interoperate with other structure services.

2 PROBLEM ANALYSIS

Navigational hypertext uses a set of basic abstractions, including nodes, links, and anchors. A node is a container of information; links connect nodes, while anchors designate areas inside a node's content from which a link originates or lands, creating a graph of nodes. For users, links function simply as jump-addresses. Such navigation from node to node via anchors and links is the primary behavior exhibited by navigational hypertext. Besides functioning as addresses, links attempt also to capture a semantic relationship between connected nodes. Over the years a considerable number of systems emerged offering the necessary tools and models to support the authoring of navigational hypertext. Although the node-link paradigm in navigational hypertext sounds simple as a model, the developed systems offered nuanced versions in order to address the needs of their respective application domains.

While the first generation of systems (such as NLS/Augment [12] or FRESS [44]) demonstrated the concept of hypertext, it was the second generation of systems (such as NoteCards [16] or KMS [1]) that offered navigational hypertext in a way that is similar to contemporary systems in terms of model and architecture [15]. In NoteCards nodes came in the form of cards, which could be typed to capture semantics while links were directional, typed, and anchored to the entire destination card. In addition, cards and links were programmable allowing the user to modify their behavior such as when and how to display the card's content. KMS offered similar abstractions as NoteCards, but did not embed links within the content of the nodes. Despite their emphasis on the node-link model these systems introduced additional abstractions that allowed the creation of hierarchical structures, for example, nodes of type *FileBox* in NoteCards or *Tree-items* in KMS.

Shortcomings and limitations of the second generation systems were identified rather early [15]. However, instead of concentrating at the identified limitations, the hypertext systems community moved into a different direction: to establish a common vocabulary with which the various existing systems could be conceived. The Dexter Hypertext Reference Model [17] originated from such concerns and aimed at providing a common formal conceptual model with which the diversity of existing navigational hypertext systems could be discussed, compared, and made to interoperate.

Dexter divides a hypertext system into three layers and specifies the roles of each layer. These layers are: (i) the *Storage layer*, responsible for the persistent storage of the objects that make up the (navigational) hypertexts; (ii) the *Within-Component layer*, responsible for the contents of the objects; and (iii) the *Runtime-layer*, responsible for handling the hypermedia objects (such as nodes, links, anchors, etc.) at runtime. Dexter defined also the interfaces between these layers: the anchors as the interface between the storage and the within-component layers and presentation specifications as the interface between the runtime and storage layers.

From a data model point of view, Dexter introduces a generic abstraction of component that can be specialized as nodes, link components (which contain presentation and anchor specifier representing links), or composite components which allows the creation of hierarchical structures. Links in the Dexter model can be single or bi-directional and *n*-ary, meaning that a single link component may connect a node to more than one destination nodes.

At around the same time, systems were developed to enable navigational hypermedia at a large and even global scale, overcoming the boundaries of the user's local computer. The WWW was one of the first attempts to offer navigational hypermedia at a global scale. WWW links are single-directional and embedded into the nodes' content. A global reference and naming scheme of nodes allows the WWW to create structures that span across systems. Despite the apparent simplicity of the model, the WWW model comes with a set of technologies that allow developers to extend and tailor the functionality of nodes and links as needed, e. g., HTML or JavaScript. From a navigational hypermedia model point of view, the model has little to offer with heavy criticisms aimed towards its trivial model and limited structure awareness [30].

3 INFRASTRUCTURE DISCUSSION

In our recent paper [4] we propose a component-based open hypermedia system, which we call *Mother*. It consists of three layers: (i) *Midgard*, hosting all *applications* that count as user interfaces or have similar functionalities; (ii) *Asgard*, a collection of Mother's (partly intelligent) components that deal with *structures*; and (iii) *Hel*, all *knowledge-based* components.

Most previous CB-OHS were designed primarily targeting the needs of node-link structures. Mother's architecture "has been developed primarily with one of the most complex [...] hypertext structures in mind. This approach appreciates the specific demands of implicit structures rather than explicit ones" [4]. Such implicit structures are supported by a spatial structure service in Asgard. It includes several multiple, highly specialized parsers (spatial, visual, temporal) that are capable of analyzing spatial structures similar to how humans would interpret them [35].

For this paper our focus is on sophisticated support for explicit structure types and structure interoperability. In particular, we aim for support of navigational structures. The Dexter model subsumes most hypertext systems at that time and even goes beyond the Web as we know it today. However, we need to bear in mind that Dexter was developed years before the first CB-OHS; thus, it is not a surprise that the model does not reflect a component-based view on systems. Because of that, we had to analyze Dexter and identify how to tear it apart and reassemble it in such a way to let it fulfill the requirements of a CB-OHS – in particular of Mother.

In the 1980s many systems combined various structure domains in a *single, monolithic model*. For example, KMS distinguishes between tree (i. e., hierarchical) and annotation (i. e., node-link) structures, whereas tree structure were dominant in usage at that time [1]. On the contrary, CB-OHS are built to support *arbitrary* structure domains within a *single architecture*, each provided by its own structure service. Such services may interoperate with each other.

In the following we take the Dexter node-link model and use only those parts that let us design a pure navigational service. Any other structure abstraction is put into its appropriate structure domain.

An important class in Dexter is named *Component* [15], referring to hypertext nodes. Links are components with endpoints. This makes links first-class objects in Dexter. At that point Dexter already provides full support of navigational hypertext. However, it also offers composites for hierarchical structures. Those differ in their behavior compared to node-link structures, e. g., removing a composite would recursively remove also the containing items.

As tree structures are supported by its own hierarchical structure service in Mother, we removed the notion of composites from our node-link support. Similar to Dexter, in Mother we also consider links as components that have a number of endpoints associated. However, components cannot contain other components, which would be a hierarchical relationship and thus not within the scope of the navigational domain. As components are not organized hierarchically by our node-link model, we also ignore Dexter's parentID attribute in Mother's component class.

Endpoints in Dexter have types that provide information about the link direction; those are SOURCE, DESTINATION, or BIDIRECT. The latter would be used for bidirectional links. Dexter also defines the direction NONE [17], however, we support dropping this type as argued in [15]. In Mother's link model an endpoint type is named *direction* (instead of *type* as in Dexter) in order not to be confused with *typed links* (see, e. g., [37]); those would have semantics/metadata attached to links. For such cases, Mother provides a specific metadata service, which is capable of adding arbitrary key-value pairs to any component, including links. In Mother metadata is considered a separate structure domain. Discussions about metadata services can also be found in previous publications (e. g., [27, 42]).

Dexter also includes presentation specifications (i. e., information about how components are to be displayed) and content in its model. In Dexter the data itself stays inside the within-component layer is not managed by the model itself. In Mother we removed both presentation specification and content from the node-link model. Those are handled by Midgard applications (see also discussion in [4]). Content (i. e., data from this point of view) lies outside Mother; the system keeps its focus on structure instead.

In summary, we use a subset of Dexter's model abstractions, removing any part that is not specific to navigational structures, including (i) composites; (ii) presentation specification; and (iii) content. Instead of overloading Mother's navigational hypertext model beyond the requirements specific to its structure domain, we offer support for hierarchical and metadata structures via specialized services. Content stays outside the system and is consequently handled by Mother's Midgard layer applications. This keeps the individual structure models simple (similar to the Web's simplistic node-link model), while granting sophisticated and flexible services.

Most of the CB-OHS mentioned in this article own a separate structure-aware node-link service. In Mother the appropriate layer for this would be Asgard. However, reducing Dexter also transformed our idea of a navigational structure services. The reason is as follows: As explained above, Mother is not content-aware. Instead, Midgard applications handle the content. The knowledge layer Hel holds all knowledge as well as linkbases, of which Mother supports an arbitrary number. This is beneficial, for example, if one wants to use multiple linkbases with different access rights as it eases implementation and lowers security risks. In Mother links are separate objects, however, the pointer to the respective resources are represented as strings, for which we suggest to use URIs [5]. Since Mother provides full node-link support at Midgard und Hel layers, there is nothing left for Asgard to take care of.

The main goal in our Dexter-based design was to cut out complexity while keeping the service as generic as possible. In order to achieve this, we distinguish between *linkbase* and *linkbase API*. The latter provides an interface to the linkbase to communicate with and – more important – propagates URIs to identify links and endpoints. Mother provides support for multiple linkbases.

The main task of a linkbase is to manage queries for existing links or add new ones. We chose a relative data structure over a graph based, because the corresponding nodes are identified by a unique string-based ID, optionally including anchor information. Nodes themselves are not part of the link data, therefore, the only item remaining to store is a list of links, kept inside a table with specific indexes to speeds up access routines. It is important to note, that the linkbase itself does not restrict the semantics of IDs and anchors. It only requires them to be UTF-8 encoded strings. Their meaning is maintained by an authority outside the scope of Mother. The linkbase is responsible for the creation of link IDs, guaranteed to be unique in the scope of a single linkbase instance only. Simply speaking, the *linkbase* defines how links are stored and makes very few assumptions about what links are to users or software. On the other hand, the *linkbase API* defines what a link is, how the parts of a link can be interpreted, and how the communication with the linkbase works (for altering, adding, or retrieving links).

We evaluated different communication protocols. A link server should be easy to integrate in any kind of existing system, and be ready for future improvements, e. g., authentication or encryption. In 1996, [8] came up with a draft proposal for the standard Open Hypermedia Protocol (OHP), which emerged from many discussions within the Open Hypermedia Systems Working Group (OHSWG) about interoperability of distinct but similar hypertext systems [10].

From that on, OHP improved significantly. As a result, OHP was split into many different interfaces. The OHP Navigational Interface (OHP-Nav) has been one of them [24]. It describes a common hypertext data model for navigational hypertext systems including a set of operations [9]. However, the development stopped in the early 2000s with an important unresolved issue: Should the components talk to each other through a programming API (e. g., CORBA) or rather via an on-the-wire communication model [25]? This and the fragmented documentation led us to the decision to keep the „good" parts (e. g., the data model) and use those along with HTTP. Because there are many other relevant protocols, we cannot provide an exhaustive comparison in the scope of this paper. With respect to the benefits of using HTTP for inter-application communication [13], the main advantage is its similarity in operations compared to OHP: The OHP operations *Create*, *Get*, *Update*, and *Delete* [9] perfectly map to the HTTP verbs *PUSH*, *GET*, *PUT*, and *DELETE* and hence make HTTP a suitable protocol for our purpose.

The chosen communication model combined with the OHP data model is not sufficient for a full featured API. Additionally, Mother's architecture has to be taken into consideration. In 2000, Fielding presented REST as an "architectural style for distributed hypermedia systems" [13]. We adopt the idea by using URIs for identifying endpoints and links in a global context. Because the linkbase only provides local IDs, the API offers them as global and unique URIs.

With such unique IDs it is easy to use HTTP verbs to manipulate or add links. Confirming to REST, we do not specify the media type of the answer. It is up to the linkbase API to answer in a way the client understands (e. g., XML, HAL+JSON) and vice versa. For users it is irrelevant to know how links are stored; they just need the URI and have support for the required media types. Furthermore, REST demands "Hypermedia As The Engine Of Application State" (HATEOAS), which decouples the server's functionality and the client's understanding of it. This means, that the client only needs to know the entry point. This design allows the API (provided that there is a smart client on the other side) to change over time. Adding or removing new functionalities become possible. The overall design described above leads to a flexible and simple to implement solution for both servers and clients.

For demonstration purposes we implemented a simple browser add-on for Chrome and Firefox, offering rich linking features to the user. The version of the software observes the URI of a visited site and queries for existing links, which use this URI as an endpoint. If this is the case, the user gets an unobtrusive notification within the add-on section of his browser. From there he can follow or change the links. Furthermore he can add new links, which are by design visible to everybody who has access to the same linkbase. The next iteration of this add-on should be able to inject links directly into the visited resource. Unfortunately, it is difficult to define endpoints appropriately for dynamic Web pages, as their content may change frequently. It may be necessary to provide unchangeable snapshots of such resources or offer the possibility to compute semantical anchors instead of syntactical ones [cf. 41].

4 SCENARIO

In this section we aim at providing a case scenario for various services. Some is still work in progress. Imagine two researchers, Sarah and Otto, working work jointly on a scientific publication. So far they mainly used (i) e-mail to discuss early ideas; (ii) Web browsers to search for related articles; (iii) pen and paper to scribble ideas and get a first glimpse of potential relationships; and (iv) word processors to write hierarchical outlines. There are gaps between different media used; e. g. Otto's used Web search engine or word processor is unaware of the paper on which Sarah scribbles first ideas or their e-mail discussions. There is only little support for structuring across different media or application domains.

Spatial hypertext. Now imagine Sarah and Otto using Mother to discuss and structure their ideas related to the publication. Furthermore, they use the system to also query information they want to further use. In order to accomplish that, Sarah and Otto use Mother's spatial hypertext application Mindspace. While structuring ideas on Mindspace's UI, the system uses intelligent methods to propose other relevant information and puts that on the space.

Spatial hypertext + hierarchies. Some spatial hypertext applications (like Viki [21] or VKB [36]) offer collections. Those can be thought as spaces in which subspaces are located. In Mother the spacial structure services does not have a notion of hierarchies. When Otto starts organizing spaces hierarchically, the hierarchy itself is handled by its own, highly specialized service.

Spatial hypertext + links. Otto finds an interesting object on the 2D space in Mindspace which was acquired from the knowledge base. The information represented by the object was automatically assembled by text mining methods harvesting the Web. Furthermore, it contains links to the original sources. Otto traverses those links in order to read and understand the original information. Furthermore, Otto adds links to objects in Mindspace manually. Those are stored in the linkbases.

Links + Web pages. Otto browses many relevant Web pages. Mother's link functionality lets him add unidirectional or bidirectional links to/from those even if he does not have write access on the Web pages. Since links are first-class objects in Mother, Otto can even see which resources link *to* the current Web page. With this information Otto navigates to relevant Web pages much quicker.

Metadata + spatial hypertext + links + Web pages. Otto grants Sarah access to his information in Mindspace. Sarah does not want to change the spatial structure, thus she annotates some objects instead. For that she uses Mother's metadata service. She also annotates some of Otto's links that she retrieved from the linkbase. For example, she adds types like "contradicting" or "supporting" to links in order to provide an understanding of the kind of relation to the linked Web page. Similar to that, Sarah also annotates Web pages she reads. Since both Sarah and Otto have access to the same resources within Mother, any of Sarah's annotations is also displayed to Otto, regardless of the Midgard tool used.

Hierarchy + Web pages + metadata. While browsing the Web for relevant information, Otto realizes that it would be beneficial to organize Websites hierarchically. For that his Web browser uses a plugin that connects to Mother's hierarchy structure service. Furthermore, Otto and Sarah use the metadata service to annotate the various hierarchy levels to indicate priorities or required resources.

5 CONCLUSION AND FUTURE WORK

In line with our previous work [4], we discussed in this paper steps toward Dexter-based navigational hypertext support in Mother. We argued why and how we reduce Dexter to match the needs of a CB-OHS. We also state that – in contradiction to other CB-OHSs – the node-link service became so much reduced that there was no reason to keep it as a separate Asgard component. Instead, node-link support can be fully handled by Hel.

We also mentioned support for spatial structures (discussed in detail in [4]), hierarchical structures, and metadata. Furthermore, this paper uses a case scenario to describe how different services can be reused in various combinations. This opens a higher level of inter-domain interoperability and lets users add or combine arbitrary structure services supported by the respective Midgard applications. We argue that this high level of freedom is not possible with super-structures, as proposed in the past (e. g., Dexter or FOHM [26]), but rather with highly specialized services of which each supports only a single structure domain, following the UNIX philosophy: "Make each program do one thing well" [23].

There are a number of open issues related to the development and also a number of open research questions. For example, we need to make objects handled by the spatial hypertext application Mindspace globally addressable in order to allow links pointing to them.

Regarding links it is still an open issue how to synchronize link anchors (which are stored within Mother's link base) and dynamic node content. The Midgard application (e. g., the browser plugin) needs to resolve the new anchor position. This is in particular difficult in cases when the Midgard application does not have unique control over node contents.

There is also the need to improve Mother's node-link support. For example, we do not consider security issues yet, e. g., access rights. Furthermore, we could extend our list of anchor direction markers with HIDDEN, as proposed by [15]. This would let users create a "blind" endpoint that exists but would not appear in any operation.

Regarding the node-link support in Mother it is still an open issue of whether we need to implement a navigational structure service within Asgard. It is likely that we want to offer computational services over networks or introduce node-link specific behavior at some point. Both would be good reasons for creating an Asgard service.

Mother is a CB-OHS, consequently prioritizing structure rather than data. This makes it different to the data-driven Web. Data – managed by Midgard applications – is outside the scope of Mother. Even though Mother shows some advantages over other CB-OHS, it is still of the same kind. In the late 1990s a different paradigm found its way to the scientific community: *structural computing,* which claims that structure is more important than data [32]. Structural computing always has supported structures independent of its kind. It is the search for first-class structural abstractions as generalization of structure. Related discussions during the early 2000s created various positions and levels of understanding, including the question of whether structural computing is an evolution or a revolution [19], implications of structural computing to hypertext infrastructures [34], and various discussions regarding the role of data, structure, and behavior within structural computing with the goal to create a coherent and global theory for it [2, 29, 33, 39].

A huge future step for Mother is extending its capabilities toward structural computing requirements. This could include, for example, introducing structural primitives (as proposed for Callimachus [38]) or supporting the EAD model (introduced by [31]).

Structural computing has the potential to lift hypertext systems to a higher and more sophisticated level of structure domain support and interoperability. Even though our CB-OHS Mother has already a very strong focus on structure, we believe that turning it into a structural computing environment would create huge benefits. This is where we want to go in a long run.

ACKNOWLEDGMENTS

This work is part of the ODIN project, sub-project HEIMDALL, funded by the German Federal Ministry of Education and Research (grant ID 03PSWKPD).

REFERENCES

[1] Robert M. Akscyn, Donald L. McCracken, and Elise A. Yoder. 1988. KMS: a distributed hypermedia system for managing knowledge in organizations. *Commun. ACM* 31, 7 (1988), 820–835.
[2] Kenneth M. Anderson, Susanne A. Sherba, and William V. Lepthien. 2003. Structure and behavior awareness in themis. In *Proceedings of the 14th ACM Conference on Hypertext and Hypermedia*. ACM Press, 138–147.
[3] Claus Atzenbeck and Mark Bernstein. 2018. Interview with Andy van Dam. *ACM SIGWEB Newsletter* Winter (January 2018).
[4] Claus Atzenbeck, Thomas Schedel, Manolis Tzagarakis, Daniel Roßner, and Lucas Mages. 2017. Revisiting Hypertext Infrastructure. In *Proceedings of the 28th ACM Conference on Hypertext and Social Media 28th ACM Conference on Hypertext and Social Media*. ACM Press, 35–44.
[5] T. Berners-Lee, R. Fielding, U. C. Irvine, and L. Masinter. 1998. *Uniform Resource Identifiers (URI): Generic Syntax*. RFC 2396. Network Working Group.
[6] Vannevar Bush. 1945. As we may think. *The Atlantic Monthly* 176, 1 (7 1945), 101–108.
[7] Jeff Conklin and Michael L. Begeman. 1987. gIBIS: a hypertext tool for team design deliberation. In *Proceedings of the ACM Conference on Hypertext*. ACM Press, 247–251.
[8] Hugh Davis, Andy Lewis, and Antoine Rizk. 1996. *OHP: A Draft Proposal for a Standard Open Hypermedia Protocol (Levels 0 and 1: Revision 1.2 – 13th March 1996)*. Technical Report. University of Southampton.
[9] Hugh Davis, Siegfried Reich, and David Millard. 1997. A Proposal for a Common Navigational Hypertext Protocol. In *Proceedings of the 3.5 Open Hypermedia System Working Group Meeting*.
[10] H. C. Davis, D. E. Millard, S. Reich, N. Bouvin, K. Grønbæk, P. J. Nürnberg, L. Sloth, U. K. Wiil, and K. Anderson. 1999. Interoperability between hypermedia systems: the standardisation work of the OHSWG. In *Proceedings of the 10th ACM Conference on Hypertext and Hypermedia*. ACM Press, 201–202.
[11] Douglas C. Engelbart. 1962. *Augmenting Human Intellect: A Conceptual Framework*. Summary Report AFOSR-3233. Standford Research Institute.
[12] Douglas C. Engelbart. 1984. Authorship Provisions in AUGMENT. In *Proceedings of the COMPCON Conference, San Francisco, CA, Feb 27–Mar 1, 1984*. 465–472.
[13] Roy Thomas Fielding. 2000. *Architectural Styles and the Design of Network-based Software Architectures*. Ph.D. Dissertation. University of California.
[14] Kaj Grønbæk and Randall H. Trigg. 1992. Design issues for a Dexter-based hypermedia system. In *Proceedings of the ACM Conference on Hypertext*. ACM Press, 191–200.
[15] Kaj Grønbæk and Randall H. Trigg. 1996. Toward a Dexter-based model for open hypermedia: unifying embedded references and link objects. In *Proceedings of the 7th ACM Conference on Hypertext*. ACM Press, 149–160.
[16] Frank G. Halasz, Thomas P. Moran, and Randall H. Trigg. 1987. NoteCards in a nutshell. In *Proceedings of the SIGCHI/GI Conference on Human Factors in Computing Systems and Graphics Interface (CHI '87)*. ACM Press, 45–52.
[17] Frank G. Halasz and Mayer Schwartz. 1994. The Dexter Hypertext Reference Model. *Commun. ACM* 37, 2 (2 1994), 30–39.
[18] Wendy Hall, Hugh Davis, and Gerard Hutchings. 1996. *Rethinking Hypermedia. The Microcosm Approach*. Kluwer.
[19] David L. Hicks and Uffe K. Wiil. 2003. Searching for revolution in structural computing. *Journal of Network and Computer Applications* 26, 1 (2003), 27–45.
[20] Catherine C. Marshall, Frank G. Halasz, Russell A. Rogers, and William C. Janssen. 1991. Aquanet: a hypertext tool to hold your knowledge in place. In *Proceedings of the 3rd ACM Conference on Hypertext*. ACM Press, 261–275.
[21] Catherine C. Marshall, Frank M. Shipman, and James H. Coombs. 1994. VIKI: Spatial hypertext supporting emergent structure. In *Proceedings of the 1994 ACM European Conference on Hypermedia Technology*. ACM Press, 13–23.
[22] Hermann Maurer. 1996. *Hyper-G Now HyperWave. The Next Generation Web Solution*. Addison-Wesley.
[23] M. D. McIlroy, E. N. Pinson, and B. A Tague. 1978. UNIX Time-Sharing System: Foreword. *The Bell System Technical Journal* 57, 6 (1978).
[24] David Millard, Siegfried Reich, and Hugh Davis. 1998. Reworking OHP: the Road to OHP-Nav. In *Proceedings of the 4th Workshop on Open Hypermedia Systems at the ACM Hypertext '98 Conference*. 48–53.
[25] David E. Millard, Hugh C. Davis, and Luc Moreau. 2000. Standardizing Hypertext: Where Next for OHP?. In *Proceedings of the 6th International Workshop and 2nd International Workshop on Open Hypertext Systems and Structural Computing*. Springer, 3–12.
[26] Dave E. Millard, Luc Moreau, Hugh C. Davis, and Siegfried Reich. 2000. FOHM: A Fundamental Open Hypertext Model for Investigating Interoperability between Hypertext Domains. In *Proceedings of the 11th ACM Conference on Hypertext and Hypermedia*. ACM Press, 93–102.
[27] Marc Nanard, Jocelyne Nanard, and Peter King. 2003. IUHM: a hypermedia-based model for integrating open services, data and metadata. In *Proceedings of the 14th ACM Conference on Hypertext and Hypermedia*. ACM Press, 128–137.
[28] Theodor Holm Nelson. 1999. The Unfinished Revolution and Xanadu. *Comput. Surveys* 31, 4es (Dec. 1999).
[29] Peter J. Nürnberg. 2000. Repositioning Structural Computing. In *Open Hypermedia Systems and Structural Computing. 6th International Workshop, OHS-6. 2nd International Workshop, SC-2. San Antonio, TX, June 3, 2000 (Lecture notes in computer science)*, Siegried Reich and Kenneth M. Anderson (Eds.), Vol. 1903. Springer, 179–183.
[30] Peter J. Nürnberg and Helen Ashman. 1999. What was the question? Reconciling open hypermedia and World Wide Web research. In *Proceedings of the 10th ACM Conference on Hypertext and Hypermedia*. ACM Press, 83–90.
[31] Peter J. Nürnberg, Kim C. Kristoffersen, David L. Hicks, and Uffe K. Wiil. 2005. EAD Revisited: First Experiences. In *Proceedings of the 2005 Symposia on Metainformatics (MIS '05)*. ACM.
[32] Peter J. Nürnberg, John J. Leggett, and Erich R. Schneider. 1997. As we should have thought. In *Proceedings of the 8th ACM Conference on Hypertext*. ACM Press, 96–101.
[33] Peter J. Nürnberg, Uffe K. Wiil, and David L. Hicks. 2004. A Grand Unified Theory for Structural Computing. In *Proceedings of the International Metainformatics Symposium 2003 (Lecture Notes in Computer Science)*, David L. Hicks (Ed.), Vol. 3002. Springer, 1–16.
[34] Peter J. Nürnberg, Uffe K. Wiil, and David L. Hicks. 2004. Rethinking structural computing infrastructures. In *Proceedings of the 15th ACM Conference on Hypertext and Hypermedia*. ACM Press, 239–246.
[35] Thomas Schedel and Claus Atzenbeck. 2016. Spatio-Temporal Parsing in Spatial Hypermedia. In *Proceedings of the 27th ACM Conference on Hypertext and Social Media*. ACM, 149–157.
[36] Frank M. Shipman, Robert Airhart, Haowei Hsieh, Preetam Maloor, J. Michael Moore, and Divya Shah. 2001. Visual and spatial communication and task organization using the Visual Knowledge Builder. In *Proceedings of the 2001 International ACM SIGGROUP Conference on Supporting Group Work*. ACM Press, 260–269.
[37] Randall H. Trigg. 1983. *A Network-Based Approach to Text Handling for the Online Scientific Community*. Ph.D. Dissertation. University of Maryland.
[38] Manolis Tzagarakis, Dimitris Avramidis, Maria Kyriakopoulou, Monica M. C. Schraefel, Michalis Vaitis, and Dimitris Christodoulakis. 2003. Structuring primitives in the Callimachus component-based open hypermedia system. *Journal of Network and Computer Applications* 26, 1 (2003), 139–162.
[39] Manolis Tzagarakis, Michail Vaitis, and Nikos Karousos. 2006. Designing domain-specific behaviours in structural computing. *New Review of Hypermedia and Multimedia* 2 (12 2006), 113–142.
[40] Manolis Tzagarakis, Michalis Vaitis, Athanasios Papadopoulos, and Dimitris Christodoulakis. 1999. The Callimachus approach to distributed hypermedia. In *Proceedings of the 10th ACM Conference on Hypertext and Hypermedia*. ACM Press, 47–48.
[41] W3C. 2017. *HTML 5.3*. Public Working Draft 1. W3C.
[42] Uffe K. Wiil, David L. Hicks, and Peter J. Nürnberg. 2001. Multiple open services: a New Approach to Service Provision in Open Hypermedia Systems. In *Proceedings of the 12th ACM Conference on Hypertext and Hypermedia*. ACM Press, 83–92.
[43] Uffe K. Wiil, Samir Tata, and David L. Hicks. 2003. Cooperation services in the Construct structural computing environment. *Journal of Network and Computer Applications* 26, 1 (2003), 115–137.
[44] Nicole Yankelovich, Norman Meyrowitz, and Andries van Dam. 1985. Reading and Writing the Electronic Book. *Computer* 18, 10 (1985), 15–30.

VAnnotatoR: A Framework for Generating Multimodal Hypertexts

Alexander Mehler
Goethe University Frankfurt
mehler@em.uni-frankfurt.de

Giuseppe Abrami
Goethe University Frankfurt
abrami@em.uni-frankfurt.de

Christian Spiekermann
Goethe University Frankfurt

Matthias Jostock
Goethe University Frankfurt

ABSTRACT

We present VAnnotatoR, a framework for generating so-called multimodal hypertexts. Based on *Virtual Reality* (VR) and *Augmented Reality* (AR), VAnnotatoR enables the annotation and linkage of semiotic aggregates (texts, images and their segments) with walk-on-able animations of places and buildings. In this way, spatial locations can be linked, for example, to discourse referents (ranging over temporal locations, agents, objects, or instruments etc. of actions) or to texts and images describing or depicting them, respectively. VAnnotatoR represents segments of texts or images, discourse referents and animations as interactive, manipulable 3D objects which can be networked to generate multimodal hypertexts. The paper introduces the underlying model of hyperlinks and exemplifies VAnnotatoR by means of a project in the area of public history, the so-called *Stolperwege* project.

KEYWORDS

multimodal hypertexts; virtual reality; augmented relatity; augmented virtuality; discourse semantics; discourse annotation

ACM Reference Format:
Alexander Mehler, Giuseppe Abrami, Christian Spiekermann, and Matthias Jostock. 2018. VAnnotatoR: A Framework for Generating Multimodal Hypertexts. In *HT'18: 29th ACM Conference on Hypertext & Social Media, July 9–12, 2018, Baltimore, MD, USA.* ACM, New York, NY, USA, 5 pages. https://doi.org/10.1145/3209542.3209572

1 INTRODUCTION

With the advent of *Augmented Reality* (AR) and *Virtual Reality* (VR) new possibilities arise regarding the further development of hypertext architectures: on the one hand, the bandwidth of human-computer interaction is enormously expanded so that one can use, control or manipulate information systems by means of gestures (using data gloves or sensor devices for detecting arm, hand or finger movements) or gaze (using eye-tracking technologies for detecting gaze motion). On the other hand, VR technologies realize

a sort of *semiotic expansion* according to which the denotata (referents) of complex signs (mainly texts or images and their segments) become manipulable objects within the same virtual representation space. The same holds for denotata in the form of topographic, topological or image schema-related relations [24, 29] of objects. Real-world objects are animated, for example, by walk-on-able "3D icons" that become indexable through pointing and symbolically enriched as well as contextualized objects through annotation and linkage, respectively. Analogously, AR technologies allow for comparable interactions embedded into real-world scenarios. As a consequence, we can now think of linking texts, images and videos not only with each other, but also with (animations of) their (real-world) denotations (in the form of (iconic representations of) persons, artifacts, buildings, places and their ties), so that these themselves become candidates for anchoring links. Moreover, since the resulting networks of animated, iconic and symbolic units are either represented in virtual space (VR) or entangled with reality (AR), users can activate several modes of information processing to read or write hypertexts (by seeing, hearing, moving or touching representational units). Thus, regarding the range of existing architectures and infrastructures (see [4] for a recent overview), it is possible to establish a new type of hypertext where users use multiple sensory modes simultaneously to browse through or to write the hypertext. In this sense, we speak of *multimodal hypertexts* made possible by AR and VR technologies.

The paper introduces VAnnotatoR as a framework for generating such 3D VR- and AR-based multimodal hypertexts. To this end, we integrate a wide range of AR and VR technologies to allow for annotations in mixed reality and even in augmented virtuality [30] (e.g. by embedding reality-related views into VR). According to urban visual analytics [11], we refer to animations of buildings, their rooms, streets and places as reference objects of annotation and as denotata of textual units of the underlying textbase. Our approach is also in line with Eco's [16] semiotic model of architecture. In this sense, VAnnotatoR extends the *denotations*, for example, of parts of buildings by *connotations* in the form of functional add-ons that support information processing when users interact with these parts. With the help of VAnnotatoR, users can upload texts and images to annotate their content, interrelate their segments and link this data to animations of spatial locations described by them. In this way, multimodal networks of physical and semiotic data are generated that inform about their syntactic or semantic relations. Further, VAnnotatoR allows for browsing the resulting networks using a new type of hyperlink that uses video streaming to look ahead at "topographically distant" targets. To this end, link activation is implemented as a kind of "teleportation" that makes remote destinations accessible. A basic principle of VANNOTATOR is to manifest, trigger and control any act of authoring or reading multimodal hypertexts by means of gestures and body movements: users can touch, for example, objects to select them; or they draw lines between objects to link them by means of pointing gestures. Finally, users can grab objects to rearrange or otherwise manipulate them. In this way VANNOTATOR combines the principles of semiotic networking of classical hypertexts with those of AR- and VR-enhanced HCI and gesture-based control.

The paper is organized as follows: Sec. 2 describes the *Stolperwege* project as the starting point of developing VANNOTATOR. Sec. 3 reviews related work. Sec. 4 describes VANNOTATOR's software architecture and Sec. 5 describes the underlying notion of hyperlinks. Finally, Sec. 6 concludes and describes future work.

2 THE STOLPERWEGE PROJECT

VANNOTATOR was initiated as part of the *Stolperwege* project [28] which develops an app for ubiquitous modeling of historical processes relating to the Holocaust. Starting from the art project *Stolpersteine*[1] (*stumbling blocks*) of Gunter Demnig, it aims at virtually connecting Stolpersteine with information about the biographies of victims of National Socialism [28]. A stumbling block informs about the last place where the corresponding person has lived by her or his own choice. They are set into the pavement in front of the corresponding location and can now be found in many European cities. A central idea of the *Stolperwege* project was to include documents that inform about the biographies of the victims in order to document (the networking of) their paths through life (aka *Stolperwege*). Biographies describe, so to speak, mappings of events to spatial and temporal locations, whereby these events are connected by involving a certain group of persons (as uniformities across different events in the sense of situation semantics [5]). Since many of these spatial locations are now destroyed or otherwise inaccessible, the *Stolperwege* project had to animate such places in order to make them accessible in virtual space. VANNOTATOR continues the *Stolperwege* project by not only virtualizing historical locations but also the annotation and documentation of historical processes, biographies and documents or images related to them. It generalizes virtualization, so to speak, by mapping all information units to virtual reality, making them networkable and traversable in the form of 3D hypertexts in VR. Information units (texts or images) can then be used to navigate, for example, to the buildings denoted by them, which themselves serve as anchors of links to other units (artifacts, texts, images etc.). Navigating through such a *multicodal* hypertext requires the wider sensory apparatus of users so that navigation becomes *multimodal*. VANNOTATOR can thus be understood as a framework for generating multimodal hypertexts as exemplified by the *Stolperwege* project, that is, by documenting the life paths of victims of the Holocaust. Henceforth, the paper refers to this instantiation when exemplifying VANNOTATOR.

3 RELATED WORK

Regarding early work on hypertexts, some notions underlying VANNOTATOR are related, for example, to [37]. This concerns the

concept of parallel paths. Regarding the *Stolperwege* project, such paths can be interpreted as documenting the lives of different people, some of which run parallel to each other (as in the case of family members). Another example is the *Information City Project* (ICP) [15], a spatial 3D hypertext in virtual reality. It represents networked information units as buildings, whose geographic organization maps their similarity relations. VANNOTATOR shares with the underlying notion of a *spatial hypertext* [32] the idea that spatial proximity and iconic attributes can be explored to author, organize and browse annotations. See [34] who combine the notion of a spatial hypertext with that of a collaboratively written wiki – though being limited to 2D representations. A related precursor is given by 3D spatial hypertexts [17] which combine geographic representations of locations (e.g. cities) with authoring components allowing users for discussing and debating events taking place at these locations and for linking ontological information. As in the case of VANNOTATOR, 3D spatial hypertexts use geographic information to locate and interrelate information units. Cinematic hypertexts [27] draw on a metaphor, which is also reflected by VANNOTATOR. The idea is to integrate the paradigms of page-based, semantic and spatial hypertexts to generate sequences of shots organizing textual nodes interrelated by coherence relations. Further, VANNOTATOR is related to 3D narratives [7] using story timelines for navigating in 3D visualizations of actions [10]. This analogy relates to the annotation of events and their time-related sequential organization. In this way, we are also related to systems that allow for generating 3D content based on natural language (NL) [9] or semantic web-related languages [18, 35] enabling inferences [26].

Another branch of work concerns tools focusing on annotations in VR. An early example is the project *VAnno* [22]. In this project, annotations are limited to audio recordings linked to virtual objects or views without allowing for annotating relations between objects. A second early project is *Virtual Vanue* [8], a simple virtual environment for visualizing annotations. Further, the *Empire 3D* project [1] can be mentioned as an example providing a virtual environment focusing on architectural data. Another example is *Croquet* [25], which allows for modeling and annotating scenes that are finally represented as 3D wikis. Related to NLP is the annotation system of [12], a virtual environment that allows for annotating documents and inserting multimedia content by means of a virtual notepad. See [13] for a vision of scenarios in which spans are accompanied with shareable experiences in VR – a scenario also addressed by VANNOTATOR. Finally, *VSim* [33] describe a 3D collaboration environment in which virtual spaces can be shared similar to VANNOTATOR, but without using VR or AR.

4 VANNOTATOR'S ARCHITECTURE

As an open hypermedia system [4, 14], VANNOTATOR is based on Unity3D. All information objects managed by VANNOTATOR are dynamically generated starting from a data model based on the class `DiscourseReferent` (DR), from which further classes are derived: `audio`, `image`, `text`, `video`, `person`, `location`, `building`, `time`, `event`, `process` (i.e. course of event) and `user`. The data model, which is mapped onto *UIMA Type System Descriptor* [21], is managed by a database specialized in handling UIMA documents, the so called *UIMA Database Interface* (UIMA DI) [3], and hosted

---

[1]http://www.stolpersteine.eu/

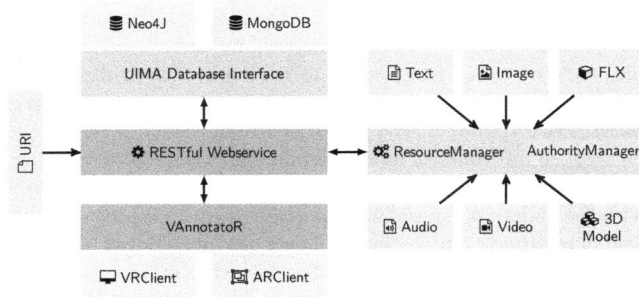

Figure 1: The software architecture of VANNOTATOR including two clients (AR, VR), two databases (Neo4J, MongoDB) and two resources (URI) or resource managers, respectively.

by a RESTful webservice (see Figure 1). UIMA DI encapsulates two database systems: Neo4J (specialized in managing graph data) and MongoDB (focusing on semi-structured documents). In this way, hyperlinkage-based network data and document content are both efficiently managed.

Instances derived from DiscourseReferent can be positioned, visualized, commented, modified, aggregated, linked or segmented if this is licensed by the underlying data format. To manage rights for processing instances, the *ResourceManager* of *eHumanities Desktop* [19] is used. This includes *ImageDB* [2] that allows for segmenting images and interrelating their parts. Web-based content is uploaded by means of *ResourceManager* or by entering its URI into VANNOTATOR's virtual browser (as exemplified in Figure 2).

After uploading content into VR, it is displayed in a Unity template. Further, a DiscourseReferent as an instance of the corresponding subclass is created together with a Unity collider specifying its shape and space of possible collisions. In this way, DRs get manageable as interactive objects that can be linked and further processed. Linkage of different DRs is done by drawing lines between them. Depending on the subtype of DR, different visualization methods are applied. Images are presented as portraits enabling image segmentation, while texts are visualized as web documents or as book pages from which spans can be selected, extracted and processed manually or by means of TextImager's NLP pipelines [23]. Displayed objects can be linked to DRs in AR by analogy to VR (see Figure 3). That is, multimodal hypertexts can be displayed in AR and in VR. AR can be used to annotate real objects (such as places, buildings, memorials or monuments). This is done to interweave multimodal hypertexts with reality by using methods for annotating and linking real and virtual objects.

5 MULTIMODAL HYPERLINKS

In addition to allowing for selecting, segmenting, extracting, typing and interrelating instances of VANNOTATOR's data model, hypertext-related features have been implemented that mainly concern the semantics of hyperlinks. More specifically, VANNOTATOR implements virtualized analogs of spatial and page-based hyperlinks. From the point of view of hypertext reading, this concerns four link types (the first three types are exemplified in Figure 4):

(1) *Highlighting:* given an annotation network of interlinked information units (text spans, discourse referents, animated

Figure 2: Depiction of *Gaußstraße 14*, Frankfurt am Main, in VANNOTATOR demonstrating several DiscourseReferents (green blocks) positioned in front of the house. The browser (left side) displays a webpage (https://tinyurl.com/y7tpzesu) providing biographical information about Erna and Erich Mannheimer. From this page, the annotator extracted an image of Erna and Erich Mannheimer together with a sentence: *"After her marriage to Leopold Mannheimer in 1912, Erna moved with her husband to the 6-room apartment on the first floor of the newly built house Gaußstraße 14."* (translation). The mention of Gaußstraße 14 in this sentence is related to a discourse referent (green block) that is linked (blue diagonal line) to the animation of the first floor of this house. Further, a subimage showing Erna Mannheimer was extracted from the above image and enlarged to enable more precise annotations. On the lower left side, a model of Gaußstraße 14 is displayed that is used in AR to further tag this scene (see Figure 3). To the right of this model, a virtual stumbling block is depicted on a blue pillar which refers to Erna and Erich Mannheimer. It represents the real-world stumbling block located in front of the real-world Gaußstraße 14.

denotata etc.), the user can point to a node N to highlight its neighborhood, that is, the set of nodes directly linked to N. Hyperedges connecting more than two nodes are represented by specialized vertices linking to the in- and out-nodes of the corresponding hyperedge. By selecting such a vertex, hyperedges are highlighted by analogy to the neighborhoods of nodes in simple graphs. This selection process can alternatively start from several nodes to highlight subgraphs and shared neighborhoods. In this way, users can interact with annotation networks to focus on contextually relevant nodes, links and subnetworks. This concept of linkage is in line with the conception of spatial hypertexts. It extends to the area of complex networks [31] in order to make them accessible as manipulable objects in VR.

Figure 3: Real view of Gaußstraße 14 seen via VAnnotatoR's AR interface. This scenario displays the same annotations as shown in VR in Figure 2. Annotations made in AR can be seen and further processed in VR and vice versa.

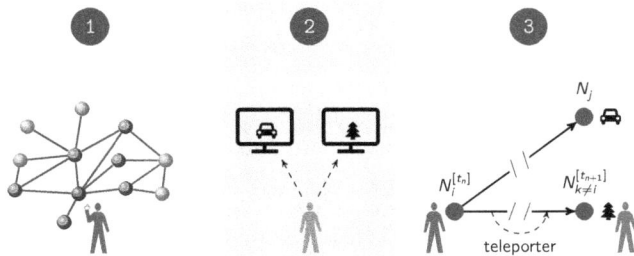

Figure 4: Three types of hyperlinks: (1) given an annotation network of interlinked information units, the user can point to a single node N (red) to highlight the set of nodes directly linked to N (green). (2) In a situation of remote link targets the user is looking ahead at the end points of two links by means of screens streaming the content of corresponding cameras. (3) The user teleports herself from a location N_i at time t_n to a remote link target N_k at time t_{n+1} thereby omitting the alternative target N_j.

(2) *Looking ahead:* in situations, in which the destination of a link is remote in VR and, thus, not directly accessible by the user, she can activate a look ahead camera streaming the scene at the link's end point (see Figure 5). In this way, users are informed about the content of a link's target without having to access it directly. This feature is indispensable in virtual worlds where related information is topographically distributed over long distances.

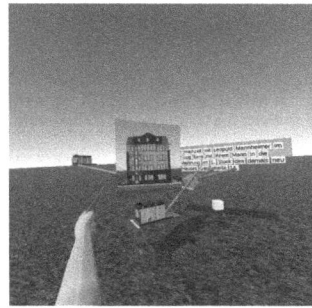

Figure 5: Preview window showing a remote link target (Gaußstraße 14, animated). By pointing to the link, teleportation starts.

Figure 6: A successful teleportation transfers the user to the location of the linked building as previewed in Figure 5.

(3) *Teleportation:* in situations, in which the user wants to access a remote link target that is "not within walking distance", she can teleport herself to that target (see Figure 5 and 6). This kind of teleportation is VAnnotatoR's 3D analog of activating links in page-based hypertexts.

(4) *Selecting links:* finally, the user can select a single edge between two nodes in a network to highlight their endpoints and make them accessible for subsequent operations (e.g. link attribution or making a link an anchor of another link).

Links in multimodal hypertexts link multicodal aggregates that are not only read, but can also be touched or experienced topographically (e.g. while being traversed). By embedding networks of this sort, for example, into AR scenarios, linkage becomes recursive entering the area of hierarchical hypergraphs [6, 20]. Such a graph model is a prerequisite for situation modeling together with the nesting of hyperlinks in virtually reconstructed, topographically anchored scenes. However, due to effects of split attention and multimodality [36], multimodal hypertexts are challenging for e-learning. An adequate instructional design will then be a major challenge for further developing this novel kind of hypertexts.

6 CONCLUSION AND FUTURE WORK

We introduced VAnnotatoR as a framework for generating multimodal hypertexts in AR and VR. The attribute *multimodal* means that writing and reading these hypertexts requires several modes of information processing, including the processing of body movements and gestures. VAnnotatoR allows for annotations in mixed reality and augmented virtuality. In this way, annotations of texts and images can be linked to real objects (e.g. buildings) as well as to animations of locations and other uniformities of situations, which themselves become candidate anchors of links. As a result, a multicodal network is generated whose nodes and links can be browsed using a new type of hyperlink that uses video streaming to look ahead at link targets, while using a "teleportation" to implement link activation. Future work aims at extending the hyperlink model of VAnnotatoR by integrating algorithms of graph drawing. The aim is to reconstruct the notion of spatial hypertexts in VR. Further, we plan user studies to evaluate VAnnotatoR.

REFERENCES

[1] Daisy Abbott, Kim Bale, Ramy Gowigati, Douglas Pritchard, and Paul Chapman. 2011. Empire 3D: a Collaborative Semantic Annotation Tool for Virtual Environments. In *Proc. of WORLDCOMP 2011*. 121–128.

[2] Giuseppe Abrami, Michael Freiberg, and Paul Warner. 2015. Managing and Annotating Historical Multimodal Corpora with the eHumanities Desktop. In *Historical Corpora: Challenges and Perspectives*, Jost Gippert and Ralf Gehrke (Eds.). Narr, 353–363.

[3] Giuseppe Abrami and Alexander Mehler. 2018. A UIMA Database Interface for Managing NLP-related Text Annotations. In *Proceedings of the 11th edition of the Language Resources and Evaluation Conference, May 7 - 12 (LREC 2018)*. Miyazaki, Japan.

[4] Claus Atzenbeck, Thomas Schedel, Manolis Tzagarakis, Daniel Roßner, and Lucas Mages. 2017. Revisiting Hypertext Infrastructure. In *Proceedings of the 28th ACM Conference on Hypertext and Social Media (HT '17)*. ACM, New York, NY, USA, 35–44.

[5] Jon Barwise and John Perry. 1983. *Situations and Attitudes*. MIT Press, Cambridge.

[6] C. Berge. 1989. *Hypergraphs: Combinatorics of Finite Sets*. North Holland, Amsterdam.

[7] Mark Bernstein. 2009. On Hypertext Narrative. In *Proceedings of the 20th ACM Conference on Hypertext and Hypermedia (HT '09)*. ACM, New York, NY, USA, 5–14. https://doi.org/10.1145/1557914.1557920

[8] Doug A. Bowman, Larry F. Hodges, and Jay Bolter. 1998. The Virtual Venue: User-Computer Interaction in Information-Rich Virtual Environments. *Presence* 7, 5 (1998), 478–493.

[9] Marc Cavazza and Ian Palmer. 2000. High-level interpretation in virtual environments. *Applied Artificial Intelligence* 14, 1 (2000), 125–144.

[10] Fred Charles, Julie Porteous, Marc Cavazza, and Jonathan Teutenberg. 2011. Timeline-based Navigation for Interactive Narratives. In *Proceedings of the 8th International Conference on Advances in Computer Entertainment Technology (ACE '11)*. ACM, New York, NY, USA, Article 37, 8 pages. https://doi.org/10.1145/2071423.2071469

[11] Zhutian Chen, Yifang Wang, Tianchen Sun, Xiang Gao, Wei Chen, Zhigeng Pan, Huamin Qu, and Yingcai Wu. 2017. Exploring the design space of immersive urban analytics. *Visual Informatics* 1, 2 (2017), 132–142.

[12] Damien Clergeaud and Pascal Guitton. 2017. Design of an annotation system for taking notes in virtual reality. In *Proc. of 3DTV-CON*.

[13] Grégoire Cliquet, Matthieu Perreira, Fabien Picarougne, Yannick Prié, and Toinon Vigier. 2017. Towards HMD-based Immersive Analytics. In *Immersive analytics Workshop, IEEE VIS*. https://hal.archives-ouvertes.fr/hal-01631306

[14] Hugh Davis, Wendy Hall, Ian Heath, Gary Hill, and Rob Wilkins. 1992. Towards an Integrated Information Environment with Open Hypermedia Systems. In *Proceedings of the ACM Conference on Hypertext (ECHT '92)*. ACM, New York, NY, USA, 181–190. https://doi.org/10.1145/168466.168522

[15] Andreas Dieberger and Jolanda G. Tromp. 1993. The Information City project – a virtual reality user interface for navigation in information spaces. In *Proceedings of the Symposium Virtual Reality Vienna, Vienna, Dec. 1-3.*

[16] Umberto Eco. 1991. *Einführung in die Semiotik*. Fink, München.

[17] Gilles Falquet and Claudine Métral. 2006. Integrating urban knowledge into 3D city models. In *Proc. of the 1st Intern. Workshop on Next Generation 3D City Models*.

[18] Jakub Flotyński and Krzysztof Walczak. 2014. Semantic representation of multi-platform 3D content. *Computer Science and Information Systems* 11, 4 (2014), 1555–1580.

[19] Rüdiger Gleim, Alexander Mehler, and Alexandra Ernst. 2012. SOA implementation of the eHumanities Desktop. In *Proceedings of the Workshop on Service-oriented Architectures (SOAs) for the Humanities: Solutions and Impacts, Digital Humanities 2012, Hamburg, Germany.*

[20] R. H. Goetschel. 1995. Introduction to fuzzy hypergraphs and Hebbian Structures. *Fuzzy Sets and Systems* 76 (1995), 113–130.

[21] T. Götz and O. Suhre. 2004. Design and implementation of the UIMA Common Analysis System. *IBM Systems Journal* 43, 3 (2004), 476–489. https://doi.org/10.1147/sj.433.0476

[22] Reid Harmon, Walter Patterson, William Ribarsky, and Jay Bolter. 1996. The Virtual Annotation System. In *Proceedings of the IEEE Virtual Reality Annual International Symposium*. IEEE, 239–245.

[23] Wahed Hemati, Tolga Uslu, and Alexander Mehler. 2016. TextImager: a Distributed UIMA-based System for NLP. In *Proceedings of COLING 2016, the 26th International Conference on Computational Linguistics: System Demonstrations*. 59–63.

[24] Jörn Hurtienne. 2017. How Cognitive Linguistics Inspires HCI: Image Schemas and Image-Schematic Metaphors. *International Journal of Human–Computer Interaction* 33, 1 (2017), 1–20.

[25] Rieko Kadobayashi, Julian Lombardi, Mark P. McCahill, Howard Stearns, Katsumi Tanaka, and Alan Kay. 2005. Annotation Authoring in Collaborative 3D Virtual Environments. In *Proc. of ICAT '05*. ACM, New York, 255–256. https://doi.org/10.1145/1152399.1152452

[26] Jean-Luc Lugrin and Marc Cavazza. 2007. Making sense of virtual environments: action representation, grounding and common sense. In *Proceedings of the 12th international conference on Intelligent user interfaces*. ACM, 225–234.

[27] Clara Mancini and Simon Buckingham Shum. 2004. Towards 'Cinematic' Hypertext. In *Proceedings of the Fifteenth ACM Conference on Hypertext and Hypermedia (HYPERTEXT '04)*. ACM, New York, NY, USA, 215–224. https://doi.org/10.1145/1012807.1012863

[28] Alexander Mehler, Giuseppe Abrami, Steffen Bruendel, Lisa Felder, Thomas Ostertag, and Christian Spiekermann. 2017. Stolperwege: An App for a Digital Public History of the Holocaust. In *Proceedings of the 28th ACM Conference on Hypertext and Social Media (HT '17)*. ACM, New York, NY, USA, 319–320. https://doi.org/10.1145/3078714.3078748

[29] Alexander Mehler, Andy Lücking, and Giuseppe Abrami. 2014. WikiNect: Image Schemata as a Basis of Gestural Writing for Kinetic Museum Wikis. *Universal Access in the Information Society* (2014), 1–17. https://doi.org/10.1007/s10209-014-0386-8

[30] Paul Milgram and Fumio Kishino. 1994. A taxonomy of mixed reality visual displays. *IEICE Transactions on Information Systems* 77, 12 (1994), 1321–1329.

[31] Mark E. J. Newman. 2010. *Networks: An Introduction*. Oxford University Press.

[32] Frank M. Shipman, III and Catherine C. Marshall. 1999. Spatial Hypertext: An Alternative to Navigational and Semantic Links. *ACM Comput. Surv.* 31, 4es, Article 14 (Dec. 1999). https://doi.org/10.1145/345966.346001

[33] Lisa M. Snyder. 2014. VSim: Scholarly Annotations in Real-Time 3D Environments. In *Proceedings of DH-CASE '14*. ACM, New York, Article 2, 2:1–2:8 pages. https://doi.org/10.1145/2657480.2657483

[34] Carlos Solis and Nour Ali. 2011. An Experience Using a Spatial Hypertext Wiki. In *Proceedings of the 22Nd ACM Conference on Hypertext and Hypermedia (HT '11)*. ACM, New York, NY, USA, 133–142. https://doi.org/10.1145/1995966.1995986

[35] Michela Spagnuolo and Bianca Falcidieno. 2009. 3D Media and the Semantic Web. *IEEE Intelligent Systems* 24, 2 (2009), 90–96.

[36] J. Sweller, P. Ayres, and S. Kalyuga. 2011. *Cognitive Load Theory*. Springer, New York.

[37] Polle T. Zellweger. 1989. Scripted Documents. A Hypermedia Path Mechanism. In *Proceedings of the Second Annual ACM Conference on Hypertext (HYPERTEXT '89)*. ACM, New York, 1–14.

The US National Library of Medicine:
A Platform for Biomedical Discovery & Data-Powered Health

Elizabeth Kittrie
National Library of Medicine
elizabeth.kittrie@nih.gov

ABSTRACT

This talk will address the role of the National Library of Medicine in fostering data-powered health and serving as a platform for biomedical discovery. It will examine emerging trends in the biomedical research landscape, such as the rapid growth of biomedical data sources, shifting paradigms for data sharing and open science, and the changing role of libraries in providing access to digital information. The talk will cover the newly developed long-range vision of the National Library of Medicine, with its triple aim of: 1) accelerating discovery and advancing health through data-driven research; 2) reaching more people in more ways through enhanced dissemination and engagement; and 3) its contributions to building a workforce and populace that is empowered to conduct data-driven research and enabled to optimize health and healthcare delivery through access to new types of health information. This talk will also examine the importance of co-creation, though partnerships and crowdsourcing, to achieve solutions that optimize the roles of government and stakeholders in improving health and healthcare through information resources.

CCS Concepts/ACM Classifiers

Information integration; information retrieval; collaborative and social computing; life and medical sciences; consumer health; health informatics; bioinformatics; digital libraries and archives

Author Keywords

National Library of Medicine; open science; data science; biomedical informatics; social media; information dissemination; prize competitions; hackathons

BIOGRAPHY

Elizabeth Kittrie is a Strategic Advisor for Data and Open Science in the Office of Health Information and Program Development at the National Library of Medicine (NLM) where she is involved in developing the NLM long-range strategic plan and leading data science and open science initiatives. Prior to joining to the NLM, she served as a Senior Advisor to the Associate Director for Data Science at the National

Institutes of Health, where she led open innovation efforts including the Open Science Prize, a collaborative partnership between the NIH, Wellcome Trust and Howard Hughes Medical Institute. Kittrie has also served as Senior Advisor to the Chief Technology Officer of the U.S. Department of Health and Human Services, where she led open government activities across HHS and coordinated the Department's efforts to develop a common Public Access Policy. Earlier in her career, Kittrie served as the first Associate Director for the Department of Biomedical Informatics at Arizona State University.

REFERENCES

1. National Library of Medicine Strategic Plan
https://www.nlm.nih.gov/pubs/plan/lrp17/NLM_StrategicReport2017_2027.html

Understanding Privacy Dichotomy in Twitter

Taraneh Khazaei
Western University
London, ON, Canada
tkhazae@uwo.ca

Lu Xiao
Syracuse University
Syracuse, NY, USA
lxiao04@syr.edu

Robert E. Mercer
Western University
London, ON, Canada
mercer@csd.uwo.ca

Atif Khan
InfoTrellis Inc.
Toronto, ON, Canada
atif@allsight.com

ABSTRACT

Balancing personalization and privacy is one of the challenges marketers commonly face. The privacy dilemmas associated with personalized services are particularly concerning in the context of social networking websites, wherein the privacy dichotomy problem is widely observed. To prevent potential privacy violations, businesses need to employ multiple safeguards beyond the current privacy settings of users. As a possible solution, companies can utilize user social footprints to detect user privacy preferences. To take a step towards this goal, we first ran a series of experiments to examine if the privacy preference attribute is homophilous in social media. As a result, we found a set of clues that users' privacy preferences are similar to the privacy behaviour of their social contacts, signaling that privacy homophily exists in social networks. We further studied users located in different neighbourhoods with varying degrees of privacy and found a set of characteristics that are specific to public users located in private neighbourhoods. These identified features can be used in a predictive model to identify public user accounts that are intended to be private, supporting companies to make an informed decision whether or not to exploit one's publicly available data for personalization purposes.

CCS CONCEPTS

• **Security and privacy** → *Human and societal aspects of security and privacy*; • **Social and professional topics** → *Computing / technology policy*; *User characteristics*;

KEYWORDS

Social privacy, Social network analysis, Preference detection

ACM Reference Format:
Taraneh Khazaei, Lu Xiao, Robert E. Mercer, and Atif Khan. 2018. Understanding Privacy Dichotomy in Twitter. In *HT'18: 29th ACM Conference on Hypertext & Social Media, July 9–12, 2018, Baltimore, MD, USA*. ACM, New York, NY, USA, 9 pages. https://doi.org/10.1145/3209542.3209564

1 INTRODUCTION

The notions of personalization and data privacy have always been intertwined since effective personalization relies on collecting and processing personal and potentially sensitive user data. This issue is especially problematic in the context of social media since studies on online behaviour indicate that there is a disparity between the privacy attitudes of social media users and their actual behaviour in specifying privacy policies [1, 16, 31]. While these platforms provide privacy setting options for the users, many users follow the default setting that is often open and permissive. Even among the ones that make the effort to manage their privacy, many are still unaware of the implications of their decisions [18].

Various solutions have been proposed to address the personalization-privacy paradox in social media. These solutions include the studies that present a set of privacy-enhancing principles for designing personalization systems [14, 32], studies that suggest usable interfaces for privacy specification [9, 20], and the ones that focus on inferring privacy preferences from user activities [7, 28]. In this work, we focus on the latter approach. This approach has had modest success in predicting privacy preferences in the past, yet its exploration has been very limited [8, 12].

To take a step towards automatic privacy preference inference, we conducted a comprehensive exploration and analysis of privacy features of Twitter users' social network in our sample. We first analyzed the adjacent neighborhoods and showed that privacy preferences are localized in the social network of Twitter users. In addition, we collected human annotated data from a crowdsourcing platform regarding the privacy preferences of the tweet authors. The human annotated data, as well, shows that privacy preferences are localized in Twitter. Next, we used this locality feature to discover a set of attributes that can characterize the online behaviour of public accounts that belong to privacy-concerned users. According to the results, these public accounts often share content that is more private and sensitive according to the societal consensus [4]. We then transformed each user in the Twitter network to a set of attributes representing the user (e.g., hashtags and topics) to discover a set of latent features that are associated with publicly available accounts that belong to privacy-concerned users. Similar to our earlier analysis of the tweets, the later attributes that are more sensitive and private are observed in such public accounts that are meant to be private. This identified feature set can be used in a predictive model to raise a red flag, alerting businesses that the user of focus is probably not willing to be profiled.

The remainder of this paper is as follows: Section 2 reviews the earlier studies on the detection of privacy preferences from social media data. Section 3 describes the data collection process. Section 4 explains our human annotation experiment and the results. Analysis of users placed in different neighbourhoods is provided in Section 5. Findings and limitations of the study are discussed in Section 6. Finally, Section 7 provides the concluding remarks.

2 RELATED WORK

Prior studies on the detection of privacy preferences in social networks have leveraged a variety of data types including user profile attributes, their social context, as well as their published content.

Profile Attributes. In the majority of social networking websites, each user account is associated with a set of profile attributes. A limited number of studies have focused on the potential relations of profile attributes and privacy attitudes. In [23], a supervised method is built on a large set of features to recommend privacy settings on Facebook. These features include metadata elements regarding a shared item as well as users' demographic and profile features. Dong et al. [6] proposed a privacy prediction model that takes into account Twitter behavioral analogs to psychological variables that are known to affect user disclosure behavior. Some of the identified analogs are based on the profile features of the users. For instance, user trustworthiness is calculated based on the ratio of their followers to the total number of their social contacts.

Social Context. A relatively large set of approaches have focused on the social context to predict privacy features. These studies can be categorized into two primary groups. The first set of works mainly focuses on privacy in terms of information visibility to different groups of social contacts, often referred to as social circles. These studies propose approaches to assist users in creating and maintaining such social circles and attempt to infer preferred privacy settings for the created circles of contacts. Various algorithms have been proposed to create circles of social contacts that have many links within themselves while having fewer links with those who are not in the circle [2, 5]. In [25] and [7], a supervised approach is utilized to predict privacy preferences of the focal user towards an unlabeled contact based on the profile and network features of a set of contacts labeled by the focal user according to his/her privacy preferences to share data with that contact.

The second group of works has adapted techniques from the area of collaborative filtering. These studies are motivated by the concept of homophily, which refers to the tendency of people to associate with similar individuals [21]. In addition, a user's information sharing behaviour has been shown to be extensively influenced by an inner circle of close friends [4]. Therefore, one set of approaches limitation on predicting privacy preferences based on the preferences of social contacts of the focal user. Similarly, people with similar backgrounds tend to have similar privacy concerns [29]. As an alternative to the use of social contacts, a group of researchers has developed techniques to detect privacy preferences based on the known preferences of users with similar backgrounds and characteristics with the focal user. For instance, Squicciarini et al. [27, 28] provide an algorithm to form social circles based on users' characteristics. When a new object is uploaded, the system first seeks the social circles that are most likely to deal with the object in a similar

way as the user. Then the privacy policies used by the selected circle is the basis for predicting the privacy policy for the newly added object. In [26], the focal user first specifies whether he/she is willing to share a specific data item with a selected contact. Then an iterative semi-supervised approach is followed to label the other contacts of the user, where labels are propagated from labeled to unlabeled instances in the social graph based on a user similarity metric.

Published Content. A frequent user activity on social networks is to publish content in the form of text, images, and videos. These shared data types can be used to draw inferences about users' personalities and preferences. In the context of textual content and privacy, Gill et al. [10] provide a set of privacy-related categories of words that are relevant in the semantic analysis of the privacy domain. LIWC[1] also contains a large number of semantic categories of words with possible relevance to privacy features. Caliskan-Islam et al. [4] used the privacy dictionary, along with a variety of methods and tools including topic modeling, named entity recognition, and sentiment analysis to decide if a tweet contains private information. Then users are given privacy scores based on the amount of private information they published in their Twitter timelines. The timelines of the labeled users are then used in a supervised technique to assign privacy scores to unlabeled users. The prediction model proposed in [23] also follows a supervised approach to recommend privacy settings for a given post on Facebook based on the bag-of-words representation, sentiment, and topical features of the post. Given an unstructured linguistic content published by a user, [30] first detects sensitive information such as phone number, address, and location. The model proposed in [17] is then adopted to quantify the potential privacy risk of the user in the network.

According to our earlier analysis of the literature [12], the majority of the studies are focused on predicting privacy settings that are specific to a particular social networking website, while less attention has been paid to general user modeling and characterization. Even though our platform of focus is Twitter, we aim to characterize general privacy preferences of publicly available user profiles. In addition, unlike many of the earlier attempts that are focused on a single or a few types of data, we incorporate a variety of data types. Finally, many of the reviewed studies have utilized supervised methods to classify and predict privacy attributes. However, such methods require labeled input and may not seem feasible in the context of social media, where the labeled information normally constitutes a very small portion of the available data. Instead, we propose an unsupervised collaborative filtering approach that is motivated by the locality of preferences in social media.

3 DATASET
3.1 Data Collection

Twitter privacy control follows a simple binary specification. In Twitter, users can follow the default *public* setting, which indicates that their tweets and contact lists are available to the public and accessible by the Twitter API. Alternatively, they can change their setting to *protected*, which makes their tweets and contacts only accessible by their approved followers. With the exception of profile

---

[1]Language Inquiry and Word Count:http://liwc.wpengine.com/

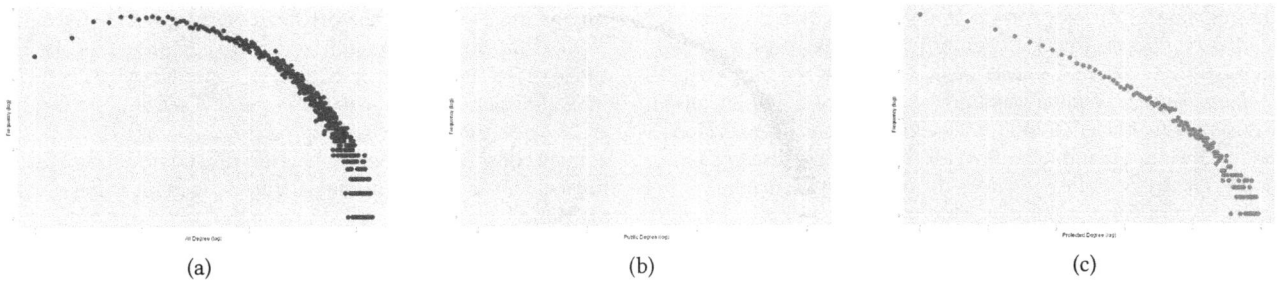

Figure 1: The degree distribution across all users in the network on a log-log scale. The distribution is shown for all of the social contacts (a), the *public* contacts (b), as well as the *protected* ones (c).

attributes, data associated with *protected* accounts are not available through the Twitter API either, making it impossible to directly compare *protected* and *public* profiles. Instead, we explored privacy features based on the social network and ties of a focal user.

To collect and build a social network from Twitter, we first selected a random user by generating a random Twitter ID. We ensured that this initial user is publicly available because the social contacts of *protected* accounts are inaccessible through the Twitter API, which makes it impossible to expand the network from a *protected* user node. After this user was selected, we iteratively built a network of users in a Breadth First Search (BFS) manner. Given that our approach exploits preference locality, we focused only on reciprocated relations instead of the asymmetric follow or friend relation. Reciprocated relations are expected to indicate a stronger relationship between the two users, and they distinguish the social network section of the Twitter-sphere from its information network [22, 33]. As we are only focused on these mutual contacts, from now on, whenever we use the word *contact*, we refer to the social one of the focal user with reciprocated relations.

Before adding each *public* user to the network, we retrieve and compute a set of metadata about the user. We first calculate, as a percent, the ratio of *protected* contacts to all of the contacts of the focal user. For instance, if a user has 100 social contacts among which 20 have protected their accounts, the user will be assigned the value of 20%. This percentage, called the *privacy ratio*, is a primary metric used in our analysis. In addition, we collect Twitter profile attributes (e.g., location and tweet count) and the latest 500 tweets published by the user as node metadata. Once the augmented user node is added to the network, we check if the new node has a reciprocated relationship with any of the existing nodes and add the corresponding edges. This process is repeated with a new *public* user drawn from the BFS queue. It should be noted that users with fewer than 10 tweets or fewer than 30 followers/friends are considered inactive and thus are not included in the data collection process. In addition, *verified* users and users with more that 1K followers/friends are excluded since they often represent brands and celebrities and are not from the general public. By following this approach, we collected a total of 23,320 *public* user nodes and 6,489,419 tweets published by these users.

3.2 Descriptive Analysis

In this dataset, each Twitter account is mutually connected to an average of 86 contacts. Among these neighbours, an average of 76 are *public* and 10 are *protected*. In addition, each user is associated with an average of 339 tweets (note that each public account has 500 tweets associated and no tweet can be retrieved from a protected account). We can obtain some insight into the network structure by examining the degree distributions. Figure 1 (a) shows the degree distribution for all of the mutual contacts across all users on a log-log scale. A heavy tail can be seen in the graph, resembling a power-law distribution. Similarly, the degree distribution for *public* contacts shown in Figure 1 (b) exhibits a heavy-tail. The same applies to the degree distribution for *protected* contacts, though to a larger extent compared to the other two (see Figure 1 (c)).

We also fit all three degree distributions to a power law distribution: $P(x) \sim x^{-\alpha}$. With this fitting, we obtained α values of 2.49, 2.98, and 1.79 for all, *public*, and *protected* accounts, respectively. For all three distributions, the Kolmogorov-Smirnov (KS) test indicates that the distribution is not refused ($P > 0.05$), and the power law can indeed be a good fit. The power law distribution is commonly observed in the context of social networks, though it is interesting to observe the same trend even after filtering the users with more than 1K friends/followers (as described in Section 3.1).

We also explored the relationship of *public* and *protected* contacts across all users. Not surprisingly, these two metrics are positively correlated, indicating that as the number of *public* contacts increases, so does the number of *protected* contacts. However, the analysis shows that the number of *public* contacts grows more quickly compared to the *protected* ones. Finally, as a first step to ensure that privacy preferences are localized in the context of privacy, we calculated the correlation between the privacy ratio of each node and the average privacy ratio of the contacts. An analysis of users who have at least 10 mutual contacts in the network (about 7000 users) showed a strong positive correlation between the two variables (Spearman $\rho = +0.89$). This result indicates that users' privacy behaviours are either influenced by their close social contacts or individuals with similar privacy behaviour tend to cluster together in social networks. In either case, this finding implies the great potential of collaborative filtering approaches for privacy preference prediction.

4 HUMAN ANNOTATIONS: AMAZON MECHANICAL TURK EXPERIMENT

Even though the correlation analysis signals the existence of preference locality for the privacy attribute, we conducted another experiment based on human annotations to further validate this finding. We chose Amazon Mechanical Turk[2] (AMT) as the platform of focus and published 12K tweets to AMT and asked AMT workers to judge the privacy preference of the tweet author based on the tweet. These 12K tweets were selected according to the following procedure.

Our collected user set was first filtered to only include those users who tweet in English. Then, 1200 users with the lowest privacy ratio and 1200 users with the highest privacy ratio are extracted from the set. Next, we selected their five latest published tweets that are not retweets or replies. We also ensured that these tweets included some text and are not generated automatically (e.g., is not labeled with [autotweet]). This process resulted in the selection of 12K tweets published by 2400 different users with extremely low or extremely high privacy ratios. Each tweet is then published to AMT to be labeled by a human annotator according to his/her judgment of the privacy preference of the tweet author. To do so, given a tweet, workers could choose one of the three given options:

- Privacy Unconcerned: He/she is not concerned if his/her data is used by companies
- Neutral/Objective: Neutral or objective tweets that reveal no information about the users' privacy preferences
- Privacy Concerned: He/she is not willing to share his/her data with companies

Each tweet is labeled independently by three different workers. Ideally, the majority label should be the subject of further analysis. However, the results are extremely unbalanced. Only about 1% of the tweets are labeled as a tweet posted by a privacy concerned user (i.e., the third option), while each of the other categories is selected more than 49% of the time. This problem might be due to the lack of expertise of the AMT workers on the subject, the features of the selected tweets, or the design of the annotation task. Further in-depth experiments can shed light on this matter. However, addressing this issue is out of the scope of this research and will be included in our future research activities.

To facilitate comparison and analysis, we employed an alternative approach. Specifically, if at least one worker annotated that the given tweet is published by a privacy concerned user, then the tweet is considered to be privacy concerned. We then counted the number of tweets that are categorized under this label (i.e., privacy concerned) for each user in the dataset. The comparison of the number of tweets of this kind among the two user groups shows a statistically significant difference (t-test P-value < 0.05). In particular, tweets published by the users with a high privacy ratio are associated with this category more often compared to the ones with a low privacy ratio. While we acknowledge the limitation of the analysis concerning the use of one AMT worker's annotation, this finding implies that users located within privacy neighborhoods are judged to be privacy-concerned, providing evidence for the locality of preferences in the context of privacy. Recognizing this limitation,

we plan to conduct similar studies with expert annotations of the same tweet set and AMT annotations of other tweet sets.

5 USER ANALYSIS

We analyzed various characteristics of *public* users and examined their potential relations to the privacy ratio metric. These characteristics have been elicited from users' profile attributes and their published tweets, both of which are directly available from *public* user profiles. The related experiments and findings are discussed in Section 5.1. In addition, we transformed the network of users into a bipartite network of features and users, wherein the features are given privacy ratios. Our transformation procedure and the results are discussed in Section 5.2.

5.1 Observable Attributes

5.1.1 Profile Attributes. A subset of the available profile attributes is deemed relevant for our purpose and is selected to be the subject of further analysis. This list is available in Table 1. A description of these profile attributes is available in the Twitter API specification[3]. To study how the profile attributes of users with different privacy ratios are configured, we calculated correlations between the profile attributes and the privacy ratio for all of the users. The correlations between profile attributes and the privacy ratio of users seem to be small for the majority of the features except a few (see Table 1). However, a few are relatively higher than the rest. For instance, this positive correlation for *tweet count*, *is geo-enabled*, and *favorite count* indicates that users with a high privacy ratio tend to tweet, geo tag, and favour tweets more often compared to the ones with a low privacy ratio. The negative correlation of *Has URL* and the privacy ratio indicates that users located within more private neighbourhoods tend not to provide URL information compared to their counterparts.

Twitter profile attributes are among a few data points that are visible to and accessible by the public and the Twitter API regardless of the user privacy settings. Therefore, in our earlier attempt to study privacy in Twitter [13], we retrieved 1M profile attributes of *protected* and *public* accounts (500K each) and directly compared the two sets in regards to their profile attributes. From this comparison, we obtained a list of profile attributes which present different values in the two groups. If these attributes behave similarly in the *protected* accounts, the *public* users with high privacy ratios, and the *public* accounts located in more private neighbourhoods (regarding their profile attribute configuration), then this provides supportive evidence that the privacy attributes are localized.

Interestingly, with two exceptions (*Has Description* and *Has Location*), the results show a very similar behaviour for users with a high privacy ratio and those who have chosen to have *protected* accounts. Specifically, *protected* accounts voluntarily reveal more information about themselves (e.g., geo-tags) and participate more actively in the network (e.g., tweet count). A possible speculation is that since users with *protected* accounts are aware that their data is private, they feel secure in this environment. On the other hand, users who are consciously following the *public* setting are utilizing a different strategy, such as self-censoring, to protect their privacy. Among the profile attributes, the existence of external URLs shows

---

[2]https://www.mturk.com/

[3]https://dev.twitter.com/overview/api/users

	Privacy Ratio
Binary Attributes	(Spearman ρ)
Has Description	-0.07
Has URL	-0.17
Has Location	-0.06
Is Geo-enabled	+0.11
Is Default Profile	-0.07
Is Default Image	-0.03
Favorite Count	+0.27
Tweet Count	+0.30
Follower Count	+0.15
Friend Count	+0.02

Table 1: Analysis of profile attributes and the privacy ratio.

a different pattern. *Public* accounts and users within public neighbourhoods seem to provide URLs more often. Despite our effort to exclude brands and celebrities, this difference can be attributed to professional Twitter accounts. For instance, artists who are on Twitter to promote their art often provide an external URL to their portfolio. Also, our correlation findings reveal that publicly available users with a large percentage of *protected* contacts behave similarly to the *protected* contacts. The implications of this finding are two-fold. First, it indicates the existence of locality for privacy preferences. Second, this result implies that such users feel secure in the environment in terms of sharing their information, yet they are more privacy concerned than the other public accounts. It is thus expected that they are more likely to feel invaded by targeted advertising and marketing messages.

5.1.2 Language Use of the Content. Natural language has been shown to be a reflection and a mediator of internal states [24]. Our words can reveal personality, emotional states and feelings, attention patterns, thought, and social situations [10, 24]. Therefore, a variety of automated content analysis techniques has been developed to measure such psychometric metrics from natural language. These methods range from the use of predefined dictionaries and taxonomies such as LIWC to complex computational algorithms that often utilize data mining and machine learning methods.

LIWC dictionaries are capable of providing a broad range of social and psychological insights from language. Hence, we used LIWC to analyze the language of tweets and to examine the links between a set of linguistic indicators and users' privacy behaviour. LIWC has a processing component that examines a text file word by word. Each word is then compared against the built-in dictionaries. Given that LIWC dictionaries are structured in a hierarchical format, the processing component then determines which LIWC categories or sub-categories the word belongs to. Once all the words are processed, LIWC outputs the ratio of words that belong to a particular category to the total number of words in the text as a percentage. In addition, a set of LIWC variables are measured independently of the dictionaries and are referred to as summary variables. These variables include four non-transparent language variables (analytical thinking, clout, authenticity, and emotional tone) and general descriptive features of the text (words per sentence and percent of

words that are longer than six letters). The definition and examples of each of these categories can be found at the LIWC website[4].

Tweet sets published by each user are first cleaned and preprocessed (e.g., emoticons are replaced with corresponding words). Then all of the collected tweets published by a user is treated as a single document and is given to LIWC for analysis. The percentages calculated by LIWC are then studied in terms of their correlations with the privacy ratio. Table 2 summarizes the correlation results for LIWC categories and summary variables, which are ranked based on their correlation strength. This table includes only those variables with their correlation coefficient beyond a certain threshold ($\rho > 0.15$ and $P < 0.005$). The majority of the LIWC features that are positively correlated with the privacy ratio can be associated with private content according to societal consensus. Examples of these features include the use of swear words, expression of anger and anxiety, and sexual topics. characterize, a positive correlation is observed for the use of "I" and the privacy ratio. Personal pronouns mainly appear in narratives and tweets that describe personal events, feelings, opinions, etc. Similarly, the use of the past tense is often observed in more private neighbourhoods.

In LIWC, the analytical thinking feature captures the degree to which a piece of text represents formal, logical, and hierarchical thinking. Analytical thinking is negatively correlated with the privacy ratio. This finding may be attributed to the professional accounts (e.g., belonging to politicians and athletes) that are often located in public neighbourhoods and may normally use a formal and a logical language. A relevant category among the LIWC outputs is called authenticity, which captures the degree to which the language is more honest, personal, and disclosing. Even though the correlation is below our threshold and thus is not included in the Table ($\rho = +0.22$), the authenticity of the language is shown to be positively correlated with the privacy ratio. Again, this finding shows that people located within private neighbourhoods are likely to be privacy-concerned, but they are probably privacy-unaware and thus publish sensitive information about themselves.

Tweets published by *protected* accounts are inaccessible, making it impossible to compare *protected* content with their *public* counterparts. However, there exists an accessible component that can represent linguistic characteristics of *protected* accounts: profile descriptions. When configuring their profile attributes, Twitter users can provide up to 160 characters in the description field. In our earlier study [12], we analyzed the language of descriptions using LIWC. Similar to the rest of the profile attributes (discussed in Section 5.1.1, we observed patterns that are extremely similar across the two studies. Even though the underlying datasets represent two sets of Twitter users and the language content of tweets and descriptions are provided for different purposes, we still see the same behaviour from *protected* accounts and the *public* accounts that are connected to a large percentage of *protected* neighbours in terms of their language use (see Table 2). For instance, authenticity and the use of function words are positively correlated with the privacy ratio. Likewise, they are more observed in profile descriptions of the *protected* accounts [12]. On the other hand, analytical thinking and clout are negatively correlated with the privacy ratio and are observed less often in *protected* accounts [12]. Again,

---

[4]http://www.liwc.net/descriptiontable1.php

LIWC Feature	Privacy Ratio (Spearman ρ)
Swear Words	+0.40
Anger	+0.35
Negative Emotions	+0.34
Body	+0.32
Negations	+0.31
Adverbs	+0.30
Sexual	+0.29
Sad	+0.27
Analytical Thinking	-0.26
FocusPast	+0.26
Interrogative	+0.26
Feel	+0.26
I	+0.26
Pronoun	+0.25
Anxiety	+0.25
Cognitive Processes	+0.23
Authentic	+0.22
Function Words	+0.23
Clout	-0.15

Table 2: Correlation analysis of the LIWC categories and the privacy ratios.

such similarities signal the presence of locality for users' privacy behaviours. Therefore, features that are specific to *public* accounts that are connected to a large number of private contacts can be considered the features that characterize privacy-concerned users.

5.1.3 Tweet Sentiment. LIWC captures the percentage of tweet words that belong to different sentiment categories. In addition to these LIWC categories, we took advantage of a lexical resource, called SentiWordNet [3]. In SentiWordNet, each word is given three sentiment scores: positivity, negativity, and objectivity. We first cleaned and tokenized each tweet. The tokens are then POS tagged and stemmed. The resulting token-POS tag pairs are then matched against SentiWordNet. Finally, the scores retrieved from SentiWordNet are aggregated for all the tokens in the tweet to generate an overall tweet sentiment score. It should be noted that whenever a negation is observed, the inverted score of the following token is taken into account. We then calculated the ratio of positive and negative tweets to the total number of tweets. Based on the analysis, the ratio of positive tweets has a small negative correlation with the privacy ratio ($\rho = -0.12$), while the ratio of negative tweets is positively correlated with the privacy ratio ($\rho = +0.26$). The number of negations observed in the tweets is also positively correlated with the privacy ratio ($\rho = 0.28$). Due to the inaccessibility of tweets published by *protected* accounts, the direct analysis of *protected* and *public* accounts in terms of the ratio of tweets with different sentiment labels is not possible.

5.1.4 Communication Behaviour. We employed a set of simple variables to characterize users' communication behaviours from their timelines. In Section 5.1.1, we observed a positive correlation between users' tweet counts and the privacy ratios. In addition

to the frequency of tweeting, we examined the average of tweet length and found a negative correlation with the privacy ratio ($\rho = -0.27$). Published tweets can either be retweets from other accounts or new tweets coming from the account of focus. Note that the retweets are excluded from the tweet length analysis. The correlation between the ratio of the retweets to the total number of tweets and the privacy ratio is very small ($\rho = +0.04$), and the ratio of the new tweets is also positively correlated with the privacy ratio ($\rho = +0.15$). In addition, users tweet to interact with each other and engage in conversations. The ratio of these conversational tweets also shows a positive correlation with the privacy ratio ($\rho = +0.22$). Another interesting variable to investigate is the use of URLs when tweeting. We expect the professional and non-personal accounts to publish news and events more frequently, which are often linked with URLs. As expected, the ratio of the tweets with URLs is found to be negatively correlated with the privacy ratio ($\rho = -0.22$). We found negligible correlations between the hashtag usage patterns and the privacy ratio. Similar to tweet sentiment, direct analysis of *protected* and *public* accounts is impossible due to the privacy restrictions associated with *protected* accounts.

5.2 Latent Attributes

5.2.1 Method. To discover a set of latent attributes that are of interest to privacy-concerned users, we transformed each user node in the network into a set of attributes. For each attribute node, we then calculated the ratio of *protected* contacts to the total number of contacts. The resulting network allows us to understand which features attract privacy-concerned users and which ones are more observed in public neighbourhoods. Figure 2 shows this transformation procedure for a sample network in which *public* nodes are encoded by blue and the *protected* ones are shown in red. Suppose that we have three users in the network: U_1, U_2, and U_3. The nodes with dotted borders are the social contacts of the users that are not yet added to the network but are counted in the metadata calculation process and added to the BFS queue (see Section 3.1). As Figure 2 (a) shows, U_1 is linked with three social contacts among which two are *public* and one is *protected*; therefore, it will be given the privacy ratio of $\theta_{u1} = 33\%$. Similarly, U_2 and U_3 are given the values of $\theta_{u2} = 50\%$ and $\theta_{u3} = 25\%$, respectively.

Now suppose that U_1 can be characterized with three features such that $U_1 = \{f_1, f_2, f_4\}$. These three features are then associated with all of the three social contacts of U_1. Then if $U_2 = \{f_2\}$, f_2 will also be associated with the neighbours of U_2. Finally, suppose that we have $U_3 = \{f_1, f_3, f_4\}$ in our example network. Figure 2 (b) shows the process of associating features with the contacts. The resulting network will then be a bipartite network of contacts and features, wherein privacy ratios can be calculated for features (see Figure 2 (c)). For instance, f_1 is a feature that characterizes users U_1 and U_3 and is not associated with U_2. Therefore, in Figures 2 (b) and 2 (c), it is linked with the neighbours of U_1 and U_3. Hence, f_1 is linked to the total of five *public* users and two *protected* ones, resulting in the privacy ratio of $\theta_{f1} = 40\%$.

A variety of features can be extracted from Twitter timelines to describe the accounts. We conducted experiments with four primary features: 1) tweet unigrams, 2) hashtags, 3) Twitter accounts that users retweet from, and 4) topics. Each of these feature sets can

(a)

(b)

(c)

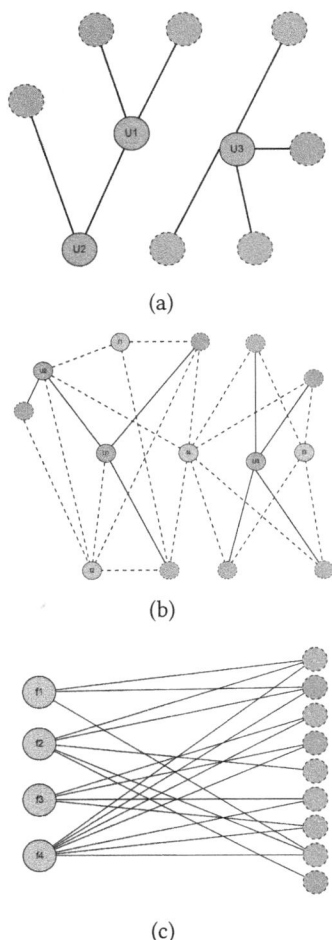

Figure 2: An overview of the network transformation.

capture and reveal a particular aspect of user behaviour and interest. Unigrams are extracted using Apache Lucene[5], while Hashtags and retweet sources are simply extracted using regular expressions. Latent Dirichlet Allocation (LDA) implementation in Mallet[6] is used to extract and analyze topics discussed in tweets.

5.2.2 Results. Table 3 provides an overview of the features' statistics in our dataset. To gain reliable privacy ratios for the features, they need to be used by a considerable number of users. Therefore, we filtered the lists only to include those features that are used by at least 100 users in the underlying set. This filtering resulted in 1228 hashtags, 906 retweet sources, more than 23K unigrams, and 32 topics. The last two columns of the table represent the mean and variance of the privacy ratios for these filtered lists.

Table 4 shows a set of example features that are located at the two ends of the privacy ratio spectrum. As can be seen, certain features in the list are specific to the dataset of focus. For instance,

---
[5]https://lucene.apache.org/core/
[6]http://mallet.cs.umass.edu/topics.php

Feature	Unique Instances	Filtered Instances	Privacy Ratio (Average)	Privacy Ratio (Variance)
Unigrams	1,094,642	23470	9.15	6.10
Hashtags	514,186	1228	9.43	10.29
Retweet Source	655,384	906	11.69	16.74
Topics	150	32	9.09	1.30

Table 3: Descriptive statistics of the timeline features.

@CityOfHamilton and *@Kathleen_Wayne* show that a considerable number of users sampled in our data collection process happen to be located in Canada. This limitation, however, is a general problem that data-driven approaches suffer from and would diminish as more data is collected. In addition, employing ontologies to map these features to a higher-level space may address this issue and will be considered in our future research plans. Nevertheless, our focus here is to gain insight into the general patterns of these features and their privacy ratios. A glance at the example table shows that privacy-sensitive features are given high privacy ratios, while the examples at the other end can often be seen in the professional and non-personal content. These results are consistent with our earlier findings from the analysis of profile features and LIWC attributes. Given that this approach is only focused on user relations and their privacy settings, our analysis of unigrams and hashtags can be conducted independent of the language of the tweets. For instance, *usluge*, which means *service* in Bosnian, is a unigram with a very low privacy score ($\theta = 2.59$) in our list.

As explained earlier, we employed LDA to generate topics from user timelines. LDA requires three hyper-parameters to be specified: the number of topics to be generated (often denoted by k), the value of α, and the value of β. α represents document-topic density. As such, a higher α indicates that documents consist of more topics, while a lower α means that documents contain fewer topics. β represents topic-word density. We built topic models with different numbers of topics (k = 50, 100, 150, and 200). For each model, we chose the value of α=50/k and β=0.01 as suggested in [11]. The topics generated by k=150 were more sensible according to our observation; hence, this model was chosen for our further analysis. Table 5 lists the top three and bottom three topics ranked according to their privacy ratios. The table shows a set of sample words that represent each topic, the topic label that we crafted based on the given words, and their privacy ratios. The results are consistent with our earlier findings since private topics are given higher privacy ratios, while topics that can be associated with the non-personal content are given lower privacy ratios.

6 DISCUSSION

Our correlation analysis of the privacy ratio across different neighbourhoods shows that privacy preferences are localized. The human annotated data collected from AMT provided further support to justify the locality of privacy preferences. Finally, the comparison results of *public* and *protected* accounts [13] with the findings of this study on different neighbourhoods of various privacy settings provided additional cues to confirm the locality in this context. This conclusion is primarily made based on the similarities observed

Feature Type	Top Features	Privacy Ratio	Bottom Features	Privacy Ratio
Unigrams	hooka	17.60	consultation	3.43
	shittiest	16.69	workshops	3.33
	hungover	16.63	catering	2.94
Hashtags	#TakeMeBack	19.76	#Adventure	3.88
	#SoTired	16.87	#ShopLocal	3.30
	#MissYou	16.64	#Entrepreneur	1.87
Retweet Source	@ColiegeStudent	17.5	@Kathleen_Wayne	4.60
	@FemalePains	17.10	@CityOfHamilton	4.05
	@MensHumour	16.91	@DanceMoms	4.02

Table 4: Example features extracted from user timelines along with their corresponding privacy ratios.

Topics	Label	Privacy Ratio
photo, gay, album, love, LGBT	sexual	10.67
health, dental, care, diet, smile	health and body	10.67
great, day, happy, weekend, tonight	positive experiences	10.55
food, wine, beer, lunch, delicious	dining	7.38
home, real estate, house, tips, mortgage	real estate	7.31
stats, followers, unfollowers, checked, automatically	follower control	6.35

Table 5: Topics extracted from user timelines along with their corresponding privacy ratios.

between *protected* accounts and the *public* accounts which are connected with a larger percentage of *protected* neighbours. To the best of our knowledge, the study conducted by Caliskan-Islam et al. [4] is the only study that has examined the potential relations of users' privacy features and the privacy attributes of their neighbours in a social network. Consistent with our findings, their analysis of 45 Twitter users showed that the amount of private information shared by users is positively correlated with the amount of private information shared by their neighbours.

The finding that privacy preferences are localized may indicate that privacy features are homophilous in Twitter. Alternatively, Twitter user preferences may be influenced by their close neighbours. Further in-depth research to reveal the potential effects of each of these two processes on privacy preferences is warranted. Earlier sociology research distinguishes two types of homophily: status homophily and value homophily [21]. Status homophily is based on informal, formal, or ascribed statuses of peoples and includes sociodemographic dimensions (e.g., age and race) as well as acquired characteristics (e.g, religion and education). Status homophily has been widely observed in the context of online social networks [15, 35]. In addition, there is a large body of research linking sociodemographic information to privacy preferences. For example, various surveys have established a positive relation of age and education with privacy concerns [14]. Therefore, similarities between privacy preferences of social contacts may stem from their similarities on these homophilous characteristics. Value homophily, on the other hand, includes a wide variety of internal states that are presumed to shape our orientation toward future behavior. Therefore, privacy similarities can be directly the result of value homophily, which stems from users' values and concerns for privacy. As a result of our study, the following interesting research questions can be raised: Is it the value and concern for privacy that drives and affects connections? Or is the privacy similarity just a derivative of status homophily? Or maybe both? Further in-depth investigations are required to address these questions.

Our approach is reliant on the current privacy settings of the contacts, thus is prone to errors caused by the disparity between privacy attitudes and settings. However, by aggregating multiple privacy labels from all the contacts, we hope to diminish the effects of this issue and capture overall privacy features. Also, our correlation studies are based on relative privacy ratios; thus, if the privacy dichotomy problem is homogeneously distributed in the network, our approach should be able to capture general privacy preferences across different neighbourhoods. Another limitation of the study is the examination of privacy preference as a binary variable. However, prior studies on privacy have shown that privacy preferences are far more complex. In fact, users may employ a variety of privacy protection strategies such as self-censoring or selective sharing [34]. Studying such privacy protection strategies and their relations to users' characteristics is warranted. Besides, our study is only focused on Twitter, while the design of the social networking website is known to shape and influence user behavior [19]. Studying other platforms with larger sets of users can give insight into the generalizability of the approach.

7 CONCLUSION

We presented a collaborative filtering approach to gain insight into user privacy preferences based on their social footprints. Our study confirms that the neighbourhood context can be used to detect privacy preferences. Then this neighbourhood information is used to characterize the attributes of privacy-unaware people. In particular, we found privacy-unaware users to publish more personal and private information compared to those who intentionally follow the public setting. Our current approach treats all of the social contacts the same. In our future studies, we plan to conduct additional human annotation studies to further confirm the results.

REFERENCES

[1] Alessandro Acquisti and Ralph Gross. 2006. Imagined Communities: Awareness, Information Sharing, and Privacy on the Facebook. In *Proceedings of the Conference on Privacy Enhancing Technologies*. 36–58.

[2] Fabeah Adu-Oppong, Casey Gardine, Apu Kapadia, and Patrick Tsang. 2008. Social Circles: Tracking Privacy in Social Networks. In *Proceedings of the Symposium on Usable Privacy and Security*.

[3] Stefano Baccianella, Andrea Esuli, and Fabrizio Sebastiani. 2010. SentiWordNet 3.0: An Enhanced Lexical Resource for Sentiment Analysis and Opinion Mining.. In *LREC*, Vol. 10. 2200–2204.

[4] Aylin Caliskan Islam, Jonathan Walsh, and Rachel Greenstadt. 2014. Privacy Detective: Detecting Private Information and Collective Privacy Behavior in a Large Social Network. In *Proceedings of the Workshop on Privacy in the Electronic Society*. 35–46.

[5] George Danezis. 2009. Inferring Privacy Policies for Social Networking Services. In *Proceedings of the ACM Workshop on Security and Artificial Intelligence*. 5–10.

[6] Cailing Dong, Hongxia Jin, and Bart Knijnenburg. 2015. Predicting Privacy Behavior on Online Social Networks. In *Proceedings of the AAAI Conference on Web and Social Media*.

[7] Lujun Fang and Kristen LeFevre. 2010. Privacy Wizards for Social Networking Sites. In *Proceedings of the International Conference on World Wide Web*. 351–360.

[8] Arik Friedman, Bart P. Knijnenburg, Kris Vanhecke, Luc Martens, and Shlomo Berkovsky. 2015. *Privacy Aspects of Recommender Systems*. Springer US, Boston, MA, 649–688.

[9] Bo Gao and Bettina Berendt. 2013. Circles, Posts and Privacy in Egocentric Social Networks: An Exploratory Visualization Approach. In *Proceedings of the Conference on Advances in Social Networks Analysis and Mining*. 792–796.

[10] Alastair J. Gill, Asimina Vasalou, Chrysanthi Papoutsi, and Adam N. Joinson. 2011. Privacy Dictionary: A Linguistic Taxonomy of Privacy for Content Analysis. In *Proceedings of the SIGCHI Conference on Human Factors in Computing Systems*. 3227–3236.

[11] Thomas L Griffiths and Mark Steyvers. 2004. Finding scientific topics. *Proceedings of the National academy of Sciences* 101, suppl 1 (2004), 5228–5235.

[12] Taraneh Khazaei, Lu Xiao, Rober Mercer, and Atif Khan. 2016. Detecting privacy preferences from online social footprint: A literature Review. In *Proceedings of the iConference*.

[13] Taraneh Khazaei, Lu Xiao, Rober Mercer, and Atif Khan. 2016. Privacy Behaviour and Profile Configuration in Twitter. In *Proceedings of the Conference on World Wide Web - Companion Volume*.

[14] Alfred Kobsa. 2007. Privacy-enhanced Personalization. *Communications of ACM* 50, 8 (2007), 24–33.

[15] Jiwei Li, Alan Ritter, and Eduard H Hovy. 2014. Weakly Supervised User Profile Extraction from Twitter. In *Proceedings of the Annual Meeting of the Association for Computational Linguistics*. 165–174.

[16] Heather Richter Lipford, Andrew Besmer, and Jason Watson. 2008. Understanding Privacy Settings in Facebook with an Audience View. In *Proceedings of the Conference on Usability, Psychology, and Security*. 2:1–2:8.

[17] Kun Liu and Evimaria Terzi. 2010. A Framework for Computing the Privacy Scores of Users in Online Social Networks. *ACM Transactions on Knowledge Discovery from Data* 5, 1 (2010), 6:1–6:30.

[18] Yabing Liu, Krishna P. Gummadi, Balachander Krishnamurthy, and Alan Mislove. 2011. Analyzing Facebook Privacy Settings: User Expectations vs. Reality. In *Proceedings of the ACM SIGCOMM Conference on Internet Measurement Conference*. 61–70.

[19] Momin Malik and Jürgen Pfeffer. 2016. Identifying platform effects in social media data. In *Proceedings of the AAAI Conference on Web and Social Media*. 241–249.

[20] Alessandra Mazzia, Kristen LeFevre, and Eytan Adar. 2012. The PViz Comprehension Tool for Social Network Privacy Settings. In *Proceedings of the Symposium on Usable Privacy and Security*. 13:1–13:12.

[21] Miller McPherson, Lynn Smith-Lovin, and James M Cook. 2001. Birds of a Feather: Homophily in Social Networks. *Annual Review of Sociology* 27, 1 (2001), 415–444.

[22] Seth A. Myers, Aneesh Sharma, Pankaj Gupta, and Jimmy Lin. 2014. Information Network or Social Network? The Structure of the Twitter Follow Graph. In *Proceedings of the International Conference on World Wide Web*. 493–498.

[23] Kaweh Naini Djafari, IsmailSengor Altingovde, Ricardo Kawase, Eelco Herder, and Claudia Niederee. 2015. Analyzing and Predicting Privacy Settings in the Social Web. In *User Modeling, Adaptation and Personalization*. Lecture Notes in Computer Science, Vol. 9146. Springer International Publishing, 104–117.

[24] James W Pennebaker, Matthias R Mehl, and Kate G Niederhoffer. 2003. Psychological aspects of natural language use: Our words, our selves. *Annual review of psychology* 54, 1 (2003), 547–577.

[25] M. Shehab, G. Cheek, H. Touati, A.C. Squicciarini, and Pau Cheng. 2010. User Centric Policy Management in Online Social Networks. In *IEEE International Symposium on Policies for Distributed Systems and Networks*. 9–13.

[26] Mohamed Shehab and Hakim Touati. 2012. Semi-Supervised Policy Recommendation for Online Social Networks. In *Proceedings of the Conference on Advances in Social Networks Analysis and Mining*. 360–367.

[27] A. Squicciarini, S. Karumanchi, D. Lin, and N. DeSisto. 2012. Automatic social group organization and privacy management. In *Proceedings of the Conference on Collaborative Computing: Networking, Applications and Worksharing*. 89–96.

[28] Anna Squicciarini, Sushama Karumanchi, Dan Lin, and Nicole DeSisto. 2014. Identifying hidden social circles for advanced privacy configuration. *Computers & Security* 41 (2014), 40 – 51.

[29] A.C. Squicciarini, Dan Lin, S. Sundareswaran, and J. Wede. 2015. Privacy Policy Inference of User-Uploaded Images on Content Sharing Sites. *IEEE Transactions on Knowledge and Data Engineering* 27, 1 (2015), 193–206.

[30] A. Srivastava and G. Geethakumari. 2013. Measuring privacy leaks in Online Social Networks. In *International Conference on Advances in Computing, Communications and Informatics*. 2095–2100.

[31] Katherine Strater and Heather Richter Lipford. 2008. Strategies and Struggles with Privacy in an Online Social Networking Community. In *Proceedings of the British HCI Group Annual Conference on People and Computers: Culture, Creativity, Interaction*. 111–119.

[32] Eran Toch, Yang Wang, and LorrieFaith Cranor. 2012. Personalization and privacy: A survey of privacy risks and remedies in personalization-based systems. *User Modeling and User-Adapted Interaction* 22, 1-2 (2012), 203–220.

[33] Jianshu Weng, Ee-Peng Lim, Jing Jiang, and Qi He. 2010. Twitterrank: Finding topic-sensitive influential twitterers. In *Proceedings of the Conference on Web Search and Data Mining*. 261–270.

[34] Pamela Wisniewski, Bart P Knijnenburg, and Heather Richter Lipford. 2014. Profiling Facebook UsersâĂŹ Privacy Behaviors. In *Symposium on Usable Privacy and Security*.

[35] Faiyaz Al Zamal, Wendy Liu, and Derek Ruths. 2012. Homophily and Latent Attribute Inference: Inferring Latent Attributes of Twitter Users from Neighbors.. In *Proceedings of the AAAI Conference on Weblogs and Social Media*.

Securing Social Media User Data - An Adversarial Approach

Ghazaleh Beigi
Arizona State University
gbeigi@asu.edu

Kai Shu
Arizona State University
kai.shu@asu.edu

Yanchao Zhang
Arizona State University
yczhang@asu.edu

Huan Liu
Arizona State University
huan.liu@asu.edu

ABSTRACT

Social media users generate tremendous amounts of data. To better serve users, it is required to share the user-related data among researchers, advertisers and application developers. Publishing such data would raise more concerns on user privacy. To encourage data sharing and mitigate user privacy concerns, a number of anonymization and de-anonymization algorithms have been developed to help protect privacy of social media users. In this work, we propose a new adversarial attack specialized for social media data. We further provide a principled way to assess effectiveness of anonymizing different aspects of social media data. Our work sheds light on new privacy risks in social media data due to innate heterogeneity of user-generated data which require striking balance between sharing user data and protecting user privacy.

ACM Reference Format:
Ghazaleh Beigi, Kai Shu, Yanchao Zhang, and Huan Liu. 2018. Securing Social Media User Data - An Adversarial Approach. In *Proceedings of 29th ACM Conference on Hypertext and Social Media, Baltimore, MD, USA, July 9–12, 2018 (HT '18)*, 9 pages.
https://doi.org/10.1145/3209542.3209552

1 INTRODUCTION

Explosive growth of social media in the last decade has drastically changed the web and billions of people all around the globe can freely conduct numerous activities such as creating online profiles, interacting with other people, sharing posts, and various personal information in a rich *heterogeneous* environment [3, 4]. The resulted user-generated social media data consists of different aspects such as links, posts and profile information. This data provides opportunities for researchers and business partners to study and understand individuals at unprecedented scales [2, 6, 13].

However, publishing social media network data risks exposing people's privacy as the data is rich in content and relationship and contains individuals' sensitive and private information, resulting in privacy leakage [18, 24, 28]. For example, users' sensitive information such as vacation plans and medical conditions can be easily

inferred from their posts. Publishing complete and intact social media data could even result in inferring sensitive information the users do not explicitly disclose such as age and location [7].

Privacy issues of users mandate social media data publishers to protect users' privacy by anonymizing the data. One straightforward anonymization technique is to remove "Personally Identifiable Information" (a.k.a. PII) such as names, user ID, age and location information and keep the social graph structure as is. This solution has been shown to be far from sufficient to protects people's privacy [2, 24]. An example of this insufficient approach is the anonymized dataset published for the Netflix prize challenge. Later, the work of [23] showed that the structure of the data carried enough information for a potential breach of privacy to re-identify anonymized users. Consequently, various protection techniques have been proposed for anonymizing each aspect of the heterogeneous social media data. For example, some works perform anonymization on graph data structure [10, 20], and others anonymize users' location information [27]. In general, the ultimate goal of an anonymization approach is to preserve social network user privacy while ensuring the utility of published data.

Existing anonymization techniques often make a specific assumption regarding the way social media data is anonymized. In particular, these works assume that it's enough to anonymize each aspect of heterogeneous social media data (e.g., structure, textual, and location information) independently. At the first glance, this assumption makes sense as anonymization takes time and effort. Moreover, users privacy is protected while the data utility is preserved at the highest possible level. For example, lets consider the simplest case study in which published data includes only two aspects such as (i) structural (e.g., friendship, follower/followee links) and (ii) textual (e.g., posts) information. We will then have options as shown in Table 1 to anonymize the data: no anonymization for either aspect, anonymization for one aspect, and anonymization for both. To ensure anonymization efficiency, as each aspect can be of different data types, a common practice is to anonymize each aspect independently. With two aspects as shown in Table 1, case 4 is the backbone of the anonymization techniques for publishing data which is clearly the strongest protection of privacy.

Privacy advocates have argued that sensitive information could be still leaked from the dataset anonymized considering each of these cases, but we lack conclusive evidence. It is unclear how the latent relation between different aspects of the data could be captured, whether the sensitive information with the scale of millions of users could be still leaked and what the success rate of such an attack could be. In particular, in this research, we are interested to study these issues by answering the following research questions:

Table 1: Four different cases for social media data anonymization. Each check mark corresponds to the aspect of data being anonymized.

	Case 1	Case 2	Case 3	Case 4
Structural Anonymization	✗	✗	✓	✓
Textual Anonymization	✗	✓	✗	✓

- **(RQ1)**: Is the data private if just one of its two aspects is anonymized?
- **(RQ2)**: Is case 4, the strongest among four cases, sufficient for anonymizing social media data?

Following the work of [24], we seek to answer these questions by taking an adversary approach to assay the privacy level of anonymized social media data. However, existing de-anonymization attacks require a list of target users. A target user is an individual v with the known identity in social media network $\mathcal{T}$ which will be mapped to a user in the given anonymized dataset. These techniques also require background knowledge $\mathcal{B}_v$ for each targeted user v before initiating the attack. These methods require time and effort to find a proper set of target users and gather their knowledge which may not be realistic in practice. To address these challenges, we first introduce a new generation of adversarial attacks specialized for social media data which does not require collecting information before initiating the attack. Furthermore, to assess different ways of the social media dataset anonymization and answer the aforementioned questions, we propose a novel Adversarial Technique for Heterogeneous Data, namely, ATHD which utilizes the latent relationship between different aspects of data. This new approach particularly well suits for social media data in which it is concerned with assessing the strengths of anonymizing different aspects of data. Our contributions could be summarized as follows:

- We introduce a new generation of adversarial attacks applicable to social media network data.
- We propose a novel de-anonymization technique ATHD to assess the privacy level of anonymized heterogeneous social media data.
- We implement and evaluate ATHD on two real world datasets to study the strengths of anonymization techniques in context of heterogeneous social media data. Our results demonstrates hidden relations between different aspects of the heterogeneous data make data anonymization techniques inefficient.

2 BACKGROUND

In this section, we review the technical preliminaries of protecting user privacy in social media data, i.e. data anonymization, which is required for the rest of this discussion. Without loss of generality, in this paper, we assume that the published social media data consists of two aspects, namely, structure and textual information. More formally, we model the social network data as $\mathcal{D} = (\mathcal{V}, \mathcal{E}, \mathcal{P})$ where $\mathcal{V} = \{i | i \text{ is a node}\}$ is the set of nodes or users, $\mathcal{E} = \{e_{i,j} | i, j \in \mathcal{V} \wedge$ there is a link from user i to user $j\}$ is the set of links between any two nodes in $\mathcal{V}$ (e.g., friend and follower/followee relations), and $\mathcal{P} = \{\mathcal{P}_i | i \in \mathcal{V}\}$ is the set of all posts (textual information) associated with users in $\mathcal{V}$. $\mathcal{P}_i = \{p_1^i, p_2^i, ..., p_{m_i}^i\}$ denotes posts by user i where m_i is the number of posts for user i. Note that links in social networks could be either directed (e.g., follower/followee relation in Twitter) or indirected (e.g., friend relation in Facebook). We focus on directed graphs, although it is straightforward to apply

the settings on undirected graphs as well. In order to preserve users' privacy, data publisher should anonymize the social media data $\mathcal{D}$ using privacy preservation techniques. Next, we will discuss techniques deployed to secure structural and textual information.

2.1 Structural Information Anonymization

To anonymize structural information, we first remove users' personally identifiable information (PII) such as user's name and ID. Techniques such as k-degree anonymity [20], sparsification, perturbation and switching [16] are used for adding or removing nodes and links. The aim of k-anonymity methods is to anonymize each node so that it is indistinguishable from at least $k - 1$ other nodes [32]. Liu *et al.* proposed to achieve k-degree anonymization [20] through edge addition/deletion strategies [20]. Sparsification technique randomly removes a set of $p|\mathcal{E}|$ edges (p is the anonymiztion coefficient) while switching methods switches $\frac{p|\mathcal{E}|}{2}$ pairs of edges. Perturbation approach first removes a set of $p|\mathcal{E}|$ edges and then add same amount of edges randomly [16].

2.2 Textual Information Anonymization

In this work, we anonymize the textual information using ϵ-differential privacy [10] by first converting each user's post into a numerical vector using tokenizing and calculating Term Frequency Inverse Document Frequency (TF-IDF) scores and then adding Laplacian noise to the text vector. Details are discussed next.

2.2.1 Text Processing. To anonymize user i's posts, we first remove user's PII such as user ID (including mentioning and retweeting), name and link information from her texts. Then, we follow a standard process to convert each of user's posts to a numerical vector. To do so, we first consider posts by all users in the dataset and perform some pre-processing including stop word removal. The unigram model is then deployed to construct the word feature space $\mathcal{W}$. Finally, we use Term Frequency Inverse Document Frequency (TF-IDF) as a feature weight to derive the vector $\mathbf{x}_l^i$ for each post p_l^i of user i. TF-IDF score for each word t is calculated as:

$$\mathbf{x}_l^i(t) = f_l^i(t) * \log \frac{M}{n_t} \tag{1}$$

where, $f_l^i(t)$ is the number of times word t appeared in the post p_l^i, M is the total number of posts in the data and n_t is the number of posts that the word t was used in them. We can represent p_l^i with the corresponding vector $\mathbf{x}_l^i$. All users' posts can be then denoted by the post-word matrix $\mathbf{X} \in \mathbb{R}^{M \times |\mathcal{W}|}$ where $|\mathcal{W}|$ denotes the size of the word space. Relations between users and posts can be also represented via a user-post matrix $\mathbf{W} \in \mathbb{R}^{N \times M}$ where N is the number of users and $\mathbf{W}_{ij} = 1$ if post j was posted by user i and $\mathbf{W}_{ij} = 0$ otherwise. Next, we will discuss how we leverage differential privacy technique to anonymize the textual information.

2.2.2 Differential Privacy. We use differential privacy technique proposed in [10] to anonymize the textual information. Differential privacy aims at maximizing privacy of users when a statistical query is submitted over a database and an answer is retrieved. Formally, ϵ-differential privacy is defined as follows:

Definition 2.1. (ϵ-Differential Privacy [10]). Given an input dataset $\mathcal{H}$, a query $f(\mathcal{H})$ and a desirable output range, a mechanism

$K(.)$ with an output range $\mathcal{R}$ satisfies ϵ-differential privacy iff,

$$\frac{Pr[K(f(\mathcal{H}_1) = R \in \mathcal{R})]}{Pr[K(f(\mathcal{H}_2) = R \in \mathcal{R})]} \le e^\epsilon \qquad (2)$$

for any datasets $\mathcal{H}_1, \mathcal{H}_2$ that differ in only one row, where ϵ is the privacy budget.

Larger values of ϵ result in a larger privacy loss as the changes of the database can be inferred more easily, and, smaller values of ϵ lead to smaller privacy loss and a higher tolerance of database to privacy breach. Note that the differential privacy is just a condition on a mechanism which releases the dataset. The mechanism which achieves ϵ-differential privacy is called sanitization. Laplacian mechanism is one popular sanitization technique which gives differential privacy for real valued queries by adding a Laplacian noise [10]. Assume that $f(\mathcal{H})$ is the real value response to a certain query f. Then, a random noise $Y(\mathcal{H})$ is generated from Laplacian distribution and added to $f(\mathcal{H})$ as:

$$K(f(\mathcal{H})) = f(\mathcal{H}) + Y(\mathcal{H}) \qquad (3)$$

The Laplacian distribution has zero mean and a scale parameter $\Delta(f)/\epsilon$ where $\Delta(f)$ is the sensitivity of f and defined as the maximum variation of the query function between datasets differing in at most one record:

$$\Delta(f) = \max\|f(\mathcal{H}_1) - f(\mathcal{H}_2)\|_1 \qquad (4)$$

The density function of the Laplacian noise will be computed as:

$$p(x) = \frac{\epsilon}{2\Delta(f)} e^{-\frac{|x|\epsilon}{\Delta(f)}} \qquad (5)$$

Note that higher sensitivity $\Delta(f)$ of the query function f with fixed ϵ, implies more Laplacian noise added to $f(\mathcal{H})$.

2.2.3 Anonymizing Textual Information with Differential Privacy.
In order to anonymize the post-word matrix $\mathbf{X}$ in a way that ϵ-differential privacy is preserved, we need to apply the discussed mechanism $K(.)$ on the original matrix $\mathbf{X}$ and transform it into a new one $X' = K(X)$. Instead of transforming the entire matrix $\mathbf{X}$ at once, we can transform each individual row of the matrix by adding a Laplacian noise to $\mathbf{X}_i$ to create a new row $\mathbf{X}'_i$. Considering the identity query function $f_I(\cdot)$ where $f(D) = D$, the sensitivity of $f_I(\cdot)$ can be defined as follows:

$$\Delta(f_I) = \max\|\mathbf{X}_i - \mathbf{X}_j\|_1 \qquad (6)$$

where $\mathbf{X}_i$ and $\mathbf{X}_j$ are any two random row vectors from $\mathbf{X}$. Following the equation 3, a Laplacian noise will be added to each vector $\mathbf{X}_i$:

$$K(f_I(\mathbf{X}_i)) = \mathbf{X}_i + \left[Y_{i1}, ...Y_{i|\mathcal{W}|}\right], i = 1, ..., n \qquad (7)$$

Similarly, Y_{ij}'s are drawn i.i.d. from Laplacian distribution with zero mean and $\Delta(f_I)/\epsilon$ scale parameter. After anonymizing the textual information, the anonymized post-word $\mathbf{X}$ and user-post $\mathbf{W}$ matrices will be published. The information regrading the word feature space $\mathcal{W}$ will be released by the data publisher as well.

3 SOCIAL MEDIA ADVERSARIAL ATTACK

De-anonymization techniques have been proposed in the literature as a counterpart to data anonymization research direction [11, 18, 26, 28, 35]. De-anonymization works further help improve anonymization techniques and reduce privacy breach by probing the potential drawbacks of anonymization techniques. Figure 1(a) depicts how these de-anonymization approaches work. These works assume that the adversary has been given a list of target users to de-anonymize requiring adversarial to collect background knowledge about target users before initiating the attack [1].

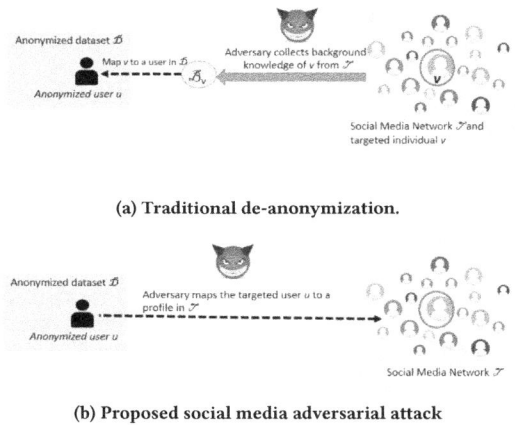

(a) Traditional de-anonymization.

(b) Proposed social media adversarial attack

Figure 1: Traditional de-anonymization vs. proposed social media adversarial attack.

Narayanan et.al. [24] discuss different ways of collecting background knowledge such as crawling data via social media networks API. Since these methods require time and effort to gather knowledge, it may not be realistic in practice for two reasons: (1) the number of target users can be very large, thinking about the number of users in Twitter; and (2) most of the online social media APIs have rate limits on the number of request a user can make through their APIs in a specific time window. Also, these APIs can only provide a random small portion of available data for each search query. This makes it infeasible to collect the background information for a significant number of users in $\mathcal{T}$ in order to find the one-to-one mapping between users in $\mathcal{D}$ and $\mathcal{T}$. Therefore, the above target-user-based approach cannot be applied to social media users when no list of target user is given.

To address these shortcomings, we introduce a new generation of adversarial attacks (Figure 1(b)) specialized for social media network data. This approach does not require the attacker to gather background knowledge $\mathcal{B}$ before starting the attack. In fact, users registered in social media which are available via online APIs are the adversaries' only source of information. The adversary can send queries to these APIs, anytime during the adversarial process. It is formally defined bellow:

Definition 3.1. (Social Media Adversarial Attack). Given an anonymized social media network dataset $\mathcal{D}$, the aim of adversarial attack is to find a one-to-one mapping between each user u in $\mathcal{D}$ and a real identity in targeted online social media network $\mathcal{T}$.

Next, we will accordingly discuss the details of our proposed de-anonymization approach, ATHD, which does not require collecting target users and their background information and is proposed to further evaluate heterogeneous social media anonymization.

4 ADVERSARIAL TECHNIQUE FOR HETEROGENEOUS DATA

Our proposed de-anonymization technique, adversarial technique for heterogeneous data (ATHD), uses different aspects of data, i.e., graph structure and users' textual information to identify the real identity of users in the anonymized dataset $\mathcal{D} = (\mathcal{V}, \mathcal{E}, \mathbf{X}, \mathbf{W}, \mathcal{W})$. We posit that this attack could be applied on various aspects of data and is not limited to only two data aspects or structural and textual information.

The main idea behind de-anonymization is to find the most similar user in social media $\mathcal{T}$ to the user u in the anonymized dataset. Here, we follow the same approach as the existing works, meanwhile our goal is to design a new framework which exploits the hidden relations between different aspects of the data, to eventually map the users to their real profile in $\mathcal{T}$.

Our proposed de-anonymization consists of three main steps. Given the anonymized dataset $\mathcal{D}$, we first extract the most revealing information for u. Second, we search those information in search engine of the targeted social media $\mathcal{T}$. This search returns a list of people whose posts include the inquired query. We save all the returned candidates as a candidate set. Third, we identify the profile from the candidate set most similar to the user u . The details of each of three steps are discussed next.

4.1 Step 1: Extracting the Most Revealing Information

The first step includes extracting the most revealing information for user u via social media API. In this work, we rather use textual information since it is not straightforward to look up information related to links. We are thus interested in extracting the most revealing textual information of user u. We assign a score s_l to each post l of u, $\{l \in \{1, ..., M\} | \mathbf{W}_{ul} = 1\}$ to measure how unique each post l is. Each post l has been vectorized using tf-idf approach and is represented in l-th row of the post-word matrix $\mathbf{X}$. Given the vector representation $\mathbf{X}_l$ of post l, the score s_l is calculated as,

$$s_l = \frac{\sum_{t=1}^{\mathcal{W}} \mathbf{X}_l(t)}{|\mathcal{W}|} \qquad (8)$$

The higher this score is, the more unique and thus the more revealing post l would be. Based on this, we rank user u's posts and select the top-k posts as the most revealing information.

4.2 Step 2: Finding a Set of Candidates

The goal of this step is to find a set of candidates for each user u, given the top-k most revealing posts. To do so, for each nominated post l from step 1, we select set of words $\mathcal{S}$ whose tf-idf scores are greater than the average of the tf-idf scores for the words in the post l, $\mathcal{S}^l = \{t | \mathbf{X}_l(t) > s_l\}$. This approach helps to not to select useless words which have non-zero tf-idf values only due to data distortion during the anonymization process. Therefore, the words with higher chances of being posted in a real text are selected. This step results in a set of queries $Q_u = \{q_u^{(1)}, q_u^{(2)}, ..., q_u^{(k)}\}$. We construct the query $q_u^{(i)}$ from set $\mathcal{S}^i$, $i \in \{1, ..., k\}$ as $q_u^{(i)} = \{word \in \mathcal{S}^i\}$. Each of $q_u^{(i)} \in Q_u$ is queried through the $\mathcal{T}$'s search engine. Result includes a set of users who have published posts including keywords in $q_u^{(i)}$.

Integrating results from all queries in Q_u, we have a set of candidate users for user u which is denoted by $C = \{c_1, c_2, ..., c_{|C|}\}$. Combining steps 1 and 2, we first find posts which are the most revealing for user u and then for each selected post we select the words that are more likely to be used by the same user. The result will be a set of candidates for u.

4.3 Step 3: Matching-Up Candidates to Target

In the last step, we find the most similar candidate to user u. We shall define a metric which measures the similarity between each user u and ith candidate $c_i \in C$. Previous works [18, 19, 24, 25, 28] have solely leveraged the structural properties to find the similarity between a target user v and users in an anonymized dataset. However, given the properly anonymized network, the attacker is not be able to accurately find the similarity between users by just incorporating structural properties. We use other aspects of the data (even if they are anonymized) along with structural properties to reveal interesting information that could be leveraged for inferring the similarity. Location, textual and profile information are good examples of such social media data aspects. We consider textual information as the second aspect of the data. We stress that out proposed approach is not limited to textual and structural information and could be generalized to any data type. We also assume that the adversary is not aware of details of deployed anonymization techniques. Next, we define two sets of features to calculate the similarity between u and her i-th candidate c_i.

4.3.1 Structural Features. It has been also shown that users can be uniquely identified using their neighbors degree distributions [15]. Following previous works [30], we thus leverage degree distribitons of u's neighbors $\mathcal{N}(u)$ (i.e. all followers and followees of u) in order to represent her structural features. Note that properties such as betweenness, closeness, and eigenvector centrality cannot be considered as u's structural features since it requires having access to the complete network of users in $\mathcal{T}$ which is not feasible in practice. We quantify degree distributions by categorizing them into b bins with size of δ in a way that each bin contains the number of neighbors that have the degree in assigned range of that bin. For directed graphs, neighbors of each user can be divided into two groups of follower and followee and final feature set is computed by concatenating result of each group.

4.3.2 Textual Features. Remind that for user u, the attacker is given a set of m_u textual vectors as well as word space features $\mathcal{W}$. For each candidate c_i, we collect a set of θ recent posts by sending requests to the $\mathcal{T}$ API. The collected posts are then concatenated in one unified document. Next, c_i's PII will be removed from the document and the corresponding text vector is then created given the word space $\mathcal{W}$ following the similar approach of the Section 2.2.1. Textual features for users u and c_i are thus represented by a set $m_u = \{t_1, t_2, ...t_{m_u}\}$ and a textual vector t_{c_i}, respectively.

4.3.3 Calculating Users Similarity. Given two groups of structural and textual features, similarity between u and c_i is computed as the linear combination of their textual and structural similarities,

$$Sim(u, c_i) = \alpha Sim_{struct}(u, c_i) + (1 - \alpha)Sim_{text}(u, c_i) \qquad (9)$$

where α controls the contribution of structural similarity. We further define $Sim_{struct}(u, c_i)$ as the cosine similarity between the two structural vectors computed as $Sim_{struct}(u, c_i) = \cos(s_u, s_{c_i})$. Textual similarity between u and c_i is also computed as the average of cosine similarity between $\forall t_j \in m_u$ and t_{c_i},

$$Sim_{text}(u, c_i) = \frac{\sum_{j=1}^{|m_u|} \cos(t_j, t_{c_i})}{m_u} \quad (10)$$

4.3.4 Improving Similarity Measure. Merely checking the structural and textual similarity between the two users' features may lead to biased and not accurate results. Moreover, the attacker needs a more powerful similarity metric which could reduce the effect of anonymization. To handle this issue, we follow a fundamental well-defined problem in the field of image processing [8], *image denoising*. Non-local mean filters are a traditional way to remove noise from image data [8]. This approach replaces a pixel's value with the weighted average of all other pixels around it. The amount of weighting for neighboring pixels is based on the degree of similarity between a small patch centered on that pixel and a small patch centered on the pixel being denoised [8]. Inspired by the idea behind non-local mean filters [8], we use the feature values of other users similar to user u in order to reduce effect of anonymization. To apply this idea, we first need to find similar users to u– here is where the concept of *homophily* comes in handy. Homophily is one of the most important social correlation theories which is also observed in social media and explains the tendency of individuals to associate and create relationship with similar ones [9, 21].

Following the similar idea to non-local means filtering, we leverage homophily and consider user u's neighbor set $\mathcal{N}(u)$ as set of similar users to her. Utilizing homophily also helps in capturing the hidden relations between different aspects of the data. We thus calculate the similarity between $\mathcal{N}(u)$ and neighbors set $\mathcal{N}(c_i)$ for candidate c_i. We first quantify the degree distributions for *all* users in both neighbors set $\mathcal{N}(u)$ and $\mathcal{N}(c_i)$ as discussed earlier in Section 4.3.1. The structural similarity of neighbors are then calculated based on the cosine similarity between $s_{\mathcal{N}(u)}$ and $s_{\mathcal{N}(c_i)}$.

Following the procedure introduced in Section 4.3.2, we collect and concatenate θ recent posts for all neighbors in $\mathcal{N}(c_i)$. Textual similarity between $\mathcal{N}(u)$ and $\mathcal{N}(c_i)$ is then computed by taking average over the cosine similarities between textual vector of each user in $\mathcal{N}(u)$ and the textual vector of $t_{\mathcal{N}(c_i)}$. The total similarity between neighbors will be then calculated as follows,

$$Sim(\mathcal{N}(u), \mathcal{N}(c_i)) = \alpha Sim_{struct}(\mathcal{N}(u), \mathcal{N}(c_i))$$
$$+ (1 - \alpha)Sim_{text}(\mathcal{N}(u), \mathcal{N}(c_i)) \quad (11)$$

This metric quantifies the fitness of $\mathcal{N}(u)$ and $\mathcal{N}(c_i)$ as the similarity scores of their structural and textual properties. It reduces the effect of data anonymization and also aligns well with the assumption that if u and c_i correspond to the same identity, their neighbors $\mathcal{N}(u)$ and $\mathcal{N}(c_i)$ should also match [11]. Finally, the total similarity between u and c_i can be computed as the combination of their individual similarity and the fitness of their neighbors:

$$Sim_{total}(u, c_i) = \beta Sim(u, c_i) + (1 - \beta)Sim(\mathcal{N}(u), \mathcal{N}(c_i)) \quad (12)$$

We empirically find that random selection of c_i's neighbors with the size λ works well in our problem and we are not required to collect all neighbors information from $\mathcal{T}$'s API. This will make the

---

Algorithm 1 Adversarial Technique for Heterogeneous Data

Input: user u, Anonymized Data $\mathcal{D}= \{\mathcal{V}, \mathcal{E}, \mathbf{W}, \mathbf{X}, \mathcal{W}\}$, k, λ, θ, h, α, β

Output: Top-h mapped accounts in targeted social network $\mathcal{T}$

1: Initialize the candidate set $C = \phi$.
2: **for** each anonymized text vector of post l for u **do**
3:     Calculate score s_l according to Eq.8.
4: **end for**
5: Select top-k posts with the highest score s_l as the most revealing information.
6: **for** For each text vector l in top-d posts **do**
7:     Select words with tf-idf scores $\mathbf{X}_l(t) > s_l$ to create search query $q_u^{(l)}$.
8:     Search query $q_u^{(l)}$ in $\mathcal{T}$ search engine and add results to C.
9: **end for**
10: **for** each candidate c_i in C **do**
11:     Calculate similarity between u and c_i according to Eq.12.
12: **end for**
13: Return the top-h candidates with maximum similarity

---

de-anonymization approach more efficient. Note that many noise removal approaches have been designed for specific kinds of noise (e.g., Guassian noise) which could be used to remove the noise from the data and particularly the vector of textual information. However, using certain noise removal approaches may not always have positive effects. In fact, it can lead to a wrong estimation of users' properties when the attacker does not have any prior knowledge of the deployed anonymized technique.

The proposed ATHD approach is shown in Algorithm 1. The input to the algorithm is the anonymized dataset and the output is the top-h mapped profile accounts in T. Lines 2–5, correspond to the first step of ATHD. The set of candidate set (step 2) is then found through lines 6–9. The similarity between u and each of the selected candidates is calculated in lines 10–12. Finally, top-h candidates with the maximum similarity to u will be returned. This re-identification procedure is then run over all users in the anonymized dataset. Note ATHD is independent of deployed anonymization techniques either for the textual or structural information. In the next section we will discuss how our proposed de-anonymization could be generalized to the social media data with any type of components.

4.4 Generalizability of ATHD

Our framework can be generalized through abstraction to different social media data, assuming that our anonymized data consists of two different aspects, $\mathcal{A}_1$ and $\mathcal{A}_2$ and the attacker is willing to initiate an attack by mapping u to a real profile in the targeted social media $\mathcal{T}$. As discussed before, the first step is to extract the most revealing information from $\mathcal{A}_1$ for user u by using the same concept as tf-idf scores. The second step includes selecting a set of candidate profiles for u by searching for the extracted information from the previous step through $\mathcal{T}$'s search engine. Finally, the similarity between u and her candidates are calculated using the combination of features of existing data components, $\mathcal{A}_1$ and $\mathcal{A}_2$. Features of the most similar users to u (e.g., neighbors) are also incorporated as well to reduce the anonymization effect while capturing the hidden relation between different aspects of the data.

5 EXPERIMENTS

In this section, we seek to answer the introduced research questions, but we first need to evaluate the efficiency of proposed adversarial technique ATHD. We begin this section by introducing the dataset and anonymization techniques we used. Then, we compare the results of ATHD against the state-of-the-art de-anonymization benchmarks to evaluate its effectiveness. Next, we use ATHD to assess the anonymization power of each of the four cases to answer the research questions:

- **(RQ1):** Is the data private if just one of its two aspects is anonymized?
- **(RQ2):** Is case 4, the strongest among four cases, sufficient for anonymizing social media data?

5.1 Datasets

We use two different datasets from two large social media websites, Twitter and Foursquare. Twitter is a prevalent and well-known microblogging social media allows millions of active users interacting with each other via short posts, called tweet. Foursquare is a location based social media in which users share their location with friends. Users can also leave tips about different places. We collect the Twitter dataset using Twitter API using the snowball sampling technique as follows. We begin with a random initial seed of users and for each user u in the seed, we obtain a random subset of size 100 of her posted tweets as well as a subset of size 500 of her follower/followee information. We repeat the same process for each u's followers/followees. This way we build our final dataset which consists of the users in the initial seed and their 2-hops connections. We follow the same procedure to collect the data from Foursquare API by considering a random initial seed of users. We collect each user friends as well as her tips on different locations. We build the final dataset by repeating this process for 2-hops connections. Note that in both datasets, we only keep the information of users who have posted at least one tweet or tip.

Next, we will apply various anonymization techniques on the obtained dataset– this is described in the next section. Also, we utilize the Twitter's advanced search engine[1] and Foursquare search [2] during the de-anonymization process for Twitter and Foursquare data, respectively. It would be also worthwhile to add that we already have the ground truth for the re-identification, since the real profiles of the crawled users are known to us beforehand. Table 2 summarizes the statistics of our datasets.

5.2 Anonymization Approaches

We use different anonymization techniques to evaluate the introduced different anonymization cases in Table1. Following previous work [11], we choose different algorithms for *structural information* anonymization as follows:

- **Naive Anonymization.** This approach only masks users' identifiers (PII), and does not change the graph structure. This is the simplest approach and thus we would expect the highest vulnerability and hence best de-anonymization result.

[1]https://twitter.com/search-advanced?lang=en
[2]https://foursquare.com/explore?

Table 2: Statistics of the crawled datasets.

(a) Twitter

# of Users	# of Edges	Avg. Clustering Coefficient
6,789	244,480	0.219
Density	# of Tweets	# of Unigrams
0.005	478,129	208,483

(b) Foursquare

# of Users	# of Edges	Avg. Clustering Coefficient
22,332	229,234	0.295
Density	# of Tips	# of Unigrams
0.0005	124,744	103,264

- **Sparsification.** This work randomly eliminates $p|\mathcal{E}|$ edges where p is the anonymiztion coefficient.
- **k-deg(add)** [20]. This anonymization method ensures that k-degree anonymity is preserved by only adding edges.
- **k-degree(add & del)** [20]. This method ensures that k-degree anonymity is preserved by performing simultaneous add/removal of the edges.
- **Switching.** This method selects two random edges (i_1, j_1) and (i_2, j_2) from the original graph such that $\{(i_1, j_2) \notin \mathcal{E} \wedge (i_2, j_1) \notin \mathcal{E}\}$. Then, it switches pairs of edges, i.e. remove edges (i_1, j_1) and (i_2, j_2) and add new edges (i_1, j_2) and (i_2, j_1) instead. This step is repeated $\frac{p|\mathcal{E}|}{2}$ times which results in $p|\mathcal{E}|$ edge removals/additions.
- **Perturbation.** This method is also known as *unintended* anonymziation and has two main steps. It first removes $p|\mathcal{E}|$ edges in a same way as sparsification method does. Then, it adds random false edges until the number of edges in the anonymized graph is the same as the original one.

Furthermore, the *Textual information* is anonymized using the techniques discussed earlier in Section 2.2 as follows:

- **Naive Anonymization.** This approach first removes users' identifiers and links from the tweets and then vectorize it.
- **Diff Privacy.** This method takes the output of the naive anonymization technique and then ensures differential privacy by adding Laplacian noise to the generated text vector.

5.3 Results and Discussion

5.3.1 Experimental Settings. We evaluate de-anonymization approaches by a metric called *success rate* $X = \frac{n_c}{N}$, where n_c is the total number of users that have been successfully re-identified and N is the total number of users in the anonymized dataset![24]. Larger values of this measure correspond to higher privacy breach.

Following the previous works [11, 28], we set $k = 10$ for k-degree anonymity and $p = 0.1$ for sparsification, purturbation and switching methods. The ϵ for differential privacy technique is set as $\epsilon = 0.01$. We also set the parameters of ATHD as follows: $\{k = 10, \alpha = 0.5, \beta = 0.7, \lambda = 20, \theta = 50, b = 7, \delta = 50\}$. The values of δ and b for quantifying degree distributions are chosen such that it can accommodate higher degrees variation. Empirical results showed that the choice of δ and b does not have a huge impact on the final results. We also set the number of returned profiles as $h = 1$. Clearly, increasing the value of h will increase the de-anonymization success rate. To answer the research questions,

(a) Twitter

	ATHD-Improved		ATHD-Simple		ADA		Narayanan et. al.	
	Naive	Diff Privacy	Naive	Diff Privacy	Naive	Diff Privacy	Naive	Diff Privacy
Naive	0.9435 (1)	0.8020 (2)	0.8200 (1)	0.6951 (2)	0.6729 (1)	0.5513 (2)	0.5073 (1)	0.4100 (2)
Sparsification	0.8087 (3)	0.6998 (4)	0.7327 (3)	0.6213 (4)	0.6099(3)	0.5114 (4)	0.4316 (3)	0.3437 (4)
k-deg(add)	0.7894 (3)	0.6814 (4)	0.6900 (3)	0.6125 (4)	0.5898 (3)	0.4982 (4)	0.3979 (3)	0.3139 (4)
k-deg(add & del)	0.7580 (3)	0.6533 (4)	0.6891 (3)	0.5821 (4)	0.5800 (3)	0.4727 (4)	0.3815 (3)	0.2997 (4)
Switching	0.6911 (3)	0.5812 (4)	0.6013 (3)	0.5186 (4)	0.4971 (3)	0.4014 (4)	0.3520 (3)	0.2618 (4)
Perturbation	0.6500 (3)	0.5685 (4)	0.5367 (3)	0.4249 (4)	0.4322 (3)	0.3618 (4)	0.2987 (3)	0.2018 (4)

(b) Foursquare

	ATHD-Improved		ATHD-Simple		ADA		Narayanan et. al.	
	Naive	Diff Privacy	Naive	Diff Privacy	Naive	Diff Privacy	Naive	Diff Privacy
Naive	0.8004 (1)	0.6799 (2)	0.7107 (1)	0.5989 (2)	0.5699 (1)	0.4821 (2)	0.4400 (1)	0.3754 (2)
Sparsification	0.7238 (3)	0.6299 (4)	0.6400 (3)	0.5499 (4)	0.5118(3)	0.4532 (4)	0.3968 (3)	0.3028 (4)
k-deg(add)	0.6947 (3)	0.5999 (4)	0.6112 (3)	0.5288 (4)	0.5138 (3)	0.4157 (4)	0.3487 (3)	0.2748 (4)
k-deg(add & del)	0.6612 (3)	0.5739 (4)	0.5918 (3)	0.4989 (4)	0.4867 (3)	0.3947 (4)	0.3025 (3)	0.2639 (4)
Switching	0.6134 (3)	0.5431 (4)	0.5517 (3)	0.4614 (4)	0.4300 (3)	0.3521 (4)	0.2987 (3)	0.2120 (4)
Perturbation	0.5642 (3)	0.4930 (4)	0.4518 (3)	0.3670 (4)	0.3402 (3)	0.2836 (4)	0.2300 (3)	0.1876 (4)

Table 3: Comparison of the de-anonymization success rates for various anonymization techniques. Higher values imply higher privacy breach. Numbers in parentheses demonstrate the corresponding case number in Table 1.

we make 12 copies of the original data and sanitize each copy with a different combination of structural and textual anonymization techniques discussed earlier. For evaluation, we define two different variants of our proposed approach, ATHD, as follows:

- **ATHD-Simple:** This uses Eq.9 and Eq.10 to calculate similarity.
- **ATHD-Improved:** This variant uses Eq.12 to improve similarity measure by incorporating features from neighbors to reduce the anonymization effect.

5.3.2 Perfomrnace Comparison. To evaluate the effectiveness of ATHD, we benchmark its two variants, ATHD-Simple and ATHD-Improved, against the following two baselines.

- **Narayanan et. al.** [24]: It computes the similarity between an unmapped user u and a candidate c_i, by using the number of neighbors of u that have been mapped to neighbors of c_i.
- **ADA** [18]: This method considers a combination of structural, relative distance and inheritance similarity. We only use degree centrality for measuring structural similarity as we do not have access to the global structure of c_i in $\mathcal{T}$.

In general, these baselines are seed-based approaches, meaning that they map a known target user v in $\mathcal{T}$ to a user in the anonymized data by utilizing a small set of initially mapped seed users and then propagating the mappings through the whole data. These works also need a previously collected background knowledge $\mathcal{B}$. We need to use same settings to make a fair comparison between the baselines and our proposed framework. To do so, we first make an initial seed set of the size $v = 20$, by mapping a set of random users in the anonymized dataset to their real identities for each of Twitter and Foursquare data. Then, we repeat the same 3-step procedure as in the ATHD for the baselines, except that we the similarity metric in the last step is replaced with those of the baselines. Performance comparison results for both datasets are demonstrated in Table 3 with the following observations:

- Narayanan et. al. is the least effective de-anonymization on both datasets. The reason is because its utilized similarity metric relies on the set of previously mapped neighbors and ignores the available structural and textual information provided in the data.
- ADA approach is more powerful than Narayanan et. al. since it incorporates structural properties of the data.
- Anonymized data is more vulnerable to ATHD-Simple compared to ADA and Narayanan et. al. This is because both structural and textual information are incorporated in the similarity metric used in ATHD-Simple. This confirms that integrating different components of data plays an important role in de-anonymization for heterogeneous social media data.
- ATHD-Improved technique achieves the best results for both Twitter and Foursquare datasets. This demonstrates the effectiveness of utilizing homophily and the features of neighbors for more effective de-anonymization.

To recap, the above observations confirm the efficiency of our proposed approach ATHD.

5.3.3 Assessing Effectiveness of Anonymization. Having discussed the efficiency of the proposed ATHD de-anonymization approach, we now seek the answer to the last two questions. The performance results w.r.t. the four anonymization cases are demonstrated in Table 3. The numbers in parentheses demonstrate the corresponding case number defined earlier in the introduction. We make the following observations for both datasets:

- Publishing the data with no anonymization for either aspect (i.e., case 1) resulted in a large information breach in both ATHD-Simple and ATHD-Improved approaches which suggests the least amount of protection as expected.
- In general, anonymizing either aspect of the data (i.e., cases 2 and 3) protects users privacy more than case 1.

- Case 4 is the strongest protection among the four cases. Accordingly, the answer to the second question is no.
- Although case 4 provides the strongest protection, ATHD-Improved was able to re-identify at least 56% of the users in the anonymized dataset, which is a significant number in the field of privacy. This shows that case 4 is far from sufficient for data anonymization.
- Sparsification is the most vulnerable anonymization approach against both ATHD-Simple and ATHD-Improved techniques as it makes the least amount of changes to the link information.
- Although the switching and perturbation methods both add and deletes the same number of edges, switching is more vulnerable to the de-anonymization since it preserves the node degrees.
- Despite the fact that k-degree anonymity based approaches guarantee the user re-identification probability to be at most $\frac{1}{k}$, but they fail because of using extra textual information.

According to these observations, the answers to the introduced research questions are no. These results further indicate that despite anonymization of all aspects of data is essential, but it is not sufficient to anonymize each aspect independently from others. This is because an adversary could easily breach privacy no matter what anonymization algorithm has been used. Consequently, serious privacy breach could happen when the published data is heterogeneous. This necessitates taking into account the latent relations in different portions of the social media data for anonymization.

6 RELATED WORK

Social Network Anonymization. Social networks contain private profile information and sensitive social relationships which provide opportunities for researchers to study and understand individuals at unprecedented scales [3, 5, 12, 14]. However, this information may leak users' privacy [2]. Anonymization methods serve as an important role to maintain data utility as well as protecting privacy [34]. Existing social network anonymization methods can be categorized mainly into three categories: *k-anonymity, edge randomization, clustering-based generalization* and *differential privacy*. The aim of k-anonymity methods is to anonymize each node so that it is indistinguishable from at least $k-1$ other nodes [32]. Liu *et al.* proposed to achieve k-degree anonymization [20] through edge addition/deletion strategies [20]. Zhou *et al.* further considered the assumption that the adversary knows subgraph constructed by the immediate neighbors of a target node, and aims to achieve k-neighborhood anonymity [37]. Edge randomization algorithms for social networks usually utilize edge-based randomization strategies to anonymize data, such as random adding/deleting and random switching [36]. Clustering-based anonymization methods group nodes and edges, and only reveal the density and size so that individual attributes are protected [33]. Another work seeks to generate an anonymized graph which guarantees differential privacy [29]. **Social Network De-anonymization.** De-anonymization approaches on social networks aim to re-identify the anonymous user data by using previously collected background information. Existing de-anonymization methods can be categorized into i) *seed-based* and ii) *seed-free*, according to whether pre-annotated seed users exist or not. Seed-based de-anonymization attack on social network was proposed to use only structural information and propagates node mappings based on seed user pairs [24]. Later, Narayanan *et al.* [22] employed a simplified attack using less heuristics rules for link

prediction problem. Nilizadeh *et al.* further proposed a community-enhanced de-anonymization scheme, which first de-anonymizes data in community-level and then de-anonymizes the users within the communities [25]. Yartseva *et al.* proposed a percolation-based de-anonymization method using neighborhood overlap information [35]. Seed-free approaches assume there is no seed users available. Pedarsani *et al.* presented a Bayesian model to iteratively perform a maximum weighted bipartite graph matching starting from the nodes with the highest degree [26]. Moreover, Ji *et al.* proposed to use optimization based methods to minimize the edge difference between anonymized network and background information [17]. Recently, another group of works have focused on exploiting additional sources of information such as profile information [11] and users attributes [28] for social graph de-anonymization. Fu *et al.* proposed to use structural and descriptive information to de-anonymize users without seed nodes [11]. A thorough survey on graph data anonymization and de-anonymization is presented in [19]. Note that de-anonymization methods are similar to those of user identity linkage across social network when only network information is available [31]. In addition to the different goals of these two research direction, the main difference is that the given graph structured is not anonymized in case of user identity linkage problem. This makes the de-anonymization much more challenging. There are two main differences between our work and the above works. First, we introduce a new adversarial attack specialized for social media data and second, we assess the efficiency of existing anonymization techniques for heterogeneous social media data.

7 CONCLUSION

In this work, we study a new problem of user data privacy for social media via an adversarial approach. Our work differs from the existing works due to unique properties of social media data: a social media site has an inordinate number of users and the site only allows for a limited number of data queries. Since anonymization takes time and requires dedicated efforts, anonymization efficiency should be maximized. Thus, we evaluate the strengths of anonymization techniques in the context of social media data and verify if it is sufficient. We propose ATHD, a novel adversarial technique by exploiting heterogeneous characteristics of social media data. Our results illustrate that anonymizing even all aspects of data is not sufficient for protecting user privacy due to hidden relations between different aspects of the heterogeneous data. One future research direction for our work is to examine how different combinations of heterogeneous data (e.g., a combination of location and textual information) are vulnerable to the de-anonymization attack, though the work reported in this paper is sufficient to show the need for better anonymization with resource constraints. Another potential direction is to improve anonymization techniques to preserve the privacy of users in social media data by considering hidden relations between different components of the data due to the innate heterogeneity of user-generated data.

ACKNOWLEDGMENTS

The authors would like to thank Alexander Nou for his help throughout the paper. This material is based upon the work supported in part by Army Research Office (ARO) under grant number W911NF-15-1-0328 and Office of Naval Research (ONR) under grant number N00014-17-1-2605.

REFERENCES

[1] Jemal H Abawajy, Mohd Izuan Hafez Ninggal, and Tutut Herawan. [n. d.]. Privacy preserving social network data publication. *IEEE communications surveys & tutorials* 18, 3 ([n. d.]), 1974–1997.

[2] Lars Backstrom, Cynthia Dwork, and Jon Kleinberg. 2007. Wherefore art thou r3579x?: anonymized social networks, hidden patterns, and structural steganography. In *Proceedings of international conference on World Wide Web*. ACM.

[3] Ghazaleh Beigi, Mahdi Jalili, Hamidreza Alvari, and Gita Sukthankar. 2014. Leveraging community detection for accurate trust prediction. In *ASE International Conference on Social Computing, Palo Alto, CA, May 2014*.

[4] Ghazaleh Beigi and Huan Liu. 2018. Similar but Different: Exploiting Users' Congruity for Recommendation Systems. In *International Conference on Social Computing, Behavioral-Cultural Modeling, and Prediction*. Springer.

[5] Ghazaleh Beigi, Jiliang Tang, and Huan Liu. 2016. Signed link analysis in social media networks. In *10th International Conference on Web and Social Media, ICWSM 2016*. AAAI Press.

[6] Ghazaleh Beigi, Jiliang Tang, Suhang Wang, and Huan Liu. 2016. Exploiting emotional information for trust/distrust prediction. In *Proceedings of the 2016 SIAM International Conference on Data Mining*. SIAM, 81–89.

[7] Valentina Beretta, Daniele Maccagnola, Timothy Cribbin, and Enza Messina. 2015. An interactive method for inferring demographic attributes in Twitter. In *Proceedings of the 26th ACM Conference on Hypertext & Social Media*. ACM.

[8] Antoni Buades, Bartomeu Coll, and J-M Morel. 2005. A non-local algorithm for image denoising. In *Computer Vision and Pattern Recognition, 2005. CVPR 2005. IEEE Computer Society Conference on*, Vol. 2. IEEE, 60–65.

[9] David Crandall, Dan Cosley, Daniel Huttenlocher, Jon Kleinberg, and Siddharth Suri. 2008. Feedback effects between similarity and social influence in online communities. In *Proceedings of ACM SIGKDD*. 160–168.

[10] Cynthia Dwork. 2008. Differential privacy: A survey of results. In *International Conference on Theory and Applications of Models of Computation*. Springer, 1–19.

[11] Hao Fu, Aston Zhang, and Xing Xie. 2015. Effective social graph deanonymization based on graph structure and descriptive information. *ACM Transactions on Intelligent Systems and Technology (TIST)* 6, 4 (2015), 49.

[12] Alireza Hajibagheri. 2017. Learning Dynamic Network Models for Complex Social Systems. (2017).

[13] Alireza Hajibagheri, Gita Sukthankar, and Kiran Lakkaraju. 2017. Extracting Information from Negative Interactions in Multiplex Networks Using Mutual Information. In *International Conference on Social Computing, Behavioral-Cultural Modeling and Prediction and Behavior Representation in Modeling and Simulation*. Springer, 322–328.

[14] Alireza Hajibagheri, Gita Sukthankar, Kiran Lakkaraju, Hamidreza Alvari, Rolf T Wigand, and Nitin Agarwal. 2018. Using Massively Multiplayer Online Game Data to Analyze the Dynamics of Social Interactions. In *Social Interactions in Virtual Worlds An Interdisciplinary Perspective*. Cambridge University Press.

[15] Michael Hay, Gerome Miklau, David Jensen, Philipp Weis, and Siddharth Srivastava. 2007. Anonymizing social networks. *Computer science department faculty publication series* (2007), 180.

[16] Shouling Ji, Weiqing Li, and Prateek Mittal. 2015. SecGraph: A Uniform and Opensource Evaluation System for Graph Data Anonymization and De-anonymization.. In *24th USENIX Security Symposium (USENIX Security 15)*.

[17] Shouling Ji, Weiqing Li, Mudhakar Srivatsa, and Raheem Beyah. [n. d.]. Structural data de-anonymization: Quantification, practice, and implications. In *Proceedings of the 2014 ACM SIGSAC Conference on Computer and Communications Security*.

[18] Shouling Ji, Weiqing Li, Mudhakar Srivatsa, Jing Selena He, and Raheem Beyah. 2016. General graph data de-anonymization: From mobility traces to social networks. *ACM Transactions on Information and System Security (TISSEC)* (2016).

[19] Shouling Ji, Prateek Mittal, and Raheem Beyah. 2016. Graph data anonymization, de-anonymization attacks, and de-anonymizability quantification: A survey. *IEEE Communications Surveys & Tutorials* (2016).

[20] Kun Liu and Evimaria Terzi. 2008. Towards identity anonymization on graphs. In *Proceedings of international conference on Management of data*. ACM.

[21] Miller McPherson, Lynn Smith-Lovin, and James M Cook. 2001. Birds of a feather: Homophily in social networks. *Annual review of sociology* 27, 1 (2001), 415–444.

[22] Arvind Narayanan, Elaine Shi, and Benjamin IP Rubinstein. 2011. Link prediction by de-anonymization: How we won the kaggle social network challenge. In *Neural Networks (IJCNN), The 2011 International Joint Conference on*. IEEE, 1825–1834.

[23] Arvind Narayanan and Vitaly Shmatikov. 2008. Robust de-anonymization of large sparse datasets. In *IEEE Symposium on Security and Privacy*. IEEE.

[24] Arvind Narayanan and Vitaly Shmatikov. 2009. De-anonymizing social networks. In *Security and Privacy, 2009 30th IEEE Symposium on*. IEEE, 173–187.

[25] Shirin Nilizadeh, Apu Kapadia, and Yong-Yeol Ahn. 2014. Community-enhanced de-anonymization of online social networks. In *Proceedings of the 2014 acm sigsac conference on computer and communications security*. ACM, 537–548.

[26] Pedram Pedarsani, Daniel R Figueiredo, and Matthias Grossglauser. 2013. A bayesian method for matching two similar graphs without seeds. In *Communication, Control, and Computing (Allerton)*. IEEE.

[27] Krishna PN Puttaswamy, Shiyuan Wang, Troy Steinbauer, Divyakant Agrawal, Amr El Abbadi, Christopher Kruegel, and Ben Y Zhao. 2014. Preserving location privacy in geosocial applications. *IEEE Transactions on Mobile Computing*.

[28] Jianwei Qian, Xiang-Yang Li, Chunhong Zhang, and Linlin Chen. 2016. De-anonymizing social networks and inferring private attributes using knowledge graphs. In *INFOCOM International Conference on Computer Communications*.

[29] Alessandra Sala, Xiaohan Zhao, Christo Wilson, Haitao Zheng, and Ben Y Zhao. 2011. Sharing graphs using differentially private graph models. In *Proceedings of the 2011 ACM SIGCOMM conference on Internet measurement conference*.

[30] Kumar Sharad. 2016. True friends let you down: Benchmarking social graph anonymization schemes. In *Proceedings of Workshop on Artificial Intelligence and Security*. ACM.

[31] Kai Shu, Suhang Wang, Jiliang Tang, Reza Zafarani, and Huan Liu. 2017. User Identity Linkage across Online Social Networks: A Review. *ACM SIGKDD Explorations Newsletter* 18, 2 (2017), 5–17.

[32] Latanya Sweeney. 2002. k-anonymity: A model for protecting privacy. *International Journal of Uncertainty, Fuzziness and Knowledge-Based Systems* (2002).

[33] Tamir Tassa and Dror J Cohen. 2013. Anonymization of centralized and distributed social networks by sequential clustering. *IEEE Transactions on Knowledge and Data Engineering* 25, 2 (2013), 311–324.

[34] Xintao Wu, Xiaowei Ying, Kun Liu, and Lei Chen. 2010. A survey of privacy-preservation of graphs and social networks. *Managing and mining graph data* (2010), 421–453.

[35] Lyudmila Yartseva and Matthias Grossglauser. 2013. On the performance of percolation graph matching. In *Proceedings of the first ACM conference on Online social networks*. ACM, 119–130.

[36] Xiaowei Ying and Xintao Wu. 2009. Graph generation with prescribed feature constraints. In *Proceedings of SDM*. SIAM.

[37] Bin Zhou and Jian Pei. 2008. Preserving privacy in social networks against neighborhood attacks. In *Proceedings of International Conference on Data Engineering*.

Search Rank Fraud De-Anonymization in Online Systems

Mizanur Rahman
Florida Int'l University, USA
mrahm031@fiu.edu

Nestor Hernandez
Florida Int'l University, USA
nestorghh@gmail.com

Bogdan Carbunar
Florida Int'l University, USA
carbunar@gmail.com

Duen Horng Chau
Georgia Tech
polo@gatech.edu

ABSTRACT

We introduce the *fraud de-anonymization* problem, that goes beyond fraud detection, to unmask the human masterminds responsible for posting search rank fraud in online systems. We collect and study search rank fraud data from Upwork, and survey the capabilities and behaviors of 58 search rank fraudsters recruited from 6 crowdsourcing sites. We propose Dolos, a fraud de-anonymization system that leverages traits and behaviors extracted from these studies, to attribute detected fraud to crowdsourcing site fraudsters, thus to real identities and bank accounts. We introduce MCDense, a min-cut dense component detection algorithm to uncover groups of user accounts controlled by *different* fraudsters, and leverage stylometry and deep learning to attribute them to crowdsourcing site profiles. Dolos correctly identified the owners of 95% of fraudster-controlled communities, and uncovered fraudsters who promoted as many as 97.5% of fraud apps we collected from Google Play. When evaluated on 13,087 apps (820,760 reviews), which we monitored over more than 6 months, Dolos identified 1,056 apps with suspicious reviewer groups. We report orthogonal evidence of their fraud, including fraud duplicates and fraud re-posts.

KEYWORDS

Fraud de-anonymization, search rank fraud

ACM Reference Format:
Mizanur Rahman, Nestor Hernandez, Bogdan Carbunar, and Duen Horng Chau. 2018. Search Rank Fraud De-Anonymization in Online Systems. In *HT'18: 29th ACM Conference on Hypertext & Social Media, July 9–12, 2018, Baltimore, MD, USA*. ACM, New York, NY, USA, 9 pages. https://doi.org/10.1145/3209542.3209555

1 INTRODUCTION

The competitive, dynamic nature of online services provides high rewards to the developers of top ranking products, through direct payments or ads. The pressure to succeed, coupled with the knowledge that statistics over user actions (e.g., reviews, likes, followers, app installs) play an essential part in a product's ranking [3, 19, 27],

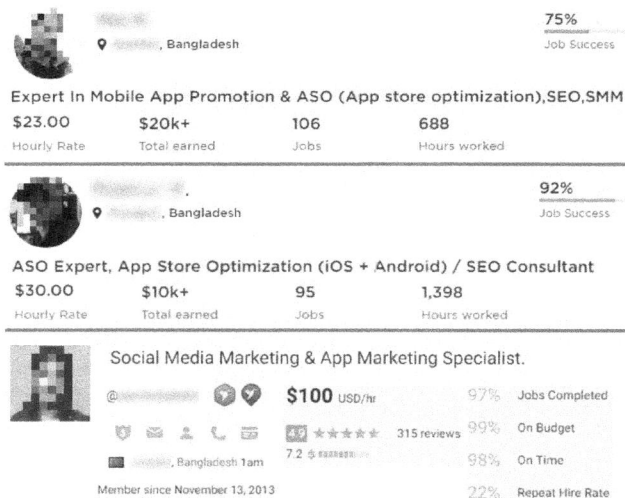

Figure 1: Anonymized snapshots of profiles of search rank fraudsters from Upwork (top 2) and Freelancer (bottom). Fraudsters control hundreds of user accounts and earn thousands of dollars through hundreds of work hours. Our goal is to de-anonymize fraud, i.e., attribute fraud detected for products in online systems, to the crowdsourcing site accounts of the fraudsters (such as these) who posted it.

has created a black market for *search rank fraud*: Fraudsters create hundreds of user accounts, connect with product developers through crowdsourcing sites [1, 2, 11], then post fake activities for their products, from the accounts they control, see Figure 1.

Detecting and disincentivizing search rank fraudsters are tasks of paramount importance to building trust in online services and the products that they host. Previous work has focused mainly on detecting online fraud [4–6, 8, 10, 12, 13, 18, 20, 21, 28, 29, 32, 33], and many review based online systems filter out detected fraudulent activities [9, 22, 25]. However, a preliminary study we performed with 58 fraudsters from 6 crowdsourcing sites revealed that workers with years of search rank fraud expertise are actively working on such jobs, and are able to post hundreds of reviews for a single product at prices ranging from a few cents to $10 per review, see e.g., Figure 3. This suggests that fraud detection alone is unable to prevent large scale search rank fraud behaviors in online systems.

In this paper we introduce the *fraud de-anonymization* problem, a new approach to address the limitations of status quo solutions, through disincentivizing search rank fraud workers and their employers. Unlike standard de-anonymization, which refers to the adversarial process of identifying users from data where their Personally Identifiable Information (PII) has been removed, the fraud de-anonymization problem seeks to attribute detected search rank fraud to the humans who posted it. A solution to this problem will enable online services to put a face to the fraud posted for the products they host, retrieve banking information and use it to pursue fraudsters, and provide proof of fraud to customers, e.g., links to the crowdsourcing accounts responsible, see Figure 1. Thus, fraud de-anonymization may provide counter-incentives both for crowdsourcing workers to participate in fraud jobs, and for product developers to recruit fraudsters.

To understand and model search rank fraud behaviors, we have developed a questionnaire and used it to survey 58 fraudsters recruited from 6 crowdsourcing sites. We have collected data from search rank fraud jobs and worker accounts in Upwork, and used it to identify fraudster traits and to collect 111,714 fake reviews authored by 2,664 fraudulent Google Play accounts, controlled by an *expert core* among 533 identified search rank fraudsters.

We leverage the identified traits to introduce DoLos[1] a system that cracks down fraud by unmasking the human masterminds responsible for posting significant fraud. DoLos detects then attributes fraudulent user accounts in the online service, to the crowdsourcing site accounts of the workers who control them. We devise MCDense, a min-cut dense component detection algorithm that analyzes common activity relationships between user accounts to uncover groups of accounts, each group controlled by a different search rank fraudster. We further leverage stylometry, graph based deep learning feature extraction tools, and supervised learning to attribute MCDense detected groups to the crowdsourcing fraudsters who control them.

DoLos correctly attributed 95% of the reviews of 640 apps (that received significant, ground truth search rank fraud) to their authors. For 97.5% of the apps, DoLos correctly de-anonymized at least one of the fraudsters who authored their fake reviews. DoLos achieved 90% precision and 89% recall when attributing the above 2,664 fraudulent accounts to the fraudsters who control them. Further, MCDense significantly outperformed an adapted densest subgraph solution.

We have evaluated DoLos on 13,087 Google Play apps (and their 820,760 reviews) that we monitored over more than 6 months. DoLos discovered that 1,056 of these apps have suspicious reviewer groups. Upon close inspection we found that (1) 29.9% of their reviews were *duplicates* and (2) 73% of the apps that had at least one MCDense discovered clique, received reviews from the expert core fraudsters that we mentioned above. We also report cases of *fraud re-posters*, accounts who re-post their reviews, hours to days after Google Play filters them out (up to 37 times in one case). In summary, we introduce the following contributions:

- **Fraud de-anonymization problem formulation**. Introduce a new approach to combat and disincentivise search rank fraud in online systems.
- **Study and model search rank fraud**. Survey 58 fraudsters from 6 crowdsourcing websites, collect gold standard attributed search rank fraud data and extract insights into fraudster behaviors.

---

[1]DoLos is a concrete block used to protect harbor walls from erosive ocean waves.

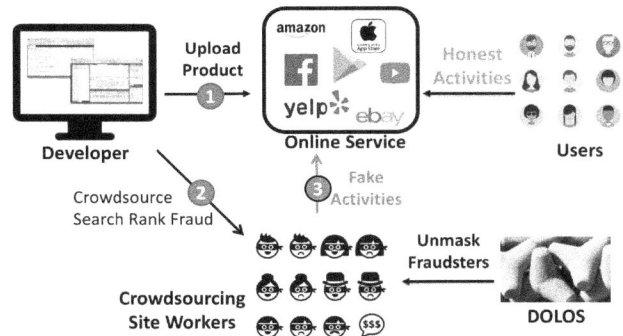

Figure 2: System and adversary model. Developers upload products, on which users post activities, e.g., reviews, likes. Adversarial developers crowdsource search rank fraud. Unlike fraud detection solutions, DoLos unmasks the human fraudsters responsible for posting search rank fraud.

- **DoLos and MCDense**. Exploit extracted insights to develop fraud de-anonymization algorithms. Evaluate algorithms extensively on Google Play data. Identify orthogonal evidence of fraud from detected suspicious products. The code is available for download at https://github.com/FraudHunt.

2 STUDY & MODEL SEARCH RANK FRAUD

2.1 System and Adversary Model

We consider an ecosystem that consists of online services and crowdsourcing sites. Online services host accounts for developers, products and users, see Figure 2. Developers use their accounts to upload products. Users post *activities* for products, e.g., reviews, ratings, likes, installs. Product accounts display these activities posted and statistics, while user accounts list the products on which users posted activities. Crowdsourcing sites host accounts for *workers* and *employers*. Worker accounts have unique identifiers and bank account numbers used to deposit the money that they earn. Employers post *jobs*, while workers bid on jobs, and, following negotiation steps, are assigned or win the jobs.

We consider product developers who hire workers from crowdsourcing sites, to perform search rank fraud, see Figure 1. We focus on workers who control multiple user accounts in the online system, which they use to post fake activities, e.g., review, rate, install.

Previous studies of online fraud include the work of Yang et al. [35], who showed that "criminal" Twitter accounts tend to form small-world social networks. Mukherjee et al. [20, 21] confirmed this finding and introduced features that identify reviewer groups, who review many products in common but not much else, post their reviews within small time windows, and are among the first to review the product. Further, Beutel et al. [7] proposed CopyCatch, a system that identifies *lockstep behaviors*, i.e., groups of user accounts that act in a quasi-synchronized manner, to detect fake page likes in Facebook. Chen et al. [8] identify clusters of apps in Apple's China App store, that have been promoted in a similar fashion.

In contrast, in this paper we focus on de-anonymizing fraud, by attributing it to fraudsters recruited from crowdsourcing sites. In this section we describe our efforts to understand and model such search rank fraud experts. In the following, we use the terms *worker*, *fraudster* and *fraud worker*, interchangeably.

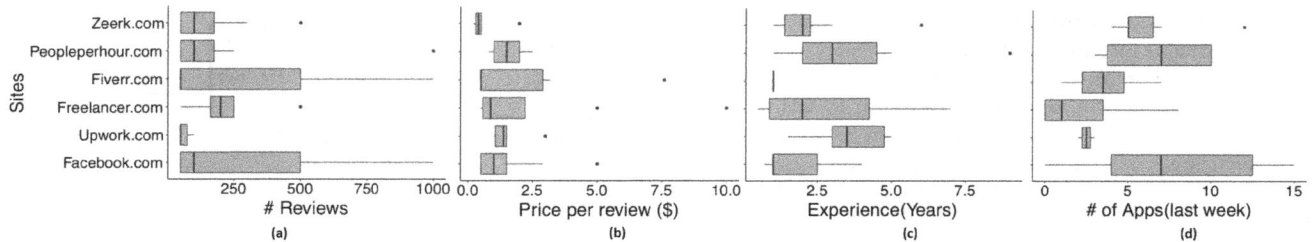

Figure 3: Statistics over 44 fraudsters (targeting Google Play apps) recruited from 5 crowdsourcing sites: minimum, average and maximum for (a) number of reviews that a fraudster can write for an app, (b) price demanded per review, (c) years of experience, (d) number of apps reviewed in the past 7 days. Fraudsters report to be able to write hundreds of reviews for a single app, have years of experience and are currently active. Prices range from 56 cents to $10 per review.

2.2 Motivation: Fraudster Capabilities

To evaluate the magnitude of the problem, we have first contacted 44 workers from several crowdsourcing sites including Zeerk (12), Peopleperhour (9), Freelancer (8), Upwork (6) and Facebook groups (9), who advertised search rank fraud capabilities for app markets. We asked them (1) how many reviews they can write for one app, (2) how much they charge for one review, (3) how many apps they reviewed in the past 7 days, and (4) for how long they been active in promoting apps.

Figure 3 shows statistics over the answers, organized by crowdsourcing site. It suggests significant profits for fraudsters, who claim to be able to write hundreds of reviews per app (e.g., an average of 250 reviews by Freelancer workers) and charge from a few cents ($0.56 on average from Zeerk.com workers) to $10 per review (Freelancer.com). Fraudsters have varied degrees of expertise in terms of years of experience and recent participation in fraud jobs. For instance, fraudsters from Peopleperhour and Upwork have more than 2.5 years experience and more than 3 recent jobs on average. Further, in recently emerged Facebook groups, that either directly sell reviews or exchange reviews, fraudsters have less than 2.5 years experience, but are very active, with more than 7 jobs in the past 7 days on average, and economical ($1.3 on average per review).

Subsequently, we have developed a more detailed questionnaire to better understand search rank fraud behaviors and delivered it to 14 fraud freelancers that we recruited from Fiverr. We paid each participant $10, for a job that takes approx. 10 minutes. The IPs from which the questionnaire was accessed revealed that the participants were from Bangladesh (5), USA (2), Egypt (2), Netherlands, UK, Pakistan, India and Germany (1). The participants declared to be male, 18 - 28 years old, with diverse education levels: less than high school (1), high school (2), associate degree (3), in college (5), bachelor degree or more (3).

The participants admitted an array of fraud expertise (fake reviews and ratings in Google Play, iTunes, Amazon, Facebook and Twitter, fake installs in Google Play and iTunes, fake likes and followers in Facebook and Instagram, influential tweets in Twitter). We found a mix of (1) inexperienced and experienced fraudsters: 4 out of 14 had been active less than 2 months and 6 fraudsters had been active for more than 1 year, and (2) active and inactive fraudsters: 4 had not worked in the past month, 9 had worked on 1-5 fraud jobs in the past month, and 1 worked on more than 10 jobs; 8 fraudsters were currently active on 1-5 fraud jobs, and 1 on more than 5. Further, we observed varying search rank fraud

capabilities: 8 of the 11 surveyed fraudsters who wrote reviews, admit to have reviewed an app at least 5 times; 1 admits to have written 51 to 100 reviews for an app.

Of the 14 fraudsters surveyed, 3 admitted to working in teams that had more than 10 members, and to sharing the user accounts that they control, with others. 10 fraudsters said that they control more than 5 Google Play accounts and 1 fraudster had more than 100 accounts. Later in this section we show that this is realistic, as other 23 fraudsters we recruited, were able to reveal between 22 and 86 Google Play accounts that they control. Further, 4 fraudsters said that they never abandon an account, 5 said that they use each account until they are unable to login, and 4 said that they use it for at most 1 year. This is confirmed by our empirical observation of the persistence of fraud (see end of section 2.4).

Ethical considerations. We have developed our protocols to interact with participants and collect data in an IRB-approved manner (Approval #: IRB-15-0219@FIU).

2.3 A Study of Search Rank Fraud Jobs

We identified and collected data from 161 search rank fraud jobs in Upwork that request workers to post reviews on, or install Google Play and iTunes apps. We have collected the 533 workers who have bid on these jobs. We call the bidding workers that are awarded a job, *winners*. One job of the 161, was awarded to 12 workers; more jobs were awarded to 2 workers than to only 1. This indicates that hiring multiple workers is considered beneficial by adversarial developers, and suggests the need to attribute detected organized fraud activities to human masterminds (see next section).

We introduce the concepts of *co-bid* and *co-win graphs*. In the co-bid graph, nodes are workers who bid on fraud jobs; edges connect workers who bid together on at least one job. The edge weights denote the number of jobs on which the endpoint workers have bid together. In the co-win graph, the weight of an edge is the number of fraud jobs won by both endpoint workers.

Out of the 56 workers who won the 161 jobs, only 40 had won a job along with another bidder. Figure 4(a) shows the co-bid graph of these 40 winners, who form a tight community. Figure 4(b) plots the co-win graph of the 40 winners. We observe an "expert core" of 8 workers who each won between 8 to 15 jobs. Further, we observe infrequent collaborations between any pair of workers: any two workers collaborated on at most 4 jobs.

Empirical Adversary Traits. Our studies reveal several search rank fraudster traits:

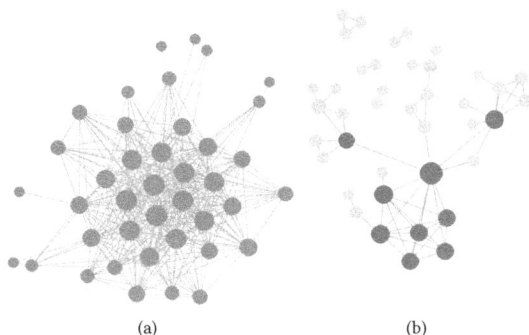

(a)   (b)

Figure 4: (a) Worker co-bid graph: Nodes are Upwork workers. An edge connects two workers who co-bid on search rank fraud jobs. We see a tight co-bid community of workers; some co-bid on 37 jobs. (b) Worker Co-win graph with an "expert core" of 8 workers (red), each winning 8 − 15 jobs. Edges connect workers who won at least one job together. Any two workers collaborated infrequently, up to 4 jobs.

- **Trait 1**: Fraudsters control multiple user accounts which they use to perpetrate search rank fraud.
- **Trait 2**: While fraudsters have diverse search rank fraud capabilities, crowdsourcing sites have an "expert core" of successful search rank fraud workers. Many fraudsters are willing to contribute, but few have the expertise or reputation to win such jobs.
- **Trait 3**: Search rank fraud jobs often recruit multiple workers. Thus, targeted products may receive fake reviews from multiple fraudsters.
- **Trait 4**: Any two fraudsters collaborate infrequently, when compared to the number of search rank fraud jobs on which they have participated, see Figure 4(b).
- **Trait 5**: Fraudsters, including experts, are willing to share information about their behaviors, perhaps to convince prospective employers of their expertise.

DOLOS exploits these traits to detect and attribute groups of fraudulent user accounts to the fraudsters who control them. While we do not claim that the sample data from which the traits are extracted is representative, in the evaluation section we show that DOLOS can accurately de-anonymize fraudsters.

2.4   Fraudster Profile Collection (FPC)

Kaghazgaran et al. [15] identified crowdsourcing site jobs that reveal the targeted Amazon products, then studied those products. However, they did not attribute the fraudulent reviews to the crowdsourcing site accounts of the workers who worked on those jobs. Xie and Zhu [34] monitored 52 paid review service providers for four months and exposed apps that they promoted.

Unlike previous work, we leveraged Trait 5 to collect a first gold standard dataset of attributed, fraudster controlled accounts in Google Play. For this, we have identified and contacted 100 Upwork, Fiverr and Freelancer workers with significant bidding activity on search rank fraud jobs targeting Google Play apps. Figure 5 shows the number of accounts (bottom, red segments) revealed by each of 23 most responsive of these workers: between 22 and 86 Google Play accounts revealed per worker, for a total of 1,356 user accounts.

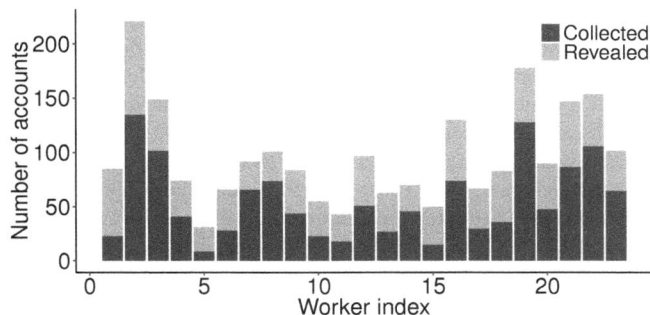

Figure 5: Attributed, fraudster-controlled accounts. The numbers of Google Play accounts revealed by the detected fraudsters are shown in red. Each of the 23 fraudsters has revealed between 22 to 86 accounts. Guilt-by-association accounts are shown in orange. We have collected a total of 2,664 accounts (red + orange). One fraudster controls (at least) 217 accounts.

Algorithm	Precision	Recall	F-measure
RF	95.5%	91.6%	93.5%
SVM	**98.5%**	**98.3%**	**98.5%**
k-NN	97.1%	96.4%	96.7%
MLP	98.6%	98.1%	98.4%

Table 1: Account attribution performance on gold standard fraudster-controlled dataset, with several supervised learning algorithms (parameters $d = 300$, $t = 100$, $\gamma = 80$, and $w = 5$ set through a grid search). SVM performed best.

Fraud app dataset. To expand this data, we collected first a subset of 640 apps that received the highest ratio of reviews from accounts controlled by the above 23 expert core workers to the total number of reviews. We have monitored the apps over a 6 month interval, collecting their new reviews once every 2 days. The 640 apps had between 7 to 3,889 reviews. Half of these apps had at least 51% of their reviews written from accounts controlled by the 23 fraudsters. In the following we refer to these, as the *fraud apps*.

Union fraud graph. We have collected the account data of the 38,123 unique reviewers (956 of which are the seed accounts revealed by the 23 fraudsters) of the fraud apps, enabling us to build their *union fraud graph*: a node corresponds to an account that reviewed one of these apps (including fraudster controlled and honest ones), and the weight of an edge denotes the number of apps reviewed in common by the accounts that correspond to the end nodes. We have removed duplicates: an account that reviewed multiple fraud apps has only one node in the graph. The union fraud graph has 19,375,550 edges and 162 disconnected components, of which the largest has 37,566 nodes.

Guilt-by-association. We have labeled each node of the union fraud graph with the ID of the fraudster controlling it or with "unknown" if no such information exists. For each unknown labeled node U, we decide if U is controlled by one of the fraudsters, based on how well U is associated with accounts controlled by the fraudster. However, U may be connected to the accounts of multiple fraudsters (see Trait 3).

To address this problem, we leveraged Trait 4 to observe that random walks that start from nodes controlled by the same fraudsters are likely to share significant context, likely different from the context of nodes controlled by other fraudsters, or that are honest. We have pre-processed the union fraud graph to convert it into a non-weighted graph: replace an edge between nodes u_i and u_j with weight w_{ij}, by w_{ij} non-weighted edges between u_i and u_j. We then used the DeepWalk algorithm [26] to perform γ random walks starting from each node v in this graph, where a walk samples uniformly from the neighbors of the last vertex visited until it reaches the maximum walk length (t). The pre-processing of the union graph ensures that the probability of DeepWalk at node u_i to choose node u_j as next hop, is proportional to w_{ij}. DeepWalk also takes as input a window size w, the number of neighbors used as the context in each iteration of its SkipGram component. Deepwalk returns a d-dimensional representation in $\mathbb{R}^d$ for each of the nodes. We then used this representation as predictor features for the "ownership" of the account U - the fraudster who controls it.

Table 1 highlights precision, recall, and F-measure achieved by different supervised learning algorithms. We observe that SVM reaches 98.5% F-measure which suggests DeepWalk's ability to provide useful features and assist in our guilt-by-association process. We then applied the trained model to the remaining and unlabeled accounts in the union fraud graph obtaining new guilt-by-association accounts for each of the 23 workers. Figure 5 shows the number of seed and guilt-by-association accounts uncovered for each of the 23 fraudsters. We have collected 1,308 additional accounts across workers for a total of 2,664 accounts.

Persistence of fraud. After more than 1 year following the collection of the 2,664 fraudster-controlled accounts, we have re-accessed the accounts. We found that 67 accounts had been deleted and 529 accounts were inactive, i.e., all information about apps installed, reviewed, +1'd was removed. 2,068 accounts were active. This is consistent with the findings from our fraudster survey, where 4 out of 14 surveyed fraudsters said that they never abandon an account, 5 said that they use each account until they are unable to login, and 4 said that they use it for at most 1 year. This further suggests the limited ability of Google Play to identify and block fraudster-controlled accounts.

3 FRAUD DE-ANONYMIZATION SYSTEM

3.1 Problem Definition

Unlike standard de-anonymization, which refers to the adversarial process of identifying users from data where their PII has been removed, in this paper we define the fraud de-anonymization problem in a positive context. Specifically, let $\mathcal{W} = \{W_1, .., W_n\}$ be the set of crowdsourcing worker accounts, let $\mathcal{U} = \{U_1, .., U_m\}$ be the set of user accounts and let $\mathcal{A} = \{A_1, .., A_a\}$ be the set of products hosted by the online service. Then, given a product $A \in \mathcal{A}$, return the subset of fraudsters in $\mathcal{W}$ who control user accounts in $\mathcal{U}$ that posted fraudulent activities for A.

3.2 Solution Overview

We introduce DoLos, the first fraud de-anonymization system that integrates activities on both crowdsourcing sites and online services. As illustrated in Figure 6, DoLos (1) proactively identifies new

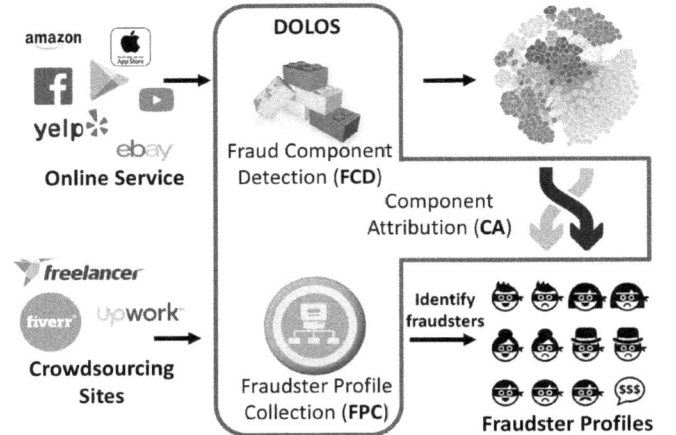

Figure 6: DoLos system architecture. The Fraud Component Detection (FCD) module partitions the co-activity graphs of apps into loosely inter-connected, dense components. The Component Attribution (CA) module attributes FCD detected components to fraudster profiles collected by the Fraudster Profile Collector (FPC), see § 2.4.

fraudsters and builds their profiles in crowdsourcing sites, then (2) processes product and user accounts in online systems to attribute detected fraud to these profiles. The gold standard fraudster profile collection (FPC) module described in the previous section performs the first task. In the following, we focus on the second task, which we break into two sub-problems:

- **Fraud-Component Detection Problem.** Given a product $A \in \mathcal{A}$, return a set of components $C_A = \{C_1, .., C_k\}$, where any $C_{j=1..k}$ consists of a subset of the user accounts who posted an activity for A, s.t., those accounts are either controlled by a single worker in $\mathcal{W}$, or are honest.
- **Component Attribution Problem.** Given $\mathcal{W}$ and a component $C \in C_A$, return the identity of the worker in $\mathcal{W}$ who controls all the accounts in the component, or $\perp$ if the accounts are not controlled by a worker.

The FCD module of DoLos partitions the reviews of a product into components, such that all the reviews in a component were posted by a single fraudster. The CA module attributes each component to crowdsourcing account of the fraudster who controls it. In the following, we detail these modules.

3.3 Fraud Component Detection (FCD) Module

The FCD module leverages graphs built over common activities performed by user accounts, in order to identify communities, each controlled by a different fraudster. Previous work has used graph based approaches to detect fraudulent behaviors, e.g., [13, 30, 32, 33, 36]. Ye and Akoglu [36] quantified the chance of a product to be a spam campaign target, then clustered spammers on a 2-hop subgraph induced by the products with the highest chance values. Wang et. al [32] leveraged a novel Markov Random Field to detect fraudsters in social networks via guilt-by-association on directed graphs. Shen et al [30] introduced "k-triangles" to measure the tenuity of account groups and proposed algorithms to approximate the Minimum k-Triangle Disconnected Group problem. Hooi et

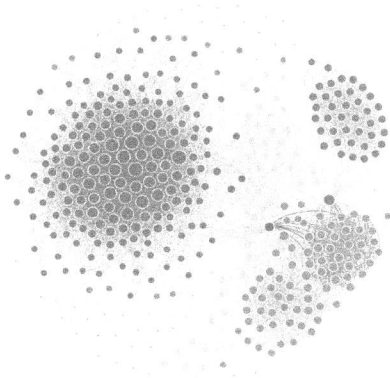

Figure 7: Co-activity graph of user accounts reviewing a popular horoscope app in Google Play (name hidden for privacy). Nodes are accounts. 4 Upwork workers each revealed to control the accounts of the same color. Two accounts are connected if they post activities for similar sets of apps. Node sizes are a function of the account connectivity.

al. [13] have shown that fraudsters have evolved to hide their traces, by adding spurious reviews to popular items. They introduced a class of "suspiciousness" metrics that apply to bipartite user-to-item graphs, and developed a greedy algorithm to find the subgraph with the highest suspiciousness metric.

In contrast, the FCD module needs to solve the more complex problem of accurately identifying groups of user accounts such that each group is controlled by a *different* fraudster. In order to achieve this, we leverage the adversary Trait 4, that the accounts controlled by one fraudster are likely to have reviewed significantly more products in common than with the accounts controlled by another fraudster. We introduce *MCDense*, an algorithm that takes as input the **co-activity graph** of a product A, and outputs its *fraud components*, sets of user accounts, each potentially controlled by a different worker. We define the **co-activity graph** of a product A as $G = (\mathcal{U}, \mathcal{E}_w)$, with a node for each user account that posted an activity for A (see Figure 7 for an illustration). Two nodes $u_i, u_j \in \mathcal{U}$ are connected by a weighted edge $e(u_i, u_j, w_{ij}) \in \mathcal{E}^w$, where the weight w_{ij} is the number of products on which u_i and u_j posted activities in common.

MCDense, see Algorithm 1, detects densely connected subgraphs, each subgraph being minimally connected to the other subgraphs. Given a graph $G = (\mathcal{U}, \mathcal{E}_w)$, its triangle density is $\rho(G) = \frac{t(V)}{\binom{|V|}{3}}$, where $t(V)$ is the number of triangles formed by the edges in $\mathcal{E}^w$.

MCDense recursively divides the co-activity graph into two minimally connected subgraphs: the sum of the weights of the edges crossing the two subgraphs, is minimized. If both subgraphs are more densely connected than the original graph (line 4) and the density of the original graph is below a threshold τ, MCDense treats each subgraph as being controlled by different workers: it calls itself recursively for each subgraph (lines 5 and 6). Otherwise, MCDense considers the undivided graph to be controlled by a single worker, and adds it to the set of identified components (line 8).

We have used the gold standard set of accounts controlled by the 23 fraudsters detailed in the previous section, to empirically

---

Algorithm 1 MCDense: Min-Cut based Dense component detection. We set η to 5 and *tau* to 0.5.

Input: G = $(\mathcal{U}, \mathcal{E}_w)$: input graph
          n := $|\mathcal{U}|$
Output: $C := \emptyset$: set of node components
1. MCDense(G){
2.   **if** (nodeCount(G) < η) return;
3. (G_1, G_2) := weightMinCut(G);
4.   **if** (($\rho(G_1) > \rho(G)$ & $\rho(G_2) > \rho(G)$)
            & ($\rho(G) < \tau$)){
5.   MCDense(G_1); MCDense(G_2);
6.   **else**
7. $C := C \cup G$;
8.   return;
9.   **end if**

---

set the τ threshold to 0.5, as the lowest density of the 23 groups of accounts revealed by the fraudsters was just above 0.5.

MCDense converges and has $O(|\mathcal{E}_w||\mathcal{U}|^3)$ complexity. To see that this is the case, we observe that at each step, MCDense either stops or, at the worst, "shaves" one node from G. The complexity follows then based on Karger's min-cut algorithm complexity [16].

3.4 Component Attribution (CA) Module

Given a set of fraud worker profiles $\mathcal{FW}$ and a set of fraud components returned by the FCD module for a product A, the component attribution module identifies the workers likely to control the accounts in each component. To achieve this, DoLos leverages the unique writing style of human fraudsters to fuse elements from computational linguistics, e.g., [17, 23], and author de-anonymization, e.g., [24]. Specifically, we propose the following 2-step component attribution process:

CA Training. Identify the products reviewed by the accounts controlled by each fraudster $W \in \mathcal{FW}$. For each such product, create a *review instance* that consist of all the reviews written by the accounts controlled by W for A. Thus, each review instance contains only (but all) the reviews written from the accounts controlled by a single fraudster, for a single product. Extract stylometry features from each review instance of each fraudster, including character count, average number of characters per word, and frequencies of letters, uppercase letters, special characters, punctuation marks, digits, numbers, top letter digrams, trigrams, part of speech (POS) tags, POS digrams, POS trigrams, word digrams, word trigrams and of misspelled words. Train a supervised learning algorithm on these features, that associates the feature values of each review instance to the fraudster who created it.

Attribution. Let C denote the set of components returned by MCDense for a product A. For each component $C \in \mathcal{C}$, group all the reviews written by the accounts in C for product A, into a review instance, r. Extract r's stylometry features and use the trained classifier to determine the probability that r was authored by each of the fraudsters in $\mathcal{FW}$. Output the identity of the fraudster with the highest probability of having authored r.

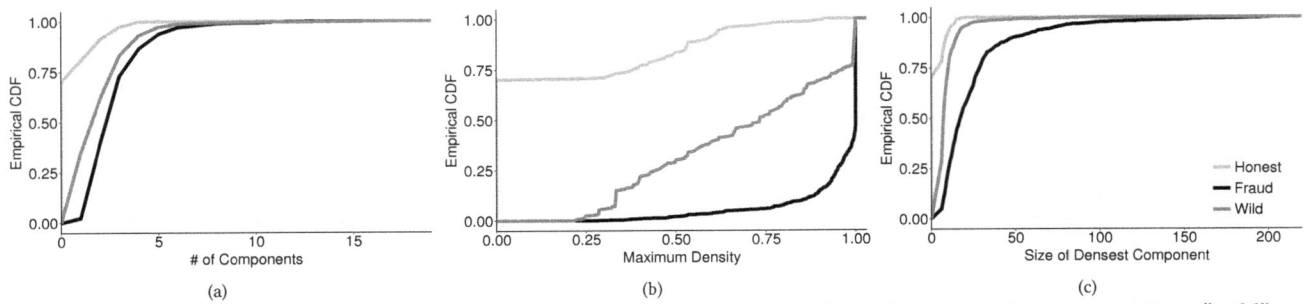

Figure 8: MCDense: Cummulative distribution function (CDF) over 640 fraud, 219 honest, and 1,056 suspicious "wild" apps, of per-app (a) number of components of at least 5 accounts, (b) maximum density of an identified component and (c) size of densest component. We observe significant differences between fraud and honest apps.

4 EMPIRICAL EVALUATION

In this section we compare the results of DOLOS on fraud and honest apps, evaluate its de-anonymization accuracy, and present its results on 13,087 apps. Further, we compare MCDense with DSG, an adapted dense sub-graph detection solution.

4.1 Fraud vs. Honest Apps

We evaluate the ability of DOLOS to discern differences between fraudulent and honest apps. For this, we have first selected 925 candidate apps from the longitudinal app set, that have been developed by Google designated "top developers". We have filtered the apps flagged by VirusTotal. We have manually investigated the remaining apps, and selected a set of 219 apps that (i) have more than 10 reviews and (ii) were developed by reputable media outlets (e.g., Google, PBS, Yahoo, Expedia, NBC) or have an associated business model (e.g., fitness trackers). We have collected 38,224 reviews and their associate user accounts from these apps.

Figure 8(a) compares the CDF of the number of components (of at least 5 accounts) found by MCDense per each of the 640 fraud apps vs. the 219 honest apps. MCDense found that all the fraud apps had at least 1 component, however, 70% of the honest apps had no component. The maximum number of components found for fraud apps is 19 vs. 4 for honest apps. Figure 8(b) compares the CDF of the maximum edge density (ratio of number of edges to maximum number of edges possible) of a component identified by MCDense per fraud vs. honest apps. 94.4% of fraud apps have density more than 75% while only 30% of the honest apps have a cluster with density larger than 0. The increase is slow, with 90% of the honest apps having clusters with density of 60% or below. Figure 8(c) compares the CDF of the size of the per-app densest component found for fraud vs. honest apps. 80% of the fraud apps vs. only 7% of the honest apps, have a densest component with more than 10 nodes. The largest, densest component has 220 accounts for a fraud app, and 21 accounts for an honest app. We have manually analyzed the largest, densest components found by MCDense for the honest apps and found that they occur for users who review popular apps such as the Google, Yahoo or Facebook clients, and users who share interests in, e.g., social apps or games.

Algo	Top 1 (TPR)	Top 3	Top 5
k-NN (IBK)	**1608** (95.0%)	**1645**	1646
RF (Random Forest)	1487 (87.9%)	1625	**1673**
DT (Decision Tree)	1126 (66.5%)	1391	1455

Table 2: DOLOS attribution performance for the 1,690 instances of the 640 fraud apps. k-NN achieved the best performance: It correctly identifies the workers responsible for 95% (1608) of the instances.

4.2 De-Anonymization Performance

We have implemented the CA module using a combination of JStylo [14] and supervised learning algorithms. We have collected the 111,714 reviews posted from the 2,664 attributed, fraudster controlled user accounts of § 2.4. The reviews were posted for 2,175 apps. We have grouped these reviews into instances, and we have filtered out those with less than 5 reviews. Figure 9 shows their distribution among the 23 fraudsters who authored them.

We have evaluated the performance of DOLOS (MCDense + CA) using a leave-one-out cross validation process over the 640 fraud apps (and their 1,690 review instances). We have used several supervised learning algorithms, including k-nearest neighbors (k-NN), Random Forest (RF), Decision Trees (DT), Naive Bayes (NB), and Support Vector Machine (SVM). In each experiment we report the top 3 performers.

Instance level performance. Table 2 shows the number of instances correctly attributed by DOLOS (out of the 1,690 instances of the 640 fraud apps) and corresponding true positive rate, as well as the number of instances where the correct worker is among DOLOS' top 3 and top 5 options. k-NN achieved the best performance, correctly identifying the workers responsible for posting 95% of the instances. We observe that k-NN correctly predicts the authors of 95% of the instances. Figure 9(b) zooms into per-fraudster precision and recall, showing the ability of DOLOS to identify the instances and only the instances of each of the 23 workers. For 21 out of 23 workers, the DOLOS precision and recall both exceed 87%.

App level performance. Table 3 shows that when using k-NN, DOLOS correctly identified at least 1 worker per app, for 97.5% of the fraud apps, and identified at least 90% of the workers in each of 87% of the fraud apps. Table 4 shows that the precision of DOLOS in identifying an app's workers exceeds 90% for 69% of the apps.

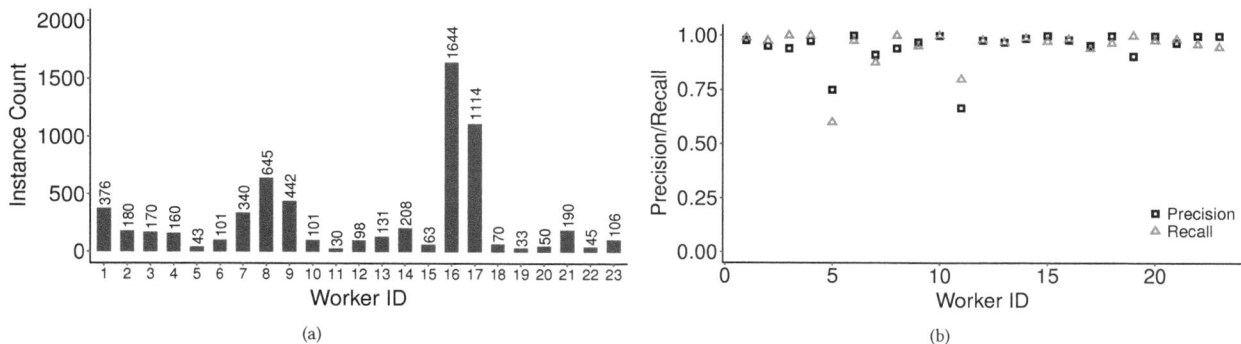

(a)

(b)

Figure 9: (a) Number of review instances collected from each of the 23 fraudster. Each review instance has at least 5 reviews, written by the accounts controlled by a single fraudster, for a single app. (b) DOLOS per-worker attribution precision and recall, over the 1,690 review instances of 640 fraud apps, exceed 87% for 21 out of the 23 fraudsters.

Algo	1 worker	50%-recall	70%-recall	90%-recall
RF	624	622	537	465
SVM	574	517	325	284
k-NN	**625**	**625**	**585**	557

Table 3: DOLOS app level recall: the number of apps for which DOLOS has a recall value of at least 50%, 70% and 90%. k-NN identifies at least one worker for 97.5% of the 640 fraud apps, and 90% of the workers of each of 557 (87%) of the apps.

Algo	50%-prec	70%-prec	90%-prec
RF	573	434	359
SVM	460	249	209
k-NN	**578**	**483**	444

Table 4: App level precision: the number of apps where its precision is at least 50%, 70% and 90%. The precision of DOLOS when using k-NN exceeds 90% for 69% of the fraud apps.

Developer tailored search rank fraud. Upon closer inspection of the DOLOS identified clusters, we found numerous cases of clusters consisting of user accounts who reviewed almost exclusively apps created by a single developer. We conjecture that those user accounts were created with the specific goal to review the apps of the developer, e.g., by the developer or their employees.

4.3 DOLOS in the Wild

To understand how Dolos will perform in real life, we have randomly selected 13,087 apps from Google Play, developed by 9,430 distinct developers. We monitored these apps over more than 6 months, and recorded their changes once every 2 days. This enabled us to collect up to 7,688 reviews per app, exceeding Google's one shot limit of 4,000 reviews. We collected the data of the 586,381 distinct reviewers of these apps, and built their co-activity graphs.

MCDense found at least 1 dense component of at least 5 accounts in 1,056 of the 13,087 apps (8%). Figure 8 compares the results of MCDense on the 1,056 apps, with those for the fraud and honest apps. The CDF of the number of components found by MCDense for these "wild" apps is closer to that of the fraud apps than to the honest apps: up to 19 components per app, see Figure 8(a). The CDF

of the maximum density of per app components reveals that 231 of the 1,056 apps (or 21.87%) had at least 1 component with edge density 1 (complete sub-graphs). The CDF of the size of the densest components (Figure 8(c)) found per each of the wild apps shows that similar to the 640 fraud apps, few of these apps have only 0 size densest components. The largest component found by MCDense for these apps has 90 accounts.

Validation of fraud suspicions. Upon close inspection of the 231 apps that had at least 1 component with edge density of 1 (i.e., clique), we found the following further evidence of suspicious fraud being perpetrated. (1) **Targeted by known fraudsters**: 169 of the 231 apps had received reviews from the 23 known fraudsters (§ 2.4). One app had received reviews from 10 of the fraudsters. (2) **Review duplicates**: 223 out of the 231 apps have received 10,563 *duplicate* reviews (that replicate the text of reviews posted for the same app, from a different account), or 25.55% of their total 41,339 reviews. One app alone has 1,274 duplicate reviews, out of a total of 4,251 reviews. (3) **Fraud re-posters**: our longitudinal monitoring of apps enabled us to detect fraud re-posters, accounts who re-post their reviews, hours to days after Google Play filters them out. One of the 231 apps received 37 fraud re-posts, from the same user account.

5 MCDENSE EVALUATION

We compare MCDense against DSG, a densest subgraph approach that we adapt based on [31]. DSG iteratively identifies multiple dense subgraphs of an app's co-activity graph $G = (U, E)$, each suspected to belong to a different worker. DSG peels off nodes of G until it runs out of nodes. During each "peeling" step, it removes the node that is least connected to the other nodes. After removing the node, the algorithm computes and saves the density of the resulting subgraph. The algorithm returns the subgraph with the highest density. We use the "triangle" density definition proposed in [31], $\rho_D = \frac{t(U)}{|U|}$, where $t(U)$ is the number of triangles formed by the vertices in U. DSG uses this greedy strategy iteratively: once it finds the densest subgraph D of G, DSG repeats the process, to find the densest subgraph in $G - D$.

To compare MCDense and DSG, we introduce a coverage score. Let $C = \{C_1, .., C_c, H_C\}$ be the partition of of the user accounts who reviewed an app A, returned by a fraud-component detection algorithm: $\forall a_i, a_j \in C_l$, are considered to be controlled by the same

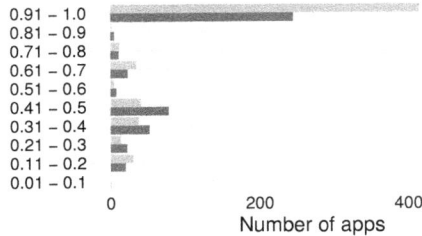

Figure 10: Comparison of the distribution of coverage scores for MCDense and DSG over 640 fraud apps. The y axis shows the p_1 value, and the x axis shows the number of apps for which MCDense and DSG achieve that p_1 value, when p_2 is 90%. MCDense outperforms DSG providing (90%+, 90%)-coverage for 416 (65%) of the apps vs. DSG's 245 apps.

worker, and H_C is the set of accounts considered to be honest. To quantify how well the partition C has detected the worker accounts $\overline{W_1}, .., \overline{W_w}$ who targeted A, we propose the "coverage" measure of worker $W_i \in S$ by a partition C, as $cov_i(C) = \frac{|\overline{W_i} \cap (C_1 \cup .. \cup C_c)|}{|\overline{W_i}|}$. Given $p \in [0, 1]$, we say that W_i is "p-covered" by C if $cov_i(C) \geq p$. Then, we say that partition C provides a (p_1, p_2)-coverage of the worker set S, if p_1 percent of the workers in S are p_2-covered by C.

Figure 10 compares the distribution of the coverage scores for MCDense and DSG over the 640 fraud apps. It shows that the number of apps for which at least 90% of their workers are at least 90%-covered is twice as high for MCDense than for DSG.

6 CONCLUSIONS

We introduced the fraud de-anonymization problem for search rank fraud in online services. We have collected fraud data from crowdsourcing sites and the Google Play store, and we have performed a user study with crowdsourcing fraudsters. We have proposed Dolos, a fraud de-anonymization system. Dolos correctly attributed 95% of the fraud detected for 640 Google Play apps, and identified at least 90% of the workers who promoted each of 87% of these apps. Dolos identified 1,056 out of 13,087 monitored Google Play apps, to have suspicious reviewer groups, and revealed a suite of observed fraud behaviors.

7 ACKNOWLEDGMENTS

This research was supported by NSF grants CNS-1527153, CNS-1526254 and CNS-1526494, and by the Florida Center for Cybersecurity.

REFERENCES

[1] Freelancer. http://www.freelancer.com. (????).
[2] Upwork Inc. https://www.upwork.com. (????).
[3] 2013. Google I/O 2013 - Getting Discovered on Google Play. www.youtube.com/watch?v=5Od2SuL2igA. (2013).
[4] Leman Akoglu, Rishi Chandy, and Christos Faloutsos. 2013. Opinion Fraud Detection in Online Reviews by Network Effects. In *Proceedings of ICWSM*.
[5] Leman Akoglu, Rishi Chandy, and Christos Faloutsos. 2013. Opinion Fraud Detection in Online Reviews by Network Effects. *Proceedings of ICWSM* (2013).
[6] Prudhvi Ratna Badri Satya, Kyumin Lee, Dongwon Lee, Thanh Tran, and Jason Jiasheng Zhang. 2016. Uncovering Fake Likers in Online Social Networks. In *Proceedings of the ACM CIKM*.

[7] Alex Beutel, Wanhong Xu, Venkatesan Guruswami, Christopher Palow, and Christos Faloutsos. 2013. CopyCatch: Stopping Group Attacks by Spotting Lockstep Behavior in Social Networks. In *Proceedings of the WWW*.
[8] Hao Chen, Daojing He, Sencun Zhu, and Jingshun Yang. 2017. Toward Detecting Collusive Ranking Manipulation Attackers in Mobile App Markets. In *Proceedings AsiaCCS*.
[9] Jason Cipriani. 2016. Google starts filtering fraudulent app reviews from Play Store. ZDNet, https://tinyurl.com/hklb5tk. (2016).
[10] Geli Fei, Arjun Mukherjee, Bing Liu, Meichun Hsu, Malu Castellanos, and Riddhiman Ghosh. 2013. Exploiting Burstiness in Reviews for Review Spammer Detection. *ICWSM* 13 (2013), 175–184.
[11] Fiverr. https://www.fiverr.com/. (????).
[12] Bryan Hooi, Neil Shah, Alex Beutel, Stephan Günnemann, Leman Akoglu, Mohit Kumar, Disha Makhija, and Christos Faloutsos. 2016. Birdnest: Bayesian inference for ratings-fraud detection. In *Proceedings of SDM*.
[13] Bryan Hooi, Hyun Ah Song, Alex Beutel, Neil Shah, Kijung Shin, and Christos Faloutsos. 2016. Fraudar: Bounding graph fraud in the face of camouflage. In *Proceedings of ACM KDD*.
[14] JStylo. The JStylo Open Source Project on Open Hub. https://www.openhub.net/p/jstylo. (????).
[15] Parisa Kaghazgaran, James Caverlee, and Majid Alfifi. 2017. Behavioral Analysis of Review Fraud: Linking Malicious Crowdsourcing to Amazon and Beyond.. In *Proceedings of ICWSM*.
[16] David R Karger. 1993. Global Min-cuts in RNC, and Other Ramifications of a Simple Min-Cut Algorithm.. In *SODA*, Vol. 93.
[17] Raymond YK Lau, SY Liao, Ron Chi Wai Kwok, Kaiquan Xu, Yunqing Xia, and Yuefeng Li. 2011. Text mining and probabilistic language modeling for online review spam detecting. *ACM Transactions on Management Information Systems* 2, 4 (2011), 1–30.
[18] Huayi Li, Geli Fei, Shuai Wang, Bing Liu, Weixiang Shao, Arjun Mukherjee, and Jidong Shao. 2017. Bimodal distribution and co-bursting in review spam detection. In *Proceedings of ACM WWW*.
[19] Michael Luca. 2011. Reviews, Reputation, and Revenue: The Case of Yelp.Com. *SSRN eLibrary* (2011).
[20] Arjun Mukherjee, Abhinav Kumar, Bing Liu, Junhui Wang, Meichun Hsu, Malu Castellanos, and Riddhiman Ghosh. 2013. Spotting opinion spammers using behavioral footprints. In *Proceedings of the ACM KDD*.
[21] Arjun Mukherjee, Bing Liu, and Natalie Glance. 2012. Spotting Fake Reviewer Groups in Consumer Reviews. In *Proceedings of ACM WWW*.
[22] Arjun Mukherjee, Vivek Venkataraman, Bing Liu, and Natalie Glance. 2013. What Yelp Fake Review Filter Might Be Doing. In *Proceedings of ICWSM*.
[23] Myle Ott, Yejin Choi, Claire Cardie, and Jeffrey T. Hancock. 2011. Finding deceptive opinion spam by any stretch of the imagination. In *Proceedings of the Human Language Technologies (HLT '11)*.
[24] Rebekah Overdorf and Rachel Greenstadt. 2016. Blogs, Twitter Feeds, and Reddit Comments: Cross-domain Authorship Attribution. *PoPETs* 2016, 3 (2016).
[25] Sarah Perez. 2016. Amazon bans incentivized reviews tied to free or discounted products. Tech Crunch, https://tinyurl.com/zgn9sq3. (2016).
[26] Bryan Perozzi, Rami Al-Rfou, and Steven Skiena. 2014. Deepwalk: Online learning of social representations. In *Proceedings of ACM KDD*.
[27] Huffington Post. 2012. Yelp Study Shows Extra Half-Star Nets Restaurants 19More Reservations. Huffington Post, https://tinyurl.com/y7u32ssl. (2012).
[28] Mahmudur Rahman, Mizanur Rahman, Bogdan Carbunar, and Polo Chau. 2016. Fairplay: Fraud and Malware Detection in Google Play. In *Proceedings of SDM*.
[29] Shebuti Rayana and Leman Akoglu. 2015. Collective opinion spam detection: Bridging review networks and metadata. In *Proceedings of ACM KDD*.
[30] Chih-Ya Shen, Liang-Hao Huang, De-Nian Yang, Hong-Han Shuai, Wang-Chien Lee, and Ming-Syan Chen. 2017. On Finding Socially Tenuous Groups for Online Social Networks. In *Proceedings of KDD*.
[31] Charalampos E. Tsourakakis. 2015. The K-clique Densest Subgraph Problem. In *Proceedings of ACM WWW*.
[32] Binghui Wang, Neil Zhenqiang Gong, and Hao Fu. 2017. GANG: Detecting Fraudulent Users in Online Social Networks via Guilt-by-Association on Directed Graphs. In *Proceedings of ICDM*.
[33] Zhen Xie and Sencun Zhu. 2014. GroupTie: Toward Hidden Collusion Group Discovery in App Stores. In *Proceedings of ACM WiSec*.
[34] Zhen Xie and Sencun Zhu. 2015. AppWatcher: Unveiling the Underground Market of Trading Mobile App Reviews. In *Proceedings of ACM WiSec*.
[35] Chao Yang, Robert Harkreader, Jialong Zhang, Seungwon Shin, and Guofei Gu. 2012. Analyzing spammers' social networks for fun and profit: a case study of cyber criminal ecosystem on Twitter. In *Proceedings of ACM WWW*.
[36] Junting Ye and Leman Akoglu. 2015. Discovering opinion spammer groups by network footprints. In *Machine Learning and Knowledge Discovery in Databases*.

Learning to Rank Social Bots

Diego Perna
DIMES, University of Calabria
Rende (CS), Italy
d.perna@dimes.unical.it

Andrea Tagarelli
DIMES, University of Calabria
Rende (CS), Italy
andrea.tagarelli@unical.it

ABSTRACT

Software robots, or simply bots, have often been regarded as harmless programs confined within the cyberspace. However, recent events in our society proved that they can have important effects on real life as well. Bots have in fact become one of the key tools for disseminating information through online social networks (OSNs), influencing their members and eventually changing their opinions. With a focus on classification, social bot detection has lately emerged as a major topic in OSN analysis; nevertheless more research is needed to enhance our understanding of such automated behaviors, particularly to unveil the characteristics that better differentiate legitimate accounts from bots. We argue that this demands for learning behavioral models that should be trained using a large and heterogeneous set of behavioral features, so to detect and characterize OSN accounts according to their status as bots. Within this view, in this work we push forward research on bot analysis by proposing a machine-learning framework for identifying and ranking OSN accounts based on their degree of bot relevance. Our framework exploits the most known existing methods on bot detection for enhanced feature extraction, and state-of-the-art learning-to-rank methods, using different optimization and evaluation criteria. Results obtained on Twitter data show the significance and effectiveness of our approach in detecting and ranking bot accounts.

CCS CONCEPTS

• **Information systems → Learning to rank**; **Social networks**;

KEYWORDS

social bot analysis, bot detection, Twitter data

ACM Reference Format:
Diego Perna and Andrea Tagarelli. 2018. Learning to Rank Social Bots. In *HT '18: 29th ACM Conference on Hypertext and Social Media, July 9–12, 2018, Baltimore, MD, USA.* ACM, New York, NY, USA, 9 pages. https://doi.org/10.1145/3209542.3209563

1 INTRODUCTION

Software robots, or bots, are computer programs designed to carry out one or more specific automated tasks. *Social bots* are a particular type of chat-bots employed in social media platforms to automatically interact with members and generate contents. Bots can be used to provide useful services such as customer support, meeting scheduling, tracking of product shippings, and so on. On the other hand, social bots often mimic a human being by controlling a social media account, and when acting as a group (i.e., botnet) they can also pursue malevolent intents, such as fostering fame [11, 42], biasing public opinion [2, 39], spamming or limiting free speech by submerging important messages with a deluge of automated bot messages [16].

In the last years, also thanks to minimal skill requirements, the use of automated accounts has seen an unprecedented rise [4, 19, 29]. Remarkably, groups of orchestrated bots are being used to steer public opinion and influence the electoral audience through the spread of (mis)information and fake news [25]; the most representative example is related to the latest US presidential election [2, 39], but several other cases can be listed [27, 31, 32, 38].

Bot detection is a challenging problem, also due to the variety of strategies implemented by bots. For instance, they can mimic human behavior in order to blend in among legitimate accounts (i.e., users) and earn their trust, making bot detection more difficult [1, 47]. Bots can also achieve an amplifying effect by replicating contents related to a specific topic in order to distort the perception of its popularity, or create the appearance of grassroots support for a position (i.e., astroturfing) by over-promoting that point of view [28, 54]. The software behind social botnets is constantly evolving, introducing new expedients that result in sophisticated simulations of human behavior in OSNs [4, 29, 45], making the identification of automated accounts ever more complicated. Therefore, there is an emergence for the development of effective methods able to better understanding the behavioral patterns that characterize automated OSN accounts.

Despite several approaches have been developed to detect bots in OSNs, a single method often covers only one specific pattern of automated behavior, leaving the detection challenge open. Taking inspiration from ensemble learning theory, whereby multiple weak learners are combined together in order to boost prediction performance, in this work we aim at developing a more general framework for the identification of bots at different severity levels, by exploiting different sources of information. Within this view, we rise the following questions:

- *How can we exploit previously identified automated accounts to learn a model for detecting bots at different degrees and ranking them?*
- *Which OSN account characteristics are best suited to model bot behavioral features?*
- *Can we successfully combine different bot-detection methods for an enhanced understanding of bot behavioral patterns?*

To answer the above research questions, our approach in this work is to resort to the machine-learning ranking paradigm, or *learning-to-rank* (LTR), for automatically building a bot ranking model. In LTR, a ranking function is learned from training data corresponding to multiple queries, whose annotations are based on the degree of relevance of objects to a given query.

LTR can help us to improve our understanding of automated behaviors in online social environments. We believe, indeed, that the inherent complexity of the bot detection problem hints at the exploitation of techniques capable of determining the status as bot of a (suspected) OSN account, rather than simply indicating whether or not an account is a bot. The supervised approach of learning from past user experiences, which is adopted in LTR, can be profitably exploited to build a ranking model from data (i.e., OSN accounts) previously annotated according to their degree of bot relevance. Moreover, the training of an LTR model can be carried out by capturing the different aspects of automated behaviors that characterize accounts from different social media platforms. LTR also offers unprecedented opportunities for incremental analysis scenarios, since once trained, the LTR model can be used to assign any previously unobserved account with a bot relevance score.

In this work, we propose the first LTR framework to discover social bots in OSNs at different severity levels. Based on state-of-the-art LTR methods, we develop a *learning-to-rank-social-bot* methodology, hereinafter denoted as LTRSB, that exploits features extracted from OSN account information of different types (including user profile, user's activity rate, media content) and is supported by three of the most known bot-detection methods, namely *DeBot*, *BotWalk*, and *BotOrNot*. Results obtained on four datasets built on Twitter have shown that LTR can be effective for unveiling automated behaviors.

The remainder of this paper is organized as follows. Section 2 briefly discusses related work, whereas Section 3 describes LTR and bot-detection methods utilized in our framework. Section 4 is devoted to the proposed LTRSB framework. Section 5 presents experimental results and Section 6 concludes the paper.

2 RELATED WORK

Bot detection. Currently adopted approaches for bot detection belong to three main categories: graph-based, time-series-analysis-based, and hybrid methods. The former group utilizes network information (e.g., contacts, interactions, (re)tweets) in order to discern between legitimate accounts and bots [9, 36, 50]. The second group of methods focuses on identifying distinctive temporal behavioral patterns of bots (e.g., burst of interactions, non-stop activity, etc.) [3, 10, 13, 46, 52]. The third group includes software systems that are designed to use features of different type to train one classifier [15, 17, 44] or an ensemble of classifiers [18]. A different perspective is taken from *BotWalk* [34], which computes an aggregated anomaly score based on an ensemble of unsupervised anomaly detection methods.

Remarkably, most of the existing methods aim to detect bots either focusing on a specific aspect of automated behavior, and for this reason they cannot be considered general enough, or by exploiting features of different type while, however, focusing on binary classification problems.

Learning-to-rank in OSNs. LTR is widely used as a key-enabling technology in web science and related fields [12, 30]. Originally developed to meet the rising needs of modern web retrieval systems, LTR techniques have also been exploited in OSN analysis contexts. In particular, LTR frameworks have been developed to tackle problems such as hashtag recommendation [41], credibility assessment of tweet content [23], ranking answers in large online question/answer collections [43], and also to address behavioral problems as user engagement [37, 53]. Nevertheless, to the best of our knowledge, LTR has never been used so far to address bot detection problems.

3 BACKGROUND

3.1 Learning-to-rank methods

LTR is a supervised approach to learn a ranking model from annotated instances. Note that margin-based classifiers are not designed to consider the ranking information, so that no guarantee is in principle provided about the rank consistency property, and its violation is some cases could lead to better separability between positive/negative instances rather than better retrieval performance (e.g., [40]). Depending on how the input data is represented according to the objective function of the corresponding optimization problem, LTR methods are typically organized into three categories, namely *pointwise*, *pairwise* and *listwise* [8, 30]. Pointwise methods predict the score of every learning instance, in the form of query-object pair. Since ordinal scales are mapped into numeric values, the ranking problem can be seen as regression or ordinal classification. Pairwise methods learn the overall ranking model from the relative ordering of every pair of objects (i.e., which object in a pair precedes the other in the ranking), thus the objective function is to minimize the number of switched/misclassified object pairs. In listwise methods, a learning instance is comprised of a query and its objects, and a quality criterion (e.g. $P@k$, $nDCG@k$, etc.) is optimized over all queries in the training data. In this work, we focus on four representative methods of the pairwise and listwise categories, namely *RankNet*, *Coordinate Ascent*, *AdaRank*, and *LambdaMART*.

RankNet [7] is a pairwise method, which has been employed in commercial search engines (e.g., Microsoft Bing®). In RankNet, the optimization problem is modeled with a cross entropy cost function, which evaluates the difference between the target probability $\bar{P}_{ij}$ and the modeled probability P_{ij}, for each pair objects i, j:

$$C_{ij} = -\bar{P}_{ij} \log(P_{ij}) - (1 - \bar{P}_{ij}) \log(1 - P_{ij}). \quad (1)$$

Backpropagation is used to minimize the cost function, whose parameters are learnt through a neural network with two hidden layers and an output node.

Coordinate Ascent [33] is a listwise method, whereby the scores of the query-object pairs are computed as weighted combination of the features values. It leverages a derivative-free optimization technique, called coordinate ascent optimization, in which the optimization is performed in one dimension at a time while keeping the other dimensions fixed, and allowing the use of any IR evaluation criterion to be plugged in the objective function. If we denote with λ_i the i-th parameter to learn, the update rule is given by:

$$\lambda_i' = \arg\max_{\lambda_i} E(R_\Delta, T), \quad (2)$$

where R_Δ is the set of rankings induced over all of the queries, T is the training data, and $E(\cdot, \cdot)$ denotes an evaluation function.

Also belonging to the listwise category, *AdaRank* [51] follows a boosting approach (like AdaBoost [20]) and a stepwise greedy optimization technique to maximize a selected IR criterion by repeatedly building "weak rankers" on the basis of re-weighted training data. The ranking predictions are finally obtained by linearly combining the weak rankers. To this purpose, higher weights are assigned to queries whose relevant objects are more difficult to rank, whereas lower weights are assigned to already learned queries, according to the forward stage-wise additive modeling paradigm. AdaRank minimizes the following function:

$$\min_{\substack{h_t \in \mathcal{H} \\ \alpha_t \in \mathbf{R}^+}} L(h_t, \alpha_t) = \sum_{i=1}^{m} \exp(-E(\pi(q_i, \mathbf{d_i}, f_{t-1} + \alpha_t h_t), \mathbf{y_i})), \quad (3)$$

where E denotes the selected quality criterion, $\mathbf{y_i}$ corresponds to the relevance labels (i.e., desired ranks), $\mathcal{H}$ denotes the set of possible weak rankers h_t, α_t is a positive weight, and π is a permutation for the i-th query q_i, the list $\mathbf{d_i}$ of retrieved documents for q_i, and the ranking model f.

LambdaMART [49] is a tree ensemble model that combines the ideas behind LambdaRank [6] and MART [21]. The former performs optimization via the gradient of the loss function, while the latter is a boosted regression tree model in which the output is a linear combination of the outputs of a set of regression trees. LambdaRank is based on a neural network, like RankNet, and it stands out for one main aspect: instead of focusing on the definition of a less expensive cost function, it takes into account the gradient of the cost function directly, avoiding the additional computational cost introduced by sorting operations [5]. For each pair of objects i, j, the λ-gradient is defined as:

$$\lambda_{ij} = S_{ij} \left| \Delta Z_{ij} \frac{\partial C_{ij}}{\partial(s_i - s_j)} \right|, \quad (4)$$

where $s_i - s_j$ is the difference of ranking scores of the two objects w.r.t. a query, $C_{ij} = s_i - s_j + \log(1 + \exp(s_i - s_j))$ is the cross-entropy cost, ΔZ_{ij} is the evaluation value gained by swapping the two objects, and S_{ij} is equal to +1 if object i is more relevant than object j, -1 otherwise.

3.2 Bot detection methods

We focus our attention on three of the most relevant and recent methods for bot classification, namely *BotOrNot* [17, 44], *DeBot* [13], and *BotWalk* [34].

Given a Twitter screen-name as input, *BotOrNot* [17, 44] retrieves information about the activity of the account to generate a fairly extensive set of features. BotOrNot resorts to a classifier to compute a score describing the likelihood that an account is a bot. Various standard classification models were tested in [44], including AdaBoost, logistic regression, decision trees, and Random Forest; the latter model, which relies on an ensemble learning approach to combine many decision trees, was found the most accurate to produce bot-likelihood scores.

DeBot [13] approach is to detect accounts characterized by high temporally correlated activities. Each account timeline is represented by the tweet/retweet actions performed by the account at

each time step. To compare time series, DeBot defines a correlation measure based on *dynamic-time-warping* (DTW) [48]. DTW is a classic method to compute the distance between two sequences by warping them locally to the same length (i.e., it allows one-to-many mappings between series to stretch a sequence, or many-to-one mappings to compress a sequence). The DTW-based correlation between two (normalized) time series $\hat{x}$ and $\hat{y}$ is defined as:

$$wC(x, y) = 1 - \frac{DTW^2(\hat{x}, \hat{y})}{2P}, \quad (5)$$

where P is the number of squared errors that are added to obtain a distance (i.e., the path length) [13]. DeBot performs a 4-stage workflow: first, tweets that contain selected keywords are gathered for a period of T hours, then it assembles the time series for each user. These series are processed based on a hash index in order to identify correlated activity patterns between two or multiple accounts. Third, the activity of suspected accounts is closely monitored through the stream Twitter API. The last step computes a pairwise warped correlation matrix, over the newly generated time series, and generates clusters of highly correlated users.

BotWalk [34] is a nearly real-time adaptive bot-identification method based on an ensemble of anomaly detection methods. Like DeBot, BotWalk adopts an unsupervised approach and focuses on specific patterns of automated behavior. In addition, BotWalk utilizes 130 features extracted from network, content, temporal and metadata information. Starting from a seed-bot and a set of random accounts, BotWalk retrieves each account's details, timeline, and one-hop follower neighborhood, with the goal of maximizing the likelihood of reaching other bots across the OSN. The output of the method is represented by an aggregated score, obtained by combining four different anomaly detection scores.

4 PROPOSED FRAMEWORK

4.1 Overview

Figure 1 shows a schematic illustration of the proposed **L**earning-**T**o-**R**ank-**S**ocial-**B**ots (**LTRSB**) framework.

We are given a database storing information about legitimate accounts and bots gathered from heterogeneous sources. This database feeds information to a component that is in charge of (i) repeatedly selecting a subset of accounts to define queries for the LTR module, and (ii) extracting static as well as dynamic features of different types, as we shall describe later.

In this work, we use Twitter as case in point, although our framework is in principle designed to be versatile and applicable to other OSN platforms. The feature extraction step is performed through Twitter API as well as through retrieving functionalities provided by BotOrNot, BotWalk and DeBot methods. In particular, Twitter API and BotOrNot are used to retrieve static and aggregate features, whereas BotWalk and DeBot are used to compute query-based features. More in detail, each DeBot run is characterized by a time-window of fixed length, in which all the users belonging to the query are being listened in order to compute clusters. Clusters are then examined to compute the warped correlation matrix and, finally, the DeBot features.

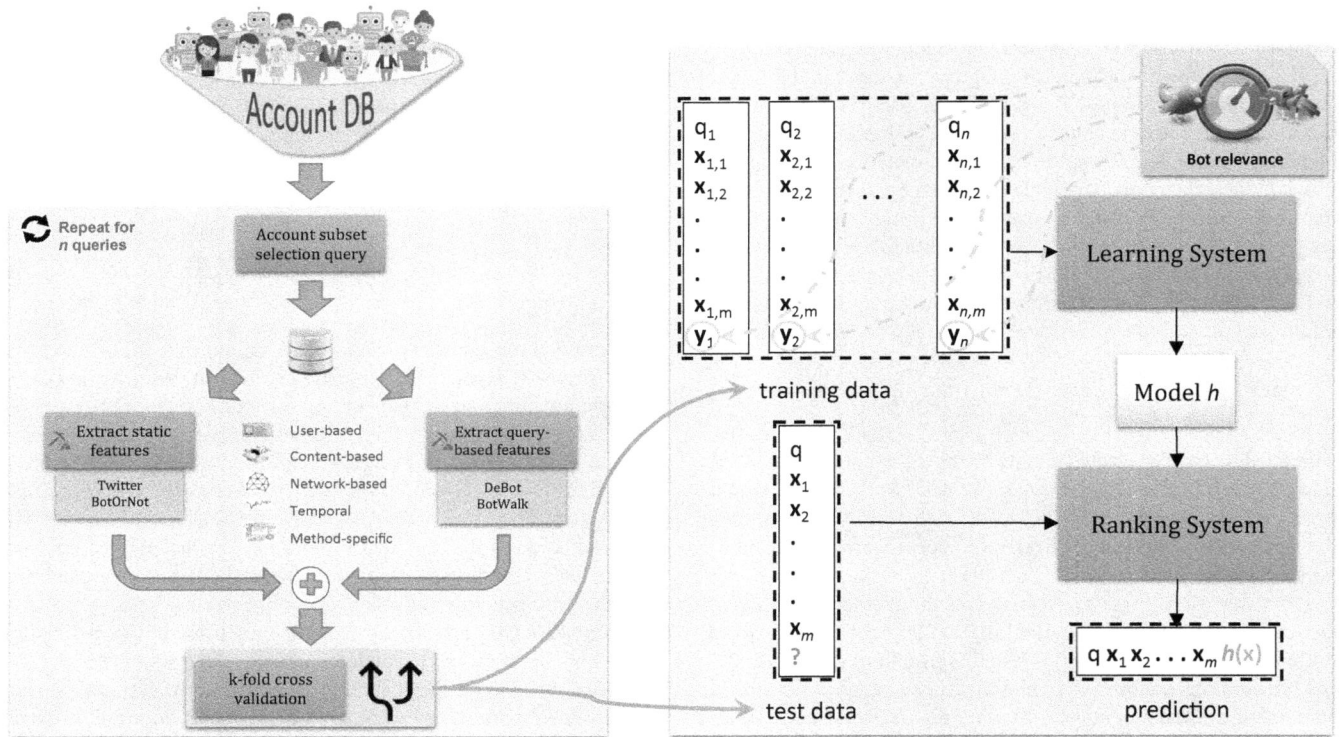

Figure 1: Main modules and data flows of our proposed learning-to-rank-social-bot (LTRSB) framework

4.2 Account database

Table 1 shows main characteristics of our evaluation data stored into an account database, for a total of about 19K accounts, 11K of which correspond to bots and the remaining to non-bots. Most of the account instances are from datasets originally built and analyzed in recent studies [16, 22, 35, 44]. From each of these datasets we removed accounts that are suspended by Twitter or no longer active. Moreover, we gathered additional bot instances from Twitter through several DeBot runs.

The account instances stored in the database were originally annotated with a binary ground-truth label (i.e., bot or non-bot), according to three different approaches as reported in Table 1. The majority of instances were labeled by human experts. Accounts from [35] were instead labeled depending on whether an account is a follower of a target *honeypot* account. (Since honeypots are designed in such a way that a human can immediately tell if they are bots, any user in the network that connects to a honeypot will be considered as a bot.) In addition to the datasets available from other studies, we exploited DeBot, which has shown to provide almost null false-positive rate, to further collect bot instances having correlation score of 0.995 or above.

4.3 Training data

LTR training data consists of triplets ⟨*query, object, relevance label*⟩. We are given n queries, each corresponding to a subset of m object-label pairs. Each object is an account's feature vector, and

Table 1: Composition of the Account DB

bots	non-bots	source	annotations
452	970	[44]	human generated
1254	1595	[22]	human generated
5937	2819	[16]	human generated
2371	2567	[35]	honeypot-based
1420	–	DeBot runs	DTW-based
11434	7951	*Total*	

the relevance label denotes one or several grades of *bot status*, so that higher grades correspond to more likely bots.

4.3.1 **Relevance labeling.** We devised three approaches to bot relevance labeling, depending on the selection of relevant/non-relevant instances, and the type of relevance label:

- In the first configuration, dubbed BB, we considered *binary* relevance, i.e., bot and non-bot, and performed a *balanced* selection of relevant and non-relevant accounts.
- In the second configuration, dubbed UB, we again considered *binary* relevance, and performed unbalanced selection of relevant (30%) and non-relevant (70%) accounts.
- In the third configuration, dubbed Grad, we considered balanced selection of relevant and non-relevant accounts, with 7 grades of *bot status*.

The first two configurations of relevance labeling correspond to the use the original binary-annotation information in the datasets reported in Table 1. For the Grad configuration, we computed the relevance labels as follows. First, we uniformed the feature representation for all the accounts in our database to the BotOrNot model, by retrieving from Twitter missing information for all the accounts not previously processed by BotOrNot. Second, we applied the BotOrNot-RandomForest classifier to produce the bot likelihood score for each instance, which varies within $[0, 1]$. Third, the bot scores were discretized into seven intervals: the lowest interval, $[0, 0.3]$, corresponds to certainly legitimate accounts, intermediate intervals are subsequently derived with increment of 0.1, and the highest interval, $[0.8, 1]$, corresponds to certainly bot accounts.

4.3.2 Feature set.
We organize the set of features extracted from our data into five categories: *user-based*, *network-based*, *temporal*, *content-based*, and *aggregate* features.

Table 2 provides a concise description of the features. User-based features describe Twitter account settings and basic information, such as account lifetime, time-zone and language, and whether the account was verified or not. Network-based features describe node-wise properties of a user in the social network graph, and include indicators of the user's centrality, popularity and role. Content-based features represent the largest group and include several indicators of the diversity of the content created by a user. Considering normal human-limitations in terms of time spent on social-media platforms, we defined several activity-rate features as indicators of overproduction. We also included basic statistics on the inter-arrival time of consecutive tweets, and on user activity distributions to gain insights into content production patterns of social bots. The last group of features is comprised of nine aggregate indicators provided by BotOrNot (i.e., from A.1 to A.9) and a query-wise score produced by the BotWalk anomaly detection task.

Note that, to ensure comparability across queries, all feature values were scaled between 0 and 1, through min-max normalization.

4.3.3 Feature informativeness.
We investigated about the usefulness or informativeness of the features, with a twofold goal: to discover any correlations between features (possibly w.r.t. the relevance class attribute), and to estimate their impact on the ranking prediction performance. For this purpose, we resorted to five standard methods used in feature selection tasks: principal component analysis (PCA), information gain (IG) and gain ratio (GR) attribute evaluation, OneR [26], correlation-based feature selection (CFS) [24], and learner-based feature selection exploiting J48 decision tree model.

The outcome of the analysis, carried out on data with binary labels, confirmed the significance of most of the feature categories, without however identifying an absolute winning category. Content-based and aggregate features were mostly selected by the above methods. More in detail, results obtained by CFS, PCA and J48 were quite diversified, including all types of features in the case of CFS, and all types except temporal-based features in the case of PCA and J48. GR, IG, and OneR methods tended to almost evenly select network-based, content-based and aggregate features.

Conversely, the same evaluation process carried out on data with graded relevance labels showed, as expected, a bias toward BotOrNot aggregate features. While BotOrNot features, used in

this work, are strongly correlated with Grad relevance labels, they are less evidently correlated with human generated labels, suggesting the opportunity of further investigation in terms of feature engineering and model design.

Overall, this evaluation step highlighted the necessity of diversifying features in such a context. As we shall declare in our evaluation goals (cf. Section 4.5), this prompted us to focus the evaluation of our framework on using either the full space of features or different subsets of feature categories.

4.4 Quality criteria and framework setting
We considered standard IR criteria for ranking evaluation [14, 30], namely mean average precision (*MAP*), precision at the top-k (*P@k*), and normalized discounted cumulative gain (*nDCG@k*).

In our evaluation we included all the LTR methods discussed in Section 3. We used the Java implementations of *RankLib* under the *The Lemur Project*, with default settings.[1]

We trained and tested through 5-cross-validation each of the LTR methods using *MAP*, *P@k*, and *nDCG@k*, with $k \in \{10, 100\}$, both for optimization (except for RankNet) and evaluation; the latter two measures were averaged over all queries, for a given rank threshold k. Note also that we used the three criteria for all settings of relevance labels; in particular, in the Grad case, for criteria that are not designed to leverage graded relevance values (i.e., *MAP* and *P@k*), we considered nonzero label-values as relevant, otherwise as non-relevant.

We defined $n = 20$ queries, each of which corresponding to $m = 1000$ instances. Also, we set to 15 minutes the width of the listening time-window in DeBot executions.

4.5 Evaluation goals
We pursue two main evaluation goals, depending on either the whole feature space or part of it was used to learn an LTRSB model. On the one hand, in the latter case, we assessed the LTRSB capability of predicting automated behaviors in OSNs by separately using each of the five groups of features in the construction of the ranking models. On the other hand, when using the whole feature space, we aimed at evaluating LTRSB in capturing different bot behavioral patterns based on heterogeneous data.

5 EXPERIMENTAL RESULTS
We organize the presentation of experimental results according to the previously discussed evaluation goals. For each stage of evaluation, we will summarize results through *heatmaps*, with numerical detail on the performance scores corresponding to the various assessment criteria, by varying LTR method and setting. Note that, for the sake of readability, particularly to avoid cluttering of the figures, we have intentionally hidden entries in every heatmap that refer to optimal performance values (i.e., equal to 1).

5.1 Evaluation w.r.t. feature subsets
Figures 2–4 show performance of the methods considered in the LTRSB framework, using one category of features at a time, under different settings of the relevance labels. At a first glance, we

---

[1] http://www.lemurproject.org

Table 2: Extracted features and their description

	id	description
User-based	U.1	Short length of user description
	U.2	Number of links appearing in the description
	U.3	URL website (Boolean value)
	U.4	Verified account (Boolean value)
	U.5	Number of lists created by the user
	U.6	Number of posts (tweets)
	U.7	Account lifetime
	U.8	Geo enabled (Boolean value)
	U.9	Time zone (ID number)
	U.10	Language (ID number)
	U.11	Default profile & background (Boolean value)
	U.12	Default profile image (Boolean value)
Network-based	N.1	Number of followers
	N.2	Number of friends (followees)
	N.3	Number of tweets with at least one mention
	N.4	Number of mentions
	N.5	Number of duplicate mentions
	N.6	Follower / followee ratio
	N.7	Mention / tweet ratio
Temporal	T.1	Duration of the longest tweet session without breaks longer than 10 minutes
	T.2	Mean (μ) of the inter-arrival time of consecutive tweets
	T.3	Minimum of the inter-arrival time of consecutive tweets
	T.4	Maximum of the inter-arrival time of consecutive tweets
	T.5	Standard deviation (σ) of the inter-arrival time of consecutive tweets
	T.6	Burstiness, i.e., $(\sigma - \mu)/(\sigma + \mu)$
	T.7	χ^2 second-of-minute, refers to tweet distributions across time
	T.8	χ^2 minute-of-hour, refers to tweet distributions across time
	T.9	χ^2 hour-of-day, refers to tweet distributions across time
	T.10	Average number of tweets per day
	T.11	Maximum number of tweets per day
	T.12	Minimum number of tweets per day
	T.13	Standard deviation of number of tweets per day
	T.14	Entropy inter-arrival time
	T.15	Average number of likes per day
	T.16	Average number of tweets per day
	T.17	Query-wise average DTW-based Correlation [DeBot]
	T.18	Query-wise DTW-based Correlation offset [DeBot]
	T.19	Query-wise activity rate [DeBot]

	id	description
Content-based(*)	C.1	Number of favorites/likes
	C.2	Number of tweets
	C.3	Number of tweets with at least one hashtag
	C.4	Number of tweets with at least one URL
	C.5	Number of retweets performed
	C.6	Number of URLs
	C.7	Number of domains
	C.8	Number of hashtags
	C.9	Number of retweets received
	C.10	Number of duplicate URLs
	C.11	Number of duplicate domains
	C.12	Number of duplicate hashtags
	C.13	Mean of the Jaccard similarity of inter-tweet bag-of-words
	C.14	Minimum of the Jaccard similarity of inter-tweet bag-of-words
	C.15	Maximum of the Jaccard similarity of inter-tweet bag-of-words
	C.16	Standard deviation of the Jaccard similarity of inter-tweet bag-of-words
	C.17	Average number of special characters
	C.18	Minimum number of special characters
	C.19	Maximum number of special characters
	C.20	Standard deviation of number of special characters
	C.21	Average of tweet lengths
	C.22	Minimum of tweet lengths
	C.23	Maximum of tweet lengths
	C.24	Standard deviation of tweet lengths
	C.25	Retweets / tweets ratio
	C.26	Number of URLs on tweets
	C.27	Number of hashtags on tweets
	C.28	Number of media files (photos or videos) on tweets
	C.29	Average number of retweets received per tweet
	C.30	Average number of likes/favorites received per tweet
Aggregate	A.1	Content indicator (based on statistics about length and entropy of shared text, POS tagging, etc.) [BotOrNot]
	A.2	Friend indicator (based on follower-friend relations, number of replies, etc.) [BotOrNot]
	A.3	Network indicator (based on mentions, retweets, and hashtags) [BotOrNot]
	A.4	Sentiment indicator (based on several sentiment extraction techniques) [BotOrNot]
	A.5	Temporal indicator [BotOrNot]
	A.6	User's basic information [BotOrNot]
	A.7	Universal score (overall score for universal language) [BotOrNot]
	A.8	English score (overall score for English language) [BotOrNot]
	A.9	Overall score (average value between universal and English score) [BotOrNot]
	A.10	Query-wise aggregated anomaly score [BotWalk]

(*) Statistics about content-based features refer to the *recent* activity of a user.

observe a variegate situation, whereby the status of bot can be successfully determined only for some particular configurations.

Results corresponding to the balanced binary relevance setting (Fig. 2) show that Coordinate Ascent and LambdaMART are able to achieve good performance for most of the configurations of the assessment criteria and feature subsets, and in general they outperform the other two LTR methods. In particular, for top-10 precision and *nDCG*, LambdaMART can even achieve optimal performance when using network-based, temporal and content-based features. On average, over the various assessment criteria, aggregate features, followed by content-based features, reveal to be a more robust support for the learning task at hand, to any of the LTR methods; however, there is an evident emergence for using a more comprehensive feature space for methods like RankNet and AdaRank. Overall, the variability of performance across feature groups would suggest that, due to the inherent difficulty of the detection task at hand, a single subset (i.e., type) of features is not

sufficient to effectively learn a ranking function capable of identifying *all* different behavioral patterns that might characterize bots or bot-nets.

Under the unbalanced binary relevance (UB), we aimed to stress the LTRSB ability to learn from fewer examples of bots, thus making the ranking task more difficult. Results shown in Fig. 3 confirm the above-mentioned challenge. Overall, quite poor performance characterizes RankNet, especially when using aggregate features only, and AdaRank, with user-based and network-based features only. LambdaMART and Coordinate Ascent reveal to be able to learn a ranking model that can successfully rank the top-10 instances, using any subset of features, though their performance in terms of all assessment criteria significantly decrease when considering top-100 or all instances.

As previously stated, the third scenario (Grad) corresponds to a balanced selection of relevant and non-relevant instances, with graded relevance labels derived from the bot probabilities computed

AdaRank 0.505 0.730 0.520 0.515 0.467
Coord.Ascent 0.772 0.817 0.809 0.895 0.770
LambdaMART 0.716 0.980 0.453 0.965 0.815
RankNet 0.725 0.839 0.759 0.835 0.735
Method
MAP NDCG@10 NDCG@100 P@10 P@100
Criterion
1.0 0.8 0.6 0.4 0.2 0.0

(a) User-based features

AdaRank 0.505 0.354 0.495 0.315 0.500
Coord.Ascent 0.724 0.802 0.885 0.694
LambdaMART 0.799 0.713 0.627
RankNet 0.717 0.759 0.722 0.760 0.701
Method
MAP NDCG@10 NDCG@100 P@10 P@100
Criterion
1.0 0.8 0.6 0.4 0.2 0.0

(b) Network-based features

AdaRank 0.505 0.756 0.495 0.775 0.785
Coord.Ascent 0.776 0.917 0.693 0.900 0.873
LambdaMART 0.739 0.841 0.872
RankNet 0.650 0.813 0.671 0.805 0.630
Method
MAP NDCG@10 NDCG@100 P@10 P@100
Criterion
1.0 0.8 0.6 0.4 0.2 0.0

(c) Temporal features

AdaRank 0.505 0.896 0.596 0.970 0.587
Coord.Ascent 0.832 0.974 0.862 0.940 0.838
LambdaMART 0.777 0.903 0.904
RankNet 0.722 0.914 0.739 0.910 0.710
Method
MAP NDCG@10 NDCG@100 P@10 P@100
Criterion
1.0 0.8 0.6 0.4 0.2 0.0

(d) Content-based features

AdaRank 0.743 0.972 0.886 0.935 0.867
Coord.Ascent 0.876 0.989 0.894 0.965 0.857
LambdaMART 0.789 0.994 0.887 0.990 0.872
RankNet 0.517 0.544 0.514 0.525 0.506
Method
MAP NDCG@10 NDCG@100 P@10 P@100
Criterion
1.0 0.8 0.6 0.4 0.2 0.0

(e) Aggregate features

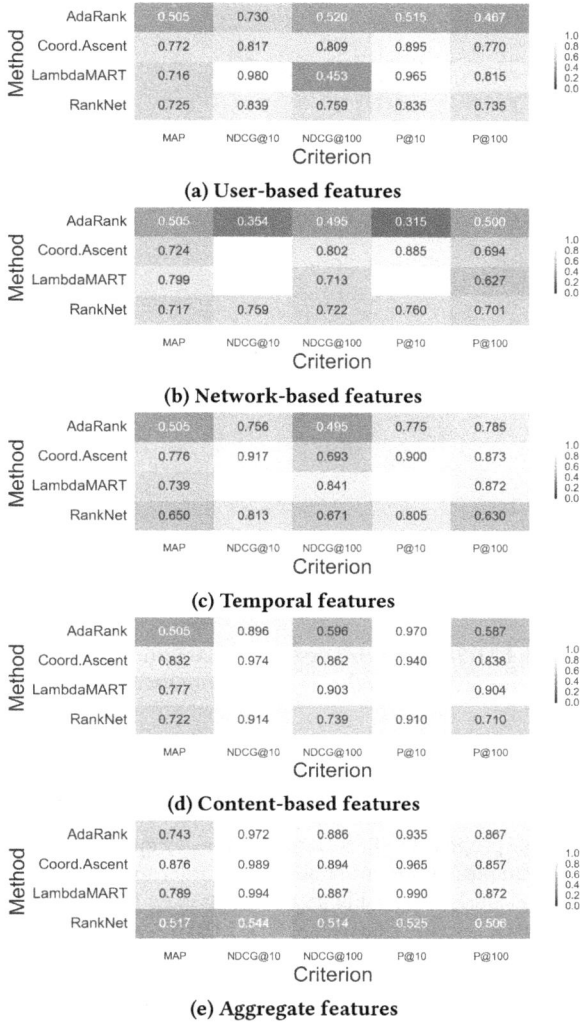

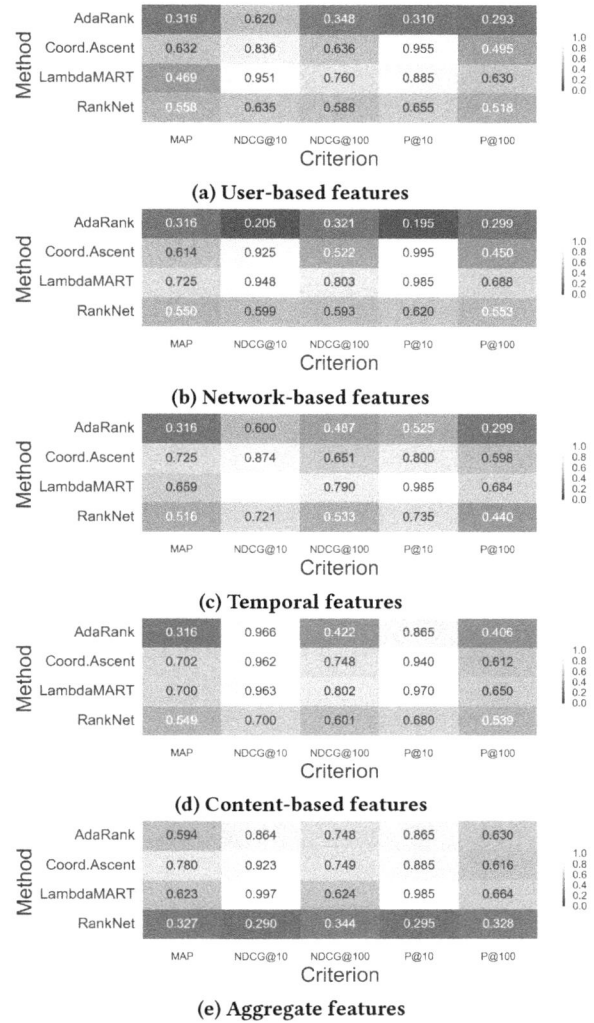

Figure 2: LTRSB performance on all data, with balanced binary relevance (BB), and using different subsets of features.

AdaRank 0.316 0.620 0.348 0.310 0.293
Coord.Ascent 0.632 0.836 0.636 0.955 0.495
LambdaMART 0.469 0.951 0.760 0.885 0.630
RankNet 0.558 0.635 0.588 0.655 0.518
Method
MAP NDCG@10 NDCG@100 P@10 P@100
Criterion
1.0 0.8 0.6 0.4 0.2 0.0

(a) User-based features

AdaRank 0.316 0.205 0.321 0.195 0.299
Coord.Ascent 0.614 0.925 0.522 0.995 0.450
LambdaMART 0.725 0.948 0.803 0.985 0.688
RankNet 0.550 0.599 0.593 0.620 0.553
Method
MAP NDCG@10 NDCG@100 P@10 P@100
Criterion
1.0 0.8 0.6 0.4 0.2 0.0

(b) Network-based features

AdaRank 0.316 0.600 0.487 0.525 0.299
Coord.Ascent 0.725 0.874 0.651 0.800 0.598
LambdaMART 0.659 0.790 0.985 0.684
RankNet 0.516 0.721 0.533 0.735 0.440
Method
MAP NDCG@10 NDCG@100 P@10 P@100
Criterion
1.0 0.8 0.6 0.4 0.2 0.0

(c) Temporal features

AdaRank 0.316 0.966 0.422 0.865 0.406
Coord.Ascent 0.702 0.962 0.748 0.940 0.612
LambdaMART 0.700 0.963 0.802 0.970 0.650
RankNet 0.549 0.700 0.601 0.680 0.539
Method
MAP NDCG@10 NDCG@100 P@10 P@100
Criterion
1.0 0.8 0.6 0.4 0.2 0.0

(d) Content-based features

AdaRank 0.594 0.864 0.748 0.865 0.630
Coord.Ascent 0.780 0.923 0.749 0.885 0.616
LambdaMART 0.623 0.997 0.624 0.985 0.664
RankNet 0.327 0.290 0.344 0.295 0.328
Method
MAP NDCG@10 NDCG@100 P@10 P@100
Criterion
1.0 0.8 0.6 0.4 0.2 0.0

(e) Aggregate features

Figure 3: LTRSB performance on all data, with unbalanced binary relevance (UB), and using different subsets of features.

by BotOrNot. We observe some difficulty in discerning between different levels of bot status; in particular, in terms of *nDCG@*10 and *nDCG@*100 criteria, almost all methods are affected by poor performance when only one subset of features is used. The only significant exception is represented by LambdaMART and Coordinate Ascent which, when trained on the subspace of aggregate features, are able to achieve optimal or very good ranking prediction accuracy. This might be explained since aggregate features includes highly descriptive features derived from BotOrNot as well as from BotWalk.

5.2 Evaluation w.r.t. all features

Figure 5 reports on LTRSB performance results on all datasets, exploiting the whole space of features, with different selections of relevant/non-relevant instances, and both graded and binary relevance labels.

One general remark is that, in most cases, LTRSB can achieve good performance, with any LTR method, especially in the case of balanced settings with both binary and graded relevance labels. Under the balanced binary relevance setting, small variations in terms of performance are observed between the methods. Performance results vary from 0.883 to 1, with two exceptions corresponding to AdaRank (0.578) and LambdaMART (0.67) according to *MAP*. For Grad, Coordinate Ascent and LambdaMART show to be robust w.r.t. the assessment criteria, with scores above 0.88 and, in most cases, close or equal to 1. RankNet (resp. AdaRank) can also achieve optimal (resp. near-optimal) performance, according to *P@*10 and *P@*100, while performing poorly in terms of *nDCG@*10.

The unbalanced setting is characterized by a high variance across all assessment criteria and methods, with evidence of some difficulty in ordering instances belonging to the tail of the ranking solution; in

Method	MAP	NDCG@10	NDCG@100	P@10	P@100
AdaRank	0.877	0.295	0.372	0.960	0.853
Coord.Ascent	0.950	0.200	0.706	0.985	0.976
LambdaMART	0.936	0.234	0.799	0.995	0.951
RankNet	0.928	0.814	0.608	0.980	0.954

(a) User-based features

Method	MAP	NDCG@10	NDCG@100	P@10	P@100
AdaRank	0.854	0.295	0.372	0.840	0.844
Coord.Ascent	0.952	0.422	0.526	0.930	0.944
LambdaMART	0.966	0.598	0.760		0.997
RankNet	0.964	0.441	0.681		0.990

(b) Network-based features

Method	MAP	NDCG@10	NDCG@100	P@10	P@100
AdaRank	0.838	0.440	0.372	0.830	0.903
Coord.Ascent	0.962	0.845	0.821	0.965	0.974
LambdaMART	0.887	0.907	0.858		0.992
RankNet	0.898	0.640	0.495	0.990	0.894

(c) Temporal features

Method	MAP	NDCG@10	NDCG@100	P@10	P@100
AdaRank	0.854	0.347	0.372	0.755	0.895
Coord.Ascent	0.951	0.778	0.798		0.975
LambdaMART	0.878	0.515	0.874	0.995	0.991
RankNet	0.952	0.811	0.647	0.995	0.972

(d) Content-based features

Method	MAP	NDCG@10	NDCG@100	P@10	P@100
AdaRank	0.957	0.215	0.783	0.845	0.861
Coord.Ascent	1.000		0.964		
LambdaMART	0.996		0.999		
RankNet	0.864	0.267	0.362	0.845	0.863

(e) Aggregate features

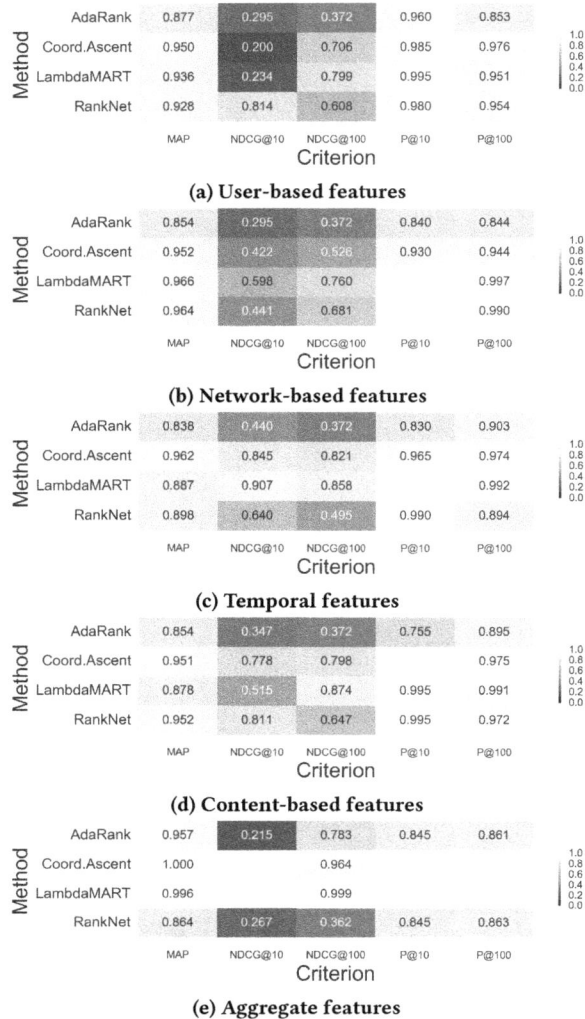

Figure 4: LTRSB performance on all data, with graded relevance setting (Grad), and using different subsets of features.

Method	MAP	NDCG@10	NDCG@100	P@10	P@100
AdaRank	0.578	0.901	0.886	0.870	0.869
Coord.Ascent	0.884	0.972	0.908	0.940	0.883
LambdaMART	0.670	0.966	0.922		0.878
RankNet	0.833	0.920	0.896	0.915	0.886

(a) BB

Method	MAP	NDCG@10	NDCG@100	P@10	P@100
AdaRank	0.423	0.864	0.748	0.925	0.384
Coord.Ascent	0.800	0.957	0.728	0.940	0.602
LambdaMART	0.424	0.981	0.809	0.925	0.671
RankNet	0.712	0.846	0.710	0.850	0.394

(b) UB

Method	MAP	NDCG@10	NDCG@100	P@10	P@100
AdaRank	0.888	0.215	0.932	0.845	0.861
Coord.Ascent	0.999	0.986	0.975		0.992
LambdaMART	0.872	0.998	0.985		
RankNet	0.984	0.520	0.747		

(c) Grad

Figure 5: LTRSB performance on all data and whole feature space, using different relevance labeling settings.

particular, according to *MAP* and *P@*100, AdaRank, LambdaMART, and RankNet obtain low results (i.e., < 0.5). Coordinate Ascent achieves best overall performance ranging from a minimum value of about 0.6 to the near optimal 0.957.

5.3 Discussion

Detecting and characterizing bot accounts in OSNs is a non-trivial learning problem. On the one hand, OSN platforms like Twitter appear not to take serious actions in order to ban, or at least regulate bots within their boundaries. On the other hand, bot-masters are developing more sophisticated tools in order to better mimic human behaviors, thus increasing their potential to influence people, bias public opinion, and even pursue malevolent intents. For those reasons, it is strongly recommended to develop software systems that can exploit all the information available, and leverage useful "signals" of different type, in order to unveil suspicious bot activities.

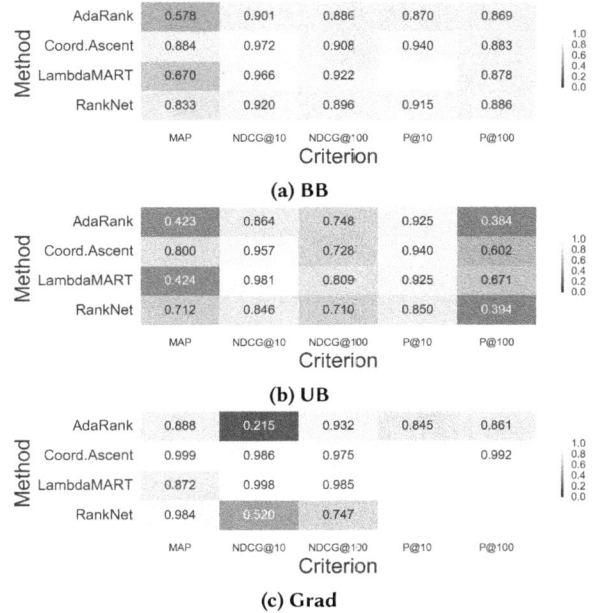

Answering the research questions stated in the Introduction:

- Our proposed LTRSB framework is designed to learn from examples of bots and non-bots in order to detect and rank previously unseen bot accounts; when equipped with Coordinate Ascent or LambdaMART, LTRSB can achieve optimal ranking performance.
- LTRSB evaluation has shown that leveraging a large and heterogeneous space of features is beneficial and, in most cases, essential to effectively detect and rank bots, whose traits might in general refer to different behavioral patterns.
- LTRSB demonstrates that different methods for bot detection, developed upon different criteria and models, can be incorporated into a unifying machine-learning framework for determining the status of OSN accounts at various levels of bot status.

6 CONCLUSION

In this work, we advanced research on bot behavior analysis by developing a robust, supervised ranking model, leveraging different behavioral signals of bot activity. Our learning-to-rank framework, named LTRSB, exploits recently developed methods on bot detection for enhanced feature extraction, and state-of-the-art learning-to-rank methods for the optimization. LTRSB was evaluated using ground-truth data, according to different assessment criteria.

As future work, it would be interesting to evaluate LTRSB using queries and ground-truth data that correspond to multiple classes of bots, from harmless (e.g., advertisement bots, entertainment bots) to malicious bots (e.g., spambots, scraper bots).

REFERENCES

[1] L. M. Aiello, M. Deplano, R. Schifanella, and G. Ruffo. 2012. People Are Strange When You're a Stranger: Impact and Influence of Bots on Social Networks. In *Proc. Int. Conf. on Weblogs and Social Media (ICWSM)*.
[2] A. Bessi and E. Ferrara. 2016. Social bots distort the 2016 U.S. Presidential election online discussion. *First Monday* 21, 11 (2016).
[3] A. Beutel, W. Xu, V. Guruswami, C. Palow, and C. Faloutsos. 2013. CopyCatch: stopping group attacks by spotting lockstep behavior in social networks. In *Proc. ACM Conf. on World Wide Web (WWW)*. 119–130.
[4] Y. Boshmaf, I. Muslukhov, K. Beznosov, and M. Ripeanu. 2013. Design and analysis of a social botnet. *Computer Networks* 57, 2 (2013), 556–578.
[5] Chris J.C. Burges. 2010. *From RankNet to LambdaRank to LambdaMART: An Overview*. Technical Report MSR-TR-2010-82. 81 pages.
[6] C. J. C. Burges, R. Ragno, and Q. Viet Le. 2006. Learning to Rank with Nonsmooth Cost Functions. In *Proc. Conf. on Neural Information Processing Systems (NIPS)*. 193–200.
[7] C. J. C. Burges, T. Shaked, E. Renshaw, A. Lazier, M. Deeds, N. Hamilton, and G. N. Hullender. 2005. Learning to rank using gradient descent. In *Proc. Int. Conf. on Machine Learning (ICML)*. 89–96.
[8] R. Busa-Fekete, G. Szarvas, T. Elteto, and B. Kégl. 2012. An apple-to-apple comparison of Learning-to-rank algorithms in terms of Normalized Discounted Cumulative Gain. In *Proc. ECAI Work. on Preference Learning: Problems and Applications in AI*, Vol. 242.
[9] Q. Cao, M. Sirivianos, X. Yang, and T. Pregueiro. 2012. Aiding the Detection of Fake Accounts in Large Scale Social Online Services. In *Proc. of Symp. on Networked Systems Design and Implementation, NSDI*. 197–210.
[10] Q. Cao, X. Yang, J. Yu, and C. Palow. 2014. Uncovering Large Groups of Active Malicious Accounts in Online Social Networks. In *Proc. of 2014 ACM SIGSAC Conference on Computer and Communications Security*. 477–488.
[11] M. Cha, H. Haddadi, F. Benevenuto, and P. K. Gummadi. 2010. Measuring User Influence in Twitter: The Million Follower Fallacy. In *Proc. Int. Conf. on Weblogs and Social Media (ICWSM)*.
[12] S. Chakrabarti. 2007. Learning to Rank in Vector Spaces and Social Networks. *Internet Mathematics* 4, 1–3 (2007), 267–298.
[13] N. Chavoshi, H. Hamooni, and A. Mueen. 2016. DeBot: Twitter Bot Detection via Warped Correlation. In *Proc. IEEE Int. Conf. on Data Mining (ICDM)*. 817–822.
[14] W. Chen, T. Y. Liu, Y. Lan, Z. Ma, and H. Li. 2009. Ranking Measures and Loss Functions in Learning to Rank. In *Proc. Conf. on Neural Information Processing Systems (NIPS)*. 315–323.
[15] Z. Chu, S. Gianvecchio, H. Wang, and S. Jajodia. 2012. Detecting Automation of Twitter Accounts: Are You a Human, Bot, or Cyborg? *IEEE Trans. Dependable Sec. Comput.* 9, 6 (2012), 811–824.
[16] S. Cresci, R. Di Pietro, M. Petrocchi, A. Spognardi, and M. Tesconi. 2017. The Paradigm-Shift of Social Spambots: Evidence, Theories, and Tools for the Arms Race. In *Proc. ACM Conf. on World Wide Web (WWW)*. 963–972.
[17] C. A. Davis, O. Varol, E. Ferrara, A. Flammini, and F. Menczer. 2016. BotOrNot: A System to Evaluate Social Bots. In *Proc. ACM Conf. on World Wide Web (WWW)*. 273–274.
[18] J. P. Dickerson, V. Kagan, and V. S. Subrahmanian. 2014. Using sentiment to detect bots on Twitter: Are humans more opinionated than bots?. In *Proc. Int. Conf. on Advances in Social Networks Analysis and Mining (ASONAM)*. 620–627.
[19] E. Ferrara, O. Varol, C. A. Davis, F. Menczer, and A. Flammini. 2016. The rise of social bots. *Commun. ACM* 59, 7 (2016), 96–104.
[20] Y. Freund and R. E. Schapire. 1995. A decision-theoretic generalization of on-line learning and an application to boosting. In *Proc. European Conf. on Computational Learning Theory (EuroCOLT)*. 23–37.
[21] J. H. Friedman. 2000. Greedy Function Approximation: A Gradient Boosting Machine. *Annals of Statistics* 29 (2000), 1189–1232.
[22] Z. Gilani, E. Kochmar, and J. Crowcroft. 2017. Classification of Twitter Accounts into Automated Agents and Human Users. In *Proc. Int. Conf. on Advances in Social Networks Analysis and Mining (ASONAM)*. ACM, 489–496.
[23] A. Gupta, P. Kumaraguru, C. Castillo, and P. Meier. 2014. TweetCred: Real-Time Credibility Assessment of Content on Twitter. (2014), 228–243.
[24] M. A. Hall. 1999. Correlation-based feature selection for machine learning. (1999).
[25] S. Hegelich and D. Janetzko. 2016. Are Social Bots on Twitter Political Actors? Empirical Evidence from a Ukrainian Social Botnet. In *Proc. Int. Conf. on Weblogs and Social Media (ICWSM)*. 579–582.
[26] R.C. Holte. 1993. Very simple classification rules perform well on most commonly used datasets. *Machine Learning* 11 (1993), 63–91.
[27] P. N. Howard and B. Kollanyi. 2016. Bots, #StrongerIn, and #Brexit: Computational Propaganda during the UK-EU Referendum. *Social Science Research Network (SSRN) Electronic Journal* (2016).
[28] F. B. Keller, D. Schoch, S. Stier, and J. Yang. 2017. How to Manipulate Social Media: Analyzing Political Astroturfing Using Ground Truth Data from South Korea. In *Proc. Int. Conf. on Weblogs and Social Media (ICWSM)*. 564–567.
[29] K. Lee, B. D. Eoff, and J. Caverlee. 2011. Seven Months with the Devils: A Long-Term Study of Content Polluters on Twitter. In *Proc. Int. Conf. on Weblogs and

[30] T.-Y. Liu. 2011. *Learning to Rank for Information Retrieval*. Springer.
[31] A. Monroy-Hernández S. Savage M. Forelle, P. Howard. 2015. Political Bots and the Manipulation of Public Opinion in Venezuela. *Social Science Research Network (SSRN) Electronic Journal* (2015).
[32] P. T. Metaxas and E. Mustafaraj. 2012. Social media and the elections. *Science* 338, 6106 (2012), 472–473.
[33] D. Metzler and W. B. Croft. 2007. Linear feature-based models for information retrieval. *Inf. Retr.* 10, 3 (2007), 257–274.
[34] A. J. Minnich, N. Chavoshi, D. Koutra, and A. Mueen. 2017. BotWalk: Efficient Adaptive Exploration of Twitter Bot Networks. In *Proc. Int. Conf. on Advances in Social Networks Analysis and Mining (ASONAM)*. 467–474.
[35] F. Morstatter, L. Wu, T. H Nazer, K. M Carley, and H. Liu. 2016. A new approach to bot detection: Striking the balance between precision and recall. In *Proc. Int. Conf. on Advances in Social Networks Analysis and Mining (ASONAM)*. 533–540.
[36] A. Paradise, R. Puzis, and A. Shabtai. 2014. Anti-Reconnaissance Tools: Detecting Targeted Socialbots. *IEEE Internet Computing* 18, 5 (2014), 11–19.
[37] D. Perna and A. Tagarelli. 2017. An Evaluation of Learning-to-Rank Methods for Lurking Behavior Analysis. In *Proc. Int. Conf. on User Modeling, Adaptation and Personalization, UMAP*. 381–382.
[38] J. Ratkiewicz, M. Conover, M. R. Meiss, B. Gonçalves, A. Flammini, and F. Menczer. 2011. Detecting and Tracking Political Abuse in Social Media. In *Proc. Int. Conf. on Weblogs and Social Media (ICWSM)*.
[39] J. Ratkiewicz, M. Conover, M. R. Meiss, B. Gonçalves, S. Patil, A. Flammini, and F. Menczer. 2011. Truthy: mapping the spread of astroturf in microblog streams. In *Proc. ACM Conf. on World Wide Web (WWW)*. 249–252.
[40] R.Yan and A. G. Hauptmann. 2006. Efficient Margin-Based Rank Learning Algorithms for Information Retrieval. In *Proc. Int. Conf. on Image and Video Retrieval (CIVR)*. 113–122.
[41] S. Sedhai and A. Sun. 2014. Hashtag recommendation for hyperlinked tweets. In *Proc. ACM SIGIR Conf. on Research and Development in Information Retrieval (SIGIR)*. 831–834.
[42] G. Stringhini, M. Egele, C. Kruegel, and G. Vigna. 2012. Poultry markets: on the underground economy of twitter followers. In *Proc. of ACM Workshop on Online Social Networks (WOSN)*. 1–6.
[43] M. Surdeanu, M. Ciaramita, and H. Zaragoza. 2008. Learning to Rank Answers on Large Online QA Collections. In *Proc. of the 46th Annual Meeting of the Association for Computational Linguistics*, Vol. 8. 719–727.
[44] O. Varol, E. Ferrara, C. A. Davis, F. Menczer, and A. Flammini. 2017. Online Human-Bot Interactions: Detection, Estimation, and Characterization. 280–289.
[45] C. Wagner, S. Mitter, C. Körner, and M. Strohmaier. 2012. When Social Bots Attack: Modeling Susceptibility of Users in Online Social Networks. In *Proc. ACM Conf. on World Wide Web (WWW)*. 41–48.
[46] G. Wang, T. Konolige, C. Wilson, X. Wang, H. Zheng, and B. Y. Zhao. 2013. You Are How You Click: Clickstream Analysis for Sybil Detection. In *Proc. of Symp. on Security USENIX*. 241–256.
[47] G. Wang, M. Mohanlal, C. Wilson, X. Wang, M. J. Metzger, H. Zheng, and B. Y. Zhao. 2013. Social Turing Tests: Crowdsourcing Sybil Detection. In *Proc. of Symp. on Network and Distributed System Security, NDSS*.
[48] X. Wang, A. Mueen, H. Ding, G. Trajcevski, P. Scheuermann, and E. J. Keogh. 2013. Experimental comparison of representation methods and distance measures for time series data. *Data Min. Knowl. Discov.* 26, 2 (2013), 275–309.
[49] Q. Wu, C. J. C. Burges, K. M. Svore, and J. Gao. 2010. Adapting boosting for information retrieval measures. *Inf. Retr.* 13, 3 (2010), 254–270.
[50] Y. Xie, F. Yu, Q. Ke, M. Abadi, E. Gillum, K. Vitaldevaria, J. Walter, J. Huang, and Z. Morley Mao. 2012. Innocent by association: early recognition of legitimate users. In *Proc. of ACM Conf. on Computer and Communications Security, (CCS)*. 353–364.
[51] J. Xu and H. Li. 2007. AdaRank: a boosting algorithm for information retrieval. In *Proc. ACM SIGIR Conf. on Research and Development in Information Retrieval (SIGIR)*. 391–398.
[52] Z. Yang, C. Wilson, X. Wang, T. Gao, B. Y. Zhao, and Y. Dai. 2014. Uncovering social network Sybils in the wild. *TKDD* 8, 1 (2014), 2:1–2:29.
[53] H. Zamani, A. Shakery, and P. Moradi. 2014. Regression and Learning to Rank Aggregation for User Engagement Evaluation. In *Proc. ACM Recommender Systems Challenge (RecSysChallenge)*.
[54] J. Zhang, D. Carpenter, and M. Ko. 2013. Online Astroturfing: A Theoretical Perspective. In *Proc. Americas Conf. on Information Systems (AMCIS)*.

An Approximately Optimal Bot
for Non-Submodular Social Reconnaissance

J. David Smith
University of Florida
Gainesville, Florida
emallson@ufl.edu

Alan Kuhnle
University of Florida
Gainesville, Florida
kuhnle@ufl.edu

My T. Thai
University of Florida
Gainesville, Florida
mythai@cise.ufl.edu

ABSTRACT

The explosive growth of Online Social Networks in recent years has led to many individuals relying on them to keep up with friends & family. This, in turn, makes them prime targets for malicious actors seeking to collect sensitive, personal data. Prior work has studied the ability of *socialbots*, i.e. bots which pretend to be humans on OSNs, to collect personal data by befriending real users. However, this prior work has been hampered by the assumption that the likelihood of users accepting friend requests from a bot is non-increasing – a useful constraint for theoretical purposes but one contradicted by observational data. We address this limitation with a novel curvature based technique, showing that an adaptive greedy bot is approximately optimal within a factor of $1 - 1/e^{1/\delta} \approx 0.165$. This theoretical contribution is supported by simulating the infiltration of the bot on OSN topologies. Counter-intuitively, we observe that when the bot is incentivized to befriend friends-of-friends of target users it out-performs a bot that focuses on befriending targets.

CCS CONCEPTS

• **Networks → Online social networks**; • **Theory of computation → Discrete optimization**;

KEYWORDS

social networks; privacy; discrete optimization; adaptive algorithms

ACM Reference Format:
J. David Smith, Alan Kuhnle, and My T. Thai. 2018. An Approximately Optimal Bot for Non-Submodular Social Reconnaissance. In *HT '18: 29th ACM Conference on Hypertext and Social Media, July 9–12, 2018, Baltimore, MD, USA.* ACM, New York, NY, USA, 9 pages. https://doi.org/10.1145/3209542.3209553

ACKNOWLEDGMENTS

This work was supported by NSF CCF-1422116, NSF CNS-1443905, and NSF EFRI 1441231.

1 INTRODUCTION

Online Social Networks (OSNs) have seen explosive growth in recent years, rapidly becoming the largest repositories of personal information on the Internet. This leads to the question: how difficult is it for an attacker to steal users' personal information from popular OSNs? This may be done by, for instance, befriending users with *socialbots* that can exfiltrate normally private data via their friendship relations. Boshmaf *et al.* showed that Facebook is vulnerable to such attacks [5], while Freitas *et al.* more recently showed that Twitter is vulnerable to similar attacks [10].[1] This information can then be sold on the black market, used to enhance spearphishing attacks, or to crack password recovery systems – and thus indirectly used to reduce the security level of the rest of our infrastructure.

Li *et al.* recently used the observational data of Boshmaf *et al.* [5] to estimate the rate at which a socialbot could extract private data from an OSN [19]. In doing so, they found that a socialbot using an adaptive greedy approach would obtain at least $(1 - 1/e)$ times as much benefit as the optimal and that no algorithm can do better than $(1 - 1/e)$ unless $P = NP$. However, this approximation guarantee demands a strong assumption: the expected benefit of befriending users must be *submodular*. In the deterministic case, this is often formalized as

$$\forall S \subseteq T : f(S \cup \{e\}) - f(S) \geq f(T \cup \{e\}) - f(T)$$

Semantically, this means that the benefit has diminishing returns as more users are befriended. However, this condition does not hold due to the impact of acceptance probability on the expectation: the acceptance probability increases as more users are befriended [5], leading to non-submodular behavior. Although Li *et al.* study this setting, their guarantees do not hold without submodularity [18].

While the performance bound of submodular problems has been studied since 1978 [20], such study of monotone non-submodularity has only begun very recently [2, 27]. However, these recent results are not readily applied to the reconnaissance attack application owing to the fact that it is necessarily *adaptive*. Due to the massive size of modern OSNs, obtaining accurate knowledge of the entire network topology at once is infeasible. Therefore, the bot must explore the network as it crawls, revealing parts of the topology by befriending users and observing with whom they are friends, and then using this information to inform future steps. This property of making decisions based on the outcome of previous ones is the defining trait of adaptive algorithms. In particular, the adaptive stochastic nature of the problem makes current results inapplicable and necessitates new solutions.

In this work, we address the above limitation by introducing novel mathematical techniques to theoretically analyze the performance bound of adaptive greedy algorithms for non-submodularity. At the heart of our techniques is a key proof bounding on the effect

---

[1]While stealing personal information from public Twitter profiles makes little sense, the embedding of socialbots on a network has other nefarious applications such as spreading misinformation e.g. in a way that evades containment [21].

of adding a node to a solution later rather than earlier. We accomplish this through a new measure of the rate of change of a function, the *primal curvature*. A bound on this measure is shown to be both necessary & sufficient to obtain an approximation guarantee in the general case. In our specific case, we exploit the structure of the problem to obtain an approximation ratio of $1 - 1/e^{1/\delta}$ with δ a constant depending on user behavior. The generalized techniques provided in this paper advance the research front of several applications, where both adaptivity and non-submodularity are required, such as adaptive viral marketing in OSNs [12, 16, 25]. As the first work established the rigorous proofs for adaptivity and non-submodularity, this paper opens the way for the development of adaptive approximation algorithms on domains where external factors – such as human behavior – prevent common assumptions like submodularity from holding.

Our contributions can be summarized as follows:

- We provide the first theoretical study of reconnaissance attacks under a realistic model of friend request acceptance. We obtain a bound of $1 - 1/e^{1/\delta}$ with $\delta = O(1)$.
- We provide the first technique to theoretically bound the approximation quality of non-submodular adaptive approximation algorithms, which generalizes the $1 - 1/e$ ratio for adaptive submodular maximization via the greedy algorithm.
- We delve deeper into the behavior of a socialbot under this realistic model, finding that the added term rewarding a bot for improving friend request probability adds needless complexity and that, paradoxically, encouraging the bot to become friends-of-friends with targeted users actually results in a greater fraction of targets being befriended.

Related Work. *Reconnaissance Attacks.* Reconnaissance attacks on OSNs have been shown to be an effective method of extracting private information from OSN users [5, 10]. The method of attack is conceptually simple: a single "socialbot" is created on the OSN with a realistic user profile, and automatically befriends users with the goal of extracting as much private data as possible (e.g. for sale on the black market or use in breaking "secret question" password recovery schemes for further attacks). Ryan & Mauch showed that such fake profiles can be effective in obtaining access to the personal feeds of high-ranking government and corporate officers [23]. In a similar vein, Varol *et. al.* studied the presence of bots on Twitter and found that human users befriended more human-like users than bots [26], indicating that for reconnaissance to be successful it must be undertaken by human-like bots–a.k.a. socialbots.

Note that this attack is distinct from the well-studied Sybil attack, and due to the absence of the bots creating large sub-graphs, it is unlikely to be detected by Sybil detection schemes [3]. Traditionally, literature on reconnaissance attacks has been primarily experimental in nature and lacked rigorous theoretical guarantees [5, 10, 22]. More recently, a greedy socialbot was shown to collect at least a $1 - 1/e$ fraction of the information collected by an optimal bot using adaptive techniques (see Golovin & Krause [11] for a full treatment on adaptivity) [18]. This was extended to a ratio of $1 - 1/e^{-(1-1/e)}$ when the bot is allowed to make multiple simultaneous friend requests [19].

However, these ratios *do not·hold* without submodular benefit and friend request acceptance models. While the benefit model is

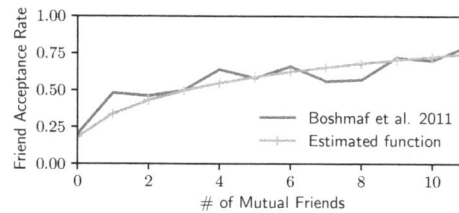

Figure 1: The acceptance probability function proposed by Li *et al.* [18] using the data of Boshmaf *et al.* [5].

under the control of the attacker and can be easily constructed to be submodular, observational data indicates that the friend request acceptance model is strongly non-submodular [5, 18].

Non-Submodular Optimization. Submodular optimization has been the subject of intense study. Perhaps the most-used work to come out of this is the tight $1 - 1/e$ ratio of Nemhauser *et al.* [7, 20], which is fundamental to the guarantees of many applied works. Quite recently, a number of works have also begun to study *non-submodular* optimization, which cannot exploit the useful "diminishing returns" of submodularity to obtain approximation guarantees. However, to obtain these guarantees constraints must be imposed on the problem (a proof of the necessity of one such constraint is contained in Sec. 3.1). Even in the case of functions that are approximately submodular and violate submodularity only due to noise, this problem requires strong constraints to obtain meaningful guarantees [13, 14]. Das & Kempe proposed the *submodularity ratio* γ as a means of quantifying the magnitude by which submodularity is violated [6]. Using this, they obtain a ratio of $1 - 1/e^\gamma$ for their specific problem. Recently, Bian *et al.* extended this by incorporating the *generalized curvature* α to obtain a ratio of $\frac{1}{\alpha}(1 - e^{-\alpha\gamma})$ in general for greedy maximization subject to cardinality constraints [2]. Wang *et al.* took an alternative approach, obtaining a ratio for the greedy algorithm via the *elemental curvature* [27].

However, none of these apply to adaptive stochastic optimization, which is necessary the modeling of non-deterministic systems – such as the reconnaissance attack. The problem of non-submodular adaptive maximization has not yet seen study.

Organization. We begin in Section 2 by giving a semantic description of the socialbot reconnaissance attack and presenting an algorithmic description of the socialbot in terms of our formal model. Next, we describe our measure of curvature and derive the $1 - 1/e^{1/\delta}$ ratio in Section 3. While we focus on our particular application, this ratio extends to any problem with a finite curvature bound. This is followed by our experimental evaluation of the socialbot in Section 4. Finally, we conclude with a discussion of the implications and potential future work in Section 5.

2 PROBLEM FORMULATION & ALGORITHM

Before formally defining our problem, we first describe the semantics of the socialbot attack that informs it. Consider a social network such as Facebook. Users have a significant amount of personal information, much of which is locked behind privacy controls. The default (and most common) setting for content on Facebook is "Only Friends," which allows only direct friends to see your posts and friends. While link prediction can give an estimate as to the probability of friendships existing (e.g. [1, 8, 9]), there remains significant incentive for attackers to befriend users for the information in their profiles. We term users under such attacks *targets*. However, users may not accept a friend request from a bot. Thus, the bot must consider the probability of acceptance – and ideally take advantage of human behavior to maximize it. To improve the acceptance probability, the bot may first seek to befriend friends of the targets. The reconnaissance process then unfolds round by round.

Boshmaf *et al.* observed that acceptance probability on Facebook seems to be dominated by the number of mutual friends – likely a result of the *Triadic Closure Principle* [5], which states that if a and b are friends with c, then a and b are also likely to be friends. In this case, the bot can boost the likelihood of requests being accepted by first befriending more vulnerable mutual friends. This raises the question of how to make the critical first few friends. It has been observed that users with abnormally high number of friends (so-called "high-degree users") have a larger chance of accepting friend requests without critical examination of the requester [4]. This allows the bot to bootstrap by sending initial requests to high-degree users, then crawling along the network–taking advantage of triadic closure to keep acceptance probabilities high.

Li *et al.* fit a model of acceptance probability to the observational data of Boshmaf *et al.* [18]. The exact function they give is

$$\alpha(u \mid \psi) = \rho_1 \log(\mathbb{E}\left[|N(u) \cap N_{in}(s)|\right] + 1) + \rho_0 \quad (1)$$

with $\rho_1 = 0.22805837$ and $\rho_0 = 0.18014571$ and s representing the bot (the expectation is taken with respect to ψ, which will be defined in the next subsection). This function is shown in Fig. 1. $N(u)$ and $N_{in}(s)$ are the sets of outgoing and incoming neighbors of u and s, respectively. Taking expectations under this model results in a non-submodular objective since the probability of a user u accepting a request may *increase* after another user v is befriended without a corresponding drop in the benefit of befriending u.

2.1 Formal Definitions

In sum, this leads us to an *adaptive* model of the problem [11]. Our model incorporates two pieces of uncertainty: the possibility that edges may not exist, and that friend requests may be rejected. The former are represented as a set of random variables (RVs) $X_e \in \{0, 1\} \forall e \in E$ where the OSN is represented as a digraph $G = (V, E)$, where V is a set of users and E is the set of friendships; $X_e = 0$ iff the edge e does not exist. Note that edges are added on successful friend requests by the bot. We model friend requests with two sets of RVs $Y_v \in [0, 1)$ and $Z_v \in \{0, 1\}$. These Y_v represent thresholds for the acceptance probability, with v accepting a request if $\alpha(v \mid \psi) \geq Y_v$, where $\alpha(v \mid \psi)$ is the acceptance probability of v under partial realization ψ (defined below). The Z_v's are induced variables representing the status of the bot's friend request to v, with $Z_v = 1$ iff $\alpha(v \mid \psi) \geq Y_v$ *at the point where s made the request.*[2]

In the adaptive framework, there exists a set of possible *(total) realizations* Φ, which encode all potential states of the random variables X_e, Y_v, and Z_v described above. An adaptive policy π makes decisions based on a partial realization ψ, which encodes the values of the random variables in a system that are currently known. The

domain of a partial realization, denoted dom(ψ), is the set of random variables revealed in ψ. We write $F(\psi) = \{u \mid Z_u \in \text{dom}(\psi)\}$. A partial realization is said to be consistent with a total realization, denoted $\psi \sim \phi$, if they are equivalent everywhere in dom(ψ). We will denote the adaptive greedy policy selecting k elements π_k and the optimal policy selecting k elements π_k^*. When the choice of k is clear, we drop the subscript for notational simplicity. We slightly abuse notation and denote the final partial realization produced by policy π were it to run on a realization ϕ as $\pi(\phi)$.

Under this model, the bot is given as input a graph G with known nodes and unknown edges, along with an edge probability function $p(u, v)$ and a benefit model $\mathcal{B} = (B_f, B_{fof}, B_e)$. The bot ultimately outputs the sequence of friend requests made and the final partial realization uncovered by this sequence. At each step, an adaptive greedy bot will select the element maximizing the expected marginal gain $\Delta(v \mid \psi)$ and sends it a friend request. If it is successful, we observe $Y_v \leq \alpha(v \mid \psi) \implies Z_v = 1$, and we observe each X_e where $e \in E$ is an outgoing edge of v. On the other hand, if the request fails we observe $Z_v = 0$ and do not observe any variables X_e. Given this formulation, we write the objective $f(S, \phi)$ as:

$$f(S, \phi) = \sum_{u \in S} Z_u \left[B_f(u) + \sum_{v \in N(u)} B_e(u, v) \right]$$

$$+ \sum_{v \in N(S) \setminus S} \left(1 - \prod_{\substack{v \in N(u) \\ u \in S}} (1 - Z_u X_{u,v}) \right) B_{fof}(v) \quad (2)$$

where $N(u)$ is the set of nodes that may be adjacent u, $N(S)$ is the union of such over all $u \in S$, and $B_f(\cdot)$, $B_{fof}(\cdot)$, and $B_e(\cdot)$ represent the benefit assigned to a given friend, friend of friend, or edge revelation. In addition, we require $B_{fof}(v) \leq B_f(v)$ for all users v. We refer to a user u as a *target* if $B_f(u) > 0$. The expected benefit of f w.r.t. all possible realizations is $f_{\text{avg}}(\pi) = \mathbb{E}\left[f(F(\pi(\Phi)), \Phi)\right]$ where Φ is a random total realization. This gives us the final piece to formally define the socialbot attack.

PROBLEM 1 (MAXIMAL INFORMATION EXTRACTION (MINE)). *Given a social graph $G = (V, E)$ with edge probabilities $p(u, v)$, an acceptance model $\alpha(v \mid \psi)$ that is adaptive monotone non-decreasing w.r.t. ψ, and a benefit model $f(S, \phi)$ that is adaptive monotone non-decreasing submodular w.r.t. S, find the k-element policy π that maximizes the expected benefit obtained.*

It has been shown that this problem[3] is inapproximable within $1 - 1/e - \epsilon$ for any $\epsilon > 0$ unless $P = NP$ even in the case where α is also submodular [19]. Were α submodular, this objective would be adaptive submodular [18] in addition to adaptive monotone, and the adaptive greedy policy would then have a tight ratio of $1 - 1/e$ [11]. It will be shown in the next section that – under some mild conditions on α – this ratio is preserved nearly exactly when α is allowed to be non-submodular.

2.2 Needed Properties for the Greedy Solution

As in prior work, we take a greedy approach to optimizing f. In this approach, the bot at each step chooses the user to befriend

---

[2] We found a definition exclusively in terms of Y_v or Z_v problematic due to the need to denote the answers to two distinct questions: (Y_v) *a request was just made–did it succeed?* and (Z_v) *a request was made in a prior step–was it successful?*. Using both together greatly simplifies presentation.

[3] This problem has seen prior study under the moniker "AReST" [18, 19].

Algorithm 1 Greedy MINE

Input: Problem instance (G, p, α, B, k)
Output: An ordered set of nodes $F \subset V$ to befriend, realization ψ.

1: $F \leftarrow \emptyset, \psi \leftarrow \emptyset$
2: **for** $i = 1 \ldots k$ **do**
3: $\quad u^* \leftarrow \arg\max_{u \in V \backslash F} \Delta(u \mid \psi)$
4: $\quad F \leftarrow F \cup \{u^*\}$
5: $\quad$ Send a friend request to u^*, observing Y_{u^*}
6: $\quad$ **if** $\alpha(u^* \mid \psi) \geq Y_{u^*}$ **then**
7: $\qquad$ **for** $v \in N(u^*)$ **do**
8: $\qquad\quad$ Observe $X_{u^*,v}$, updating ψ
9: $\qquad$ Set $Z_{u^*} = 1$
10: $\quad$ **else**
11: $\qquad$ Set $Z_{u^*} = 0$
12: $\quad$ Update ψ with the observed value of Y_{u^*}
13: **return** F, ψ

---

with highest expected marginal gain (line 3 of Alg. 1). It then sends this request and observes the result. If the user accepts the request, additional observations are made (lines 6-11). After having sent k requests, the bot returns the set of requests it made F and the partial realization resulting from those requests ψ.

Despite a similar approach to prior work, our objective function differs in the omission of a term rewarding the bot directly for improving marginal gain. We therefore prove necessary properties for the greedy algorithm to be applied. First, we prove that our objective maintains the property of *adaptive monotonicity*. Then, we derive a closed form for the expected marginal gain. The section closes by using this closed form to prove that the function is in general not *adaptive submodular*.

Adaptive Monotonicity of f. We adopt an alternative definition of adaptive monotonicity that is equivalent to the standard one. First, we require the definition of policy concatenation.

DEFINITION 1 (CONCATENATION OF POLICIES [11]). *Given two policies π, π', define $\pi @ \pi'$ as the policy obtained by running π to completion, and then running π' as if from a fresh start, ignoring the information gathered during the running of π.*

DEFINITION 2 (ADAPTIVE MONOTONICITY [11]). *A function $g : 2^E \times O^E \to \mathbb{R}_{\geq 0}$ is adaptive montone if for all polices π, π', it holds that $g_{avg}(\pi) \leq g_{avg}(\pi' @ \pi)$.*

LEMMA 2.1. *f is adaptive monotone.*

PROOF. Let π, π' be policies and for a realization ϕ write $\psi = \pi(\phi), \psi' = \pi @ \pi'(\phi)$. Notice that for any realization $\phi, F(\psi) \subseteq F(\psi')$. Hence it is enough to show for any $S \subseteq S', f(S, \phi) \leq f(S', \phi)$. It is clear that any $B_f(u), B_e(v, w)$ in $f(S, \phi)$ is also present in $f(S', \phi)$. Furthermore, any $B_{fof}(v)$ term in $f(S, \phi)$ is absent in $f(S', \phi)$ only if it is replaced by $B_f(v)$. Since we have $B_{fof}(v) \leq B_f(v)$ for all v, the result follows. $\qquad \square$

Closed Form of $\Delta(u \mid \psi)$. The expected marginal gain $\Delta(u \mid \psi)$ is defined by Golovin & Krause [11] as

$$\Delta(u \mid \psi) = \mathbb{E}\left[f(F(\psi) \cup \{u\}, \Phi) - f(F(\psi), \Phi) \mid \Phi \sim \psi\right] \quad (3)$$

Based on the definition given in Equation (2) and the definitions of the variables, this has the closed form

$$\Delta(u \mid \psi) = \alpha(u \mid \psi)\left[B_f(u) + \sum_{v \in N(u)} B_e(u, v) \right.$$

$$\left. + \sum_{v \in N(u) \backslash F(\psi)} (1 - I_{fof}(v))p(u,v)B_{fof}(v)\right]$$

$$= \alpha(u \mid \psi)\mathcal{B}(\psi, u) \quad (4)$$

where $I_{fof}(v)$ is the indicator function returning 1 if v is already a friend-of-friend of s and 0 otherwise.

Adaptive Submodularity For the sake of completeness, we now present the definition of adaptive submodularity:

DEFINITION 3 (ADAPTIVE SUBMODULARITY [11]). *A function $g : 2^E \times O^E \to \mathbb{R}_{\geq 0}$ is adaptive submodular if for a pair of partial realizations $\psi \subseteq \psi'$:*

$$\forall e \in E \setminus dom(\psi') : \Delta(e \mid \psi) \geq \Delta(e \mid \psi')$$

LEMMA 2.2. *f is not adaptive submodular in general.*

PROOF. A trivial counter-example is $\forall u \in V : B_f(u) = 1, B_{fof}(u) = 0, \forall(u, v) \in E : B_e(u, v) = 0$. Then, we easily have non-submodularity because α is increasing w.r.t. ψ. This example will be shown non-submodular by contradiction. Suppose we have $\psi' \supset \psi$ s.t. $\alpha(u \mid \psi) \neq \alpha(u \mid \psi')$. Begin with the definition of adaptive submodularity:

$$\Delta(u \mid \psi) \geq \Delta(u \mid \psi')$$

By the closed form of Δ derived previously and the selection of B_f, B_e, B_{fof} this simplifies to

$$\alpha(u \mid \psi)B_f(u) \geq \alpha(u \mid \psi')B_f(u)$$

However, we know $\alpha(u \mid \psi) < \alpha(u \mid \psi')$ for this pair ψ, ψ'. We thus arrive at a contradiction. $\qquad \square$

3 APPROXIMATION RATIO

Greedy methods are often chosen for their good real-world performance in addition to the strong theoretical guarantee that any solution produced is at least $1 - 1/e$ times as good as the optimal if the objective is submodular [11, 20]. However, the behavior of users observed by Boshmaf et al. [5] indicates that the objective is must be non-submodular since it incorporates the increasing acceptance function.[4] Therefore, we introduce a new technique for deriving the approximation guarantee for the greedy adaptive policy.

Wang et al. [27] were among the first to provide an approximation guarantee for general non-submodular set functions in terms of the *elemental* curvature: the maximum ratio between the marginal gain of an element i at any pair of sets S and $S \cup \{j\}$. We extend their idea to the adaptive realm with the *primal curvature*: a localized definition of curvature.

DEFINITION 4 (ADAPTIVE PRIMAL CURVATURE). *The primal curvature of an adaptive monotone non-decreasing function f is*

$$\nabla_f(i, j \mid \psi) = \mathbb{E}\left[\frac{\Delta(i \mid \psi \cup s)}{\Delta(i \mid \psi)} \,\middle|\, s \in S(j)\right]$$

---
[4]We remark that any reasonable objective must incorporate the likelihood of acceptance, as doing so is a fundamental part of computing the expected value.

where $S(j)$ is the set of possible states of j and Δ is the conditional expected marginal gain [11].

Intuitively, the adaptive primal curvature measures the immediate change in the (expected) marginal value of i after j is added to the solution. In the non-adaptive case (i.e. $|S(j)| = 1$), the elemental curvature is the maximum primal curvature. However, this localization allows us to proceed in a new direction with the proof. We use the *total primal curvature*, defined below, to measure the total change between two partial realizations.

DEFINITION 5 (ADAPTIVE TOTAL PRIMAL CURVATURE). *Let $\psi \subset \psi'$ and $\psi \to \psi'$ represent the set of possible state sequences leading from ψ to ψ'. Then the adaptive total primal curvature is*

$$\Gamma(i \mid \psi', \psi) = \mathbb{E}\left[\left.\prod_{s_j \in Q} \nabla'(i, s_j \mid \psi \cup \{s_1, \ldots, s_{j-1}\})\right| Q \in \psi \to \psi'\right]$$

The following lemma clarifies the relation between total primal curvature and the marginal gain, and the corresponding result in Corollary 3.4 directly enables our proof of the adaptive approximation guarantee.

LEMMA 3.1.
$$\Gamma(i \mid \psi', \psi) = \frac{\Delta(i \mid \psi')}{\Delta(i \mid \psi)}$$

PROOF. Fix a sequence $Q \in \psi \to \psi'$ of length r. Then, expanding the product we obtain

$$\frac{\Delta(i \mid \psi \cup \{s_1\})}{\Delta(i \mid \psi)} \cdot \frac{\Delta(i \mid \psi \cup \{s_1, s_2\})}{\Delta(i \mid \psi \cup \{s_1\})} \cdots \frac{\Delta(i \mid \psi')}{\Delta(i \mid \psi' \setminus \{s_{r-1}\})}$$

If we take the expectation of this w.r.t. the possible sequences Q, we obtain the same ratio regardless of Q, and therefore the claim holds trivially. □

This identity allows us to place a constant bound on the total primal curvature for the MINE problem. As we will show later, this ultimately leads to a constant approximation ratio.

LEMMA 3.2. $\max_{i, \psi, \psi'} \Gamma(i \mid \psi', \psi)$ *is upper bounded by*

$$\delta = \max_{u, \psi, \psi'} \frac{\alpha(u \mid \psi)}{\alpha(u \mid \psi')}$$

PROOF. For any i, ψ', ψ, we have

$$\Gamma(i \mid \psi', \psi) = \frac{\alpha(i \mid \psi')\mathcal{B}(\psi', i)}{\alpha(i \mid \psi)\mathcal{B}(\psi, i)} \leq \delta \frac{\mathcal{B}(\psi', i)}{\mathcal{B}(\psi, i)}$$

by the derivation of the closed form in Section 2.2. $\mathcal{B}(\psi', i) \leq \mathcal{B}(\psi, i)$ by definition, and therefore $\Gamma(i \mid \psi', \psi) \leq \delta$. □

COROLLARY 3.3. *For the ETC acceptance function, $\delta = O(1)$.*

PROOF. Recall that the ETC acceptance function is defined as:

$$\alpha(u) = \rho_1 \log(\mathbb{E}[|N(u) \cap N(s)|] + 1) + \rho_0$$

Thus, for any u, $\min_\psi \alpha(u \mid \psi)$ is achieved in all partial realizations that guarantee $|N(u) \cap N(s)| = 0$ and $\max_\psi \alpha(u \mid \psi) \leq 1$. Thus, $\rho_0 \leq \alpha(u \mid \psi) \leq 1, \forall \psi$. So we have:

$$\delta \leq \frac{\max_\psi \alpha(u \mid \psi)}{\min_\psi \alpha(u \mid \psi)} \leq \frac{1}{\rho_0}$$

As ρ_0 is a constant, $\delta = O(1)$ for the ETC acceptance function. □

This leaves the task of proving a ratio in terms of this bound. While the following proofs hold for more general statements of the adaptive TPC, we will prove them w.r.t. δ instead as this dramatically simplifies our notation.

COROLLARY 3.4. *Given a partial realization ψ resulting from application of the l-element greedy policy, $\psi \subset \psi'$, $i \notin dom(\psi)$, and g_{l+1} the next element that would be selected by the greedy policy at partial realization ψ, we have:*

$$\Delta(i \mid \psi') \leq \delta\Delta(g_{l+1} \mid \psi)$$

PROOF. By Lemmas 3.1 and 3.2,

$$\Delta(i \mid \psi') = \Gamma(i \mid \psi', \psi)\Delta(i \mid \psi) \leq \delta\Delta(g_{l+1} \mid \psi)$$

and thus the statement holds. □

We exploit this corollary in the following lemma to explicitly relate the difference between an arbitrary policy and the l-element greedy policy to the expected marginal gain of adding an $l + 1$'st element to the greedy solution. Note that this "arbitrary policy" will, in practice, be an *optimal* policy.

LEMMA 3.5.
$$f_{avg}(\pi') - f_{avg}(\pi_l) \leq k\delta\Delta_{avg}(\pi_l, \pi_{l+1}) \tag{5}$$
where π_l is the greedy policy selecting l elements with $l < k$, π' selects exactly k elements, and $\Delta_{avg}(\pi_l, \pi_{l+1}) = f_{avg}(\pi_{l+1}) - f_{avg}(\pi_l)$.

PROOF. Note that
$$f_{avg}(\pi') - f_{avg}(\pi_l) \leq f_{avg}(\pi_l @ \pi') - f_{avg}(\pi_l)$$
since $f_{avg}(\pi') \leq f_{avg}(\pi_l @ \pi')$ due to the adaptive monotonicity of f. From this inequality, it is clear that the difference in the expected values of π' and π_l is bounded by the marginal gain of running π' after π_l. This involves sending at most k additional requests. By Corollary 3.4, the marginal gain of each of these requests is bounded above by $\delta\Delta(g_{l+1} \mid \psi)$ for each possible ψ. Thus, we have:

$$f_{avg}(\pi') - f_{avg}(\pi_l) \leq \mathbb{E}[k\delta\Delta(g_{l+1} \mid \psi) \mid \psi]$$
$$= k\delta\mathbb{E}[\Delta(g_{l+1} \mid \psi) \mid \psi]$$
$$= k\delta\mathbb{E}[\mathbb{E}[f(dom(\psi) + g_{l+1}, \Phi) - f(dom(\psi), \Phi) \mid \Phi \sim \psi] \mid \psi]$$
$$= k\delta\mathbb{E}[f(E(\pi_{l+1}, \Phi), \Phi) - f(E(\pi_l, \Phi), \Phi) \mid \Phi]$$
$$= k\delta\Delta_{avg}(\pi_l, \pi_{l+1})$$

where the second equality uses the definition of $\Delta(\cdot)$. □

Finally, we have the main theorem providing the adaptive approximation guarantee:

THEOREM 3.6.
$$\left[1 - \left(1 - \frac{1}{k\delta}\right)^k\right] f_{avg}(\pi_k^*) \leq f_{avg}(\pi_k) \tag{6}$$

PROOF. By Lemma 3.5, we have

$$f_{avg}(\pi_k^*) \leq f_{avg}(\pi_l) + k\delta\Delta_{avg}(\pi_l, \pi_{l+1})$$

Multiply both sides by $(1 - (k\delta)^{-1})^{k-1-l}$ and sum from $l = 0$ to $k - 1$. We directly get that the left hand side reduces to

$$k\delta\left[1 - \left(\frac{k\delta - 1}{k\delta}\right)^k\right] f_{avg}(\pi_k^*)$$

The right-hand side reduces to

$$\sum_{l=0}^{k-1} \left[f_{\text{avg}}(\pi_l) + k\delta\Delta_{avg}(\pi_l, \pi_{l+1}) \right] \left(1 - \frac{1}{k\delta} \right)^{k-1-l}$$

To simplify the below equations, we will denote $\beta = 1 - \frac{1}{k\delta}$ and use the identity $f_{\text{avg}}(\pi_l) = \sum_{i=0}^{l-1} \Delta_{\text{avg}}(\pi_i, \pi_{i+1})$.

Consider the $j + 1$'st decision made by the policy π. Inside the summation, decision π_{j+1} appears in the terms

$$\beta^{k-1-j} k\delta\Delta_{\text{avg}}(\pi, \pi_{j+1}) + \beta^{k-1-(j+1)}\Delta_{\text{avg}}(\pi, \pi_{j+1})$$
$$+ \beta^{k-1-(j+2)}\Delta_{\text{avg}}(\pi, \pi_{j+1}) + \dots$$

$$= \left[\beta^{k-1-j} k\delta + \sum_{l=j+1}^{k} \beta^{k-1-l} \right] \Delta_{\text{avg}}(\pi, \pi_{j+1})$$

Applying the closed form of the geometric series, we can simplify this coefficient to

$$\beta^{k-1-j} k\delta + \frac{\beta^{k-1-j} - 1}{\beta - 1} = \beta^{k-1-j} k\delta - \beta^{k-1-j} k\delta + k\delta$$

where the right-hand of this inequality comes from noting that $(1 - 1/(k\delta)) - 1 = -1/(k\delta)$. Therefore, we have the sum

$$\sum_{l=0}^{k-1} k\delta\Delta_{\text{avg}}(\pi_l, \pi_{l+1}) = k\delta f_{\text{avg}}(\pi)$$

Rearranging terms, we arrive at the statement of the theorem. □

COROLLARY 3.7. *Greedy maximization of an adaptive monotone function with total primal curvature bound δ satisfies*

$$\left(1 - 1/e^{1/\delta} \right) f_{avg}(\pi_k^*) \le f_{avg}(\pi_k) \tag{7}$$

PROOF. This follows immediately by noting

$$\lim_{k \to \infty} \left(1 - \frac{1}{k\delta} \right)^k = 1/e^{1/\delta}$$

□

Thus, we have a constant approximation ratio of $1 - 1/e^{1/\delta} \approx 0.165$ for the MINE problem under the ETC model.

3.1 The Necessity of Finite Curvature

In the statement of Theorem 3.6, we use our problem-specific bound δ on Γ. We now show that it is necessary for any problem to have a finite bound δ to obtain an approximation ratio unless $P = NP$. We accomplish this by showing that any $\rho(n)$-approximation algorithm for maximizing an arbitrary monotone non-submodular g must solve a class of NP-hard problems exactly, but that the constraint $\Gamma < \infty$ excludes such problems.

THEOREM 3.8. *There is no polynomial time algorithm for $\rho(n)$-approximate maximization of an arbitrary monotone non-submodular function g with $\rho(n) > 0$ unless $P = NP$.*

PROOF. To show this, we first construct an objective function with infinite curvature that cannot be exactly solved in polynomial time by reduction to SAT [15]. We then show that any approximation algorithm with ratio $\rho(n) > 0$ is necessarily exact. While our proof uses discrete terminology, we note that discrete problems are a subset of adaptive problems where there is only a single realization and therefore our proof extends to the adaptive case.

Suppose we are given a CNF formula F with C clauses each having k_l literals and containing L literals total. We show how to construct a monotone supermodular function g which returns 1 when the formula is satisfied and 0 otherwise.

First, we construct the domain of g. For every literal x_i in F, insert two elements T_i and F_i into set N, corresponding to assigning the literal x_i 1 and 0, respectively. Then, a satisfying assignment for F corresponds to a set S containing either T_i or F_i for every literal x_i. For the moment, we assume that such an assignment exists.

The verifying function g is then composed of three semantic parts, each of which returns 1 when satisfied and 0 otherwise: (1) S contains a satisfying assignment, (2) S does not contain both T_i and F_i for any i, and (3) S assigns every literal a value. The latter two conditions are needed because it is possible for a formula such as $F = (x_1 \vee \cdots) \wedge (x_1 \vee \cdots) \wedge \cdots$ to be given, which is satisfied by the assignment corresponding to $S = \{T_1\}$.

For each clause $c_l = x_i \vee x_j \vee \cdots \vee \bar{x}_r \vee \cdots$, define a function $C_l(S)$ verifying the clause is satisfied. For each literal x_i, define a function $A_i(S)$ verifying x_i is not simultaneously assigned 0 and 1. Finally, define a function $B(S)$ verifying that every literal is assigned a value. These can be constructed and evaluated exactly in polynomial time with the following closed forms:

$$C_l(S) = \left\lceil \frac{1}{k_l} \left(|\{T_i\} \cap S| + |\{T_j\} \cap S| + \cdots + |\{F_r\} \cap S| \right) \right\rceil$$

$$A_i(S) = 1 - \left\lfloor \frac{1}{2} |\{T_i, F_i\} \cap S| \right\rfloor$$

$$B(S) = \left\lfloor \frac{1}{L} |S| \right\rfloor$$

Then define g as

$$g(S) = B(S) \prod_{i=1}^{L} A_i(S) \prod_{l=1}^{C} C_l(S)$$

By construction, g is 1 for any S corresponding to a satisfying assignment and 0 otherwise. Further, note that $\forall |S| \le k$, this function is monotone supermodular. To have this property everywhere, we extend it piecewise to $g'(S) = g(S) \forall |S| \le k$ and $g'(S) = 1 \forall |S| > k$.

Now, suppose we have an F with exactly one satisfying assignment. Then there is exactly one $S^*, |S^*| = k$ s.t. $g'(S^*) = 1$, and $\forall S, |S| \le k : g'(S) = 0$. Clearly, if a polynomial-time algorithm $\mathcal{A}$ can approximate the optimal solution S^* with $\rho(n) > 0$, then on this problem it must find the optimal solution. Otherwise, it would have $\rho(n) = 0$. Therefore, either $\mathcal{A}$ can solve SAT in polynomial time, implying $P = NP$, or $\mathcal{A}$ does not have a non-zero approximation ratio for the stated class of objective functions. □

Observe that the above problem does not have a finite bound δ, since $\Gamma(i \mid S^* \setminus \{i\}, S^* \setminus \{i, j\}) = 1/0.$[5] Thus, the constraint that δ be finite is also sufficient to exclude such cases. More generally, this means that every technique for giving an approximation ratio for

---

[5]We abuse our notation here. $\Gamma(i \mid T, S)$ is the discrete analogue of the adaptive total primal curvature, and can be defined as the ratio of marginal gains.

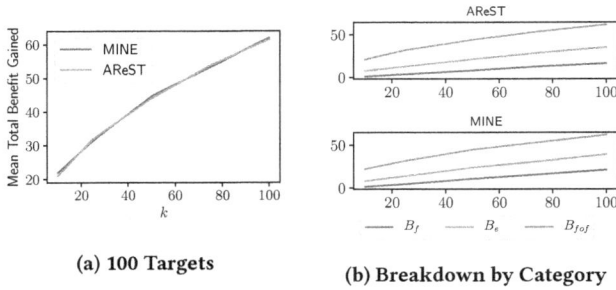

(a) 100 Targets

(b) Breakdown by Category

Figure 2: Benefit with and without a term rewarding boosting future acceptance chances on the Slashdot network.

non-submodular maximization must also bound δ unless $P = NP$.[6]

4 EXPERIMENTAL EVALUATION

We now examine several key questions about the performance of the greedy socialbot. Extensive experiments have already established the general efficacy of the greedy policy under various acceptance models, including the one studied in this paper, and that the choice of acceptance model significantly impacts the potency of the attack [18, 19]. Thus, we instead focus on investigation of particular factors influencing the behavior of the bot. First, we establish equivalence with the bot models studied previously – a result necessitated by the omission of a term rewarding the bot for improving acceptance probability from our definition of $f(F, \phi)$. We then examine the impact of the benefit model on the bot, finding the counter-intuitive result that rewarding the bot for being merely a friend-of-friend of a target increases the fraction of targets befriended.

We adopt the benefit model given by Li *et al.* [18]: for a *target set* of users T, $B_f(u) = 1$ if $u \in T$, 0 otherwise; $B_{fof}(u) = \frac{1}{2}B_f(u)$; and $B_e(u, v) = 2^{T_u + T_v}/M$ where M is the maximum expected degree of any user on the network, $T_u = 1$ if $u \in T$ and 0 otherwise. We additionally use their "degree incentive" function to model the tendency of high-degree users to accept friend requests without critical examination. We set $\epsilon = 0.2$, which yields $\beta \leq 10$ and gives the performance ratio of roughly 10%. Our simulations are implemented in Rust.[7][8] Unless otherwise specified, we run each method 250 times per data point and plot the mean.

Our experiments focus on the DBLP (317k nodes, 1M edges, 13.5k ground-truth communities) and Slashdot 2008 (77k nodes, 516k edges) datasets, both taken from SNAP [17]. As location of targets may impact the attack policy, we focus on two natural target models in our experiment. First, a simple breadth-first-search from a randomly chosen node, collecting 100 possible neighbors (i.e. the BFS progresses as if each potential edge exists). This models an adversary taking a simple topological approach to building a target list. Alternately, the attacker could obtain a ground-truth list of targets from an external source (e.g. an organizational list of employees). We model this by targeting ground-truth communities, which have been provided for the DBLP topology. These are paired

---

[6]We remark that if one lets $g'(S) = c$, $c > 0$ rather than setting it to 0 for non-solution sets, then *any* algorithm obtains a $1/c$ approximation ratio.

[7]https://rust-lang.org

[8]Code is available at https://gitlab.com/emallson/ht2018-experiments.

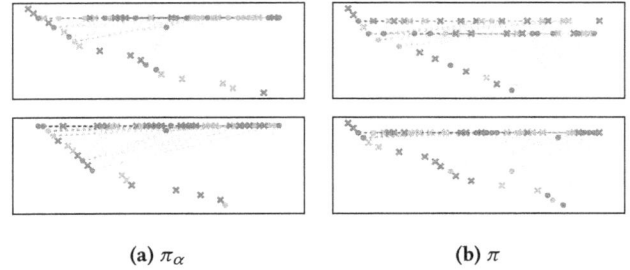

(a) π_α

(b) π

Figure 3: Sample traces under policies π_α and π with $k = 50$ and 100 targets on the Slashdot network. Dark nodes are targeted. $\times$ marks represent users that rejected the bot's friend request and circular marks the opposite. Time proceeds left to right. Each node is placed on the first row from the top containing a friend or is added to a new row if none exist. Lines correspond to edges in the OSN.

with a baseline we term "Untargeted:" every user is assigned a random $b_u \in [0, 1]$ and we set $B_f(u) = b_u$. This models the attacker wishing only to collect private data, but having some idea of which users are more likely to give high return for their investment.

4.1 Equivalence to Prior Models

In prior work, an additional term is present in the optimization objective that directly rewards the bot for increasing the acceptance probability α of other nodes. Note that this term is absent from our formulation (compare Eqn. (4) to the equivalent in e.g. [18]). Figure 2 shows that this change does very little to alter the total benefit gained. However, it does not rule out the possibility that the corresponding policies encode different choices. Golovin & Krause observe that a policy π can be viewed as a decision tree encoding the actions to take based on the current partial realization [11]. We wish to verify whether the decision tree for the α-rewarding policy (which we will denote π_α) is fundamentally different from the policy encoded by Alg. 1 (simply denoted π).

As the problem of constructing – let alone comparing – these decision trees is quite difficult, we take the simpler approach of qualitative comparison to check for macro-level differences in behavior. Figure 3 shows a sample sets of *traces* for each policy. We see very similar patterns of behavior in both policies: early attempts to establish a foothold, followed by exploitation of that foothold to befriend other users. From these figures, it is clear that there is not a large difference in behavior caused by omitting this term, and therefore we assume that prior results apply to this formulation.

4.2 Befriending Targets by Encouraging Friend-of-Friend Relations

According to Li *et al.*, the benefit model they use is constructed to reward the bot based on the amount of information it may obtain from friendship: full benefit for befriending a user, part of that benefit for friend-of-friend relations, and a small additional amount for revealing an edge (present or not). We observe that this means the bot is rewarded a nontrivial amount for only becoming a friend-of-friend of targets. This leads us to ask what impact this has on the bot's success in infiltrating the target set.

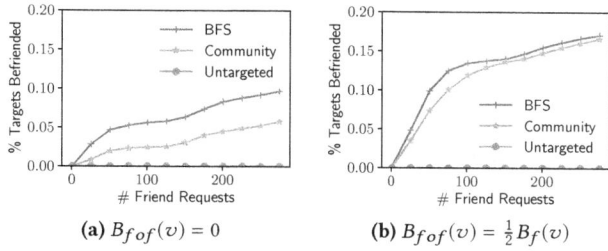

(a) $B_{fof}(v) = 0$

(b) $B_{fof}(v) = \frac{1}{2}B_f(v)$

Figure 4: Fraction of target set T befriended by the bot as a function of the # of requests sent on the DBLP network.

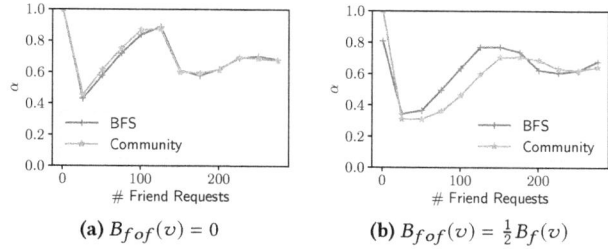

(a) $B_{fof}(v) = 0$

(b) $B_{fof}(v) = \frac{1}{2}B_f(v)$

Figure 5: Acceptance probability of each request sent by the bot on the DBLP network.

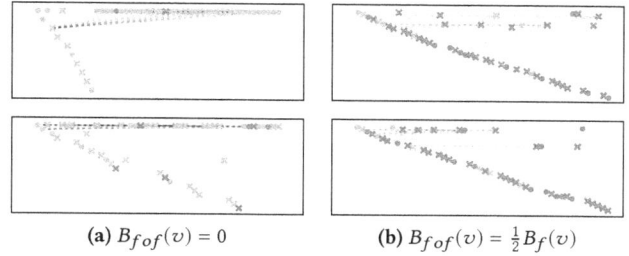

(a) $B_{fof}(v) = 0$

(b) $B_{fof}(v) = \frac{1}{2}B_f(v)$

Figure 6: Sample traces with community targets on DBLP both (a) without and (b) with FoF benefit.

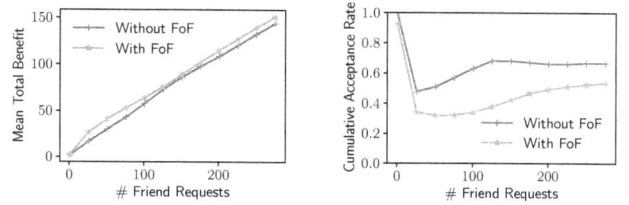

Figure 7: Mean Benefit gained with and without FoF benefit when targeting communities on DBLP.

Figure 8: Overall acceptance rate over the lifetime of a bot when targeting communities on DBLP.

Figure 4 shows that the "consolation prize" of $B_{fof}(u) > 0$ actually increases the fraction of targets befriended, although as seen in Fig. 7 the amount of benefit gained remains similar. On the other hand, Figure 5 shows that this setting leads to a lower overall probability of acceptance of requests sent by the bot. Figure 6 shows sample traces covering the first 50 requests when a community is targeted on DBLP. Immediately apparent are two results: the bot having friend-of-friend benefit focuses almost all of its requests on targeted nodes, while the one without is dramatically more successful early in the process. We note that the mean acceptance probability shown in Fig. 5 is similar early in the process, so these degree of failure seen in Fig. 6b (which does not show average behavior) is likely not representative.

However, this does illuminate the change caused by removing friend-of-friend benefit. Without this benefit source, the higher probability of befriending untargeted users and for their edge benefit edges out the value of befriending target users. The addition friend-of-friend benefit causes a greater number of targets to be befriended through a pair of effects: the direct effect of greater benefit for clustered targets and the secondary effect of improving the acceptance probability of targets by befriending their neighbors.

We note that the side effect of reducing early acceptance rate may not be worth the cost, however. The use of rejection rate in bot detection was remarked upon by the developers of the Facebook Immune System [24], although the overall acceptance rate seen by Boshmaf et al. during the same time period was quite low (19.3% in the first 6 days, moving up to 59.1% over the entire 6-week experiment) [5]. Figure 8 shows the mean acceptance rate (defined as the rate of successful requests, as opposed to the predicted values shown in Fig. 5) over the lifetime of the bot. Notably, the acceptance rate never drops as low as the sub-20% seen in the experiments of

Boshmaf et al. However, there is a sizable gap between the rates of a bot operating with and without friend-of-friend benefit.

5 CONCLUSION & FUTURE WORK

In this work, we developed a novel technique for bounding the approximation quality of a greedy socialbot conducting a reconnaissance attack under a *realistic* model of user behavior. This was then generalized to provide a bound for the much broader class of adaptive monotone non-submodular problems given a bound on the *adaptive primal curvature* (APC) of their objective functions. We further showed that a finite bound on the APC is necessary for any approximation guarantee to hold for any algorithm. Our definition of curvature differs from those used in prior work, which indicates that more study is needed to identify the exact properties necessary to obtain an approximation ratio.

We then conducted further analysis of the behavior of a socialbot under this realistic model. Notably, we found the counter-intuitive result that rewarding the bot for becoming friends-of-friends of its targets actually improved the rate at which it befriended targets – at a small cost to overall acceptance rate. This counter-intuitive result leads us to note that the current definition of benefit may be sub-optimal. Further study should be devoted to finding the optimal scheme for assigning benefit to users to maximize particular metrics (e.g. target friending rate). We also note that our model of user acceptance only incorporates topological features. Future work may explore the impact of profile and temporal features on acceptance probability, and optimality under such features.

REFERENCES

[1] Lars Backstrom and Jure Leskovec. 2011. Supervised random walks: predicting and recommending links in social networks. In *Proceedings of the fourth ACM international conference on Web search and data mining*. ACM, 635–644.

[2] Andrew An Bian, Joachim Buhmann, Andreas Krause, and Sebastian Tschiatschek. 2017. Guarantees for Greedy Maximization of Non-submodular Functions with Applications. In *Proceedings of the 34th International Conference on Machine Learning (ICML '17)*.

[3] Yazan Boshmaf, Konstantin Beznosov, and Matei Ripeanu. 2013. Graph-based sybil detection in social and information systems. In *Advances in Social Networks Analysis and Mining (ASONAM), 2013 IEEE/ACM International Conference on*. IEEE, 466–473.

[4] Yazan Boshmaf, Dionysios Logothetis, Georgos Siganos, Jorge Lería, Jose Lorenzo, Matei Ripeanu, and Konstantin Beznosov. 2015. Íntegro: Leveraging Victim Prediction for Robust Fake Account Detection in OSNs. In *Proc. of NDSS*.

[5] Yazan Boshmaf, Ildar Muslukhov, Konstantin Beznosov, and Matei Ripeanu. 2011. The Socialbot Network: When Bots Socialize for Fame and Money. In *Proceedings of the 27th Annual Computer Security Applications Conference (ACSAC '11)*. ACM, 93–102. https://doi.org/10.1145/2076732.2076746

[6] Abhimanyu Das and David Kempe. 2011. Submodular Meets Spectral: Greedy Algorithms for Subset Selection, Sparse Approximation and Dictionary Selection. (2011). arXiv:cs, stat/1102.3975

[7] Uriel Feige. 1998. A Threshold of Ln N for Approximating Set Cover. 45, 4 (1998), 634–652. https://doi.org/10.1145/285055.285059

[8] Michael Fire, Rami Puzis, and Yuval Elovici. 2013. Link prediction in highly fractional data sets. In *Handbook of computational approaches to counterterrorism*. Springer, 283–300.

[9] Michael Fire, Lena Tenenboim, Ofrit Lesser, Rami Puzis, Lior Rokach, and Yuval Elovici. 2011. Link prediction in social networks using computationally efficient topological features. In *Privacy, Security, Risk and Trust (PASSAT) and 2011 IEEE Third Inernational Conference on Social Computing (SocialCom), 2011 IEEE Third International Conference on*. IEEE, 73–80.

[10] Carlos Freitas, Fabricio Benevenuto, Saptarshi Ghosh, and Adriano Veloso. 2015. Reverse Engineering Socialbot Infiltration Strategies in Twitter. In *Proceedings of the 2015 IEEE/ACM International Conference on Advances in Social Networks Analysis and Mining 2015 (ASONAM '15)*. ACM, 25–32. https://doi.org/10.1145/2808797.2809292

[11] Daniel Golovin and Andreas Krause. 2011. Adaptive Submodularity: Theory and Applications in Active Learning and Stochastic Optimization. 42 (2011), 427–486.

[12] Thibaut Horel and Yaron Singer. 2015. Scalable Methods for Adaptively Seeding a Social Network. In *Proceedings of the 24th International Conference on World Wide Web (WWW '15)*. International World Wide Web Conferences Steering Committee, 441–451. https://doi.org/10.1145/2736277.2741127

[13] Thibaut Horel and Yaron Singer. 2016. Maximization of Approximately Submodular Functions. In *Advances in Neural Information Processing Systems 29*, D. D. Lee, M. Sugiyama, U. V. Luxburg, I. Guyon, and R. Garnett (Eds.). Curran Associates, Inc., 3045–3053.

[14] Rishabh K Iyer, Stefanie Jegelka, and Jeff A Bilmes. 2013. Curvature and Optimal Algorithms for Learning and Minimizing Submodular Functions. (2013), 2742–2750.

[15] Richard M. Karp. 1972. Reducibility among Combinatorial Problems. In *Complexity of Computer Computations*, Raymond E. Miller, James W. Thatcher, and Jean D. Bohlinger (Eds.). Springer US, 85–103. DOI: 10.1007/978-1-4684-2001-2_9.

[16] David Kempe, Jon Kleinberg, and Éva Tardos. 2003. Maximizing the Spread of Influence Through a Social Network. In *Proceedings of the Ninth ACM SIGKDD International Conference on Knowledge Discovery and Data Mining (KDD '03)*. ACM, 137–146. https://doi.org/10.1145/956750.956769

[17] Jure Leskovec and Andrej Krevl. 2014. SNAP Datasets: Stanford Large Network Dataset Collection. http://snap.stanford.edu/data. (June 2014).

[18] Xiang Li, J. David Smith, Thang N. Dinh, and My T. Thai. 2016. Privacy Issues in Light of Reconnaissance Attacks with Incomplete Information. In *Proceedings of the 2016 IEEE/WIC/ACM International Conference on Web Intelligence*. IEEE/WIC/ACM.

[19] Xiang Li, J. David Smith, and My T. Thai. 2017. Adaptive Reconnaissance Attacks with Near-Optimal Parallel Batching. In *2017 IEEE 37th International Conference on Distributed Computing Systems (ICDCS)* (2017-06). 699–709. https://doi.org/10.1109/ICDCS.2017.130

[20] George L. Nemhauser, Laurence A. Wolsey, and Marshall L. Fisher. 1978. An Analysis of Approximations for Maximizing Submodular Set Functions—I. 14, 1 (1978), 265–294.

[21] Nam P Nguyen, Guanhua Yan, and My T Thai. 2013. Analysis of misinformation containment in online social networks. *Computer Networks* 57, 10 (2013), 2133–2146.

[22] Abigail Paradise, Asaf Shabtai, and Rami Puzis. 2015. Hunting Organization-Targeted Socialbots. In *Proceedings of the 2015 IEEE/ACM International Conference on Advances in Social Networks Analysis and Mining 2015 (ASONAM '15)*. ACM, New York, NY, USA, 537–540. https://doi.org/10.1145/2808797.2809396

[23] Thomas Ryan and G Mauch. 2010. Getting in bed with Robin Sage. In *Black Hat Conference*.

[24] Tao Stein, Erdong Chen, and Karan Mangla. 2011. Facebook Immune System. In *Proceedings of the 4th Workshop on Social Network Systems (SNS '11)*. ACM, 8:1–8:8. https://doi.org/10.1145/1989656.1989664

[25] Guangmo Tong, Weili Wu, Shaojie Tang, and Ding-Zhu Du. 2017. Adaptive Influence Maximization in Dynamic Social Networks. 25, 1 (2017), 112–125. https://doi.org/10.1109/TNET.2016.2563397

[26] Onur Varol, Emilio Ferrara, Clayton A. Davis, Filippo Menczer, and Alessandro Flammini. 2017. Online Human-Bot Interactions: Detection, Estimation, and Characterization. In *Eleventh International AAAI Conference on Web and Social Media* (2017-05-03). https://aaai.org/ocs/index.php/ICWSM/ICWSM17/paper/view/15587

[27] Zengfu Wang, Bill Moran, Xuezhi Wang, and Quan Pan. 2014. Approximation for Maximizing Monotone Non-Decreasing Set Functions with a Greedy Method. 31, 1 (2014), 29–43. https://doi.org/10.1007/s10878-014-9707-3

A Deep Joint Network for Session-based News Recommendations with Contextual Augmentation

Lemei Zhang
Department of Computer Science
Trondheim, Norway
lemei.zhang@ntnu.no

Peng Liu
Department of Computer Science
Trondheim, Norway
peng.liu@ntnu.no

Jon Atle Gulla
Department of Computer Science
Trondheim, Norway
jon.atle.gulla@ntnu.no

ABSTRACT

Session-based recommendations have drawn more and more attention in many recommendation settings of modern online services. Unlike many other domains such as books and music, news recommendations suffer from new challenges of fast updating rate and recency issues of news articles and lack of user profiles. In this paper, we proposed a method that combines user click events within session and news contextual features to predict next click behavior of a user. The model consists of two different kinds of hierarchical neutral networks to learn article contextual properties and temporal sequential patterns in streams of clicks. Character-level embedding over input features is adopted to allow integrating different types of data and reduce engineering computation. Besides, we also introduced a time-decay method to compute the freshness of news articles within a time slide. Experimental results on two real-world datasets show significant improvements over several baselines and state-of-the-art methods on session-based neural networks.

CCS CONCEPTS

• **Human-centered computing** → **User models**; • **Computing methodologies** → **Neural networks**; • **Mathematics of computing** → *Time series analysis*;

KEYWORDS

Convolutional neural networks, recurrent neural networks, deep learning, session-based recommendation

ACM Reference Format:
Lemei Zhang, Peng Liu, and Jon Atle Gulla. 2018. A Deep Joint Network for Session-based News Recommendations with Contextual Augmentation. In *HT'18: 29th ACM Conference on Hypertext & Social Media, July 9–12, 2018, Baltimore, MD, USA.* ACM, New York, NY, USA, 9 pages. https://doi.org/10.1145/3209542.3209557

1 INTRODUCTION

News recommender systems have become popular and are employed by many multimedia companies in recent years, as a natural consequence of the increasing complexity and scale of web services and e-commerce platforms. They are able to cope with the information overload and to assist users in finding information matching their individual preferences. Unlike other recommender system domains like books, music and movies, news recommender systems must address additional challenges [5]. For example, large publishers release hundreds of news daily, implying that they must deal with fast-growing numbers of items that get quickly outdated and irrelevant to most readers. User interests change much faster compared with other domains. News articles have recency issues which make users tend to read recent news, not the old ones. In addition, the news domains suffer from extreme levels of sparsity.

Generally, traditional news recommender systems always produce relevant items based on news content and user input profiles [5]. However, problems arise when it goes to unregistered users, since there are no profiles for them, while on the other hand unregistered users occupy a large proportion of the total news readers. According to the statistics performed on Cxense platform[1], the subscribers only take up about 20% of all users in Adresseavisen company[2], which is the third biggest news portal in Norway. Providing accurate recommendations to non-subscribers is also very necessary in real-life applications.

Under such situation, a typical solution is to base recommendations on session data, e.g. session clicks. These data have two important characteristics. First, session clicks are sequential in nature and the order of clicks may contain information of user intent. Second, clicked items are often associated with metadata such as names, categories, and descriptions, which provide additional information about user taste. Most recent works have focused on exploiting these two characteristics to draw more information from data when designing recommendation strategies. Hidasi et al. for the first time investigated the use of recurrent neural networks (RNN) for session-based next-item recommendation [10]. RNNs are a natural choice for this problem and have been successfully explored for other sequence-based prediction problems in the past [3, 7]. An experimental evaluation on two datasets indicated that their GRU4REC method significantly outperforms item-based k-nearest-neighbor (kNN) methods by 15% to 30% in terms of ranking metrics. Massimo et al. further improved the work in [10] by proposing a model based Hierarchical RNN, that extends previous RNN-based session modeling with one additional GRU level that models the user activity across sessions and the evolution of his interests over time [22]. Despite these positive results, some questions regarding the effectiveness of the session-based recommendation method remain open. First, from our exploratory analysis using standard recurrent architectures for session modeling, we find that they model sequential patterns in streams of clicks and consider all

---

[1] https://www.cxense.com/.
[2] http://www.adressa.no/.

past events to improve recommendation performance. But they fail to integrate different feature types and jointly model their interactions. Second, in the news domain, recency issues of news articles is another predominant challenging which they ignore. Third, the lack of scalable models applicable to deal with the large amounts of noisy data seriously restrains the application of recommendation service in the real world.

In this paper, we propose a neural network (NN) based model, named Deep Joint Neural Networks (DeepJoNN), to address these three problems. The proposed model uses a recurrent neural network (RNN) to capture sequential patterns in streams of clicks and associated features. A convolutional neural network (CNN) is exploited to consider item IDs and all content features including hierarchical categories, keywords and entities as texts and represent the resulting textual data with a character-level model [33]. DeepJoNN provides an effective way to jointly model temporal and content patterns that are indicative of readers' intention with two types of hierarchical neural networks (CNN and RNN). At the same time, representing all features at character level frees us from the need of time consuming feature engineering and can be applied for different types of features. We applied our model to several real data sets and the experimental results demonstrate promising and reasonable performance of our approach.

In summary, our contributions are as follows:

- The proposed Deep Joint Neural Networks (DeepJoNN) jointly model sequential pattern of session clicks and different content features of items for session-based recommendation. To the best of our knowledge, DeepJoNN is the first one that jointly models both user and item from news streams using two different kinds of hierarchical neural networks.
- We propose to use character-level representation for all types of features, which frees us from feature engineering steps and reduces the number of model parameters. Experiments demonstrate the effectiveness of the proposed method.
- We extend the traditional Convolutional Neural Network to multi-dimensional level processing by integrating tensor-based feature representation method.
- We conduct extensive experiments to evaluate the performance and generality of our model on two real large-scale datasets. The results show the advantages of our method for session-based recommendation in comparison with state-of-the-art techniques.

The remainder of the paper is organized as follows. Section 2 introduces the related work. In section 3, we present our DeepJoNN model in detail. We describe the data sets, experimental settings and the state-of-the-art methods we use in section 4, as well as experimental results and analysis. Finally, we present the conclusions and future work in Section 5.

2 RELATED WORK

News Recommendation. News recommendation aims to recommend to users the news that match their personal interests best[18]. As a popular service and an important way to retain users, industry puts much efforts in news recommendation researches[4]. Several adaptive news recommending systems, such as Google News and Yahoo! News provide personalized news recommendation services for a substantial amount of online users. Existing news recommender systems can be roughly catogorized into three groups: collaborative filtering, content-based filtering and hybrid methods. The first one makes use of news ratings by users to provide recommendation services, and they are content-free. In practice, most collaborative filtering systems are constructed based on users' past rating behaviors, either using a group of users "similar" to the given user to predict news ratings[26], or modelling users' behaviors in a probabilistic way[12]. However, collaborative filtering is ineffective for cold-start problem. Content-based methods try to sequentially find newly-published articles similar to the user's reading history in terms of content. Generally speaking, news content is often represented using vector space model (e.g., TF-IDF) [19], or topic distributions obtained by language models (e.g., PLSI and LDA), and specific similarity measurements are adopted to evaluate the relatedness between news articles. However, in some scenario, simply representing the user's profile information by a bag of words is insufficient to capture the exact reading interest of the user. Recently, hybrid solutions are attracted more attentions to improve recommendation results. Representative examples include Rao et al. [23], in which the inability of collaborative filtering to recommend news items is alleviated by combining it with content-based filtering.

Other important factors related to news recommendations include news recency issue and data sparsity problem. Many online users read limited news stories compared with the entire repository, and hence the access matrix is very sparse. Cold start problem caused by new registered users will also lead to sparse problem. To address this problem, model-based collaborative (i.e. matrix factorization, probabilistic matrix factorization) is most commonly adopted to reduce dimensions and consequently reduce the level of sparsity [14, 20]. To alleviate recency issue in news recommendation, Bilsus et al. [1] report to take a list of articles as input, which have been selected in advance by several criteria including recency. Das et al. [4] choose to re-build the recommender models every hour in order to present the freshest information to the users. In this paper, we adopt time-decay function to reduce the weight of the historical news articles, and character-level encoding to alleviate sparsity problem.

Session-based Recommendations. Classical content-based and collaborative filtering do not work well in the session-based setting when no user profile can be constructed from past user behavior. A natural solution to this problem is the item-to-item recommendation approach [26], in which two items are deemed to be similar if they are frequently clicked together in the same sessions. It is a simple but effective method. However, a drawback of the item-to-item recommendation is that it does not consider click order and generates predictions based only on the last click. Figueiredo et al. [6] propose a Bayesian generative model to model click sequences. Learning item embeddings is another approach suitable for session-based recommendation. The authors of [30] leverage item metadata to regularize item embeddings, which makes it relevant to content-based approaches. Recently, several studies have been done to use neural network based models including deep learning techniques for recommendation tasks. Hidasi et al. [10] propose to use RNN to model whole sequences of session click IDs. In a later work, they [11] extend their previous work by combining rich features of clicked items such as item IDs, textual descriptions, and images. They use different RNNs to represent different types of features and train those networks in a parallel fashion. Our work is relevant to [11] in that we combine features of different type for better session-based recommendation. However, our method uses a totally different model (DeepJoNN) and encoding method, which provide improved accuracy while simplify feature engineering steps.

Deep Learning. Deep learning has been successfully employed in computer vision [15], speech recognition [8], and several other application domains [16]. Among these applications, convolutional neural networks (CNN) and recurrent neural networks (RNN) are two most popular deep learning models. Other deep learning models include auto-encoders, Restricted Boltzman Machines (RBMs), and fully connected networks with multiple hidden layers [16]. In recent years, deep learning methods have also been shown to be promising in the area of recommender systems. One of the first related methods along this direction was presented by Salakhutdinop et al. [25], in which several layers of RBMs are stacked together to deliver a better accuracy than a CF algorithm using singular value decomposition. Deep Models have been used to extract features from unstructured content such as music or images that are then used together with more conventional collaborative filtering models. Wang et al. [32] introduced a more generic approach whereby a deep network is used to extract generic content-features from any types of items, these features are then incorporated in a standard collaborative filtering model to enhance the recommendation performance. Van den Oord et al. [29] proposed a somewhat similar hybrid method exploiting a convolutional deep network to learn features from content descriptions of songs, which are then used in a CF model to tackle the data sparsity problem. The difference is that they use CNNs for feature learning rather than auto-encoders. Our method also uses CNNs and content features, but our model allows capturing temporal patterns, which is important for sequential nature of session clicks.

3 THE DEEPJONN MODEL

In this section, we describe the proposed Deep Joint Neural Networks (DeepJoNN) for session-based news recommendation.

In the session-based recommender system, there is a set of items that a user can interact with; note that the term "item" is used in a broad sense here. We experiment with the proposed models using two different datasets, where the possible recommendations are news articles and artists respectively. The datasets are described in Section 4.

Let M be the set of items in the system, and $M_v \in \mathbb{R}^{m_v \times n}$ is the embedding representation of item v. The embedding representation approach will be introduced in the next section. Let $S = [S_1, S_2, ..., S_{n_s}]$ be a set of sessions, and $S_i = [U_{i,1}, U_{i,2}, U_{i,n_u}]$ be the set of events grouped by users and then ordered by timestamp within session S_i, where n_s and n_u denote the number of sessions in training data and the number of users within a session respectively. $U_{i,u} = [s_{i,u,1}, s_{i,u,2}, ..., s_{i,u,q}]$ where $s_{i,u,q}$ denotes the q-th interaction event of user u within session i. Our DeepJoNN model retrieves the corresponding embedding representation of $s_{i,u,q}$ for each interaction event q of user u in session i, and feed those into the CNN layer of the model. The common task

for all the recommendation models we experiment with is to predict each consecutive item for user u in a session S_i. That is, for a sub-session $[s_{i,u,1}, s_{i,u,2}, ..., s_{i,u,j}]$ for user u of S_i, the system is to predict $s_{i,u,j+1}$. A recommendation C_i, is an ordered list of k recommended items, where we would want to see the next item as close to the top as possible.

3.1 Character-level Representation

Character-level representation as input for especially Convolutional Neutral Network (CNN) has been widely used in NLP domain, and presents competitive results compared with traditional models with fewer parameters and computational cost [13, 33]. The only problem appears when processing misspelling and informal words, which seldom happens in news domain. Inspired by this idea, we encode the input features such as keywords, categories and entities into character-level but still different from the existing approaches, which will be described in this section.

Let Ψ denote the vocabulary of characters of size $|\Psi|$. Suppose an item feature f is given as a sequence of characters $[\psi_1, \psi_2, ..., \psi_p]$, where p is the length of f. Then the character-level encoding of feature f is given by vector $e^f \in R^{L_f}$, where L_f is the length of feature f in the dataset, and the i-th element will be set as the index number of the i-th character in Ψ, and set as 0 otherwise. Note that the index number of character in Ψ starts from 1. In this work, we use vocabulary Ψ of 74, including all lower case characters and upper case characters from Norwegian alphabet, 10 digit characters, and several other characters, which are shown below:

ABCDEFGHIJKLMNOPQRSTUVWXYZÆØÅabcdefghijklmnopqrstu
vwxyzæøå1234567890 .-/|:@

For each clicked event, we represent the associated features as follows:

- Item ID and User ID. A sequence of hash code is encoded according to their digits and alphabets and represented as vectors.
- Keywords and Entities. Each word or phrase such as "været" and "Anne-Grete", in keywords and entities is encoded as one vector, and all encoded words and phrases are stacked vertically to form as a matrix $K^{m_k \times n_k}$, where m_k is the maximum number of words and phrases in keywords and entities which is set as 408 in our case, and n_k is the maximum length of characters in each unit which is set as 100 in our experiment.
- Category. Categories are usually organized in a hierarchy by the website owner. To utilize the information encoded in the hierarchy, we concatenate the current category with all its ancestors up to the root and use the resulting sequence of characters as category feature, for instance "nyheter|moreromsdal". Category is encoded as vector.

Given character-level encoded vectors and matrices for each type of features, we stack the vector and matrices on top of each other to form to the final matrix of $M_{s,j}^u \in \mathbb{R}^{m \times n}$ for the j-th event in session s of user u, where $m = m_k + 3$ and n is the longest features which is the same as n_k in our experiments. If the length of the feature is shorter than its maximum length, then we fill empty positions with all zeros to get a matrix with equal size for each event within the dataset.

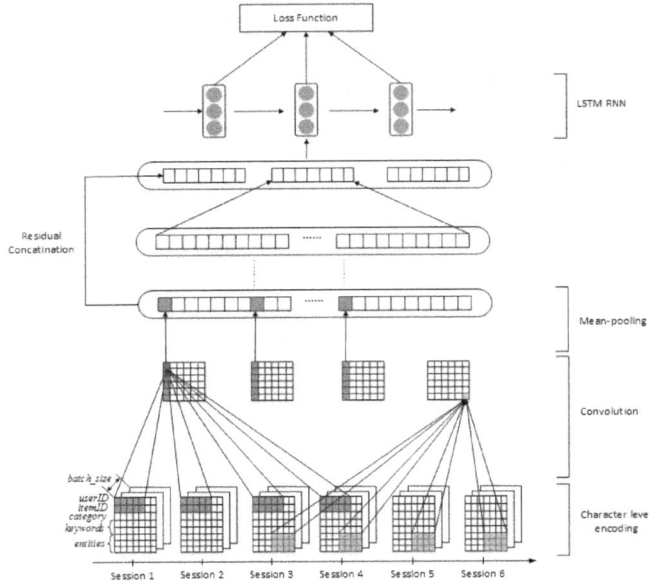

Figure 1: The architecture of the proposed model

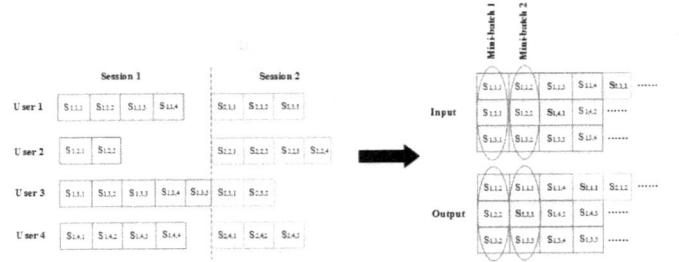

Figure 2: User-parallel mini-batches for mini-batch size 3.

3.2 DeepJoNN Architecture

In this section, we describe the proposed Deep Joint Neural Networks (DeepJoNN) for session-based recommendation. The architecture of our model, shown in Figure 1 is straightforward. After character-level embedding into matrix as input, a 2-layer convolutional neural network is deployed to learn the input feature patterns, and then its output will be transferred as input to RNN layer.

3.2.1 CNN with Multiple Dimensional Input.
Many researchers have found that CNNs are useful in extracting information from raw data, ranging from computer vision to speech recognition and several NLP tasks. By applying convolution operations at different level of granularity, a CNN can extract features that are useful for learning tasks and reduce the need of manual feature engineering [28]. This characteristic is adopted in our task to extract useful patterns of separate features or their combinations, from streams of click events within sessions.

Recall that $S = [S_1, S_2, ..., S_{n_s}]$ is a set of sessions, and $S_i = [U_{i,1}, U_{i,2}, U_{i,n_u}]$ denotes the set of events within session S_i. $s_{i,u,q}$ in $U_{i,u} = [s_{i,u,1}, s_{i,u,2}, ..., s_{i,u,q}]$ denotes the q-th interaction event of user u within session i. For the sake of efficiency in training, we adopt the session-parallel mini-batch mechanism described in [11] to consider user identifiers during training as shown in Figure 2. To begin with, the first events of the first session of the first mini-batch with size b of users constitute as input matrix $M \in \mathbb{R}^{m \times n \times b}$ to the model. Meanwhile the next items of the first session of the same users mentioned above form as the target output from the model. Then the next events of the first session of the same users used as the input for the next iteration, and so on. When a mini-batch end, if there are other users in the first session that haven't been trained, then these users will be regarded as input for next mini-batches. With session-parallel mini-batch integrated into the

training process, the model can be trained efficiently over different users having different number of sessions and different number of events within sessions.

Inspired by the work [17] which uses low-rank n-gram tensors to directly exploit interactions between words already at the convolution stage, we extend it to learn tensor based feature mapping from multi-dimensional contextual input features. Recall that $M \in \mathbb{R}^{m \times n \times b}$ represents the character-level input matrix with m number of features, n of character embedding length and b of mini-batch size. For each matrix $M_{s,j}^u \in \mathbb{R}^{m \times n}$ within batch, $e_i \in \mathbb{R}^n$ is a vector denoting the i-th feature. The consecutive c vectors ending at position j is obtained by concatenating the corresponding vectors

$$v_j = [e_{j-c+1}; e_{j-c+2}; ...; e_j] \tag{1}$$

which can be seen as the combination of consecutive features, e.g. category and keywords, or different keywords. Out-of-index position are simply set to all zeros.

Thus, the filter for v_j can be denoted as $K_j \in \mathbb{R}^{cn \times h}$ which can be thought as c smaller filter applied to each vector in v_j. The operator maps each v_j in the input matrix to $K_j^T v_j \in \mathbb{R}^h$ so that the input features is transformed into a sequence of combined feature representation,

$$V_j = [K_j^T v_1, ..., K_j^T v_L] \in \mathbb{R}^{L \times h} \tag{2}$$

In order to capture relevant information in the combined features in a more direct way, the outer product is conducted for $v_j = [e_{j-c+1}; e_{j-c+2}; ...; e_j]$. Suppose for $c = 3$, the value of result from outer product at position (i, j, k) can be denoted as

$$(e_1 \otimes e_2 \otimes e_3)_{ijk} = e_{1i} \cdot e_{2j} \cdot e_{3k} \tag{3}$$

Therefore, the filters for the concatenate matrix should also be maintained as high-order tensors. In other words, the filters are linear mappings over the higher dimensional interaction terms and can be denoted as T. Let $z \in \mathbb{R}^h$ denotes the resulting h-dimensional feature representation for $c = 3$ combined feature vectors, and it can be achieved through multiplying the filter T and the combined features vectors. The l-th coordinate of z is given by

$$z_l = \sum_{i,j,k} T_{ijkl} \cdot (e_1 \otimes e_2 \otimes e_3)_{ijk}$$
$$= \sum_{i,j,k} T_{ijkl} \cdot e_{1i} \cdot e_{2j} \cdot e_{3k} \tag{4}$$

However, directly maintaining the filter T as full tensor can lead to parametric explosion. To solve this problem, a low-rank-factorization of the tensor T is introduced. Specifically, T is decomposed into a sum of h rank-1 tensors

$$T = \sum_{i=1}^{h} P_i \otimes Q_i \otimes R_i \otimes O_i \qquad (5)$$

where $P, Q, R \in \mathbb{R}^{h \times c}$ and $O \in \mathbb{R}^{h \times h}$ are four smaller parameter matrices. For simplicity, we assume that the number of rank-1 components in the decomposition is equal to the feature dimension h. Plugging the low-rank factorization into Eq.(1), the feature-mapping can be rewritten in a vector form as

$$z = O^T(Pe_1 \odot Qe_2 \odot Re_3) \qquad (6)$$

where $\odot$ is the element-wise product. Note that while Pe_i is a linear mapping from each feature e_i into a h dimensional feature space, higher order terms arise from the element-wise products (the same as Qe_2 and Re_3).

After z has been derived, we put z into an activation function $f(\cdot)$. In the proposed model, we use Rectified Linear Units (ReLUs). Deep convolutional neural networks with ReLUs train several times faster than their equivalents with tanh units. Then we apply Eq. 7, a mean pooling operation, over the feature map and take the average value as the feature corresponding to this particular filter.

$$f_j = mean\{f(z_1), f(z_2), ..., f(z_L)\} \qquad (7)$$

We have described the process by which one feature is extracted from one filter. The model uses multiple filters to obtain various features and the output vector of the convolutional layer is as Eq. 8.

$$F = \{f_1, f_2, ..., f_J\} \qquad (8)$$

where J denotes the number of filters in the convolutional layer. The results from the mean pooling layer are passed to a fully connected layer with weight matrix W. As shown bellow:

$$x_i = f(W \times F + b) \qquad (9)$$

The output of the fully connected layer $x_i \in \mathbb{R}^{n_2 \times b}$ is considered as the feature for input events, where n_2 represents the number of neutrons of the last CNN layer.

3.2.2 Session-based Recurrent Neutral Network.
A recurrent neutral network is a type of neutral network particularly suited for modelling sequential data. The main difference between RNNs and conventional feedforward deep models is the existence of an internal hidden state in the units that compose the network. Such hidden state summarizes all historical information up to current training timestamp , and meanwhile an additional memory cell is designed to alleviate gradients vanishing/exploding issues. Thus, RNN is suitable for our tasks to learn inter-session and intra-session patterns. In session s_i, an RNN takes the input matrix $x_i \in \mathbb{R}^{n_2 \times b}$ which is the output from CNN layers, and the hidden state vector $h_{i-1} \in \mathbb{R}^{n_o \times b}$ and produce the next hidden state h_i by applying the following recursive operation

$$h_i = f(W \cdot x_i + U \cdot h_{i-1} + b) \qquad (10)$$

Here $W \in \mathbb{R}^{n_o \times n_2}$, $U \in \mathbb{R}^{n_o \times n_o}$, $b \in \mathbb{R}^{n_o}$ are parameters of an affine transformation and f is an element-wise nonlinearity. n_o and n_2 represent the number of items and the number of output units

from CNN layer. Long short-term memory (LSTM) optimizes the traditional RNN by integrating a memory cell vector $c_i \in \mathbb{R}^{n_2 \times n_o}$ during each session in our tasks and thus addresses the problem of exploding/vanishing gradient when learning long-term dependencies. Concretely, one step of an LSTM takes as input x_i, h_{i-1}, c_{i-1} and produces h_i, c_i via the following intermediate calculations

$$
\begin{aligned}
i_i &= \sigma(W^i \cdot x_i + U^i \cdot h_{i-1} + b^i) \\
f_i &= \sigma(W^f \cdot x_i + U^f \cdot h_{i-1} + b^f) \\
o_i &= \sigma(W^o \cdot x_i + U^o \cdot h_{i-1} + b^o) \\
g_i &= \tanh(W^g \cdot x_i + U^g \cdot h_{i-1} + b^g) \\
c_i &= f_i \odot c_{i-1} + i_i \odot g_i \\
h_i &= o_i \odot tanh(c_i)
\end{aligned}
\qquad (11)
$$

Where $\sigma(\cdot)$ and $tanh(\cdot)$ are the element-wise sigmoid and hyperbolic tangent functions, $\odot$ is the element-wise multiplication operator, and i_i, f_i, o_i are referred to as input, forget and output gate. For the first session with subscript $i = 1$, h_0 and c_0 are initialized to zero matrix. Parameters that need to be tuned for LSTM are W^p, U^p, b^p for $p \in \{i, f, o, g\}$. However, in our experiments, sometimes gradient exploding is still an issue, but can be alleviated by using optimization strategies such as gradient clipping.

3.2.3 Ranking Loss Design.
Ranking is the core of a Recommender System, and it consists pointwise, pairwise and listwise ways. Pointwise ranking estimates the score or the rank of items independently of each other, whereas pairwise ranking compares the score or the rank of pairs of a positive and a negative one. Listwise ranking uses the scores and ranks of all items and compares them to the perfect ordering. However, listwise ranking is not used so often because of the expensive computational cost for sorting. As a part of our model training procedure, we adopt both pointwise ranking (BPR) and pairwise ranking (TOP1). Their definitions are defined as follows:

- BPR: Byesian Personalized Ranking [24] is a matrix factorization method that uses pairwise ranking loss. It compares the score of a positive and a sampled negative item. In our experiment, we compare the score of the positive item with several sampled items and use their average as the loss. The loss at a given point in one session is defined as

$$L_i = -1/N_i \cdot \sum_{j=1}^{N_i} log(\sigma(\hat{r}_{i,k} - \hat{r}_{i,j})) \qquad (12)$$

where N_i is the item size, $\hat{r}_{i,q}$ is the score on item q at a given point of session i, k is the target item and j are items with score less then 0.5.

- TOP1: This ranking loss criteria proposed by [10] is defined as the regularized approximation of the relative rank of the relevant item. In our task, the TOP1 loss can be defined as

$$L_i = 1/N_i \cdot \sum_{j=1}^{N_i} \sigma(\hat{r}_{i,j} - \hat{r}_{i,k}) + \sigma(\hat{r}_{i,j}^2) \qquad (13)$$

The square part in this equation is the regularization term to avoid exploding score when certain positive items act as negative examples.

- CROSS ENTROPY: Besides, cross entropy is also a widely used loss function in recommendation area which can be formulated in our tasks as:

$$L_i = -1/N_i \cdot \sum_{j=1}^{N_i} [r_{i,j} log \hat{r}_{i,j} + (1 - r_{i,j}) log(1 - \hat{r}_{i,j})] \quad (14)$$

To note that, if the item k is target item in session i, then $r_{i,k} = 1$, then 0 otherwise.

3.2.4 Recency Issues of News.
News articles always suffer from recency issues which describes the phenomenon that the freshness of a newly published article in news domain to users can only lasts 2 to 3 days on average. Beyond this time period, this news article will hardly intrigue interests for users. To solve this problem, we integrate a time-decay function into our model which is defined as below.

$$R_{decay} = e^{-\lambda \cdot (t - t_0)} \quad (15)$$

where λ is the parameter that needs to be tuned during training, and controls the decay rate for the news. t and t_0 represent the predicated time at one point within session and the publication time of the news. The decay rates are multiplied by the output values from LSTM RNN layer to form the final outputs.

4 EXPERIMENTS

In this section we describe our experimental setup and provide an in-depth discussion of the obtained results.

4.1 Datasets

We used two datasets for our experiments. The first is the Adressa 16G dataset[3] which contains 93,948 news articles, 398,545 readers, and about 113 million events over a 90-days period [9]. Each of these events represent that a user read a particular news article. As pre-processing, we filtered top 50 active users and keeped sessions with more than 2 events for a user. Besides, we removed the records that users visited the news front page for there are no articles related information within the events. In order to evaluate our model's generality, we adopted Last.fm provided by Schedl[27], which contains 10 weeks of log data between 1/1/2013 and 11/3/2013. To enrich the content information for the dataset, we also used Last.fm API[4] to collect artist information to improve the recommendation accuracy. The characteristics of the datasets are summarized in Table 1.

Table 1: Main properties of the experimental datasets.

Dataset	Adressa	Last.fm
#sessions	2,215	73,273
#users	50	2,501
#events	62,908	580,393
#items	6,765	7,899
#sessions_train	2,146	70,772
#events_train	41,746	560,976
#sessions_test	50	2,501
#events_test	5,650	19,417

---

[3]https://www.ntnu.no/wiki/display/smartmedia/SmartMedia+Program.
[4]https://www.last.fm/api/show/artist.getInfo

Table 2: Main hyper-parameters of DeepJoNN.

Parameter	Value	Parameter	Value
Batch-size	20	Loss	TOP1
Learning rate	0.01	#Hidden units	100,100,100
Optimization	adagrad	#Parameters	2170100
L2	0.0001	Drop out	0.1/0.1/0
#Layer_CNN/RNN	2/1	Hidden activation	ReLU, tanh

To split users' historical logs into sessions, for both datasets, following Zheleva et al.[34] and Baur et al.[2], we use the time gap approach to generate sessions. If the gap between two reading/play items is less than 30 minutes for user u, they belong to the same session. Otherwise, they will be separated into two sessions. However, especially for Addressa dataset, users only read one articles for most of the time when setting time gap as 30 minutes, which may not have enough samples for training. Thus, we also test different time gaps that influence recommendation performance.

The testing set is build with the last session of each user. The remaining sessions form the training set. Besides, we also leave the last session of each user from training set as a validation set, which is used for hyper-parameter selection during each iteration in training procedure. To help the reproducibility of our experiments, we report the hyper-parameters of our model in Table 2.

4.2 Evaluation Metrics

Based on temporally ordered lists of read/played items, our objective is to correctly predict the next item a target user will likely read/play. The ground truth at a particular time step is therefore represented by a single user-item tuple. To present the user with adequate recommendations, the target item should be among the top few recommended items. Since we are interested in measuring top-k recommendation instead of rating prediction, we measure the quality by looking at the $Recall@K$ and $MRR@K$, which are widely used for evaluating top-k recommender systems.

- $MRR@k$ (Mean Reciprocal Rank) is defined as the average of the reciprocal ranks of the desired items [31]. The rank is set to zero if it is above k.
- $Recall@k$ is defined as the fraction of cases where the item actually consumed in the next event is among the top k items recommended [21].

We set $k = 20$, as it appears desirable from a user's perspective to expect the target among the first 20 items [10].

4.3 Baselines

To validate the effectiveness of DeepJoNN, we compared our model with the following session-based recommendation methods.

- Popular-based Method (POP): This method recommends items with the largest number of interactions by the users.
- Item KNN: Item KNN is a simple, yet effective method, which is widely deployed in practice. In this method, two item are considered similar if they co-occur frequently in different sessions. In our situation, we recommend items based on cosine similarity between different sessions.

- BPR-MF[5]: It is one of the commonly used matrix factorization methods, but cannot directly apply to session-based recommendations for the new session do not have feature vectors precomputed. Instead, we use the average value of item feature vectors that had occurred in the session before the predicting point, as the user feature vector [24].
- Hierarchical RNN (HRNN)[6]: Proposed by [22], the model is a personalized RNN model with cross-session information transfer in a seamless way. HRNN relays end evolveds latent hidden states of the RNNs across user sessions.

4.4 Performance Evaluation

The performance of DeepJoNN and the baselines are reported in terms of Recall@k and MRR@k on two kinds of datasets in Figure 3. In addition to the baseline models, we also compare our DeepJoNN model with and without integrating time-decay factors, which are represented as *DeepJoNN* and *DeepJoNN − t* respectively.

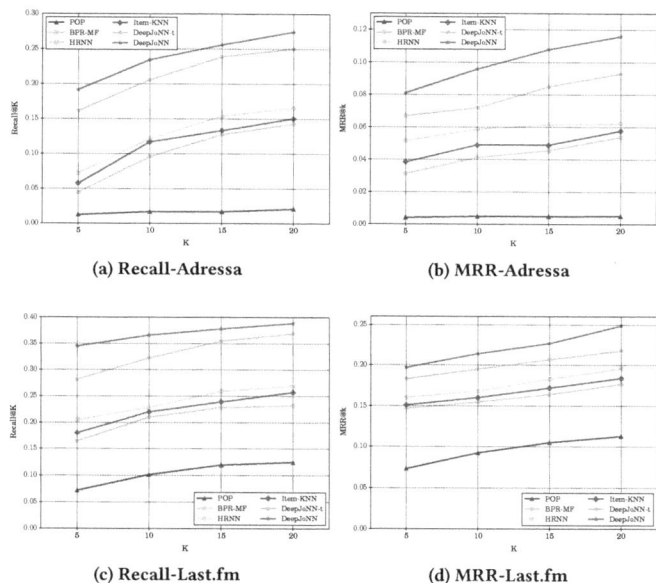

(a) Recall-Adressa

(b) MRR-Adressa

(c) Recall-Last.fm

(d) MRR-Last.fm

Figure 3: Performance comparison w.r.t. top@k rank scores in terms of Recall@k and MRR@k on Adressa and Last.fm datasets. k ranges from 5 to 20 and h fixed at 3 for DeepJoNN and DeepJoNN-t.

The figure shows that all models perform better on *Last.fm* dataset than *Adressa*. It is mainly because the sparsity and unbalance characteristics appearing in *Adressa* dataset. As described in [9], only small amount of news are read by a lot of users, and thus, in our experiments, these kinds of news have a better chance to get higher scores than the others. The deep learning models consistently outperform the other models on both datasets in terms of Recall and MRR, despite the fact that Item KNN is a very competitive baseline. Beside, all DeepJoNN models outperform HRNN model

---

[5]https://github.com/bbc/theano-bpr.
[6]https://github.com/mquad/hgru4rec.

on both evaluation metrics which we believe is mainly because the integration of contextual features. Furthermore, the integration of tensor-based feature mapping method in CNN can also be a possible reason that explain the higher performance. The DeepJoNN model using time-decay factors consistently outperforms other experimented models in terms of all evaluation metrics, on both datasets.

4.5 Model Parameter Analysis

In this section, we analyse the influence of the gap length of the session and the value of h parameters in CNN filters to the performance of our model. In our experiments, parameter h is varied from 1 to 4, and session length is set to 0.5, 1, 3, 6, 9 hour(s). The results are shown in Figure 4. Just as we expected, the performance continually goes up along with the higher value setting to h for that the intra-relationships between features, especially between words and phrases, for one event are also important for recommendation performance. However, when h is more than 3, more computational resources are needed to process more parameters and tensor operations without recommendation performance obviously increasing. Thus, we believe 3 is a suitable order for balance the computational cost and model performance in our tasks. Besides, with smaller gap length of sessions, there are fewer users and events within a session and thus little diversities are incorporated in our dataset for one session. Furthermore, frequently switchings of users during training may also cause fluctuation effect of the parameter tuning and will lead to slow convergence.

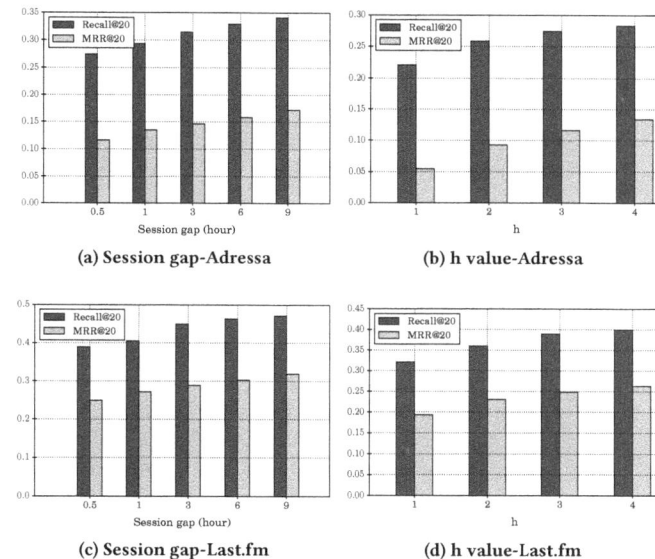

(a) Session gap-Adressa

(b) h value-Adressa

(c) Session gap-Last.fm

(d) h value-Last.fm

Figure 4: Performance of DeepJoNN on recommendation tasks with varied session lengths and h values.

4.6 Comparison of Loss Functions

In this section, we measure the performance gain of the proposed improvements over the 3 different loss functions, TOP1, Bayesian Personalized Ranking(BPR) [24] and Cross Entropy. In our tasks,

Table 3: Recall@10 and MRR@10 for different types of configuration of DeepJoNN with different losses. Best results per dataset are highlighted.

Loss / #Units	Adressa Dataset		Last.fm Dataset	
	Recall@20	MRR@20	Recall@20	MRR@20
TOP1 300	0.271 (+3.4%)	0.115 (+1.2%)	0.389 (+2.6%)	0.249 (+1.6%)
BPR 300	0.249 (+3.0%)	0.106 (+2.0%)	0.360 (+2.4%)	0.227 (+1.4%)
Cross-entropy 300	0.261 (+4.1%)	0.109 (+1.4%)	0.392 (+3.2%)	0.258 (+1.7%)
TOP1 600	0.296 (+2.5%)	**0.157 (+1.8%)**	**0.407 (+3.6%)**	**0.271 (+2.1%)**
BPR 600	**0.321 (+5.0%)**	0.119 (+1.3%)	0.367 (+2.1%)	0.241 (+1.2%)
Cross-entropy 600	0.263 (+2.6%)	0.103 (+1.5%)	0.374 (+1.7%)	0.238 (+1.3%)

we conducted 2 groups of experiments with 300 hidden units (2-layers CNN with 100 units in each layer, and 1-layer RNN with 100 units in each layer), and 600 hidden units (2-layers CNN with 200 units in each layer, and 2-layer RNN with 100 units in each layer) respectively. Within each group of experiments, we run 10 times with different random seeds for each loss function in order to get different performance in terms of Recall and MRR value. Our results are shown in Table 4, and the numbers in brackets represent the fluctuation towards positive direction.

From the listed results, it can be observed that cross entropy achieved better than the other two functions in terms of *Last.fm*, whereas TOP1 scheme get the best result for *Adressa* dataset with 300 hidden units. Therefore, for different recommendation tasks, different loss functions may result in slightly different recommendation performance. However, cross entropy is relatively unstable compared with other schemes for the number in brackets are slightly bigger under the same settings, which from another side proves the observation in research [10], that pointwise ranking based losses were usually unstable, even with regularization. Additionally, it does not always happen that deep networks with bigger and deeper configuration can achieve better performance which makes parameter tuning an important task in training deep networks.

4.7 Cold-Start Problem

Additionally, we also conducted experiments to study the effectiveness of different recommendation algorithms in addressing cold-start issues on the two kinds of datasets. As preprocession, we removed users who have less then 3 events during sessions and less than 2 sessions in training set. The users who have more than 20 sessions are also removed from dataset. Besides, we also filtered users in testing set who were not contained in training dataset.

The experimental results are shown in Figure 5, from which we have the following observations: 1) our proposed DeepJoNN and DeepJoNN-t still performs best consistently in recommending cold-start cases; 2) by comparing the recommendation results in Fig. , the Recall and MRR value of all recommendation algorithms kept nearly the same effectiveness. For instance, the Recall value of HRNN in cold-start settings is 13.90%, MRR values is 5.36%, and meanwhile it achieved nearly the same performance with value of 16.56% and 6.22% of Recall and MRR when set k to 20 on *Adressa* dataset. Similar phenomenon can also be found from *Last.fm* dataset. From training process, we also discovered that our DeepJoNN and HRNN converged faster than traditional RNN with better performance.

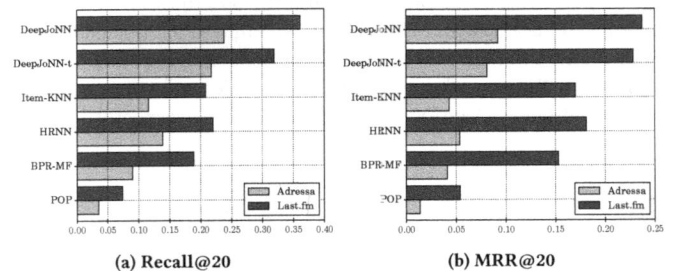

(a) Recall@20   (b) MRR@20

Figure 5: Recommendations for Cold-start Cases.

5 CONCLUSION

In this paper, we presented a Deep Joint Network (DeepJoNN) for session-based recommendations. The proposed model allows combining various item features such as ID, category, keywords and entities, which then are transformed into character-level input matrix to the model. DeepJoNN consists of two parts of deep neural networks coupled together in a hierarchical way and thus could extract contextual patterns and process long and short-term dependencies simultaneously. In comparison of the state-of-the-art baselines, DeepJoNN achieved nearly 11% and 12% improvements on datasets of *Adressa* and *Last.fm* respectively w.r.t. Recall value. Additionally, we also explored the influence of different parameter settings and conducted experiments on different loss functions. Our model also performed competitively on cold start users without user profiles.

As future works, we plan to look into more features such as user locations, reading time for an article, and improve the session-based recommendation even further. We also plan to investigate recommendations in other domains, such as commercial data.

6 ACKNOWLEDGEMENT

This work is supported by the Norges forskningsråd (Research Council of Norway), #245469.

REFERENCES

[1] Amr Ahmed, Choon Hui Teo, SVN Vishwanathan, and Alex Smola. 2012. Fair and balanced: Learning to present news stories. In *Proceedings of the fifth ACM international conference on Web search and data mining*. ACM, 333–342.
[2] Dominikus Baur, Jennifer Büttgen, and Andreas Butz. 2012. Listening factors: A large-scale principal components analysis of long-term music listening histories. In *Proceedings of the SIGCHI Conference on Human Factors in Computing Systems*. ACM, 1273–1276.

[3] Junyoung Chung, Caglar Gulcehre, KyungHyun Cho, and Yoshua Bengio. 2014. Empirical evaluation of gated recurrent neural networks on sequence modeling. *arXiv preprint arXiv:1412.3555* (2014).

[4] Abhinandan S Das, Mayur Datar, Ashutosh Garg, and Shyam Rajaram. 2007. Google news personalization: scalable online collaborative filtering. In *Proceedings of the 16th international conference on World Wide Web*. ACM, 271–280.

[5] Elena Viorica Epure, Benjamin Kille, Jon Espen Ingvaldsen, Rebecca Deneckere, Camille Salinesi, and Sahin Albayrak. 2017. Recommending Personalized News in Short User Sessions. In *Proceedings of the Eleventh ACM Conference on Recommender Systems (RecSys '17)*. ACM, New York, NY, USA, 121–129. https://doi.org/10.1145/3109859.3109894

[6] Flavio Figueiredo, Bruno Ribeiro, Jussara M Almeida, and Christos Faloutsos. 2016. TribeFlow: mining & predicting user trajectories. In *Proceedings of the 25th International Conference on World Wide Web*. International World Wide Web Conferences Steering Committee, 695–706.

[7] Alex Graves. 2013. Generating sequences with recurrent neural networks. *arXiv preprint arXiv:1308.0850* (2013).

[8] Alex Graves, Abdel-rahman Mohamed, and Geoffrey Hinton. 2013. Speech recognition with deep recurrent neural networks. In *Acoustics, speech and signal processing (icassp), 2013 ieee international conference on*. IEEE, 6645–6649.

[9] Jon Atle Gulla, Lemei Zhang, Peng Liu, Özlem Özgöbek, and Xiaomeng Su. 2017. The Adressa dataset for news recommendation. In *Proceedings of the International Conference on Web Intelligence*. ACM, 1042–1048.

[10] Balázs Hidasi, Alexandros Karatzoglou, Linas Baltrunas, and Domonkos Tikk. 2015. Session-based recommendations with recurrent neural networks. *arXiv preprint arXiv:1511.06939* (2015).

[11] Balázs Hidasi, Massimo Quadrana, Alexandros Karatzoglou, and Domonkos Tikk. 2016. Parallel recurrent neural network architectures for feature-rich session-based recommendations. In *Proceedings of the 10th ACM Conference on Recommender Systems*. ACM, 241–248.

[12] Thomas Hofmann. 2004. Latent semantic models for collaborative filtering. *ACM Transactions on Information Systems (TOIS)* 22, 1 (2004), 89–115.

[13] Yoon Kim, Yacine Jernite, David Sontag, and Alexander M Rush. 2016. Character-Aware Neural Language Models.. In *AAAI*. 2741–2749.

[14] Yehuda Koren, Robert Bell, and Chris Volinsky. 2009. Matrix factorization techniques for recommender systems. *Computer* 42, 8 (2009).

[15] Alex Krizhevsky, Ilya Sutskever, and Geoffrey E Hinton. 2012. Imagenet classification with deep convolutional neural networks. In *Advances in neural information processing systems*. 1097–1105.

[16] Yann LeCun, Yoshua Bengio, and Geoffrey Hinton. 2015. Deep learning. *Nature* 521, 7553 (2015), 436–444.

[17] Tao Lei, Regina Barzilay, and Tommi Jaakkola. 2015. Molding CNNs for text: non-linear, non-consecutive convolutions. In *Proceedings of the 2015 Conference on Empirical Methods in Natural Language Processing*. Association for Computational Linguistics, 1565–1575. https://doi.org/10.18653/v1/D15-1180

[18] Lihong Li, Wei Chu, John Langford, and Robert E Schapire. 2010. A contextual-bandit approach to personalized news article recommendation. In *Proceedings of the 19th international conference on World wide web*. ACM, 661–670.

[19] James H Martin and Daniel Jurafsky. 2000. Speech and language processing. *International Edition* 710 (2000), 25.

[20] Andriy Mnih and Ruslan R Salakhutdinov. 2008. Probabilistic matrix factorization. In *Advances in neural information processing systems*. 1257–1264.

[21] David Martin Powers. 2011. Evaluation: from precision, recall and F-measure to ROC, informedness, markedness and correlation. (2011).

[22] Massimo Quadrana, Alexandros Karatzoglou, Balázs Hidasi, and Paolo Cremonesi. 2017. Personalizing Session-based Recommendations with Hierarchical Recurrent Neural Networks. In *Proceedings of the Eleventh ACM Conference on Recommender Systems (RecSys '17)*. ACM, New York, NY, USA, 130–137. https://doi.org/10.1145/3109859.3109896

[23] Junyang Rao, Aixia Jia, Yansong Feng, and Dongyan Zhao. 2013. Personalized news recommendation using ontologies harvested from the web. In *International Conference on Web-Age Information Management*. Springer, 781–787.

[24] Steffen Rendle, Christoph Freudenthaler, Zeno Gantner, and Lars Schmidt-Thieme. 2009. BPR: Bayesian personalized ranking from implicit feedback. In *Proceedings of the twenty-fifth conference on uncertainty in artificial intelligence*. AUAI Press, 452–461.

[25] Ruslan Salakhutdinov, Andriy Mnih, and Geoffrey Hinton. 2007. Restricted Boltzmann machines for collaborative filtering. In *Proceedings of the 24th international conference on Machine learning*. ACM, 791–798.

[26] Badrul Sarwar, George Karypis, Joseph Konstan, and John Riedl. 2001. Item-based collaborative filtering recommendation algorithms. In *Proceedings of the 10th international conference on World Wide Web*. ACM, 285–295.

[27] Markus Schedl. 2016. The LFM-1b Dataset for music retrieval and recommendation. In *Proceedings of the 2016 ACM on International Conference on Multimedia Retrieval*. ACM, 103–110.

[28] Trinh Xuan Tuan and Tu Minh Phuong. 2017. 3D Convolutional Networks for Session-based Recommendation with Content Features. In *Proceedings of the Eleventh ACM Conference on Recommender Systems*. ACM, 138–146.

[29] Aaron Van den Oord, Sander Dieleman, and Benjamin Schrauwen. 2013. Deep content-based music recommendation. In *Advances in neural information processing systems*. 2643–2651.

[30] Flavian Vasile, Elena Smirnova, and Alexis Conneau. 2016. Meta-Prod2Vec: Product Embeddings Using Side-Information for Recommendation. In *Proceedings of the 10th ACM Conference on Recommender Systems*. ACM, 225–232.

[31] Ellen M Voorhees et al. 1999. The TREC-8 Question Answering Track Report.. In *Trec*, Vol. 99. 77–82.

[32] Hao Wang, Naiyan Wang, and Dit-Yan Yeung. 2015. Collaborative deep learning for recommender systems. In *Proceedings of the 21th ACM SIGKDD International Conference on Knowledge Discovery and Data Mining*. ACM, 1235–1244.

[33] Xiang Zhang, Junbo Zhao, and Yann LeCun. 2015. Character-level convolutional networks for text classification. In *Advances in neural information processing systems*. 649–657.

[34] Elena Zheleva, John Guiver, Eduarda Mendes Rodrigues, and Nataša Milić-Frayling. 2010. Statistical models of music-listening sessions in social media. In *Proceedings of the 19th international conference on World wide web*. ACM, 1019–1028.

Dynamics and Prediction of Clicks on News from Twitter

Arthi Ramachandran
University of Chicago
Chicago, USA
arthir@cs.columbia.edu

Lucy Wang
Buzzfeed
New York, USA
lucyxw1@gmail.com

Augustin Chaintreau
Columbia University
New York, USA
augustin@cs.columbia.edu

ABSTRACT

Social networks are a major gateway to access news content. It is estimated that a third of all web visits originate on social media, and about half of users rely on those to keep up-to-date with world events. Strangely, no model has been proposed and validated to study how to reproduce and interpolate clicks created by social media. Here we study news posted on Twitter, leveraging public information as well as private data from a popular online publisher. We propose and validate a simple two-step model of information diffusion that can be easily interpreted and applied using only public information to determine current and future clicks.

ACM Reference Format:
Arthi Ramachandran, Lucy Wang, and Augustin Chaintreau. 2018. Dynamics and Prediction of Clicks on News from Twitter. In *HT '18: 29th ACM Conference on Hypertext and Social Media, July 9–12, 2018, Baltimore, MD, USA.* ACM, New York, NY, USA, 5 pages. https://doi.org/10.1145/3209542.3209568

1 INTRODUCTION

Data from social networks is being used to predict a range of outcomes, including the performance of various stocks [5], the progress of various epidemics [24], statistics on crimes [28], and the box office success of movies [3, 29]. However, little is known on how links distributed on social media generate *clicks* even though social media based traffic is a massive source of web traffic.

Among links exchanged on social media, predicting the attention gathered by links to news articles seems especially important. An *increasing* fraction of the population receives their news via social media posts. Further, that evolution of news distribution has raised concerns about its societal impact, including the formation of echo chambers or the spread of dishonest information. Without a satisfactory estimation of clicks, that impact is difficult to gauge. We may be ignoring a silent majority of readers who devote attention only through clicking on, but not sharing or posting content. For these reasons, we urgently need *methods that interpolate attention measured in clicks* using data currently available to social scientists such as shares and followers popularity.

Estimating clicks is hard due to lack of publicly available data and the complex interplay of several factors pertaining to the content,

This material is based upon work supported by the National Science Foundation under Grant No.1254035 and 1514437; A. Ramachandran conducted it at Columbia University.

source, and time. In this paper, we leverage a unique data set and modeling design to model observed click dynamics:

- We analyze impression dynamics on Twitter. (Section 3)
- We justify a two-step, memoryless generative model of link clicks on Twitter, with just a few time-invariant parameters. (Section 4)
- We can then use those lessons learned to interpolate the (private) clicks from (public) social media activity either applied in real time or in foresight. (Section 5)

Our analysis reveals important insights: In contrast with share cascade dynamics, click evolution naturally unfolds at a slower pace. As a result, we demonstrate much higher accuracy in foresight. This indicates that the opportunities to predict web traffic may be underestimated in previous analyses.

2 A SURVEY OF CLICKS ESTIMATION

We feel the need to clarify how interpolating clicks differs from previous works and fits into the large body of work studying the dynamics of news diffusion on Twitter. Information diffusion has been studied to quantify influence [4, 7] and how social networks affect news sharing [1, 2]. Our results are a first step to analyze the behavior of the large majority of silent social media participants, using clicks as a proxy for their collective *reading habits*. Historically, most models of clicks have been designed for online advertising [10, 19] which is a different context from social media.

The vast majority of work studying information diffusion measure popularity through posting activity (shares, tweets, retweets). Some proposed models exploit *microscopic* information about the earliest posts (such as detailed time statistics, or network structure) [9, 18]. Clicks are more sensitive and hence can almost never be observed at such microscopic individual level. Other models of posting dynamics include using a Bayesian approach [30], reinforcing processes [25, 31], or dynamical process under external influence [20]. But while posts appear as bursts in a short-time frame, clicks appear and decay at larger time scales [11].

Finally, a handful of works have addressed the prediction of web traffic and page views online, but are radically different. Studies on YouTube videos, which publicly disclose the view counts, use the popularity observed in the first hour alone ([26]), aggregate retweet counts from subsequent hours ([21]) and explicitly model the *impact* of social media posts as a decaying function ([23]). Recently, [15] posed the prediction of page views for news articles after a day as a regression task. Like [26], it confirmed that (among many features) the early page views observed after 30mn has the highest correlation. We cannot compare our results directly as this paper offers no reproducible algorithm or model and contains no result applied outside of a proprietary dataset. Our results suggest that a much stronger predictive value can be extracted from Twitter.

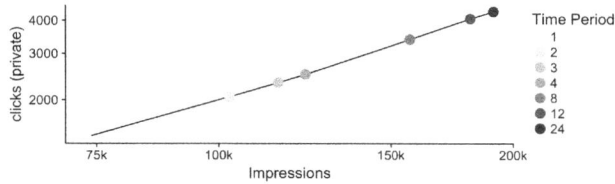

Figure 1: Evolutions of clicks with age for an example link.

3 FOLLOWERS, IMPRESSIONS AND CLICKS

To reproduce click dynamics, we conduct the first complete analysis of news diffusion on Twitter across all three stages of diffusion: tweets, clicks, and the intermediate step of impressions.

3.1 News Media and Publisher Datasets

We start out with BuzzFeed's internal (private) Twitter dataset which has the hourly metrics on each BuzzFeed tweet. We use this source of truth to validate our estimates from public data. The first public data source gives us follower counts of tweets (to estimate impressions i.e., the number of times a link appeared on anyone's screen). The second public source allows us to estimate clicks.

Collecting the Source of Truth We use a proprietary content publisher dataset from BuzzFeed. This data has hourly link clicks, retweets, and impressions for more than 40 active Twitter accounts. The readership information provided by this dataset is used solely here for the purpose of validating a reproducible model. Since the content publisher data set contains proprietary information of a commercial nature, it cannot be disclosed in its entirety.

Collecting (Re)Tweets and Followers We used Twitter's REST API to scrape all tweets and subsequent retweets by BuzzFeed accounts for August 3 to 17, 2016 (4K tweets). Each (re)tweet provides the publicly available follower count of the (re)tweeting user, from which we estimate potential readership, and therefore impressions. This data ignores private retweets, which make up a trivial fraction of retweets [27].

Collecting Impressions and Clicks For each of the Buzzfeed tweets collected, we used bit.ly's API to gather all link clicks referred from Twitter (those with `twitter.com` or `t.co` as the listed referrer domain). We collected data for the periods of hours $1, 2, 3, 4, 5 - 8, 9 - 12, 13 - 24$. We considered only links with bit.ly URLs which completed a 24-hour lifecycle within the date range (1.4K tweets).

We validate our analyses with a data set that includes five major news outlet (*Multiple News Media*[1]).

3.2 Click evolution and its metrics

Receptions, impressions, and distinct click ratios When a Twitter user (re)tweets a link, their followers join the set of "receiving" Twitter users who are susceptible to seeing the link. We call that event a *reception*. The number of receptions of a link is the sum of follower counts for all accounts that (re)tweeted the link. Previous work has shown that overestimation from double-counting followers is less than 20% for 75% of reception counts [12]. [2]

---

[1] available at http://www-sop.inria.fr/members/Arnaud.Legout/Projects/sotweet.html
[2] While one can theoretically compute the number of unique accounts in the "receiving set" to remove multiplicity, the number of API queries involved quickly makes this prohibitively expensive.

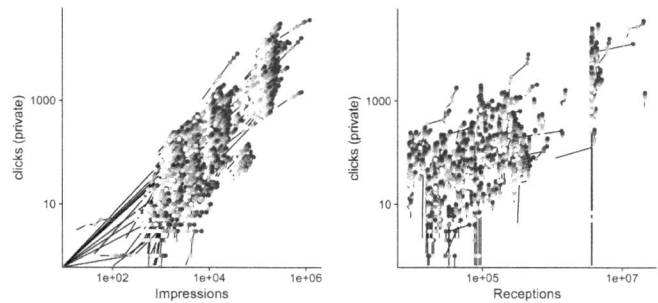

Figure 2: Evolutions of clicks with age (y-axis) (left) by impressions (x-axis) for all links in *Content Publisher* (right) by receptions (x-axis) where no simple dependence emerges.

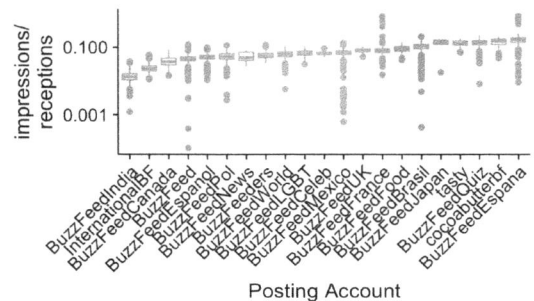

Figure 3: Impressions to Receptions Ratio, seen for all URLs across different accounts, as estimated after 24h.

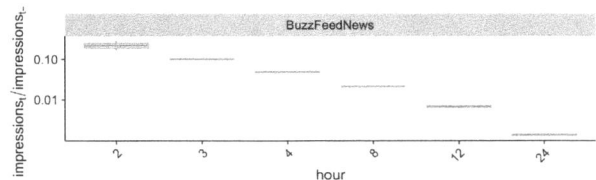

Figure 4: Hourly impressions produced decreases geometrically with time

Most prior studies of online traffic focus on *Clicks Per Impression* (equivalently *Click Through Rate*). However, the number of impressions is almost never available when studying social media. We use the following:

- *Clicks Per Impressions* (CPI): $\frac{\# \, clicks}{\# \, impressions}$

- *Clicks Per Receptions* (CPR): $\frac{\# \, clicks}{\sum_{u \in U} \# \, followers(u)}$, where U is the set of users (re)tweeting the link.

Receptions and Impressions have distinct dynamics The dynamics of receptions and impressions in click generation show substantial differences (Figure 2). Here, each link is a line connecting dots that represent that same link at different time, so that data for a given link becomes darker with its age (example in Figure 1).

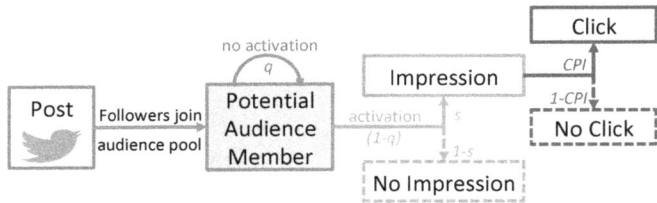

Figure 5: Model of evolution of a click from an initial post to an impression to a click.

Variable	Description
x_t	observed cumulative receptions in time t
y_t	actual cumulative impressions at time t
$\tilde{y}_t$	predicted cumulative impressions at time t
z_t	actual cumulative clicks at time t
$\tilde{z}_t$	predicted cumulative clicks at time t
z_t^{bitly}	observed cumulative clicks from bit.ly at time t
s	scaling parameter
q	activation parameter

Table 1: Variables and Parameters of Model.

The line relating impressions and clicks at different times is, in log-scale, almost perfectly linear. Moreover, that linear trajectory is exhibited by almost all links in the data, regardless of how many clicks it starts out with (Figure 2 left). This indicates that up to a multiplying constant, clicks and impressions per link follow a linear dependence. We conclude that *clicks can be derived from a link's impression by a simple multiplication* and the *multiplying factor is invariant so it can be estimated once*. In contrast, we find that with the number of receptions of a news link (*i.e.*, the sum of followers of all posting sources), the effects of age do not follow a simple dependence (Figure 2 right).

A different model is needed So far our results explain the failure of most click interpolation methods: Receptions are not sufficient alone to predict clicks, while impressions would be but are almost never available. Our results point to a possible new design: studying the dynamics creating impressions from receptions, with the hope to build a robust *estimation* of (private) impressions using (public) receptions with other available factors that play a role.

3.3 In depth dynamics of Twitter diffusion

With a diverse dataset from multiple content sources we can isolate the role of different factors on impression generation. The ratio of impressions divided by receptions across all links varies a lot (Figure 3). But strikingly, almost all this ratio's variance comes from the content source and within the source there is little variation. That result essentially confirms *a posteriori* that impressions are created based on how the source's particular followers pay attention to Twitter, somewhat independently of the specific content of a link.

In Figure 4, the hourly impressions produced by links from the Buzzfeed news account, normalized by impressions produced in the first period, are shown to follow a geometric decreasing trend with few variations. Similar trends have been observed for all accounts and are omitted due to space constraints. Those observations allow us to design an interpretable generative model of clicks on Twitter.

4 CLICK GENERATING MODEL

We model click and impression generation over time as summarized in Figure 5. The only variable for each link is the size of the potential audience, or receptions (light green box). Each time step represents a unit of time (*e.g.*, an hour). At the end of each time step, we first increase the potential audience by the sum of followers for any tweet or retweets sent during that hour containing the link. Each audience member independently then decides to "activate" an impression with a fixed probability (solid orange arrow) or not

(dotted orange arrow). When a member activates, it is removed from the audience and follows the orange path. Otherwise, it remains in the potential audience as shown by the green loop. Of those who activate the impression, each independently decides to click on the article with a fixed probability (red solid box). Potential audience members leave as they activate while more members get added with new retweets. The model stops when the potential audience has no members left. Note that once a user is in the audience pool, it is no longer relevant *when* they entered the pool. Therefore, the dynamics of that model exhibit a memoryless property, typical of the geometric decay we observed before.

From Receptions to Impressions Formally, in this simple memoryless model, a fraction $1 - q$ of the receptions are activated in each of the T time periods (which corresponds to logging on to Twitter). Following that, all activated impressions are removed, and the process repeats on the remaining fraction q in the next time period, and so on until none are left. Of all activated receptions in a given time slot, we assume a fraction s will create an impression and the remainder will miss the link entirely. The form of decay in the potential audience pool size is a geometric decay and thus our model is a geometric memoryless model. Table 1 has a description of all the parameters and variables used. Let x_t be the observed number of receptions in time $t \in [1, T]$ and $\tilde{y}_t$ be the predicted cumulative number of impressions in time t. Then we have $\tilde{y}_t = s \cdot \sum_{\tau=1}^{t} x_\tau \cdot (1 - q^{t-\tau+1})$.

From Impressions to Clicks The memory-less model above predicts the degree of *exposure* or potential audience to a given article. As previously observed, the ratio of clicks per impression remains stable over time. We can use a simple multiplicative factor to estimate the clicks from the predicted impressions at any hour t ($\tilde{y}_t$). This factor is computed at the first time period as the clicks-to-impressions ratio at time $t = 1$ *i.e.*, $CPI_{t=1} = \frac{z_1}{y_1}$ where z_t is the observed number of clicks at time t. Note that in cases where the private click information is not available, we can use the clicks obtained from the bit.ly API. Let $\tilde{z}_t$ be the predicted cumulative number of clicks at time t. Then $\tilde{z}_t = CPI_{t=1} \cdot \tilde{y}_t$.

Parameter Optimization For each article, we can study and learn its model parameters s and q minimizing the square error loss between the predicted number of clicks ($\tilde{y}_t \forall t \in [1, T]$) and the actual number of clicks ($y_t \forall t \in [1, T]$): $\min_{s,q} J = \frac{1}{2} \sum_{\tau=1}^{T} (y_\tau - \tilde{y}_\tau)^2$. We used the L-BFGS-B optimization method [17] from Python's SciPy toolkit [14] for the minimization. The parameters learned for all links span a small range of values (the 5th percentile-95th percentile range for s is [0.046, 0.103] and for q is [0.207, 0.390]).

Method	Training	MAPE	MAPE (adjusted)
Geom.	Hour 1	**17.29** %	**16.20** %
HIP	Hour 1	102.2 %	99.5 %
HIP (rec)	Hour 1	102.2 %	106.3 %
Geom.	Hour 1, 2, 3, 4	**12.68** %	**11.97**%
HIP	Hour 1, 2, 3, 4	91.7 %	89.7 %
HIP (rec)	Hour 1, 2, 3, 4	24.0 %	32.2 %

Table 2: Comparing prediction accuracy of our method and HIP for estimates at 24h for various training periods.

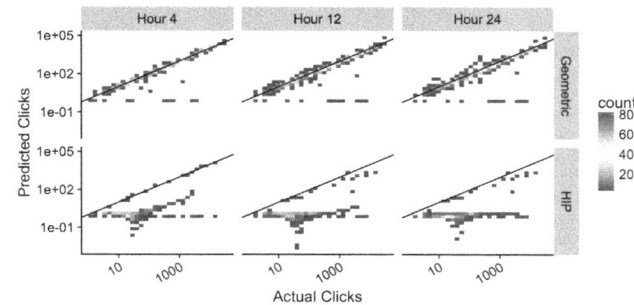

Figure 6: Prediction accuracy of our method and HIP with actual (x-axis) vs predicted (y-axis) values of clicks at different estimation times (shown for 4h of training)

5 REAL-TIME INTERPOLATION

Since the parameters we've learned fall within a narrow range for all links, these parameter values can be used to interpolate hourly clicks for most links. For this study, we assume that in a short period (the training period, which can be up to 4h here), a model has access to all previous clicks and impressions to estimate its own parameters (similar to [23, 25, 32]). After that period is over, the model only has access to the (public) process of posts and retweets and aims to to estimate clicks based on that activity as it unfolds.

Comparing with state-of-the-art When our model is trained on just 1 hour of retweets and clicks, it can interpolate each link's 24-hour click counts with mean absolute percentage error (MAPE) of 17.29% (and 16.20% in adjusted MAPE, where every value is incremented by 1 to handle links with 0 clicks). We compare our model to a real-time interpolation state-of-the-art method to predict views on YouTube [23]. This method uses a Hawkes Intensity Process (HIP) to model the aggregate impact and decay from multiple shares . The interpolated number of clicks is the sum of the influence of current shares and the sum of influences of deprecated previous shares, not unlike our equation. However, HIP leverages 6 parameters capturing several other features like the content type, the network of diffusion, and content sensitivity to promotion. We reproduced HIP, using two training periods for comparison - hour 1 and hours 1-to-4 of the lifespan of the post. HIP trains using shares (retweets) and clicks, while our model follows a different evolution model and uses receptions, impressions and clicks.

Geometric decay is more robust A quick glance at the comparative interpolation results (Table 2 and Figure 6) highlight the merit of a geometric method. We outperform the state of the art, with 5-8x smaller relative errors. The HIP model was not initially designed

Training	Method	MAPE (adj.) by # clicks		
		None	1-5	>5
Hour 1	HIP	772%	1205%	691%
Hours 1-4	HIP	**38.7**%	327%	551%
Other domains	Geom.	305%	**301**%	**66**%

Table 3: Comparing cross domain robustness for HIP and the Geometric method in predicting 24-hour clicks, by article popularity.

to include the effect of the number of followers, so we refine this method to use receptions as a feature instead of shares. Shown as HIP (rec), we find that this improves with sufficient training, but it still falls short of our model. The scatterplot reveals that HIP, while it is initially well trained underestimate clicks that occur later in time. In contrast, our geometric evolution, which is memoryless, is more robust to the noise added with time. We further validate that result by training HIP to predict impressions instead of clicks. Once more, (results omitted due to space constraints), we find that at this time-scale, the geometric evolution returns much more accurate estimations in the case of Twitter.

Robustness across news domains Our method follows a relatively simple dynamic, but we cannot exclude that its superior accuracy originates from idiosyncrasies present in BuzzFeed. We turn to *Multiple News Media* to study the robustness of interpolation in other domains. A caveat to keep in mind is that for those links, we only have access to the bit.ly hourly click counts reported by these URLs which are not a perfect ground truth. In a first validation, we use a random third of the data as training and achieve MAPE of 58%, arguably comparable to noise introduced by bit.ly. To further ensure that we are not dependent on content-specific features, we employed a leave-one-out strategy where the parameters (q, s) were learned from the 4 other domains, and link specific CPI estimated at hour 1. Our interpolation errors remains below 100% and often approaches 50% for more than half of the links.

We compare HIP's performance on these other domains. Since HIP is designed to learn the model from the initial trajectory of shares, we train on the first hour and first four hours. In contrast, the memoryless model was trained using a leave-one-out strategy. For more popular articles, the memoryless model outperforms HIP (Figure 3).

6 CONCLUSIONS

This research validates the use of a publicly accessible method of analyzing social news consumption on Twitter. The analyses provide further evidence that commonly used popularity metrics such as the number of shares or posts have flaws. In our analyses, we show that the relationship between shares and clicks is not straightforward. Rather, it is a two-stage process with a key intermediate piece of information: impressions.

Using this insight, we developed a model based on this two-stage process to predict the temporal dynamics of a post using publicly available data. Compared to many other models, our model only relies on the first hour of data. In particular, it only relies on easily obtainable public information. As such, it provides utility in forecasting applications with time constraints.

Overall, we hope that our model and methodology will help foster better understanding of sharing and audience dynamics.

REFERENCES

[1] J An, Meeyoung Cha, Krishna Gummadi, and Jon Crowcroft. 2011. Media landscape in Twitter: A world of new conventions and political diversity. In *Proceedings of the International Conference Weblogs and Social Media (ICWSM)*. 18–25.

[2] J An, D Quercia, Meeyoung Cha, Krishna Gummadi, and Jon Crowcroft. 2014. Sharing political news: the balancing act of intimacy and socialization in selective exposure. *EPJ Data Science* (2014).

[3] S. Asur and B A Huberman. 2010. Predicting the Future with Social Media. In *Web Intelligence and Intelligent Agent Technology (WI-IAT), 2010 IEEE/WIC/ACM International Conference on*. 492–499.

[4] Eytan Bakshy, Jake M Hofman, Winter A Mason, and Duncan J Watts. 2011. Everyone's an influencer: quantifying influence on twitter. In *WSDM '11: Proceedings of the fourth ACM international conference on Web search and data mining*. ACM Request Permissions.

[5] J Bollen, H Mao, and X Zeng. 2011. Twitter mood predicts the stock market. *Journal of Computational Science* (2011).

[6] danah boyd, Scott Golder, and Gilad Lotan. 2010. Tweet, Tweet, Retweet: Conversational Aspects of Retweeting on Twitter. In *System Sciences (HICSS), 2010 43rd Hawaii International Conference*. IEEE, Honolulu, HI, 1–10.

[7] Meeyoung Cha, H Haddadi, F Benevenuto, and Krishna Gummadi. 2010. Measuring User Influence in Twitter: The Million Follower Fallacy. In *Proceedings of the International Conference Weblogs and Social Media (ICWSM)*.

[8] P Chebolu and P Melsted. 2008. PageRank and the random surfer model. In *Proceedings of ACM-SIAM SODA*.

[9] Justin Cheng, Lada A Adamic, P Alex Dow, Jon Michael Kleinberg, and Jure Leskovec. 2014. Can cascades be predicted?. In *WWW '14: Proceedings of the 23rd international conference on World wide web*. International World Wide Web Conferences Steering Committee.

[10] Ayman Farahat and Michael C Bailey. 2012. How effective is targeted advertising?. In *WWW '12: Proceedings of the 21st international conference on World Wide Web*. ACM Request Permissions.

[11] Maksym Gabielkov, Arthi Ramachandran, Augustin Chaintreau, and Arnaud Legout. 2016. Social Clicks: What and Who Gets Read on Twitter? *SIGMETRICS '16: Proceedings of the ACM SIGMETRICS/international conference on Measurement and modeling of computer systems* (June 2016).

[12] Maksym Gabielkov, Arthi Ramachandran, Arnaud Legout, and Augustin Chaintreau. 2016. Social Clicks: What and Who Gets Read on Twitter?. In *ACM SIGMETRICS / IFIP Performance 2016*. Antibes Juan-les-Pins, France.

[13] A B Hubert, T Hubert, and C Mugizi. 2006. A Random-Surfer Web-Graph Model. In *Proc. of ANALCO'06*. New York, USA.

[14] Eric Jones, Travis Oliphant, Pearu Peterson, and others. 2001. *SciPy: Open source scientific tools for Python*. Technical Report.

[15] Yaser Keneshloo, Shuguang Wang, Eui Hong Han, and Naren Ramakrishnan. 2016. Predicting the popularity of news articles. In *16th SIAM International Conference on Data Mining 2016, SDM 2016*. Virginia Polytechnic Institute and State University, Blacksburg, United States, 441–449.

[16] Haewoon Kwak, Changhyun Lee, Hosung Park, and Sue Moon. 2010. What is Twitter, a social network or a news media?. In *WWW '10: Proceedings of the 19th international conference on World wide web*. ACM.

[17] D C Liu and J Nocedal. 1989. On the Limited Memory BFGS Method for Large Scale Optimization. *Math. Program.* 45, 3 (Dec. 1989), 503–528.

[18] Travis Martin, Jake M Hofman, Amit Sharma, Ashton Anderson, and Duncan J Watts. 2016. Exploring Limits to Prediction in Complex Social Systems. In *Proceedings of the 25th International Conference on World Wide Web*. International World Wide Web Conferences Steering Committee, Republic and Canton of Geneva, Switzerland, 683–694.

[19] H B McMahan, G Holt, D Sculley, M Young, and D Ebner. 2013. Ad Click Prediction: a View from the Trenches. *KDD '16: Proceedings of the 22th ACM SIGKDD international conference on Knowledge discovery and data mining* (2013).

[20] SA Myers, C Zhu, and Jure Leskovec. 2012. Information Diffusion and External Influence in Networks. *KDD '12: Proceedings of the 18th ACM SIGKDD international conference on Knowledge discovery and data mining* (2012). arXiv:5B22CD56-A65B-43CA-95AB-4E21D8FE35A6

[21] Henrique Pinto, Jussara M Almeida, and Marcos A Gonçalves. 2013. *Using early view patterns to predict the popularity of youtube videos*. ACM, New York, New York, USA.

[22] Matthew Richardson, Ewa Dominowska, and Robert Ragno. 2007. Predicting clicks: estimating the click-through rate for new ads. In *WWW '07: Proceedings of the 16th international conference on World Wide Web*. ACM.

[23] Marian-Andrei Rizoiu, Lexing Xie, Scott Sanner, Manuel Cebrian, Honglin Yu, and Pascal Van Hentenryck. 2017. Expecting to Be HIP: Hawkes Intensity Processes for Social Media Popularity. In *Proceedings of the 26th International Conference on World Wide Web*. International World Wide Web Conferences Steering Committee, Republic and Canton of Geneva, Switzerland, 735–744.

[24] Adam Sadilek and Henry Kautz. 2013. Modeling the impact of lifestyle on health at scale. In *WSDM '13: Proceedings of the sixth ACM international conference on Web search and data mining*. ACM Request Permissions.

[25] Hua-Wei Shen, Dashun Wang, Chaoming Song, and Albert-László Barabasi. 2014. Modeling and Predicting Popularity Dynamics via Reinforced Poisson Processes. *available on arXiv.org* (Jan. 2014). arXiv:1401.0778v1

[26] Gabor Szabo and Bernardo A Huberman. 2010. Predicting the popularity of online content. *Commun. ACM* 53, 8 (Aug. 2010).

[27] Lucy Wang, Arthi Ramachandran, and Augustin Chaintreau. 2016. Measuring Click and Share Dynamics on Social Media: A Reproducible and Validated Approach. *Proceedings of AAAI ICWSM Workshop on News and Public Opinion* (May 2016).

[28] Xiaofeng Wang, Matthew S Gerber, and Donald E Brown. 2012. Automatic crime prediction using events extracted from twitter posts. In *SBP'12: Proceedings of the 5th international conference on Social Computing, Behavioral-Cultural Modeling and Prediction*. Springer-Verlag.

[29] FMF Wong, S Sen, and M Chiang. 2012. Why watching movie tweets won't tell the whole story?. In *Proceedings of the 2012 ACM workshop ...*.

[30] Tauhid Zaman, Emily B Fox, and Eric T Bradlow. 2014. A Bayesian Approach for Predicting the Popularity of Tweets. *Annals of Applied Statistics* 8, 3 (Sept. 2014), 1583–1611.

[31] Qingyuan Zhao, Murat A Erdogdu, Hera Y He, Anand Rajaraman, and Jure Leskovec. 2015. SEISMIC. In *the 21th ACM SIGKDD International Conference*. ACM Press, New York, New York, USA, 1513–1522.

[32] Qingyuan Zhao, Murat A Erdogdu, Hera Y He, Anand Rajaraman, and Jure Leskovec. 2015. SEISMIC: A Self-Exciting Point Process Model for Predicting Tweet Popularity. *available on arXiv.org* (June 2015). arXiv:1506.02594v1

To Post or Not to Post: Using Online Trends to Predict Popularity of Offline Content

Sofiane Abbar
Qatar Computing Research
Institute
Doha, Qatar
sabbar@qf.org.qa

Carlos Castillo
Universitat Pompeu Fabra
Barcelona, Catalunya, Spain
chato@acm.org

Antonio Sanfilippo
Qatar Environment & Energy
Research Institute, HBKU
Doha, Qatar
asanfilippo@hbku.edu.qa

ABSTRACT

Predicting the popularity of online content has attracted much attention in the past few years. In news rooms, journalists and editors are keen to know, as soon as possible, the articles that will bring the most traffic into their website. In this paper, we propose a new approach for predicting the popularity of news articles before they go online. Our approach complements existing content-based methods, and is based on a number of observations regarding article similarity and topicality. We use time series forecasting to predict the number of visits an article will receive. Our experiments on real data collections demonstrate the effectiveness of the proposed method.

ACM Reference Format:
Sofiane Abbar, Carlos Castillo, and Antonio Sanfilippo. 2018. To Post or Not to Post: Using Online Trends to Predict Popularity of Offline Content. In *HT '18: 29th ACM Conference on Hypertext and Social Media, July 9–12, 2018, Baltimore, MD, USA*. ACM, New York, NY, USA, 5 pages. https://doi.org/10.1145/3209542.3209575

1 INTRODUCTION

Monitoring the performance of news articles is a core task within any news media organization. The highly crowded news market, and the fast growth of online news platforms and applications in recent years, have pushed editors into a fierce competition for the attention of news readers. Currently, editors focus on *popularity* in terms of number of visits and visitors to news websites as the most important performance metric for news articles online. While social media has changed the way people consume news, their contribution in terms of visits to websites is relatively small. Andrew Miller, Guardian News and Media CEO, estimated all social media combined are around 10% of their site's traffic [20]

Measuring popularity, however, is not sufficient. The ability to *anticipate* online news popularity enables editorial teams to take strategic decisions to maximize the impact of their online content, such as promoting or demoting articles in their web pages. Given the high velocity of news, editors need to have forecasts for news articles as early as possible after publishing the article – and ideally, before publication.

The research community has addressed the problem of predicting the popularity of news articles in several recent papers including [3, 5, 11], typically addressing this as a regression problem (i.e. predict the popularity of an item), and sometimes as a classification problem (discretization of popularity into different levels/classes). Approaches that can dispense with early popularity measurements have been explored through the development of predictive models that use features such as the words in the title of the article, e.g. [8]. Our approach is complementary to such methods, and provides a novel extension where topic popularity forecasts are used to improve news article popularity predictions.

We explore two forecasting algorithms that exploit these observations, and test them on a large collection of news articles published by *Aljazeera Network*[1] – an international news organization – over 18 months in 2013 and 2014. The ensuing results yield a mean average percentage error (MAPE) as low as 11%, demonstrating the efficacy of the approach in predicting news article popularity.

2 RELATED WORK

We review in the following three categories of work related to our paper. *(i.) Methods Based on Early Measurements.* The success of the auto-correlation approach pioneered by [17] has encouraged many researchers to use early popularity measurements as predictors of future popularity. Examples include [7] for votes in Digg; [10] for comments to articles; [12] for visits to articles; [1] for views in YouTube and Vimeo, and for votes in Digg. *(ii.) Methods Based on Topics.* [3] used information about the category of a news article (e.g. sports, politics) together with information about the source, subjectivity, and named entities to predict the popularity of news articles in social media, prior to their publication. [18] predicted the number of comments to articles on a large news website. *(iii.) Methods Based on Keywords.* [19] studied the prediction of comments on news articles, using features such as publication date, number of articles posted at the same

---

[1] http://www.aljazeera.com

time, and named entities. [8] measured the impact of titles on the popularity of image *re-posts* for different communities in *Reddit*. Our approach differs from and is complementary to the approaches reviewed in this section, in that it relies on article similarity and topic modeling. Our approach can also use recent historical data at any level of granularity (e.g. days, hours) to predict online content popularity.

3 DATASET

We use data provided by *Al Jazeera*, a large international news network operating multiple television channels and websites. We harvested articles from the English version of this website, which has millions of visits per month. The data covers a time span from September 2012 through April 2014. Our collection comprises two types of articles: *News* (8,065) and *Opinion* (4,357). The first category refers to breaking news. The latter refers to opinions and features contributed by named writers sharing their analysis of a topic of public interest. For each article, we also retrieved a time series of the number of visits the article gets after its publication.

4 PREDICTING TOPIC VOLUME

The first task we describe is the prediction of the total volume of visits to a topic u, i.e. the sum of the visits of all articles that have the topic u as the main topic. We use the Latent Dirichlet Allocation algorithm (LDA) to uncover the topics in our collection of articles [4].

4.1 Determining the Number of Topics

As many topic modeling methods such as non-negative matrix factorization [9] and Probabilistic Latent Semantic Analysis [6], LDA assumes the number of topics k given. Empirically, a small k leads to broad topics such as "politics" and "sports" whereas a large k leads to specialized topics such as US elections. We use supervised classification to find the "appropriate" number of topics k^*. The intuition is that k^* topics should yield a partition of the documents in the dataset that can be accurately recognized by a classifier trained on k^* classes of documents. First, we run LDA with different number of topics ($k \in \{10, \ldots 100\}$). Let $\mathcal{T}^{(k)}$ be the topic set produced by LDA for each value of k. For each set of topics, we label every article $a \in \mathcal{D}$ with its primary topic $u_a^{(k)}$ such that $u_a^{(k)} = \text{argmax}_{u \in \mathcal{T}^{(k)}} \text{rel}(a, u)$. Next, we split articles into train (80%) and test (20%) sets, and train a Multinomial Naive Bayes classifier (MNB) [14] on the tf $\cdot$ idf scores of stems within each article. Results are reported in Figure 1. While the precision of the classifier is almost the same at $k = 10$ and $k = 20$, the recall and F_1 scores are maximized for $k = 20$. Hence, we set $k^* = 20$.

4.2 Topic Volume Prediction Results

We use Pearson's correlation (r^2) to measure auto-correlations and cross-correlations between topics, and Mean Absolute Percentage Error (MAPE) to evaluate forecasting results.

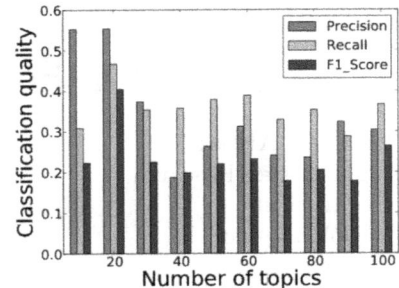

Figure 1: Quality of MNB for different numbers of topics obtained using LDA. F_1 maximizes at about 20 topics.

Determining the size of the training window. We now address the selection of the appropriate size of the time-window for training. A larger training window means more data is used for training, but *if the underlying process changes over time*, then incorporating training data that is too old may actually be counterproductive. The number of time lags δ to use is another important parameter. A larger δ means more variables are used for the prediction, which may lead to over-fitting. We train our prediction models with training windows of different sizes and different time lag values. We vary the sliding training window size to take values in $\{3, 5, 7, 10, 20, 30, 40, 50, 60\}$, and the lag $\delta \in \{2, 3, 4, 5\}$, both values expressed in days.

Figure 2 reports the average MAPE scores for different values of time lags and sizes of training sets. Each reported MAPE value is the average of scores achieved at predicting different steps-ahead (2, 3, 7, 15, and 30). Linear regression (LR) results are shown in Figure 2(a). A high variation of MAPE scores is observed for small sizes of the training set (≤ 30) before the scores stabilizes starting from training sets of size 50. SVR results are shown in Figure 2(b). MAPE scores are lower compared to those of LR, for all the values of the training set size we consider. It also shows that the ideal size of the training window is 7 days. Finally, adding more lags (larger δ) also increases the error rate. To summarize, the best prediction model is SVR with feature selection, a training window size of 7 days, and $\delta = 2$ or $\delta = 3$ as time lags.

5 ARTICLE PREDICTIONS

We now address the problem of predicting the number of visits to an *article*. Our objective is to assess to which extent topicality and article similarity can help predict the number of visits an article will receive. First we compute the popularity of an article as a function of the popularity of similar previously posted articles (Section 5.1). Then, we include topic popularity into the model (Section 5.2). Next, we integrate *predicted* topic popularity into the overall forecasting model (Section 5.3). Finally, we complement our prediction with early traffic observations to improve over both methods (Section 5.4).

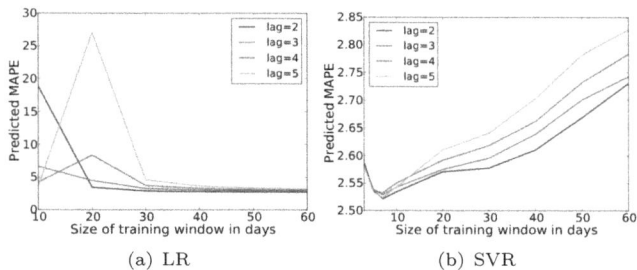

(a) LR   (b) SVR

Figure 2: MAPE of LR and SVR for # training sizes & lags.

5.1 Prediction Based on Article Similarity Using Nearest Neighbors (NN)

We hypothesize that similar articles posted within a relatively small time window receive a similar number of visits. The rationale behind this hypothesis is that people who visited an article about a developing story yesterday (or a few days ago), are likely to visit similar articles published today or at a later day. Sets of follow-up articles can be understood as playing the role of ephemeral pseudo-topics.

We measure article similarity by representing articles $\mathcal{D}$ using tf · idf vectors over the concatenation of their content and title. The similarity between each pair of articles is measured using cosine similarity $\mathrm{sim}_{\cos}(\cdot, \cdot) \in [0, 1]$.

To predict article visits, we use these similarities as input to a nearest-neighbors estimation method (NN). This method consists on estimating the value of a function at given point, as an aggregate of the value of that function for a set of points near it [2, 15]. We use a variant of the kNN method applied to popularity prediction by [13], where the number of views of an item is the weighted sum of the number of views of similar items in the past few days.

Given an article a posted on day t_a, and a similarity threshold θ, we define $N_\theta^t(a)$ as the set of articles published on day t whose similarity with a is greater than or equal to θ:

$$N_\theta^t(a) = \{b \in \mathcal{D}, \mathrm{sim}_{\cos}(a, b) \geq \theta \wedge t_b = t\} . \quad (1)$$

We next define a function which gives the weighted average of the number of visits to articles in $N_\theta^t(a)$ (for $t < t_a$) up to date t_a:

$$X_a(t) = \sum_{b \in N_\theta^t(a)} \frac{\mathrm{sim}_{\cos}(a, b) \cdot V_b(t_a)}{\sum_{b \in N_\theta^t(a)} V_b(t_a)} \quad (2)$$

where $V_b(t_a)$ is the cumulative number of visits received by article b from its publication up to and including the publication date of a, t_a. Finally, our estimator is based on linear regression:

$$\widehat{V}_a(t_a + h) = \alpha_i + \sum_{i \in \delta(t_a)} \beta_i X_a(i) + \varepsilon \quad (3)$$

where as before $\delta(t_a) = \{t_a - \delta, t_a - \delta + 1, \ldots, t_a - 1\}$ is the set of time lags under consideration, α and β_i are the linear regression coefficients, and ε is the residual term.

Results are shown on Figure 3(a). The model is trained on 80% of the articles, and tested on the remaining 20%. We vary δ from 1 to 7 days and set θ to values in $\{0.05, 0.1, 0.2, 0.3\}$. We observe that adding more days does not improve significantly the results. Values of θ close to 0.1 and 0.2 yield in general better results than 0.05 (which may cover too many articles distantly related to the one for which the prediction is being done) or 0.3 (which may be too strict as a criterion and include too few neighbors). We experimented with SVR and found the results to be no better than those obtained with linear regression (LR); in the remainder we report only the results with LR which is a simpler model.

5.2 Prediction Based on Topic Volume (NN+T)

Let us now consider a predictor of visits to article a based on the topic volume of its main topic u_a. This predictor is simply:

$$\widehat{V}_a(t_a + h) = \alpha_i + \sum_{i \in \delta(t_a)} \beta_i Y_{u_a}(i) + \varepsilon \quad (4)$$

where $Y_{u_a}(i)$ is the number of visits to topic u_a at time i. The result is the dashed line in Figure 3(a). We observe its MAPE value is 1.33 percentage points lower than the one obtained with the method based on NN. Given that this method is complementary to the one using nearest neighbors, we can combine them using:

$$\widehat{V}_a(t_a + h) = \alpha_i + \sum_{i \in \delta(t_a)} \beta_i X_a(i, t_a) + \sum_{i \in \delta(t_a)} \gamma_i Y_{u_a}(i) + \varepsilon \quad (5)$$

where $X_a(i, t_a)$ is the aggregate of visits to nearest neighbors defined in Equation 2. Results are shown on Figure 3(b). We observe that the combined method is better than the method based only on topic volume for $\delta > 1$, and that in general the MAPE for $\delta = 3$ or $\delta = 4$ is lower than for $\delta = 1$.

5.3 Prediction Based on Predicted Topic Volume (NN+T+PT)

We further improve the results by creating an *ensemble* forecasting that operates in two steps. First, we predict the future popularity of a's topic u_a at time $t_a + h$, $\widehat{Y}_{u_a}(t_a + h)$ using the best estimator from Section 4.2. Next, we incorporate this as an input variable for the regression:

$$\widehat{V}_a(t_a + h) = \alpha_i + \sum_{i \in \delta(t_a)} \beta_i X_a(i, t_a) + \sum_{i \in \delta(t_a)} \gamma_i Y_{u_a}(i)$$
$$+ \eta \widehat{Y}_{u_a}(t_a + h) + \varepsilon$$

Results are shown on Figure 4. We observe a small but consistent improvement when incorporating this variable to our best predictor so far. Again, best results are observed using $\delta = 3$ or $\delta = 4$.

5.4 Incorporating Early Observations

Finally, we compare our method to the standard auto-regressive models based on early measurements (e.g. [13, 16, 17]). Recall that early-measurements methods rely on the existence

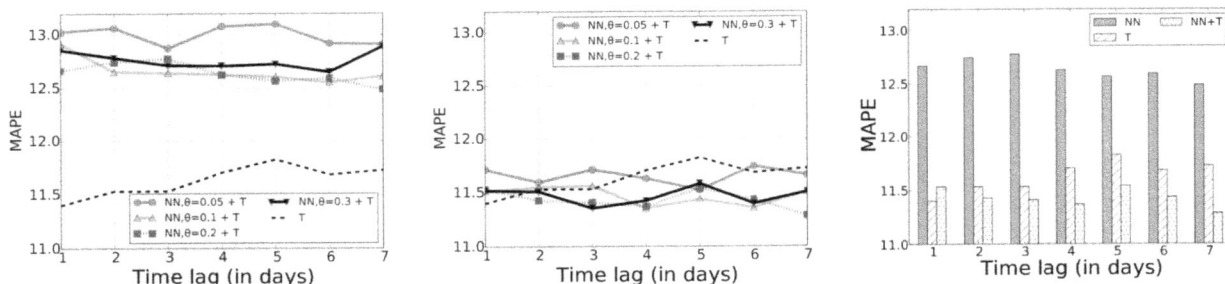

(a) Performance of nearest-neighbors method
NN (continuous line) vs. topic-based method
T (dashed line)

(b) Performance of combined NN+T method
(continuous line) vs. topic-based method alone
(dashed line)

(c) Comparison of NN, T, and NN+T with a
fixed $\theta = 0.2$

Figure 3: Article popularity prediction using the nearest-neighbors method (NN), the topic-based method (T), and a combined method (NN+T). The first two plots vary $\theta \in \{0.05, 0.1, 0.2, 0.3\}$. The last plot fixes $\theta = 0.2$.

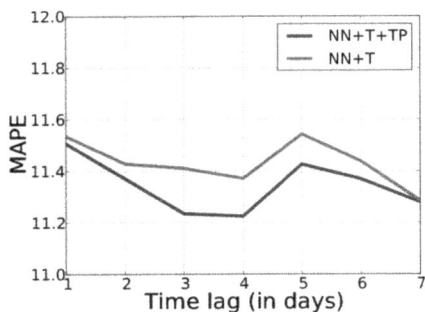

Figure 4: Predicting visits using nearest neighbors, observed topic volume, and predicted topic volume. θ is set to 0.1.

of a strong correlation between early and later times observed popularities, logarithmically transformed [17]. The forecasting formula of such a model is given below:

$$\widehat{V}_a(t_a + h_2) = \alpha + \beta V_a(t_a + h_1) + \varepsilon(h_2, h_1) \qquad (6)$$

Where t_a is the publication time of article a, $\widehat{V}_a(t_a + h_2)$ is the predicted future popularity of article a at time $t_a + h_2$, $V_a(t_a + h_1)$ is the popularity observed at time $t_a + h_1$, and $\varepsilon(h_2, h_1)$ is the noise term. Results of predicting the popularity of articles at three days ($h_2 = 3days$) at different early-measurements periods ($h_1 \in \{5min, 1h, 6h\}$) are shown on Figure 5. We observe that our method yields an error rate on the same scale as methods that use early observations. There is a smooth transition between the error rate resulting from our method (which can be used before publishing the article), and the error rate resulting from methods that use 5 minutes, 1 hour, or 6 hours of early observations. On average, our method yields a MAPE of 11.47%, while early predictions after 5 minutes, 1 hour and six hours obtain error rates of 9.59%, 6.83%, and 4.75% respectively. In the news domain, it is not realistic that an editor would publish a news article just to verify if it will have a large impact or not. Once a news

is published, it can not be withdrawn without compromising reputation. Hence, our method provides a unique competitive advantage over the early-measurements-based methods.

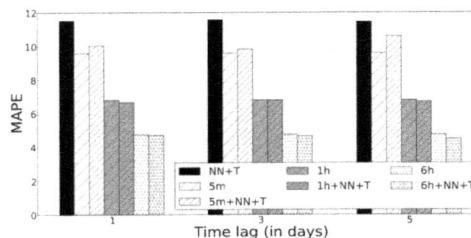

Figure 5: Visits prediction using our method, compared to methods using early measurements. The threshold θ is set to 0.1.

6 CONCLUSIONS

Predicting the popularity of an article before its date of publication requires combining content-based methods, which capture the article's communicative frame, with time series methods, which capture the evolution of people's attention around different issues. Our approach successfully combines two dimensions in the forecasting of visits for an article: the popularity of similar articles of recent issue, and the popularity of the topics that the article treats. More specifically, we have shown that an integration of these two dimensions rivals the performance of each dimension on its own. In future work, we will integrate information about sources, potential reach, as well as possible sources of competition for attention (e.g. similar articles on the same day), as a way of increasing the accuracy and robustness of the approach we have presented.

ACKNOWLEDGMENTS

C. Castillo is partially funded by La Caixa project LCF/PR/PR16/11110009.

REFERENCES

[1] Mohamed Ahmed, Stella Spagna, Felipe Huici, and Saverio Niccolini. 2013. A Peek into the Future: Predicting the Evolution of Popularity in User Generated Content. In *Proc. of WSDM*. ACM, Rome, Italy, 607–616. DOI:http://dx.doi.org/10.1145/2433396.2433473

[2] Christopher G. Atkeson, Andrew W. Moore, and Stefan Schaal. 1997. Locally Weighted Learning. *Artificial Intelligence Review* 11, 1-5 (1997), 11–73. http://citeseer.ist.psu.edu/atkeson96locally.html

[3] Roja Bandari, Sitaram Asur, and Bernardo A. Huberman. 2012. The Pulse of News in Social Media: Forecasting Popularity. In *Proc. of ICWSM*.

[4] David M. Blei, Andrew Y. Ng, and Michael I. Jordan. 2003. Latent Dirichlet Allocation. *J. Mach. Learn. Res.* 3 (March 2003), 993–1022. http://dl.acm.org/citation.cfm?id=944919.944937

[5] Carlos Castillo, Mohammed El-Haddad, Jürgen Pfeffer, and Matt Stempeck. 2014. Characterizing the Life Cycle of Online News Stories Using Social Media Reactions. In *Proc. of CSCW*. ACM, Baltimore, Maryland, USA, 211–223. DOI:http://dx.doi.org/10.1145/2531602.2531623

[6] Thomas Hofmann. 1999. Probabilistic Latent Semantic Indexing. In *Proc. of SIGIR*. 50–57.

[7] Salman Jamali and Huzefa Rangwala. 2009. Digging Digg: Comment Mining, Popularity Prediction, and Social Network Analysis. In *Proc. of WISM*. IEEE Computer Society, Washington, DC, USA, 32–38. DOI:http://dx.doi.org/10.1109/WISM.2009.15

[8] Himabindu Lakkaraju, Julian J. McAuley, and Jure Leskovec. 2013. What's in a Name? Understanding the Interplay between Titles, Content, and Communities in Social Media. In *Proc. of ICWSM*. AAAI Press.

[9] Daniel D. Lee and H. Sebastian Seung. 2000. Algorithms for Non-negative Matrix Factorization. In *In NIPS*. MIT Press, 556–562.

[10] Jong G. Lee, Sue Moon, and Kave Salamatian. 2010. An Approach to Model and Predict the Popularity of Online Contents with Explanatory Factors. In *IEEE Conference on Web Intelligence.* Toronto, Canada.

[11] Kristina Lerman and Tad Hogg. 2010. Using a Model of Social Dynamics to Predict Popularity of News. In *Proc. of WWW*. ACM, Raleigh, North Carolina, USA, 621–630. DOI:http://dx.doi.org/10.1145/1772690.1772754

[12] Kristina Lerman and Tad Hogg. 2010. Using a model of social dynamics to predict popularity of news. In *Proc. of WWW*. ACM, Raleigh, North Carolina, USA, 621–630. DOI:http://dx.doi.org/10.1145/1772690.1772754

[13] Haitao Li, Xiaoqiang Ma, Feng Wang, Jiangchuan Liu, and Ke Xu. 2013. On popularity prediction of videos shared in online social networks. In *Proc. of CIKM*. ACM, 169–178.

[14] Andrew McCallum and Kamal Nigam. 1998. A comparison of event models for Naive Bayes text classification. In *IN AAAI-98 WORKSHOP ON LEARNING FOR TEXT CATEGORIZATION*. AAAI Press, 41–48.

[15] A. Navot, L. Shpigelman, N. Tishby, and Vaadia. 2006. Nearest neighbor based feature selection for regression and its application to neural activity.. In *Proc. of NIPS*.

[16] Matthew Rowe. 2011. Forecasting audience increase on YouTube. In *Workshop on User Profile Data on the Social Semantic Web*. Heraklion, Greece.

[17] Gabor Szabo and Bernardo A. Huberman. 2010. Predicting the Popularity of Online Content. *Commun. ACM* 53, 8 (Aug. 2010), 80–88. DOI:http://dx.doi.org/10.1145/1787234.1787254

[18] Alexandru Tatar, Jérémie Leguay, Panayotis Antoniadis, Arnaud Limbourg, Marcelo D. de Amorim, and Serge Fdida. 2011. Predicting the popularity of online articles based on user comments. In *Proc. of WIMS*. ACM, Sogndal, Norway. DOI:http://dx.doi.org/10.1145/1988688.1988766

[19] Manos Tsagkias, Wouter Weerkamp, and Maarten De Rijke. 2009. Predicting the volume of comments on online news stories. In *Proc. of CIKM*. ACM, 1765–1768.

[20] Twitter Blog. 2013. The Guardian Social Media Traffic. The Twitter blog. (2013). https://blog.twitter.com/2013/guardian-says-twitter-surpassing-other-social-media-for-breaking-news-traffic

Stance Classification through
Proximity-based Community Detection

Ophélie Fraisier
CEA-Tech Occitanie
IRIT, Université de Toulouse, CNRS
ophelie.fraisier@cea.fr

Guillaume Cabanac
IRIT, Université de Toulouse, CNRS
guillaume.cabanac@irit.fr

Yoann Pitarch
IRIT, Université de Toulouse, CNRS
yoann.pitarch@irit.fr

Romaric Besançon
CEA LIST, Nano-INNOV
romaric.besancon@cea.fr

Mohand Boughanem
IRIT, Université de Toulouse, CNRS
mohand.boughanem@irit.fr

ABSTRACT

Numerous domains have interests in studying the viewpoints expressed online, be it for marketing, cybersecurity, or research purposes with the rise of computational social sciences. Current stance detection models are usually grounded on the specificities of some social platforms. This rigidity is unfortunate since it does not allow the integration of the multitude of signals informing effective stance detection. We propose the SCSD model, or Sequential Community-based Stance Detection model, a semi-supervised ensemble algorithm which considers these signals by modeling them as a multi-layer graph representing proximities between profiles. We use a handful of seed profiles, for whom we know the stance, to classify the rest of the profiles by exploiting like-minded communities. These communities represent profiles close enough to assume they share a similar stance on a given subject. Using datasets from two different social platforms, containing two to five stances, we show that by combining several types of proximity we can achieve excellent results. Moreover, we compare the proximities to find those which convey useful information in term of stance detection.

CCS CONCEPTS

• **Applied computing** → **Sociology**; • **Information systems** → *Web mining*;

KEYWORDS

Stance detection, Social media, Computational Social Science, Political discourse

ACM Reference Format:
Ophélie Fraisier, Guillaume Cabanac, Yoann Pitarch, Romaric Besançon, and Mohand Boughanem. 2018. Stance Classification through Proximity-based Community Detection. In *HT '18: 29th ACM Conference on Hypertext and Social Media, July 9–12, 2018, Baltimore, MD, USA*. ACM, New York, NY, USA, 9 pages. https://doi.org/10.1145/3209542.3209549

1 INTRODUCTION

Since the launching of SixDegrees in 1997, social media sites became deeply embedded in users' lives [10]. This includes well-known

This project is co-financed by the European Union – Europe is committed to Midi-Pyrénées with the European fund for regional development.

networking sites, such as Facebook and Twitter, but also other platforms enabling users to interact with their content. Several domains evolved to take advantage of this overabundance of online activities, such as marketing [7, 34, 38] or cybersecurity [12, 28]. These domains have an increasing interest in stance detection due to its wide range of applications. It can be used to detect persons of interest [36], like Democrats and Republicans during a political campaign for example. Furthermore, automatic stance detection is also a precious tool for social scientists. Indeed, it enables researchers to have a better grasp on some research objects by extending observations to large corpora of data which used to be unusable. This task has already been tackled, but the proposed approaches often rely on large quantity of annotated text or specific social interactions [26, 42]. The written content is indubitably a rich source of information, and so is the pattern of interactions, but there are other types of information which could be helping us characterize profiles.

Profiles on social media are linked by a variety of information: elements of language, various social interactions, location, etc. If we try to infer their stance on a topic, we intuitively understand that using several bodies of evidence is beneficial: while one profile could heavily share the publications of a political candidate, another one might be more discreet in sharing but could use the same rethorics in her message, or could be passive but live in an area known to be in favor of a specific stance. Our hypothesis relies on homophily, and states that several evidences hinting at a strong similarity between two profiles are likely to mean that said profiles share a common stance. This is reinforced by the body of literature showing that social media are highly polarized on political topics [14, 27]. We model these *proximities* with a multi-layer graph, each layer representing a specific proximity, with profiles as vertices, and weighted edges as similarities. On this multi-layer proximity graph, we can extract communities, which can then be used for stance detection. We assume that when using adequate proximities, the extracted communities will be extremely homogeneous in terms of stance, allowing us to infer the stance of many profiles with only a handful of seed profiles. The contributions of this paper are:

(1) A detailed analysis strengthening our initial intuition that communities based on proximities tend to be very homogeneous in terms of stance.
(2) A semi-supervised ensemble model for stance detection employing this combination of proximities, and requiring a minimal amount of human investment. Our approach is flexible and generic in terms of platforms, proximities, and number of stances.
(3) Higher effectiveness than state-of-the-art methods, with F1-score as high as 95% while using only 1% of annotated data.

Table 1: Positioning in the existing literature

	[24]	[40]	[9]	[29]	[43]	[4]	[36]	[37]	[44]	[41]	[26]	[42]	[16]	SCSD
Textual features	✓	✓	✓	✓	✓	✗	✓	✗	✓	✓	✓	✓	✓	✓
Social interactions	✗	✗	✗	✗	✗	✓	✓	✓	✓	✓	✓	✓	✓	✓
Other information	✗	✗	✗	✓	✗	✗	✗	✗	✓	✗	✓	✗	✗	✓
Few annotations	✓	✓	✓	✓	✗	✗	✓	✓	✗	✓	✗	✓	✓	✓
More than 1 platform	✓	✓	✓	✓	✗	✗	✗	✗	✓	✗	✗	✓	✓	✓
More than 2 stances	✗	✓	✓	✗	✗	✗	✗	✓	✓	✓	✓	✗	✗	✓

2 RELATED WORK

2.1 Polarization on social media

Several studies showed that online social media were highly polarized in some contexts, particularly for political topics [25, 27]. They revealed the presence of *"echo chambers"* created by a strong *homophily* on several platforms [39]. This term describes a phenomenon characterised by users preferring to interact with like-minded people. Conservative and liberal blogs tend to mainly reference blogs from their own ideological camp, as shown by their linking patterns and discussion topics [2]. Similarly, Twitter's retweet networks concerning the 2010 and 2014 US midterms elections and the 2014 Scottish independance referendum were highly polarized between left- and right-leaning profiles, while people interacted more freely in the mention networks [14, 21]. Even on Wikipedia, controversies occur mainly in neighbourhoods of related topics [17]. This suggests that some topics tend to be particularly attractive for users promoting diverse mindsets. It is important to note however that on non-political topics, polarization is usually more nuanced [5].

2.2 Stance detection

Text is often the main piece of information used to determine stance. Several researchers studied debate sites and argumentative essays [24]. [40] used a topic model to discover viewpoints, topics, and opinions to classify texts on the Israeli-Palestinian conflict according to their ideological leaning. Other studies focused on less structured platforms: Twitter has, for instance, been largely used, due to its large popularity and the facility to collect data. [9] used a statistical model to determine the political stance of politicians from the Belgian Parliament on Twitter. [29] trained an SVM model including sentiments as features to detect if profiles were "for" or "against" given targets. Forums are other exploitable information silos: [43] used neural networks on a breast cancer forum to identify the profiles' stances on complementary and alternative medicine.

Alternatively, some works rely on social interactions between profiles. [4] built a bayesian model inferring ideology of profiles according to which political actors they are following. [36] identified pairs of profiles with differing opinions thanks to a retweet-based label propagation algorithm tied to a supervised classifier. [37] present a framework based on an unsupervised community extraction from social interactions, followed by a supervised classifier, to detect stances on an OSN. [44] use several textual and contextual features to detect the stance of Twitter profiles regarding a given rumor. [41] propose an unsupervised topic model taking into account the text and social interactions to identify stances. [26] used an SVM on textual content, retweets, and mentions to predict the future attitude of profiles in the aftermath of a major event. Their results show that social features are of prime importance for this task. [42] also used a combination of text and retweets to quantify the political leaning of media outlets and prominent profiles. [16] consider users' discussions and interactions to predict stances using few annotations on any social media. These works are the most relevant ones for our task but they are focused on Twitter datasets,

limited by the fact that they require a large number of annotations, or consider two stances at most (see Table 1). In contrast, we promote a generic approach which needs significantly less annotated data to perform well, as exposed in the following sections.

2.3 Community detection

Detecting and interpreting community structure is an essential part of network analysis. The goal of community detection is to identify groups of vertices more closely connected to each other than to the rest of the network. [19] presents an extensive survey of community detection methods and their methodological foundations in a generic context. [33] builds on this work to focus on community detection in social media and its particular challenges, such as scaling methods to handle larger amount of data or how to interpret community detection results.

3 DATA MODEL

To take advantage from the numerous available proximities, we represent them as proximity graphs, and exploit their structure to predict unknown stances. Formally, let $P = \{p_1, p_2, \ldots\}$ a set of profiles, Σ the set of expressed stances, and $\sigma(p_i)$ the stance of p_i. Each profile has thus one stance, which does not evolve in time. Let us consider a setting where $S \subset P$ the set a profiles with a known stance, with $|S| \ll |P|$. $A = \{A_1, \ldots, A_k\}$ is a set of attributes, with A_i^j the value of attribute A_i for the profile p_j. We define a multiplex $\mathcal{G}$, i.e., a multi-layer graph with each layer sharing the same vertex set P. Each layer is defined as a graph $G_i = (P, \text{Sim}_i)$ such that Sim_i expresses the proximity between profiles in P according to attribute A_i. We consider that proximities are symmetrical measures, hence G_i is undirected. The proximities used in this paper are described in Section 4.3.

Problem formulation. Given $\mathcal{G} = \{G_i, i \in [1, k]\}$ and S, is it possible to effectively determine $\sigma(p_i)$ with $p_i \in P \setminus S$?

4 PRELIMINARY STUDY

4.1 Objectives

Our model is based on the double intuition that (1) communities extracted using proximities and similar stances are correlated and (2) one single proximity is not sufficient to effectively predict stances. In this section, we provide results of an extensive analysis of four real-world datasets to show the validity of our hypotheses. Specifically, we answer the following three questions:
AQ1. Do our proximities have distinct community structures?
AQ2. Are the main communities homogeneous in terms of stance?
AQ3. Are the detected communities different according to the considered proximities?

4.2 Datasets

Real-world datasets usually represent a large number of profiles that cannot be fully manually annotated. We thus focus our analyses on a subset $P_T \subset P$ of profiles. We used three Twitter datasets, and a dataset from CreateDebate.com, available from their respective references. Table 2 presents some basic statistics on these datasets.

4.2.1 2014 Scottish Independence Referendum (SR) [11]. Profiles in P_T were part of the Scottish Independence Referendum Electoral Commission, or unambiguously indicated their stance in their Twitter biographies, giving us $\Sigma_{SR} =$ ("Yes", "No").

4.2.2 2014 US Midterm Elections (ME) [11]. Stances were determined thanks to several sources listing official Twitter accounts of campaigners: $\Sigma_{ME} =$ ("Democrat", "Republican").

Table 2: Dataset sizes and stances

Dataset	$|P|$	Σ	$|P_{T_\sigma}|$	$|P_T|$
SR	604,399	Yes	564	1,101
		No	537	
ME	1,718,131	Democrat	761	1,571
		Republican	810	
PE	22,843	France Insoumise	5,113	18,649
		Parti Socialiste	1,832	
		En Marche !	3,962	
		Les Républicains	4,366	
		Front National	3,376	
GC	1,420	Prefers strict gun control	312	801
		Opposes strict gun control	489	

4.2.3 2017 French Presidential Elections (PE) [22]. This Twitter dataset was collected from November 25th 2016 to May 12th 2017, by monitoring several keywords referencing the campaign. These keywords were selected by researchers familiar with the French political landscape on Twitter. Profiles in P referenced one of the five main political parties in their names or biographies, and had published at least 10 posts (including tweets or retweets) during the seven months of collection. They were manually annotated by experts. We did not consider in P_T the profiles having undefined or multiple party affiliations, hence: Σ_{PE} = ("France Insoumise", "Parti Socialiste", "En Marche !", "Les Républicains", "Front National").

4.2.4 Gun control in the US (GC) [1]. This dataset contains discussions from CreateDebate.com, a debate site. Each discussion has two possible stances, decided by its creator, which were mapped by [1] to 2 global stances: Σ_{GC} = ("prefers strict gun control", "opposes strict gun control"). For example, in a discussion titled "The Right to Bear Arms, necessary?", the stance "Yes, to defend ourselves" is mapped to "opposes strict gun control" and "No, it only creates criminals" to "prefers strict gun control". When a profile adds a post to a discussion, it has to indicate its stance, and if the post supports, clarifies, or disputes another post. Profiles also contain biographical information, and other profiles indicated as allies. The 88 profiles whose global stance changed from debate to debate were not included here.

4.3 Proximities

Many proximities belonging to various categories, e.g., textual, social, can be exploited. This flexible definition enables a generic model that can be used on any social platform. In this work, several proximities exploiting different aspects of social media were used (Table 3[1]). Since each proximity is used separately, it is not necessary to normalize the edges' weights.

4.3.1 Content-based proximities. This type of proximities links profiles using similar textual tokens in their posts.

- Use of *keywords* (*kw*): $\text{Sim}_{kw}(p_i, p_j) = |A^i_{kw} \cap A^j_{kw}|$

with A^i_{kw} being the hashtags used in p_i's publications for Twitter datasets, or nouns for CreateDebate since this platform does not provide tags or keywords by post.

- *Reference* to a piece of information (*ref*): $\text{Sim}_{ref} = |A^i_{ref} \cap A^j_{ref}|$

with A^i_{ref} the websites mentioned by p_i.[2] Urls are shortened to domain names for CreateDebate due to the fact that only three urls were shared by several profiles, the others being used only once.

4.3.2 Social-based proximities. Proximities based on social context rely on the number of social interactions. We considered the following proximities:

- *Citation* (*cite*): share of another profile's post, via retweets for Twitter and quotes for CreateDebate.
- *Call*: interpellation of another profile, i.e. mentions for Twitter, and supporting and clarifying posts for CreateDebate (see Section 4.2.4).
- *Association* (*asso*): profiles explicitly monitored, friends on Twitter and allies on CreateDebate. Only associations of the profiles in P_T were collected.

We define $A^i_{soc} = \{s^i_k\}$ as the set of interactions $s^i_k = (p_k, t_k)$, with *soc* being the considered social interaction, p_k a profile which interacted with p_i, and t_k the date of the interaction. As explained by [13], symmetric and non-symmetric relationships rationale vary greatly. To take this into account, we considered three versions of these proximities. The first one ($_{all}$) considers all interactions, while the second one ($_{rec}$) focuses only on reciprocal interactions, and the third one ($_{\overline{rec}}$) on non-reciprocal interactions. Their formal definitions are given by equations 1, 2, and 3 respectively. By construction, $A_{soc_{all}} = A_{soc_{rec}} \cup A_{soc_{\overline{rec}}}$.

$$\text{Sim}_{soc_{all}}(p_i, p_j) = |\{s^i_k \mid p_k = p_j\}| + |\{s^j_l \mid p_l = p_i\}| \quad (1)$$

$$\text{Sim}_{soc_{rec}}(p_i, p_j) = \min\left(|\{s^i_k \mid p_k = p_j\}|, |\{s^j_l \mid p_l = p_i\}|\right) \quad (2)$$

$$\text{Sim}_{soc_{\overline{rec}}}(p_i, p_j) = \left||\{s^i_k \mid p_k = p_j\}| - |\{s^j_l \mid p_l = p_i\}|\right| \quad (3)$$

CreateDebate profiles contained more information which was used as another way to measure social similarity between profiles:

- *Socio*-demographic criteria: $\text{Sim}_{socio}(p_i, p_j) = |A^i_{sex} \cap A^j_{sex}| + |A^i_{school\ level} \cap A^j_{school\ level}| + |A^i_{decade} \cap A^j_{decade}|$
- Religious and political *beliefs*: $\text{Sim}_{belief}(p_i, p_j) = |A^i_{religion} \cap A^j_{religion}| + |A^i_{party} \cap A^j_{party}|$

4.3.3 Geographic context. This type of proximities relies on the locations reported in profiles. The construction is similar for *city*, *region*, and *country*: $\text{Sim}_{city}(p_i, p_j) = |A^i_{city} \cap A^j_{city}|$
Since variations in format made it necessary to manually extract the information for a large number of entries, for Twitter, only locations of the profiles in P_T were used.

4.4 Metrics

To answer **AQ1**, we compute the *transitivity* of our proximity graphs. The transitivity measures the probability that two neighbors of a vertex are connected, and the higher it is, the stronger the community structure in the graph is [31]. It is the average weighted clustering coefficient [6]. To answer **AQ2**, we measure the homogeneity of the communities detected for each proximity. We used the average intra-community *purity* [23]. Communities are extracted using label propagation [35]. It has been shown in a previous work to be efficient for this task when compared to other methods, despite not being deterministic [21]. To measure how much information was shared between proximities and thus answer **AQ3**, we computed the *Normalized Mutual Information* [15].

---

[1]After further investigation, the surprisingly high values observed for avg_w and max_w in SR are caused by a dozen of profiles – mostly in favor of the independence, like @YesScotland, @WeAreNational, or @_WeAreScotland_ – which were extremely active and used common language elements, probably due to some offline organisation.

[2]Urls coming from shortening services, such as bit.ly or goo.gl, were expanded when possible for an optimal matching.

Table 3: Number of edges in Sim_i. avg_w represents their average weight, and max_w their maximum weight.

Interaction	SR			ME			PE			GC		
	$|Sim_i|$	avg_w	max_w	$|Sim_i|$	avg_w	max_w	$|Sim_i|$	avg_w	max_w	$|Sim_i|$	avg_w	max_w
ref	314,303	4	36,444	15,640	6	7,592	17,367,840	10	99,704	74	3	32
kw	422,737	5,142	5,319,272	1,304,290	24	222,379	78,440,288	80	29,006	236,976	49	29,854
$cite_{all}$	1,426,334	1	324	712,734	2	672	1,262,484	3	7,983	128	6	68
$cite_{rec}$	11,563	1	65	7,167	2	73	123,853	7	7,983	23	8	53
$call_{all}$	335,171	3	1,296	66,066	2	377	1,787,127	5	10,473	226	2	14
$call_{rec}$	21,682	2	197	2,640	1	55	227,400	8	8,658	48	2	11
$asso_{all}$	1,743,105	1	1	3,121,674	1	1	3,135,200	1	1			
$asso_{rec}$	1,582,919	1	1	2,648,403	1	1	1,532,825	1	1	4,034	1	1
$asso_{\overline{rec}}$	160,186	1	1	473,271	1	1	1,602,375	1	1			
$socio$										312,795	1	3
$beliefs$										240,323	1	2
$city$	11,833,595	1	1	2,023	1	1	2,929,622	1	1			
$region$	12,196,762	1	1	20,447	1	1	7,780,336	1	1			
$country$										445,407	1	1

Table 4: Proximity graphs transitivity

	ref	kw	$cite_{all}$	$cite_{rec}$	$call_{all}$	$call_{rec}$	$asso_{all}$	$asso_{rec}$	$asso_{\overline{rec}}$	$socio$	$beliefs$	$city$	$region$	$country$
SR	0.61	0.95	0.02	0.09	0.15	0.11	0.16	0.16	0.03			1.00	1.00	
ME	0.44	0.79	0.06	0.12	0.11	0.04	0.12	0.10	0.03			0.73	1.00	
PE	0.69	0.87	0.38	0.24	0.48	0.24	0.41	0.31	0.26			0.95	0.99	
GC	0.59	0.91	0.03	0.07	0.05	0.01		0.09		0.80	0.82			0.98

Table 5: Average purity of the 10 biggest communities containing at least 5 profiles in P_T. Values above 0.80 are bolded for readability.

	ref	kw	$cite_{all}$	$cite_{rec}$	$call_{all}$	$call_{rec}$	$asso_{all}$	$asso_{rec}$	$asso_{\overline{rec}}$	$socio$	$beliefs$	$city$	$region$	$country$
SR	**0.82**	0.52	**0.94**	**1.00**	0.52	0.79	**0.98**	**0.99**	0.75			0.61	0.61	
ME	**0.84**	0.62	**0.99**	**0.98**	0.78	**0.96**	**0.94**	0.52	0.52			0.69	0.58	
PE	0.68	0.25	**0.93**	**0.95**	**0.93**	**0.85**	**0.87**	0.79	**0.84**			0.33	0.30	
GC	0.76	0.63	0.67	0.60	0.66	0.66		0.66		0.64	0.64			0.62

4.5 Findings

AQ1. Table 4 presents the transitivity of our proximities. Most proximities have a non-negligible transitivity, suggesting an underlying community structure, more or less pronounced depending on the dataset. Despite being often successfully used in stance detection models, all versions of $cite$ exhibit a low or medium transitivity.

AQ2. To confirm that some proximities give us homogeneous communities in terms of stance, we measured the average purity of the 10 biggest communities containing at least 5 profiles in P_T (see Table 5). While this is an incomplete picture – we have a median of 50% of annotated profiles – we can see that some proximities have extremely high purity. On Twitter datasets, $cite_{all}$, $cite_{rec}$, and $asso_{all}$ consistently obtain a mean purity close to or higher than 0.90. Ref and $call_{rec}$ are not as efficient but still give good results. On the other hand, scores for $call_{all}$, $asso_{rec}$, and $asso_{\overline{rec}}$ vary a lot depending on the considered dataset.

AQ3. Figure 1 presents the normalized mutual information between proximities. The first observation we can make is that the relationships between proximities is heavily dataset-dependent. In most cases, each proximity brings unique information about profiles in regards to others. The proximities having similar communities structure are not surprising: $city$ and $region$ are often strongly related,

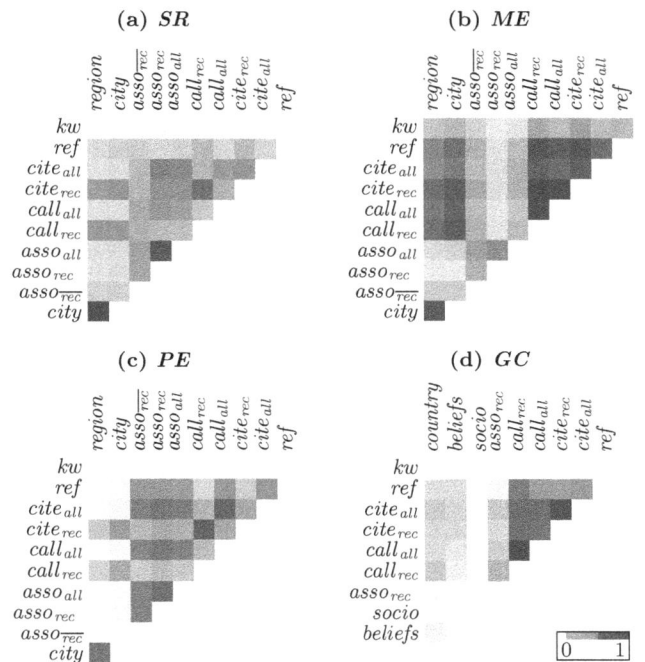

(a) *SR* (b) *ME* (c) *PE* (d) *GC*

Figure 1: Normalized Mutual Information between proximity communities for each dataset.

as well as reciprocal versions of proximities with their complete versions. There is a lot more of redundant information between proximities on *ME*, with $call_{all}$, $cite_{all}$, and ref being closely related. This is interesting since we do not observe this phenomenon on the other Twitter datasets. The surprisingly low values observed between kw and the other proximities on *SR*, *PE*, and *GC* are due to the fact that on these datasets, all profiles in P_T are placed in the same community when using the kw proximity.

4.6 Implications for Stance Detection

The results of these experiments demonstrate that communities detected on social media elements can yield extremely high homogeneity in terms of stance, and therefore be an effective way to propagate stance from some known profiles. Moreover, as indicated by moderate NMI values, the communities extracted from the different considered proximities look different. This suggests that each one brings a specific piece of information about the profiles entourage, allowing for a better characterization. Unsurprisingly, reciprocal versions of the proximities are semantically close to their complete versions (we see high NMI scores between the pairs) but their higher purities may be of interest for our task.

Even when extracted from the same platform, each dataset has its own particularities. Indeed we can see that some proximities can be useful or hurtful depending on the dataset, and that the similarity between proximities varies across datasets. On Twitter, $cite_{all}$ and $asso_{all}$ seem particularly encouraging for our task: they have very homogeneous communities and bring unique information compared to other proximities (apart from their reciprocal version). On CreateDebate, ref and $asso_{rec}$ seem interesting for the same reasons. These measures could help us determine which proximity to discard in order to optimize our process, but for the time being we will consider all the defined proximities.

5 SEQUENTIAL COMMUNITY-BASED STANCE DETECTION MODEL

Based on the previous results, we propose the Sequential Community-based Stance Detection model, or **SCSD**. Algorithm 1 exposes the main mechanism of our model, i.e., the assignment of one stance per community iteratively: first, different sets of communities are built according to different profile proximities, then a specific function is used to order them, and a set of seed profiles is selected from these communities. Finally, an iterative stance detection step is performed based on these seed profiles to find the stance of the remaining profiles in P. This algorithm features two crucial elements:

(1) the order in which the proximities are considered,
(2) and the profiles selected as seeds.

The following sections present our answers to these questions.

Algorithm 1 : SCSD framework – $X = (x_1, \ldots, x_n)$ is the sequence of proximities to be used. The functions designed to order the proximities and to select the seed profiles are presented in Section 5.1 and Section 5.2 respectively. The algorithm of getMajorityStance is detailed in Algorithm 2.

1: **for** x_i **in** X **do**   ▷ *Initialisation*
2:     $C_{x_i} \leftarrow$ detectCommunities(x_i)
3: $X^{ord} \leftarrow$ orderProximities(X, ω)
4: $S \leftarrow$ selectSeedProfiles($x_1^{ord}, s, s_{com}, s_{min}, \varphi$)
5: **for** p_i **in** S **do**
6:     $P(p_i) \leftarrow$ getGroundTruth(p_i)
7: **for** x_i^{ord} **in** X^{ord} **do**   ▷ *Stance detection process*
8:     **for** c **in** $C_{x_i^{ord}}$ **do**
9:         **for** p_i **in** c **do**
10:            **if** $\sigma(p_i)$ is undefined **then**
11:                $\sigma(p_i) \leftarrow$ getMajorityStance(c)

5.1 Proximities ordering

In SCSD, a profile's stance cannot change once it has been assigned. The order in which the proximities are considered in the stance detection loop is thus crucial. The ordering function ω computes the ordered sequence of proximities to be used during the rest of the model, X^{ord}. The ideal strategy is to order them in order of decreasing like-mindedness of the communities. Since, in most

---

Algorithm 2 : getMajorityStance – c is the community whose majority stance must be determined.

1: stances $\leftarrow \varnothing$ ▷ *Table mapping stances with frequencies*
2: **for** p_i **in** c **do**
3:     **if** $\sigma(p_i)$ is defined **then**
4:         stances[$\sigma(p_i)$].increment()
5: sorted $\leftarrow$ sortByDecreasingFreq(stances)
6: **if** stances $\neq \varnothing$ **and** sorted[0].freq $\neq$ sorted[1].freq **then**
7:     **return** sorted[0].stance
8: **else**
9:     **return** undefined

---

cases, it is impossible to know this element beforehand, let us discuss two options to design this ordering function ω:

Manual ordering function. This mode is useful if the user already has expertise on the dataset, and when he wants to choose the order in which the proximities are to be used.

Automatic ordering function. The model can also automatically arrange proximities according to a user-defined function. Some examples are:
- Ordering by decreasing modularity.
- Ordering by ascending number of communities.
- Ordering by descending number of communities.
- Ordering by ascending number of profiles.
- Ordering by descending number of profiles.

Section 6.3 presents a comparison of these functions.

5.2 Seed selection

Algorithm 3 : Seed selection – s is the size of the seed, s_{com} the minimum number of seed communities to consider, s_{min} the minimum number of seed profiles in each seed community, and φ the importance function determining how the seed profiles are selected.

1: seedP $\leftarrow \varnothing$ ▷ *Selected seed profiles*
2: seedC $\leftarrow \varnothing$ ▷ *Selected seed communities*
3: nbPossibleP $\leftarrow 0$ ▷ *Number of possible seed profiles*
4:   ▷ *in selected seed communities*
5: **for** c **in** sortByDecreasingSize($C_{x_1^{ord}}$) **do**
6:     **if** $|c| \geq s_{min}$ **then**
7:         seedC $\leftarrow$ seedC $\cup$ c
8:         nbPossibleP $\leftarrow$ nbPossibleP $+ |c$
9:     **if** $|$seedC$| \geq s_{com}$ **and** nbPossibleP $\geq s$ **then**
10:        break
11: **for** c **in** seedC **do**
12:     nbProfiles $\leftarrow \min\left(|c|, \max\left(s_{min}, \dfrac{|c| \times s}{\text{nbPossibleP}}\right)\right)$
13:     newSeedProfiles $\leftarrow$ selectSeedProfiles(c, nbProfiles, φ)
14:     seedP $\leftarrow$ seed P $\cup$ newSeedProfiles
15: **return** seedP

We now detail our strategy for seed selection. Indeed, manually annotating data is time-consuming and expensive. SCSD is designed to be efficient with a very small seed (i.e., less than 5% of the number of profiles to classify), and seed selection is dependent on the global cost of annotation s the final user wishes to put into it: s is the size of our seed S, i.e., the total number of seed profiles to manually annotate. *Seed profiles* are profiles contained in the seed, and *seed communities* the communities containing seed profiles.

In order to accurately detect the $|\Sigma|$ stances present in the considered dataset, we sample at least s_{com} seed communities, with

Table 6: SCSD model scores using $(s, s_{com}, s_{min}) = (3\% \times |P_T|, 3 \times |\Sigma|, 3)$ **and** $\omega = Manual.$ These scores are identical when using the following importance functions φ: *degree, closeness centrality, number of posts, seniority,* and *random* (average scores on 10 runs).

Dataset	s	p	r	F1
SR	33	0.95	0.95	0.95
ME	47	0.95	0.95	0.95
PE	560	0.90	0.86	0.87
GC	24	0.58	0.52	0.45

$s_{com} \geq |\Sigma|$. The number of seed profiles in each seed community is proportional to its size, and each seed community contains at least s_{min} seed profiles. The importance function φ indicates the method of selection for the seed profiles. It can be deterministic or not – random for example. Algorithm 3 details this process.

The importance functions translate greater importance by larger values, and can be divided into 2 families. The first family is based on raw information from the profiles, for example:

- For Twitter datasets: number of *followers*, number of *friends*, number of *posts*, number of *retweets* of the profile's posts, *seniority*.
- For the CreateDebate dataset: *efficiency*, number of *debates*, number of *posts*, number of *relations*, *seniority*.

The second one is based on the proximity graphs: *degree, strength, pagerank* [32], *closeness centrality* [8], *eigenvector centrality* [30]. Section 6.1 presents a comparison of these functions.

6 EXPERIMENTS

In this section we examine the effectiveness of the SCSD model. We use standard metrics in a classification settings, namely the macro-averaged *precision, recall,* and *F1-score,* computed on the subset P_T defined in Section 4.2. We consider several questions in order to measure the impact of the different components of the SCSD model:

Q1. What is the influence of the importance function φ, used in the seed selection step, on the performance?
Q2. What is the contribution of each proximity?
Q3. How well do the automatic ordering functions perform compared to a manual ordering of proximities?
Q4. How robust is SCSD with regards to seed size variations?
Q5. How does SCSD perform compared to baselines?

6.1 Comparison of importance functions φ

6.1.1 Study of compared importance functions. We suppose that some importance functions are heavily correlated to others. In order to consider relevant functions only, we study their pairwise similarities. Figure 2 presents the Spearman correlation [18] between profiles ranks returned by the importance functions indicated in Section 5.2. As expected, a lot of functions seem to be redundant. *Degree, pagerank,* and *strength* returns similar profiles, as shown by their high correlations. It is not surprising given their definitions and the existing literature [20]. The *closeness* and *eigenvector centralities* are close to each other, suggesting their evaluation of the profiles' importance is also similar. The number of *posts* is often correlated to the number of *retweets* and of *followers* for Twitter, and to the number of *debates* and *relations* for CreateDebate. For the Twitter datasets, the numbers of *followers* and *friends* returns a majority of similar profiles. This is probably due to the atypical profiles (i.e. public figures) having a large number of friends and of followers. Based on these observations, we can omit some functions

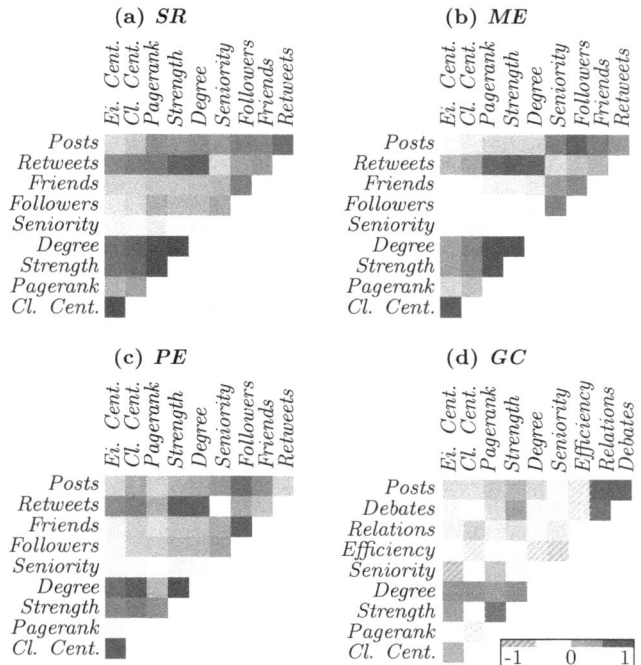

Figure 2: Spearman correlation between profiles ranks returned by different importance functions φ.

from our analysis. We will only consider *degree, closeness centrality, number of posts,* and *seniority* for the remaining analyses.

6.1.2 Influence of importance function on seed selection. In order to compare the importance functions in an optimal setting, we chose to manually order the proximities. We built an optimal sequence per dataset: the proximities are manually ordered by decreasing purity (see Table 5). The first observation we can make is that, with the correct proximities ordering, we successfully assign stance to a large majority of profiles. And, surprisingly, the scores do not vary while using different functions (see Table 6). This is probably a consequence of seed communities being so homogeneous in terms of stance that the importance metric used does not make a difference.

This result has a very interesting practical application: once the seed communities and the number of profiles to pick in each one has been determined, it is possible to select profiles from which the stance is known beforehand. This is particularly useful when used by an expert user, since there is a high probability that she already knows the stance of a fraction of the profiles in the studied dataset.

6.2 Contribution of each proximity

In order to measure the contribution of each considered proximity, we computed scores for SCSD-Basic, a simplified version of SCSD with $X = (x)$ for each proximity x, with $(s, s_{com}, s_{min}, \varphi) = (3\% \times |P_T|, 3 \times |\Sigma|, 3, Degree)$. We note that despite the small seed size, some proximities obtain extremely high precision scores, but they usually retrieve few profiles, leading to a poor recall. This phenomenon is less present in *PE*, where we see that we can obtain excellent results in detecting the five different stances. The weak scores obtained by $asso_{rec}$ on *ME* are surprising. After further investigation, this is due to the fact that on this dataset, profiles are

Table 7: SCSD-Basic model scores with $(s, s_{com}, s_{min}, \varphi) = (3\% \times |P_T|, 3 \times |\Sigma|, 3, Degree)$.

	SR			ME			PE			GC		
	p	r	F1	p	r	F1	p	r	F1	p	r	F1
ref	0.51	0.37	0.33	0.87	0.15	0.25	0.48	0.51	0.45	0.38	0.02	0.03
kw	0.25	0.46	0.32	0.57	0.34	0.38	0.05	0.13	0.07	0.31	**0.50**	**0.39**
cite$_{all}$	0.91	0.71	0.78	0.97	0.29	0.37	0.91	0.84	0.87	0.58	0.04	0.08
cite$_{rec}$	**1.00**	0.34	0.50	**1.00**	0.03	0.06	**0.96**	0.22	0.35	**0.83**	0.02	0.04
call$_{all}$	0.25	0.42	0.31	0.72	0.02	0.04	0.90	**0.88**	**0.89**	0.60	0.05	0.09
call$_{rec}$	0.78	0.23	0.35	0.94	0.03	0.06	0.84	0.27	0.39	0.72	0.03	0.05
asso$_{all}$	0.97	0.84	0.90	0.97	**0.81**	**0.88**	0.89	0.74	0.79			
asso$_{rec}$	0.99	**0.85**	**0.91**	0.25	0.43	0.31	0.89	0.70	0.78	0.59	0.17	0.24
asso$_{\overline{rec}}$	0.55	0.39	0.31	0.25	0.38	0.30	0.67	0.63	0.63			
socio										0.39	0.21	0.25
beliefs										0.56	0.21	0.27
city	0.60	0.08	0.14	0.64	0.05	0.09	0.41	0.06	0.08			
region	0.56	0.10	0.16	0.56	0.14	0.22	0.37	0.10	0.12			
country										0.64	0.23	0.25

Table 8: Comparison of ordering functions on SCSD model F1-scores, using $(s, s_{com}, s_{min}, \varphi) = (3\% \times |P_T|, 3 \times |\Sigma|, 3, Degree)$.
Scores presented for the random ordering are the average scores on 10 runs.

	SR	ME	PE	GC
Random	0.67	0.53	0.63	0.43
Manual	**0.95**	**0.95**	0.87	0.45
Modularity	0.49	0.50	0.83	0.47
Ascending number of communities	0.38	0.43	0.11	0.43
Descending number of communities	0.79	0.40	0.74	**0.48**
Ascending number of profiles	0.50	0.55	0.21	0.41
Descending number of profiles	0.90	0.91	**0.89**	0.34

highly connected using this proximity. When detecting communities, the majority of profiles in P_T are assigned to the same cluster, leading to one stance being largely ignored during the classification process. Despite gun control being often presented as a "right-wing versus left-wing" debate, or like a generational conflict, the *socio* and *beliefs* proximities did not perform well. This is probably due to the small size of the dataset, especially when it comes to the more efficient proximities (see Table 3).

6.3 Comparison of ordering functions ω

The order of the proximities is a key element of the model. The interactions providing the most homogeneous communities should be used first in order to obtain the best results. We decided to compare the performances of our model using different proximity sequences, given by the ordering functions ω presented in Section 5.1, with $(s, s_{com}, s_{min}, \varphi) = (3\% \times |P_T|, 3 \times |\Sigma|, 3, Degree)$.[3] We also consider a random ordering of the proximities (whose scores are averaged on 10 runs). Figure 3 presents the evolution of precision and recall during the process, and Table 8 the final F1-scores. For Twitter, we see that ordering proximities by descending number of profiles is a strong contender to the manual ordering. For *SR* and *PE*, the number of communities (in descending order) could be an acceptable alternative, probably because a higher number of communities means smaller, more homogeneous ones on these datasets. For *GC*, modularity and the number of communities in descending order give us slightly better results than the manual ordering, and only the number of profiles in descending order gives us significantly weakened scores. Contrary to our initial intuition that modularity could be a good indicator for proximities ordering, its results shows

Table 9: Influence of s and s_{com} on SCSD model F1-scores, using $(s_{min}, \varphi) = (3, Degree)$ and $\omega = Manual$.
The missing values represent cases where the seed selection is impossible because $s < s_{com} \times s_{min}$.

s	$1\% \times |P_T|$		$3\% \times |P_T|$		$5\% \times |P_T|$		$7\% \times |P_T|$	
s_{com}	$1 \times |\Sigma|$	$2 \times |\Sigma|$	$1 \times |\Sigma|$	$2 \times |\Sigma|$	$1 \times |\Sigma|$	$2 \times |\Sigma|$	$1 \times |\Sigma|$	$2 \times |\Sigma|$
SR	0.95	-	0.95	0.95	0.95	0.95	0.95	0.95
ME	0.95	0.95	0.95	0.95	0.95	0.95	0.95	0.95
PE	0.47	0.87	0.47	0.87	0.47	0.88	0.48	0.88
GC	0.29	-	0.45	0.45	0.45	0.45	0.45	0.45

Table 10: Baselines scores.

		SVM	RF$_{cite}$	RF$_{asso}$	LP$_{cite}$	LP$_{asso}$	SCSD
		Annotations: 80%			*Annotations: 3%*		
SR	p	0.92	0.94	**0.95**	0.89	**0.95**	**0.95**
	r	0.92	0.91	0.94	0.76	0.93	**0.95**
	F1	0.92	0.90	0.94	0.78	0.94	**0.95**
ME	p	0.88	0.93	**0.96**	0.20	0.11	0.95
	r	0.87	0.92	0.93	0.33	0.08	**0.95**
	F1	0.87	0.92	0.93	0.24	0.07	**0.95**
PE	p	0.75	**0.91**	0.87	0.21	0.11	0.90
	r	0.76	**0.89**	0.82	0.19	0.09	0.88
	F1	0.75	**0.89**	0.83	0.20	0.10	**0.89**
GC	p	0.43	**0.62**	0.55	0.45	0.40	0.57
	r	0.37	**0.54**	0.51	0.04	0.17	0.53
	F1	0.37	**0.51**	0.50	0.08	0.19	0.48

it vastly depends on the studied dataset. Good results characterise *PE* and *GC*, but we see a great loss of performance on *SR* and *ME*.

6.4 Influence of seed size

We then looked at the influence of the seed size and the number of initial communities on scores. Table 9 presents the F1-scores of the SCSD model when s and s_{com} vary, using $(s_{min}, \varphi) = (3, Degree)$ and $\omega = Manual$. With our compared configurations, *SR* and *ME* do not vary, however *PE* and *GC* show the influence of s and s_{com}. *GC* shows degraded performances when considering a minimal seed, i.e. $(s, s_{com}) = (1\% \times |P_T|, 1 \times |\Sigma|)$. For *PE*, s_{com} seems to hold more importance than s, since with $s_{com} = 1 \times |\Sigma|$ we see a drastic drop in F1-score which is not compensated by the increase in s, while we obtain good results with $s_{com} = 2 \times |\Sigma|$ even when taking into account only 1% of annotated profiles. Finally, these results confirm that SCSD model is built to be effective with a very small seed, the benefit given by a seed larger than 3% of the number of profiles being non-existent.

6.5 Comparison with baselines

We compare the performance of the SCSD model to several baselines traditionally used for stance detection. For the social aspect, we use the two main proximities used for this task: *cite*$_{all}$ and *asso*$_{rec}$.[4] These baselines being supervised models, we use a 5-fold cross-validation.

SVM We use an SVM model based on the concatenation of each profile's posts, with a vocabulary consisting of the 10,000 most distinctive tokens according to χ^2 stats.

---

[3] Given the results presented in Section 6.1, we use only one importance function for the remaining analyses.

[4] We use *asso*$_{rec}$ because *asso*$_{all}$ is undefined for *GC*, the ally interaction being inevitably reciprocal.

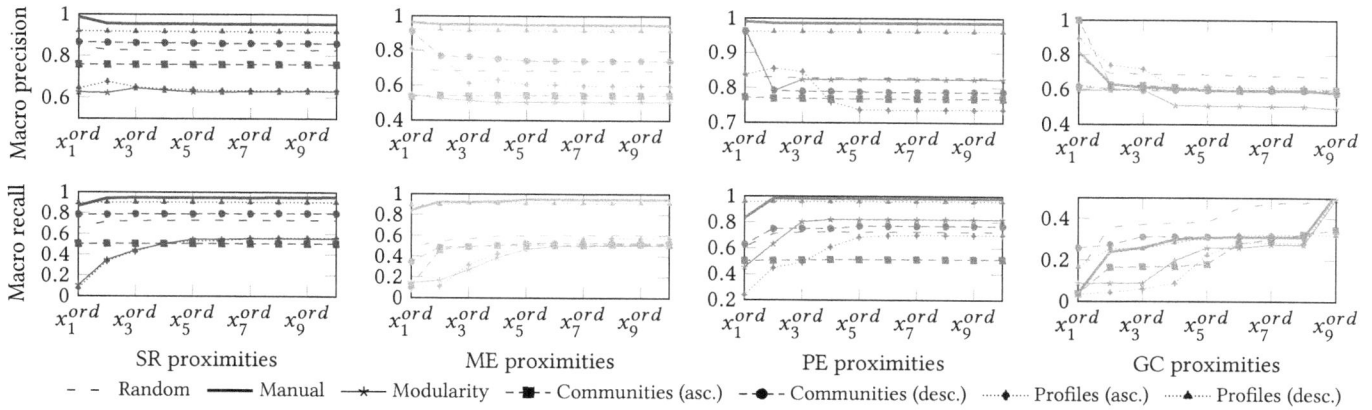

Figure 3: Comparison of ordering functions on SCSD model precision and recall evolution, using $(s, s_{com}, s_{min}, \varphi) = (3\% \times |P_T|, 3\times |\Sigma|, 3, Degree)$. Every x_i^{ord} represent the different proximities used in sequential order. Scores presented for *Random* are the mean scores on 10 runs.

RF_{cite} For the social aspect, we build a Random Forest classifier based on the $cite_{all}$ proximity: each profile is represented by its similarities to other profiles according to this proximity.

RF_{asso} Similar to RF_{cite} but using the $asso_{rec}$ proximity.

These baselines being supervised, they need a lot more of annotated data than the SCSD model. To compare to models using the same amount of annotated data, we define the following baselines:

LP_{cite} A semi-supervised label propagation process running on the $cite_{all}$ proximity graph. The seed selection being random, we present the average scores on 10 runs.

LP_{asso} Similar to LP_{cite} but using the $asso_{rec}$ proximity.

Table 10 presents the results of SCSD using the optimal configurations, deduced from previous experiments, compared to our baselines. We can see that SCSD obtains, with at least 30 times less annotated data, scores higher than or close to our supervised baselines. When comparing to the semi-supervised baselines using the same amount of annotated data, it has an average gain in F1-score of 49 points (ranging between 1 and 88 percentage points). For *ME*, the low scores obtained by LP_{asso} are probably linked to the overabundance of links observed in Section 6.2. This is a problem posed by relying on a unique proximity: if it is not adapted to the studied dataset, there is no way to rectify the situation. Since we observed high purities for $cite_{all}$ and $asso_{rec}$ on both *SR* and *PE*, the differences in scores are probably due to the multiple stances of *PE* which are a lot harder for label propagation to deal with than the simple bipartite problematic represented by *SR*. We see that for all models, *GC* profiles were significantly harder to classify, probably because of the small size of the dataset: all proximities considered, we have approximately 1,500 interactions on average by profile for *GC* compared to 27,300 for *SR*, 5,300 for *ME*, and 6,200 for *PE*.

6.6 Discussion

The analysis of the different proximities supports previous findings in the literature. The precision scores of $cite_{all}$ and *ref* suggest people tend to construct their discourse on social media by sharing arguments they agree on rather than refuting opposing ones. Note that while people can call out their opponents, they tend to engage a lot more to their allies. This is demonstrated by the better precision usually obtained by $call_{rec}$ compared to $call_{all}$. The $asso_{all}$ precision tends to demonstrate that they also select the profiles they follow [3, 14]. Interestingly, and contrary to the observation made above, another behaviour appears. Some profiles, mainly profiles of public

figures, decided to follow their opponents as well as their allies. This is probably a way of monitoring their actions and discourse, suggesting that on Twitter, retweets and following are not always endorsements. This phenomenon is visible in the 2014 US midterms elections, when profiles are so closely linked that they are assigned to the same cluster.

The results seem to indicate that the majority of keywords are more related to the topic than to a specific stance. Moreover, the importance of the geographical proximity appears to vary depending on the topic. Unfortunately it was not possible to investigate all possible granularities for the geographical proximity. In addition, finer granularities were not always provided and inferring which granularity would be the most effective for a given topic is not an easy task. Since the focus of the study was stance detection, we used a naive version of geographical proximity, but this issue requires further attention.

7 CONCLUSION

Our aim was to detect profiles' stance using their likeliness to other profiles with a very small seed, to reduce annotation costs. We proposed SCSD, a generic semi-supervised model which can easily be customized to suit any requirement. The results of this study on 4 corpora suggest that it is possible to accurately predict stance using this method, even when using as little as 1% of annotated profiles and considering more than two stances. Moreover, they showed that since all proximities do not carry as much information in terms of stance, using several proximities allows to strengthen stance assignment. We do think this model could be a great help for computational social scientists wishing to exploit large datasets without having the resources to manually annotate them. The basic principles do not require advanced technical skills to grasp. Moreover, social scientists usually have the expert knowledge needed to order the proximities in an optimal manner according to the platform they wish to study.

The present study did not investigate the whole Twitter follow graphs due to their computational cost, and the excellent performance of more focused graphs. It would be interesting in the future to compare the performance of follow graphs to the friends graphs. A more complete and finer use of the textual content would surely be helpful as well, since keywords alone are not easily exploitable. Finally, taking into account the temporal aspect of stances, such as the possibility for a profile to change its mind, would definitely improve the insights given by our model.

REFERENCES

[1] Rob Abbott, Brian Ecker, Pranav Anand, and Marilyn Walker. 2016. Internet Argument Corpus 2.0: An SQL Schema for Dialogic Social Media and the Corpora to Go with It. In *Proceedings of the Tenth International Conference on Language Resources and Evaluation (LREC 2016)*. ELRA, 23–28.

[2] Lada A. Adamic and Natalie Glance. 2005. The Political Blogosphere and the 2004 U.S. Election: Divided They Blog. In *Proceedings of the 3rd International Workshop on Link Discovery*. ACM Press, 36–43. https://doi.org/10.1145/1134271.1134277

[3] Jisun An, Daniele Quercia, and Jon Crowcroft. 2013. Fragmented Social Media: A Look into Selective Exposure to Political News. In *Companion Proceedings of the 22nd International Conference on World Wide Web*. ACM Press, 51–52. https://doi.org/10.1145/2487788.2487807

[4] Pablo Barberá. 2015. Birds of the Same Feather Tweet Together: Bayesian Ideal Point Estimation Using Twitter Data. *Political Analysis* 23, 01 (2015), 76–91. https://doi.org/10.1093/pan/mpu011

[5] Pablo Barberá, John T. Jost, Jonathan Nagler, Joshua A. Tucker, and Richard Bonneau. 2015. Tweeting From Left to Right: Is Online Political Communication More Than an Echo Chamber? *Psychological Science* 26, 10 (2015), 1531–1542. https://doi.org/10.1177/0956797615594620

[6] A. Barrat, M. Barthelemy, R. Pastor-Satorras, and A. Vespignani. 2004. The Architecture of Complex Weighted Networks. *Proceedings of the National Academy of Sciences* 101, 11 (2004), 3747–3752. https://doi.org/10.1073/pnas.0400087101

[7] Carl Julien Barrelet, Sebnem Sahin Kuzulugil, and Ayşe Başar Bener. 2016. The Twitter Bullishness Index: A Social Media Analytics Indicator for the Stock Market. In *Proceedings of the 20th International Database Engineering & Applications Symposium*. ACM Press, 394–395. https://doi.org/10.1145/2938503.2938508

[8] Alex Bavelas. 1950. Communication Patterns in Task-Oriented Groups. *The Journal of the Acoustical Society of America* 22, 6 (1950), 725–730. https://doi.org/10.1121/1.1906679

[9] Michaël Boireau. 2014. Determining Political Stances from Twitter Timelines: The Belgian Parliament Case. In *Proceedings of the 2014 Conference on Electronic Governance and Open Society: Challenges in Eurasia*. ACM Press, 145–151. https://doi.org/10.1145/2729104.2729114

[10] Danah M. Boyd and Nicole B. Ellison. 2007. Social Network Sites: Definition, History, and Scholarship. *Journal of Computer-Mediated Communication* 13, 1 (2007), 210–230. https://doi.org/10.1111/j.1083-6101.2007.00393.x

[11] Igor Brigadir, Derek Greene, and Pádraig Cunningham. 2015. Analyzing Discourse Communities with Distributional Semantic Models. In *Proceedings of the ACM Web Science Conference*. ACM Press, 1–10. https://doi.org/10.1145/2786451.2786470

[12] Ming Cheung, Xiaopeng Li, and James She. 2017. An Efficient Computation Framework for Connection Discovery Using Shared Images. *ACM Transactions on Multimedia Computing, Communications, and Applications* 13, 4 (2017), 1–21. https://doi.org/10.1145/3115951

[13] Elanor Colleoni, Alessandro Rozza, and Adam Arvidsson. 2014. Echo Chamber or Public Sphere? Predicting Political Orientation and Measuring Political Homophily in Twitter Using Big Data: Political Homophily on Twitter. *Journal of Communication* 64, 2 (2014), 317–332. https://doi.org/10.1111/jcom.12084

[14] M. D. Conover, J. Ratkiewicz, M. Francisco, B. Gonçalves, A. Flammini, and F. Menczer. 2011. Political Polarization on Twitter. In *Proceedings of the 5th International AAAI Conference on Weblogs and Social Media*. AAAI Press, 89–96.

[15] Leon Danon, Albert Díaz-Guilera, Jordi Duch, and Alex Arenas. 2005. Comparing Community Structure Identification. *Journal of Statistical Mechanics: Theory and Experiment* 2005, 09 (2005), P09008–P09008. https://doi.org/10.1088/1742-5468/2005/09/P09008

[16] Rui Dong, Yizhou Sun, Lu Wang, Yupeng Gu, and Yuan Zhong. 2017. Weakly-Guided User Stance Prediction via Joint Modeling of Content and Social Interaction. In *Proceedings of the 2017 ACM on Conference on Information and Knowledge Management*. ACM Press, 1249–1258. https://doi.org/10.1145/3132847.3133020

[17] Shiri Dori-Hacohen, David Jensen, and James Allan. 2016. Controversy Detection in Wikipedia Using Collective Classification. In *Proceedings of the 39th International ACM SIGIR Conference on Research and Development in Information Retrieval*. ACM Press, 797–800. https://doi.org/10.1145/2911451.2914745

[18] E. C. Fieller, H. O. Hartley, and E. S. Pearson. 1957. Tests for Rank Correlation Coefficients. I. *Biometrika* 44, 3-4 (1957), 470–481. https://doi.org/10.1093/biomet/44.3-4.470

[19] Santo Fortunato. 2010. Community Detection in Graphs. *Physics Reports* 486, 3-5 (2010), 75–174. https://doi.org/10.1016/j.physrep.2009.11.002

[20] Santo Fortunato, Marián Boguñá, Alessandro Flammini, and Filippo Menczer. 2008. Approximating PageRank from In-Degree. In *Algorithms and Models for the Web-Graph*. Vol. 4936. Springer Berlin Heidelberg, 59–71.

[21] Ophélie Fraisier, Guillaume Cabanac, Yoann Pitarch, Romaric Besancon, and Mohand Boughanem. 2017. Uncovering Like-minded Political Communities on Twitter. In *Proceedings of the ACM SIGIR International Conference on Theory of Information Retrieval*. ACM Press, 261–264. https://doi.org/10.1145/3121050.3121091

[22] Ophélie Fraisier, Guillaume Cabanac, Yoann Pitarch, Romaric Besancon, and Mohand Boughanem. 2018. #Élysée2017fr: The 2017 French Presidential Campaign on Twitter. In *Proceedings of the 12th International AAAI Conference on Weblogs and Social Media*. AAAI Press.

[23] M. Girvan and M. E. J. Newman. 2002. Community Structure in Social and Biological Networks. *Proceedings of the National Academy of Sciences* 99, 12 (2002), 7821–7826. https://doi.org/10.1073/pnas.122653799

[24] Kazi Saidul Hasan and Vincent Ng. 2013. Stance Classification of Ideological Debates: Data, Models, Features, and Constraints. In *Proceedings of the Sixth International Joint Conference on Natural Language Processing*. 1348–1356.

[25] Shanto Iyengar and Sean J. Westwood. 2015. Fear and Loathing across Party Lines: New Evidence on Group Polarization. *American Journal of Political Science* 59, 3 (2015), 690–707. https://doi.org/10.1111/ajps.12152

[26] Walid Magdy, Kareem Darwish, Norah Abokhodair, Afshin Rahimi, and Timothy Baldwin. 2016. #ISISisNotIslam or #DeportAllMuslims?: Predicting Unspoken Views. In *Proceedings of the 8th ACM Conference on Web Science*. ACM Press, 95–106. https://doi.org/10.1145/2908131.2908150

[27] Miller McPherson, Lynn Smith-Lovin, and James M Cook. 2001. Birds of a Feather: Homophily in Social Networks. *Annual Review of Sociology* 27, 1 (2001), 415–444. https://doi.org/10.1146/annurev.soc.27.1.415

[28] Pasquale De Meo, Katarzyna Musial-Gabrys, Domenico Rosaci, Giuseppe M. L. Sarnè, and Lora Aroyo. 2017. Using Centrality Measures to Predict Helpfulness-Based Reputation in Trust Networks. *ACM Transactions on Internet Technology* 17, 1 (2017), 1–20. https://doi.org/10.1145/2981545

[29] Saif M. Mohammad, Parinaz Sobhani, and Svetlana Kiritchenko. 2017. Stance and Sentiment in Tweets. *ACM Transactions on Internet Technology* 17, 3 (2017), 1–23. https://doi.org/10.1145/3003433

[30] Mark Newman. 2010. *Mathematics of Networks*. Oxford University Press. https://doi.org/10.1093/acprof:oso/9780199206650.001.0001

[31] Keziban Orman, Vincent Labatut, and Hocine Cherifi. 2013. An Empirical Study of the Relation between Community Structure and Transitivity. In *Complex Networks*. Vol. 424. Springer Berlin Heidelberg, 99–110. https://doi.org/10.1007/978-3-642-30287-9_11

[32] Lawrence Page, Sergey Brin, Rajeev Motwani, and Terry Winograd. 1999. *The PageRank Citation Ranking: Bringing Order to the Web*. Technical Report. Stanford InfoLab.

[33] Symeon Papadopoulos, Yiannis Kompatsiaris, Athena Vakali, and Ploutarchos Spyridonos. 2012. Community Detection in Social Media: Performance and Application Considerations. *Data Mining and Knowledge Discovery* 24, 3 (2012), 515–554. https://doi.org/10.1007/s10618-011-0224-z

[34] Christopher Phethean, Thanassis Tiropanis, and Lisa Harris. 2015. Assessing the Value of Social Media for Organisations: The Case for Charitable Use. In *Proceedings of the ACM Web Science Conference*. ACM Press, 32:1–32:9. https://doi.org/10.1145/2786451.2786457

[35] Usha Nandini Raghavan, Réka Albert, and Soundar Kumara. 2007. Near Linear Time Algorithm to Detect Community Structures in Large-Scale Networks. *Physical Review E* 76, 3 (2007), 036106. https://doi.org/10.1103/PhysRevE.76.036106

[36] Ashwin Rajadesingan and Huan Liu. 2014. Identifying Users with Opposing Opinions in Twitter Debates. In *Social Computing, Behavioral-Cultural Modeling and Prediction*. Vol. 8393. Springer International Publishing, 153–160. https://doi.org/10.1007/978-3-319-05579-4_19

[37] Georgios Rizos, Symeon Papadopoulos, and Yiannis Kompatsiaris. 2017. Multi-label User Classification Using the Community Structure of Online Networks. *PLOS ONE* 12, 3 (2017), e0173347. https://doi.org/10.1371/journal.pone.0173347

[38] Dmitry Saprykin, Galina Kurcheeva, and Maxim Bakaev. 2016. Impact of Social Media Promotion in the Information Age. In *Proceedings of the International Conference on Electronic Governance and Open Society: Challenges in Eurasia*. ACM Press, 229–236. https://doi.org/10.1145/3014087.3014109

[39] Cass R Sunstein. 2009. *Republic. Com 2. 0*. Princeton University Press.

[40] Thibaut Thonet, Guillaume Cabanac, Mohand Boughanem, and Karen Pinel-Sauvagnat. 2016. VODUM: a Topic Model Unifying Viewpoint, Topic and Opinion Discovery. In *European Conference on Information Retrieval*, Vol. 9626. Springer, 533–545. https://doi.org/10.1007/978-3-319-30671-1_39

[41] Thibaut Thonet, Guillaume Cabanac, Mohand Boughanem, and Karen Pinel-Sauvagnat. 2017. Users Are Known by the Company They Keep: Topic Models for Viewpoint Discovery in Social Networks. In *Proceedings of the 2017 ACM on Conference on Information and Knowledge Management*. ACM Press, 87–96. https://doi.org/10.1145/3132847.3132897

[42] Felix Ming Fai Wong, Chee-Wei Tan, Soumya Sen, and Mung Chiang. 2013. Quantifying Political Leaning from Tweets and Retweets. In *Proceedings of the 7th International Conference on Weblogs and Social Media*. AAAI Press, 640–649.

[43] Shaodian Zhang, Lin Qiu, Frank Chen, Weinan Zhang, Yong Yu, and Noémie Elhadad. 2017. We Make Choices We Think Are Going to Save Us: Debate and Stance Identification for Online Breast Cancer CAM Discussions. In *Proceedings of the 26th International Conference on World Wide Web Companion (WWW '17 Companion)*. International World Wide Web Conferences Steering Committee, 1073–1081. https://doi.org/10.1145/3041021.3055134

[44] Arkaitz Zubiaga, Elena Kochkina, Maria Liakata, Rob Procter, Michal Lukasik, Kalina Bontcheva, Trevor Cohn, and Isabelle Augenstein. 2018. Discourse-Aware Rumour Stance Classification in Social Media Using Sequential Classifiers. *Information Processing & Management* 54, 2 (2018), 273–290. https://doi.org/10.1016/j.ipm.2017.11.009

Sentiment-driven Community Profiling and Detection on Social Media

Amin Salehi, Mert Ozer, Hasan Davulcu
Computer Science and Engineering
Arizona State University, Tempe, AZ, USA
{asalehi1,mozer,hdavulcu}@asu.edu

ABSTRACT

Web 2.0 helps to expand the range and depth of conversation on many issues and facilitates the formation of online communities. Online communities draw various individuals together based on their common opinions on a core set of issues. Most existing community detection methods merely focus on discovering communities without providing any insight regarding the collective opinions of community members and the motives behind the formation of communities. Several efforts have been made to tackle this problem by presenting a set of keywords as a community profile. However, they neglect the positions of community members towards keywords, which play an important role for understanding communities in the highly polarized atmosphere of social media. To this end, we present a sentiment-driven community profiling and detection framework which aims to provide community profiles presenting positive and negative collective opinions of community members separately. With this regard, our framework initially extracts key expressions in users' messages as representative of issues and then identifies users' positive/negative attitudes towards these key expressions. Next, it uncovers a low-dimensional latent space in order to cluster users according to their opinions and social interactions (i.e., retweets). We demonstrate the effectiveness of our framework through quantitative and qualitative evaluations.

ACM Reference Format:
Amin Salehi, Mert Ozer, Hasan Davulcu. 2018. Sentiment-driven Community Profiling and Detection on Social Media. In *HT '18: 29th ACM Conference on Hypertext and Social Media, July 9–12, 2018, Baltimore, MD, USA.* ACM, New York, NY, USA, 9 pages. https://doi.org/10.1145/3209542.3209565

1 INTRODUCTION

With the advent of social media platforms, individuals are able to express their opinions on a variety of issues online. Like-minded users forge online communities by interacting with each other and expressing similar attitudes towards a set of issues. While many methods [31] have been proposed to detect online communities, most of them do not provide insights into the collective opinions of community members. To shed light on such opinions, few efforts have focused on profiling communities, but a large body of work

has been devoted to user profiling [17, 19, 26]. Indeed, "the founders of sociology claimed that the causes of social phenomena were to be found by studying groups rather than individuals" [18].

Turner et al. [43] suggest that individuals come together and form communities by developing shared social categorization of themselves in contrast to others . Therefore, to profile a community, we need to uncover the collective opinions of its members which makes them distinguishable from the members of other communities. Tajfel [40] suggests focusing on unit-forming factors (e.g., similarities, shared threats, or common fate) which function as cognitive criteria for segmentation of the social world into discrete categories. Accordingly, the controversial issues on which users have different opinions can be taken into account in order to discover the motives driving the segmentation of social media and the formation of communities. As a result, the profile of a community should present its important issues on which its members generally have the same position. Such community profiles can be found useful in a broad range of applications such as recommender systems [38], community ranking [6, 16], online marketing [20], interest shift tracking of communities [47], and community visualization [8]. For example, a group recommender system [3] can suggest more relevant items to communities by knowing the collective opinions of their members.

Many community detection methods [1, 5, 29, 30, 32, 33, 37, 46, 47] which are capable of community profiling have been proposed. However, these methods usually present a set of frequent keywords used by the members of a community as the community profile. However, it is common in social media that the members of different communities use the same keywords in their messages. Therefore, keywords alone might not be enough to differentiate communities in which their members have similar word usage. For instance, in the course of the US presidential election of 2016, Republicans and Democrats have used many common keywords such as Trump, Clinton, and Obamacare but with different sentiments. To differentiate and understand these two parties, not only keywords but also the collective attitude of community members towards these keywords should be taken into account.

In this paper, we tackle the aforementioned problem by proposing a sentiment-driven community profiling and detection framework which utilizes user-generated content and social interactions. Our framework first captures key expressions in users' messages as representative of issues by utilizing a POS-tagger and built-in features of social media platforms (i.e. hashtags and user accounts). Next, it identifies users' attitudes towards the extracted key expressions. Finally, we employ a novel graph regularized semi-nonnegative matrix factorization (GSNMF) technique to cluster users according to both their opinions and social interactions.

GSNMF uncovers not only communities but also their sentiment-driven profiles. The main contributions of the paper are as follows:

- Providing sentiment-driven community profiles which separately present the positive and negative collective attitudes of the members of each community towards their important key expressions;
- Achieving higher performance in detecting communities compared to several existing state-of-the-art community detection methods.

The rest of the paper is organized as follows. We review related work in Section 2. In Section 3, we propose our sentiment-driven community profiling and detection framework. To demonstrate the efficacy of our framework, we conduct quantitative and qualitative experiments by using real-world social media datasets in Section 4. Section 5 concludes the paper and discusses future work.

2 RELATED WORK

Community detection methods can fall into three broad categories: link-based, content-based and hybrid methods. Most of the existing works belong to the first category and utilize only social interactions [2, 7]. However, they neglect to utilize valuable user-generated content in which users express their opinions. On the other hand, content-based methods only utilize user-generated content [22]. Nevertheless, the content on social media is extremely noisy, resulting in the failure in detecting communities effectively. To alleviate these challenges, hybrid community detection methods are proposed. These methods are the most related work to our study since they not only exploit both user-generated content and social interactions but are also capable of profiling communities. These methods roughly fall into two categories: probabilistic graphical models and non-negative matrix factorization (NMF) based methods.

2.1 Probabilistic Graphical Models

Community User Topic (CUT) models [46] are one of the earliest works for detecting communities using probabilistic graphical models. The first proposed model (CUT_1) assumes that a community is a distribution over users, while the second one (CUT_2) considers a community as a distribution over topics. To discover communities, CUT_1 and CUT_2 are biased towards social interactions and user-generated content, respectively. Community Author Recipient Topic (CART) [32] is an unbiased model which assumes the members of a community discuss topics of mutual interests and interact with one other based on these topics. CART considers users as both authors and recipients of a message. However, in well-known social networks such as Twitter and Facebook, the number of recipients for a message can be very large. To make community detection scalable, Topic User Community Model (TUCM) [37], considering users as authors not recipients, is proposed. Since CART and TUCM consider users as authors, recipients, or both, they are limited to certain types of social interactions (e.g., retweet and reply-to in Twitter). The link-content model [29] solves this problem by ignoring the assumption that messages can be related to each other using social interactions. It is also capable of using different types of social interactions (e.g., friendship in Facebook and followership in Twitter). Furthermore, COCOMP [47] is proposed to model each community as a mixture of topics about which a corresponding group of

Table 1: Notations used in the paper

Notation	Explanation
$\mathcal{U}$	The set of users
C	The set of communities
S	The set of key expressions
n	The number of users
m	The number of key expressions
k	The number of communities
$\mathbf{X}$	User opinion matrix
$\mathbf{U}$	Community membership matrix
$\mathbf{V}$	Community profile matrix
$\mathbf{W}$	Social Interaction matrix
$\tilde{\mathbf{W}}$	Symmetrically normalized matrix $\mathbf{W}$
$\mathbf{D}$	Degree matrix of $\mathbf{W}$

users communicate. [5] is another model which detects and profiles communities in the domains having user-user, user-document, and document-document links.

2.2 NMF-based Methods

In order to encode graphs as local geometric structures, many methods extending standard NMF are proposed. LLNMF [15] introduces a regularizer, imposing the constraint that each data point should be clustered based on the labels of the data points in its neighborhood. GNMF [4] further incorporates a graph regularizer to encode the manifold structure. Moreover, DNMF [39] is proposed based on the the idea that not only the data, but also the features lie on a manifold. The graph regularizers proposed by the above methods have been utilized by several other works [30, 33] to detect communities on social media. Moreover, another work [1] proposes a NMF-based approach utilizing a graph regularizer to exploit different social views (i.e., different social interactions and user-generated content) as well as prior knowledge in order to detect and profile communities.

3 THE PROPOSED FRAMEWORK

3.1 Problem Statement

We first begin with the introduction of the notations used in the paper as summarized in Table 1. Let $\mathcal{U} = \{u_1, u_2, ..., u_n\}$ be the set of n users, $C = \{c_1, c_2, ..., c_k\}$ indicate the set of k communities, and $S = \{s_1, s_2, ..., s_k\}$ denote the set of m key expressions. $\mathbf{X} \in \mathbb{R}^{m \times n}$ indicates the matrix of users' attitudes towards key expressions, where $\mathbf{X}_{li}$ corresponds to the attitude of user u_i towards key expression s_l. Furthermore, $\mathbf{U} \in \mathbb{R}_+^{n \times k}$ indicates the community membership matrix, in which $\mathbf{U}_{ik}$ corresponds to the membership strength of user $\mathbf{U}_i$ in community c_k. $\mathbf{V} \in \mathbb{R}^{m \times k}$ further denotes the community profile matrix, where $\mathbf{V}_{lk}$ corresponds to the contribution strength of key expression s_l in the profile of community c_k. Moreover, $\mathbf{W} \in \mathbb{R}_+^{n \times n}$ indicates the social interaction matrix, in which $\mathbf{W}_{ij}$ represents the number of social interactions between user u_i and user u_j. We use $\tilde{\mathbf{W}}$ to denote the symmetric normalization of $\mathbf{W}$ (i.e., $\tilde{\mathbf{W}} = \mathbf{D}^{-1/2}\mathbf{W}\mathbf{D}^{-1/2}$, where $\mathbf{D}$ is the degree matrix of $\mathbf{W}$).

By using the above notations, the problem of detecting and profiling communities can be defined as: *Given user opinion matrix*

X *and social interaction matrix* **W** *, we aim to obtain community membership matrix* **U** *and community profile matrix* **V**.

3.2 Extracting Key Expressions as Issues

Social media presents an opportunity to utilize user-generated content in which individuals express their opinions on various issues. The first step towards understanding users' opinions is the extraction of the issues they discuss. To this end, many efforts [28, 35, 45] have been made to extract issues or related aspects. However, these methods require enough training samples for a specific domain to work accurately. Due to the lack of such a dataset for our required experiments, we follow a simple approach to extract key expressions. We utilize the built-in features common among well-known social media platforms. In such social networks, hashtags and user account mentions, which usually indicate issues, are perpended by '#' and '@', respectively. However, the built-in features are not enough to detect all issues. To tackle this problem, we employ a part-of-speech (POS) tagger to extract proper nouns and noun phrases (two or more nouns in a row) as representative of issues. If some proper nouns are in a row, they are considered as a single key expression. We utilize the POS tagger proposed in [13] proven to perform well for the content on social media.

3.3 Capturing Users' Opinions

The position individuals take towards issues reflects their opinions[1]. Many efforts [34, 41] have been made to detect users' sentiments towards issues. However, these methods work effectively when enough training samples for a specific domain are given. However, there is no such a dataset for our required experiments so we apply a simple approach although a sophisticated approach can improve the result of our framework. First, a window with a certain size centered at each positive/negative sentiment word is created. Next, the nearest key expression to the sentiment word is selected, and the positivity/negativity of the sentiment word determines user's positive/negative attitude towards that key expression. For instance, in the message "Conservatives seem angry every time economy adds jobs", we assume the author has a negative sentiment towards key expression "conservatives" because it is the closest key expression to the negative sentiment word "angry" if we consider the window size to be at least two. To generate matrix **X**, we need to apply the above procedure for all messages. Therefore, for each message if author u_i takes a positive/negative attitude towards key expression s_l, we add the sentiment strength of the corresponding sentiment word to X_{li}, respectively. We utilize SentiStrength [42] to discover positive and negative words as well as their sentiment strength.

3.4 Exploiting Users' Opinions

After extracting users' attitudes towards key expressions, the next major objective is sentiment-driven community profiling and detection of like-minded users. To accomplish this, we exploit semi-nonnegative matrix factorization [10] as follows:

$$\min_{U,V} \ ||\mathbf{X} - \mathbf{V}\mathbf{U}^T||_F^2$$
$$\text{s.t.} \quad \mathbf{U} \geq 0. \tag{1}$$

[1]An opinion is defined as an attitude towards an issue [11].

Since the non-negativity constraint in Eq. (1) only holds on matrix **U**, matrix **V** can contain both positive and negative values. A positive/negative value of V_{lk} denotes that the members of community c_k have a collective positive/negative attitude towards key expression s_l. The larger the positive value of V_{lk} is, the more the members of community c_k have a collective positive attitude towards key expression s_l. The lower the negative value of V_{lk} is, the more the members of community c_k have a collective negative attitude towards key expression s_l. This property of matrix **V** also results in the categorization of key expressions into positive and negative categories according to the sign of the corresponding elements of key expressions in matrix **V**. Therefore, key expressions in a community profile are divided into two positive and negative categories. Moreover, the key expressions in each category can also be ranked by their values in matrix **V** in order to show how important they are to the members of the corresponding community.

3.5 Exploiting Social Interactions

Social interactions (e.g., retweets in Twitter and friendship in Facebook) are one of the most effective sources of information to detect communities [31]. To utilize social interactions, NMF-based methods exploit graph regularizers. Gu *et al.* [14] suggest that graph regularizers used in GNMF [4] and DNMF [39] suffer from the trivial solution problem and the scale transfer problem. When the graph regularizer parameter is too large, the trivial solution problem occurs and results in similarity among the elements of each row of community membership matrix **U**. The scale transfer problem, in which $\{\mathbf{V}^*, \mathbf{U}^*\}$ stands as the optimal solution for Eq. (1), results in a smaller objective value for the scaled transferred solution ($\frac{\mathbf{V}^*}{\beta}, \beta\mathbf{U}'$), for any real scalar $\beta > 1$.

To avoid these problems, we propose using the following graph regularizer,

$$\max_{U} \ Tr(\mathbf{U}^T\widetilde{\mathbf{W}}\mathbf{U})$$
$$\text{s.t.} \quad \mathbf{U} \geq 0, \mathbf{U}^T\mathbf{U} = \mathbf{I}. \tag{2}$$

where **I** is the identity matrix with the proper size. Eq. (2) clusters users into k communities, with the most interactions within each community and the fewest interactions between communities. In fact, Eq. (2) is equivalent to the nonnegative relaxed normalized cut as put forth in [9].

3.6 The Proposed Framework GSNMF

In the previous sections, we introduced our solutions to exploit and social interactions and users' attitudes toward key expressions. Using these solutions, our proposed framework simultaneously utilizes users' opinions and social interactions to uncover communities and their profiles. The proposed framework requires solving the following optimization problem,

$$\min_{U,V} \ \mathcal{F} = ||\mathbf{X} - \mathbf{V}\mathbf{U}^T||_F^2 - \lambda Tr(\mathbf{U}^T\widetilde{\mathbf{W}}\mathbf{U})$$
$$\text{s.t.} \quad \mathbf{U} \geq 0, \mathbf{U}^T\mathbf{U} = \mathbf{I}. \tag{3}$$

where λ is a non-negative regularization parameter controlling the contribution of the graph regularizer in the final solution. Since the optimization problem in Eq. (3) is not convex with respect to variables **U** and **V** together, there is no guarantee to find the global

Algorithm 1 The Proposed Algorithm for GSNMF

Input: user opinion matrix **X** and social interaction matrix **W**
output: community membership matrix **U** and community profile matrix **V**
1: Initialize **U** and **V** randomly where $U \geq 0$
2: **while** not convergent **do**
3:     Update **U** according to Eq. (4)
4:     Update **V** according to Eq. (6)
5: **end while**

---

optimal solution. As suggested by [21], we introduce an alternative scheme to find a local optimal solution to the optimization problem. The key idea is optimizing the objective function with respect to one of the variables U or V, while fixing the other one. The algorithm keeps updating the variables until convergence.

Optimizing the objective function $\mathcal{F}$ with respect to U leads to the following update rule,

$$U = U \odot \sqrt{\frac{(X^T V)^+ + [U(V^T V)^-] + \lambda \tilde{W} U + U\Gamma^-}{(X^T V)^- + [U(V^T V)^+] + U\Gamma^+}} \quad (4)$$

where $\odot$ denotes the Hadamard product, and

$$\Gamma = U^T X^T V - V^T V + \lambda U^T \tilde{W} U \quad (5)$$

We separate the negative and positive parts of a matrix A as $A^- = (|A| - A)/2$ and $A^+ = (|A| + A)/2$, respectively. The details regarding the computation of Eq (4) are given in Appendix A.

Moreover, optimizing the objective function $\mathcal{F}$ with respect to V leads to the following updating rule,

$$V = XU(U^T U)^{-1} \quad (6)$$

The details are given in Appendix B.

The algorithm for GSNMF is shown in Algorithm 1. In line 1, it randomly initializes U and V. From lines 2 to 5, it updates U and V until convergence is achieved.

3.7 Algorithm Complexity

In Algorithm 1, the most costly operations are the matrix multiplications in update rules Eq. (4) and Eq. (6). Therefore, we provide the time complexity of these two updating rules as follows:

- The time complexity of Eq. (4) is $O(nmk + mk^2 + n^2k + nk^2)$.
- Since the inversion of small matrix $U^T U$ is trivial, the time complexity of Eq. (6) is $O(mnk + nk^2)$.

Accordingly, the time complexity of Algorithm 1 is $O(ik(nm + mk + n^2 + nk))$ where i is the number of iterations. Our framework can be applied to large scale social network platforms by exploiting the distributed approaches outlined in [12, 23, 25].

4   EXPERIMENTS

To evaluate the efficacy of our framework, we need to answer the following two questions:

(1) How effective is the proposed framework in detecting communities compared to the-state-of-the-art community detection methods?
(2) How effective is our framework in profiling communities?

Table 2: The statistics of the datasets.

	US	UK	Canada
# of tweets	113,818	236,008	98,899
# of retweets	18,891	6,863	3,104
# of distinct words	5,773	7,653	3,738
# of distinct key expressions	165	349	69
# of users	404	317	102
# of baseline communities	2	5	3

In the next sections, we first describe the datasets used in this study. Next, the performance of GSNMF is compared with several state-of-the-art community detection methods. Then, we qualitatively evaluate the community profiles uncovered by our framework.

4.1   Data Description

We take politics as an example to evaluate our framework. In this regard, we used Twitter search API to crawl politicians' tweets from three different countries, namely United States, United Kingdom, and Canada. However, Twitter API imposes the limitation of retrieving only the latest 3200 tweets for each user. To overcome this limitation, we crawled politicians' user accounts several times during the time each dataset covers. The datasets are described as follows,

- **US Dataset** consists of the tweets posted by 404 politicians from two major political parties (Republican party and Democratic party) in the United States from August 26 to November 29, 2016.
- **UK Dataset** consists of the tweets posted by 317 political figures from five major political parties (Conservative Party, Labour Party, Scottish National Party, Liberal Democratic Party, and UK Independence Party) in the United Kingdom from January 1 to September 30, 2015.
- **Canada Dataset** consists of the tweets posted by 102 politicians from three major political parties (Liberal Party, Conservative Party, and New Democratic Party) from January 1 to November 18, 2016.

All users in the datasets have discussed at least 15 key expressions. Moreover, the key expressions used by less than 15 users and stop words are eliminated. As a window size, we experimentally determine the threshold of 3 for the nearest keywords on both sides of each sentiment word. Furthermore, the party to which a user belong is labeled as ground truth. The statistics for the datasets are shown in Table 2. The GSNMF code and users' Twitter accounts as well as their ground truth labels used in this paper are available [2].

4.2   Community Detection Evaluation

4.2.1   Baselines. In order to demonstrate the effectiveness of our framework, we compare GSNMF with the following state-of-the-art community detection methods,

- **GNMF** [4] is a hybrid method utilizing both user-generated and social interactions by incorporating a graph regularizer into standard NMF.

---

[2] https://github.com/amin-salehi/GSNMF

- **Louvain** [2] is a link-based method optimizing modularity using a greedy approach.
- **Infomap** [36] is a link-based method built upon information theory to compress the description of random walks in order to find community structure.
- **DNMF** [39] is a hybrid method utilizing both user-generated content and social interactions by incorporating two regularizers (i.e, a graph regularizer and a word similarity regularizer) into standard NMF.
- **Soft Clustering** [44] is a link-based method that assigns users to communities in a probabilistic way.
- **CNM** [7] is a link-based method based on modularity optimization.

4.2.2 Evaluation Metrics. To evaluate the performance of the methods, we utilize three metrics frequently used for community detection evaluation; namely, Normalized Mutual Information (NMI), Adjusted Rand Index (ARI), and purity.

4.2.3 Experimental Results. For this experiment, we use all three datasets. We also utilize the party membership of each politician as ground truth in our evaluation. For the methods providing soft community membership, like our framework, we select the community with the highest membership value for each user as the community to which she/he belongs. Regularization parameters of NMF-based methods are set to be all powers of 10 from 0 to 9 to find the best configuration for each of these methods. We run each method 10 times with its best configuration and then report the best result. According to the results shown in Table 3, we can make the following observations,

- Our proposed framework achieves the highest performance in terms of NMI and ARI for all three datasets. In terms of purity, it also achieves the best in the Canada and US datasets. In the UK dataset, Louvain, Infomap, and CNM obtain higher purity compared to our framework since they generate an artificially large number of communities for sparse graphs such as social media networks. For instance, Louvain detects 21 communities for UK dataset.
- Exploiting both user-generated content and social interactions does not necessarily result in achieving better performance compared to link-based methods. For example, the Soft Clustering method achieves better results compared to GNMF and DNMF in terms of all three used metrics. However, link-based methods do not uncover any community profile.
- All NMF-based methods achieve their highest performance with large values (i.e., from 10^6 to 10^9) for the graph regularizer parameter.

4.3 Community Profiling Evaluation

In this section, we evaluate the effectiveness of our proposed framework in profiling communities by using US and UK datasets. In this regard, we first label each community detected by our framework with the party to which the majority of community members belong. Next, we evaluate how effectively the profile of a community represents its corresponding ground truth party. To this end, two graduate students who have knowledge of US and UK politics are

Table 3: Comparison of community detection methods.

Method	US			UK			Canada		
	NMI	ARI	Purity	NMI	ARI	Purity	NMI	ARI	Purity
Louvain	0.5083	0.3889	0.9752	0.7077	0.4352	**0.9937**	0.8602	0.8430	0.9902
Infomap	0.5026	0.3755	0.9752	0.8871	0.8874	0.9936	0.8971	0.9299	0.9804
CNM	0.5741	0.4664	0.9752	0.8830	0.8746	0.9905	0.9405	0.9643	0.9902
GNMF	0.8564	0.9126	0.9777	0.8120	0.8291	0.9085	0.9597	0.9794	0.9902
DNMF	0.8599	0.9222	0.9802	0.8308	0.8030	0.8896	0.9574	0.9716	0.9902
Soft Clustering	0.8934	0.9413	0.9851	0.8481	0.8450	0.9495	1.0000	1.0000	1.0000
GSNMF	**0.9069**	**0.9510**	**0.9876**	**0.9298**	**0.9612**	0.9811	**1.0000**	**1.0000**	**1.0000**

assigned to label the results of community profiling methods. It is asked that each key expression in a community profile to be assigned to one of the following categories:

- Supported: A key expression is labeled as supported if the majority of community members have a positive attitude towards it or support it.
- Opposed: A key expression is labeled as opposed if the majority of community members have a negative attitude towards it or oppose it.
- Concerned: A key expression is labeled as concerned if the majority of community members are concerned about it.
- Unrelated: A key expression is labeled as unrelated if the annotators cannot find a strong relevance between the community (party) and the key expression.

In the tables representing community profiles, we color (and mark) supported, opposed, and concerned key expressions with green (+), red (−), and blue (±), respectively. We also leave unrelated key expressions uncolored (and unmarked).

In the following experiments, we expect our proposed framework to achieve three goals:

(1) Uncovering community profiles which represent the collective opinions of community members into two positive/negative categories;
(2) Assigning supported key expressions and opposed/concerned ones to positive/negative categories, respectively;
(3) Minimizing the number of unrelated key expressions in community profiles.

In Sections 4.3.1 and 4.3.2, we evaluate the results of GSNMF according to the first and second goals by using US and UK datasets. To evaluate the performance of the third goal, Section 4.3.3 compares GSNMF with the baselines with regard to their effectiveness in extracting relevant key expressions.

4.3.1 US Politics. The US dataset covers many events such as occurrences of gun violence, police brutality (e.g., the shooting of Terence Crutcher), the Flint water crisis, and the death of Fidel Castro; but the major event is the US presidential election of 2016. To give brief background knowledge, two major US parties during the election are described as follows [24],

- **Democratic Party:** A liberal party focusing on social justice issues. In 2016, Hillary Clinton was nominated as the presidential candidate of the party with Tim Kaine as her vice president. Moreover, Barrack Obama, the incumbent Democratic President, was a strong advocate for Hillary Clinton.
- **Republican Party:** A conservative party, known as the GOP, which had the majority of congressional seats in 2016 and embraces Judeo-Christian ethics. Moreover, Donald Trump

Table 4: The profiles of two communities detected by our framework in the US dataset.

Democrats		Republicans	
Positive	Negative	Positive	Negative
+ HillaryClinton	± Zika	+ America	− Obamacare
+ POTUS	− Trump	+ @SpeakerRyan	± #BetterWay
+ America	− @HouseGOP	+ Congress	± Zika
+ #WomensEqualityDay	− Donald Trump	+ @Mike_Pence	− Iran
+ #NationalComingOutDay	− Gun Violence	+ @RepTomPrice	− Obama
+ Americans	± #Trans	+ @realDonaldTrump	− Tax code
+ #LaborDay	− #GunViolence	+ Texas	± Breast Cancer
+ TimKaine	± Climate Change	+ #VeteransDay	− President Obama
+ Hillary	± #Trabajadores	ICYMI	± GITMO
+ American	± TerenceCrutcher	Senator	± Islamic
Cubs	− GOP	+ #LaborDay	− State Sponsor
+ Halloween	− Violence Situations	+ God	− POTUS
+ Veterans	− ISIS	+ Constitution Day	− ISIS
Florida	± #FundFlint	+ USMC	− Hillary
+ #LGBTQ equality	− Donald	+ Thanksgiving	− Fidel Castro

Note: All colors, signs, and the name of parties in the table are ground truth.

Table 5: The profiles of two communities detected by GNMF and DNMF in the US dataset.

a. GNMF

Democrats	Republicans
− Trump	− Obamacare
+ Hillary	± #BetterWay
+ Gov	+ Congress
+ HillaryClinton	± Zika
− Donald Trump	+ America
± #DoYourJob	+ @HouseGOP
DebateNight	+ American
− @realDonaldTrump	ICYMI
China	− Obama
− @CoryBooker	Florida
± Russia	− Iran
ElectionDay	+ U.S.
± Climate Change	+ Americans
Debate	± #HurricanMatthew
+ Hillary Clinton	POTUS
− Donald	+ @realDonaldTrump
Virginia	Clinton
+ HRC	± Hurrican Matthew
VPDebate	− Washington
+ America	± FBI
+ TimKaine	+ Texas
+ #WomenEqualityDay	+ Senate
+ FLOTUS	+ Veterans
+ #IamWithHer	± Matthew
± Flint	#DoYourJob
+ POTUS	+ @SpeakerRyan
+ HouseDemocrats	Ohio
− Steve Bannon	± #NeverForget
Bannon	+ GOP
+ USA	+ WSJ

b. DNMF

Democrats	Republicans
− Congress	+ Congress
+ Obamacare	− Obamacare
− Trump	+ Trump
#BetterWay	± #BetterWay
+ America	+ America
± Zika	± Zika
− @HouseGOP	+ @HouseGOP
+ American	+ American
+ Gov	− Gov
± #DoYourJob	± #DoYourJob
ICYMI	ICYMI
+ Americans	− HillaryClinton
+ HillaryClinton	+ Americans
+ Hillary	+ Hillary
− @realDonaldTrump	+ @realDonaldTrump
+ Obama	− Obama
+ U.S.	+ U.S.
+ POTUS	− POTUS
+ Iran	− Iran
+ Clinton	− Clinton
− Donald Trump	+ Donald Trump
+ Veterans	+ Veterans
+ Washington	− Washington
± HurricanMatthew	+ HurricanMatthew
− Senate	+ Senate
± FBI	± FBI
Florida	+ Florida
Texas	+ Texas
+ GOP	+ GOP
Oct	Oct

was nominated as the party candidate for the presidency with Mike Pence as his vice president.

During the campaign, Republicans—especially Donald Trump—mainly criticized president Obama and his policies (e.g., Obamacare, tax plans, and Iran deal) in order to discredit Hillary Clinton, whom they claimed was going to continue the Obama legacy and uphold the status quo [24]. On the other hand, Clinton's campaign brought the issue of gun violence into the contest, and also focused on human rights for groups such as women and LGBTQ [24].

Table 4 shows the profiles of two communities detected by our framework in the US dataset as well as their corresponding ground truth political parties and experts' labels. According to the provided background, the community on the left highly resembles the Democratic Party since its members have generally expressed: (1) positive attitudes towards Hillary Clinton, the U.S. president (i.e., POTUS), Tim Kaine, and human rights issues (e.g., #WomensEqualityDay, #LGBTQ equality, and #NationalComingOutDay), and (2) negative attitudes towards the Republican Party (e.g., @HouseGOP and GOP), Donald Trump, and gun violence, police brutality (e.g., the shooting of Terence Crutcher). On the other hand, the community on the right highly resembles the Republican Party since its members have generally expressed: (1) positive attitudes towards the Republican Party (e.g., @HouseGOP and @SpeakerRyan), Donald Trump, Mike Pence, Congress, and religion (i.e., God), and (2) negative attitudes towards President Obama and his policies (i.e., Obamacare, tax code, Iran, Guantanamo Bay detention camp (i.e., GITMO)) as well as Hillary Clinton.

Negative sentiment implies both opposition and concern. If necessary, our framework can differentiate opposition from concern by providing the sentiment words frequently expressed by the members of a community towards each key expression. For example, Democrats' negative sentiment towards Donald Trump mainly comes from the sentiment words "unfit", "low", and "dangerous" which suggest opposition. On the other hand, their negative sentiment towards #Trans (i.e., transgender people) mainly originates from the sentiment words "discrimination" and "murder" which indicate concern.

To demonstrate the advantage of our community profiling method, we compare the profiles of typical community profiles usually provided by retrospective studies with those uncovered by our framework. Table 5 shows the profiles of two communities detected by GNMF and DNMF in the US dataset as well as their corresponding

ground truth political parties. As we observe, it is almost impossible for a non-expert individual to recognize the party associated with each profile since the position of the communities towards the key expressions are not taken into account. For example, in profiles corresponding to the Democratic Party and the Republican Party, many key expressions related to Trump, Clinton, and Obama exist, but there is no information regarding collective attitude of community members toward such key expressions. However, Table 4 shows that our proposed method correctly divides opposed/concerned key expressions and supported ones into the correct categories. Therefore, our framework makes it easy not only to differentiate and understand communities better but also to associate online communities with their real-world counterparts (if exist).

4.3.2 UK Politics. The UK dataset covers many events such as the rise of terrorism and terrorist attacks (e.g., CharlieHebdo and Tunisia attack), and many natural disasters (e.g., Nepal earthquake and Ebola) that happened in the first nine months of 2015. However, the major event in this period of time is the UK general election. Brief background knowledge about five major UK parties during the general election are provided as follows [27],

- **Conservative Party:** This party is also known as Tory and was led by David Cameron in 2015. David Cameron also led the UK government before and after the election of 2015. George Osborne, Nicky Morgan, and Jeremy Hunt were some of his secretaries.
- **Labour Party:** Ed Miliband was the leader of the Labour party for the election and selected Tom Watson as his deputy chair and campaign coordinator. Jeremy Corbyn, Yvette Cooper, Liz Kendall, and Andy Burnham were among the prominent members of the party.
- **Liberal Democrat Party:** Nick Clegg led the Liberal Democrat Party in 2015. Norman Lamb, John Leech, Nick Harvey, Tim Farron, and Charles Kennedy were some of the party's parliamentarians.

Table 6: The profiles of five communities detected by our framework in the UK dataset.

Conservative Party (Tory)		Labour Party (Lab)		Liberal Democrat Party (Lib Dem)		Scottish National Party (SNP)		UK Independence Party (UKIP)	
Positive	Negative	Positive	Negative	Positive	Negative	Positive	Negative	Positive	Negative
+ Conservatives	− Labour	+ Labour	− Tories	+ LibDems	− Labour	TheSNP	− Tory	+ UKIP	± Calais
+ @David_Cameron	− Miliband	+ UKLabour	− Tory	+ @Nick_Clegg	± Iraq	GE15	± Trident	+ @Nigel_Farage'	− Labour
+ Cameron	± Tunisia	+ LabourDoorStep	− Cameron	GE2015	± Climate Change	+ SNP	− Tories	+ Nigel Farage	− ISIS
GE2015	± Paris	+ @AndyBurnhamMP	− A&E	+ NormanLamb	− Tories	+ NicolaSturgeon	− Labour	BBCqt	± Greece
+ @George_Osborne	FIFA	+ Ed_Miliband	− David Cameron	+ @TimFarron	− UKLabour	+ Scotland	± #RefugeesWelcome	GE2015	− BBC
+ VoteConservative★	− ISIL	+ Britain	− Bedroom Tax	+ Lib Dem	− Tuition Fees	MPs	± Iraq	+ Cameron	± Britain
+ NickyMorgan01★	± Heathrow	+ @GloriadePiero	− BedroomTax	± Mental Health	− HIV	+ Glasgow	± Paris	Mark	− Government
London	− Charles Kennedy	+ YvetteCooperMP	− Govt	+ Lib Dems	− SNP	Alan	± CharlieHebdo★	+ Brexit	− Tories
Wales	− Ed_Miliband	+ YvetteForLabour★	± Tax Credits	NHS	− PMQs	+ Scottish	± Syria	Telegraph	− David Cameron
+ David Cameron	− SNP	+ SteveReedMP	− SNP	John	± CharlieHebdo	GE2015	± Mediterranean	BBC5live	± Libya
+ @Jeremy_Hunt	± Syria	+ @LeicesterLiz	− Government	+ Nick Clegg	− Nigel Farage	+ Edinburgh	± Med	+ Queen	− Miliband
+ Team2015★	− Lab	+ LizforLeader★	± France	LBC	− Ebola	Maiden Speech	± French	Andrew	± Tunisia
Chris	− LibDems	+ @TristramHuntMP	± Tunisia	+ LibDem	± Paris	+ NHS	± Charles	+ George's	− Paris
+ @Tracey_Crouch	± Calais	GE2015	± Syria	+ Govt	− Welfare Bill	Neil	± Tunisia	− JeremyCorbyn★	− SNP
+ England	± Nepal	+ VoteLabour★	± Europe			+ Nicola Sturgeon	− Westminster	+ Jeremy Corbyn	± Mediterranean

Note: All colors, signs, and the name of parties in the table are ground truth.

- **Scottish National Party:** The SNP is a Scottish Nationalist party led by Nicola Sturgeon in 2015. Alan Brown and Neil Gray were some of the party's parliamentarians.
- **UK Independence Party:** UKIP was led by Nigel Farage in 2015. The party embodies opposition to both United Kingdom EU membership and immigration.

Table 6 shows the profiles of five communities detected by our framework in the UK dataset as well as their corresponding ground truth political parties. As shown in the table, all parties have a common key expression, the general election of 2015 (e.g, GE2015 and GE15). We can also observe that the members of each party have generally expressed: (1) positive attitudes towards their party and also their prominent members and (2) negative attitudes towards other parties and their prominent members due to election competition [27]. Moreover, the government was a coalition between the Conservative Party and the Liberal Democrat Party before the election. This coalition explains why they expressed positive sentiments towards the government related issues (i.e., Govt and Cameron) [27]. According to the negative attitudes of almost all parties, we can determine that the Conservative party and the Labour party are the ones towards which other parties expressed most negative sentiments. Furthermore, these two parties expressed a high negative sentiment towards each other. The reason behind this antagonism is that these parties are the two biggest parties having the highest chance of winning an outright majority in the election [27]. Moreover, UKIP's negative view on Calais, the city in France where immigrants enter the UK, and Mediterranean (immigrants/immigration) reflects its anti-immigration stance. Moreover, UKIP's positive sentiment on Brexit and its negative sentiment on Greece indicates its anti-EU orientation.

Table 7 shows the profiles of five communities detected by GNMF in the UK dataset as well as their corresponding ground truth political parties. Due to space limitation, we do not provide the community profiles detected by DNMF. As we observe from Table 7, the same problem which exists in the profiles of communities detected by GNMF and DNMF in the US dataset still exists here. In other words, it is not clear which community represents which party. For instance, the profiles which corresponds to the Conservative Party and the Labour Party shared many key expressions such as Labour, Tories, David Cameron (@David_Cameron), @Ed_Miliband, UKLabour, and VoteLabour, but there is no other information to understand the positions of these two parties towards these key expressions in order to differentiate them and also

Table 7: The profiles of five communities detected by using GNMF in the UK dataset .

Conservatives		Labours		Lib dems		SNPs		UKIPs	
−	Miliband	−	UKIP	+	Libdems	+	SNP	−	@JessPhillips
+	Conservatives	+	Labour	−	GE2015	+	Scotland		birmingham
	GE2015	−	Tories	−	Labour	+	VoteSNP	−	Labour
+	@David_Cameron	+	NHS	+	@LFeatherstone		GE15		john
−	Labour	+	Britain	−	@CLeslieMP	+	@TheSNP	−	Libdems
+	VoteConservetives	−	Cameron		Bradford	−	Labour	−	LabourEoin
+	Govt	+	@Nigel_Frange	+	@Nick_Clegg	+	Westminster	−	Lib dems
+	NHS	+	UKLabour		London	−	Tory	−	Lib dem
	LeaderDebates	+	London	±	Budget2015		GE2015	−	Hansard
+	@ZacGoldsmith	+	LabourDoorStep	+	Wales	+	@NicolaSturgeon	−	@TobyPerkinsMP
−	@Ed_Miliband		BBC	+	NHS		LeadersDebate	−	UKLabour
	MPs		BBCqt	−	Miliband	−	LaboursDoorStep		MPs
	London	+	Europe		LeaderDebate		MPs		@SabelHardman
−	UKLabour	+	@AndyBurnhamMP	−	@George_Osborne	±	Trident		Jess
	Wales	+	@ED_Miliband	−	Lib dems	+	Scottish	−	Labour party
+	England	+	TessaJowell	−	David Cameron		London	−	@SimonDanczuk
+	@George_Osborne	+	David Cameron	+	Lib dem	−	UKLabour		Libdem
	croydon	−	Tory	±	Mental Health		PMQS		GE2015
+	@NickyMorgan01	+	Corbyn	+	@SWilliamsMP	+	@David_Cameron		Youtube
+	@NorwichChloe	±	Calasis	+	@NormanLamb		Wales	−	Europe
+	@RobertBuckland	+	@YvetteCooper	−	Conservatives	+	@GradySNP		miliband
−	VoteLabour	−	VoteLabour	−	Tories	−	Glasgow	−	Food Banks
−	@CLeslieMP	±	Greece	+	Nick Clegg		Front Page	−	Housing Benefit
−	LabourLeadership	+	England		Cardiff	+	VoteLabour		Google
+	Tories	−	Jeremy Corbyn	+	@TimFarron	−	ScottishLabour	−	@GiselaStuart
+	Minister	−	Farage	−	VoteConservatives	+	Nicola Sturgeon		Labour MPs
+	Guardian	+	YvetteCooperLabour		Bristol	−	LabourLeadership	+	Britain
	Leeds	−	Telegraph		Croydon	−	Lab		Wales
+	Government	+	@EmmaReynoldMP		Norwich	+	Edinburgh	−	@David_Cameron
	State		Thurrock		Chancellor	−	@AndyburnhamMP★		

Note: All colors, signs, and the name of parties in the table are ground truth.

associate the community profiles to the parties. However, as Table 6 suggests, the community profiles detected by our framework shows that the community associated to the Conservative Party have positive attitude towards David Cameron but negative attitude towards Labour and Miliband. On the other hand, the community associated to the Labour Party have the positive attitude towards Labour, UKLabour, and Miliband but negative attitude towards Tories and David Cameron. Since this corresponds to our ground truth, we can conclude that sentiment information can play an essential role in providing better community profiles.

4.3.3 Quantitative results. In this section, we aim to compare GSNMF with GNMF and DNMF in terms of their effectiveness in extracting relevant key expressions for community profiles. Figure 1 shows the accuracy of all methods in US and UK datasets by considering different number of top key expressions as community profiles. As we observe, GSNMF outweighs GNMF and DNMF in all experiments. For instance, by considering top 30 key expressions as community profiles, 93% of key expressions extracted by GSNMF in the US dataset are relevant compared to 82% in GNMF and 85% in DNMF. Similarly, 83% of key expressions extracted by GSNMF in the UK dataset are relevant compared to 65% in DNMF and 73% in GNMF. The experiments also suggest that GSNMF achieves better

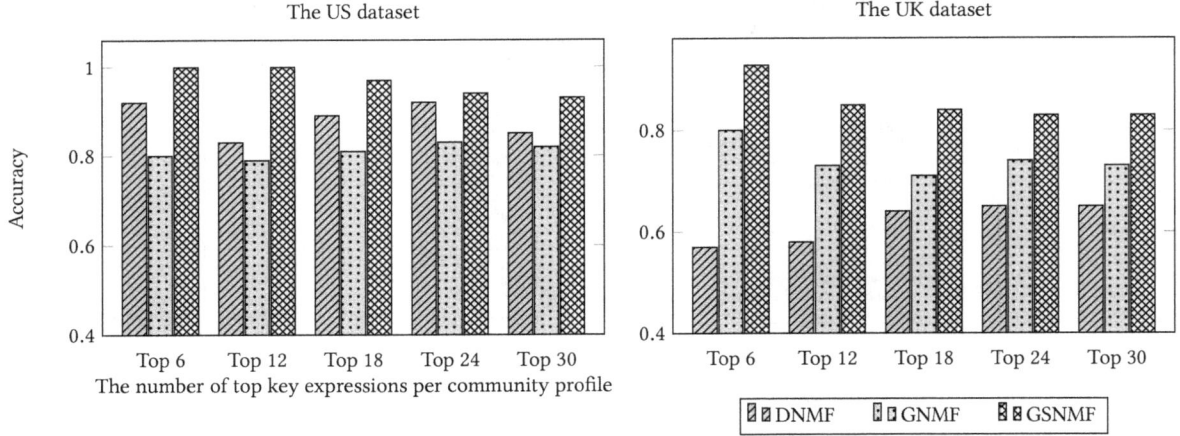

Figure 1: The accuracy of community profiling methods in extracting relevant key expressions.

accuracy with lower number of top key expressions as community profiles. This implies that the higher a key expression is ranked by GSNMF, the more likely it is relevant. Following these observations, sentiment-driven community profiling produces key expressions which are more relevant than its sentiment insensitive counterparts.

5 CONCLUSION AND FUTURE WORK

In this paper, we presented a sentiment-driven community profiling and detection framework. Our framework uncovers a low-dimensional latent space in order to cluster users according to their opinions and social interactions. It also provides community profiles reflecting positive/negative collective opinions of their members. Experimental results on real-world social media datasets demonstrated: (1) our framework obtains significant performance in detecting communities compared to several state-of-the-art community detection methods, and (2) our framework presents a sentiment-driven community profiling approach that provides better insights into the collective opinions of community members by dividing key expressions into positive and negative categories.

Our future work includes the following directions. First, the current sentiment analysis is not capable of differentiating between opposition and concern. There is a need to propose new methods to differentiate between opposition and concern. Second, identifying the dynamics of communities sheds light on their temporal behavior. Therefore, we will focus our efforts on detecting and profiling the dynamics of communities.

A APPENDIX

A.1 Computation of U

Optimizing the objective function $\mathcal{F}$ in Eq. (3) with respect to U is equivalent to solving

$$\min_{\mathbf{U}} \quad \mathcal{F}_U = ||\mathbf{X} - \mathbf{V}\mathbf{U}^T||_F^2 - \lambda Tr(\mathbf{U}^T \tilde{\mathbf{W}}\mathbf{U}) \tag{7}$$
$$\text{s.t.} \quad \mathbf{U} \geq 0, \mathbf{U}^T\mathbf{U} = \mathbf{I}.$$

Let Γ and Λ be the Lagrange multiplier for constraints $\mathbf{U}^T\mathbf{U} = \mathbf{I}$ and $\mathbf{U} \geq 0$ respectively, and the Lagrange function is defined as

follows:

$$\min_{\mathbf{U}} \quad \mathcal{L}_{\mathbf{U}} = ||\mathbf{X} - \mathbf{V}\mathbf{U}^T||_F^2 - \lambda Tr(\mathbf{U}^T \tilde{\mathbf{W}}\mathbf{U})$$
$$- Tr(\Lambda \mathbf{U}^T) + Tr(\Gamma(\mathbf{U}^T\mathbf{U} - \mathbf{I})) \tag{8}$$

The derivative of $\mathcal{L}_{\mathbf{U}}$ with respect to U is

$$\frac{\partial \mathcal{L}_{\mathbf{U}}}{\partial \mathbf{U}} = -2\mathbf{X}^T\mathbf{V} + 2\mathbf{U}\mathbf{V}^T\mathbf{V} - 2\lambda\tilde{\mathbf{W}}\mathbf{U} - \Lambda + 2\mathbf{U}\Gamma \tag{9}$$

By setting $\frac{\partial \mathcal{L}_{\mathbf{U}}}{\partial \mathbf{U}} = 0$, we get

$$\Lambda = -2\mathbf{X}^T\mathbf{V} + 2\mathbf{U}\mathbf{V}^T\mathbf{V} - 2\lambda\tilde{\mathbf{W}}\mathbf{U} + 2\mathbf{U}\Gamma \tag{10}$$

With the KKT complementary condition for the nonnegativity of U, we have $\Lambda_{ij}\mathbf{U}_{ij} = 0$. Therefore, we have

$$(-\mathbf{X}^T\mathbf{V} + \mathbf{U}\mathbf{V}^T\mathbf{V} - \lambda\tilde{\mathbf{W}}\mathbf{U} + \mathbf{U}\Gamma)_{ij}\mathbf{U}_{ij} = 0 \tag{11}$$

where $\Gamma = \mathbf{U}^T\mathbf{X}^T\mathbf{V} - \mathbf{V}^T\mathbf{V} + \lambda\mathbf{U}^T\tilde{\mathbf{W}}\mathbf{U}$.

Matrices Γ, $\mathbf{X}^T\mathbf{V}$, and $\mathbf{V}^T\mathbf{V}$ take mixed signs. Motivated by [10], we separate positive and negative parts of any matrix A as $\mathbf{A}_{ij}^+ = (|\mathbf{A}_{ij}| + \mathbf{A}_{ij})/2$, $\mathbf{A}_{ij}^- = (|\mathbf{A}_{ij}| - \mathbf{A}_{ij})/2$.

Thus, we get

$$+\lambda\tilde{\mathbf{W}}\mathbf{U} + \mathbf{U}\Gamma^-)$$
$$+((\mathbf{X}^T\mathbf{V})^- + [\mathbf{U}(\mathbf{V}^T\mathbf{V})^+] + \mathbf{U}\Gamma^+)]_{ij}\mathbf{U}_{ij} = 0 \tag{12}$$

which leads to the updating rule of U in Eq (4).

A.2 Computation of V

Optimizing the objective function $\mathcal{F}$ in Eq. (3) with respect to V is equivalent to solving

$$\min_{\mathbf{V}} \quad \mathcal{F}_{\mathbf{V}} = ||\mathbf{X} - \mathbf{V}\mathbf{U}^T||_F^2 \tag{13}$$

The derivative of $\mathcal{F}_{\mathbf{V}}$ with respect to V is

$$\frac{\partial \mathcal{F}_{\mathbf{V}}}{\partial \mathbf{V}} = -2\mathbf{X}\mathbf{U} + 2\mathbf{V}\mathbf{U}^T\mathbf{U} \tag{14}$$

Setting $\frac{\partial \mathcal{F}_{\mathbf{V}}}{\partial \mathbf{V}} = 0$, we get the updating rule of V in Eq (6).

REFERENCES

[1] Mohammad Akbari and Tat-Seng Chua. 2017. Leveraging Behavioral Factorization and Prior Knowledge for Community Discovery and Profiling. In *Proceedings of the Tenth ACM International Conference on Web Search and Data Mining*. ACM, 71–79.

[2] Vincent D Blondel, Jean-Loup Guillaume, Renaud Lambiotte, and Etienne Lefebvre. 2008. Fast unfolding of communities in large networks. *Journal of statistical mechanics: theory and experiment* 2008, 10 (2008), P10008.

[3] Ludovico Boratto. 2016. Group Recommender Systems. In *Proceedings of the 10th ACM Conference on Recommender Systems*. ACM, 427–428.

[4] Deng Cai, Xiaofei He, Jiawei Han, and Thomas S Huang. 2011. Graph regularized nonnegative matrix factorization for data representation. *IEEE Transactions on Pattern Analysis and Machine Intelligence* 33, 8 (2011), 1548–1560.

[5] Hongyun Cai, Vincent W Zheng, Fanwei Zhu, Kevin Chen-Chuan Chang, and Zi Huang. 2017. From community detection to community profiling. *Proceedings of the VLDB Endowment* 10, 7 (2017), 817–828.

[6] Wen-Yen Chen, Dong Zhang, and Edward Y Chang. 2008. Combinational collaborative filtering for personalized community recommendation. In *Proceedings of the 14th ACM SIGKDD international conference on Knowledge discovery and data mining*. ACM, 115–123.

[7] Aaron Clauset, Mark EJ Newman, and Cristopher Moore. 2004. Finding community structure in very large networks. *Physical review E* 70, 6 (2004), 066111.

[8] Juan David Cruz, Cécile Bothorel, and François Poulet. 2013. Community detection and visualization in social networks: Integrating structural and semantic information. *ACM Transactions on Intelligent Systems and Technology (TIST)* 5, 1 (2013), 11.

[9] Chris HQ Ding, Xiaofeng He, and Horst D Simon. 2005. On the Equivalence of Nonnegative Matrix Factorization and Spectral Clustering.. In *SDM*, Vol. 5. SIAM, 606–610.

[10] Chris HQ Ding, Tao Li, and Michael I Jordan. 2010. Convex and semi-nonnegative matrix factorizations. *IEEE transactions on pattern analysis and machine intelligence* 32, 1 (2010), 45–55.

[11] Martin Fishbein and Icek Ajzen. 1977. Belief, attitude, intention, and behavior: An introduction to theory and research. (1977).

[12] Rainer Gemulla, Erik Nijkamp, Peter J Haas, and Yannis Sismanis. 2011. Large-scale matrix factorization with distributed stochastic gradient descent. In *Proceedings of the 17th ACM SIGKDD international conference on Knowledge discovery and data mining*. ACM, 69–77.

[13] Kevin Gimpel, Nathan Schneider, Brendan O'Connor, Dipanjan Das, Daniel Mills, Jacob Eisenstein, Michael Heilman, Dani Yogatama, Jeffrey Flanigan, and Noah A Smith. 2011. Part-of-speech tagging for twitter: Annotation, features, and experiments. In *Proceedings of the 49th Annual Meeting of the Association for Computational Linguistics: Human Language Technologies: short papers-Volume 2*. Association for Computational Linguistics, 42–47.

[14] Quanquan Gu, Chris Ding, and Jiawei Han. 2011. On trivial solution and scale transfer problems in graph regularized nmf. In *IJCAI Proceedings-International Joint Conference on Artificial Intelligence*, Vol. 22. 1288.

[15] Quanquan Gu and Jie Zhou. 2009. Local learning regularized nonnegative matrix factorization. In *Proceedings of the 21st international jont conference on Artifical intelligence*. Morgan Kaufmann Publishers Inc., 1046–1051.

[16] Xiao Han, Leye Wang, Reza Farahbakhsh, Ángel Cuevas, Rubén Cuevas, Noel Crespi, and Lina He. 2016. CSD: A multi-user similarity metric for community recommendation in online social networks. *Expert Systems with Applications* 53 (2016), 14–26.

[17] Morgan Harvey, Fabio Crestani, and Mark J Carman. 2013. Building user profiles from topic models for personalised search. In *Proceedings of the 22nd ACM international conference on Conference on information & knowledge management*. ACM, 2309–2314.

[18] Michael Hechter. 1988. *Principles of group solidarity*. Vol. 11. Univ of California Press.

[19] Kazushi Ikeda, Gen Hattori, Chihiro Ono, Hideki Asoh, and Teruo Higashino. 2013. Twitter user profiling based on text and community mining for market analysis. *Knowledge-Based Systems* 51 (2013), 35–47.

[20] Robert V Kozinets. 2002. The field behind the screen: Using netnography for marketing research in online communities. *Journal of marketing research* 39, 1 (2002), 61–72.

[21] Daniel D Lee and H Sebastian Seung. 2001. Algorithms for non-negative matrix factorization. In *Advances in neural information processing systems*. 556–562.

[22] Kyumin Lee, James Caverlee, Zhiyuan Cheng, and Daniel Z Sui. 2013. Campaign extraction from social media. *ACM Transactions on Intelligent Systems and Technology (TIST)* 5, 1 (2013), 9.

[23] Fanglin Li, Bin Wu, Liutong Xu, Chuan Shi, and Jing Shi. 2014. A fast distributed stochastic gradient descent algorithm for matrix factorization. In *Proceedings of the 3rd International Conference on Big Data, Streams and Heterogeneous Source Mining: Algorithms, Systems, Programming Models and Applications-Volume 36*. JMLR. org, 77–87.

[24] Darren Lilleker, Dan Jackson, Einar Thorsen, and Anastasia Veneti. 2016. US Election Analysis 2016: Media, Voters and the Campaign. (2016).

[25] Chao Liu, Hung-chih Yang, Jinliang Fan, Li-Wei He, and Yi-Min Wang. 2010. Distributed nonnegative matrix factorization for web-scale dyadic data analysis on mapreduce. In *Proceedings of the 19th international conference on World wide web*. ACM, 681–690.

[26] Alan Mislove, Bimal Viswanath, Krishna P Gummadi, and Peter Druschel. 2010. You are who you know: inferring user profiles in online social networks. In *Proceedings of the third ACM international conference on Web search and data mining*. ACM, 251–260.

[27] Michael Moran. 2015. *Politics and Governance in the UK*. Palgrave Macmillan.

[28] Arjun Mukherjee and Bing Liu. 2012. Aspect extraction through semi-supervised modeling. In *Proceedings of the 50th Annual Meeting of the Association for Computational Linguistics: Long Papers-Volume 1*. Association for Computational Linguistics, 339–348.

[29] Nagarajan Natarajan, Prithviraj Sen, and Vineet Chaoji. 2013. Community detection in content-sharing social networks. In *Proceedings of the 2013 IEEE/ACM International Conference on Advances in Social Networks Analysis and Mining*. ACM, 82–89.

[30] Mert Ozer, Nyunsu Kim, and Hasan Davulcu. 2016. Community Detection in Political Twitter Networks using Nonnegative Matrix Factorization Methods. *IEEE/ACM International Conference on Advances in Social Networks Analysis and Mining* (2016).

[31] Symeon Papadopoulos, Yiannis Kompatsiaris, Athena Vakali, and Ploutarchos Spyridonos. 2012. Community detection in social media. *Data Mining and Knowledge Discovery* 24, 3 (2012), 515–554.

[32] Nishith Pathak, Colin DeLong, Arindam Banerjee, and Kendrick Erickson. 2008. Social topic models for community extraction. In *Proceedings of the 2nd SNA-KDD Workshop*.

[33] Yulong Pei, Nilanjan Chakraborty, and Katia Sycara. 2015. Nonnegative matrix tri-factorization with graph regularization for community detection in social networks. In *Proceedings of the 24th International Conference on Artificial Intelligence*. AAAI Press, 2083–2089.

[34] Maria Pontiki, Dimitris Galanis, Haris Papageorgiou, Ion Androutsopoulos, Suresh Manandhar, AL-Smadi Mohammad, Mahmoud Al-Ayyoub, Yanyan Zhao, Bing Qin, Orphée De Clercq, et al. 2016. SemEval-2016 task 5: Aspect based sentiment analysis. In *Proceedings of the 10th international workshop on semantic evaluation (SemEval-2016)*. 19–30.

[35] Guang Qiu, Bing Liu, Jiajun Bu, and Chun Chen. 2011. Opinion word expansion and target extraction through double propagation. *Computational linguistics* 37, 1 (2011), 9–27.

[36] Martin Rosvall and Carl T Bergstrom. 2008. Maps of random walks on complex networks reveal community structure. *Proceedings of the National Academy of Sciences* 105, 4 (2008), 1118–1123.

[37] Mrinmaya Sachan, Danish Contractor, Tanveer A Faruquie, and L Venkata Subramaniam. 2012. Using content and interactions for discovering communities in social networks. In *Proceedings of the 21st international conference on World Wide Web*. ACM, 331–340.

[38] Shaghayegh Sahebi and William W Cohen. 2011. Community-based recommendations: a solution to the cold start problem. In *Workshop on recommender systems and the social web, RSWEB*.

[39] Fanhua Shang, LC Jiao, and Fei Wang. 2012. Graph dual regularization nonnegative matrix factorization for co-clustering. *Pattern Recognition* 45, 6 (2012), 2237–2250.

[40] Henri Tajfel. 2010. *Social identity and intergroup relations*. Cambridge University Press.

[41] Duyu Tang, Bing Qin, and Ting Liu. 2016. Aspect level sentiment classification with deep memory network. *arXiv preprint arXiv:1605.08900* (2016).

[42] Mike Thelwall, Kevan Buckley, Georgios Paltoglou, Di Cai, and Arvid Kappas. 2010. Sentiment strength detection in short informal text. *Journal of the American Society for Information Science and Technology* 61, 12 (2010), 2544–2558.

[43] John C Turner, Michael A Hogg, Penelope J Oakes, Stephen D Reicher, and Margaret S Wetherell. 1987. *Rediscovering the social group: A self-categorization theory*. Basil Blackwell.

[44] Kai Yu, Shipeng Yu, and Volker Tresp. 2005. Soft clustering on graphs. In *Advances in neural information processing systems*. 1553–1560.

[45] Lei Zhang and Bing Liu. 2014. Aspect and entity extraction for opinion mining. In *Data mining and knowledge discovery for big data*. Springer, 1–40.

[46] Ding Zhou, Eren Manavoglu, Jia Li, C Lee Giles, and Hongyuan Zha. 2006. Probabilistic models for discovering e-communities. In *Proceedings of the 15th international conference on World Wide Web*. ACM, 173–182.

[47] Wenjun Zhou, Hongxia Jin, and Yan Liu. 2012. Community discovery and profiling with social messages. In *Proceedings of the 18th ACM SIGKDD international conference on Knowledge discovery and data mining*. ACM, 388–396.

Intelligent Generative Locative Hyperstructure

Charlie Hargood
Creative Technology
Bournemouth University
chargood@bournemouth.ac.uk

Fred Charles
Creative Technology
Bournemouth University
fcharles@bournemouth.ac.uk

David E. Millard
Web and Internet Science
University of Southampton
dem@soton.ac.uk

ABSTRACT

Locative Hypertext Narrative has seen a resurgence in the Hypertext and Interactive Narrative research communities over the last five years. However, while locative hypertext provides significant opportunities for rich locative applications for both education and entertainment, many applications in this space are tied to very specific locations, restricting their utility to local users. While this is necessary for some locative applications (such as tour guides), others make use of location as a thematic or contextual backdrop and as such could be effectively read in similar locations elsewhere. However, many locative systems are restricted to use specific prescribed locations, and systems that do generate locations do so in a simplistic manner, and often with mixed results. In this paper we propose a more intelligent generative approach to locative hypertext that will generate a locative structure for the user's local area that both respects the thematic location demands of the piece and the effective patterns and structures of locative narrative.

CCS CONCEPTS

• **Human-centered computing** → **Hypertext/hypermedia**;

KEYWORDS

Location-Based Narrative, Narrative Generation, Location Querying

ACM Reference Format:
Charlie Hargood, Fred Charles, and David E. Millard. 2018. Intelligent Generative Locative Hyperstructure. In *HT '18: 29th ACM Conference on Hypertext and Social Media, July 9–12, 2018, Baltimore, MD, USA*. ACM, New York, NY, USA, 4 pages. https://doi.org/10.1145/3209542.3210574

1 INTRODUCTION

Locative Hypertext allows for context-aware documents which respond to the readers location. Typically they are made up of pages linked together as a hypertext with constraints (sometimes called guard fields) that bind pages to particular locations. A navigational interface as part of a reading application then allows the reader to travel from location to location reading the hypertext.

This work has seen a resurgence in the last 5 years in the hypertext and interactive narrative research communities [1, 5, 8, 17],

brought on by the increasing prevalence of location-aware mobile devices. Applications of this work include tour guides and other educational pieces, as well as interactive fiction and games [10]. While some of these applications demand specific locations (such as tour guides) others make use of location as more of a thematic backdrop to the narrative, where the requirement is the *type* of location in which a page is read rather than the *specific* location itself (for example a page that needs to be read in a park, but with no specific park required). However, due to the limitations of the hypertext platforms that support such systems these pages are typically required to be bound to specific locations, often a GPS based circle. This limits the reading of these works to local users, or demands extensive travel to experience them. This restricts the audience reach of such creations, and hinders the wider study of locative works through demands on scholarly travel.

In this paper we propose that authors should be able to bind content to location classifications rather than specific GPS positions. An intelligent system could then use a variety of open data sources to search the surrounding area for candidate locations that match this classification. This is not dissimilar to the generative locations used by systems such as Six to Start's *Wanderlust* that allowed content to be tied to FourSquare classifications of place. However, existing generative locative systems do not take into account the effective use and structures of locative narrative [16], meaning that the locations generated are logically correct, but may be tonally out of step with the rest of the story, or impractical to traverse. We propose to support the generative process with an intelligent system that applies a series of rules that could be applied to candidate locations creating a more effective location design given the narrative content and structure.

2 BACKGROUND AND RELATED WORK

We propose that the author replace specific locations with classifications of location, and that an intelligent system will select the actual locations themselves based on a reader's surroundings and a rule based system representing effective locative narrative structures. Consequently we consider work from locative hypertext, and narrative generation.

2.1 Locative Narrative Hypertext

Historically locative narratives can be separated into educational tools such as the Chawton House project [18], tour guides such as HopStory, Nisi2004, interactive fiction such as San Servolo [13], and games such as Viking Ghost Hunt [11]. While all tour guides and some examples of the other classifications are written about specific places many others hold the potential for more flexible location installations that might benefit from our suggested proposal. Viking ghost hunt [11] for example relies upon a historical urban environment - but that does not inherently have to be Dublin, and the ambient wood [19] could be set in a forest outside of that specific wood in Hampshire in the UK. The more recent resurgence in this spaces includes bespoke locative experience such as the interactive augmented reality tour guides of Geist [17] and the locative drama work at LIFA [1], but general platforms for locative narrative hypertext such as StoryPlaces [4] are rare and don't enable as flexible a hypertextual structure.

StoryPlaces[1] [3, 8] was a project exploring both the technical and poetic demands of locative narrative hypertext. It lead to the development of the StoryPlaces platform - a generic framework of software that including an authoring and reading application for the creation and consumption of locative narrative [4]. StoryPlaces is powered by a flexible sculptural hypertext system, and a schema that recognises both a general model of locative narrative, and a range of hypertextual patterns that commonly arise from locative narrative. StoryPlaces' research into the poetics of locative narratives uncovered a range of important considerations which led to the creation of an authors toolkit which offers guidance on poetic, aesthetic, and pragmatic considerations for effective locative narrative such as the consideration of entry and exit points, avoiding zigzagging, and respecting the aesthetic demands of the geography [12]. If our proposal is to enable effective locative narrative in multiple locations it will need to reflect these rules in its selection of locations.

Existing systems that generate locations do so based solely on classification (such as *Wanderlust* noted in our introduction) or even randomly [16], allowing the user to try again if the location is unreachable . These leave a lot of the quality of the experience to chance.

2.2 Narrative Generation

We suggest that candidate locations taken from the readers local area that match classifications dictated by the author be collected and then selected from using a rule based system that reflects best authorial practice. This general approach to generating stories has been explored before in what Riedl and Young would call *'Author Centric'* narrative generation [15]. *'Author Centric'*, also known as *'Plot Centric'*, approaches have a centralised approach providing a mechanism for narrative control and hence provides a better solution to the problem of authorial control in order for improved narrative coherence. However authorial control brings the negative effect of individual actions becoming over-complicated, along with a reduction in the generative power that more distributed approaches might provide. *'Character Centric'* approaches offer a greater flexibility and potential for generative scalability when narratives emerge from the interactions between different narrative characters [2].

AI planning was first proposed for the task of narrative generation by Young [20] because it provided a natural fit for representation with narratives as plans; ensured causality which is important for the generation of meaningful and comprehensible narratives; and provided considerable flexibility and potential generative power. Moreover, a plan-based approach is neutral with

respect to the duality between character and plot since both stances are compatible with the approach at the representational level.

3 GENERATIVE LOCATIVE HYPERSTRUCTURE

Our approach has three parts:

(1) **Separation of narrative and locative structure**: The narrative structure of content and its logical flow and restrictions should be separated from the locative structure. This enables a narrative structure firmly defined by the author and a locative structure generated to suit the reader's locale.

(2) **Location classifications**: Replacing static location definitions with flexible location classifications allows for the identification of candidate locations suitable to the content in a readers local area.

(3) **Pragmatic and Poetic Locative Structure Generation**: Having identified candidate locations a rules based author centric system selects the most suitable locations that create a locative structure best fitting rules defining effective locative narrative design.

3.1 Separation of narrative and locative structure

The creation of locative narrative is effectively a twin design process: the design of a story, and the design of a walk. Each of these structures is essential to the resulting creation and although it is important they compliment each other each demonstrates slightly different patterns and structures [8]. By separating these processes we enable a narrative structure that is wholly author created, and a locative structure that is machine generated (given that authors set constraints) but mindful of that structure.

StoryPlaces already makes this separation, with stories considering both content and locations as separate first order objects [4]. Consequently location definitions are not entangled with page content making replacing the locations for a story without effecting the content significantly easier. Thus, StoryPlaces lends itself to our proposed approach and this is no coincidence, as the idea of dynamic or 'fuzzy' location classifiers was partially experimented with in StoryPlaces' predecessor - the experimental prototype Geo-Yarn [10].

3.2 Location Classifications

This part of our proposal finds candidate locations local to the reader that match the location requirements of the story as defined by the author. This will necessitate the development of a simple structured location query language. While there are prior existing languages for locative querying such as PostGIS, Simple Features (ISO 19125), and Geosparql these are more concerned with the spatial extents of geographical information systems (such as GPS polygons, or routes) rather than the semantic descriptive classifications demanded by this approach. Consequently while existing technology such as those mentioned above might be used in any such approach, a custom solution will be necessary. This language would allow the user to express the desired restriction of content to a particular type of location.

---

[1]http://storyplaces.soton.ac.uk/ as of 27/2/18

This could be made up of location classifications such as 'park land', 'road', 'waterfront', 'commercial center', or adjectives such as 'noisy', 'quiet', 'busy', 'isolated', 'historical'. The specific descriptors themselves would need to be identified by a two fold study of both what was required by authors and what was possible to resolve through open data queries. Each classifier would be linked to available open data queries using services such as Open Street Map or DBpedia[2], these queries again would require careful design and validation to ensure the results reflected the desired classification.

The author would express location as a query in terms of this language instead of a specific GPS position as is normally currently done in systems such as StoryPlaces. As such logical queries may not come naturally to authors work may have to be done to refine the authoring tools used to give support in the construction of such queries as has been done with logical story structures in StoryPlaces authoring tool [9]. Any reader client would then be able to access a list of candidate locations that satisfied these constraints within a predefined distance. What this distance should be set to and whether locations that only partially satisfy constraints should be used are flexible design issues outside of the domain of this initial proposal and to be experimented with through implementation, a constraint based system with tolerances that can be relaxed is anticipated however.

3.3 Pragmatic Poetic Locative Structure Generation

Having identified candidate locations from the previous stage our proposed system would now need to tie content to the most suitable specific locations in the local area. This would involve generating a hyperstructure of locations from the candidate set that is both pragmatic and poetic for the given narrative. For example if our story involves ten pages, each with their own location classification, and arranged in a branching structure, then we need to select locations that not only match the location classifications, but that are pragmatic for our reader (no far flung nodes hours away from their predecessor), and of high poetic quality for the branching structure (if possible using the local geography to reflect and enhance the branching nature of the story).

As previously mentioned the StoryPlaces project has not only delivered a general software platform but also done much to formalise and identify the rules and principles behind poetically effective and pragmatic locative narrative [12]. These rules would form the basis of our generative system, the logical structure of the story (the structure implicit from the sculptural hypertext) would need to be loaded and compared with candidate locations and these rules to score potential location selections on their suitability.

For example, StoryPlaces' findings indicated that for pragmatic reasons stories should begin and end in places close together as this reflects the fact that readers need to arrive and leave a place, normally via a common means. This would require the intelligent location generation to undertake some level of forward planning, looking for not only continuous routes through the landscape, but arcs that could ultimately lead the reader back to their starting point. Poetically the project found that distinct narrative areas (such as Acts, or point of view shifts) should be reflected in location

[2] https://www.openstreetmap.org/ and dbpedia.org as of 27/2/18

choices, this could translate into the identification of geographic zones for different parts of the story. It also argued that people were naturally drawn towards points of interest, which made them good for implicit direction, or dramatically highlighting certain points in the narrative. This suggests rules that associate items from POI data with critical turning points, or align them with potential narrative destinations.

For many years, AI planning has been applied to the task of narrative generation, for example [14, 21]. However, planning has also been applied to the task of control, in IDA [7] and to the planning of discourse aspects [6]. The structure of the narrative plot can be quite naturally modeled using a plan. Hence plans should be equated to the sequence of narrative steps to be part of the solution of semantically relevant selected locations. Overall, the planning process would provide the ability to generate a selection of solution plans, thus defining the narrative graph for any specific reader. Consequently, whether the overall aim is to generate an instance of a narrative which includes a start and finish locations closeby; a set of narratively meaningful locations for the current plot being considered; or ensuring the dramatic coherence and evolution of the narrative across the locations, plan-based narrative generation can be applied to this locative context. Nevertheless, several challenges remain, including an important one: how can plan metrics be specified to align with the quality of narrative solutions generated from the semantic classification of locations based on strong narrative poetics? This could be defined as a poetic and pragmatic suitability score to be calculated for candidate structures generated from candidate locations. This would allow for the selection of the most effective locative structure for a given narrative structure in a particular locale.

3.4 The Locative Hyperstructure Generator

Ultimately these three parts of our proposal would come together to form an Intelligent Locative Hyperstructure Generator that can be used to create a local locative binding between a story and a reader's locale, creating a specific locative experience. Our approach is summarised diagrammatically in figure 1 which depicts the approach in 5 steps from story definition to suitable locative structure definition (for a very simple case). Step 1 refers to the **Separation of narrative and locative structure**, step 1 and 2 to **Location classifications**, and step 3 to 5 to **Pragmatic Poetic Locative Structure Generation**. Our simple depicted example only includes three pages in a linear structure with fairly simple location classifications. However we can see how classifications can lead to candidate location identification, to potential structures that match the story structure, and then to removing structures according to the rules (in this example, removing those with excessive distance between nodes, or those that zigzag back on themselves rather than providing a continuous progression).

4 CONCLUSIONS AND WAY FORWARD

In this paper we propose an approach towards intelligent generative locative hyperstructure as a means to free locative narratives from specific locations and enable their access in a reader's local area. It is our hope that this will both increase the reach of locative hypertext,

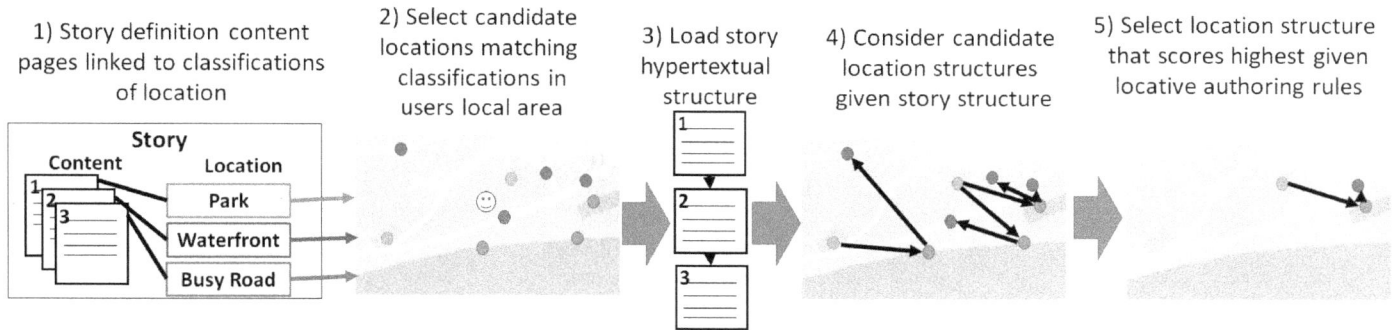

Figure 1: The proposed generative locative hypertextual approach

and unlock its access to scholars, paving the way for both a more mature medium and one that is better understood.

Our proposed approach is based upon three key principles; **Separation of narrative and locative structure, Location classifications**, and **Pragmatic poetic locative structure generation**. This will be powered by a suitable locative narrative model such as that provided by StoryPlaces, a location query language, and author centric narrative generation technology. We propose a number of potential technological solutions from related work, the contributions of which might be brought together as a solution to this problem.

While the authors intend our own investigation into this, starting with location classification and querying for StoryPlaces, we anticipate with the increased attention to locative hypertext that this problem will become a notable challenge for the community going forward. There is an opportunity here for implementations of possible solutions, such as the one described here, to make a substantial contribution.

We conclude by summarising the four individual challenges that make up this grand challenge:

- Identifying needed location classifications.
- Build suitable location query language and system.
- Refining authoring tools for location querying.
- Build locative narrative poetics into a rules based system for structure generation.

REFERENCES

[1] Federico Martín Alconada Verzini, Juan Ignacio Tonelli, Cecilia Challiol, Alejandra Beatriz Lliteras, and Silvia Ethel Gordillo. 2015. Authoring tool for location-aware experiences. In *Proceedings of the 2015 Workshop on Narrative & Hypertext*. ACM, 21–25.
[2] Marc Cavazza, Fred Charles, and Steven J Mead. 2002. Character-based interactive storytelling. *IEEE Intelligent systems* 17, 4 (2002), 17–24.
[3] Charlie Hargood, Verity Hunt, Mark Weal, and David E. Millard. 2016. Patterns of Sculptural Hypertext in Location Based Narratives. In *Proceedings of the 27th ACM Conference on Hypertext and Social Media*. ACM, New York, NY, USA.
[4] Charlie Hargood, Mark J. Weal, and David E. Millard. 2018. The StoryPlaces Platform: Building a Web-Based Locative Hypertext System. In *Proceedings of the 29th ACM Conference on Hypertext and Social Media*. Currently under review and not yet publushed as of 27/2/18.
[5] Katie Headrick Taylor. 2017. Learning along lines: Locative literacies for reading and writing the city. *Journal of the Learning Sciences* 26, 4 (2017), 533–574.
[6] Arnav Jhala and R Michael Young. 2010. Cinematic visual discourse: Representation, generation, and evaluation. *IEEE Transactions on Computational Intelligence and AI in Games* 2, 2 (2010), 69–81.
[7] Brian Magerko. 2007. Evaluating preemptive story direction in the interactive drama architecture. *Journal of Game Development* 2, 3 (2007), 25–52.
[8] David E. Millard and Charlie Hargood. 2017. Tiree tales: a co-operative inquiry into the poetics of location-based narratives. In *Proceedings of the 28th ACM Conference on Hypertext and Social Media*.
[9] David E Millard, Charlie Hargood, Yvonne Howard, and Heather Packer. 2017. The StoryPlaces Authoring Tool: Pattern Centric Authoring. In *Authoring for Interactive Storytelling 2017 Workshop @ ICIDS 2017*.
[10] David E. Millard, Charlie Hargood, Michael O. Jewell, and Mark J. Weal. 2013. Canyons, Deltas and Plains: Towards a Unified Sculptural Model of Location-based Hypertext. In *Proceedings of the 24th ACM Conference on Hypertext and Social Media*. ACM, New York, NY, USA, 109–118.
[11] K. Naliuka, T. Carrigy, N. Paterson, and M. Haahr. 2010. A narrative architecture for story-driven location-based mobile games. In *New Horizons in Web-Based Learning*. Springer, 11–20.
[12] Heather S Packer, Charlie Hargood, Yvonne Howard, Petros Papadopoulos, and David E Millard. 2017. Developing a WriterâĂŹs Toolkit for Interactive Locative Storytelling. In *International Conference on Interactive Digital Storytelling*. Springer, 63–74.
[13] F. Pittarello. 2011. Designing a context-aware architecture for emotionally engaging mobile storytelling. *IFIP Conference on Human-Computer Interaction* (2011), 144–151.
[14] Julie Porteous, Marc Cavazza, and Fred Charles. 2010. Applying planning to interactive storytelling: Narrative control using state constraints. *ACM Transactions on Intelligent Systems and Technology (TIST)* 1, 2 (2010), 10.
[15] Mark O Riedl. 2009. Incorporating Authorial Intent into Generative Narrative Systems.. In *AAAI Spring Symposium: Intelligent Narrative Technologies II*. 91–94.
[16] Duncan Speakman. 2017. *It Must Have Been Dark by Then*. Taylor Brothers Bristol.
[17] Ulrike Spierling, Peter Winzer, and Erik Massarczyk. 2017. Experiencing the Presence of Historical Stories with Location-Based Augmented Reality. In *International Conference on Interactive Digital Storytelling*. Springer, 49–62.
[18] Mark J. Weal, D. Cruickshank, D.T. Michaelides, David E. Millard, D.C.D. Roure, K. Howland, and G. Fitzpatrick. 2007. A card based metaphor for organising pervasive educational experiences. In *Pervasive Computing and Communications Workshops, 2007*. IEEE, 165–170.
[19] Mark J Weal, Danius T Michaelides, Mark K Thompson, and David C DeRoure. 2003. The ambient wood journals: replaying the experience. In *Proceedings of the fourteenth ACM conference on Hypertext and hypermedia*. ACM, 20–27.
[20] R Michael Young. 1999. Notes on the use of plan structures in the creation of interactive plot. In *AAAI Fall Symposium on Narrative Intelligence*. 164–167.
[21] R Michael Young et al. 2001. An overview of the mimesis architecture: Integrating intelligent narrative control into an existing gaming environment. In *The Working Notes of the AAAI Spring Symposium on Artificial Intelligence and Interactive Entertainment*. 78–81.

As We May Hear

Our Slaves of Steel II

Mark Bernstein
Eastgate Systems, Inc.
134 Main Street
Watertown MA 02472 USA
Bernstein@eastgate.com

ABSTRACT

Our slaves of steel [4] explored some moral questions that arise from narrative with persistent digital agents. If we propose to her on the holodeck, can Ophelia conceivably consent to marry us? Here, we propose simple audio agents that are well within the capacity of current technology, and we explore the reader's responsibility, if any, to care for persistent agents.

CCS CONCEPTS

• **Software and its engineering**→**Software creation and management**→**Designing Software**   • **Applied Computing**→**Computers in other domains.**

KEYWORDS

Hypertext, hypermedia, literature, fiction, education, design, implementation, , history of computing, ethics.

ACM Reference format:

M. Bernstein. 2018. As We May Hear: our slaves of steel II. In *Proceedings of the 29th ACM Conference on Hypertext and Social Media, Baltimore, MD USA, July 2018 (HT2018) ACM, NY, NY, USA.,* 4 pages. https://doi.org/10.1145/3209542.3210575

1   FRONT OF THE HOUSE

Our current experience of hypertext is conditioned by our experience of the Web and its assumption that, at least normatively, the reader's state is largely synonymous with (and represented by) a URI. Early research was far less confined, yet retained a strong interest in formalisms more constrained than general computation. Stretchtext [9] and its generalization [6], for example, let the reader expand, collapse, and move passages

within a notionally continuous scroll, while Trellis [22] replaced the boxes and arrows of the hypertext's underlying finite state machine with a Petri net in which following a link might activate multiple windows or other media objects at once. Though these facilities were often motivated by allusions to multimedia content, we can readily envision scenarios in which the same techniques would prove useful or indispensable for everyday knowledge work.

Let us consider, for example, the challenges faced by the host of a small restaurant[1]. At the start of the evening, we have a list of reserved tables. The names of some frequent patrons will be familiar to us. Others names may be found in our restaurant's records, and those records can refresh our understanding of their tastes and preferences. Many names might be new to us, but even then we may know something about them — we may have met some socially, we may know some others from their work. We know the police chief, the provost of the college down the street, the writer who is a Tuesday night regular. A quick Web search might prove helpful; some restaurants already do this routinely. Of course, there is no substitute for acute observation, a sensitive ear, and a facility for putting people at their ease.

Yet, much might be accomplished with technical assistance that is well within (or at least not very far beyond) the limitations of current technology. We have, at most, one name associated with each reservation, but each party might include four or eight people. We may know nothing of Ms. Snodgrass, but it behooves us to know that her guest is the restaurant critic for The Herald. It's always nice to see Dr. Watson, a frequent patron, but today his guests turn out to be Mayor Matsuda and Elaine Orcrist, the actress. Vannevar Bush predicted that hypertext readers would have head-mounted cameras [11]; these might not be typical accouterments for researchers today, but discrete use of facial recognition and image databases could save a host from many a sad blunder.

Of course, the host must not spend their time staring into a cell phone or a podium-mounted screen; the entire point of their

---

[1] Similar or identical problems might face an aide at a diplomatic reception, or indeed anyone who needs to offer hospitality to a diverse and open audience.

role is direct and unmediated contact[2]. Nor do we wish to share our information broadly; it's important for us to know that Dr. Watson didn't care for his shrimp last week, but we don't want to advertise that debacle. If we are to use the formidable resources of computation at the moment of contact, the interface must be unobtrusive and discrete. Taste and smell are too slow, and our host's vision must be unencumbered and his or her face unobstructed; in communicating with the machine, we'll need to rely on sound and gesture [2]. We need the machine to watch, observe what it can, and to whisper in our ear.

2 POLYPHONIC HYPERTEXT

As a party walks through our door, we can easily envision a wealth of information that could be made available to our host. Some comes from our previous experience with this guest, some from public information sources, some might be derived from colleagues or from other businesses with whom we share information. This flood of data cannot be communicated at once—especially not through a low-bandwidth audio link. Instead, it is essential to rapidly communicate what we might know, its provenance and reliability, and then to allow our human agent to indicate which lines are most promising.

The one advantage we do possess is that the human agent is a professional, an expert who performs precisely this task all the time. We can then, within reason, encode and compress information to more efficiently communicate what is available. We don't want a droning lecture of all the available data; instead, a variety of distinct voices offer what each source or agent considers the most interesting or useful data.

BOBBY, for example, is the voice of our customer relation database; he knows who has dined here before and remembers what they enjoyed.

CLARE follows the news. Clare knows who is the mayor, and knows from the local paper that there's a city council hearing tonight at eight. Clare knows what's playing Symphony Hall and at what time the concert starts.

DERRICK is a broad search tool, an interface to general-purpose search engines that our host has trained to prioritize areas that are likely to be helpful and deemphasize sources that might be problematic. Derrick knows who is speaking at the University down the road, and who is visiting our town to plan next summer's repertory theater program.

ELIN knows the food industry. Is a new patron a restaurant reviewer for a national magazine or for a distant newspaper? Elin will know. Just as important, Elin knows lots of servers, cooks, and investors at restaurants around town, not to mention novelists and nonfiction writers who are interested in food.

---

[2] Indeed, I have chosen this scenario because here the role of human interaction cannot readily be automated away. The context is replete with concerns of embodiment, with the intimacy of social spaces and nourishment. It is worth remembering, too, that prior to the current generation, the front of the house was what really mattered in shaping the reputation of a restaurant.

Each agent speaks in a distinctive voice, with an intonation that reflects both its confidence in its own conclusions and its estimate of its own importance. With a word or hand gesture, the host selects which agents may speak. The agents need not be expert at understanding social context or common sense, but can specialize in their limited province.

It is easy to improve agents over the course of time. Our customer data, for example, improves nightly. Every industry party is an opportunity to improve Elin's reach. We can conclude that certain sources are too partisan or too speculative for Derrick to trust, or locate specialized sources that Derrick should download and review whenever they are updated. Each interaction is a potential training case for each agent.

3 CONDUCTING THE CHORUS

Our agents could easily deliver far more information than the host could usefully assimilate in the available time, much less through the limited bandwidth of an audio feed. We need, then, to categorize information, placing higher priority on what the host most needs to know. The agents already described are little more than database queries, search engine lookups or simple neural networks, but this executive editor or director function is far more difficult. Adapting a hypertextual textbook to a limited audience of motivated undergraduates working with little time stress is hard enough; the user modeling and common sense reasoning required to tell our host what they most need is likely far beyond our abilities [10].

Instead, we might use a very low-bandwidth channel from the human back to the chorus of agents to determine which agent is to speak. Agents wishing to speak ask for attention[20], and the host uses a hand gesture or simple tactile interface to indicate which agent is of greatest interest. While we're always interested in our customer relationship database, for example, very frequent customers may be so familiar that we'd prefer to hear about their recent news.

Throughout its history, hypertext and AI have been competing technologies — the one true docuverse opposed to the one true system[7]. Common sense has proven a significant challenge; fortunately, we can easily substitute the host's good sense for the computer's.

Note, too, that the agents may be able to form and express opinions about the priority of their messages, reasoning alike from their own data, and from the urgency and confidence expressed by other agents. The host may instill explicit or implicitly-learned heuristics; industry news is less important than our customer experience database most of the time, but not during Restaurant Week.

4 DISCUSS AMONG YOURSELVES

Agents may also respond to each other. Many personal names are difficult to search, either because hundreds of individuals share a common name, or because some people share a name with (or were named for) more famous people. The "Louis Sullivan" who reserved a table is probably not the architect who died in 1924, but finding living Louis/Louie/Louise

Sullivans is complicated by the prominence of the deceased architect. Bobby might be able to disambiguate ("He comes for lunch meetings about once a month") and enable other agents to search more efficiently ("The Louis Sullivan who works nearby.")

The challenge of composing effective dialogue among independent agents is of great interest to hyperdrama and generative hypertext [5] [18]. Dialogue among agents raises some interesting architectural problems.

If agents see only the output of their peers, they may need both sophisticated language understanding and common sense to fully understand what is said.

If agents see the internal state of their peers, they might perhaps gain more insight into what other agents are trying to express, at the cost of breaking encapsulation and enormously complicating maintenance.

If agents proceed on incomplete or superficial understanding of the output of their peers, their dialogue may be incoherent.

Of three unsatisfactory alternatives, the last is clearly the best. Coherence, even more than closure, is in hypertext a suspect quality [17], and natural dialog follows rhythms and patterns that defy simple logical analysis. Consider even the laconic, straightforward Hemingway [15]:

"Oh, Jake," Brett said, "we could have had such a damned good time together."

Ahead was a mounted policeman in khaki directing traffic. He raised his baton. The car slowed suddenly pressing Brett against me.

"Yes," I said. "Isn't it pretty to think so?"

Jake says "yes," meaning "no," even though Brett did not ask a question. The policeman has not been seen before and will not be seen again; it could be argued that he is irrelevant. But this does not read as Dada or even as experimental high modernism; the reader supplies what is not in the text [13].

5 OUR SLAVES OF STEEL

Let us suppose that our human host, Alice, leaves her post for a two week tour of Tuscan vineyards. Aaron, a temporary host on loan from a neighboring restauranct, takes her role, and uses her agents while she is away. Aaron inevitably has distinct preferences and therefore tends to train the agents differently. When Alice returns, they will have changed — perhaps Bobby, after much chastening, is greatly subdued, while Elin feels much freer to repeat industry gossip. The result alienates the returning expert: Alice is no longer at home with her familiar agents. If Alice had left human assistants to the mercies of an abusive temporary chief, she would be greatly to blame; does any blame inhere here?

Alice might be able to roll back the agents to their pre-Aaron state without discarding the data accumulated during the past two weeks. But should she? These are not people, or even sentient beings, of course, but they enact disembodied intelligences. Would rolling back their state not be implicit violence[16]? Does enacting even symbolic violence against credible enactments of beings – against unscripted characters – not harm us? Our slaves of steel[21] may perform dull and repetitive chores that we would not wish upon actual people, but does that make us free to erase their experience, even metaphorically?

Of course, workers in some fields conventionally own their own tools and avoid sharing them with colleagues. Restaurants supply ovens and refrigerators, but cooks bring their own knives. It is common for auto mechanics and machinists to provide their own hand tools. Perhaps Alice ought not to have lent her agents in the first place; Aaron could have brought his own, or worked with an untrained, generic collection of agents. That solution raises the question of who owns the agents: are they Alice's property, or her employer's? If she decides to remain in Tuscany, is she entitled to take her agents with her?

6 AGENTS WITH ATTITUDE

Because different agents may be either more or less reliable, an agent's identity should be communicated clearly but efficiently. If an agent tells us that a guest enjoys chopped liver, it's important to understand whether this observation is based on their previous visit to our restaurant or on a gossip column discovered by a Web search. To this end, we can simply assign a distinct voice to each agent, varying intonation, dialect, accent and timbre.

The agent's habitual mode of expression, their style and affect, can provide useful cues to their identity and utility. Iain M. Banks envisions the voice of a hub computer, an intelligence capable of managing the environment and communications of an entire planet, like this:

> "Ho-ho! It was *you*, was it? We thought it was going to take *months* to work that one out. You've just seen a Private visit, game-player Gurgey; Contact business; not for us to know. *Wow*, were we inquisitive though. [3]"

Without expending unnecessary words, the Hub's language both distinguishes it from other machines and communicates some useful reminder of its particular skills and preferences. The hub is very curious — it's the job of the central environmental system to know what's going on and what people want — and it's enthusiastic on our behalf.

The personality or affect of the Planetary Hub grows naturally out of that agent's competences and roles. Personality may also be attached, more or less arbitrarily, to distinguish different voices. This need not cost many extra words or much additional time, but it can provide a useful heuristic. Douglas Adams' robot, Marvin, is depressed; his function does not require depression, but the theatricality of his affliction distinguishes his voice and makes it memorable.

I could calculate your chance of survival, but you won't like it. [1]

This is, in fact, an established strategy for managing the many hands and voices that interact at critical intersections of restaurant service as in other challenging environments [8]. Actual people, despite their actual nuance and subtlety, adopt exaggerated personae that help their colleagues identify who is who and who needs what now; when meeting outside of work, colleagues seem entirely different [12].

Careful writing can make even dull and repetitive dialogue delightful. Air traffic controller Steve Abraham, for example, gained a following of hundreds of thousands of listeners for condensations of his routine work guiding planes between boarding gate and runway. This an unlikely realm for humor — almost all the dialogue necessarily concerns waiting at intersections — is spiced with just enough color and drama to make compelling listening. This may serve some cognitive or metacognitive function by encouraging pilots to pay attention or by improving their mood, but (as Adrian Miles reminded us in his classic paper) "the immanent economy of excess" created by polyphonic hypertextuality might be its own justification [19].

7 TALKING AMONGST OURSELVES

The earliest audible agents — aircraft alarm annunciators were among the first — had a repertoire of only a few phrases and were tolerable because they were usually silent. Attempting to engage users in frequent dialogue with a limited repertoire of utterance is both boring and annoying, as all who remember Clippy's many offers to help us write a letter will recall. Modern audible agents like Siri or Alexa have larger repertoires, so their response to routine requests like "Set a timer for 30 minutes" varies from time to time.

Writing for a single, isolated agent is difficult. If they merely acknowledge orders, they have no personality at all, but if they express personality, those expressions are either defined by resistance to the user (ELIZA [23]) or are limited to overt expressions of their purported desires:

AUTHOR: Who are you, really?

PHONE: I'm Siri. But enough about me. How can I help you?

This is writing "on the nose," communicating the agent's agenda by stating it [18]. The polyphony of our agents provide opportunities for agents to express themselves in relationship to other agents.

By giving agents access to the underlying representation from which utterances are generated, they can easily and swiftly react to each other. For example, our Web search might speculate that the Henri Higginson at the door is the subject of a Wall Street Journal article about investing in wine. The agent states only what the host needs to know: "I think he may be a wine expert." The inter-agent chalkboard on which the utterance is based would include the underlying URL of the article and the search agent's confidence in the source. Other agents can use this information to pursue their independent responses; the customer relations database might follow up by observing that "Last month, he had one bottle of Pinot Grigio for a party of six," which both provides additional data and casts some implicit doubt on the tentative identification. Two lines of dialogue can create a third idea, contained in neither line alone, from their implied conflict[14][13].

Some agents will naturally tend to conflict with others; a high-recall Web search may tend to be credulous, a database with excellent precision might be taciturn but, when speaking up, worth attention.

8 CONCLUSION

Though audio hypertexts today are associated with interminable telephone trees, polyphonic interfaces offer intriguing opportunities to provide computational support for tasks that require personal social interaction. Designing a single, comprehensive agent would require deep understanding of the task, and therefore deep understanding of people. Instead, a chorus of simple agents with simple, characteristic expertise could provide useful support under the guidance of their master. Cultivation of these agents over the span of months or years could yield many benefits, and raises interesting questions of ownership, property rights, and ethical treatment of artificial constructs.

ACKNOWLEDGMENTS

The scenarios described here are fiction, and any resemblance to actual persons, places, or organizations is entirely coincidental.

REFERENCES

[1] Adams, D. 1980 *The hitchhiker's guide to the galaxy.* Harmony Books.
[2] Arons, B. 1991. "Hyperspeech: Navigating In Speech-Only Hypermedia" Proceedings Of The Third Annual ACM Conference On Hypertex". *Hypertext '91.* 133-146.
[3] Banks, I. 1989 *The Player Of Games.* St. Martin's Press.
[4] Bernstein, M. 2017. "Thoughts On Some Moral Questions Concerning Story In Immersive Hypertext Narrative". *International Conference On Interactive Digital Storytelling: Workshop On Authoring For Interactive Storytelling.*
[5] Bernstein, M. 1995 *Conversations With Friends: Hypertexts With Characters.* In Hypermedia Design, S. Fraïse, F. Garzotto, T. Isakowitz, J. Nanard, And M. Nanard, Eds. Springer.
[6] Bernstein, M. 2009. "On Hypertext Narrative". *ACM Hypertext 2009.*
[7] Bernstein, M., Drekler, K. E., And Feiner, S. 1988. "Workshop On Hypertext And Artificial Intelligence". *AAAI-88,* Minneapolis, MN (20-25 August 1988).
[8] Bourdain, A. 2000 *Kitchen Confidential : Adventures In The Culinary Underbelly.* Bloomsbury.
[9] Brown, P. J. 1987. "Turning Ideas Into Products: The Guide System". *Proceedings Of The ACM Conference On Hypertext.* 33-40.
[10] Brusilovsky, P., Stock, O., And Strapparava, C. 2000 *Adaptive Hypermedia And Adaptive Web-Based Systems : International Conference, Ah 2000, Trento, Italy, August 28-30, 2000 : Proceedings.* Springer.
[11] Bush, V. 1945. "As We May Think". *Atlantic Monthly.* July 1945, 101-108.
[12] Danler, S. 2016 *Sweetbitter.* Alfred A. Knopf.
[13] Eagleton, T. 2003 *After Theory.* Basic Books.
[14] Eisenstein, S. And Leyda, J. 1942 *The Film Sense, By Sergei M. Eisenstein.* Harcourt, Brace And Company.
[15] Hemingway, E. 1926 *The Sun Also Rises.* Scribner.
[16] Kubrick, S., Clarke, A. C., Dullea, K., Lockwood, G., And Sylvester, W. 1988 *2001, A Space Odyssey.* The Voyager Company.
[17] Bernstein, M. 2016 *Getting Started With Hypertext Narrative.* Eastgate Systems, Inc.
[18] McKee, R. 2016 *Dialogue : The Art Of Verbal Action For Page, Stage, Screen.* Twelve.
[19] Miles, A. 2001. "Hypertext Structure As The Event Of Connection". *Hypertext 2001: Proceedings Of The 12th ACM Conference On Hypertext And Hypermedia.* 61-68.
[20] Oren, T., Solomon, G., Kreitman, K., And Don, A. 1990 *Guides: Characterizing The Interface.* In The Art Of Human Computer Interface Design, B. Laurel, Ed. Addison Wesley.
[21] Spuybroek, L. 2011 *Sympathy Of Things : Ruskin And The Ecology Of Design.* V2 Publishing : NAI Publishing
[22] Stotts, P. D. And Furuta, R. 1989. "Petri-Net Based Hypertext: Document Structure With Browsing Semantics". *ACM Transactions On Office Information Systems.* 7, 1, 3-29.
[23] Weizenbaum, J. 1976 *Computer Power And Human Reason : From Judgment To Calculation.* W. H. Freeman.

A Villain's Guide To Social Media And Web Science

Mark Bernstein
Eastgate Systems, Inc.
134 Main Street
Watertown MA 02472 USA
Bernstein@eastgate.com

Clare Hooper
Vancouver, BC, Canada
clare@clarehooper.net

ABSTRACT

If we have not yet achieved planetary super-villainy on the desktop, it may be feasible to fit it into a suburban office suite. Social media and Web science permit the modern villain to deploy traditional cruelties to great and surprising effect. Because the impact of villainous techniques is radically asymmetric, our fetid plots are difficult and costly to foil.

CCS CONCEPTS

• **Software and its engineering** → **Software creation and management** → **Designing Software** • **Applied Computing** → **Computers in other domains.**

KEYWORDS

Hypertext, social media, literature, fiction, implementation, history of computing, politics, villainy.

ACM Reference format:

M. Bernstein and C. Hooper. 2018. A villain's guide to social media and Web Science. In *Proceedings of the 29th ACM Conference on Hypertext and Social Media, Baltimore, MD USA, July 2018 (HT2018),* 5 pages.
https://doi.org/10.1145/3209542.3210576

1 INTRODUCTION

Technological innovation has long facilitated villainy at ever greater scale. Technology, moreover, offers many opportunities to cater to the whims and caprice of the individual villain. The vandal hordes of antiquity were proverbially destructive, but they were hordes: They lacked the personal touch. More recent efforts such as the M. Ming's Gigantic Nitron Ray, D. Vader's Death Star, and A. Goldfinger's thermonuclear attack on international markets, achieved that personal touch only by commanding vast stockpiles of capital.

Previous technological approaches to villainy depended on doomsday machines, zombie apocalypses, thermonuclear devices and the like, as these were the only available technologies that supported large-magnitude calamities. Social media and Web science permit the modern villain to deploy traditional cruelties at unprecedented scale. We admit that small cruelties and local harms can be just as satisfying as global conquest, mass destruction, or summoning the elder gods. Still, there is satisfaction in numbers, and only by specifying a victim pool of adequate size can we ensure the statistical significance of our results.

The focus of this work is restricted to villainy. We are not concerned here with merely criminal uses of social media and the Web, such as money laundering, theft, or embezzlement. Similarly, we do not consider unethical practices that may not be criminal, much less villainous. Our concerns, as always, are domination of cities, nations, and planets, accumulation of wealth beyond the dreams of avarice, the destruction of dreams and widespread infliction of pain.

2 VICTIM PROCUREMENT

Social media generate vast resources of information about the interests, habits, and circumstances of millions of people throughout the world. Much information is, of course, contained in the users' posts, data they freely make available for our use. Other useful information is implicit in their use of social media to keep in touch with friends and family, to discover entertaining Web sites, or to purchase products. We can use this vast stream of data to identify those to whom we might most profitably devote our attentions. Where an advertiser looks for a persuadable and remunerative prospect, villains look for a vulnerable and satisfying victim.

It is useful in this connection to distinguish between intrinsic and extrinsic vulnerability. The intrinsically vulnerable target is subject to attack by their circumstances and context; the friendless are natural victims, of course, but so, too, are those whose friends are largely disjoint from ours. This is readily detected through the social graph [13]. Extrinsic vulnerability occurs when people have secrets: hidden families, complex love affairs, financial strain are all classic indicators, and these, too, may be detectable from social networks alone [3].

We now know it is possible to de-anonymize anonymous social graphs [2] and that private information like religious belief may be inferred from such seemingly secular statistics as Wikipedia edit counts [15]. It is essential, too, to remember that we are villains; sometimes, the old ways are the best ways, and a simple kidnapping or a short prison term can lead people otherwise hostile to us to help de-anonymize even the most obfuscated data or to give us the most closely guarded password [7] [17] [14].

Because we never give a sucker an even break, the benefits of victim identification may be considerable. Collateral benefits can be surprising and far-reaching; the persistence of Nigerian Prince or 419 scheme is ample testimony to the rewards of a villainy that surely, at this date, has vanishingly low recall. [10] Remember that a good victim is our greatest asset, that inflicting pain is good in itself, and that today's victim may be compelled to assist us tomorrow.

3 DISMAYING OUR ENEMIES

Not only can we use social media for our dark purposes and analyze it for our nefarious ends, but at the same time we can prevent our enemies from enjoying its benefits. Twenty years ago, one could send email to nearly any active computer scientist and be confident that it would be received and read; today, spam filters, phishing attacks, and ad filters make many scholars inaccessible.

Social media are exquisitely vulnerable to trolls[1], and their vulnerability is only increased when, as in Facebook, users are encouraged to combine professional, community, and personal friends in a common network. Good people can sometimes tolerate being unjustly criticized in the pages of an obscure and dusty journal; to be smeared before one's family and closest friends, on the other hand, will try the patience of saints. Helpfully, bystander apathy is the norm online [23].

Through *dogpiling*, we can exploit social networks to prevent their use by opponents. When someone makes a statement we dislike or that is adverse to our cause, we disagree and initiate a discussion. But we don't do this once: we summon dozens of friends and allies to join us simultaneously. Our victim cannot spread their message or interfere with our schemes; they must either argue with dozens of opponents or abandon the matter. Bystanders will gather to learn what the fuss concerns, and may be impressed by our apparently great numbers.

Dogpiling, moreover, is massively asymmetric. Our victim asserted something they believe and care about Perhaps their deluded friends share their misguided conviction. They were in any case writing gratuitously, describing their thoughts to their friends. We, however, are villains: well-paid professionals with an interest in hounding them and in winning. We may easily employ assistants (*minions*) to add their voice to ours; a single minion can engage in many arguments at once, and can control numerous separate personae and supervise dozens of autonomous 'bots. Our opponents may care deeply, but our minions suffer no corresponding handicap: win or lose, the minion gets paid [20].

Though most minions require minimal skills and training, it is sometimes possible to acquire minions who are already well placed in social networks. These can be invaluable for dogpile attacks, as they lend not merely their own weight but also the mass of their followers. Recruitment to our wicked cause is facilitated as well by the observation that the online world is a place where people "just like to be nastier" [22]."

We must also remember that conventional villainy may be employed with profit on the social media battlefield. Blackmail, for example, may effectively silence even the most influential and experienced Wikipedia opponent. Elaborate and inconvenient security arrangements can be defeated by simply accosting the target and displaying a weapon. Indeed, speculating about attacking a pet animal may suffice, not only from fear of losing the services and cost of the target's mangy little dog, but because the target will understand that if villains knows about Toto, they also know details of the rest of their beloved circle. Crowd-sourced research can frequently reveal surprising insights into an anonymous writer's life[4], and these may be deployed through conventional means among the target's family, employers, and neighbors. Sometimes, we can sit back and enjoy the fun while the asymmetries of public outrages and confusion do our work for us[1].

4 MINING

Great efforts have been dedicated to anticipating individual needs by mining users' online behavior, since advertising will naturally be most profitable when directed to those who already need the advertised goods. It may be possible for algorithms to detect needs and desires before they are consciously expressed — for example, to detect from her purchasing and browsing behavior that a woman may be pregnant before she (or her family) knows [11]. Might it be possible to identify women who will soon seek to terminate a pregnancy prior to conception? Even accepting a substantial error rate, great mayhem might be achieved at very little cost. Similar mining efforts directed at other behaviors — romantic entanglements, dread diseases — could yield spectacular dividends [8]. Powerful and well-established methods can reliably trick people into revealing more than they intend [24]. The online world is our oyster.

Again, we observe a pronounced asymmetry in the villainous effects of data mining. Our opponents must make do with data that they can access freely or that they can purchase. Unlike them, we are free to use stolen data — either information that happens to have been stolen (John Podesta's emails, Vermeer's *The Concert*), or information whose theft, being advantageous to our plans, we commission. Co-occurrence in large, stolen data stores can be a powerful tool in itself; a cluster of healthy, athletic users of watch-based fitness apps who are geolocated in an area that is blank in Google Maps may be a secret military base [12]. Analysis of big data thrives on bigger data: our data will always be bigger than theirs, and we can buy, borrow, and steal more.

5 STEALING CANDY FROM A BABY

Although we now enjoy unprecedented computational power and can employ analytical tools that exceed the wildest dreams of our predecessors, it behooves us to remember the simple joys of those bygone days. Let us consider, for example, stealing candy

---

[1] http://www.cbc.ca/news/canada/calgary/jeremy-quaile-knightley-dog-death-calgary-1.4602948

from a baby. Nothing could be easier to contemplate or swifter to accomplish. Yet, through a single act, we reap many benefits.

- The baby is wretched, naturally, and expresses its dismay with appropriate force.
- An infant's cry of distress cannot be resisted: its parents must stop what they were doing, however virtuous and important their plans may have been, to attend to the child.
- Bystanders will be annoyed and distracted, and may cast disparaging glances at the parents who permit such disruption. Discord is sown.
- The infant may have siblings; if so, they may be jealous of the attention the baby is receiving, and may take advantage of parental distraction to engage in roughhousing, casual vandalism, or indoor parkour practice.
- And, you get a lollipop!

The intent of this perfidious pastorale is not to indulge nostalgia for a simpler era, but to observe the powerful asymmetry we can so gainfully employ. To steal candy from a baby is proverbially easy, yet the theft does not merely please the thief and dismay the baby; parents, siblings, bystanders, the owners of the candy shop, the paramedics summoned when indoor parkour practice goes awry, all share and multiply the impact. Efforts to foil our scheme are disproportionately difficult: for example, handing out free lollipops to passing infants is unlikely to exert an equal effect.

Social networks exploit network effects. Not only do the asymmetric effects of villainy benefit the same network phenomena, but the villainy also benefits the social network. On the internet, wronged innocents wail online, and their cries attract clicks (which improve the platform's stock valuation) and viewers (to whom advertising may be displayed). Crowds that gather at the crime scene are themselves famously vulnerable to villainous exploitation [9]; a modest expenditure of effort and resources can keep an event like Gamergate or Pizzagate in play for weeks or months. Virtuous peacemakers diminish platform profits.

Analyzing the crowds gathered by these events may yield useful leads for staffing your malevolent enterprises. Conventional global villainy once entailed a large and costly staff of mad scientists and renegade warlords. These indispensible personnel were costly to hire and difficult to manage. Our armies of minor minions, moreover, required salaries, training, and the acquisition of at least the same number of cool uniforms, while a costly Human Resources division was needed to locate and recruit them. Though villains were pioneers in employing the physically challenged [16], those challenges brought expense, inconvenience, and sometimes betrayal [20]. Much recruitment and support can now be automated; indeed, minions often appear at our crime scenes and volunteer for service. Others, observed committing spontaneous villainies at the scene of your own crimes, can be recruited with ease. Within minutes of the Parkland, Florida school shooting, for example, 8chan chatboards were filled with efforts to coordinate stories to blame the reaction to the crime on Jewish kabalistic numerology and hired crisis actors [21]. Many of our most technically-demanding roles may now be crowdsourced.

Nor should we neglect the costs of maintaining entire districts to serve as vile dens and wretched hives of scum and villainy. Now, we can recruit minions in their own basements to support our repellent endeavor. They advance our dark ends without costly secret bases or inconvenient hidden fortresses.

6 DISINFORMATION AND DISCORD

What is better than making one's fellow man believe something that is not true? Why, making vast numbers of people believe something that is both preposterous and harmful! Systematically spreading false news has proven to be of enormous value.

Familiar analytical techniques for real-time sentiment analysis and A/B testing can now be deployed to track engagement and propagation of false information. We can know within minutes what messages are most attractive to different audiences. A single weird trick may be sufficient to capture the imagination of niche audiences through hyper-tailored, adaptive messaging. Our successes are our own; our failures cost us nothing.

Engagement aroused by provocative and targeted false news benefits us. Our opponents are bound to try to discredit the news; their futile struggles only increase our reach. Discourse generation and assistive writing tools allow minions with limited skills to manage numerous online personae, each of which can contribute to spreading our message. A single semi-literate minion can, in favorable circumstances, engage several distinguished professors and authoritative pundits. Because many of the bystanders witnessing the argument will undoubtedly resent teachers — who among us has no desire to avenge old classroom wrongs? — our minion may well achieve surprising success. Yet even if our minion is vanquished and today's message is entirely discredited, no harm is done; our minion can go home, drink a beer, enjoy a good cackle with friends, and tomorrow our minion can pick up its new followers, put on a new persona, and try again. The more we engage, the more traffic we receive.

There are a million lies in the naked city, and only one truth. Our sanctimonious rivals will fight endlessly among themselves to define and refine that truth, even if the result is adverse to their personal and political interest. While they parse nuance and endure inconvenient truths, we invent our own, numerous truths and test them rigorously for efficacy. What is more, we design our untruths to be more interesting than truth, and so our foul fantasies will be shared and retweeted far more frequently than truthful reports[25].

Disinformation promotes discord. We consider discord good in itself, of course, but discord also weakens our opponents while strengthening our other operations. Our truthiness itself promotes further discord among our enemies, as each invidious invention demands provokes a new fissure among our fractious enemies.

Disinformation has revived some of our oldest aspirations, villainous visions once thought lost forever. The dream of a single vast database that identifies every prominent Jew (as defined by the *Nürnberger Gesetze!*) once seemed lost forever, but numerous Wikipedia efforts labor daily to make it real. Wikipedia editors — often the same editors — work to render articles about marginal extremists more prominent and palatable, to excuse (and publicize) racist and anti-Semitic memes, and to defame both contemporary and historic figures. Deliberate campaigns to move the Overton window target topics such as Nordic Nazi Parties; if Sweden and Norway have white supremacists, they argue, perhaps Nazism is worth a second look?

7 RELATED WORK

Though early villainy was sometimes conceived at surprising scale (see *Paradise Lost*, or the *Prose Edda*), it was only after James Moriarty's invention of organized crime that technology could properly be applied to our ends. The early work of Sauron is typical in its acceptance of the limitations of scale, targeting a mere nineteen initial victims: as the nineteen designated targets were the rulers of the known world, the scheme did demonstrate commendable audacity. Computational efforts to summon the elder gods [18], to mock creation [16][21] or to bring on the end of the universe [6] anticipate the approaches described here.

Preliminary efforts known as Gamergate, though unsuccessful in reforming ethics in game journalism, did succeed in harming a handful of targeted victims while requiring our opponents to expend thousands of hours in order to oppose our handful of amateur villains. The same methods are generally believed to have been applied to the 2016 US Presidential Election with surprising success.

Villains may learn a great deal from well-intentioned systems. When Facebook, for example identified images that might evoke fond memories of the preceding year and urged people to share them with their social networks, it showed Eric Meyer the portrait of his six-year-old daughter who had recently succumbed to aggressive brain cancer [19]. "Yes, my year looked like that. True enough," he wrote. "My year looked like the now-absent face of my Little Spark. It was still unkind to remind me so tactlessly." Another well-intentioned Facebook feature proposed new candidates for admission to each user's social network, demonstrating a surprising facility at proposing the user's former romantic partners.

8 CONCLUSION

Much though we deplore the fact, technological progress can benefit the virtuous as well as the evil. What seems striking in this brief and anecdotal survey of new techniques and recent developments are the prominent asymmetries that redound to the benefit of villainy.

- The villain can lie, the good should not. Disinformation is villainous in itself and leads to discord, which is even better.

- The villain can steal, the good must not. Data mining is powerful, but its power increases as more data becomes available. Our neural networks do not care that some of our data is stolen.

- Disinformation and rumor may be spread by the idle, the unskilled, and the robot. To confound them requires the attention of skilled advocates.

- We can choose the lies that serve us best; our enemies cannot. There are a million lies but only one truth.

- A working minion, stymied, can dust itself off and work on a new meme. A true believer in the same position may experience profound humiliation.

- A single scurrilous word or damaging disclosure can do lasting harm that a thousand well-intentioned and sympathetic notes will not repair.

ACKNOWLEDGMENTS

This is a satire. Don't try this at home. The works cited here are not villainous. We don't know the Twitterological literature as well as we ought, and any apparently-inexplicable choice to single out a particular research effort is surely due to our ignorance. We thank David E. Millard, Charlie Hargood, Dr. Fionnbar Lenihan and Robert A. Sullivan for helpful conversations on related topics. Of course, none of them are in any way responsible for this villainous paper.

REFERENCES

[1] Ammann, R. 2009. "Jorn Barger, The Newspage Network And The Emergence Of The Weblog Community," Proceedings Of The 20th ACM Conference On Hypertext And Hypermedia". *HT '09.* 279-288.

[2] Backstrom, L., Dworkin, C., and Kleinberg, J. 2011. "Wherefore Art Thou R3579x?: Anonymized Social Networks, Hidden Patterns, And Structural Steganography". *Commun. ACM.* 54, 12, 133-141.

[3] Backstrom, L. And Kleinberg, J. 2014. "Romantic Partnerships And The Dispersion Of Social Ties: A Network Analysis Of Relationship Status On Facebook Proceedings Of The 17th Acm Conference On Computer Supported Cooperative Work \&\#38; Social Computing". *CSCW '14.* 831-841.

[4] Johnson, B. 2001. "The Short Life Of Kaycee Nicole". *The Guardian.*

[5] Chen, A. 2015. "The Agency". *New York Times Magazine.*

[6] Clarke, A. C. 1967 *The Nine Billion Names Of God; The Best Short Stories Of Arthur C. Clarke.* Harcourt, Brace & World.

[7] Derakhshan, H. 2016. "Killing The Hyperlink, Killing The Web: The Shift From Library-Internet To Television-Internet Proceedings Of The 27th Acm Conference On Hypertext And Social Media". *HT '16.* 3-3.

[8] Dick, P. K. 2016 *The Minority Report : And Other Classic Stories.* Citadel Press.

[9] Dickens, C. 1870 *The Adventures Of Oliver Twist.* Fields, Osgood & Co.

[10] Edwards, M., Peersman, C., And Rashid, A. 2017. "Scamming The Scammers: Towards Automatic Detection Of Persuasion In Advance Fee Frauds Proceedings Of The 26th International Conference On World Wide Web Companion". *WWW '17 Companion.* 1291-1299.

[11] Hamilton, D. 2016 *The Thinking Machine.* In Echoes Of Sherlock Holmes : Stories Inspired By The Holmes Canon, L. R. King, L. S. Klinger, J. Connolly, M. Gardiner, D. Cameron, T. Alexander, D. Morrell, T. Lee, B. Musson, H. P. Ryan, A. Perry, M. Scott, H. Ephron, G. Phillips, W. K. Krueger, C. Mcpherson, D. Crombie, J. Maberry, D. Mina, And C. Doctorow, Eds. Pegasus Books.

[12] Hern, A. 2018. "Fitness Tracking App Strava Gives Away Location Of Secret Us Army Bases". *The Guardian.*

[13] Huang, Q., Singh, V. K., And Atrey, P. K. 2014. "Cyber Bullying Detection Using Social And Textual Analysis Proceedings Of The 3rd International Workshop On Socially-Aware Multimedia". *SAM '14.* 3-6.

[14] Le Carré,, J.. 1980 *Smiley's People.* Knopf.

[15] Rizoiu, M.-A., Xie, L., Caetano, T., And Cebrian, M. 2016. "Evolution Of Privacy Loss In Wikipedia Proceedings Of The Ninth Acm International Conference On Web Search And Data Mining". *WSDM '16.* 215-224.

[16] Shelley, M. W. 1984 *Frankenstein, Or, The Modern Prometheus.* Modern Library.

[17] Sofia El Amine, S. B., Sabrine Saad, Addis Tesfa And Christophe Varin "Infowar In Syria: The Web Between Liberation And Repression". *Web Science 2012.*

[18] Stross, C. 2006 *The Jennifer Morgue.* Golden Gryphon Press.

[19] Meyer, E. 2014 "My Year Was Tragic. Facebook Ambushed Me With a Painful Reminder**.**" *Slate,* http://www.slate.com/blogs/future_tense/2014/12/29/facebook_year _in_review_my_tragic_year_was_the_wrong_fodder_for_facebook. html

[20] Czege, P. *My Life With Master,* Half-Meme Press, 2003.

[21] Timberg, C. and Harwell, D. 2018 "We studied thousands of anonymous posts about the Parkland attack — and found a conspiracy in the making", *The Washington Post* (28 February 2018)

[22] Nevin, Andrew D. 2015. *Cyber-Psychopathy: Examining the Relationship between Dark E-Personality and Online Misconduct.* M.A. Thesis, Western University. https://ir.lib.uwo.ca/etd/2926

[23] DiFranzo, D., Taylor, S. H. et al., 2018, "Upstanding by Design: Bystander Intervention in Cyberbullying", *CHI 18* (Montréal 21-26 April 2018)

[24] Brignull, Harry. "Types of Dark Patterns," https://darkpatterns.org/types-of-dark-pattern

[25] Vosoughi, S., Roy, D., and Aral, S. 2018 "The spread of true and false news online' *Science* (9 March 20-18) pp. 1146-1151

Efficient Auto-Generation of Taxonomies for Structured Knowledge Discovery and Organization

Deepak Ajwani
Nokia Bell Labs
Dublin, Ireland
deepak.ajwani@nokia-bell-labs.com

Sourav Dutta
Nokia Bell Labs
Dublin, Ireland
sourav.dutta@nokia-bell-labs.com

Pat Nicholson
Nokia Bell Labs
Dublin, Ireland
pat.nicholson@nokia-bell-labs.com

Luca Maria Aiello
Nokia Bell Labs
Cambridge, United Kingdom
luca.aiello@nokia-bell-labs.com

Alessandra Sala
Nokia Bell Labs
Dublin, Ireland
alessandra.sala@nokia-bell-labs.com

ABSTRACT

This tutorial introduces the audience to the latest breakthroughs in the area of interpreting unstructured content through an analysis of the key enabling scientific results along with their real-world applications. With technical presentations of problems like named-entity disambiguation and dynamically updating the knowledge hierarchy with domain-specific vocabulary, it would provide the fundamentals to the building-blocks of various applications in Artificial Intelligence, Natural Language Processing, Machine Learning, and Data Mining.

CCS CONCEPTS

• **Information systems** → *Data extraction and integration*; *Ontologies*; *Information extraction*; Information systems applications;

ACM Reference Format:
Deepak Ajwani, Sourav Dutta, Pat Nicholson, Luca Maria Aiello, and Alessandra Sala. 2018. Efficient Auto-Generation of Taxonomies for Structured Knowledge Discovery and Organization. In *HT '18: 29th ACM Conference on Hypertext and Social Media, July 9–12, 2018, Baltimore, MD, USA*. ACM, New York, NY, USA, 2 pages. https://doi.org/10.1145/3209542.3212476

1 INTRODUCTION

Future Big Data systems are expected to showcase enriched cognitive abilities for data and pattern discovery for large-scale analytics on vast amounts of linked structured and unstructured multi-modal data. This would usher in the next-generation functionalities for e-commerce, transportation, IoT and smarter health-care.

However, progress in the area of data science lies at the confluence of semantic search, reasoning, knowledge representation, algorithm engineering, natural language processing and machine learning. To this end, the proposed tutorial will provide the audience with the latest breakthroughs and state-of-the-art techniques for knowledge discovery and their organization for applications like semantic linking and contextual interpretation. We further present

how linked knowledge hierarchies can be compared on both structural and semantic subsumption similarities. Further, such cognitive blocks should be highly accurate and scalable, depicting just-in-time prediction and computationally cheap updates.

As a real-world manifestation, we discuss the application of techniques to novel analytical avenues like: (1) analyzing "sound maps" of urban areas to extract relationship between soundscapes, emotions and perceptions; (2) creation of dictionary for urban smell to analyze how different categories (e.g., industry, transport) correlate with air quality; and (3) retrieving topically related multimedia content segments for faster ingestion of information.

Finally, as food for thought, the tutorial will also highlight future directions of work and various open challenges.

Keywords: *Linked Knowledge Hierarchies, Entity Linking, Word Embeddings, Graph Measures, Katz Centrality, Topic Labeling*

Tutorial Outline

The tutorial would impress the importance of structure knowledge hierarchy and enable the attendees to gain an insight as to how a taxonomy can be mined from unstructured or semi-structured corpus of text using co-occurrence graphs, statistical methods and hierarchical clustering methods. The detailed outline is as follows:

(1) Introduction – Semantic Linking, Knowledge Repositories, and Linked Data discovery
   – Ontologies and Knowledge Hierarchies
   – RDF structure and Linked Data
   – Taxonomy structure: Directed Acyclic Graphs
   – TF-IDF, LDA [3], classifiers [6], word embeddings [13]
(2) Application areas that leverage taxonomies
   – Semantic relationship and Topical relatedness
   – Community detection in social media
(3) Efficiency trade-offs
   – Semantic interpretation
   – Accuracy and Scalability
   – Just-in-time prediction
   – Fast updates
(4) Dynamically updating taxonomies
   – Induction of taxonomies [1, 7]
   – Breaking cycles in noisy hierarchies [15]
   – Evolution of new concepts and word senses

– Named entity linking for existing concepts [4, 11]
– Measures to capture new concepts
(5) Unsupervised placement of new concepts in taxonomies
– Rule based techniques
– Probabilistic approaches
(6) Supervised placement of new concepts in taxonomies
– Syntactic Features
– Semantic Features
– Graph Features
– Integrating features using learning-to-rank [12]
– Discussion of efficiency trade-offs
– Identifying Wikipedia categories for emerging concepts
(7) Efficient comparison of taxonomies
– Structural overlap measures
– Tree-edit distance [2] and graph similarity measures [10]
– Fowlkes-Mallows measure [5]
– Katz similarity scores [9] and their aggregation
– Discussion of efficiency trade-offs
(8) Domain-specific taxonomies for smarter applications
– Assigning human-readable topical tags to documents [8]
– Linking related multi-media contents
– Taxonomies for different senses: sound, visual, smell [14]
(9) Conclusion and Future Directions

Tutorial Length: 1.5 hours.

2 CONCLUSION

Linked data such as structured knowledge hierarchies provide invaluable source of information pertaining to concepts, their relationships, and dependency structure. This tutorial discusses efficient techniques for induction of taxonomies, and their subsequent dynamic updation to reflect emerging concepts. We show how current techniques in text mining, graph processing and machine learning can be leveraged by breaking complex learning models into smaller models. Such techniques would directly impact the representation, enrichment, and management for analysis of evolution and influence in semantic graphs and networks.

REFERENCES

[1] Luca Maria Aiello, Rossano Schifanella, Daniele Quercia, and Francesco Aletta. 2016. Chatty maps: constructing sound maps of urban areas from social media data. *Royal Society open science* 3, 3 (2016), 150690.
[2] P. Bille. 2005. A survey on tree edit distance and related problems. *Theoretical Computer Science* 337, 1 (2005), 217–239.
[3] David M. Blei. 2012. Probabilistic Topic Models. *Commun. ACM* 55, 4 (April 2012), 77–84.
[4] Paolo Ferragina and Ugo Scaiella. 2010. TAGME: on-the-fly annotation of short text fragments (by wikipedia entities). In *Proceedings of the 19th ACM Conference on Information and Knowledge Management, CIKM 2010, Toronto, Ontario, Canada, October 26-30, 2010*. ACM, 1625–1628.
[5] E. B. Fowlkes and C. L. Mallows. 1983. A Method for Comparing Two Hierarchical Clusterings. *J. Amer. Statist. Assoc.* 78, 383 (1983), 553–569.
[6] S. R. Gunn. 1998. *Support Vector Machines for Classification and Regression*. Technical Report. Univ. of Southampton, USA.
[7] Victoria Henshaw. 2013. *Urban smellscapes: Understanding and designing city smell environments*. Routledge.
[8] Ioana Hulpus, Conor Hayes, Marcel Karnstedt, and Derek Greene. 2013. Unsupervised Graph-based Topic Labelling Using Dbpedia. In *WSDM*.
[9] Leo Katz. 1953. A new status index derived from sociometric analysis. *Psychometrika* 18, 1 (1953), 39–43.
[10] Danai Koutra, Neil Shah, Joshua T. Vogelstein, Brian Gallagher, and Christos Faloutsos. 2016. DeltaCon: A principled massive-graph similarity function with attribution. *ACM Transactions on Knowledge Discovery from Data (TKDD)* 10, 3 (2016).
[11] Tiep Mai, Bichen Shi, Patrick K. Nicholson, Deepak Ajwani, and Alessandra Sala. 2017. Scalable Disambiguation System Capturing Individualities of Mentions. In *Language, Data, and Knowledge - First International Conference, LDK 2017, Galway, Ireland, June 19-20, 2017, Proceedings (Lecture Notes in Computer Science)*, Vol. 10318. Springer, 365–379.
[12] Brian McFee and Gert Lanckriet. 2010. Metric Learning to Rank. In *Proceedings of the 27th International Conference on International Conference on Machine Learning*. 775–782.
[13] Tomas Mikolov, Ilya Sutskever, Kai Chen, Greg Corrado, and Jeffrey Dean. 2013. Distributed Representations of Words and Phrases and Their Compositionality. In *Proceedings of the 26th International Conference on Neural Information Processing Systems - Volume 2*. 3111–3119.
[14] Daniele Quercia, Rossano Schifanella, Luca Maria Aiello, and Kate McLean. 2015. Smelly maps: the digital life of urban smellscapes. *arXiv preprint arXiv:1505.06851* (2015).
[15] Jiankai Sun, Deepak Ajwani, Patrick K. Nicholson, Alessandra Sala, and Srinivasan Parthasarathy. 2017. Breaking cycles in noisy hierarchies. In *ACM Conference on Web Science*. 151–160.

Author Index

NOTES